Get more out of your textbook with the FREE Book Companion Site.

Created to help you master key themes and concepts and build skills, the activities in this free resource help you test and broaden your knowledge.

bedfordstmartins.com/huntconcise

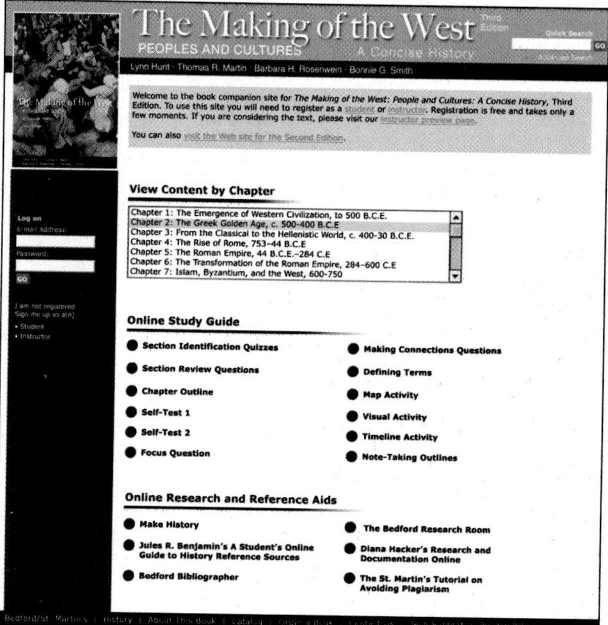

Online Study Guide. Get immediate feedback on your progress with Self-Tests and Defining Terms activities designed to check your understanding of chapter concepts and key terms. Other resources, such as map and visual activities, note-taking outlines, and more, help reinforce concepts and ideas presented in the textbook.

Make History. Access our online database with thousands of images, maps, Web links, and documents. Browse by topic, date, or resource type.

Online Research and Reference Aids. Research guides, models for documenting sources, plagiarism tutorials, and other resources provide you with the support you need to refine your research skills, effectively evaluate sources, and organize your findings.

THIRD EDITION

The Making of the West

Peoples and Cultures

A Concise History

Volume II: Since 1340

Lynn Hunt
University of California, Los Angeles

Thomas R. Martin
College of the Holy Cross

Barbara H. Rosenwein
Loyola University Chicago

Bonnie G. Smith
Rutgers University

Bedford / St. Martin's
Boston ▪ New York

For Bedford / St. Martin's

Publisher for History: Mary Dougherty
Director of Development for History: Jane Knetzger
Developmental Editor: Danielle Slevens
Senior Production Editor: Rosemary R. Jaffe
Senior Production Supervisor: Dennis J. Conroy
Executive Marketing Manager: Jenna Bookin Barry
Editorial Assistant: Robin Soule
Production Assistants: Alexis Biasell, Samuel S. Jones, and Alexandra Leach
Senior Art Director: Anna Palchik
Text Designer: Lisa Buckley
Copyeditor: Barbara Jatkola
Proofreaders: Linda McLatchie and Stella Gelboin
Indexer: Leoni Z. McVey
Photo Researcher: Gillian Speeth
Cover Designer: Donna Lee Dennison
Cover and Title Page Art: A Collective Farm Festival, 1937 (oil on canvas). Sergej Vasilevic Gerasimov (1885–1964). Tretyakov Gallery, Moscow, Russia/© DACS/Alinari/The Bridgeman Art Library International. © Estate of Sergej Vasilevic Gerasimov/RAO, Moscow/VAGA, New York.
Cartography: Mapping Specialists, Ltd.
Composition: MPS Limited, A Macmillan Company
Printing and Binding: RR Donnelley and Sons

President: Joan E. Feinberg
Editorial Director: Denise B. Wydra
Director of Marketing: Karen R. Soeltz
Director of Editing, Design, and Production: Marcia Cohen
Assistant Director of Editing, Design, and Production: Elise S. Kaiser
Managing Editor: Elizabeth M. Schaaf

Library of Congress Control Number: 2009924677

Manufactured in the United States of America.
4 3 2 1 0
f e d c

For information, write: Bedford/St. Martin's, 75 Arlington Street, Boston, MA 02116 (617-399-4000)

ISBN 10: 0-312-55458-3 ISBN 13: 978-0-312-55458-3 (combined edition)
ISBN 10: 0-312-55459-1 ISBN 13: 978-0-312-55459-0 (Vol. I)
ISBN 10: 0-312-55460-5 ISBN 13: 978-0-312-55460-6 (Vol. II)

Preface

THE DRAMATIC EVENTS OF THE LAST DECADE have pushed us to look at the history of the West in new ways. The terrorist attacks of September 11, 2001, the subsequent wars in Afghanistan and Iraq, and a global financial and economic crisis all have roots in the past. Digging down to those roots helps us make better sense of the present, and at the same time gives us a better appreciation of how the past differs from the present. We welcome the challenge of incorporating and explaining these momentous events and believe that our project's basic goal and approach are well suited to meeting the challenge presented by them. From the very beginning, we have insisted on an expanded vision of the West that includes the United States, fully incorporates eastern Europe, and emphasizes Europe's relationship with the rest of the world, whether through trade, colonization, migration, cultural exchange, or religious and ethnic conflict. This approach enables us to explain how globalization can seem both promising and problematic, now and in the past.

Textbooks, even very good ones, must constantly evolve. New developments, whether in the form of events or historical approaches, require new efforts at synthesis. This observation applies not just to the recent past, where change is evident at every level, but also to all the other epochs in history, right back to what has been called "prehistory." New archaeological discoveries and techniques for studying the remains of the past continually produce fresh evidence, even about peoples who lived before the invention of writing. Contrary to popular opinion, the past never stands still, and so authors of textbooks must constantly gather up the new evidence, consider the new approaches, and rewrite history accordingly. We relish the opportunity and take seriously the responsibility of providing a coherent narrative of the West that will enable students to understand the world they live in now.

Central Themes and Approach

Our title, *The Making of the West: Peoples and Cultures, A Concise History* makes three enduring points about our themes and approach: (1) that the history of the West is the story of a process that is still ongoing, not a finished result with only one fixed meaning; (2) that "the West" includes many different peoples and cultures; that is, that there is no one Western people or culture that has existed from the beginning until now. To understand the historical development of the West and its position in the world today, it is essential to place the West's emergence in a larger, global context that reveals the cross-cultural interactions fundamental to the shaping of Western identity. Finally, (3) that a "concise" approach is ideally suited to meet the needs of instructors who wish to assign additional supplementary readings, who need to cover the entire introduction to Western civilization in a single semester, or who find a comprehensive textbook too detailed and daunting for their students. By reworking, condensing, and combining thematically related sections throughout the text ourselves, we've created a brief edition that preserves the narrative flow, balance, and power of our full-length work. We've also provided for maximum flexibility by publishing *A Concise History* in an electronic format (see below) and three print versions. Volume I extends from the beginning of civilization to 1740; Volume II picks up at 1340, for courses on Europe from the Renaissance to the present; and a one-volume softcover edition treats the whole of Western history.

We know from our own teaching that introductory students need a solid chronological framework, one with enough familiar benchmarks to make the material readily digestible, but also one with enough flexibility to incorporate the new varieties of historical research. That is one reason we present our account in a straightforward, chronological manner. Each chapter treats all the main events, people, and themes of a period in a common context; thus students are not required to learn about political events in one chapter, and then backtrack to concurrent social and cultural developments in the next. The chronological organization also accords with our belief that it is important, above all else, for students to see the interconnections among varieties of historical experience—between politics and cultures, between public events and private experiences, between wars or economic crisis and everyday life. Our integrated approach allows students to appreciate these relationships; it captures the spirit of each age and sparks students' historical imaginations. For teachers, our chronological approach ensures a balanced account, allows the flexibility to stress themes of one's own choosing, and perhaps best of all, provides a text that reveals history not as a settled matter but as a process that is constantly alive, subject to pressures, and able to surprise. Our task as authors, moreover, is to integrate the best of social and cultural history with the enduring developments of political, military, and economic history, offering a clear, compelling narrative that sets all the key events and stages of the West's evolution in a broad, meaningful context.

In writing *The Making of the West: Peoples and Cultures, A Concise History,* it has been our aim to communicate the vitality and excitement as well as the fundamental importance of history. If we have succeeded in conveying some of the vibrancy of the past and the thrill of historical investigation, we will be encouraged to start rethinking and revising—as historians always must—once again.

Textual Changes

Unlike most scholarly books, a textbook offers historians the rare chance to revise the original work, to keep it fresh, and to make it better. It has been a privilege to bring our own scholarship and teaching to bear on this rewriting. In this third edition, we have kept our emphasis on a strong central story line that incorporates the best of new research, but we have worked to make the narrative even more concise, focused, and accessible.

In this edition, we have further highlighted thematic coverage to help students discern major developments. Coverage of the Renaissance and Reformation has been revised thoroughly, with more on Renaissance art and architecture, the Ottomans' influence on the West, and a consolidated treatment of the European Reformation. We have worked to make key developments clearer in other chapters as well. Changes to this end include refocused sections on Pompey and Julius Caesar in Chapter 4 and Romanization in Chapter 5; a new section on the political transformation of the Roman Empire in Chapter 6; a reorganized treatment of Islam and Byzantium in Chapter 7; a consolidated discussion of the medieval papacy and lay piety in Chapter 10; newly consolidated coverage of the scientific revolution in Chapter 12; refocused sections on the execution of Louis XVI in Chapter 16 and nineteenth-century social reform in Chapter 17; and consolidated and strengthened coverage of Robespierre and Napoleon in Chapter 16, and of industrialization in Chapter 17.

We have also added new material and drawn on new scholarship on topics such as the emergence of civilization, in light of recent findings in Turkey (Chapter 1); the origins of the Black Death (Chapter 11); the Atlantic system and the creation of a new public sphere (Chapter 14); and the conflict in the Middle East, the effects of increasing globalization, and the global economic crisis (Chapter 24).

A final way we have chosen to help students identify and absorb major developments is by adding and refining "signposts" to guide students' reading. New chapter-opening focus questions, posed at the end of the opening vignettes, encapsulate the essence of the era covered in the chapter and guide students toward each chapter's core message. To help students as they read, we have worked hard to ensure that chapter and section overviews outline the central points of each section clearly, and that section headings are as clear and strong as possible. We have also condensed some material to better illuminate key ideas, resulting in a textbook that is a good deal shorter than the previous edition, and—we hope—a clearer, more accessible read for students.

Pedagogy and Features

More and more is required of students these days, and not just in Western Civilization courses. We know from our own teaching that students need all the help they can get in assimilating information, acquiring skills, and learning about historical debate. With these goals in mind, we retained the class-tested learning and teaching aids that contributed to the previous edition, but we have also added more such features.

Each chapter begins with a ***vivid anecdote*** that draws readers into the atmosphere and issues of the period and raises the chapter's main themes, supplemented by a full-page illustration that echoes the anecdote and similarly reveals the temper of the times. A ***new Chapter Focus Question*** provides students with an overarching theme to help guide their reading. ***Review questions*** strategically placed at the end of each major section help students check their comprehension of main ideas. Bolded

key terms in the text are defined in the ***Glossary of Key Terms*** at the end of the book. A list of author-selected ***Suggested References,*** now present in every chapter, directs students to print and online resources for further investigation. Each chapter closes with a ***new graphical Timeline,*** which enables students to see the sequence and overlap of important events in a given period, and two ***Chapter Review Questions*** that encourage their analysis of chapter material.

The map program of *A Concise History* has been widely praised as the most comprehensive of any brief survey text. In each chapter we offer a set of three types of maps, each with a distinct role in conveying information to students. On average, three to four ***full-size maps*** show major developments; one to three ***"spot" maps***—small maps that emphasize a detailed area from the discussion—aid students' understanding of specific but crucial issues; and a ***Mapping the West*** summary map at the end of each chapter provides a snapshot of the West at the close of a transformative period and helps students visualize the West's changing contours over time. In addition to the ***more than 160 maps,*** numerous charts and graphs visually support the narrative, including innovative ***Taking Measure*** features, which highlight a chart, table, graph, or map of historical statistics that illuminates an important political, social, or cultural development.

It has been our intention to integrate art as fully as possible into the narrative and to show its value for teaching and learning. ***Over 260 illustrations,*** carefully chosen to reflect this edition's broad topical coverage and geographic inclusion, reinforce the text and show the varieties of visual sources from which historians build their narratives and interpretations. All artifacts, illustrations, paintings, and photographs are contemporaneous with the chapter; there are no anachronistic illustrations—no fifteenth-century peasants tilling fields in a chapter on the tenth century! We know that today's students are very attuned to visual sources of information, yet they do not always receive systematic instruction in how to "read" or think critically about such visual sources. Our substantive captions for the maps and art help them learn how to make the most of these informative materials, and we have frequently included specific questions or suggestions for comparisons that might be developed. Specially designed visual exercises in the *Online Study Guide* supplement this approach.

Supplements

We have taken great care in revising and augmenting the comprehensive and well-integrated set of print and electronic resources for students and instructors that support the third edition of *The Making of the West: A Concise History.*

For Students

Print Resources

***Sources of* The Making of the West, Third Edition**—Volumes I (to 1740) and II (since 1500)—by Katharine J. Lualdi, University of Southern Maine. This companion sourcebook provides written and visual sources to accompany *The Making of* *the West: A Concise History.* Political, social, and cultural documents offer a variety of perspectives that complement the textbook and encourage students to make connections between narrative history and primary sources. A correlation guide showing how the documents align with each textbook chapter appears in *Sources of The Making of the West* and on the *Book Companion Site.* The reader is available free when packaged with the text.

The Bedford Series in History and Culture. Over one hundred titles in this highly praised series combine first-rate scholarship, historical narrative, and important primary documents for undergraduate courses. Each book is brief, inexpensive, and focused on a specific topic or period. Package discounts are available.

Rand McNally Atlas of Western Civilization. This collection of over fifty full-color maps highlights social, political, and cross-cultural change and interaction from classical Greece and Rome to the post-industrial Western world. Each map is thoroughly indexed for fast reference. The Atlas is available for $3.00 when packaged with the text.

The Bedford Glossary for European History. This handy supplement for the survey course gives students historically contextualized definitions for hundreds of terms—from Abbasids to Zionism—that students will encounter in lectures, reading, and exams. The Glossary is available free when packaged with the text.

Trade Books. Titles published by sister companies Farrar, Straus and Giroux; Henry Holt and Company; Hill and Wang; Picador; St. Martin's Press; and Palgrave Macmillan are available at a 50 percent discount when packaged with Bedford/St. Martin's textbooks. For more information, visit **bedfordstmartins.com/tradeup**.

New Media Resources

The Making of the West: A Concise History *e-Book*. This electronic version of *The Making of the West: A Concise History* offers students unmatched value—the complete text of the print book, with easy-to-use highlighting, searching, and note-taking tools, at a significantly reduced price.

FREE *Online Study Guide* at bedfordstmartins.com/huntconcise. The popular *Online Study Guide for The Making of the West: A Concise History* is a free learning tool to help students master the themes and information presented in the textbook and improve their historical skills. Assessment quizzes help students to evaluate their comprehension, a flashcard activity tests students' knowledge of key terms, and a wide range of further quizzing, map, and primary document analysis activities provides them with the opportunity for further study. Instructors can monitor students' progress through the online *Quiz Gradebook* or receive e-mail updates.

***Jules R. Benjamin's A Student's Online Guide to History Reference Sources* at** bedfordstmartins.com/huntconcise. This Web site provides links to history-related databases, indexes, and journals, plus contact information for state, provincial, local, and professional history organizations.

***Bedford Bibliographer* at** bedfordstmartins.com/huntconcise. This simple but powerful Web-based tool assists students with the process of collecting sources and generates bibliographies in four commonly used documentation styles.

***Diana Hacker's Research and Documentation Online* at** bedfordstmartins.com/huntconcise. This Web site provides clear advice on how to integrate primary and secondary sources into research papers, how to cite sources correctly, and how to format in MLA, APA, *Chicago,* or CBE style.

***The St. Martin's Tutorial on Avoiding Plagiarism* at** bedfordstmartins.com/huntconcise. This online tutorial reviews the consequences of plagiarism and explains what sources to acknowledge, how to keep good notes, how to organize research, and how to integrate sources appropriately. The tutorial includes exercises to help students practice integrating sources and recognizing acceptable summaries.

For Instructors

Print Resources

Transparencies. This set of full-color acetate transparencies includes all maps and many images from the parent textbook to help instructors prepare lectures and teach students important map-reading skills. A correlation guide showing how the transparencies align with the brief text appears in the *Instructor's Resource Manual* and on the *Book Companion Site.*

New Media Resources

***Instructor's Resource Manual* at** bedfordstmartins.com/huntconcise/catalog. This manual by Dakota Hamilton, Humboldt State University, offers both experienced and first-time instructors tools for presenting textbook material in exciting and engaging ways. It includes an outline of main chapter topics, annotated chapter outlines, lecture strategies, ways to start class discussions, answer guidelines for questions in the book, tips for discussing the documents and working with visual sources, mapping exercises, suggestions for in-class activities (including using film, video, and literature), and take-home essay questions. Each chapter concludes with a guide to all the chapter-specific supplements available with *The Making of the West: A Concise History.* The manual also features essays on approaches to the Western Civilization course.

Instructor's Resource CD-ROM. This disc provides instructors with ready-made and customizable PowerPoint multimedia presentations built around chapter outlines, maps, figures, and selected images from the textbook, plus jpeg versions of all maps, figures, and selected images. Outline maps are provided in PDF format for quizzing or handouts. Also included are chapter questions formatted in PowerPoint and MS Word for use with i>clicker, a classroom response system.

Computerized Test Bank. The test bank, by Joseph Coohill, Pennsylvania State University at New Kensington, and Frances Mitilineos, Loyola University Chicago, offers over eighty exercises per chapter, including multiple-choice, fill-in-the-blank, short-answer, primary-source analysis, and essay questions. The answer key includes textbook page numbers and correct answers for all questions except the essays. Instructors can customize quizzes, add or edit both questions and answers, and export questions to a variety of formats, including WebCT and Blackboard.

***Book Companion Site* at bedfordstmartins.com/huntconcise.** The companion Web site gathers all the electronic resources for the text, including the *Online Study Guide* and *Quiz Gradebook,* at a single Web address, providing convenient links to lecture, assignment, and research materials such as PowerPoint chapter outlines and the digital libraries at *Make History.*

***Make History* at bedfordstmartins.com/huntconcise.** Comprising the content of our five acclaimed online libraries—*MapCentral, The Bedford History Image Library, DocLinks, HistoryLinks,* and *PlaceLinks*—*Make History* provides one-stop access to relevant digital content including maps, images, documents, and Web links. Students and instructors can browse this free, easy-to-use database by course, topic, date, or resource type and can download the content they find. Instructors can also create entire collections of content and store them online for later use or post their collections to the Web to share with students.

Content for Course Management Systems. A variety of student and instructor resources developed for this textbook is ready for use in course management systems such as Blackboard, WebCT, and other platforms. This e-content includes nearly all of the offerings in the book's *Online Study Guide,* as well as the book's *Test Bank.*

Videos and Multimedia. A wide assortment of videos and multimedia CD-ROMs on various topics in European history is available to qualified adopters. Contact your Bedford/St. Martin's sales representative for more information.

Acknowledgments

In the vital process of revision, the authors have benefited from repeated critical readings by many talented scholars and teachers. Our sincere thanks go to the following instructors, as well as three anonymous reviewers, whose comments often challenged us to rethink or justify our interpretations and who always provided a check on accuracy down to the smallest detail.

Marjorie Berman, *Red Rocks Community College*
Scott G. Bruce, *University of Colorado at Boulder*
Tamara Chaplin, *University of Illinois at Urbana*
Stephanie Christelow, *Idaho State University*
Marcus Cox, *The Citadel*
Jason Coy, *College of Charleston*
Cara Delay, *College of Charleston*
Gillian Hendershot, *Grand Valley State University*
David Hudson, *Texas A&M University*
Geoffrey Jensen, *University of Arkansas*
Brian Nance, *Coastal Carolina University/American Academy in Rome*
Ian Petrie, *Saint Joseph's University*
Craig Pilant, *County College of Morris*
James Sack, *University of Illinois at Chicago*
Jim Slocombe, *Champlain Regional College*
Charles Steinwedel, *Northeastern Illinois University*
Matthew Stith, *University of Arkansas*
David Tengwall, *Anne Arundel Community College*
Victor Triay, *Middlesex Community College*
Kirk Tyvela, *Sinclair Community College*
Rachelle Wadsworth, *Florida Community College at Jacksonville*
Janet Walmsley, *George Mason University*

Many colleagues, friends, and family members have helped us develop this work as well. They know how grateful we are. We also wish to acknowledge and thank the publishing team at Bedford/St. Martin's who did so much to bring this revised edition to completion: president Joan Feinberg, editorial director Denise Wydra, publisher for history Mary Dougherty, director of development for history Jane Knetzger, editor Danielle Slevens, freelance editors Jim Strandberg and Debra Michals, editorial assistant Robin Soule, executive marketing manager Jenna Bookin Barry, managing editor Elizabeth Schaaf, senior production editor Rosemary Jaffe, art researcher Gillian Speeth, permissions manager Sandy Schechter, and senior art director Donna Dennison. Our students' questions and concerns have shaped much of this work, and we welcome all our readers' suggestions, queries, and criticisms. Please contact us at our respective institutions or via history@bedfordstmartins.com.

Brief Contents

Contents

Chapter 11

Crisis and Renaissance, 1340–1500 *393*

Chapter 12

Struggles over Beliefs, 1500–1648 *435*

Chapter 13

State Building and the Search for Order, 1648–1690 *481*

Chapter 14
The Atlantic System and Its Consequences, 1690–1740 *521*

Chapter 15

The Promise of Enlightenment, 1740–1789 *561*

Chapter 17

Industrialization and Social Ferment, 1815–1850 *639*

Chapter 18

Constructing the Nation-State, c. 1850–1880 *683*

Chapter 19

Empire, Modernity, and the Road to War, c. 1880–1914 *729*

Chapter 20
War, Revolution, and Reconstruction, 1914–1929 *779*

Chapter 21

An Age of Catastrophes, 1929–1945 *825*

DAVID LEAN'S FILM OF BORIS PASTERNAK'S
DOCTOR ZHIVAGO
GERALDINE CHAPLIN · JULIE CHRISTIE · TOM COURTENAY
ALEC GUINNESS · SIOBHAN McKENNA · RALPH RICHARDSON
OMAR SHARIF (AS ZHIVAGO) ROD STEIGER · RITA TUSHINGHAM
ROBERT BOLT · DAVID LEAN
WINNER OF 6 ACADEMY AWARDS!

PALACH

Chapter 24

The New Globalism, 1989 to the Present *947*

Maps and Figures

MAPS

Chapter 11

Chapter 12

Chapter 13

Chapter 14

Chapter 15

Chapter 16

Chapter 17

Chapter 18

Chapter 19

Chapter 20

Chapter 21

FIGURES

About the Authors

LYNN HUNT (Ph.D., Stanford University) is Eugen Weber Professor of Modern European History at University of California, Los Angeles. She is the author or editor of several books, including most recently *Inventing Human Rights* (2007) and *Measuring Time, Making History* (2008). She has in press a co-authored work on religious toleration in early eighteenth-century Europe.

THOMAS R. MARTIN (Ph.D., Harvard University) is Jeremiah O'Connor Professor in Classics at the College of the Holy Cross. He is the author of *Sovereignty and Coinage in Classical Greece* (1985) and *Ancient Greece* (1996, 2000) and is one of the originators of *Perseus: Interactive Sources and Studies on Ancient Greece* (www.perseus.tufts.edu). He is currently conducting research on the career of Pericles as a political leader in classical Athens as well as on the text of Josephus's *Jewish War*.

BARBARA H. ROSENWEIN (Ph.D., University of Chicago) is professor of history at Loyola University Chicago. She is the author or editor of several books, including *A Short History of the Middle Ages* (2001, 2004, 2009) and *Emotional Communities in the Early Middle Ages* (2006). She is currently working on a general history of the emotions in the West.

BONNIE G. SMITH (Ph.D., University of Rochester) is Board of Governors Professor of History at Rutgers University. She is the author or editor of several books, including *Ladies of the Leisure Class* (1981); *The Gender of History: Men, Women and Historical Practice* (1998); and *The Oxford Encyclopedia of Women in World History* (2007). Currently she is studying the globalization of European culture and society since the seventeenth century.

THIRD EDITION

The Making of the West

Peoples and Cultures

A Concise History

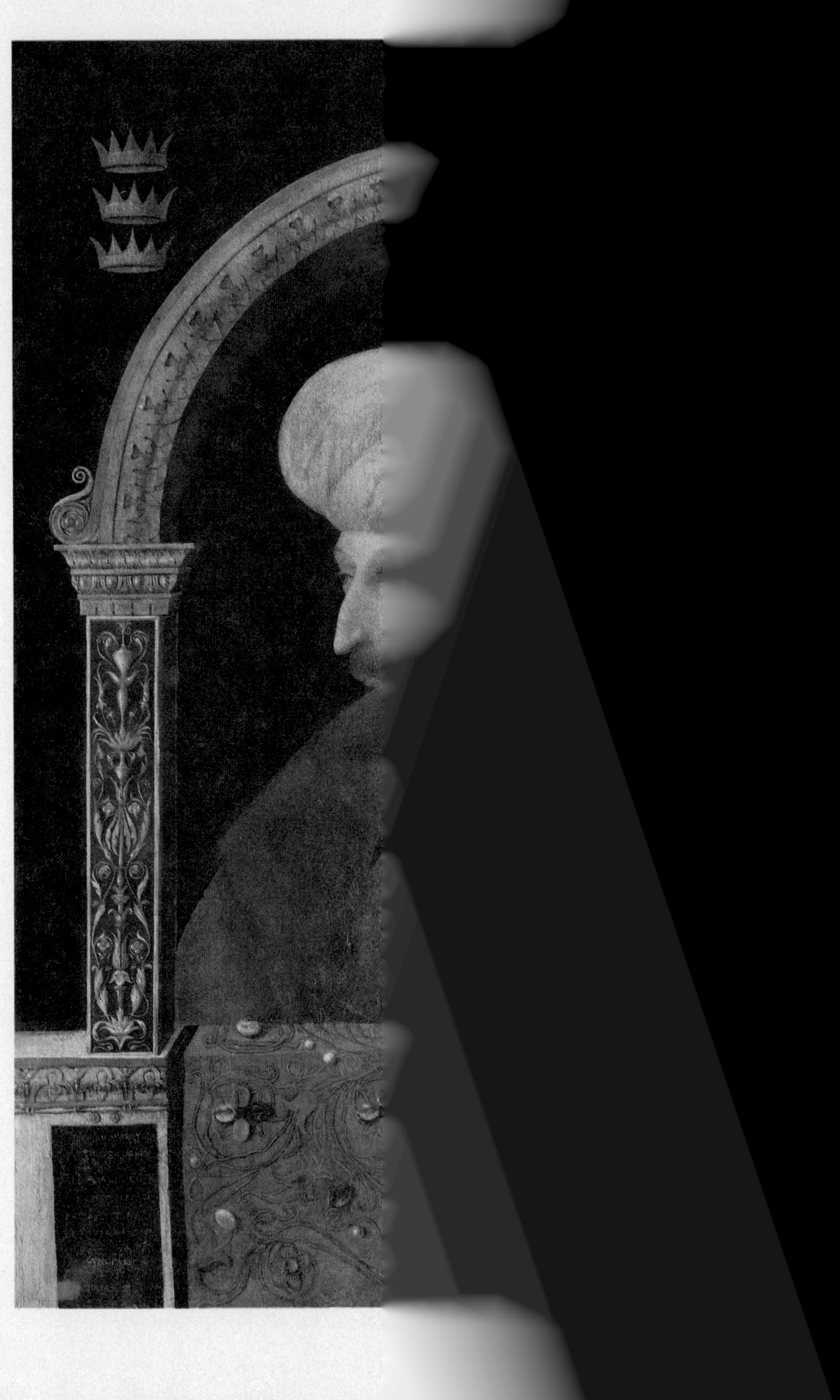

11

Crisis and Renaissance

1340–1500

IN 1453, THE OTTOMAN TURKS turned their cannons on Constantinople and blasted the city's walls. The fall of Constantinople, which spelled the end of the Byzantine Empire, was an enormous shock to Europeans. Some, like the pope, called for a crusade against the Ottomans. Others, like the writer Lauro Quirini, sneered, calling the Turks "a barbaric, uncultivated race, without established customs, or laws, [who live] a careless, vagrant, arbitrary life."

But the Ottomans didn't consider themselves uncultivated or arbitrary. In fact, they shared many of the values and tastes of the Europeans who were so hostile to them. Sultan Mehmed II employed European architects to construct his new palace, the Topkapi Saray, in the city that was once called Constantinople and was now normally called Istanbul. He also commissioned the Venetian Gentile Bellini to paint his portrait. In this, he was no different from the most fashionable European rulers of the day.

Portrait of Mehmed II
The Ottoman ruler Mehmed II (r. 1451–1481) saw himself as a Renaissance patron of the arts, and he called upon the most famous artists and architects of the day to work for him. The painter of this portrait, Gentile Bellini, was from a well-known family of artists in Venice and served at Mehmed's court in 1479–1480. The revival of portraiture, so characteristic of Renaissance tastes, was as important to the Turkish sultans as to European rulers. *(Erich Lessing/Art Resource, NY.)*

Mehmed's actions and interests sum up the three main features of the period 1340–1500: a crisis in the global order, as the Ottomans created a new and long-lived state; political consolidation; and the artistic and cultural movement known as the Renaissance.

During this period a series of crises struck Europe. The disease known as the **Black Death** tore at the fabric of communities and families, though survivors and their children reaped the benefits of higher wages and better living standards. The **Hundred Years' War**, fought between France and England from 1337 to 1453, brought untold misery to the French countryside. Following their conquest of Constantinople, the Ottoman Turks penetrated far into the Balkans. And a crisis in the church, called the **Great Schism**, pitted pope against pope and divided Europe into separate camps.

These crises were met and overcome in large measure through the policies of newly consolidated states. New political entities such as Poland-Lithuania and Muscovy rose to prominence. France and England became centralized monarchies. Italy's political mosaic began to coalesce into five territorial states. And the Iberian kingdoms of Portugal and Spain expanded European domination to Africa, Asia, and the Americas.

Meeting the needs of men and women in crisis while often catering to the wishes of newly rich and powerful rulers, the Renaissance—a word that means "rebirth" and refers to the revival of classical culture—gave Europe new styles of living, ruling, and thinking. A new vocabulary drawn from classical literature, as well as astonishing new forms of art and music based on ancient precedents, were used both to confront and to mask the crises of the day.

CHAPTER FOCUS QUESTION What were the roles of the newly consolidated states of Europe in both the crises of the period and the Renaissance?

Crisis: Disease, War, and Schism

The crises began in the mid-fourteenth century. The Black Death decimated the population; the Hundred Years' War buffeted France, England, and the Low Countries; and the Ottoman Turks began their conquest of formerly Byzantine territory. Soon two and then three rival popes divided the church. In the wake of these crises, many ordinary folk sought solace in new forms of piety, some of them heretical.

Economic Contraction and the Black Death

Bad weather and overpopulation contributed to a series of famines at the beginning of the fourteenth century. Population growth meant that peasants had to divide their plots into ever smaller parcels or farm marginal land. Their income and the quality of their diet eroded. In the great urban centers, where thousands depended on steady employment and cheap bread, a bad harvest, always followed by sharply rising food prices, meant hunger and eventual famine.

A cooling of the European climate also contributed to the crisis in the food supply. Europe entered a colder period, with a succession of severe winters beginning in 1315. Crop failures were widespread. In many cities of northwestern Europe, the price of bread tripled, and thousands starved to death. The Great Famine (1315–1322) left many people hungry, sick, and weak.

At midcentury, a terrible disease, later called the Black Death (1346–c. 1350), hit Europe. Possibly bubonic plague, possibly another as yet unidentified disease, the Black Death attacked the region between the Black and Caspian seas in 1346 (Map 11.1). In 1347, many members of the Genoese colony in Caffa, in the Crimea, fell to the disease, which then traveled westward, to Byzantium, the Middle East, the North African coast, and Europe. By January 1348, the Black Death had infected southern Italy and France. Soon it spread to all of Italy, the Balkans, and most of

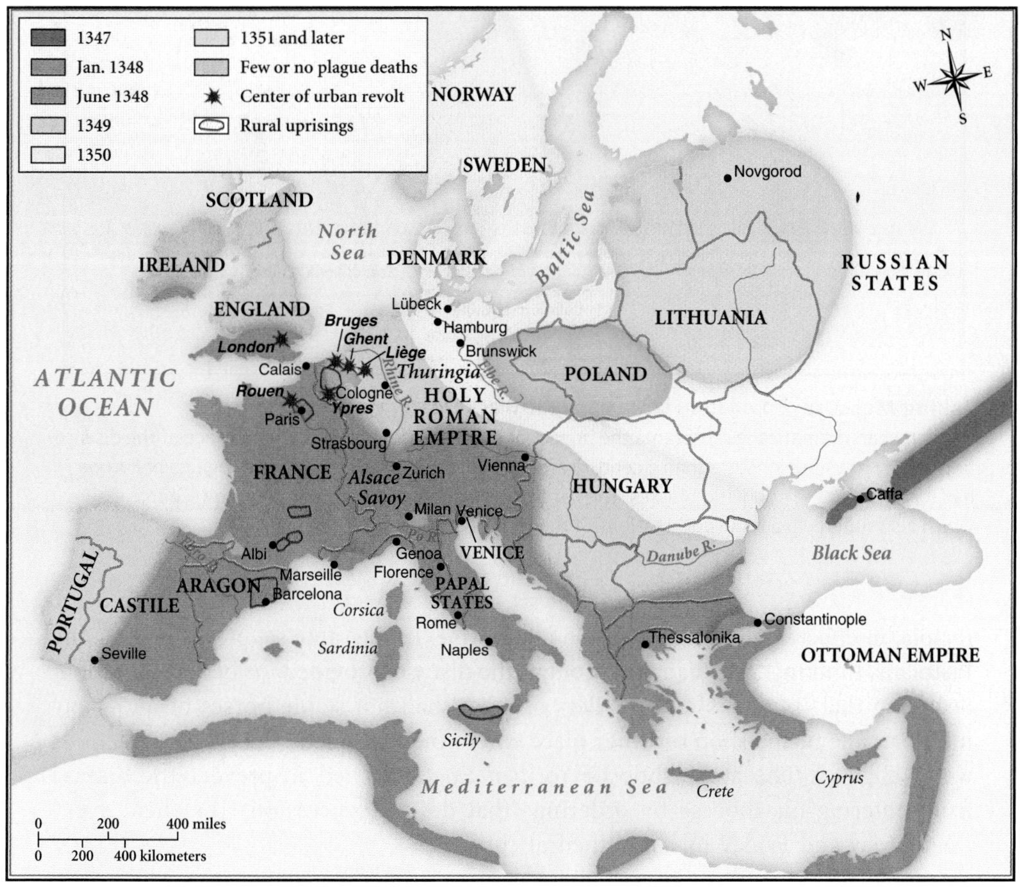

Map 11.1 Advance of the Black Death
The gradual but deadly spread of the Black Death followed the roads and waterways of Europe. **For more help analyzing this map, see the map activity for this chapter in the Online Study Guide at** bedfordstmartins.com/huntconcise.

France. The disease then crept northward to Germany, England, and Scandinavia, reaching the Russian city of Novgorod around 1350.

Nothing like this had struck Europe before. Inhabitants of cities, where crowding and filth increased the chances of contagion, died in massive numbers. Florence lost almost two-thirds of its population of ninety thousand; Siena, like most cities visited by the disease, lost half its people. Rural areas suffered fewer deaths, but regional differences were pronounced. (See "Taking Measure," page 396.) Further outbreaks of the disease, though not called the Black Death, occurred in Europe in 1361, 1368–1369, 1371, 1375, 1390, and 1405. They continued, with longer dormant intervals, into the eighteenth century.

In some places, responses to the Black Death were immediate and practical. At the Italian city of Pistoia in 1348, for example, the government decreed that no citizen could go to nearby Pisa or Lucca, nor could people from those cities enter

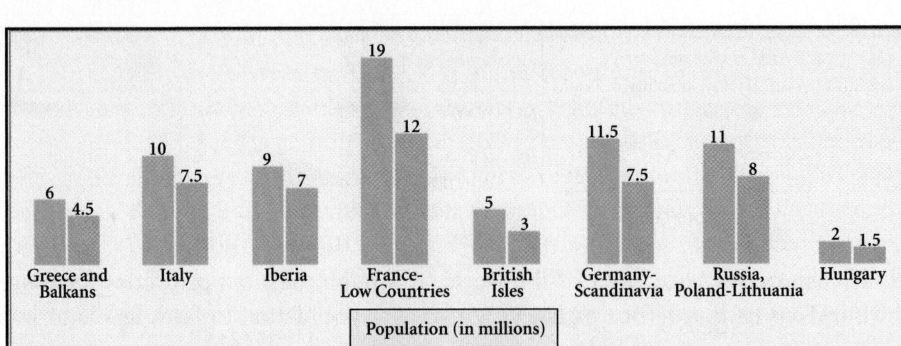

Taking Measure Population Losses and the Black Death, 1340–1450
This bar chart dramatically represents the impact of the Black Death and the recurrence of the disease between 1340 and 1450. More than a century after the Black Death, none of these regions of Europe had made up for the population losses. The hardest-hit areas were France and the Low Countries, which also suffered from the devastations of the Hundred Years' War.

Pistoia; in effect, Pistoia established a quarantine. In the same set of ordinances, the Pistoians, thinking that "bad air" brought the disease, provided for better sanitation, declaring that "butchers and retailers of meat shall not stable horses or allow any mud or dung in the shop or other place where they sell meat." Elsewhere reactions were religious. The archbishop of York in England tried to prevent the disease from entering his diocese by ordering "that devout processions [be] held every Wednesday and Friday in our cathedral church."

Some people took more extreme measures. Lamenting their sins—which they believed had brought on the Black Death and other calamities—and attempting to placate God, groups of men and women wandered from city to city with whips in their hands. Entering a church, they took off their shirts or blouses, lay down one by one on the church floor, and, according to the chronicler Henry of Hervordia (d. 1370),

> one of them would strike the first with a whip, saying, "May God grant you remission [forgiveness] of all your sins. Arise." And he would get up, and do the same to the second, and all the others in turn did the same. When they were all on their feet, and arranged two by two in procession, two of them in the middle of the column would begin singing a hymn in a high voice, with a sweet melody.

Churchmen did not approve of the flagellants, as these people were called, because they took on the preaching and penance that was supposed to be done by the clergy. Nevertheless, the flagellants aroused popular sympathy wherever they went. The religious enthusiasm they inspired often culminated in violence against Jews, as rumors circulated that Jews were responsible for the Black Death. Old charges that Jews were plotting to "wipe out all the Christians with poison and had poisoned wells and springs everywhere," as one Franciscan friar put it, revived. In Germany especially thousands of Jews were slaughtered. Many fled to Poland, which was less affected by the Black Death and where the authorities welcomed Jews as productive taxpayers. In western and central Europe, however, the persecutions impoverished Jews.

Preoccupation with death led to the popularity of a theme called the Dance of Death as a subject of art, literature, and performance. It featured a procession of people of every age, sex, and rank making their way to the grave. Preachers and poets talked and wrote on the theme. Yet at the same time the Black Death helped inspire this bleak view of the world, it brought new opportunities for those who survived its murderous path. With a smaller population to feed, less land was needed for farming. Marginal land that had been cultivated was returned to pasture, meadow, or forest. Landlords diversified their products. Wheat had been the favored crop before the Black Death, but barley—the key ingredient in beer—turned out to be more profitable afterward. Animal products continued to fetch a high price, and some landlords switched from farming to animal husbandry.

These changes in agriculture meant a better standard of living. The peasants and urban workers who survived the Black Death were able to negotiate better working conditions or higher wages from their landlords or employers. With more money to spend, people could afford a better and more varied diet that included beer and meat. Even commoners could now afford finery, a fact that threatened to erase the lines between the nobles and everyone else. Many Italian cities passed laws to prohibit ostentatious dress among every class of citizens. These laws were generally ineffective, however, as families continued to announce their rank and prestige by wearing lavish clothes.

Each attack of the disease brought with it, a few years later, a slight jump in the birthrate. It is unlikely that women became more fertile. Rather, the cause of the increased birthrate was more subtle: with good employment opportunities, couples married at younger ages and with greater frequency than they had previously. "After the end of the epidemic," one chronicler wrote, "the men and women who stayed alive did everything to get married."

The Black Death also had an effect on patterns of education. The survivors' children needed schooling, but the disease spared neither the students nor the professors of the old universities. As the disease ebbed, new local colleges and universities were built, partly to train a new generation for the priesthood and partly to satisfy local donors—many of them rulers—who, riding on a sea of wealth left behind by the dead, wanted to be known as patrons of education. Thus, in 1348, in the midst of the Black Death, Holy Roman Emperor Charles IV chartered a university at Prague. The king of Poland founded Cracow University, and a Habsburg duke created the University of Vienna. Rather than travel to Paris or Bologna, young men living east of the Rhine River now tended to study closer to home.

The Hundred Years' War, 1337–1453

In France, the misery wrought by disease was compounded by the devastation of war. Since the Norman invasion of England in the eleventh century (see page 329), the king of England had held land on the continent. The French kings continually

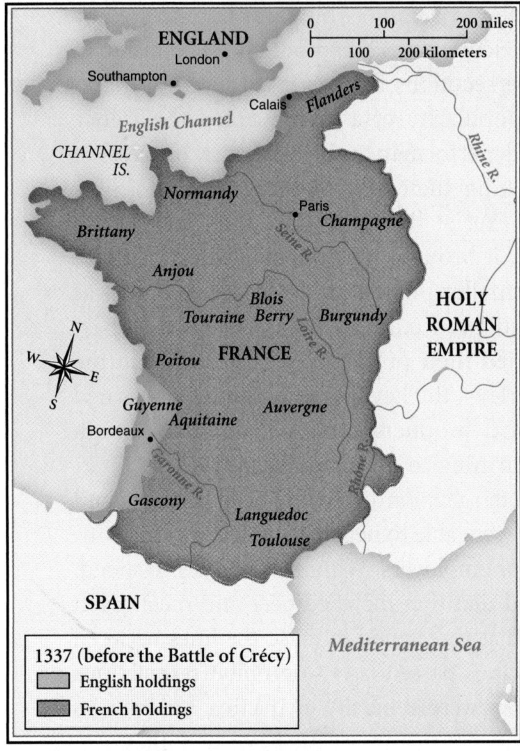
ENGLAND
London
Southampton
Calais
Flanders
English Channel
CHANNEL IS.
Rhine R.
Normandy
Paris
Champagne
Brittany
Seine R.
Anjou
Blois
Touraine
Berry
Burgundy
HOLY ROMAN EMPIRE
Poitou
FRANCE
Loire R.
Guyenne
Aquitaine
Auvergne
Bordeaux
Garonne R.
Rhône R.
Gascony
Languedoc
Toulouse
SPAIN
Mediterranean Sea
0 100 200 miles
0 100 200 kilometers
1337 (before the Battle of Crécy)
English holdings
French holdings

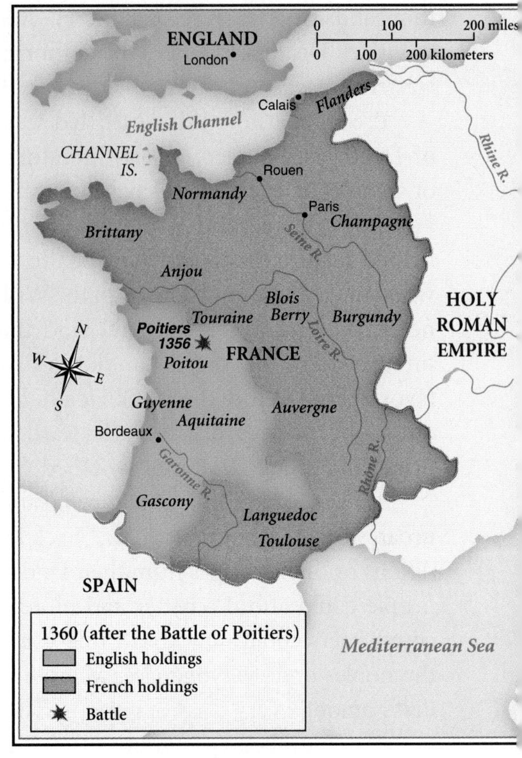
ENGLAND
London
Calais
Flanders
English Channel
CHANNEL IS.
Rhine R.
Rouen
Normandy
Paris
Champagne
Brittany
Seine R.
Anjou
Blois
Touraine
Berry
Burgundy
HOLY ROMAN EMPIRE
Poitiers 1356
Poitou
FRANCE
Loire R.
Guyenne
Aquitaine
Auvergne
Bordeaux
Garonne R.
Rhône R.
Gascony
Languedoc
Toulouse
SPAIN
Mediterranean Sea
0 100 200 miles
0 100 200 kilometers
1360 (after the Battle of Poitiers)
English holdings
French holdings
Battle

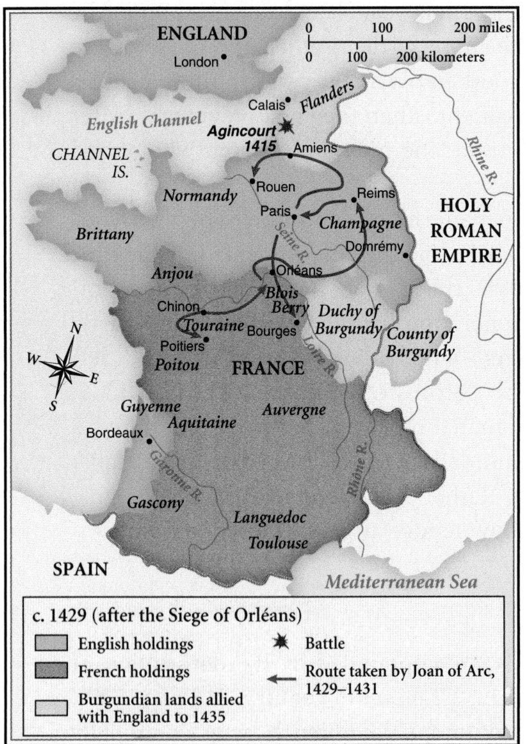
ENGLAND
London
Calais
Flanders
English Channel
Agincourt 1415
Amiens
CHANNEL IS.
Rhine R.
Rouen
Normandy
Reims
Paris
Champagne
Brittany
Seine R.
Domrémy
HOLY ROMAN EMPIRE
Anjou
Orléans
Blois
Chinon
Berry
Duchy of Burgundy
Touraine
Bourges
County of Burgundy
Poitiers
Poitou
FRANCE
Loire R.
Guyenne
Aquitaine
Auvergne
Bordeaux
Garonne R.
Rhône R.
Gascony
Languedoc
Toulouse
SPAIN
Mediterranean Sea
0 100 200 miles
0 100 200 kilometers
c. 1429 (after the Siege of Orléans)
English holdings
French holdings
Burgundian lands allied with England to 1435
Battle
Route taken by Joan of Arc, 1429–1431

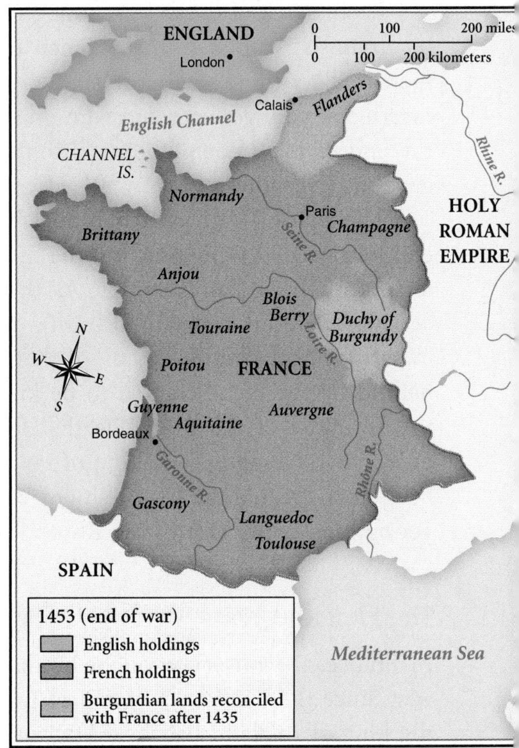
ENGLAND
London
Calais
Flanders
English Channel
CHANNEL IS.
Rhine R.
Normandy
Paris
Champagne
HOLY ROMAN EMPIRE
Brittany
Seine R.
Anjou
Blois
Berry
Touraine
Duchy of Burgundy
Loire R.
Poitou
FRANCE
Guyenne
Aquitaine
Auvergne
Bordeaux
Garonne R.
Rhône R.
Gascony
Languedoc
Toulouse
SPAIN
Mediterranean Sea
0 100 200 miles
0 100 200 kilometers
1453 (end of war)
English holdings
French holdings
Burgundian lands reconciled with France after 1435

chipped away at it, however, and by the beginning of the fourteenth century England retained only the area around Bordeaux, called Guyenne. In 1337, after a series of challenges and skirmishes, King Philip VI of France declared Guyenne to be his; King Edward III of England in turn declared himself king of France. The Hundred Years' War had begun.

The war had four phases (Map 11.2). The first three saw the progressive weakening of French power, the strengthening of England, and the creation of a new kingdom, Burgundy, which for a crucial time allied itself with England. The fourth phase, which began when King Henry V (r. 1413–1422) of England invaded France and achieved a great victory at the battle of Agincourt in 1415, ended in a complete reversal and the ousting of the English from the continent for good.

That reversal was largely begun by a woman, Joan of Arc (1412–1431). The sixteen-year-old arrived at the court of the dauphin (the uncrowned king of France) wearing armor, riding a horse, and leading a small army. Full of charisma and confidence at a desperate hour, Joan convinced the dauphin that she had been sent by God. She was allowed to fight (and win) a battle at Orléans in 1429. At her urging and under her leadership, the dauphin traveled deep into enemy territory to be anointed and crowned King Charles VII at the cathedral in Reims, following the tradition of French monarchs. Despite Joan's victory at Orléans and the anointing of Charles, the French allowed her to be captured and turned over to the English in 1431. Tried as a witch, she was burned at the stake. But her bad luck was matched by French good fortune. The duke of Burgundy recognized Charles VII as king of France, and Charles entered Paris in 1437. Skirmish by skirmish, the English were driven from French soil.

The Hundred Years' War drew other countries into its vortex. Mercenaries for both sides came from Germany, Switzerland, and the Netherlands; the best crossbowmen came from Genoa. The textile workers of Flanders rose up against their French-leaning count when the war cut off their supply of raw wool. In 1369, the marriage of the heiress of Flanders and the duke of Burgundy created a powerful new state, the duchy of Burgundy, which allied itself with England until 1435. Then, riding the wave of French victories, it switched sides. The dukes of Burgundy created a glittering court, a center of art and culture, but their state was short-lived. Clashing with the Swiss Confederation, the duchy of Burgundy began to fall apart in 1474.

The French chronicler Jean Froissart, writing around 1400, considered the Hundred Years' War to be a chivalric adventure. But even Froissart had to admit that the armies were made up mainly of mercenaries rather than knights. These men, who fought for pay and plunder, cared nothing about the king for whom they were

Map 11.2 The Hundred Years' War, 1337–1453
During the Hundred Years' War, English kings, aided by the new state of Burgundy, contested the French monarchy for the domination of France. For many decades, the English seemed to be winning, but the French prevailed in the end.

Joan of Arc, c. 1430
Painted in the style of the French-Flemish school, this manuscript illustration contrasts the metallic hardness of Joan's armor and sword with the soft, fluttering banner depicting God and two angels. With her right hand upturned and clasping a sword, and her left turned down to support the banner, Joan strikes a perfect pose as a messenger of God, similar to the angels depicted above. **For more help analyzing this image, see the visual activity for this chapter in the Online Study Guide at bedfordstmartins.com/huntconcise.** (© akg-images, London.)

supposed to be fighting. They formed "Free Companies" and during lulls in the war lived off the French countryside, terrorizing the peasants and exacting "protection" money.

Some of the soldiers recruited by both sides, both mercenaries and nonmercenaries, were archers. The French archers tended to use crossbows, whose heavy, deadly arrows were released by a mechanism that even a townsman could master. The English employed longbows, which could shoot five arrows for every one launched with a crossbow. Gunpowder was introduced during this war, and cannons were forged. Handguns also were beginning to be used, their effect about equal to that of crossbows.

The Spoils of War
This illustration from Jean Froissart's *Chronicles* depicts soldiers pillaging a conquered city. During the Hundred Years' War, looting became the main source of income for mercenary troops and contributed to the general misery of late-medieval society. Food, furniture, and even everyday household items were taken. (Bibliothèque nationale de France.)

By the end of the war, chivalry was only a dream (though one that continued to inspire soldiers even up to the First World War). Heavy artillery and foot soldiers, tightly massed together in formations of many thousands of men, were the face of the new military. The army was becoming more professional and centralized. In the 1440s the French king created a permanent army of mounted soldiers, paying them wages and subjecting them to regular inspection.

The outbreak of the Hundred Years' War led to popular revolts. Although the Flemish count supported France, the townspeople, dependent on England for the raw wool they wove into cloth, revolted in 1338. The count fled to France, but discord among and within the towns allowed his successor to return in 1348. Revolts continued to flare up thereafter, but the new count allowed the towns a measure of self-government, maintained some distance from French influence, and managed on the whole to keep the peace. Later, as we have seen, Flanders became part of the duchy of Burgundy, an ally of England.

In France, the Parisians chafed against the high taxes they were forced to pay to finance the war. When the English captured the French king John at the battle of Poitiers in 1356, Étienne Marcel, provost of the Paris merchants, and other disillusioned members of the estates of France (the representatives of the clergy, nobility, and commons) met in Paris to discuss political reform, the incompetence of the French army, and taxes. Under Marcel's leadership, the Parisians took control of the city. In response, the royal army blockaded Paris and cut off its food supply. Later that year, Marcel was assassinated, and the Parisian revolt came to an end.

In that same year, 1358, the French peasants, weary of the Free Companies that were ravaging the countryside and disgusted by the military incompetence of the nobility, rose up in protest. Their revolt, derisively called the Jacquerie (from the word *jacque,* or "peasant"), was quickly put down by the nobility.

Similar revolts took place in England. Wat Tyler's Rebellion started as an uprising in much of southern and central England after royal agents tried to collect a poll tax (a tax on each household) to finance the Hundred Years' War. Refusing to pay and refusing to be arrested, the commons (peasants and small householders) rose up in rebellion in 1381. They massed in various groups and marched to London to see the king, whom they professed to support. There they made a radical demand: an end to serfdom. Although the rebellion was put down and its leaders executed, the death knell of serfdom in England had been sounded, as the peasants returned home to bargain with their lords for better terms.

Finally, the Hundred Years' War started a period of financial hard times. During the war, the English king Edward III borrowed heavily from the largest Italian banking houses, the Bardi and Peruzzi of Florence. With many of their assets tied up in loans to the English monarchy, the Italian bankers had no choice but to extend more credit, hoping to recover their initial investments. In the early 1340s, however, Edward defaulted, and the once illustrious houses went bankrupt. Meanwhile, diminished production and trade eventually caused turmoil in northern Europe and a crisis for financiers in the Low Countries. Bruges, the financial center of northwestern Europe, saw its power fade during the fifteenth century when several of its money changers went bankrupt.

The Ottoman Conquests

The rise of the Ottoman Turks, a new Islamic group, was the most astonishing development of the late thirteenth century, when they began a holy war against Byzantium. Under Osman I (r. 1280–1324), who gave the dynasty its name, and his successors, the Ottomans became a formidable force in Anatolia and the Balkans, where political disunity opened the door for their advances (Map 11.3). By the end of the fourteenth century, they had reduced the Byzantine Empire to the city of Constantinople, Thessalonika, and a narrow strip of land in modern-day Greece. Farther to the west, the Ottomans defeated a joint Hungarian-Serbian army at the Maritsa River (1364), alerting Europe for the first time to the threat of an Islamic

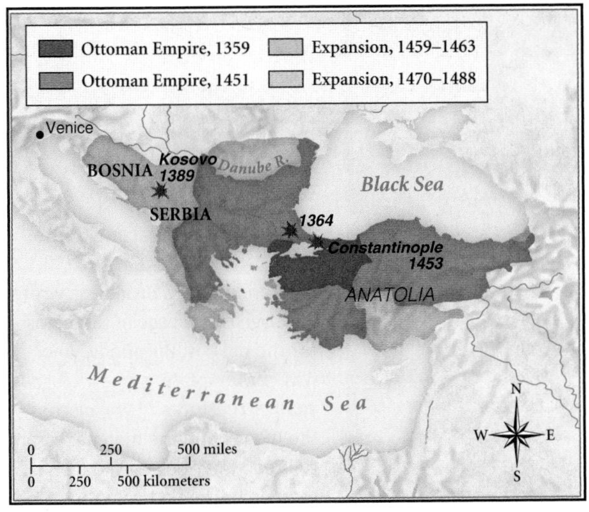

Map 11.3 Ottoman Expansion in the Fourteenth and Fifteenth Centuries
The Balkans were the major theater of expansion for the Ottoman Empire. The Byzantine Empire was reduced to the city of Constantinople and surrounded by the Ottomans before its final fall in 1453.

invasion. Pope Urban V called vainly for a crusade. In the Balkans, the Ottomans skillfully exploited Christian disunity, playing local interests against one another. An Ottoman army, allied with the Bulgarians and some Serbian princes, won the battle of Kosovo (1389), destroying the last organized Christian resistance south of the Danube. (Even today the battle remains a rallying cry for Serbian nationalists.) The Ottomans secured control of southeastern Europe after 1396, when they crushed a crusading army summoned by Pope Boniface IX.

After Mehmed II (r. 1451–1481) ascended the Ottoman throne, he laid siege to Constantinople in 1453. The Byzantine capital, a city of 100,000, could muster only six thousand defenders (including a small contingent of Genoese) against an Ottoman force estimated at between 200,000 and 400,000 men. The city's walls were no match for fifteenth-century cannons. The last Byzantine emperor, Constantine XI ("Palaeologos"), died in battle, some sixty thousand residents were carried off into slavery, and the city was sacked. Mehmed entered Constantinople in triumph and rendered thanks to God in Justinian's Church of the Holy Wisdom (Hagia Sophia), which he turned into a mosque.

Mehmed wanted to be the new ruler of the Roman Empire—a Muslim Roman Empire. We have seen that he turned to the west for his artistic commissions, such as his Topkapi palace and his portrait. The Ottoman sultan employed Christian slave children raised as Muslims to be his Janissaries, the backbone of the Ottoman army. At the sultan's court, Christian women were prominent in the harem, and as a consequence many Ottoman princes had Greek or Serbian mothers. Christian princes and converts to Islam served in the emerging Ottoman administration. In conquered areas, existing religious and social structures remained intact when local people accepted Ottoman overlordship and paid taxes. Only in areas of persistent resistance did the Ottomans drive out or massacre the inhabitants, settling Turkish tribes in their place. A distinctive pattern of Balkan history was therefore established

The Siege of Constantinople, 1453
Bertrandon de la Broquiere wrote his *Overseas Voyage* in the 1430s for the duke of Burgundy, who was contemplating a new crusade against the Turks. "I will discuss the means and the men necessary to break their power and defeat them in battle and gain their territory," he wrote, adding, "I don't think it would be very hard to break and defeat them, given their lack of arms." Within two decades, however, the Turks had taken Constantinople. When an artist was commissioned around 1455 to illustrate Bertrandon's work, he or she chose to show the siege. In this picture, you can see the tents of the Turkish captains, their cannons and cannonballs just behind them, and, across the water, the city of Constantinople with its doomed defenders. (Bibliothèque Nationale, Paris/The Bridgeman Art Library.)

at the beginning of the Ottoman conquest: extremely diverse ethnic and religious communities were woven together into the fabric of an efficient central state.

The Great Schism, 1378–1417

Even as war and disease threatened Europeans' material and physical well-being, a crisis in the church, precipitated by a scandal in the papacy, tore at their spiritual life. The move of the papacy from Rome to Avignon in 1309 (see page 375) had caused an outcry, especially among Italians, distraught by the election of French popes and anxious to see the papacy return to Rome. Some critics, such as Marsilius of Padua, were disillusioned with the institution of the papacy itself. Marsilius, a physician and lawyer by training, argued in *The Defender of the Peace* (1324) that the source of all power lay within the people: "The law-making power or the first and real effective source of law is the people or the body of citizens or the prevailing part of the people according to its election or its will expressed in general convention by vote." Applied to the papacy, Marsilius's argument meant that Christians themselves formed the church and that the pope should be elected by a general council representing all Christians.

When Pope Gregory XI (r. 1370–1378) left Avignon to return to Rome in 1377, the scandal of the Avignon papacy seemed to be over. But Rome itself presented a problem. Glad to have the papacy back, the Romans were determined never to lose it again. When the cardinals—many of whom came from Spain, Italy, and France—met to elect Gregory's successor, the Roman popolo, who controlled the city, demanded that they choose a Roman: "A Roman! A Roman! A Roman or at least an Italian! Or else we'll kill them all." Expecting to gain an important place in papal government, the cardinals chose an Italian, who took the name Urban VI. But Urban had no intention of kowtowing to the cardinals. Instead, he exalted the power of the pope and began to reduce the cardinals' wealth and privileges. The cardinals from France decided that they had made a big mistake. Many left Rome for a meeting at Anagni, where they claimed that Urban's election had been irregular and called on him to resign. When he refused, they elected a Frenchman as pope. He took the name Clement VII and soon moved his papal court back to Avignon, but not before he and Urban had excommunicated each other. The Great Schism (1378–1417) had begun.

All of Europe was drawn into the dispute. The king of France supported Clement; the king of England favored Urban. Some European states—Burgundy, Scotland, and Castile, for example—lined up on the side of France. Others—the Holy Roman Empire, Poland, and Hungary—supported Urban. Portugal switched sides four times, depending on which alliance offered it the most advantages. Each pope declared that those who followed the other were to be deprived of the rights of church membership; in effect, everyone in Europe was excommunicated by one or the other of the popes.

Contrary to the ideas of Marsilius, church law said that only a pope could summon a general council of the church—a sort of parliament of high churchmen. But given the state of confusion in Christendom, many intellectuals argued that the crisis justified calling a general council to represent the body of the faithful, even against the wishes of an unwilling pope—or popes. They spearheaded the conciliar movement—a movement to have the cardinals or the Holy Roman Emperor call a council.

In 1408, long after Urban and Clement had passed away, the conciliar movement succeeded when cardinals from both sides met and declared their resolve "to pursue the union of the Church . . . by way of abdication of both papal contenders." With support from both England and France, the cardinals called for a council to be held at Pisa in 1409. Both popes refused to attend, and the council deposed them, electing a third pope, Alexander V. The "deposed" popes refused to budge, even though most of the European powers abandoned them. Alexander's successor, John XXIII, turned to the emperor to arrange for another council.

The Council of Constance (1414–1418) met to resolve the papal crisis and to institute church reforms. The delegates deposed John XXIII and accepted the resignation of the pope at Rome. After long negotiations with rulers still supporting the Avignon pope, all allegiance to him was withdrawn, and he was deposed. The council then elected Martin V, who was recognized as pope by every important ruler of Europe. The Great Schism had come to an end.

New Forms of Piety and Heresy

The Great Schism, along with the miseries of disease and war, caused enormous anxiety among ordinary Christians. Worried about the salvation of their souls, pious men and women eagerly sought new forms of religious solace. The plenary indulgence—full forgiveness of sins, which had been originally offered to crusaders who died while fighting for the cause—was now offered to those who made a pilgrimage to Rome or one of the other designated holy places during declared Holy Years. Sins could be wiped away through confession and contrition, but some guilt remained that could be removed only through good deeds or in purgatory. As the idea of purgatory—the place where sins were fully purged—took full form, new indulgences were offered for good works to reduce the time there. Thus, for example, the duchess of Brittany was granted a hundred days off her purgatorial punishments when she allowed the Feast of Corpus Christi to be preached in her chapel. Lesser folk might obtain indulgences in more modest ways.

Both clergy and laity became more interested than ever in the education of young people as a way to deepen their faith and spiritual life. The Brethren of the Common Life—laypeople, mainly in the Low Countries, who devoted themselves to pious works—set up a model school at Deventer, and humanists in Italy emphasized primary school education. Priests were expected to teach the faithful the basics of the Christian religion.

Home was also a place for devotion. Portable images of Mary, the mother of God, and of the life and passion of Christ proliferated. They were meant to be contemplated by ordinary Christians at convenient moments throughout the day. People purchased or commissioned copies of Books of Hours, which contained prayers to be said on the appropriate day at the hours indicated in the Benedictine rule. Books of Hours included calendars, sometimes splendidly illustrated with depictions of the seasons and labors of the year. Other illustrations reminded readers of the life and suffering of Christ.

On the streets of towns, priests marched in dignified processions, carrying the sanctified bread of the Mass—the very body of Christ—in tall, splendid containers called monstrances, which trumpeted the importance and dignity of the Eucharistic wafer. Like images of the Lord's life and crucifixion, the monstrance emphasized Christ's body. Christ's blood was perhaps even more important. It was considered "wonderful blood," the blood that had brought people's redemption. The image of a bleeding, crucified Christ was seen repeatedly in depictions of the day. Viewers were meant to think about Christ's pain and feel it themselves, mentally participating in his death on the cross. Flagellants, as we have seen, literally drew their own blood.

Religious anxieties, intellectual dissent, and social unrest combined to create new heretical movements in England and Bohemia. In England the Lollards (a derisive name given to them by their opponents, from the Middle Dutch *lollaerd*, or "mumbler") were inspired by the Oxford scholar John Wycliffe (c. 1330–1384), who had come to believe that the true church was the community of believers rather than the clerical hierarchy. Wycliffe criticized monasticism, excommunication, and the Mass. He wanted people to read the Bible in the vernacular rather than in Latin, arguing that true believers, not corrupt priests, formed the church.

Wycliffe's followers included scholars and members of the gentry (lesser nobles), as well as artisans and other humbler folk. His supporters translated the Bible into English and produced many sermons to publicize his views. They influenced the priest John Ball, one of the leaders of Wat Tyler's Rebellion. Ball rallied the crowds with the chant "When Adam dug and Eve spun / Who then was the gentleman?" From questioning the church hierarchy, some Lollards advanced to challenging social inequality of every sort. After Wycliffe's death, the Lollards were persecuted in England. Groups of them remained underground, only to reemerge with the coming of the Reformation (see Chapter 12).

The Bohemian Hussites—named after one of their leaders, Jan Hus (1372?–1415)—had greater success. Their central demand—that the faithful receive not just the bread (the body) but also the wine (the blood) at Mass—brought together several passionately held desires and beliefs. The blood of Christ was particularly important to the devout, and the Hussite call to allow the laity to drink the wine from the chalice reflected this focus on its redemptive power. Furthermore, the call for communion in both bread and wine signified a desire for equality. Bohemia was an exceptionally divided country, with an urban German-speaking elite, including merchants, artisans, bishops, and scholars, and a Czech-speaking nobility and peasantry that was beginning to seek better opportunities. (Hus himself was a Czech of peasant stock who became a professor at the University of Prague.) When priests celebrated Mass, they had the privilege of drinking the wine. The Hussites, who were largely Czech laity, wanted the same privilege and, with it, recognition of their dignity and worth.

Condemned by the church as a heretic, Hus was protected by the Bohemian nobility until he was lured to the Council of Constance by the Holy Roman Emperor Sigismund "to justify himself before all men." Though promised safe conduct, Hus was arrested when he arrived at the council. After refusing to recant his views, he was declared a heretic and burned at the stake.

Hus's death caused an uproar, and his movement became a full-scale national revolt of Czechs against Germans. Sigismund called crusades against the Hussites, but all of his expeditions were soundly defeated. Radical groups of Hussites organized several new communities in southern Bohemia at Mount Tabor, named after the New Testament spot where the transfiguration of Christ was thought to have taken place (Matt. 7:1–8). Here the radicals attempted to live according to the example of the first Apostles. They recognized no secular lord, gave women some political rights, and created a simple liturgy in the Czech language. Negotiations with Sigismund and his successor led by 1450 to the Hussites' tentative incorporation into the Bohemian political system and the right to receive communion in "both kinds" (wine and bread). The Hussites made Bohemia intensely aware of its Czech, rather than its German, identity.

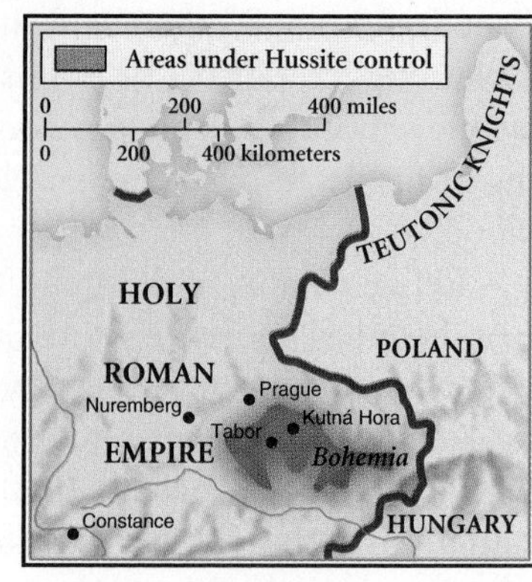

The Hussite Revolution, 1415–1436

REVIEW What crises did Europeans confront in the fourteenth and fifteenth centuries, and how did they handle them?

The New Map of Europe

As both a symptom and a result of these crises, political consolidation was taking place all across Europe in the period 1340–1500. As we have seen, the Ottoman Empire joined European powers in the Balkans. Eastern Europe took shape when the capital of the Holy Roman Empire moved to Prague and the duke of Lithuania married the queen of Poland, uniting those two states. In western Europe, the union of Aragon and Castile via the marriage of their respective rulers created Spain. In England and France, consolidation meant the strengthening of the central monarchies. The few states that organized and maintained themselves as republics—Switzerland, Venice, and Florence—were run by elites. Nowhere was the consolidation of the period clearer than in Italy. In 1340 it was dotted with numerous small city-states. By 1500 it was dominated by five major powers: Milan, Venice, and Florence in the north, the papacy in the middle, and the kingdom of Naples in the south.

New States in Eastern Europe

In the eastern half of the Holy Roman Empire, Bohemia gained new status as the seat of the Luxembourg imperial dynasty (Emperor Sigismund was its last representative). This development bred a religious and political crisis when the Hussites clashed with Sigismund. The chief beneficiary of the violence was the nobility, both Catholic and Hussite, but they quarreled among themselves, especially about who should be king. No Joan of Arc appeared to declare the national will, and most of Europe considered Bohemia a heretic state.

Farther north, it was the cities rather than the landed nobility that held power. Allied cities, such as the Hanseatic League (see page 376), were common. By the fourteenth century, the Hanseatic League linked the Baltic coast with Russia, Norway, the British Isles, France, and even (via imperial cities like Augsburg and Nuremberg) the cities of Italy. When threatened by rival powers in Denmark and Norway in 1367–1370, the league waged war and won the peace. In the fifteenth century it confronted new rivals and began a long and slow decline.

To the east of the Hanseatic cities, two new monarchies took shape in northeastern Europe: Poland and Lithuania. Poland had begun to form in the tenth century. Powerful nobles soon dominated it, and Mongol invasions devastated the land. But recovery was under way by 1300. Unlike almost every other part of Europe, Poland expanded demographically and economically during the fourteenth century. Jews migrated there to escape persecution in western Europe, and both Jewish and German settlers helped build thriving towns like Cracow. Monarchical consolidation began thereafter.

On Poland's eastern flank was Lithuania, the only major holdout from Christianity in eastern Europe. As it expanded into southern Russia, however, its grand dukes flirted with both the Roman Catholic and Orthodox churches. In 1386, Grand Duke Jogailo (c. 1351–1434), taking advantage of a hiatus in the Polish ruling dynasty, united both states when he married Queen Jadwiga of Poland, received a Catholic baptism, and was elected by the Polish nobility as King Wladyslaw II ("Jagiello"). As part of the negotiations prior to these events, he promised to convert Lithuania, and after his coronation he sent churchmen there to begin the long, slow process. The union of Poland and Lithuania lasted, with some interruptions, until 1772 (Map 11.4, page 410).

Powerful States in Western Europe

Four powerful states dominated western Europe during the fifteenth century. The kingdom of Spain and the duchy of Burgundy were created by marriage; the newly powerful kingdoms of France and England were forged in the crucible of war. By the end of the century, however, Burgundy had disappeared, leaving three exceptionally powerful monarchies.

Decades of violence on the Iberian peninsula ended when Isabella of Castile and Ferdinand of Aragon married in 1469 and restored law and order in the decades that followed. Castile was the powerhouse, with Aragon its lesser neighbor and Navarre a pawn between the two. When the king and queen joined forces, they ruled together over their separate dominions, allowing each to retain its traditional laws and privileges. The union of

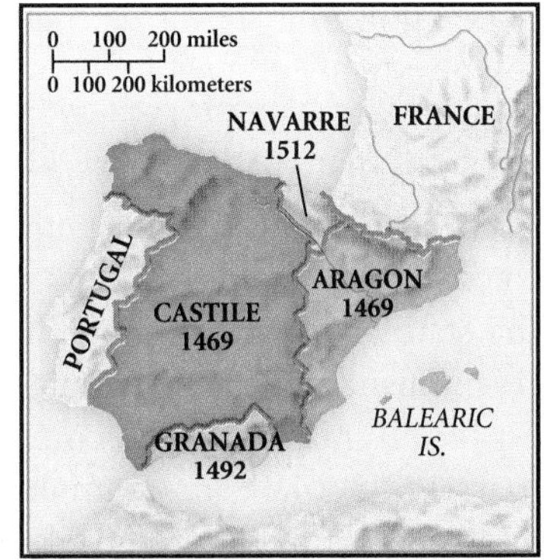

Unification of Spain, Late Fifteenth Century

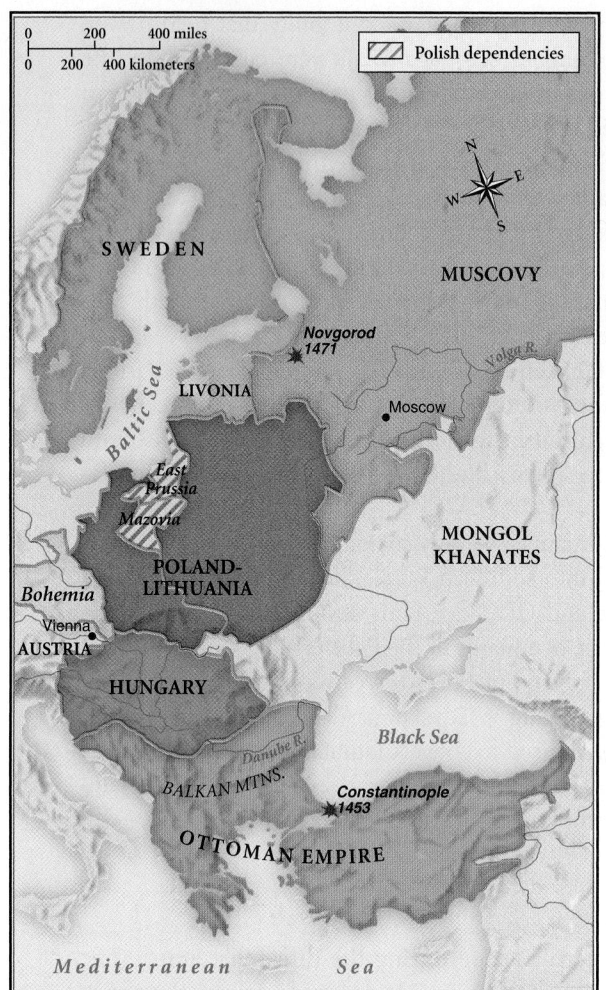

Map 11.4 Eastern Europe in the Fifteenth Century
Crucial to the new political developments of the fifteenth century was the rise of Muscovy and Poland-Lithuania.

Castile and Aragon was the first step toward a united Spain and a centralized monarchy there.

Relying on a lucrative taxation system, pliant meetings of the cortes (the representative institution that voted taxes), and an ideology that glorified the monarchy, Ferdinand and Isabella consolidated their power. They had an extensive bureaucracy to handle financial matters and a well-staffed writing office. They sent their own officials to rule over towns that had previously been self-governing, and they established regional courts of law.

Once Ferdinand and Isabella established their rule over Castile and Aragon, they sought to impose religious uniformity and purity. First they began systematically persecuting the *conversos* (converts)—Jews who had converted to Christianity in the aftermath of vicious attacks on Jews at Seville, Córdoba, Toledo, and other Spanish towns in 1391. During the first half of the fifteenth century they and their descendants (still called conversos, even though their children had been born and baptized in the Christian faith) took advantage of the opportunities open to educated Christians, in many instances rising to high positions in both the church and the state and marrying into "Old Christian" families. The conversos' success bred resentment, and their commitment to Christianity was questioned as well.

Local massacres of conversos began even before Isabella and Ferdinand married. In 1467, for example, two conversos in Toledo were hanged "as traitors and captains of the heretical conversos." The terms "traitors" and "heretical" are telling: because conversos were technically no longer Jews, their persecution was justified by branding them as heretics who undermined the monarchy. In 1478, Ferdinand and Isabella set up the Inquisition in Spain to continue, on behalf of the crown, what the towns had started. Treating the conversos as heretics, the inquisitors imposed harsh sentences, expelling or burning most of them. That was not enough (in the view of the monarchs) to purify the land. In 1492, Ferdinand and Isabella decreed that all Jews in Spain must convert or leave the country. Some did convert, but the experiences of the former conversos soured most on the prospect, and many Jews—perhaps 150,000—left Spain, scattering around the Mediterranean.

Meanwhile, Ferdinand and Isabella determined to defeat Granada, the last Muslim stronghold in Spain. Disunity within Granada's ruling family allowed the conquest to proceed, and in January 1492—just a few months before they expelled the Jews—Ferdinand and Isabella made their triumphal entry into the Alhambra, the former residence of the Muslim king of Granada. Although they initially promised freedom of religion to the Muslims who chose to remain, the royal couple also provided a fleet of boats to evacuate those who chose exile. In 1502, they demanded that all Muslims adopt Christianity or leave the kingdom.

United with less tumult, the duchy of Burgundy—created when the duke of Burgundy and heiress of Flanders married in 1369—was nevertheless disunited linguistically and geographically. Its success and expansion in the fifteenth century were the result of military might and careful statecraft. Soon, however, Burgundy fell to the militias of its neighbors. The chief importance of the duchy of Burgundy was its support of the arts; the dukes were great patrons of Renaissance culture.

By contrast, France, one of Burgundy's neighbors, became more powerful in the years before 1500. It made a quick recovery from the Hundred Years' War and expanded under Louis XI (r. 1461–1483). Soon after most of Burgundy fell to him, Louis also inherited much of southern France. After he inherited claims to the duchy of Milan and the kingdom of Naples, he was ready to invade Italy. By the end of the century, France had doubled its territory, assuming boundaries close to its modern ones, and was looking to expand even further.

To strengthen royal power at home, Louis promoted industry and commerce, imposed permanent salt and land taxes, maintained western Europe's first standing army (created by his predecessor), and suspended the meetings of the estates, which included the clergy, the nobility, and representatives from the major towns of France. The French kings had already increased their power with important concessions from the papacy. In addition, the Pragmatic Sanction of Bourges (1438) had asserted the superiority of a general church council over the pope. Claiming special sacredness because of their anointment, the kings established what would come to be known as Gallicanism (after Gaul, the ancient Roman name for France), in which the French king would effectively control ecclesiastical revenues and the appointment of French bishops.

The experience of England was only slightly less fortunate. The Hundred Years' War led to intermittent civil wars that came to be called the Wars of the Roses (1460s–1485). They ended with the victory of Henry Tudor, who took the title of Henry VII (r. 1485–1509). Though long, the Wars of the Roses caused relatively little damage; the battles were generally short, and, in the words of one chronicler, "neither the country, nor the people nor the houses, were wasted, destroyed or demolished, but the calamities and misfortunes of the war fell only upon the soldiers, and especially on the nobility."

As a result, the English economy continued to grow during the fifteenth century. The cloth industry expanded considerably, and the English used much of the raw wool they had been exporting to the Low Countries to manufacture goods at home. London merchants, taking a vigorous role in trade, also assumed greater political prominence, not only in governing London but also as bankers to kings and members of Parliament. In the countryside the landed classes—the nobility, the gentry (the lesser nobility), and the yeomanry (free farmers)—benefited from rising farm and land-rent income as the population increased slowly but steadily. The Tudor monarchs took advantage of the general prosperity to bolster both their treasury and their power.

It did not matter whether a state was run by a monarch or a small elite; consolidation was the watchword. Switzerland, Venice, and Florence were republics that prided themselves on traditions of self-rule. At the same time, however, they were in every case dominated by elites—or even by one family.

In the late thirteenth century, Swiss cantons had formed an alliance that eventually became the Swiss Confederation (see page 377). Though not united by a comprehensive constitution, the Swiss Confederation was nevertheless an effective political force. Wealthy merchants and tradesmen dominated the cities of the confederation, and in the fifteenth century they managed to supplant the landed nobility. At the same time, the power of the rural communes gave some ordinary folk political importance. No king, duke, or count ever became head of the confederation. In its fiercely independent stance against the Holy Roman Empire, it became a symbol of republican freedom. Yet it was also dominated by the wealthy. Poor Swiss foot soldiers made their living by hiring themselves out as mercenaries, fueling the wars of kings in the rest of Europe.

Similarly, Venice proudly proclaimed itself a republic but was ruled by a small elite. Built on a lagoon, Venice by 1400 ruled an extensive empire. Its merchant ships plied the waters stretching from the Black Sea to the Mediterranean and out to the Atlantic Ocean, and it had an excellent navy. Now, for the first time, it turned its attention inland, looking to conquer the cities of northern Italy. In the early fifteenth century, Venice took over Brescia, Verona, Padua, Belluno, and many other cities, eventually coming up against the equally powerful city-state of Milan to its west. Between 1450 and 1454, two coalitions—one led by Milan, the other by Venice—fought for territorial control of the eastern half of northern Italy. Financial exhaustion and fear of an invasion by France or the Ottoman Turks led to the Peace of Lodi in 1454. With that peace, it was clear that Italy was no longer a collection of small cities and their contados (the surrounding countryside) but a country of large, territorial city-states.

It is no accident that the Peace of Lodi was signed one year after the Ottoman conquest of Constantinople; Venice wanted to redirect its might against the Turks. But the Venetians also knew that peace was good for business; they traded with the Ottomans, and the two powers influenced each other's art and culture. Gentile Bellini's portrait of Mehmed is a good example of the importance of Venetian artists at the Ottoman court.

Venice was never ruled by a signore (lord). Far from being a hereditary monarch, the doge—the leading magistrate at Venice—was elected by the Great Council. But that council itself was dominated by the most important families. It is unclear why the lower classes at Venice did not rebel and demand their own political power, as happened in so many other Italian cities. The answer may be that Venice's foundation on water demanded so much central planning, citywide effort to maintain buildings and services, and the dedication of public funds to provide the population with necessities that it fostered a greater sense of community than could be found elsewhere.

Florence, like Venice, was also a republic. Unlike Venice, it came to be ruled by one family. Also unlike Venice, its society and political life were turbulent, as social classes and political factions competed for power. The most important of these civil uprisings was the Ciompi Revolt of 1378. Named after the wool workers (*ciompi*), laborers so lowly they had not been allowed to form a guild, the revolt led to the creation of a guild, along with a new distribution of power in the city. By 1382, however, the upper classes were once again monopolizing the government, and now with even less sympathy for the commoners.

By 1434, the Medici family had become the dominant power in Florence. The patriarch of this family, Cosimo de' Medici (1389–1464), founded his political power on the wealth of the Medici bank, which handled papal finances and had numerous branch offices in Italian and northern European cities. Backed by this money, Cosimo took over Florentine politics. He determined which men could take public office, and he established new committees made up of men loyal to him to govern the city. He kept the old forms of the Florentine constitution intact, governing behind the scenes not by force but through a broad consensus among the ruling elite.

Cosimo's grandson Lorenzo the Magnificent (1449–1492), who assumed power in 1467, bolstered the regime's legitimacy with his patronage of the humanities and arts. He himself was a poet and avid collector of antiquities. He intended to build a grand library made of marble at his palace but died before it was completed. More successful was his sculpture garden, which he filled with ancient works. Serving on various Florentine committees in charge of building, renovating, and adorning the churches of the city, Lorenzo employed important artists and architects to work on his own palaces as well. He probably encouraged the young Michelangelo; he certainly patronized the poet Angelo Poliziano, whose verses inspired Botticelli's *Birth of Venus* (see the illustration on page 421). No wonder writers and poets sang his praises.

But the Medici family also had enemies. In 1478, Lorenzo narrowly escaped an assassination attempt, and his successor was driven out of Florence in 1494. The Medici returned to power in 1512, only to be driven out again in 1527. In 1530, the republic fell for good as the Medici once again took power, this time declaring themselves dukes of Florence.

The Tools of Power

Whether monarchies, duchies, or republics, the newly consolidated states of the fifteenth century exercised their power more thoroughly than ever before. Sometimes they reached into the intimate lives of their subjects or citizens.

A good example of the ways in which governments peeked into people's lives—and picked their pockets—is the Florentine *catasto*. This was an inventory of households within the city and its outlying territory made for the purposes of taxation in 1427. The Domesday survey conducted in England in 1086 had been the most complete census of its day. But the catasto bested Domesday in thoroughness and inquisitiveness. It inquired about names, types of houses, and animals. It asked people to identify their trades, and their answers reveal the levels of Florentine society, ranging from agricultural laborers with no land of their own to soldiers, cooks, grave diggers, scribes, merchants, doctors, wine dealers, innkeepers, and tanners. The catasto inquired about private and public investments, real estate holdings, and taxable assets. Finally, it turned to the sex of the head of the family, his or her age and marital status, and the number of mouths to feed in the household. An identification number was assigned to each household.

The catasto shows that in 1427 Florence and its outlying regions had a population of more than 260,000. Although the city itself had only thirty-eight thousand inhabitants (about 15 percent of the total population), it held 67 percent of the wealth. Some 60 percent of Florentine households belonged to the "little people"—artisans and small merchants. The "fat people" (*popolo grosso,* what we would call the upper middle class) made up 30 percent of the urban population and included wealthy merchants, leading artisans, notaries, doctors, and other professionals. At the bottom of the hierarchy were slaves and servants, largely women from the surrounding countryside employed in domestic service. At the top, a tiny elite of wealthy patricians, bankers, and wool merchants controlled the state and owned more than one-quarter of its wealth. This was the group that produced the Medici family.

Most Florentine households consisted of at least six people, not all of whom were members of the family. Wealthier families had more children, while childless couples existed almost exclusively among the poor. The rich gave their infants to wet nurses to breast-feed, while the poor often left their children to public charity. Florence was rightly proud of its orphanage: it both provided for the city's poorer children and was built in the newest and finest Renaissance style.

REVIEW What were the chief political entities in the year 1500, and how did they come to be so powerful?

New Forms of Thought and Expression: The Renaissance

Whether monarchies, principalities, or republics, states throughout Europe used their new power and money to foster Renaissance writers, artists, and musicians. Most textbooks divide the period 1340–1500 into two chapters, one covering the crises and the other the Renaissance. But this is misleading; both phenomena happened at the same time. In many ways, the Renaissance was a response to the crises. It revived elements of the classical past—the Greek philosophers before Aristotle, Hellenistic artists, and Roman rhetoricians—in order to deal with contemporary issues. Humanists modeled their writing on the Latin of Cicero, architects looked back to ancient notions of public space, artists adopted classical forms, and musicians used classical texts. Yet they were very much involved in the movements of their own day.

Renaissance Humanism

Humanism was a literary and linguistic movement—an attempt to revive classical Latin (and later Greek), as well as the values and sensibilities that came with the language. It began among men and women living in the Italian city-states, where many saw parallels between their urban, independent lives and the experiences of the city-states of the ancient world. Humanism was a way to confront the crises—and praise the advances—of the fourteenth through sixteenth centuries. Humanists wrote poetry, history, moral philosophy, and grammar books, all patterned on classical models.

A good example of the aim of humanists is provided by three delegates to the Council of Constance—Cincius Romanus, Poggius Bracciolinus, and Bartholomaeus Politianus. One day they decided to take time off from the council for a "rescue mission." Cincius described the escapade to one of his Latin teachers back in Italy:

> In Germany there are many monasteries with libraries full of Latin books. This aroused the hope in me that some of the works of Cicero, Varro, Livy, and other great men of learning, which seem to have completely vanished, might come to light if a careful search were instituted. A few days ago, [we] went by agreement to the town of St. Gall. As soon as we went into the library [of the monastery there], we found *Jason's Argonauticon,* written by C. Valerius Flaccus in verse that is both splendid and dignified and not far removed from poetic majesty. Then we found some discussion in prose of a number of Cicero's orations.

Cicero, Varro, Livy, and Valerius Flaccus were pagan Latin writers. Even though Cincius and his friends were working for Pope John XXIII, they loved the writings of the ancients, whose Latin was, in their view, "splendid and dignified," unlike the Latin that was used in their own time, which they found debased and faulty. They saw themselves as the resuscitators of ancient language, literature, and culture. Cincius continued:

> When we carefully inspected the nearby tower of the church of St. Gall in which countless books were kept like captives and the library neglected and infested with dust, worms, soot, and all the things associated with the destruction of books, we all burst into tears. . . . Truly if this library could speak for itself, it would cry loudly: ". . . Snatch me from this prison. . . ." There were in that monastery an abbot and monks totally devoid of any knowledge of literature. What barbarous hostility to the Latin tongue! What damned dregs of humanity!

The monks were barbarians, and Cincius and his companions were heroic raiders swooping in to liberate the captive books.

That Cincius was employed by the pope yet considered the monks of St. Gall barbarians was no oddity. Most humanists combined sincere Christian piety with their new appreciation of the pagan past. Besides, they needed to work in order to live, and they took employment where they found it. Some humanists worked for the church, others were civil servants, and still others were notaries. A few were rich men who had a taste for literary subjects.

The first humanist, most historians agree, was Francis Petrarch (1304–1374). He was born in Arezzo, a town about fifty miles southeast of Florence. As a boy, he moved around a lot (his father was exiled from Florence), ending up in the region of Avignon, where he received his earliest schooling and fell in love with classical literature. After a brief flirtation with legal studies at the behest of his father, Petrarch gave up law and devoted himself to writing poetry, in both Italian and Latin. When writing in Italian, he drew on the traditions of the troubadours, dedicating poems of longing to an unattainable and idealized woman named Laura. When writing in Latin, he was much influenced by classical poetry.

On the one hand, a boyhood in Avignon made Petrarch sensitive to the failings of the church: he was the writer who coined the phrase "Babylonian captivity." On the other hand, he took minor religious orders there, which afforded him a modest living. Struggling between what he considered a life of dissipation (he fathered two children out of wedlock) and a religious vocation, he resolved the conflict at last in his book *On the Solitary Life,* in which he claimed that the solitude needed for reading the classics was akin to the solitude practiced by those who devoted themselves to God. For Petrarch, humanism was a vocation, a calling.

Less famous, but for that reason perhaps more representative of humanists in general, was Lauro Quirini (1420–1475?), the man who (as we saw at the start of this chapter) considered the Turks to be barbarians. Educated at the University of

Padua, Quirini eventually got a law degree there. He wrote numerous letters and essays, corresponding with other humanists on topics such as the nature of the state and the character of true nobility. He spent the last half of his life in Crete, where he traded various commodities—alum, cloth, wine, Greek books. Believing that the Ottomans had destroyed the libraries of Constantinople, he wrote to Pope Nicholas V, "The language and literature of the Greeks, invented, augmented, and perfected over so long a period with such labor and industry, will certainly perish." But the fact that he himself participated in the lively trade of Greek books proved his prediction wrong.

If Quirini represents the ordinary humanist, Giovanni Pico della Mirandola (1463–1494) was perhaps the most flamboyant. Born near Ferrara of a noble family, Pico received a humanist education at home before going on to Bologna to study law and to Padua to study philosophy. Soon he was picking up Hebrew, Aramaic, and Arabic. A convinced eclectic, he thought that Jewish mystical writings supported Christian Scriptures, and in 1486 he proposed that he publicly defend at Rome nine hundred theses drawn from diverse sources. The church found some of the theses heretical, however, and banned the whole affair. But Pico's *Oration on the Dignity of Man,* which he intended to deliver before his defense, summed up the humanist view of humanity: the creative individual, armed only with his (or her) "desires and judgment," could choose to become a boor or an angel. Humanity's potential was unlimited.

Christine de Pisan (c. 1365–c. 1430) exemplifies a humanist who chose to fashion herself into a writer and courtier. Born in Venice and educated in France, Christine de Pisan was married and then widowed young. Forced to support herself, her mother, and her three young children, she began to write poems inspired by classical models, depending on rich patrons to admire her work and pay her to write more. Many members of the upper nobility supported her, including Duke Philip the Bold of Burgundy, Queen Isabelle of Bavaria, and the English earl of Salisbury. But this cast of characters did not mean she sided with the English during the Hundred Years' War. On the contrary, she lamented the violence on all sides, and Joan of Arc's early victories inspired her to write a hymn to "the Maid":

> We've never heard
> About a marvel quite so great,
> For all the heroes who have lived
> In history can't measure up
> In bravery against the Maid.

Even more political was the humanist Niccolò Machiavelli (1469–1527), whose small handbook *The Prince* (1513) argued that the state was an artifice of human creation to be conquered, shaped, and administered by princes according to the principles of power politics. Was it better for a ruler to be loved or feared by his subjects? Machiavelli answered coldly: "It may be answered that one should wish to be both, but, because it is difficult to unite them in one person, it is much safer to be feared than loved." Today the word *Machiavellian* means "coldly calculating": the end justifies the means.

Some historians deny Machiavelli the status of a humanist. But when he wrote in *The Prince* about his study of the ancients, he was identifying himself with the humanist movement. His contemporaries certainly considered him one, appointing him (in 1498) chancellor of Florence, a position normally held by humanists.

Through their activities as educators, writers, and civil servants, professional humanists gave new vigor to the humanist curriculum of grammar, rhetoric, poetry, history, and moral philosophy. By the end of the fifteenth century, the Renaissance was a European-wide phenomenon, and the humanist agenda—a good command of classical Latin, with perhaps some knowledge of Greek—had come to be one of the requirements of an educated person.

The invention of the printing press in the 1440s by a German goldsmith named Johannes Gutenberg made the world of letters more accessible to a literate audience. The key to Gutenberg's innovation was movable type—reusable metal letters, numbers, and various other characters. The typesetter arranged the characters by hand, page by page, to create a printable text. The surface of the type was inked, and sheets of paper pressed against the type picked up an impression of the text. Numerous copies could be made with only a small amount of human labor. This was a revolutionary departure from the old practice of copying by hand, making possible the mass production of identical books and pamphlets.

The printing press depended on paper production. The art of papermaking came to Europe from the Islamic world (which had borrowed it from China). By the fourteenth century, paper mills were operating in Italy, producing paper that was more fragile but much cheaper than parchment or vellum, the animal skins that Europeans had previously used for writing. To produce paper, old rags were soaked in a chemical solution, beaten by mallets into a pulp, washed with water, treated, and dried in sheets—a method that still produces good-quality paper today.

After the 1440s, printing spread rapidly from Germany to other European countries. The German cities of Cologne, Strasbourg, Nuremberg, and Augsburg all had major presses. In 1467, two German printers established the first press in Rome and produced twelve thousand volumes in five years, a feat that previously would have required a thousand scribes working full-time. By 1480, many Italian cities had established their own presses. In the 1490s, the German city of Frankfurt am Main became an international meeting place for printers and booksellers. The Frankfurt Book Fair, where printers from different nations exhibited their newest titles, represented a major international cultural event and remains an unbroken tradition to this day.

The invention of mechanical printing gave rise to a communications revolution as significant as the widespread use of the personal computer today. The multiplication of standardized texts altered the thinking habits of Europeans by freeing individuals from having to memorize everything they learned; it made possible the relatively speedy and inexpensive dissemination of knowledge; and it created a wider community of scholars, no longer dependent on personal patronage or church sponsorship for texts. Printing facilitated the free expression and exchange of ideas, and its disruptive potential did not go unnoticed by political and ecclesiastical authorities. Emperors and bishops in Germany, the homeland of the printing industry, moved quickly to issue censorship regulations.

The Prestige of Renaissance Art

The lure of the classical past was as strong in the arts as in literature. Architects and artists admired ancient Athens and Rome and drew on their traditions. At the same time, they modified classical models, combining them with medieval forms. Working for patrons—churchmen, secular rulers, rich patrons, or republican governments—Renaissance artists used both past and present to express the patriotism, religious piety, and prestige of their benefactors.

The change was clear even on the streets of the cities. Medieval cities had grown without planning: streets turned back on themselves; churches sat cheek by jowl with private houses. In the Renaissance, however, the whole city was reimagined as a place of order and harmony. The Florentine architect Leon Battista Alberti (1404–1472) proposed that each building in a city be proportioned to fit harmoniously with all the others and that city spaces allow for all necessary public activities: there should be market squares, play areas, and grounds for military exercises. In Renaissance cities, the agora and forum (the public spaces of the classical world) appeared once again, but in a new guise, as the piazza (a plaza or open square). Architects carved out spaces around their new buildings, and they built graceful covered walkways (porticos) of columns and arches. The artist Pietro Perugino (1445–1523) depicted Christ giving the keys of the kingdom of heaven to the Apostle Peter in an idealized city piazza, at the center of which was a perfectly proportioned church.

The same principles applied to the architecture of the Renaissance court. At Urbino, Duke Federico, a great patron of humanists and artists, commissioned a new palace. The architect, probably Luciano Laurana, designed its courtyard as a public space, a sort of piazza within a palace. A city had both public and private spaces; similarly, public rooms at the ducal palace gave way to a modest space for the duke's private quarters: a bedroom, a bathroom, a chapel, and, most important, his study, filled with books.

The Gothic cathedral of the Middle Ages was a cluster of graceful spikes and soaring arches. Renaissance architects appreciated its vigor and energy, but they tamed it with regular geometrical forms inspired by classical buildings. Classical forms were applied to previously built structures as well as new ones. Florence's Santa Maria Novella, for example, had been a typical Gothic church when it was first built. But when Alberti, the man who believed in public spaces and harmonious buildings, was commissioned to replace its facade, he drew on Roman temple forms.

Powerful groups within the cities, whether guilds, communes, or princely families, sponsored the new art. In 1400, the Florentines held a competition for new bronze doors for their baptistery. The entry of Lorenzo Ghiberti (1378?–1455) depicted the sacrifice of Isaac, the Old Testament story in which God tests Abraham's

Pietro Perugino, *Christ Giving the Keys to St. Peter*
This fresco on one of the side walls of the Sistine Chapel in the papal palace at Rome (now the Vatican) depicts the transfer of power in Christ's church. Inspired by the architecture of the ancient world, Perugino set the action in a large piazza flanked by Roman triumphal arches. (© Vatican Museums and Galleries, Vatican City, Italy/The Bridgeman Art Library.)

faith by ordering him to sacrifice his son. Cast in one piece, a major technological feat at the time, it shows a young, nude Isaac modeled on a classical sculpture. At the same time, Ghiberti drew on medieval models for his depiction of Abraham. In this way, he gracefully melded old and new elements—and won the contest.

In addition to using the forms of classical art, Renaissance artists also mined the ancient world for new subjects. Venus, the Roman goddess of love and beauty, had numerous stories attached to her name. At first glance, *The Birth of Venus* (page 421) by Sandro Botticelli (c. 1445–1510) seems simply an illustration of the tale of Venus's rise from the sea. In fact, however, Botticelli's work is much more complicated, drawing on the ideas of Marsilio Ficino (1433–1499) and the poetry of Angelo Poliziano (1454–1494). According to Ficino, Venus was "humanitas"—the essence of the humanities. For Poliziano, she was

> fair Venus, mother of the cupids.
> Zephyr bathes the meadow with dew
> spreading a thousand lovely fragrances:
> wherever he flies he clothes the countryside
> in roses, lilies, violets, and other flowers.

In Botticelli's painting, Zephyr, one of the winds, blows, while Venus receives a fine robe embroidered with leaves and flowers.

Sandro Botticelli, *The Birth of Venus*
Venus had been depicted in art before Botticelli's painting, but he was the first artist since antiquity to portray her in the nude. (© Galleria degli Uffizi, Florence, Italy/Giraudon/The Bridgeman Art Library.)

The Sacrifice of Isaac and *The Birth of Venus* show some of the ways in which Renaissance artists used ancient models. Other artists perfected perspective—the illusion of three-dimensional space—to a degree that even classical antiquity had not anticipated. The development of the laws of perspective accompanied the introduction of long-range weaponry, such as cannons. In fact, some artists who excelled in using perspective, such as Leonardo da Vinci (1452–1519), were military engineers as well. In Leonardo's painting *The Annunciation* (page 422), sight lines meeting at a point on the horizon open wide precisely where the angel kneels and Mary responds in surprise.

Ghiberti, Botticelli, and Leonardo were all Italian artists. While they were creating their works, a northern Renaissance was taking place as well. At the court of France during the Hundred Years' War, kings commissioned portraits of themselves—sometimes unflattering ones—just as Roman leaders had once commissioned their own busts. Soon it was the fashion for everyone who could afford it to have his or her portrait made, as naturalistically as possible. Compare the image of Joan of Arc on page 400 with the painting of the Virgin Mary and Chancellor Nicolas Rolin completed by the Dutch artist Jan van Eyck around 1433 (see page 423). The artist who depicted Joan wanted to show a young woman dressed

Leonardo da Vinci, *The Annunciation*
Working with a traditional Christian theme (the moment when the angel Gabriel announced to the Virgin Mary that she would give birth to Christ), Leonardo produced a work of great originality, drawing the viewer's eye from a vanishing point in the distance to the subject of the painting. The ability to subordinate the background to the foreground was a great contribution of Renaissance perspective. (Scala/Ministero per i Beni e le Attività Culturali/Art Resource, NY.)

in armor—any young woman. The image was meant to be symbolic. By contrast, van Eyck and his patron wanted to show a particular person, Nicolas Rolin. The very wrinkles of Rolin's neck proclaim his individuality. Though shown in a pious pose, Rolin is the key figure in the picture; the Virgin and baby Jesus sit a bit to the back and in the shadows. Meanwhile, the grand view of a city spreads out behind them, underscoring Rolin's stature in the community. Van Eyck was a master of perspective, and he used it here to emphasize Rolin's gravity and importance. Rolin was indeed an eminent man: he worked for the duke of Burgundy and was the founder of a hospital at Beaune and a religious order of nurses to serve it. Van Eyck conveyed his prominence in this portrait.

The Music of the Courts

Patrons of the new arts also used music to add glamour and glory to their courts and reputations. Renaissance rulers spent as much as 6 percent of their annual revenue to support musicians and composers. The Avignon papacy, in its own way one such court, was a major sponsor of sacred music. Whether secular or religious, music was appreciated for its ability to express the innermost feelings of the individual.

Every proper court had its own musicians. Some served as chaplains, writing music for the ruler's private chapel—the place where his court and household heard Mass. When Josquin Desprez (1440–1521) served as the duke of Ferrara's chaplain,

Jan van Eyck, *The Virgin of Chancellor Rolin*
Van Eyck portrays the Virgin and Chancellor Rolin as if they were contemporaries sharing a nice chat. Only the angel, who is placing a crown on the Virgin's head, suggests that something out of the ordinary is happening. (Erich Lessing/Art Resource, NY.)

he wrote a Mass that used the musical equivalents of the letters of the duke's name (the Italian version of *do re mi*) as its theme. Isabella d'Este (1474–1539), the daughter of the duke, employed her own musicians—singers, woodwind and string players, percussionists, and keyboard players—while her husband, the duke of Mantua, had his own band. When her brother sent her poems to copy, she had her favorite musician set them to music. This was one of the ways in which humanists and musicians worked together: the poems that interested composers and rulers alike were of the newest sort, patterned on classical forms. Isabella particularly favored Petrarch's poems.

The church, too, was a major sponsor of music. Every feast required music, and the papal schism inadvertently encouraged more musical production than usual, as rival popes tried to best one another in the realm of pageantry and sound. Churches needed choirs, and many composers got their start as choirboys. But that job could last well into adulthood. In the fourteenth century, the men who sang in the choir at Reims, for example, received a yearly stipend and an extra fee every time the choir sang the Mass and the liturgical offices of the day.

When the composer Johannes Ockeghem, chaplain for three French kings, died in 1497, his fellow musicians vied in expressing their grief in song. Josquin Desprez was among them, and his composition illustrates how the addition of classical elements to very traditional musical forms enhanced music's emotive power. Josquin's work combines personal grief with religious liturgy and the feelings expressed in classical elegies. The piece uses five voices. Inspired by classical mythology, four of the voices sing in the vernacular French about the "nymphs of the wood" coming together to mourn. But the fifth voice intones the words of the liturgy: "Requiescat in pace" (May he rest in peace). At the very moment in the song when the four vernacular voices lament Ockeghem's burial in the dark ground, the liturgical voice sings of the heavenly light. The contrast makes the song more moving. By drawing on the classical past, Renaissance musicians found new ways in which to express emotion.

REVIEW How and why did Renaissance humanists, artists, and musicians revive classical traditions?

On the Threshold of Global History

Only in the fifteenth century did Europe become a major player in world history. Before the maritime explorations of Portugal and Spain, Europe had remained at the periphery of world events. Fourteenth-century Mongols had been more interested in conquering China and Persia—lands with sophisticated cultures—than in invading Europe; Persian historians of the early fifteenth century dismissed Europeans as "barbaric Franks"; and China's Ming dynasty rulers, who sent maritime expeditions to Southeast Asia and East Africa around 1400, seemed unaware of Europeans, even though Marco Polo and other Italian merchants had appeared at the court of the preceding Mongol Yuan dynasty.

In the fifteenth century, Portuguese and Spanish vessels, followed a century later by English, French, and Dutch ships, sailed across the Atlantic, Indian, and Pacific oceans, bringing with them people, merchandise, crops, and diseases in a global exchange that would shape the modern world. For the first time, the people of the Americas were brought into contact with a larger historical force that threatened to destroy not only their culture but also their existence. European exploitation and conquest defined this historical era of transition from the medieval to the modern world, as Europeans left the Baltic and the Mediterranean for wider oceans.

The Divided Mediterranean

In the second half of the fifteenth century, the Mediterranean Sea, which had dominated medieval maritime trade, began to lose its preeminence to the Atlantic Ocean. To win control over the Mediterranean, the Ottomans embarked on an ambitious naval program to transform their empire into a major maritime power. War and piracy disrupted the flow of Christian trade: the Venetians mobilized all their resources to fight off Turkish advances, and the Genoese largely abandoned the eastern Mediterranean for trade opportunities presented by the Atlantic.

Mediterranean trade used ships made with relatively backward naval technology. The most common ship, the galley—a flat-bottomed vessel propelled mainly by oarsmen with the help of a sail—dated from the time of ancient Rome. Most galleys could not withstand open-ocean voyages, although Florentine and Genoese galleys did make long journeys to Flanders and England, hugging the coast for protection. The galley's dependence on human labor was a more serious handicap. Because prisoners of war and convicted criminals toiled as oarsmen on both Christian and Muslim ships, victory in war or the enforcement of criminal penalties was crucial to a state's ability to float large numbers of galleys. Slaves, too, sometimes provided the necessary labor.

Portuguese Confrontations

The exploration of the Atlantic began with the Portuguese (Map 11.5). By 1415, they had captured Ceuta on the Moroccan coast, establishing a foothold in Africa. Thereafter, Portuguese voyages sailed farther down the West African coast. By midcentury, a chain of Portuguese forts reached Guinea, protecting the trade in gold and slaves. At home, the royal house of Portugal financed the fleets, with crucial roles played by Prince Peter, regent between 1440 and 1448; his more famous younger brother Prince Henry the Navigator; and King John II. As a governor of the noble crusading Order of Christ, Henry financed many voyages out of the order's revenues. Private monies also helped, as leading Lisbon merchants participated in financing the gold and slave trades off the Guinea coast.

In 1455, Pope Nicholas V authorized Portuguese overseas expansion, praising King John II's crusading spirit and granting him and his successors a monopoly on trade with inhabitants of the newly "discovered" regions. In 1487–1488, Bartholomeu Dias took advantage of the prevailing winds in the South Atlantic to reach the Cape of Good Hope. A mere ten years later (1497–1499), under the captainship of Vasco da Gama, a Portuguese fleet rounded the cape and reached Calicut, India, center of the spice trade. By 1517, a chain of Portuguese forts dotted the Indian Ocean. In 1519, Ferdinand Magellan, a Portuguese sailor in Spanish service, led the first expedition to circumnavigate the globe.

In many ways a continuation of the struggle against the Muslims on the Iberian peninsula, Portugal's maritime voyages displayed that country's mixed motives of piety, glory, and greed. The sailors dreamed of finding gold mines in West Africa and a mysterious Christian kingdom established by a mythical "Prester John." They hoped to reach the spice-producing lands of South and Southeast Asia by sea and to bypass the Ottoman Turks, who controlled the traditional land routes between Europe and Asia.

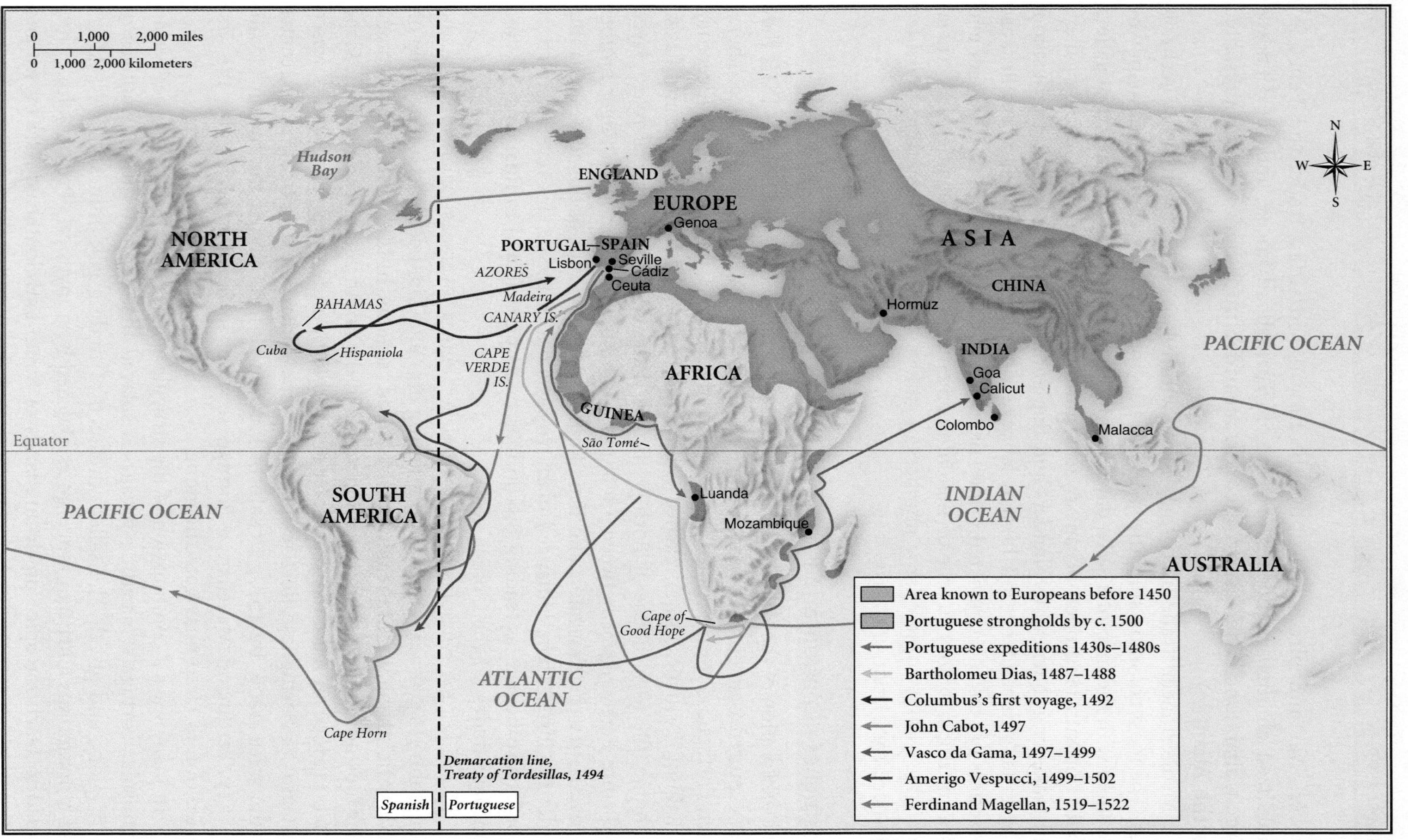

0 1,000 2,000 miles
0 1,000 2,000 kilometers
N
W
E
S
Hudson Bay
NORTH AMERICA
BAHAMAS
Cuba
Hispaniola
ENGLAND
EUROPE
Genoa
PORTUGAL
SPAIN
Lisbon
Seville
Cádiz
Ceuta
AZORES
Madeira
CANARY IS.
CAPE VERDE IS.
ASIA
CHINA
Hormuz
INDIA
Goa
Calicut
Colombo
Malacca
PACIFIC OCEAN
AFRICA
GUINEA
São Tomé
Equator
Luanda
Mozambique
SOUTH AMERICA
PACIFIC OCEAN
INDIAN OCEAN
AUSTRALIA
Cape of Good Hope
ATLANTIC OCEAN
Cape Horn
Demarcation line, Treaty of Tordesillas, 1494
Spanish
Portuguese
Area known to Europeans before 1450
Portuguese strongholds by c. 1500
Portuguese expeditions 1430s–1480s
Bartholomeu Dias, 1487–1488
Columbus's first voyage, 1492
John Cabot, 1497
Vasco da Gama, 1497–1499
Amerigo Vespucci, 1499–1502
Ferdinand Magellan, 1519–1522

The new voyages depended for their success on several technological breakthroughs. The lateen (triangular) sail permitted ships to tack against headwinds. Light caravels and heavy galleons, however different in size, were alike in using more than one mast and sail, harnessing wind—rather than human—power to move them. Better charts, maps, and instruments made long-distance voyages less risky.

After the voyages of Christopher Columbus, Portugal's interests clashed with those of Spain. Mediated by Pope Alexander VI, the 1494 Treaty of Tordesillas reconciled Portugal and Spain by dividing the Atlantic world between the two royal houses. A demarcation 370 leagues west of the Cape Verde Islands divided the Atlantic Ocean, reserving for Portugal the western coast of Africa and the route to India and giving Spain the oceans and lands to the west. Unwittingly, this agreement also allowed Portugal to claim Brazil in 1500, which Pedro Álvares Cabral (1467–1520) accidentally "discovered" on his voyage to India.

The Voyages of Columbus

Historians agree that Christopher Columbus (1451–1506) was born of Genoese parents; beyond that, we have little accurate information about this man who brought together the history of Europe and the Americas. In 1476, he arrived in Portugal, apparently a survivor in a naval battle between a Franco-Portuguese and a Genoese fleet. In 1479, he married a Portuguese noblewoman. He spent the next few years mostly in Portuguese service, gaining valuable experience in regular voyages down the west coast of Africa. In 1485, after the death of his wife, Columbus settled in Spain.

Fifteenth-century Europeans already knew that Asia lay beyond the vast Atlantic Ocean, and *The Travels of Marco Polo,* written more than a century earlier, still exerted a powerful hold on European images of the East. Columbus read it many times, along with other travel books, and proposed to sail west across the Atlantic to reach the lands of the khan, unaware that the Mongol Empire had already collapsed in eastern Asia. Vastly underestimating the distances, he dreamed of finding a new route to the East's gold and spices and partook of the larger European vision that had inspired the Portuguese voyages. (His critics had a much more accurate idea of the globe's size and of the difficulty of the venture. No one believed that the

Map 11.5 Early Voyages of World Exploration
At the end of the fifteenth century, Europeans began moving aggressively across the globe. Beginning with initial forays along the African coast, their voyages soon widened out to transatlantic crossings and, by 1522, the circumnavigation of the world. The web of arrows on this map suggests an earth bound together by many threads, and this is partly true, for never again would the two halves of the globe be isolated. At the same time, the threads pulled in one direction only—toward the Europeans. Africa was exploited for gold and slaves, while the discovery of precious metals fueled the explorations and settlements of Central and South America.

world was flat!) After the Portuguese and French monarchs rejected his proposal, Columbus found royal patronage with the recently proclaimed Catholic monarchs Isabella of Castile and Ferdinand of Aragon. In August 1492, equipped with a modest fleet of three ships and about ninety men, Columbus set sail across the Atlantic. His contract stipulated that he would claim Castilian sovereignty over any new land and inhabitants and share any profits with the crown.

Reaching what we know today as the Bahamas on October 12, Columbus mistook the islands to be part of the East Indies, not far from Japan and "the lands of the Great Khan." As the Castilians explored the Caribbean islands, they encountered communities of peaceful Indians, the Arawaks, who were awed by the Europeans' military technology, not to mention their appearance. Exchanging gifts of beads and broken glass for Arawak gold—an exchange that convinced Columbus of the trusting nature of the Indians—the crew established peaceful relationships with many communities. Yet despite many positive entries in the ship's log referring to Columbus's personal goodwill toward the Indians, the Europeans' objectives were clear: find gold, subjugate the Indians, and propagate Christianity.

Excited by the prospect of easy riches, many flocked to join Columbus's second voyage. When Columbus departed Cádiz in September 1493, he commanded seventeen ships that carried between twelve hundred and fifteen hundred men, many believing all they had to do was "load the gold into the ships." Failing to find the imaginary gold mines and spices, however, the colonial enterprise quickly switched its focus to finding slaves. Columbus and his crew first enslaved the Caribs, enemies of the Arawaks; in 1494, Columbus proposed a regular slave trade based in Hispaniola. The Spaniards exported enslaved Indians to Spain, and slave traders sold them in Seville. Soon the Spaniards began importing sugarcane from the Portuguese island of Madeira and forced large numbers of Indians to work on plantations to produce more sugar for export to Europe. Columbus himself was edged out of this new enterprise. When the Spanish monarchs realized the vast potential for material gain that lay in their new dominions, they asserted direct royal authority by sending officials and priests to the Americas, which were later named after the Italian Amerigo Vespucci, who led a voyage across the Atlantic in 1499–1502.

Columbus's place in history embodies the fundamental transformations of his age. A Genoese in the service of Portuguese and Spanish employers, Columbus's career illustrates the changing balance between the Mediterranean and the Atlantic. His voyages of 1492–1493 would eventually draw a triangle of exchange among Europe, the Americas, and Africa, an exchange gigantic in its historical impact and its human cost.

A New Era in Slavery

During the Middle Ages and Renaissance, female slaves served as domestic servants in wealthy Mediterranean homes, and male slaves toiled in the galleys of Ottoman and Christian fleets. Some were captured in war or by piracy; others, Africans, were

Dürer's Engraving of Katharina, an African Woman
Like other artists in early-sixteenth-century Europe, Albrecht Dürer would have seen in person Africans who were living in Portugal and Spain as students, servants, and slaves. (Foto Marburg/Art Resource, NY.)

sold by African and Bedouin traders to Christian buyers. In western Asia, impoverished parents sometimes sold their children into servitude. Many people in the Balkans became slaves when their land was devastated by Ottoman invasions. Slaves were Greek, Slav, European, African, and Turk.

The Portuguese maritime voyages changed this picture. From the fifteenth century on, Africans increasingly filled the ranks of slaves. Exploiting warfare in West Africa, the Portuguese traded in gold and "pieces," as African slaves were called, a practice condemned at home by some conscientious clergy. Critical voices, however, could not deny the enormous profits the slave trade brought to Portugal. Most slaves toiled on the sugar plantations of the Portuguese Atlantic islands and in Brazil. A fortunate few labored as domestic servants in Portugal, where African freedmen and slaves, some 35,000 in the early sixteenth century, constituted almost 3 percent of the population, a much higher percentage than in other European countries. In the Americas, slavery would flourish as an institution of exploitation.

Europeans in a New World

In 1500, on the eve of European invasion, the native peoples of the Americas were divided into many sedentary and nomadic societies. Among the settled peoples, the largest political and social organizations were in the Mexican and Peruvian highlands. The Aztecs and Incas ruled over subjugated Indian populations in their respective empires. With an elaborate religious culture and a rigid social and political hierarchy, the Aztecs and Incas based their civilizations in large urban capitals.

The Spanish explorers organized their expeditions to the mainland from a base in the Caribbean. Two prominent leaders, Hernán Cortés (1485–1547) and Francisco Pizarro (c. 1475–1541), gathered men and arms and set off in search of gold. Catholic priests accompanied the fortune hunters to bring Christianity to allegedly uncivilized peoples and thus to justify brutal conquests. His small band swollen by peoples who had been subjugated by the Aztecs, Cortés captured the Aztec capital, Tenochtitlán, in 1519. To the south, Pizarro conquered the Andean highlands, exploiting a civil war between rival Incan kings. By the mid-sixteenth century, the Spanish Empire stretched unbroken from Mexico to Chile.

Not to be outdone by the Spaniards, other European powers joined the scramble for gold in the New World. In 1500, a Portuguese fleet led by Pedro Álvares Cabral landed in Brazil, but Portugal did not begin colonizing there until 1532, when it established a permanent fort on the coast. In North America, the French went in search of a "northwest passage" to China. By 1504, French fishermen had appeared in Newfoundland. Thirty years later, Jacques Cartier led three voyages that explored the St. Lawrence River as far as Montreal. An early attempt in 1541 to settle Canada failed because of the harsh winter and Indian hostility, and John Cabot's 1497 voyage to find a northern route to Asia also failed. More permanent settlements in Canada and the present-day United States would succeed only in the seventeenth century.

REVIEW Which European countries led the way in maritime expansion, and what were their motives?

Conclusion

Confronted by disease, economic contraction, war, popular uprisings, and a disgraced papacy, Europe's ruling classes grasped the reins of power ever more tightly, creating more centralized and institutionalized states. Muscovy and Poland-Lithuania formed in the east, while western European kings, dukes, and even republics consolidated their rule.

Surrounding themselves with artists, musicians, and humanists, these new-style rulers supported the Renaissance—an attempt to resuscitate the classical past for the purposes of the present. The Renaissance, which emphasized human potential and achievement, was one of Europe's most brilliant periods of artistic activity, one that glorified both God and humanity. Inspired by ancient models, Renaissance humanists

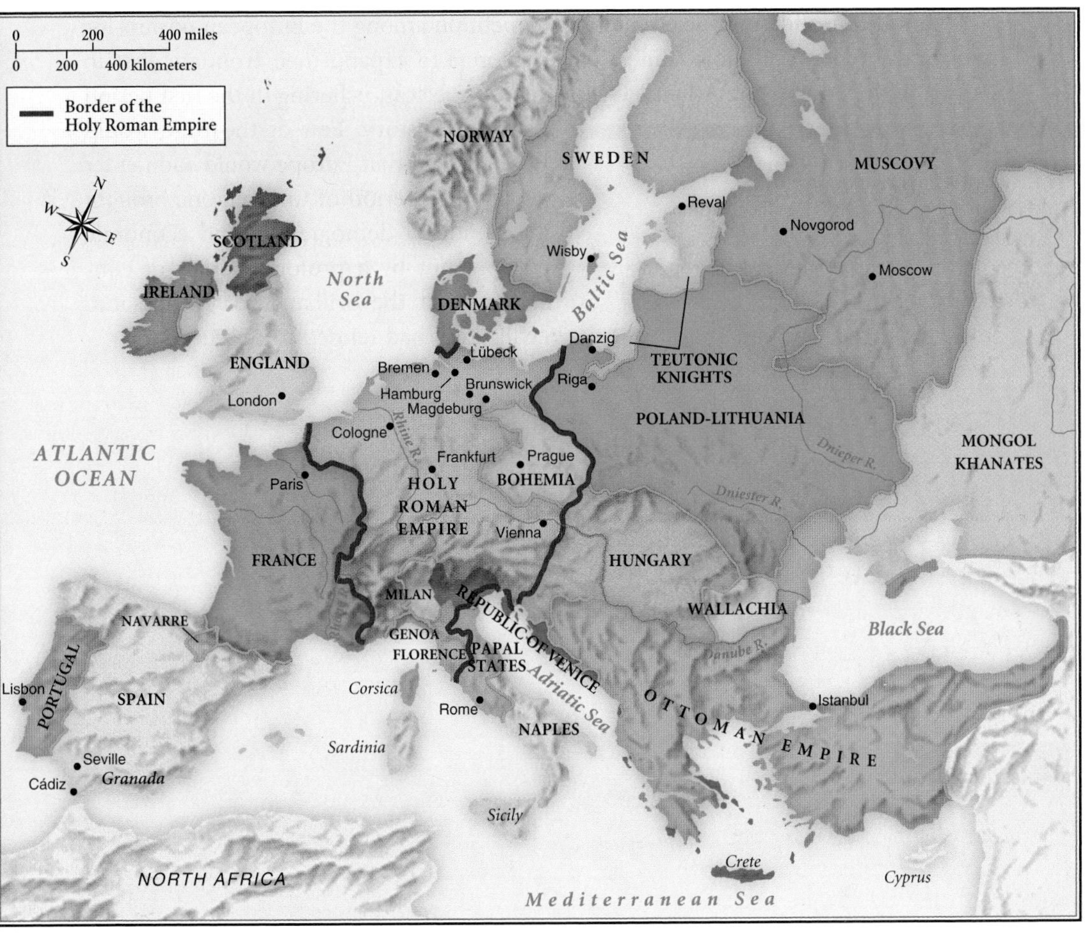

Mapping the West Renaissance Europe, c. 1500
By 1500, the shape of early modern Europe was largely set. It would remain stable until the eighteenth century, except for the disappearance of an independent Hungarian kingdom, which was conquered by the Ottomans in 1529.

revived classical literary style, Renaissance architects planned cities as well as buildings, Renaissance artists demonstrated a new appreciation for the human body and the illusion of depth, and Renaissance musicians invented new forms of polyphony. The Renaissance began mainly in the city-states of Italy, but it spread throughout much of Europe. At the courts of great kings and dukes, even the Ottoman sultan, Renaissance music, art, and literature served as a way to celebrate the grandeur of rulers who controlled more of the apparatuses of government—armies, artillery, courts, and taxes—than ever before.

Political consolidation fueled intense competition among the European powers for more land, money, and glory. Rulers paid explorers to expand their frontiers, first to Africa and then across the Atlantic Ocean to the Americas, ushering in the first period of global history. Few at the time would have guessed that Europe would soon enter yet another period of turmoil, one brought about not by demographic and economic collapse but by a profound crisis of conscience that the brilliance of Renaissance civilization had tended to obscure.

CHAPTER REVIEW QUESTIONS

1. How did Renaissance states differ from medieval monarchies?
2. How did the Ottomans' impact on Europe differ from the Mongols'?

For practice quizzes and other study tools, see the Online Study Guide at bedfordstmartins.com/huntconcise.

For primary-source material from this period, see Chapters 13 and 14 of *Sources of THE MAKING OF THE WEST*, Third Edition.

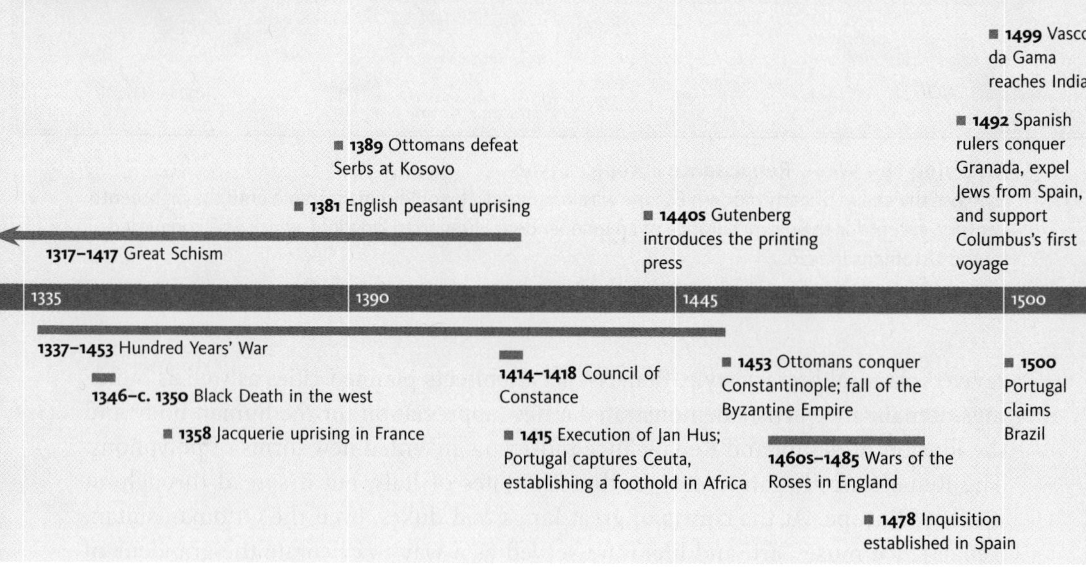

Suggested References

The old view of historians associated the Renaissance primarily with Florence, but now the Renaissance is seen as a European movement (Kirkpatrick, Knecht) and even part of Ottoman culture (Jardine and Brotton). Similarly, the traditional view of "Europe discovering the world" has been replaced by a more nuanced and complex discussion (Abulafia) that includes non-European views and uses Asian, African, and Mesoamerican sources.

Aberth, John. *From the Brink of the Apocalypse: Confronting Famine, War, Plague, and Death in the Later Middle Ages.* 2001.

Abulafia, David, ed. *The Discovery of Mankind: Atlantic Encounters in the Age of Columbus.* 2008.

Bisaha, Nancy. *Creating East and West: Renaissance Humanists and the Ottoman Turks.* 2004.

*Froissart, Jean. *Chronicles.* Trans. Geoffrey Brereton. 1968.

*Horrox, Rosemary, ed. and trans. *The Black Death.* 1994.

Jardine, Lisa, and Jerry Brotton. *Global Interests: Renaissance Art between East and West.* 2000.

Jordan, William Chester. *The Great Famine: Northern Europe in the Early Fourteenth Century.* 1996.

Kirkpatrick, Robin. *The European Renaissance, 1400–1600.* 2002.

Knecht, R. J. *The French Renaissance Court, 1483–1589.* 2008.

Plague and public health in Renaissance Europe: http://jefferson.village.virginia.edu/osheim/intro.html

Renaissance art in Italy: http://witcombe.sbc.edu/ARTHrenaissanceitaly.html

Russell-Wood, A. J. R. *A World on the Move: The Portuguese in Africa, Asia, and America, 1415–1808.* 1992.

Thomas, Hugh. *Rivers of Gold: The Rise of the Spanish Empire, from Columbus to Magellan.* 2003.

12

Struggles over Beliefs

1500–1648

HILLE FEIKEN LEFT THE NORTHERN GERMAN CITY of Münster on June 16, 1534, elegantly dressed, bedecked with jewels, and determined to kill. Münster, which religious radicals had declared a holy city, lay under siege by armies loyal to the local Catholic bishop—her intended victim. Hille crossed enemy lines and tried to persuade the commander of the besieging troops to take her to the bishop, promising to reveal a secret means of recapturing the city. When a defector from her camp recognized Hille and betrayed her, she was beheaded.

Hille Feiken belonged to the religious group known as **Anabaptists**, who wanted to form a holy community separate from the rest of society. Anabaptists organized in response to the Protestant Reformation, which was set in motion by the German friar Martin Luther in 1517 and quickly became a sweeping movement to uproot church abuses and restore early Christian teachings. Supporters of Luther were called **Protestants**, those who protested. Inspired by Luther and then by other reformers, ordinary men and women across much of Europe attempted to remake their heaven and earth. Their stories intertwined with bloody struggles among princes for domination in Europe, an age-old conflict now complicated by the clash of rival faiths.

Vincenzo Catena, *Judith*
The Book of Judith tells the story of a beautiful young Israelite who presents herself to Holofernes, the general of an army besieging Jerusalem. His guard lowered by wine and Judith's charms, Holofernes falls victim to Judith, who assassinates him and cuts off his head, thus frightening off the enemy and saving her people. In this painting from the 1520s, the Venetian artist Vincenzo Catena conveys Judith's strength, beauty, and commitment to her task—one that Hille Feiken sought to reenact so that she might free her own besieged city of Münster. *(akg-images/ Cameraphoto.)*

Struggles over religious beliefs frequently erupted into armed confrontation, culminating in the Thirty Years' War of 1618–1648, which devastated the lands of central Europe. The orgy of mutual destruction in this war left no winners in the religious struggle, and the cynical manipulation of religious issues by both Catholic and Protestant leaders showed that political interests eventually outweighed those of religion. The extreme violence of religious conflict pushed rulers and political thinkers to seek other, nonreligious grounds for governmental authority. Few would argue for genuine toleration of religious differences, but many began to insist that the interests of states had to take priority over the desire for religious conformity.

Although particularly dramatic and deadly, the church-state crisis was only one of a series of upheavals that shaped this era. After decades of rapid economic and population growth in the sixteenth century, a major economic downturn led to food shortages, famine, and disease in the first half of the seventeenth century. An upheaval in worldviews was also in the making, catalyzed by increasing knowledge of the new worlds discovered overseas and in the heavens. The development of new scientific methods of research would ultimately reshape Western attitudes toward religion and state power, as Europeans desperately sought alternatives to wars over religious beliefs.

CHAPTER FOCUS QUESTION Why did struggles over religious beliefs in the sixteenth and seventeenth centuries provoke such violence?

The Protestant Reformation

Since the mid-fifteenth century, many clerics had tried to reform the church from within, criticizing clerical abuses and calling for moral renewal, but their efforts came up against the church's inertia and resistance. At the beginning of the sixteenth century, widespread popular piety and anticlericalism existed side by side, fomenting a volatile mixture of need and resentment. A young German friar, tormented by his own religious doubts, was to become the spokesman for a generation. From its origins as a theological dispute, Martin Luther's reform movement sparked explosive protests. By the time he died in 1546, half of western Europe had renounced allegiance to the Roman Catholic church. Christian unity fractured, opening the way not only to widespread turmoil but also to a host of new attitudes about the nature of religious and political authority.

Popular Piety and Christian Humanism

Numerous signs pointed to an intense spiritual anxiety among the laity. New shrines sprang up, reports of miracles multiplied, and prayer books sold briskly. Critics complained that the church gave external behavior more weight than spiritual intentions. In receiving the sacrament of penance—one of the central pillars of the Roman church—sinners were expected to examine their consciences, sincerely confess their sins to a priest, and receive forgiveness. In practice, however, some priests abused their authority by demanding sexual or monetary favors in return for forgiveness. Priests also sold **indulgences**, which according to doctrine could alleviate suffering in purgatory after death. The faithful were supposed to earn indulgences by performing certain religious tasks—going on pilgrimage, attending Mass, doing holy works. The sale of indulgences as a substitution for performing good works suggested that the church was more interested in making money than in saving souls.

Dissatisfaction with the official church prompted some Christian intellectuals to link their scholarship to the cause of social reform and to dream of ideal societies based on peace and morality. The Dutch scholar Desiderius Erasmus (c. 1466–1536) and the English lawyer Thomas More (1478–1535) stood out as representatives of these Christian humanists, who, unlike Italian humanists, placed their primary emphasis on Christian piety. Each established close links to the powerful. Erasmus was on intimate terms with kings and popes, and his fame spread across Europe. More became lord chancellor to England's king Henry VIII.

Erasmus advocated a simple piety devoid of greed and the lust for power, but he also promoted the new humanist learning. To this end he devoted years to translating a new Latin edition of the New Testament from the original Greek. He argued ironically in *The Praise of Folly* (1509) that the wise appeared foolish, because modesty, humility, and poverty had few adherents in this world. Although Erasmus mocked the clergy's corruption and Christian princes' bloody ambitions, he emphasized the role of education in reforming individuals and through them society as a whole. Even ordinary table manners drew his attention. In the *Colloquies* (1523), a compilation of Latin dialogues intended as language-learning exercises, he advised his cultivated readers not to pick their noses at meals and not to speak while stuffing their mouths. Challenged by angry younger men and radical ideas once the Reformation took hold, Erasmus chose Christian unity over reform and schism. He died in the Swiss city of Basel, isolated from the Protestant community and condemned by many in the Catholic church, who found his writings too critical of the church's authority.

Erasmus's good friend Thomas More, to whom *The Praise of Folly* was dedicated,* met with even greater suffering for his beliefs. He would later pay with his life for upholding conscience over political expediency. Inspired by the recent voyages of discovery, More's best-known work, *Utopia* (1516), describes an imaginary ideal place that offered a stark contrast to his own society. Because utopians enjoyed public schools, communal kitchens, hospitals, and nurseries, they had no need for money. Greed and private property disappeared in this world. Dedicated to the pursuit of knowledge and natural religion, Utopia knew neither crime nor war (*Utopia* means both "no place" and "best place" in Greek). Despite a few oddities—voluntary slavery, for instance, and strictly controlled travel—Utopia seemed a paradise compared with the increasing violence in a Europe divided by religion.

Martin Luther and the German Nation

Like Erasmus and More, Martin Luther (1483–1546) pursued a life of scholarship, but a personal crisis of faith led him to break with the Roman church and establish a competing one. The son of a miner, Luther abandoned his studies in the law to enter the Augustinian order. The choice of a monastic life did not resolve Luther's doubts about his own salvation. Appalled at his own sense of sinfulness and the weakness of human nature, he lived in terror of God's justice despite frequent confessions and penance.

*The Latin title *Encomium Moriae* (*The Praise of Folly*) was a pun on More's name and the Latin word meaning "folly."

A pilgrimage to Rome only deepened his unease with the institutional church. Sent to study theology by a sympathetic superior, Luther gradually came to new insights through his study of Scripture. He later described his breakthrough experience:

> At last, by the mercy of God, meditating day and night, I gave heed to the context of the words [in Romans 1:17], namely, "In [the Gospel] the righteousness of God is revealed, as it is written, 'He who through faith is righteous shall live.'" There I began to understand that the righteousness of God is that by which the righteous live by a gift of God, namely by faith.

Luther soon came into conflict with the church authorities. In 1516, the new archbishop ordered the sale of indulgences to help cover the cost of constructing St. Peter's Basilica in Rome and also to defray his expenses in pursuing his election. Such blatant profiteering outraged many, including Luther, who now served as professor of theology at the University of Wittenberg. In 1517, Luther composed ninety-five theses—propositions for an academic debate—that questioned indulgence peddling and the purchase of church offices. Once they became public, the theses unleashed a torrent of pent-up resentment and frustration among the laypeople. This apparently ordinary academic dispute soon engulfed the Holy Roman Empire in conflict.

As Luther developed his ideas more fully, rupture became inevitable. In 1520, he published three treatises that laid out his theological position, attacked the papacy in Rome as the embodiment of the Antichrist, and called upon the German princes to reform the church themselves. Luther insisted that faith alone, not good works or penance, could save sinners from damnation. Faith came from the believer's personal relationship with God, which he or she cultivated through individual study of Scripture. Ordinary laypeople thus made up "the priesthood of all believers," who had no need of a professional caste of clerics to show them the way to salvation. The attack on the church's authority could not have been more dramatic.

Luther Triumphs over His Catholic Opponents
This 1521 woodcut by Matthias Gnidias shows Martin Luther, Bible in hand, standing above his Catholic opponent, the Franciscan friar Thomas Murner, who is depicted here as the biblical monster Leviathan. The monster breathes "ignis, fumus, & sulphur"—fire, smoke, and sulfur. The vertical Latin caption declares that the Lord will visit the earth with his sword and kill the monster. Both Protestants and Catholics used woodcuts and illustrations extensively as propaganda to appeal to the vast majority of people who were illiterate.

From Rome's perspective, the "Luther Affair," as church officials called it, was essentially a matter of clerical discipline. Rome ordered Luther to obey his superiors and keep quiet. But the church establishment had seriously misjudged the extent of Luther's influence. Luther's ideas, published in numerous German and Latin editions, spread rapidly throughout the Holy Roman Empire, unleashing forces that Luther himself could not control. Social, nationalist, and religious protests fused into an explosive mass very similar to the Czech revolution that Jan Hus had inspired a century earlier. Like Hus, Luther appeared before an emperor: in 1521, he defended his faith before Charles V (r. 1520–1558), the newly elected Holy Roman Emperor, who at the age of nineteen was the ruler of the Low Countries, Spain, Spain's Italian and New World dominions, and the Austrian Habsburg lands. At the Imperial Diet of Worms, the formal assembly presided over by this powerful ruler, Luther shocked Germans by declaring his admiration for the Czech heretic. But unlike Hus, Luther did not suffer martyrdom because he enjoyed the protection of his local lord, the elector of Saxony (one of the seven German princes entitled to elect the Holy Roman Emperor). Luther also had the support of many literate townspeople who were eager to read the Scriptures for themselves.

What began as an urban movement turned into a war in the countryside in 1525. The church was the largest landowner in the Holy Roman Empire: about one-seventh of the empire's territory consisted of ecclesiastical principalities in which bishops and abbots exercised both secular and churchly power. Peasants had to pay taxes to both the church and their lords. In the spring of 1525, many peasants in southern and central Germany rose in rebellion, sometimes inspired by wandering preachers. Urban workers and artisans joined the peasant bands, plundering monasteries, refusing to pay church taxes, and demanding village autonomy, the abolition of serfdom, and the right to appoint their own pastors. In Thuringia, the rebels were led by an ex-priest, Thomas Müntzer (1468?–1525), who promised to chastise the wicked and thus clear the way for the Last Judgment.

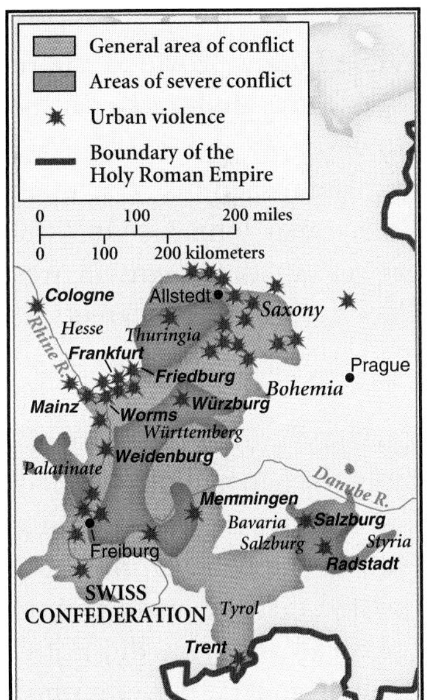

The Peasants' War, 1525

The uprising of 1525, known as the Peasants' War, split the reform movement. In Thuringia, Catholics and reformers joined hands to kill Müntzer and crush his supporters. All over the empire, princes rallied their troops to defeat the peasants and hunt down their leaders. By the end of 1525, more than 100,000 rebels had been killed and others maimed, imprisoned, or exiled. Luther had tried to mediate, criticizing the princes for their brutality toward the peasants but also warning the rebels against mixing religion and social protest.

The Progress of the Reformation

1517	Martin Luther disseminates ninety-five theses attacking the sale of indulgences and other church practices
1520	Reformer Huldrych Zwingli breaks with Rome
1525	Radical reformer Thomas Müntzer killed in the Peasants' War
1529	Lutheran German princes protest the condemnation of religious reform by Charles V; genesis of the term *Protestants*
1534	English Parliament establishes King Henry VIII as head of the Anglican church, severing ties to Rome
1534–1535	Anabaptists control the city of Münster, Germany, in a failed experiment to create a holy community
1541	John Calvin and his followers take control in Geneva, making that city the center of Calvinist reforms

Luther believed that rulers were ordained by God and thus must be obeyed even if they were tyrants. The kingdom of God belonged not to this world but to the next. When the rebels ignored his appeal to stop, Luther called on the princes to destroy "the devil's work" and slaughter the rebels. Fundamentally conservative in its political philosophy, the Lutheran church would henceforth depend on established political authority for its protection.

Emerging as the champions of an orderly religious reform, many German princes eventually confronted Emperor Charles V, who supported Rome. In 1529, Charles declared the Roman Catholic faith the empire's only legitimate religion. Proclaiming their allegiance to the reform cause, the Lutheran German princes protested and thus came to be called Protestants.

Huldrych Zwingli and John Calvin

While Luther provided the religious leadership for northern Germany, the south soon came under the influence of reformers based in Switzerland. In 1520, Huldrych Zwingli (1484–1531), the son of a Swiss village leader, broke with Rome and established his reform headquarters in German-speaking Zurich. In 1541, the Frenchman John Calvin (1509–1564) made French-speaking Geneva his center for reform campaigns in western Europe (Map 12.1). Like Luther, Zwingli and Calvin began their careers as priests, but in contrast to their predecessor, they demanded an even more radical break with the Roman Catholic church, especially on the question of the sacrament of communion. According to Catholic doctrine, during the Mass officiated by a priest the bread and wine of holy communion changed into the body and blood of Christ. Luther believed that the body and blood were actually present in the bread and wine, but only because of the faith of the believer, not because a priest officiated. Zwingli pushed further and insisted that the bread and wine simply symbolized Christ's union with believers; the bread and wine did not change in substance. Calvin took a position between Zwingli and Luther, arguing that the sacrament of communion was more than just symbolic but insisting that it was entirely in God's power, dependent neither on the priest nor on the individual's faith. All efforts to mediate between these positions failed.

Map 12.1 The Spread of Protestantism in the Sixteenth Century
The Protestant Reformation divided northern and southern Europe. From its heartland in the Holy Roman Empire, the Reformation spread to Scandinavia, England, and Scotland and made considerable inroads into the Low Countries, France, eastern Europe, the Swiss Confederation, and even parts of northern Italy. While the Mediterranean countries remained loyal to Rome, religious divisions characterized the landscape of Europe from the British Isles in the west to Poland in the east.

In Zurich, Zwingli tolerated no dissent. When laypeople secretly set up their own new sect, called Anabaptists, Zwingli immediately attacked them. The Anabaptists believed that only adults had the free will to truly understand and accept baptism and therefore had to be rebaptized (*anabaptism* means "rebaptism"). How could a baby knowingly choose Christ? Rebaptism symbolized the Anabaptists' determination to withdraw from a social order corrupted, as they saw it, by power and evil. They therefore rejected the authority of courts and magistrates and refused to bear arms or swear oaths of allegiance. When persuasion failed to convince them, Zwingli urged Zurich magistrates to impose the death sentence.

Anabaptism spread quickly from Zurich to many cities in southern Germany, despite the Holy Roman Empire's general condemnation of the movement in 1529. In 1534, one incendiary Anabaptist group, believing that the end of the world was imminent, seized control of the northwestern German town of Münster. Proclaiming themselves a community of saints and imitating the ancient Israelites, they were initially governed by twelve elders and later by Jan of Leiden, a Dutch Anabaptist tailor who claimed to be the prophesied leader—a second "King David."

The Münster Anabaptists abolished private property and dissolved traditional marriages, allowing men, like Old Testament patriarchs, to have multiple wives, to the chagrin of many women. In 1535, Münster fell to a combined Protestant and Catholic army. Many Anabaptists died in battle or, like Hille Feiken, were executed. The remnants of the Anabaptist movement survived under the determined pacifist leadership of the Dutch reformer Menno Simons (1496–1561), whose followers were eventually named Mennonites.

As a young priest, Calvin had believed it might be possible to reform the Roman Catholic church from within, but gradually he came to share Luther and Zwingli's conviction that only fundamental change could restore the true religion. While Calvin moved toward the Protestant position, his homeland of France experienced increasing turmoil over religion. On Sunday, October 18, 1534, in the so-called Affair of the Placards, Parisians found church doors posted with broadsheets denouncing the Catholic Mass. The government arrested hundreds of French Protestants and executed scores of them, precipitating the flight into exile of many others, including Calvin.

Calvin did not intend to settle in Geneva, but when he stopped there, a local reformer threatened him with God's curse if he did not stay and help organize reform in the city. After intense conflict between the supporters of reform, many of whom were French refugees, and the opposition, led by the traditional elite families, the Calvinists triumphed in 1541. Geneva soon followed the precepts laid out in Calvin's great work, *The Institutes of the Christian Religion*, first published in 1536. Calvin followed the other Protestant reformers in insisting that God is almighty and humans cannot earn their salvation by good works, and then he went a step further, arguing that no Christian can be certain of salvation. With his doctrine of **predestination**, Calvin asserted that God had foreordained every man, woman, and child to salvation or damnation—even before the creation of the world. Only God knew who was among the "elect."

In practice, however, Calvinist doctrine demanded rigorous discipline: the knowledge that a small group of "elect" would be saved should guide the actions of the godly in an uncertain world. Fusing church and society into what followers named the Reformed church, Geneva became a single theocratic community, in which dissent was not tolerated. The Genevan magistrates arrested the Spanish physician Michael Servetus when he passed through in 1553 because he had published books attacking Calvin and questioning the doctrine of the Trinity, the belief shared by virtually all Christians that God exists in three persons—the Father, Son (Christ), and Holy Spirit. Servetus was executed at Calvin's insistence. Geneva quickly became the new center of the Reformation, sending out pastors trained for mission work and exporting books that taught Calvinist doctrines. The Calvinist movement spread to France, the Netherlands, England, Scotland, the German states, Poland, Hungary, and eventually New England, becoming the established form of the Reformation in many of these countries (Map 12.1, page 441).

Protestantism in England

Until 1527, England's king Henry VIII (r. 1509–1547) firmly opposed the Reformation, even receiving the title "Defender of the Faith" from Pope Leo X for a treatise Henry wrote against Luther. Henry's family problems changed his mind. Henry had married Catherine of Aragon (d. 1536), the daughter of Ferdinand and Isabella of Spain and the aunt of Charles V, and the marriage had produced a daughter, Princess Mary (known as Mary Tudor). Henry wanted a male heir to consolidate the rule of his Tudor dynasty, and he had fallen in love with Anne Boleyn, a lady-in-waiting at court and a strong supporter of the Reformation. In 1527, Henry asked the reigning pope, Clement VII, to declare his eighteen-year marriage to Catherine invalid on the grounds that she was the widow of his older brother, Arthur. Arthur and Catherine's marriage, which apparently was never consummated, had been annulled by Pope Julius II. When Henry failed to secure a papal dispensation for his divorce, he chose two Protestants as his new loyal servants: Thomas Cromwell (1485–1540) as chancellor and Thomas Cranmer (1489–1556) as archbishop of Canterbury. Under their leadership the English Parliament declared Henry's marriage to Catherine invalid, allowing him to marry Anne Boleyn; passed the Act of Supremacy of 1534, establishing Henry as the head of the Anglican church (the Church of England); and began confiscating the properties of the Catholic monasteries. Henry thus doubled his revenues.

By 1536, Henry had grown tired of Anne Boleyn, who had given birth to the future Queen Elizabeth I but had produced no sons. The king, who would go on to marry four other wives but father only one son, Edward (by his third wife, Jane Seymour), had Anne beheaded on the charge of adultery, an act that he defined as treason. Thomas More, once Henry's chancellor, had been executed in 1535 for treason—in his case, for refusing to recognize Henry as "the only supreme head on earth of the Church of England"—and Cromwell suffered the same fate in 1540 when he lost favor. After Henry's death in 1547, the Anglican church, nominally

Queen Elizabeth I of England
The Anglican (Church of England) Prayer Book of 1569 included a hand-colored print of Queen Elizabeth saying her prayers. As queen, Elizabeth was also the official head of the Church of England (the scepter or sword at her feet symbolizes her power). She named bishops and made final decisions about every aspect of church governance. **For more help analyzing this image, see the visual activity for this chapter in the Online Study Guide at bedfordstmartins.com/huntconcise.** (HIP/Art Resource, NY.)

Protestant, still retained much traditional Catholic doctrine and ritual. But the principle of royal supremacy in religious matters would remain a lasting feature of Henry's reforms.

When Henry's Protestant son, Edward VI (r. 1547–1553), died at age sixteen, his half sister Mary Tudor (r. 1553–1558) succeeded him, and the Catholic Mass was spontaneously restored in most places without bloodshed. Mary intended to reestablish Catholicism and the authority of Rome, but she lost popularity when she ordered some three hundred Protestants burned at the stake as heretics, including Cranmer. Hundreds more fled. In 1554 she married the Catholic king of Spain, Philip II, which prompted a brief and unsuccessful rebellion. When Mary died in 1558, Anne Boleyn's daughter, Elizabeth, came to the throne and the Anglican cause again gained momentum. As Elizabeth I (r. 1558–1603) moved to solidify her personal power and the authority of the Anglican church, she had to squash uprisings by Catholics in the north and at least two serious plots against her life. She also had to hold off Calvinist **Puritans**, who pushed for more reform, and Spain's Philip II, who first wanted to be her husband and then, failing that, planned to invade her country to restore Catholicism.

The Puritans were strict Calvinists who opposed all vestiges of Catholic ritual in the Church of England. After Elizabeth became queen, many Puritans returned from exile abroad, but Elizabeth resisted their demands for drastic changes in Anglican ritual and governance. She had assumed control as "supreme governor" of the Church of England, and she therefore appointed all bishops. The Church of England's Thirty-nine

Articles of Religion, issued in 1563, incorporated elements of Catholic ritual along with Calvinist doctrines. Puritan ministers angrily denounced the Church of England's "popish attire . . . and a thousand more abominations." Puritans tried to undercut the bishops' authority by placing control of church administration in the hands of the local congregation. Elizabeth rejected this Calvinist "presbyterianism." The Puritans nonetheless steadily gained influence. Known for their emphasis on strict moral lives, the Puritans tried to close the theaters and Sunday fairs and insisted that every father "make his house a little church" by teaching the children to read the Bible. The precise nature of church government would remain a subject of contention for generations to come.

Elizabeth made the most of her limited means and consolidated the country's position as a Protestant power. In her early years, she held out the prospect of marriage to many political suitors but never married. She cajoled Parliament with references to her female weaknesses, but she showed steely-eyed determination in protecting the monarchy's interests. Her chosen successor, James I (r. 1603–1625), came to the throne as king of Scotland, England, and Ireland. Elizabeth left James secure in a kingdom of growing stature in world politics.

Reshaping Society through Religion

For all their differences over doctrine and church organization, the Protestant reformers shared a desire to instill greater discipline in Christian worship and in social behavior. As a consequence, they advocated changes in education and marriage to create a God-fearing, pious, and orderly Christian society. Some of these efforts grew out of developments that stretched back to the Middle Ages, but others, such as an emphasis on literacy, appeared first in Protestant Europe.

Prior to the Reformation, the Latin Vulgate was the only Bible authorized by the church; as a result, priests interpreted the Bible for their parishioners. In 1522, Martin Luther translated Erasmus's Greek New Testament into German because he believed that everyone should read the Bible for him- or herself. Within twelve years, printers published more than 200,000 copies of it, an immense number for the time. In 1534, Luther completed a German translation of the Old Testament. Inspired by Luther's example during a visit to Wittenberg, the Englishman William Tyndale (1495–1536) translated the Bible into English. After he had his translation printed in Germany and the Low Countries, Tyndale smuggled copies into England in 1526, while England was still Catholic.

Although the vernacular Bible was a prized possession in many Protestant households, Bible reading did not become widespread until the 1600s. To educate children in the new religious principles and replace the late medieval church schools, the Protestant reformers set up state school systems. Luther urged the German princes to use the proceeds of confiscated church properties to establish primary schools in every parish for boys and girls ages six to twelve. The Protestant churches also developed a secondary system of higher schools for boys, called gymnasia (from the Greek *gymnasion*), in which the study of Greek and Latin classics and religious instruction prepared future pastors, scholars, and officials for university study.

Like the reforms of education, Protestant efforts to reshape marriage reflected their concern to discipline individual behavior and institute an orderly Christian society. Protestant magistrates established marital courts, passed new marriage laws, closed brothels, and inflicted harsher punishments for sexual deviance. Under canon law, the Catholic church recognized any promise made between two consenting adults (with the legal age of twelve for females, fourteen for males) as a valid marriage. In rural areas and among the urban poor, most couples simply lived together as common-law husband and wife, and some couples never even registered with the church. Protestant governments declared a marriage illegitimate if the partners failed to register their marriage with a local official and a pastor. They usually also required parental consent, thus giving parents immense power in regulating marriage and the transmission of family property.

Taught to become obedient spouses and affectionate companions in Christ, women approached this new sexual regime with ambivalence. The new laws stipulated that women could seek divorce for desertion, impotence, and flagrant abuse, although in practice the marital courts encouraged reconciliation. These improvements came at a price, however: Protestant women were expected to be obedient wives, helpful companions, and loving mothers, but they could no longer join the convent and pursue their own religious paths outside the family. Luther's wife, Katharina von Bora, typified the new ideal Protestant woman. A former nun, she accepted her prescribed role in a patriarchal household: once married, Katharina ran the couple's household, feeding their children, relatives, and student boarders. Although she deferred to Luther—she addressed him as "Herr Doktor"—she nonetheless defended a woman's right as an equal in marriage. Other Protestant

The Disciplined Home
Proper table manners reflected discipline and morality in the godly household, an ideal of the religious reformers of the sixteenth century. The householder, the father-patriarch, leads his wife and children in prayer before a meal. The orderly behavior parallels the comfort (oven, smoked-glass windows, chandeliers, timbered ceiling, and cabinets) of a well-off patrician family. (Staatsbibliothek Bamberg, Germany.)

women spoke out even more decisively. Katharina Zell, wife of the Strasbourg reformer Matthew Zell, wrote hymns, fed the sick and imprisoned, and denounced the intolerance of the new Protestant clergy. Rebuking one for his persecution of dissenters, she wrote, "You young fellows tread on the graves of the first fathers of this church in Strasbourg and punish all who disagree with you, but faith cannot be forced." She also insisted that women should have a voice in religious affairs.

Catholic Renewal and Missionary Zeal

Reacting to the waves of Protestant challenge, the Catholic church mobilized for defense in a movement that is called by some the Counter-Reformation and by others Catholic Reform. Pope Paul III (r. 1534–1549) convened a general church council to codify church doctrine, and he personally approved the founding of new religious orders to undertake aggressive missionary efforts. The Council of Trent (Map 12.1, page 441) met intermittently between 1545 and 1563, when it concluded its work. Its decisions shaped the essential character of Catholicism until the 1960s. Emphatically rejecting the major Protestant positions, the council reasserted the supremacy of clerical authority over the laity and reaffirmed that the bread and wine of communion actually become Christ's body and blood. It required that all weddings take place in churches and be registered by the parish clergy and explicitly refused to allow divorce. All hopes of reconciliation between Protestants and Catholics faded.

Most important of the new Catholic religious orders was the Society of Jesus. Its founder was Ignatius of Loyola (1491–1556), a Spanish nobleman and charismatic former military officer, who abandoned his quest for military glory in favor of serving the church. Ignatius soon attracted other young men to his side, and in 1540 the pope recognized his small band of Jesuits. Over time, the Jesuits founded hundreds of colleges in Spain, Portugal, France, Italy, the German states, Hungary, Bohemia, and Poland. Among their alumni would be princes, philosophers, lawyers, churchmen, and officials—the elite of Catholic Europe. In 1544 the pope recognized a new order for women, the Company of Saint Ursula, known as the Ursulines, who devoted themselves to the education of girls. Together these new religious orders restored the confidence of the faithful in the dedication and power of the Catholic church.

Catholic missionaries set sail throughout the globe to bring Roman Catholicism to Africans, Asians, and native Americans. They saw their effort as proof of the truth of Roman Catholicism and the success of their missions as a sign of divine favor, both particularly important in the face of Protestant challenge. To ensure rapid Christianization, European missionaries focused initially on winning over local elites. A number of young African nobles went to Portugal to be trained in theology. Catholic missionaries preached the Gospel to Confucian scholar-officials in China and to the samurai (the warrior aristocracy) in Japan. Measured in numbers alone, the Catholic missionary enterprise seemed highly successful: by the second half of the sixteenth century, vast multitudes of native Americans had become

The Portuguese in Japan
In this sixteenth-century Japanese black-lacquer screen painting of Portuguese missionaries, the Jesuits are dressed in black and the Franciscans in brown. At the lower left corner is a Portuguese nobleman depicted with exaggerated "Western" features. The Japanese considered themselves lighter in skin color than the Portuguese, whom they classified as "barbarians." In turn, the Portuguese classified Japanese (and Chinese) as "whites." The perception of ethnic differences in the sixteenth century depended less on skin color than on clothing, eating habits, and other cultural signals. Color classifications were unstable and changed over time. By the late seventeenth century, Europeans no longer regarded Asians as "white." (The Granger Collection, NY.)

Christians at least in name, and thirty years after Francis Xavier's 1549 landing in Japan, the Jesuits could claim over 100,000 Japanese converts.

After an initial period of relatively little racial discrimination, the Catholic church in the Americas and Africa adopted strict rules based on color. For example, the first Mexican Ecclesiastical Provincial Council in 1555 declared that holy orders were not to be conferred on Indians, mestizos (people of mixed European-Indian parentage), or mulattoes (people of mixed European-African heritage), groups deemed "inherently unworthy of the sacerdotal [priestly] office." Europeans reinforced their sense of racial superiority with their perception of the "treachery" that native Americans and Africans exhibited whenever they resisted domination. Frustrated in his efforts to convert Brazilian Indians, a Jesuit missionary wrote to his superior in Rome in 1563 that "for this kind of people it is better to be preaching with the sword and rod of iron." The Dominican Bartolomé de Las Casas (1474–1566) criticized the treatment of the Indians in Spanish America, yet even he argued that Africans should be imported in order to relieve the indigenous peoples, who were being worked to death.

REVIEW In what ways did Luther, Zwingli, and Calvin challenge the Roman Catholic church?

State Power and Religious Conflict, 1500–1618

Even as religious disputes heightened the potential for conflict within Europe, the European powers continued to fight their traditional dynastic wars and still faced the military threat posed by the Muslim Ottoman Turks in the east. But these wars did not long deflect attention from increasing divisions within European countries. Rulers viewed religious divisions as a dangerous challenge to the unity of their realms and the stability of their regimes; a subject could very well swear greater allegiance to God than to his lord. Yet rulers often proved powerless to stem the rising tide of religious strife. Lutheranism flourished in the northern German states and Scandinavia; Calvinism spread from its headquarters in the Swiss city of Geneva all the way to England and Poland-Lithuania. The rapid expansion of Lutheranism and Calvinism created deadly political conflicts between Protestants and Catholics.

Wars among the Habsburgs, Valois, and Ottomans

While the Reformation was taking hold in the German states, the Catholic powers of Spain and France fought each other for the domination of Europe (Map 12.2). French claims over Italian territories sparked conflict in 1494, but the ensuing Italian Wars soon involved most Christian monarchs and the Muslim Ottoman sultan as well. Despite some spectacular and bloody turns of fortune, no one power ultimately emerged victorious. In 1525, the troops of the Habsburg emperor Charles V crushed the French army at Pavia, Italy, and captured the French king Francis I (r. 1515–1547). Charles treated Francis as an honored guest but held him in Spain until he agreed to renounce his claims to Italy. Furious at this humiliation, Francis repudiated the agreement the moment he returned to France, reigniting the conflict. In 1527, Charles's troops invaded and then pillaged Rome to punish the pope for allying with the French. Among the imperial troops were German Protestant mercenaries, who pillaged Catholic churches. The sack of Rome shocked the Catholic church hierarchy and helped turn it toward renewal.

Charles could not crush the French in one swift blow because he also had to counter the Muslim Ottomans in Hungary and along the Mediterranean coast. The Ottoman Empire reached its height of power under Sultan Suleiman I ("the

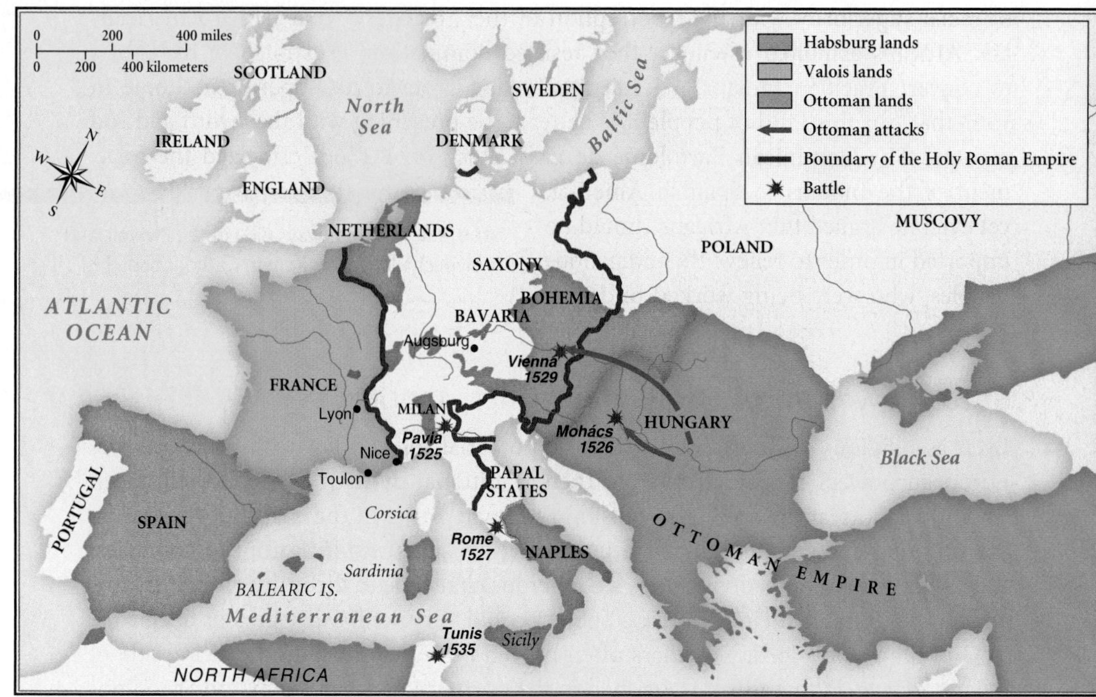

Map 12.2 The Habsburg-Valois-Ottoman Wars, 1494–1559
As the dominant European power, the Habsburg dynasty fought on two fronts: a religious war against the Islamic Ottoman Empire and a political war against the French Valois, who challenged Habsburg hegemony. The Mediterranean, the Balkans, and the Low Countries all became theaters of war.

Magnificent"; r. 1520–1566). In 1526, a Turkish force destroyed the Hungarian army at Mohács. Three years later, the Ottoman army laid siege to Vienna; though unsuccessful, the siege shocked Christian Europe. In 1535, Charles V tried to capture Tunis, the lair of North African pirates under Ottoman rule. Desperate to overcome Charles's superior forces in Europe, Francis I eagerly forged an alliance with the Turkish sultan. The Turkish fleet besieged Nice, on the southern coast of France, to help the French wrest it from imperial occupiers. Francis even ordered all inhabitants of nearby Toulon to vacate their town so that he could turn it into a Muslim colony for eight months, complete with a mosque and slave market. The Franco-Turkish alliance, however brief, showed that the age-old idea of a Christian crusade against Islam had to make way for a new political strategy that considered religion as but one factor in power politics.

In 1559, the French king finally acknowledged defeat and signed the peace treaty of Cateau-Cambrésis. By then, years of conflict had drained the treasuries of all the monarchs. Fueled by warfare, armies grew in size, firepower became ever more deadly, and costs soared. For example, heavier artillery pieces meant that the rectangular walls of medieval cities had to be transformed into fortresses with

The Siege of Vienna, 1529
This illustration from an Ottoman manuscript of 1588 depicts the Turkish siege of Vienna (the siege guns can be seen in the center of the picture). Sultan Suleiman I ("the Magnificent") led an army of more than 100,000 men against Vienna, the capital of the Austrian Habsburg lands. Several attacks on the city failed, and the Ottomans withdrew in October 1529. They maintained control over Hungary, but the logistics of moving so many men and horses kept them from advancing any farther west into Europe. (The Art Archive/Topkapi Museum, Istanbul/Dagli Orti.)

jutting forts and gun emplacements. Charles V boasted the largest army in Europe—but he could not make ends meet with the proceeds from taxation, the sale of offices, and even outright confiscation. Charles and his French opponents both relied on private bankers for funds to make ends meet. Bankers, like the Fugger family of the southern German imperial city of Augsburg, charged as much as 14 to 18 percent interest on their loans and amassed huge fortunes.

French Wars of Religion

During the 1540s and 1550s, one-third of the French nobles converted to Calvinism, usually influenced by noblewomen who protected pastors, provided money and advice, and helped found schools and establish relief for the poor. As many as twelve hundred Reformed churches were established, especially in southern and western France. The Catholic Valois monarchy tried to maintain a balance of power between Catholics and Calvinists. Francis I and his successor, Henry II (r. 1547–1559), both succeeded to a degree. But when Henry was accidentally killed during a jousting tournament, the weakened monarchy could no longer hold together the fragile realm. Henry was succeeded first by his fifteen-year-old son, Francis II, who died in 1560, and then by his ten-year-old son, Charles IX (r. 1560–1574).

Catherine de Médicis (1519–1589), the Italian wife of Henry II, acted as regent for her young son. She first urged limited toleration for the Calvinists—called **Huguenots** in

France—in an attempt to maintain political stability, but she could not prevent the eruption of civil war between Catholics and Huguenots in 1562. Although a Catholic herself, Catherine desperately tried to play the Catholic and Huguenot factions off against each other so that neither would dominate. To this end, she arranged the marriage of her daughter Marguerite to Henry of Navarre, head of the Bourbon family, which had converted to Calvinism. Just four days after the wedding in August 1572, assassins tried but failed to kill one of the Huguenot nobles allied with the Bourbons, Gaspard de Coligny. Panicked at the thought of Huguenot revenge and perhaps herself implicated in the botched plot, Catherine convinced her son to order the killing of leading Huguenots. On St. Bartholomew's Day, August 24, a bloodbath began, fueled by years of growing animosity between Catholics and Protestants. In three days, Catholic mobs murdered three thousand Huguenots in Paris. Thousands more died in the provinces over the next six weeks. The pope joyfully ordered the church bells rung throughout Catholic Europe; Spain's Philip II wrote Catherine that it was "the best and most cheerful news which at present could come to me." Protestants and Catholics alike now saw the conflict as an international struggle for survival that required aid to coreligionists in other countries. In this way, the French Wars of Religion paved the way for wider international conflicts over religion in the future.

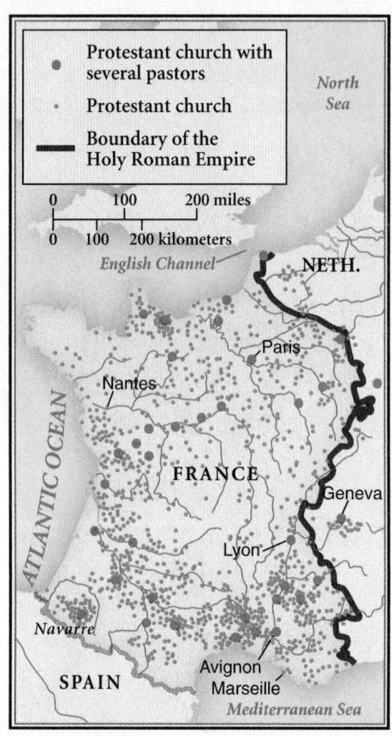

Protestant Churches in France, 1562

The religious division in France grew even more dangerous when Charles IX died and his brother Henry III (r. 1574–1589) became king. Like his brothers before him, Henry III failed to produce an heir. Next in line to succeed the throne was none other than the Calvinist Bourbon leader Henry of Navarre. Because Henry III saw an even greater threat to his authority in a newly formed Catholic League, which had requested Spain's help in rooting out Protestantism in France, he took action against the league. In 1588, he summoned two prominent league leaders to a meeting and had his men kill them. A few months later a fanatical monk stabbed Henry III to death, and Henry of Navarre became Henry IV (r. 1589–1610), despite Spain's attempt to block his way with military intervention.

The new king soon concluded that to establish control over the war-weary country, he had to place the interests of the French state ahead of his Protestant faith. In 1593, Henry IV publicly embraced Catholicism, reputedly explaining his conversion with the phrase "Paris is worth a Mass." In 1598, he made peace with Spain and issued the Edict of Nantes, in which he granted the Huguenots a large measure of religious toleration. The approximately 1.25 million Huguenots became a legally protected minority within an officially Catholic kingdom of some 20 million people. Protestants were free to worship in specified towns and were allowed their own troops, fortresses, and even courts. Few believed in religious toleration, but Henry IV followed the advice of those neutral Catholics and Calvinists called ***politiques*** who urged him to give priority to the development of a durable state. Although their opponents hated them for their compromising spirit, the politiques believed that religious disputes could be resolved only in the peace provided by strong government.

The Edict of Nantes ended the French Wars of Religion, but Henry still needed to reestablish monarchical authority. He used court festivities and royal processions to rally subjects around him, and he developed a new class of royal officials to counterbalance the fractious nobility. In exchange for an annual payment, officials who had purchased their offices could pass them on to heirs or sell them to someone else. By buying offices that eventually ennobled their holders, rich middle-class merchants and lawyers could become part of a new social elite known as the nobility of the robe (named after the robes that magistrates wore, much like those judges wear today). New income raised by the increased sale of offices reduced the state debt and helped Henry build the base for a strong monarchy. His efforts did not, however, prevent his own assassination in 1610 after nineteen unsuccessful attempts.

Challenges to Habsburg Power

Charles V proved more successful at fending off the Turks and subduing the French than he did at resolving growing religious conflicts inside his empire. After the Imperial Diet of Regensburg in 1541 failed to patch up the theological differences between Protestants and Catholics, Charles secured papal support for a war against the Schmalkaldic League, a powerful alliance of Lutheran princes and cities. Charles's army occupied the German imperial cities in the south, restoring Catholic patricians and suppressing the Reformation wherever they triumphed. In 1547, Charles defeated the Schmalkaldic League armies at Mühlberg and captured the leading Lutheran princes. Jubilant, he proclaimed the Interim, which restored Catholics' right to worship in Protestant lands while still permitting Lutherans to celebrate their own services. Riots broke out in many cities as resistance to the Interim spread. Charles's victory proved short-lived, for after one of his former allies, Duke Maurice of Saxony, joined the other side, the princes revived the war in 1552 and chased a surprised, unprepared, and practically bankrupt emperor back to Italy.

Forced to negotiate, Charles V agreed to the Peace of Augsburg in 1555. The settlement recognized the Lutheran church in the empire; accepted the secularization of church lands but kept the remaining ecclesiastical territories (mainly the bishoprics) for Catholics; and, most important, established the principle that all princes, whether Catholic or Lutheran, enjoyed the sole right to determine the religion of their lands and subjects. Significantly, the agreement excluded Calvinist, Anabaptist, and other dissenting groups from the settlement. The Peace of Augsburg preserved a fragile peace in central Europe until 1618, but the exclusion of Calvinists planted the seeds of future conflict.

Exhausted by constant war and depressed by the disunity in Christian Europe, Charles V resigned his many thrones in 1555 and 1556, leaving his Netherlandish-Burgundian and Spanish dominions to his son, Philip II, and his Austrian lands to his brother, Ferdinand, who was also elected Holy Roman Emperor to succeed Charles. Retiring to a monastery in southern Spain, the once powerful Christian monarch spent his last years quietly seeking salvation. Although Philip II of Spain (r. 1556–1598) ruled over fewer territories than his father, his inheritance still left him the most powerful ruler in Europe (Map 12.3). In addition to the western Habsburg lands in

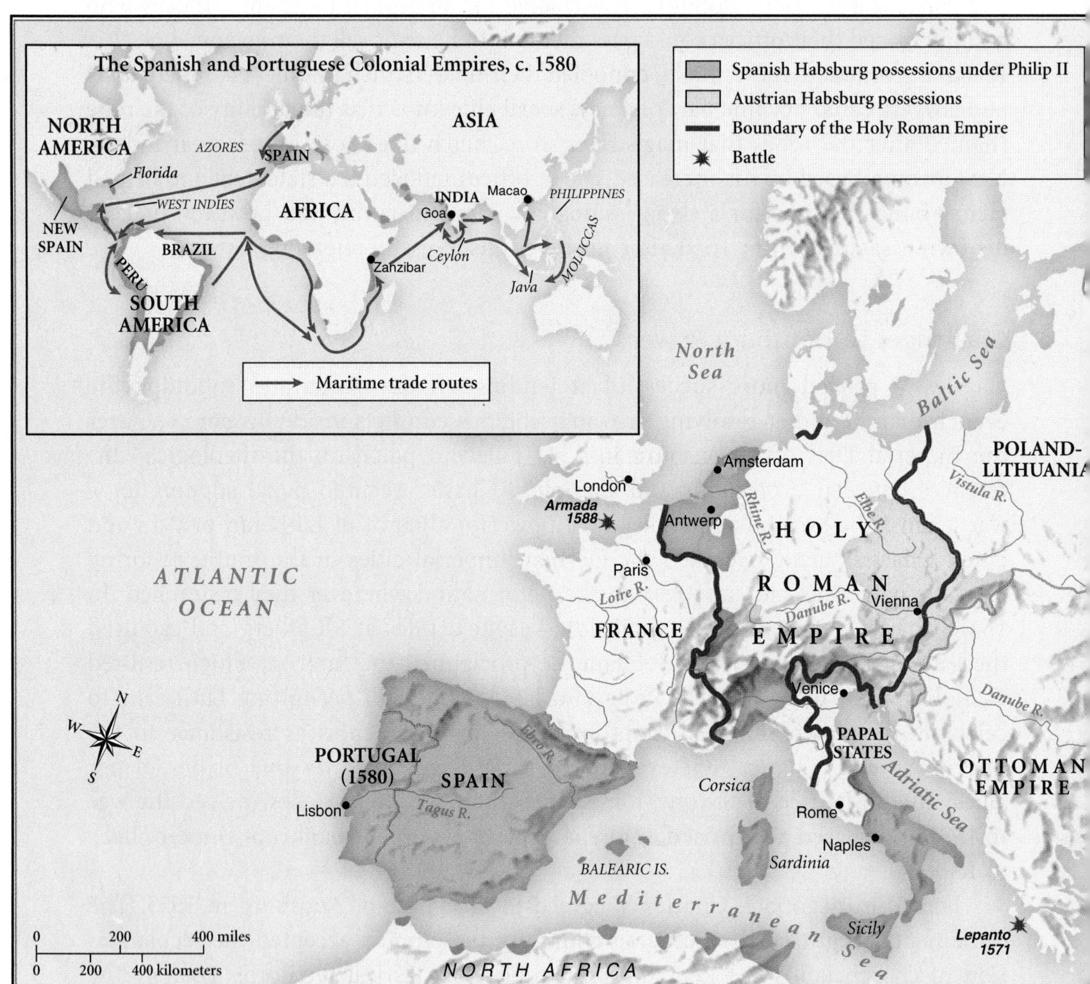

Map 12.3 The Empire of Philip II, r. 1556–1598
The Spanish king Philip II drew revenues from a truly worldwide empire. In 1580, he was the richest European ruler, but the demands of governing such far-flung territories eventually drained many of his resources. **For more help analyzing this map, see the map activity for this chapter in the Online Study Guide at** bedfordstmartins.com/huntconcise.

Spain and the Netherlands, he had inherited all the Spanish colonies recently settled in the New World of the Americas. In 1580, when the king of Portugal died without a direct heir, Philip took over this neighboring realm with its rich empire in Africa, India, and the Americas. Gold and silver funneled from the colonies supported his campaigns against the Ottoman Turks and French and English Protestants.

A deeply devout Catholic, Philip II came to the Spanish throne at age twenty-eight, determined to restore Catholic unity in Europe and lead the Christian defense against the Muslims. In 1571, Philip joined with Venice and the papacy to defeat the Turks in a great sea battle off the Greek coast at Lepanto. But Philip could not rest on his laurels. Between 1568 and 1570, the Moriscos—Muslim converts to Christianity who remained secretly faithful to Islam—had revolted in the south of Spain, killing ninety priests and fifteen hundred Christians. The victory at Lepanto destroyed any prospect that the Turks might come to their aid, yet Philip nonetheless forced fifty thousand Moriscos to leave their villages and resettle in other regions. In 1609, his successor, Philip III, ordered their expulsion, and by 1614 some 300,000 Moriscos had been forced to relocate to North Africa.

The Calvinists of the Netherlands were less easily intimidated than the Moriscos: they were far from Spain and accustomed to being left alone. In 1566, Calvinists in the Netherlands attacked Catholic churches, smashing stained-glass windows and statues of the Virgin

Philip II of Spain
The king of Spain is shown here (kneeling in black) with his allies at the battle of Lepanto, the doge of Venice on his left and Pope Pius V on his right. El Greco painted this canvas, sometimes called *The Dream of Philip II*, in 1578 or 1579. The painting is typically mannerist in the way it crowds figures into every available space, uses larger-than-life or elongated bodies, and creates new and often bizarre visual effects. What can we conclude about Philip II's character from the way he is depicted here? (© National Gallery, London/Art Resource, NY.)

Mary. Philip sent an army, which executed more than eleven hundred people during the next six years. When resistance revived, the Spanish responded with more force, culminating in November 1576, when Philip's armies sacked Antwerp, then Europe's wealthiest commercial city. In eleven days of horror known as the Spanish Fury, the Spanish soldiers slaughtered seven thousand people. Shocked into response, the ten Catholic southern provinces joined with the seven Protestant northern provinces and expelled the Spaniards. In 1579, however, the Catholic southern provinces returned to the Spanish fold. Despite the assassination in 1584 of William of Orange, the leader of the anti-Spanish forces, Spanish troops never regained control in the north.

Spain would not formally recognize Dutch independence until 1648, but by the end of the sixteenth century the Dutch Republic was a self-governing state sheltering a variety of religious groups. The princes of Orange (whose name came from family lands near the city of Orange, in southern France) resembled a ruling family in the Dutch Republic, but their powers paled next to those of local interests. Urban merchant and professional families known as regents controlled the towns and provinces. Each province (Holland was the most populous of the seven provinces) governed itself and sent delegates to the one common institution, the States General. Well situated for maritime commerce, the Dutch Republic developed a thriving economy based on shipping and shipbuilding. By 1670, the Dutch commercial fleet was larger than the English, French, Spanish, Portuguese, and Austrian fleets combined.

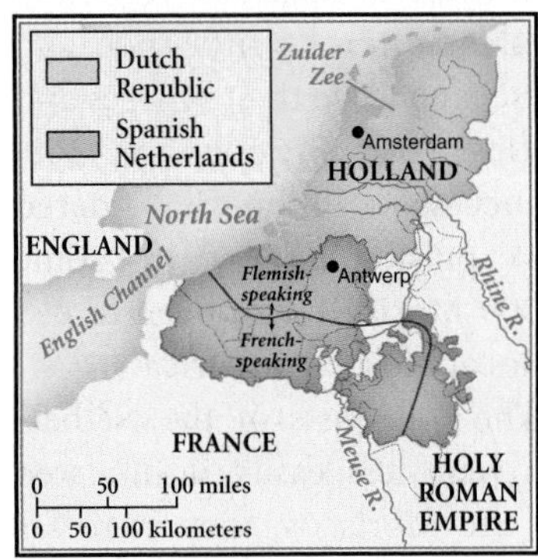

The Netherlands during the Revolt, c. 1580

The Dutch Republic tolerated more religious diversity than the other European states. One-third of the Dutch population remained Catholic, and the secular authorities allowed Catholics to worship as they chose in private. Because Protestant sects could generally count on toleration from local regents, they remained peaceful. The Dutch Republic also had a relatively large Jewish population because many Jews had settled there after being driven out of Spain and Portugal. From 1597, Jews could worship openly in their synagogues. This openness to various religions helped make the Dutch Republic one of Europe's chief intellectual and scientific centers in the seventeenth and eighteenth centuries.

The brief marriage of Philip II to Mary Tudor (Mary I of England) did not produce an heir, but it gave him reason to resist England's return to Protestantism. When Mary died, Elizabeth rejected Philip's proposal of marriage and eventually provided funds and troops to the Dutch rebels. Philip bided his time as long as Elizabeth remained unmarried and her Catholic cousin Mary Stuart—better known as Mary, Queen of Scots—stood next in line to inherit the English throne. In 1567,

Scottish Calvinists forced Mary to abdicate the throne of Scotland in favor of her year-old son, James (eventually James I of England), who was then raised as a Protestant. The Scottish Calvinists feared Mary's connections to Catholic France; her mother was French and devoutly Catholic, and Mary had earlier been married to France's Francis II (who died in 1560). After her abdication, Mary spent nearly twenty years under house arrest in England, fomenting plots against Elizabeth. In 1587, when Mary's letter offering her succession rights to Philip was discovered, Elizabeth overcame her reluctance to execute a fellow monarch and ordered Mary's beheading.

In response, Pope Sixtus V decided to subsidize a Catholic crusade under Philip's leadership against the heretical queen. At the end of May 1588, Philip II sent his armada (Spanish for "fleet") of 130 ships from Lisbon toward the English Channel. The English scattered the Spanish Armada by sending blazing fireships into its midst. A great gale then forced the Spanish to flee around Scotland. By the time the Armada limped home in September, half the ships had been lost and thousands of sailors were dead or starving. Protestants throughout Europe rejoiced. A Spanish monk lamented, "Almost the whole of Spain went into mourning." When Philip II died in 1598, his great empire was beginning to lose its luster. The costs of fighting the French, the Dutch, and the English had mounted, and an overburdened peasantry could no longer pay the taxes required to meet rising expenses. In his novel *Don Quixote* (1605), the Spanish writer Miguel de Cervantes (who had himself been wounded at Lepanto and been held captive in Algiers, then served as a royal tax collector) captured the sadness of Spain's loss of grandeur. His hero, a minor nobleman, reads so many romances and books of chivalry that he loses his wits and wanders the countryside hoping to re-create the heroic deeds of times past.

REVIEW How did the power of states depend on unity in religion?

The Thirty Years' War and the Balance of Power, 1618–1648

In 1618, a new series of violent conflicts between Catholics and Protestants erupted in the Holy Roman Empire. The final and most deadly of the wars of religion, the Thirty Years' War eventually drew in most of the European states. By the end of the war in 1648, many central European lands lay in ruins and many rulers were bankrupt. Reformation and Counter-Reformation had shattered the Christian humanist dream of peace and unity. The Thirty Years' War brought the preceding religious conflicts to a head and by its very violence effectively removed religion from future European disputes. Although religion still divided people *within* various states, after 1648 religion no longer provided the rationale for wars *between* European states. Out of the carnage would emerge centralized and powerful states that made increasing demands on ordinary people.

Origins and Course of the War

The fighting that devastated central Europe had its origins in religious, political, and ethnic divisions within the Holy Roman Empire. The Austrian Habsburg emperor and four of the seven electors who chose him were Catholic; the other three electors were Protestants. The Peace of Augsburg of 1555 was supposed to maintain the balance between Catholics and Lutherans, but it had no mechanism for resolving conflicts. Tensions rose as the Jesuits won many Lutheran cities back to Catholicism and as Calvinism, unrecognized under the agreement, made inroads into Lutheran areas. By 1613, two of the three Protestant electors had become Calvinists. When the Catholic Habsburg heir Archduke Ferdinand was crowned king of Bohemia in 1617, he began to curtail the religious freedom previously granted to Protestants. Protestants wanted to build new churches; Ferdinand wanted to stop them. Tensions boiled over when two Catholic deputy governors tried to dissolve the meetings of Protestants.

On May 23, 1618, a crowd of angry Protestants surged up the stairs of the royal castle in Prague, trapped the two Catholic deputies, dragged them screaming for mercy to the windows, and hurled them to the pavement below. Because they landed in a dung heap, the deputies survived. Although no one died, this "defenestration" (from the French for "window," *la fenêtre*) of Prague touched off a new cycle of conflict. The Czechs, the largest ethnic group in Bohemia, established a Protestant assembly to spearhead resistance. A year later, when Ferdinand was elected emperor (as Ferdinand II, r. 1619–1637), the rebellious Bohemians deposed him and chose in his place the young Calvinist Frederick V of the Palatinate (r. 1616–1623). A quick series of clashes ended in 1620 when the imperial armies defeated the

The Horrors of the Thirty Years' War

The French artist Jacques Callot produced this etching of the Thirty Years' War as part of a series called The Miseries and Misfortunes of War (1633). It shows the rape, torture, and pillaging inflicted by soldiers on noncombatants they found in their path. (The Granger Collection, NY.)

outmanned Czechs at the battle of White Mountain, near Prague (Map 12.4). Like the martyrdom of the religious reformer Jan Hus in 1415, White Mountain became an enduring symbol of the Czechs' desire for self-determination. They would not gain their independence until 1918.

White Mountain did not end the war. Private mercenary armies (armies for hire) began to form during the fighting, and the emperor had virtually no control over them. In 1625, a Czech Protestant, Albrecht von Wallenstein (1583–1634), offered to raise an army for the Catholic emperor and soon had in his employ 125,000 soldiers, who occupied and plundered much of Protestant Germany with the emperor's approval. In response, the Lutheran king of Denmark, Christian IV (r. 1596–1648), invaded to protect the Protestants and to extend his own influence.

Map 12.4 The Thirty Years' War and the Peace of Westphalia, 1648
The Thirty Years' War involved many of the major continental European powers. The arrows marking invasion routes show that most of the fighting took place in central Europe, in the lands of the Holy Roman Empire. The German states and Bohemia sustained the greatest damage during the fighting. None of the combatants emerged unscathed because even ultimate winners such as Sweden and France depleted their resources of men and money.

Wallenstein's forces defeated him. Emboldened by his general's victories, Ferdinand issued the Edict of Restitution in 1629, which outlawed Calvinism in the empire and reclaimed Catholic church properties confiscated by the Lutherans.

With Protestant interests in serious jeopardy, Gustavus Adolphus (r. 1611–1632) of Sweden marched into Germany in 1630. A Lutheran by religion, he also hoped to gain control over trade in northern Europe, where he had already ejected the Poles from present-day Latvia and Estonia. Poland and Lithuania had joined in a commonwealth (common state) in 1569, and many Polish and Lithuanian nobles converted to Lutheranism or Calvinism, but this did not ensure common cause with Sweden. Gustavus's highly trained army of some 100,000 soldiers made Sweden, with a population of only one million, the supreme power of northern Europe, even more powerful than Russia, which had barely recovered from the "Time of Troubles" that had followed on the rule of Tsar Ivan IV (r. 1533–1584). Known as "Ivan the Terrible" because of his rages, during one of which he killed his son and heir, Ivan had initiated Russian expansion eastward into Siberia, but his moves westward had run up against the Poles and the Swedes.

Although Gustavus had religious motives for intervening in German affairs, events soon showed that power politics trumped religious interests. The Catholic French government under the leadership of Louis XIII (r. 1610–1643) and his chief minister, Cardinal Richelieu (1585–1642), offered to subsidize Gustavus—and the Lutheran ruler accepted. The French hoped to counter Spanish involvement in the war and win influence and perhaps territory in the Holy Roman Empire. Gustavus defeated the imperial army and occupied the Catholic parts of southern Germany before he was killed at the battle of Lützen in 1632 (Map 12.4, page 459). Once again the tide turned, but this time it swept Wallenstein with it. Because Wallenstein was rumored to be negotiating with Protestant powers, Ferdinand dismissed his general and had his henchmen assassinate Wallenstein.

France openly joined the fray in 1635 by declaring war on Spain and soon after forged an alliance with the Calvinist Dutch to aid them in their struggle for independence from Spain. The two Catholic powers, France and Spain, pummeled each other. The Swedes kept up their pressure in Germany, the Dutch attacked the Spanish fleet, and a series of internal revolts shook the cash-strapped Spanish crown. In 1640, peasants in the rich northeastern province of Catalonia rebelled, overrunning Barcelona and killing the viceroy; the Catalans resented government confiscation of their crops and demands that they house and feed soldiers on their way to the French frontier. The Portuguese revolted in 1640 and proclaimed independence. In 1643, the Spanish suffered their first major defeat at French hands. Although the Spanish were forced to concede independence to Portugal (part of Spain only since 1580), they eventually suppressed the Catalan revolt.

France, too, faced exhaustion after years of rising taxes and recurrent revolts. In 1642, Richelieu died. Louis XIII followed him a few months later and was succeeded by his five-year-old son, Louis XIV. With the queen mother, Anne of Austria, serving as regent and depending on the Italian cardinal Mazarin for advice, French politics once again moved into a period of instability, rumor, and crisis. All sides were ready for peace.

Effects of Constant Fighting

When peace negotiations began in the 1640s, they did not come a moment too soon for the ordinary people of Europe. Some towns faced up to ten or eleven prolonged sieges during the fighting. In 1648, as negotiations dragged on, a Swedish army sacked the rich cultural capital of Prague, plundered its churches and castles, and effectively eliminated it as a center of culture and learning. Even worse suffering took place in the countryside. Peasants fled their villages, which were often burned down. War and intermittent outbreaks of plague cost some German towns one-third or more of their population. One-third of the inhabitants of Bohemia also perished.

Soldiers did not fare all that much better. Governments increasingly short of funds often failed to pay the troops, and frequent mutinies, looting, and pillaging resulted. Armies attracted all sorts of displaced people desperately in need of provisions. In the last year of the Thirty Years' War, the Imperial-Bavarian Army had 40,000 men entitled to draw rations—and more than 100,000 wives, prostitutes, servants, children, maids, and other camp followers forced to scrounge for their own food. The bureaucracies of early-seventeenth-century Europe simply could not cope with such demands: armies and their hangers-on had to live off the countryside.

Peace of Westphalia, 1648

The comprehensive settlement finally provided by the Peace of Westphalia—named after the German province where negotiations took place—would serve as a model for resolving conflict among warring European states. For the first time, a diplomatic congress addressed international disputes, and the signatories to the treaties guaranteed the resulting settlement. A method still in use, the congress was the first to bring all parties together, rather than two or three at a time.

France and Sweden gained most from the Peace of Westphalia. Although France and Spain continued fighting until 1659, France replaced Spain as the prevailing power on the European continent and acquired parts of Alsace, a region on its eastern border that would remain a source of conflict between French and German rulers well into the twentieth century. Baltic conflicts would not be resolved until 1661, but Sweden took several northern territories from the Holy Roman Empire (Map 12.4, page 459).

The Habsburgs lost the most. The Spanish Habsburgs recognized Dutch independence after eighty years of war. The Swiss Confederation and the German princes demanded autonomy from the Austrian Habsburg rulers of the Holy Roman Empire. Each German prince gained the right to establish Lutheranism, Catholicism, or Calvinism in his state, a right denied to Calvinist rulers by the earlier Peace of Augsburg. The independence ceded to German princes sustained political divisions that would remain until the nineteenth century. After losing considerable territory in the west, the Austrian Habsburgs turned eastward to concentrate on restoring Catholicism to Bohemia and wresting Hungary from the Turks.

The Peace of Westphalia permanently settled the distributions of the main religions in the Holy Roman Empire: Lutheranism would dominate in the north, Calvinism in the area of the Rhine River, and Catholicism in the south (see "Mapping the West," page 477). In the future, warfare between European states would be undertaken for reasons of national security, commercial ambition, or dynastic pride rather than to enforce religious uniformity. As the politiques of the late sixteenth century had hoped, state interests now outweighed motivations of faith in political affairs.

Growth of State Authority

Warfare increased the reach of states: as the size of armies increased, governments needed more men, more money, and more supervisory officials. Most armies in the 1550s had fewer than 50,000 men, but Gustavus Adolphus had 100,000 men under arms in 1631. In France, the rate of land tax paid by peasants doubled in the eight years after France joined the Thirty Years' War. In addition to raising taxes, governments deliberately depreciated the value of the currency, which often resulted in inflation and soaring prices; sold new offices; and manipulated the embryonic stock and bond markets. When all else failed, they declared bankruptcy. The Spanish government, for example, did so three times in the first half of the seventeenth century.

As the demand for soldiers and for the money to supply them rose, the number of state employees multiplied, paperwork proliferated, and appointment to office began to depend on university education in the law. Monarchs relied on advisers who began to take on the role of modern prime ministers. As the French king Louis XIII's chief minister, Richelieu arranged support for the Lutheran Gustavus even though Richelieu was a cardinal of the Catholic church. His priority was ***raison d'état*** (reason of state)—that is, the state's interest above all else. Richelieu silenced Protestants within France because they had become too independent, and he crushed noble and popular resistance to Louis's policies. He set up intendants—delegates from the king's council dispatched to the provinces—to oversee police, army, and financial affairs. Richelieu and his intendants still had to contend with the thousands of officials who had bought their offices and therefore owned them as personal property.

To justify the growth of state authority and the expansion of government bureaucracies, rulers carefully cultivated their royal images. James I of England explicitly argued that he ruled by divine right and was accountable only to God: "Kings are not only God's lieutenant on earth, but even by God himself they are called gods." Words rarely sufficed to make the point, however, and rulers used displays at court to overawe their subjects. Already in the 1530s, the French court of Francis I had numbered sixteen hundred people, including officials, guards, cooks, physicians, librarians, musicians, dwarfs, and animal trainers. When the court changed residence, which it did frequently, no fewer than eighteen thousand horses were required to transport the people, furniture, and documents—not to mention the dogs and falcons for the royal hunt. Hunting and mock battles honed the military skills of the male courtiers. Francis once staged a mock combat at court involving twelve hundred "warriors," and he led a party to lay siege to a model town during which several players were accidentally killed.

Just as soldiers had to learn new drills for combat, courtiers had to learn to follow precise rituals. In his influential treatise *The Courtier* (1528), the Italian diplomat Baldassare Castiglione (1478–1529) depicted the ideal courtier as a gentleman who spoke in a refined language and carried himself with nobility and dignity in the service of his prince and his lady. Spain's king Philip IV (r. 1621–1665) translated this notion of courtesy into detailed regulations that set the wages, duties, and ceremonial functions of every courtier. State funerals, public festivities, and court displays, like the acquisition of art and the building of sumptuous palaces, served to underline the power and glory of the ruler.

REVIEW Why did a war fought over religious disputes result in stronger states?

From Growth to Recession

The Protestant Reformation started in a period of economic growth, but by the time of the Thirty Years' War recession had set in. In the sixteenth century, despite religious and political turbulence, population grew, doubling in Spain and increasing 70 percent in England. The supply of precious metals swelled, too. Spanish gold imports from the American colonies peaked in the 1550s, silver in the 1590s (see "Taking Measure"). The flood of gold and silver fueled an astounding inflation in food prices in western Europe—400 percent in the sixteenth century. When recession

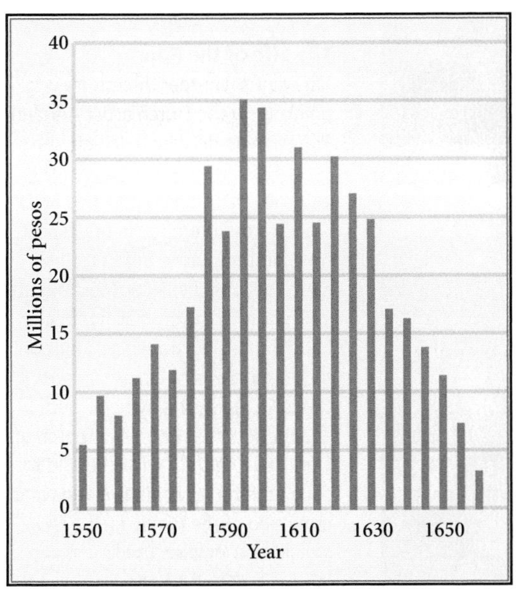

Taking Measure The Rise and Fall of Silver Imports to Spain, 1550–1660 Gold and silver from the New World enabled the king of Spain to pursue aggressive policies in Europe and around the world. At what point did silver imports, shown here, reach their highest level? Was the fall in silver imports precipitous or gradual? What can we conclude about the resources available to the Spanish king?

struck after 1600, all the economic indicators slumped: silver imports declined; textile production collapsed; agricultural prices dropped. Overall, Europe's population may actually have declined, from 85 million in 1550 to 80 million in 1650.

Causes and Consequences of Economic Crisis

Historians have long disagreed about the causes of the early-seventeenth-century recession. Some cite the inability of agriculture to support a growing population by the end of the sixteenth century. Others blame the Thirty Years' War, the states' demands for more taxes, the irregularities in money supply resulting from rudimentary banking practices, or the waste caused by middle-class expenditures in the desire to emulate the nobility. To this list of causes, recent researchers have added climate change. Global cooling translated into advancing glaciers, falling temperatures, and great storms, like the one that blocked the escape of the Spanish Armada. Bad harvests, food shortages, and famine followed in short order.

Economic crisis dramatically altered the rural landscape. As prices began to stagnate and population growth slowed, farmers converted grain-growing land to pasture or vineyards. In some places, peasants abandoned their villages and left

The Life of the Poor
This mid-seventeenth-century painting by the Dutch artist Adriaen Pietersz van de Venne depicts the poor peasant weighed down by his wife and child. An empty food bowl signifies their hunger. In retrospect, this painting seems unfair to the wife: she is shown in clothes that are not nearly as tattered as her husband's and is portrayed as a burden rather than as a helpmate in hard times. In reality, many poor men abandoned their homes in search of work, leaving their wives behind to cope with hungry children and what remained of the family farm. (Allen Memorial Art Museum, Oberlin College, Mrs. F. F. Prentiss Fund, 1960.)

land to waste, as had happened during the plague epidemic of the late fourteenth century. The only country that emerged relatively unscathed from this downturn was the Dutch Republic, principally because it had long excelled in agricultural innovation. Inhabiting Europe's most densely populated area, the Dutch developed systems of field drainage, crop rotation, and animal husbandry that provided high yields of grain for both people and animals. After the Dutch, the English fared best; unlike the Spanish, the English never depended on New World gold and silver, and unlike most continental European countries, England escaped the direct impact of the Thirty Years' War.

When grain harvests fell short, peasants immediately suffered because outside of England and the Dutch Republic, grain had replaced more expensive meat as the essential staple of most Europeans' diets. Peasants lived on bread, soup with a little fat or oil, peas or lentils, garden vegetables in season, and only occasionally a piece of meat or fish. Usually the adverse years differed from place to place, but from 1594 to 1597 most of Europe suffered from shortages that triggered revolts from Ireland to Muscovy. To head off social disorder, the English government drew up a new Poor Law in 1597 that required each community to support its poor. Many other governments also increased relief efforts.

Most people, however, did not respond to their dismal circumstances by rebelling or mounting insurrections. They simply left their huts and hovels and took to the road in search of food and charity. Overwhelmed officials recorded pitiful tales of suffering. Women and children died while waiting in line for food at convents or churches. Husbands left their wives and families to search for better conditions in other parishes or even other countries. Those left behind might be reduced to eating chestnuts, roots, bark, and grass. In eastern France in 1637, a witness reported, "The roads were paved with people. . . . Finally it came to cannibalism." Eventually compassion gave way to fear as these hungry vagabonds, who sometimes banded together to beg for bread, became more aggressive, occasionally threatening to burn a barn if they were not given food.

Successive bad harvests led to malnutrition, which weakened people and made them more susceptible to such epidemic diseases as the plague, typhoid fever, typhus, dysentery, smallpox, and influenza. Disease did not spare the rich, although many epidemics hit the poor hardest. The plague was feared most: in one year it could kill up to half a town or village's population, and it struck with no discernible pattern. Nearly 5 percent of France's population died in the plague epidemic of 1628–1632.

Economic crisis heightened the contrast between prosperity and poverty. In England, the Dutch Republic, northern France, and northwestern Germany, the peasantry was disappearing: improvements gave some peasants the means to become farmers who rented substantial holdings, produced for the market, and in good times enjoyed relative comfort and higher status. Those who could not afford to plant new crops such as buckwheat or to use techniques that ensured higher yields became simple laborers with little or no land of their own. One-half to four-fifths of the peasants in Europe did not have enough land to support a family.

They descended deeper into debt during difficult times and often lost their land to wealthier farmers or to city officials intent on developing rural estates.

Families reacted almost immediately to economic crisis. During bad harvests, they postponed marriages and had fewer children. When hard times passed, more people married and had more children. But even in the best of times, one-fifth to one-quarter of all children died in their first year, and half died before age twenty. Ten percent of women died in childbirth, and even in the richest homes childbirth often occasioned an atmosphere of panic. It might be assumed that families would have more children to compensate for high death rates, but from around 1600 to 1800, families in all ranks of society started to limit the number of children. Because methods of contraception were not widely known, they did this for the most part by marrying later; the average age at marriage during the seventeenth century rose from the early twenties to the late twenties. The average family had about four children. Poorer families seem to have had fewer children, wealthier ones more. Peasant couples, especially in eastern and southeastern Europe, had more children than urban couples because cultivation still required intensive manual labor.

The consequences of late marriage were profound. Young men and women were expected to put off marriage (and sexual intercourse) until their mid- to late twenties—if they were among the lucky 50 percent who lived that long and not among the 10 percent who never married. Because both the Reformation and the Counter-Reformation stressed sexual fidelity and abstinence before marriage, the number of births out of wedlock was relatively small (2 to 5 percent of births); premarital intercourse was generally tolerated only after a couple had announced their engagement.

The Economic Balance of Power

Just as the recession produced winners and losers among ordinary people, it also created winners and losers among the competing states of Europe. The seventeenth-century downturn ended the dominance of Mediterranean economies, which had endured since the time of the Greeks and Romans, and ushered in the new powers of northwestern Europe with their growing Atlantic economies. With expanding populations and geographical positions that promoted Atlantic trade, England and the Dutch Republic vied with France to become the leading mercantile powers. Northern Italian industries were eclipsed; Spanish commerce with the New World dropped. Amsterdam replaced Seville, Venice, Genoa, and Antwerp as the center of European trade and commerce. The plague also had differing effects. Whereas central Europe and the Mediterranean countries took generations to recover from its ravages, northwestern Europe quickly replaced its lost population, no doubt because this area's people had suffered less from the effects of the Thirty Years' War and from the malnutrition related to the economic crisis.

All but the remnants of serfdom had disappeared in western Europe, but in eastern Europe nobles reinforced their dominance over peasants, and the burden of serfdom increased. The price rise of the sixteenth century had prompted Polish and eastern German nobles to expand their holdings and step up their production of grain for western markets. Although noble landlords lost income in the economic downturn of the first half of the seventeenth century, their peasants gained nothing. Those who were already dependent became serfs—completely tied to the land. In Muscovy, the complete enserfment of the peasantry would eventually be recognized in the Code of Laws in 1649. Although enserfment produced short-term profits for landlords, in the long run it retarded economic development in eastern Europe and kept most of the population in a stranglehold of illiteracy and hardship.

Competition for colonies overseas intensified because many European states, including Sweden and Denmark, hoped it would tip the balance of power in their favor. According to the doctrine of mercantilism, governments should sponsor policies to increase national wealth and make sure new sources of wealth did not fall into the hands of their competitors. To this end, rulers chartered private joint-stock companies to enrich investors by importing fish, furs, tobacco, and precious metals, if they could be found, and to develop new markets for European products. Because Spain and Portugal had divided among themselves the rich spoils of South America, other prospective colonizers had to carve niches in seemingly less hospitable places, especially North America and the Caribbean. Eventually the English, French, and Dutch would dominate commerce with these colonies (Map 14.1, page 524).

What began as a competition for national wealth between trading companies soon evolved, sometimes by accident, into permanent colonies with whole new communities. Originally, the warm climate of Virginia made it an attractive destination for the Pilgrims, a small English sect that, unlike the Puritans, attempted to separate from the Church of England. But the *Mayflower,* which sailed for Virginia with Pilgrim emigrants, landed far to the north in Massachusetts, where in 1620 the settlers founded New Plymouth Colony. As the religious situation for English Puritans worsened, wealthier people became willing to emigrate, and in 1629 a prominent group of Puritans incorporated themselves as the Massachusetts Bay Company. They founded a virtually self-governing colony headquartered in Boston.

Colonization gradually spread. Migrating settlers, including dissident Puritans, soon founded new settlements in Connecticut and Rhode Island. Catholic refugees from England established a much smaller colony in Maryland. By the 1640s, the English North American colonies had more than fifty thousand people—not including the Indians, whose numbers had been decimated by epidemics and wars—and the foundations of representative government in locally chosen colonial assemblies.

By contrast, French Canada had only about three thousand European inhabitants by 1640. Because the French government refused to let Protestants emigrate from France and establish a foothold in the New World, it denied itself a ready population for the settling of permanent colonies abroad. Both England and France turned their attention to the Caribbean in the 1620s and 1630s when they occupied the islands of the West Indies after driving off the native Caribs. These islands would prove ideal for a plantation economy of tobacco and sugarcane.

REVIEW What were the consequences of economic recession in the early 1600s?

A Clash of Worldviews

The countries that moved ahead economically in this period—England, the Dutch Republic, and to some extent France—turned out to be the most receptive to new secular worldviews. Although secularization did not entail a loss of religious faith, it did prompt a search for nonreligious explanations for political authority and natural phenomena. During the late sixteenth and early seventeenth centuries, art, political theory, and science all began to break some of their bonds with religion. A "scientific revolution" was in the making. Yet traditional attitudes such as belief in magic and witchcraft did not disappear. People of all classes accepted supernatural explanations for natural phenomena, a view only gradually and partially undermined by new ideas.

The Arts in an Age of Religious Conflict

A new form of artistic expression—professional theater—developed to express secular values in this age of conflict over religious beliefs. In previous centuries, traveling companies made their living by playing at major religious festivals. In London, Seville, and Madrid, the first professional acting companies performed before paying audiences in the 1570s. A huge outpouring of playwriting followed. The Spanish playwright Lope de Vega (1562–1635) alone wrote more than fifteen hundred plays. Between 1580 and 1640, three hundred English playwrights produced works for a hundred different acting companies. Theaters did a banner business despite Puritan opposition in England and Catholic objections in Spain. Shopkeepers, apprentices, lawyers, and court nobles crowded into open-air theaters to see everything from bawdy farces to profound tragedies.

The most enduring and influential playwright of the time was the Englishman William Shakespeare (1564–1616), son of a glovemaker, who wrote three dozen plays and acted in one of the chief troupes. Shakespeare never referred to religious disputes in his plays and did not set the action in contemporary England. Yet his works clearly reflected the political concerns of his age: the nature of power and the crisis of authority. Three of his greatest tragedies—*Hamlet* (1601), *King Lear* (1605), and *Macbeth* (1606)—show the uncertainty and even chaos that result when power is misappropriated or misused. In each play, family relationships are linked to questions about the legitimacy of government, just as they were for Elizabeth I herself. Hamlet's mother marries the man who murdered his royal father and usurped the crown; Macbeth's wife persuades him to murder the king and seize the throne. Like many real-life people, Shakespeare's tragic characters found little peace in the turmoil of their times.

Although many rulers commissioned paintings on secular subjects for their own uses, religion still played an important role in painting, especially in Catholic Europe. The popes competed with secular rulers to hire the most talented painters and sculptors. Pope Julius II, for example, engaged the Florentine Michelangelo Buonarroti (1475–1564) to paint the walls and ceiling of the Sistine Chapel and to prepare a tomb and sculpture for himself. Michelangelo's talents served to glorify a papacy under siege, just as other artists burnished the images of secular rulers.

In the late sixteenth century, the artistic style known as **mannerism** departed abruptly from the Renaissance perspective of painters like Michelangelo. An almost theatrical style, mannerism allowed painters to distort perspective to convey a message or emphasize a theme. The most famous mannerist painter, El Greco, created new and often strange visual effects. The religious intensity of his pictures shows that faith still motivated many artists, as it did much political conflict.

The most important new style was the **baroque**, which featured exaggerated lighting, intense emotions, release from restraint, and even a kind of artistic sensationalism. *Baroque* was not used as a label by people living at the time; in the eighteenth century, art critics coined the word to mean shockingly bizarre, confused, and extravagant, and until the late nineteenth century, art historians and collectors largely disdained the baroque style. Closely tied to the Counter-Reformation, this style melodramatically reaffirmed the emotional depths of the Catholic faith and glorified both church and monarchy. The first great baroque painter was Peter Paul Rubens (1577–1640). Born in the Spanish Netherlands and trained in Italy, Rubens painted vivid, exuberant pictures on religious themes. The style spread from Rome to other Italian states and then into central Europe, Spain, and the Spanish Netherlands. The Spanish built baroque churches in their American colonies as part of their massive conversion campaign. The great Dutch Protestant painters of the next generation, such as Rembrandt van Rijn (1606–1669), sometimes used biblical subjects, but their pictures were more realistic and focused on everyday scenes. Many of them suggested the Protestant concern for an inner life and personal faith rather than the public expression of religiosity.

Differences in musical style also reflected religious divisions. The new Protestant churches developed their own distinct music, which differentiated their worship from the Catholic Mass. Unlike

Baroque Painting
The baroque painter Peter Paul Rubens used monumental canvases like this one from the Antwerp cathedral to celebrate the Catholic religion. Known as *The Elevation of the Cross,* this painting from 1610 to 1611 shows one of the most important moments in the story of the crucifixion of Jesus. (© Onze Lieve Vrouwkerk, Antwerp Cathedral, Belgium/The Bridgeman Art Library.)

Catholic services, for which professional musicians sang in Latin, Protestant services invited the entire congregation to sing, thereby encouraging participation. Martin Luther, an accomplished lute player, composed many hymns in German, including "Ein' feste Burg" ("A Mighty Fortress"). Protestants sang hymns before going into battle, and Protestant martyrs sang before their executions.

A new secular musical form, the opera, grew up parallel to the baroque style in the visual arts. First influential in the Italian states, opera combined music, drama, dance, and scenery in a grand sensual display, often with themes chosen to please the ruler and the aristocracy. Like Shakespeare, opera composers often turned to familiar stories their audiences would recognize and readily follow. One of the most innovative composers of opera was Claudio Monteverdi (1567–1643), whose work contributed to the development of both opera and the orchestra. His earliest operatic production, *Orfeo* (1607), was the first to require an orchestra of about forty instruments and to include instrumental as well as vocal sections.

The Natural Laws of Politics

In reaction to the wars over religious beliefs, jurists and scholars not only began to defend the primacy of state interests over those of religious conformity but also insisted on secular explanations for politics. Machiavelli had pointed in this direction with his prescriptions for Renaissance princes in the early sixteenth century, but the intellectual movement gathered steam in the aftermath of the religious violence unleashed by the Reformation. Religious toleration could not take hold until government could be organized on some principle other than one king, one faith. The French politiques Michel de Montaigne and Jean Bodin and the Dutch jurist Hugo Grotius started the search for those principles.

Michel de Montaigne (1533–1592) was a French magistrate who resigned his office in the midst of the wars of religion to write about the need for tolerance and open-mindedness. Although himself a Catholic, Montaigne painted on the beams of his study the words "All that is certain is that nothing is certain." In short and pointed essays filled with personal reflection, he revived the ancient doctrine of skepticism, which held that total certainty is never attainable—a doctrine, like toleration of religious differences, that was repugnant to Protestants and Catholics alike, both of whom were certain that their religion was the right one. Montaigne also questioned the common European habit of calling newly discovered peoples in the New World barbarous and savage: "Everyone gives the title of barbarism to everything that is not in use in his own country."

The French Catholic lawyer Jean Bodin (1530–1596) sought systematic secular answers to the problem of disorder in *The Six Books of the Republic* (1576). Comparing the different forms of government throughout history, he identified three basic types of sovereignty: monarchy, aristocracy, and democracy. Only strong monarchical power offered hope for maintaining order, he insisted. Bodin rejected any doctrine of the right to resist tyrannical authority: "I denied that it was the function of a good man or of a good citizen to offer violence to his prince for any reason, however great a tyrant he might be" (and, it might be added, whatever his ideas on religion). Bodin's ideas helped lay the foundation for absolutism, the idea that the monarch should be the sole and uncontested source of power. Nonetheless, the very discussion of types of governments in the abstract implied that they might be subject to choice rather than simply being God given, as most rulers maintained.

During the Dutch revolt against Spain, the jurist Hugo Grotius (1583–1645) gave new meaning to the notion of "natural law"—laws of nature that give legitimacy to government and stand above the actions of any particular ruler or religious group. Grotius argued that natural law stood beyond the reach of either secular or divine authority; it would be valid even if God did not exist. By this account, natural law—not Scripture, religious authority, or tradition—should govern politics. Such ideas got Grotius into trouble with both Catholics and Protestants. When the Dutch Protestant government arrested him, his wife helped him escape from prison by hiding him in a chest of books. Grotius was one of the first to argue that international conventions should govern the treatment of prisoners of war and the making of peace treaties.

At the same time that Grotius expanded the principles of natural law, many jurists worked on codifying the huge amount of legislation and jurisprudence devoted to legal forms of torture. Most states and the courts of the Catholic church used torture when the crime was serious and the evidence seemed to point to a particular defendant but no definitive proof had been established. The judges ordered torture—hanging the accused by the hands with a rope thrown over a beam, pressing the legs in a leg screw, or just tying the hands very tightly—to extract a confession, which had to be given with a medical expert and notary present and had to be repeated without torture. Children, pregnant women, the elderly, aristocrats, kings, and even professors were exempt.

Grotius's conception of natural law directly challenged the use of torture. To be in accord with natural law, Grotius argued, governments had to defend natural rights, which he defined as life, body, freedom, and honor. Grotius's ideas would influence John Locke and the American revolutionaries of the eighteenth century. Although Grotius did not encourage rebellion in the name of natural law or rights, he did hope that someday all governments would adhere to these principles and stop killing their own and one another's subjects in the name of religion. Natural law and natural rights would play an important role in the founding of constitutional governments from the 1640s forward and in the establishment of various charters of human rights in our own time.

The Scientific Revolution

Although the Catholic and Protestant churches encouraged the study of science and many prominent scientists were themselves clerics, the search for a secular, scientific method of determining the laws of nature eventually challenged the traditional accounts of natural phenomena. A revolution in astronomy undermined the view of the second-century Greek astronomer Ptolemy, endorsed by the Catholic church, which held that the sun revolved around the earth. Remarkable advances took place in medicine, too, which laid the foundations for modern anatomy and pharmacology. Conflicts between the new science and religion followed almost immediately, but toward the end of the seventeenth century Isaac Newton provided a new mathematical explanation for movement both on earth and in the heavens. It made the **scientific method** the new standard of truth.

The traditional account derived from Ptolemy put the earth at the center of the cosmos. Above the earth were fixed the moon, the stars, and the planets in concentric crystalline spheres; beyond these fixed spheres dwelt God and the angels. The sun revolved around the earth, the heavens were perfect and unchanging, and the earth was "corrupted." In 1543, the Polish clergyman Nicolaus Copernicus (1473–1543) attacked the Ptolemaic account in his treatise *On the Revolution of the Celestial Spheres.* He argued that it was mathematically simpler to calculate orbits if the earth and planets revolved around the sun, a view known as **heliocentrism** (a sun-centered universe).

Copernicus's views began to attract widespread attention in the early seventeenth century, when astronomers systematically collected evidence that undermined the Ptolemaic view. A leader among them was the Danish astronomer Tycho Brahe (1546–1601), whose observations of a new star in 1572 and a comet in 1577 called into question the Aristotelian view that the universe was unchanging. Brahe still rejected heliocentrism, but the assistant he employed when he moved to Prague in 1599, Johannes Kepler (1571–1630), was converted to the Copernican view. Kepler continued Brahe's collection of planetary observations and used the evidence to develop his three laws of planetary motion, published between 1609 and 1619. Kepler's laws provided mathematical backing for heliocentrism and directly challenged the claim long held, even by Copernicus, that planetary motion was circular. Kepler's first law stated that the orbits of the planets were ellipses, with the sun always at one focus of the ellipse.

The Italian Galileo Galilei (1564–1642) provided more evidence to support the heliocentric view and also challenged the doctrine that the heavens were perfect and unchanging. In 1609, he developed an improved telescope and then observed the earth's moon, four satellites of Jupiter, the phases of Venus (a cycle of changing physical appearances like that of the moon), and sunspots. The moon, the planets, and the sun were no more perfect than the earth, he insisted, and the shadows he could see on the moon could only be the product of hills and valleys like those on earth. Because he recognized the utility of the new science for everyday projects and hoped to appeal to a lay audience of merchants and aristocrats, Galileo was the first scientist to publish his studies in the vernacular (Italian) rather than in Latin.

Since his discoveries challenged the Bible as well as the commonsensical view that the sun rose and set while the earth stood still, Galileo's work alarmed the Catholic church. In 1616, the church forbade Galileo to teach that the earth moved and in 1633 accused him of not obeying the earlier order. Forced to appear before the Inquisition, he agreed to publicly recant his assertion that the earth moved to save himself from torture and death. Afterward he lived under house arrest and could publish his work only in the Dutch Republic, which had become a haven for scientists and thinkers who challenged conventional ideas.

Startling breakthroughs took place in medicine, too. Until the mid-sixteenth century, medical knowledge in Europe had been based on the writings of the second-century Greek physician Galen, a contemporary of Ptolemy. In the same year that Copernicus challenged the traditions of astronomy (1543), the Flemish scientist Andreas Vesalius (1514–1564) did the same for anatomy. He published a new illustrated anatomical text, *On the Construction of the Human Body*, that revised Galen's work by drawing on public dissections in the medical faculties of European universities. Theophrastus Bombastus von Hohenheim, better known as Paracelsus (1493–1541), went even further than Vesalius. He burned Galen's text at the University of Basel, where he was a professor of medicine. Paracelsus experimented with new drugs, performed operations (at the time most academic physicians taught medical theory, not practice), and pursued his interests in magic, alchemy, and astrology. He helped establish the modern science of pharmacology.

The Englishman William Harvey (1578–1657) also used dissection to examine the circulation of blood within the body, demonstrating how the heart worked as a pump. The heart and its valves were "a piece of machinery," Harvey claimed. They obeyed mechanical laws just as the planets and earth revolved around the sun in a mechanical universe. Nature could be understood by experiment and rational deduction, not by following traditional authorities.

In the 1630s, the European intellectual elite began to accept the new scientific views. Ancient learning, the churches and their theologians, and even cherished popular beliefs seemed to be undermined by a new standard of truth—the scientific method, which was based on systematic experiments and rational deduction. Two men were chiefly responsible for spreading the prestige of the scientific method, the English politician Sir Francis Bacon (1561–1626) and the French mathematician and philosopher René Descartes (1596–1650). Respectively, they represented the two essential processes of the scientific method: (1) inductive reasoning through observation and experimental research and (2) deductive reasoning from self-evident principles.

In *The Advancement of Learning* (1605), Bacon attacked reliance on ancient writers and optimistically predicted that the scientific method would lead to social progress. The minds of the medieval scholars, he said, had been "shut up in the cells of a few authors (chiefly Aristotle, their dictator) as their persons were shut up in the cells of monasteries and colleges." Knowledge, in Bacon's view, must be empirically based—that is, gained by observation and experiment. Claiming that God had called the Catholic church "to account for their degenerate manners and ceremonies," Bacon looked to the Protestant English state, which he served as lord chancellor, for leadership on the road to scientific advancement.

Although Descartes agreed with Bacon's denunciation of traditional learning, he saw that the attack on tradition might only replace the dogmatism of the churches with the skepticism of Montaigne—that nothing at all was certain. A Catholic who served in the Thirty Years' War, Descartes insisted that human reason could not only unravel the secrets of nature but also prove the existence of God. He aimed to establish the new science on more secure philosophical foundations, those of mathematics and logic. Not coincidentally, Descartes invented analytic geometry. In his *Discourse on Method* (1637), he argued that mathematical and mechanical principles provided the key to understanding all of nature, including the actions of people and states. All prior assumptions must be repudiated in favor of one elementary principle: "I think, therefore I am." Everything else could—and should—be doubted, but even doubt showed the certain existence of someone thinking. Begin with the simple and go on to the complex, he asserted, and believe only those ideas that present themselves "clearly and distinctly." Although Descartes hoped to secure the authority of both church and state, his reliance on human reason alone irritated authorities, and his books were banned in many places. He moved to the Dutch Republic to work in peace. Scientific research, like economic growth, became centered in the northern, Protestant countries, where it was less constrained by church control.

Building on the work of Copernicus, Kepler, and Galileo, the English scientist Isaac Newton (1642–1727) finally synthesized astronomy and physics with his **law of universal gravitation**, further enhancing the prestige of the new science. Yet Newton also aimed to reconcile faith and science. By proving that the physical universe followed rational principles, Newton argued, scientists could prove the existence of God and so liberate humans from doubt and the fear of chaos. Newton applied mathematical principles to formulate three physical laws: (1) in the absence of external force, an object in motion continues in a straight line; (2) the rate of change in the motion of an object is a result of the forces acting on it; and (3) the action and reaction between two objects are equal and opposite. The basis of Newtonian physics thus required understanding mass, inertia, force, velocity, and acceleration—all key concepts in modern science.

Extending these principles to the entire universe in his masterwork, *Principia Mathematica* (1687), Newton united celestial and terrestrial mechanics—astronomy and physics—with his law of universal gravitation. This law holds that every body in the universe exerts over every other body an attractive force directly proportional to the product of their masses and inversely proportional to the square of the distance between them. The law of gravitation explained Kepler's elliptical planetary orbits just as it accounted for the motion of ordinary objects on earth. Once set in motion, the universe operated like clockwork, with no need for God's continuing intervention. Gravity, though a mysterious force, could be expressed mathematically. Not all scientists accepted Newton's theories immediately, but within a couple of generations his work was preeminent, partly because of experimental verification. His breakthroughs remained the basis for all physics until the advent of relativity theory and quantum mechanics in the early twentieth century.

Magic and Witchcraft

Despite the new emphasis on clear reasoning, observation, and independence from past authorities, science had not yet become entirely separate from magic. Paracelsus and Newton studied alchemy alongside other scientific pursuits; magic and science were still closely linked. In a world in which most people believed in astrology, magical healing, prophecy, and ghosts, it is hardly surprising that many of Europe's learned people also firmly believed in witchcraft, the exercise of magical powers gained by a pact with the devil. The same Jean Bodin who argued against religious fanaticism insisted on death for witches—and for those magistrates who would not prosecute them. In France alone, 345 books and pamphlets on witchcraft appeared between 1550 and 1650. Trials of witches peaked in Europe between 1560 and 1640, the very time of the celebrated breakthroughs of the new science. Montaigne was one of the few to speak out against executing accused witches. "It is taking one's conjectures rather seriously to roast someone alive for them," he wrote in 1580.

Belief in witches was not new in the sixteenth century. Witches had long been thought capable of almost anything: passing through walls, flying through the air, destroying crops, and causing personal catastrophes from miscarriage to demonic possession. What was new was the official persecution, justified by the notion that witches were agents of Satan whom the righteous must oppose. In a time of economic crisis, plague, warfare, and the clash of religious differences, witchcraft trials provided an outlet for social stress and anxiety, legitimated by state power. At the same time, the trials seem to have been part of the religious reform movement itself. Denunciation and persecution of witches coincided with the spread of reform, both Protestant and Catholic. The trials concentrated especially in the German lands of the Holy Roman Empire, the boiling cauldron of the Thirty Years' War.

The victims of the persecution were overwhelmingly female: women accounted for 80 percent of the accused witches in about 100,000 trials in Europe and North

Giving a Child to Satan
This woodcut from Francesco Maria Guazzo's *Compendium Maleficarum* of 1608 shows witches giving a child to the devil. Many believed that witches made a pact with the devil to carry out his evil deeds. (The Art Archive/Dagli Orti [A].)

America during the sixteenth and seventeenth centuries. About one-third were sentenced to death. Before 1400, when witchcraft trials were rare, nearly one-half of those accused had been men. Two Catholic clergymen compiled a guide for detecting witches, the *Malleus Maleficarum* (Hammer of Witches), which was published in 1486 and reissued countless times in the sixteenth and seventeenth centuries. Official descriptions of witchcraft oozed lurid details of sexual orgies, incest, homosexuality, and cannibalism, in which women acted as the devil's sexual slaves. Social factors help explain the prominence of women among the accused. The poorest and most socially marginal people in most communities were elderly spinsters and widows. Because they were thought likely to hanker after revenge on those more fortunate, they were singled out as witches.

Witchcraft trials declined when scientific thinking about causes and effects raised questions about the evidence used in court: how could judges or jurors be certain that someone was a witch? The tide turned everywhere at about the same time, as physicians, lawyers, judges, and even clergy came to suspect that accusations were based on popular superstition and peasant untrustworthiness. In 1682, a French royal decree treated witchcraft as fraud and imposture, meaning that the law did not recognize anyone as a witch. In 1693, the jurors who had convicted twenty witches in Salem, Massachusetts, recanted, claiming, "We justly fear that we were sadly deluded and mistaken." The Salem jurors had not stopped believing in witches; they had simply lost confidence in their ability to identify them. When physicians and judges had believed in witches and persecuted them officially, with torture, witches had gone to their deaths in record numbers. But when the same groups distanced themselves from popular beliefs, the trials and the executions stopped.

REVIEW How could belief in witchcraft and the rising prestige of the scientific method coexist?

Conclusion

The witchcraft persecutions reflected the traumas of these times of religious war and economic decline. Marauding armies combined with economic depression, disease, and the threat of starvation to shatter the lives of many ordinary Europeans, while religious conflicts shaped the destinies of every European power in this period. These conflicts began with the Protestant Reformation, which dispelled forever the Christian humanist dream of peace and unity, and came to a head from 1618 to 1648 in the Thirty Years' War, which cut a path of destruction through central Europe and involved most of the European powers. Shocked by the effects of religious violence, European rulers agreed to a peace that effectively removed disputes between Catholics and Protestants from the international arena.

The growing separation of political motives from religious ones did not mean that violence or conflict had ended, however. Struggles for religious uniformity within states would continue, though on a smaller scale. Bigger armies required more state involvement, and almost everywhere rulers emerged from these decades

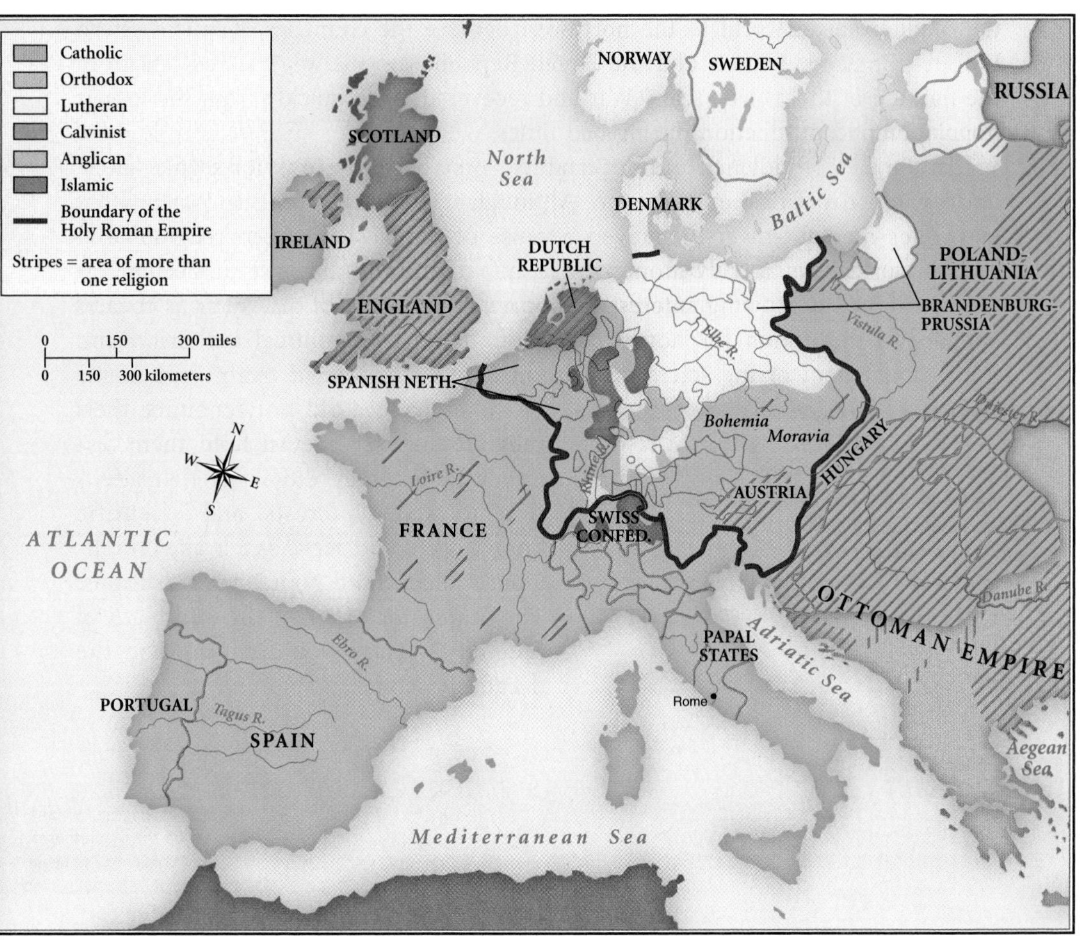

Mapping the West The Religious Divisions of Europe, c. 1648
The Peace of Westphalia recognized major religious divisions within Europe that have endured for the most part to the present day. Catholicism dominated in southern Europe, Lutheranism had its stronghold in northern Europe, and Calvinism flourished along the Rhine River. In southeastern Europe, the Islamic Ottoman Turks accommodated the Greek Orthodox Christians under their rule but bitterly fought the Catholic Austrian Habsburgs for control of Hungary.

of conflict with expanded powers. The growth of state power directly changed the lives of ordinary people: more men went into the armies, and most families paid higher taxes. The constant extension of state power is one of the defining themes of modern history; religious warfare gave it a jump start.

For all their increased power, rulers could not control economic, social, or intellectual trends, much as they often tried. The economic downturn of the seventeenth century produced unexpected consequences for European states even while it made life miserable for many ordinary people. Economic power and vibrancy shifted from the Mediterranean world to the northwest because the countries of northwestern Europe—England, France, and the Dutch Republic especially—suffered less from the fighting of the Thirty Years' War and recovered more quickly from the loss of population and production during bad times.

In the face of violence and uncertainty, some began to look for secular alternatives in art, politics, and science. Although it would be foolish to claim that everyone's mental universe changed because of the clash between religious and secular worldviews, a truly monumental shift in attitudes had begun. Secularization combined a growing interest in nonreligious forms of art, such as theater and opera; the search for nonreligious foundations of political authority; and the establishment of the scientific method as the standard of truth. Proponents of these changes did not renounce their religious beliefs or even hold them less fervently, but they did insist that attention to state interests and scientific knowledge could serve as a brake on religious violence and popular superstitions. The search for order in the aftermath of religious warfare would continue in the decades to come.

CHAPTER REVIEW QUESTIONS

1. How did the balance of power in Europe shift between 1500 and 1648? What were the main reasons for the shift?
2. Relate the new developments in the arts and sciences to the political and economic changes in this period of crisis.

TIMELINE

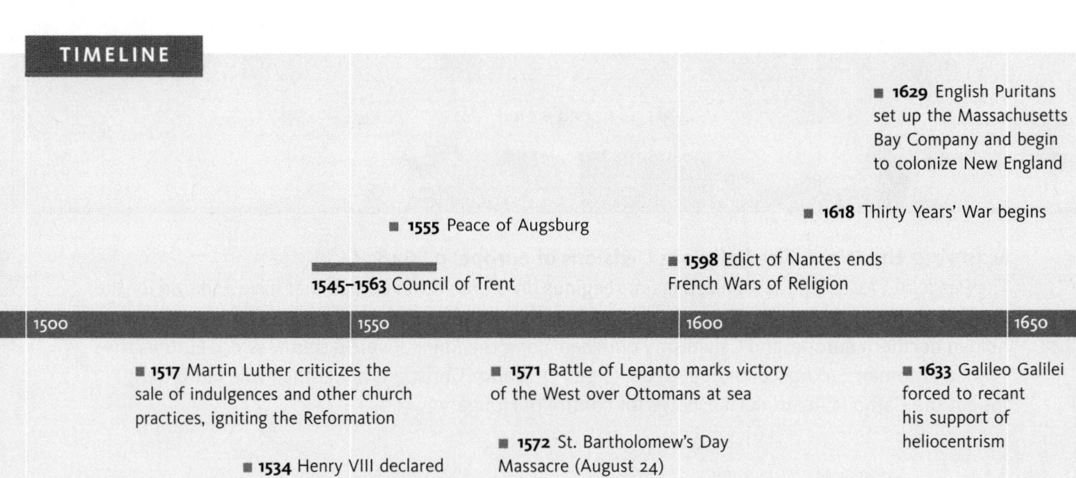

For practice quizzes and other study tools, see the Online Study Guide at bedfordstmartins.com/huntconcise.

For primary-source material from this period, see Chapters 14 and 15 of *Sources of* THE MAKING OF THE WEST, Third Edition.

Suggested References

Religion, warfare, science, witchcraft, and the travails of everyday life have all been the subject of groundbreaking research, yet the personalities of individual rulers still make for great stories, too.

Benedict, Philip. *Christ's Churches Purely Reformed: A Social History of Calvinism.* 2002.

Bonney, Richard. *The Thirty Years' War.* 2002.

Braudel, Fernand. *The Mediterranean and the Mediterranean World in the Age of Philip the Second.* Trans. Siân Reynolds. 2 vols. 1972, 1973.

Briggs, Robin. *Witches and Neighbors: The Social and Cultural Context of European Witchcraft.* 1996.

*Diefendorf, Barbara B. *The Saint Bartholomew's Day Massacre: A Brief History with Documents.* 2009.

**Erasmus: The Praise of Folly and Other Writings.* Trans. Robert M. Adams. 1989.

Galileo Project: http://galileo.rice.edu

Hsia, R. Po-chia. *The World of the Catholic Renewal.* 1997.

Jacob, James. *The Scientific Revolution.* 1998.

Luther's life and thought: http://www.luther.de/en

Lynn, John A. *Women, Armies, and Warfare in Early Modern Europe.* 2008.

Patterson, Benton Rain. *With the Heart of a King: Elizabeth I of England, Philip II of Spain, and the Fight for a Nation's Soul and Crown.* 2007.

13

State Building and the Search for Order

1648–1690

During a week in May 1664, King Louis XIV of France organized a series of entertainments for his court at Versailles, where he had recently begun the construction of a magnificent new palace. More than six hundred members of his court attended the series of spectacles called "The Delights of the Enchanted Island." The carefully orchestrated activities opened with an elaborate parade of the king and his courtiers, accompanied by an eighteen-foot-high float in the form of a chariot dedicated to Apollo, the Greek god of the sun and Louis's personally chosen emblem. During the week, the king's favorite artists presented works prepared especially for the occasion, including ballets, plays, and musical concerts. Equestrian tournaments, visits to the king's personal collection of wild animals and birds, and a huge fireworks display captivated the audience. Every detail of the festivities appeared in an official program published the same year.

Louis XIV and His Bodyguards
One of Louis XIV's court painters, Adam Frans van der Meulen, depicted the king arriving at the Palace of Versailles, still under construction (the painting dates from 1669). None of the gardens, pools, or statues had yet been installed. Louis is the only figure facing the viewer, and his dress is much more colorful than that of anyone else in the painting. *(Réunion des Musées Nationaux/Art Resource, NY.)*

Louis XIV spared no expense in promoting his image, especially to those most dangerous to him, the leading nobles of the kingdom. Other rulers either followed his example or explicitly rejected it, but they could not afford to ignore it. All governments faced the daunting task of rebuilding authority after the wars over religion and the economic recession of the early seventeenth century. As part of his campaign to emphasize his majesty, Louis encouraged leading nobles to dispense huge sums to entertain him and his court. He always spent even more in order to show that he was richer and more powerful than any noble or than any other monarch.

Louis XIV's model of state building was known as **absolutism**, a system of government in which the ruler claimed sole and uncontestable power. Although absolutism exerted great influence, especially in central and eastern Europe, it faced competition from **constitutionalism**, a system in which the ruler had to share power with parliaments made up of elected representatives. Constitutionalism led to weakness in Poland-Lithuania, but it provided a strong foundation for state power in England, the English North American colonies, and the Dutch Republic. Constitutionalism triumphed in England, however, only after one king had been executed as a traitor and another had been deposed.

Whether absolutist or constitutionalist, states faced similar challenges to state building in the mid-seventeenth century. Competition in the international arena required resources, and all states raised taxes, provoking popular protests and even rebellions. The wars over religion that had culminated in the Thirty Years' War (1618–1648) left many economies in dire straits, and, even more significant, they created a need for new explanations of political authority. Monarchs still relied on religion to justify their divine right to rule, but they increasingly sought secular defenses of their powers, too. Absolutism and constitutionalism were the two main responses to the threat of disorder and breakdown left as a legacy of the wars over religion.

The search for order took place not only at the level of states and rulers but also in intellectual, cultural, and social life. Thomas Hobbes and John Locke famously sought to ground political authority in a **social contract**. Artists looked for ways of glorifying power and expressing order and symmetry in their work. As states consolidated their power, elites endeavored to distinguish themselves more clearly from the lower orders. The upper classes emulated the manners developed at court and tried in every way to distance themselves from anything viewed as vulgar or lower-class. Officials, clergy, and laypeople all worked to reform the poor, now seen as a major source of disorder.

CHAPTER FOCUS QUESTION What were the chief differences between absolutism and constitutionalism?

Louis XIV: Model of Absolutism

The French king Louis XIV (r. 1643–1715) personified the absolutist ruler who in theory shared his power with no one. Louis personally made all important state decisions and left no room for dissent. In 1651, he reputedly told the Paris high court of justice, "*L'état, c'est moi*" (I am the state), emphasizing that state authority rested in him personally. Louis cleverly manipulated the affections and ambitions of his courtiers, chose as his ministers middle-class men who owed everything to him, built up Europe's largest army, and snuffed out every hint of religious or political opposition. Yet the absoluteness of his power should not be exaggerated. Like all other rulers of his time, Louis depended on the cooperation of many others: local officials who enforced his decrees, peasants and artisans who joined his armies and paid his taxes, creditors who loaned crucial funds, and nobles who joined court festivities organized to glorify the king rather than stay at home and cause trouble.

The Fronde, 1648–1653

Louis XIV built on a long French tradition of increasing centralization of state authority, but before he could extend it, he had to weather a series of revolts known as the **Fronde**. Derived from the French word for a child's slingshot, the term was used by critics to signify that the revolts were mere child's play. In fact, they posed an unprecedented threat to the French crown. Louis was only five when he came to the throne in 1643 upon the death of his father, Louis XIII. Louis XIV's mother, Anne of Austria, and her Italian-born adviser and rumored lover, Cardinal Mazarin (1602–1661), ruled in the young monarch's name. To meet the financial pressure of fighting the Thirty Years' War and then even after the peace to keep up a draining war against Spain, Mazarin sold new offices, raised taxes, and forced creditors to extend loans to the government. In 1648, a coalition of his opponents presented him with a charter of demands that, if granted, would have given the **parlements** (high courts) a form of constitutional power with the right to approve new taxes. Mazarin responded by arresting the coalition's leaders. He soon faced a series of revolts that at one time or another involved nearly every social group in France and lasted until 1653.

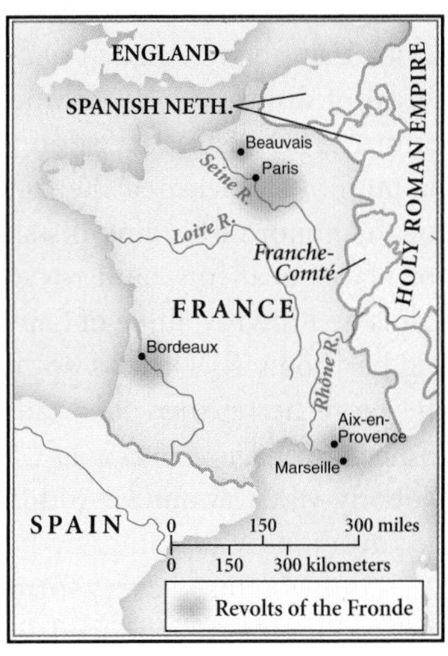

The Fronde, 1648–1653

Faced with barricades in the streets of Paris, Anne took Louis and fled the city. As civil war threatened, Mazarin and Anne agreed to compromise with the parlements. The nobles then tried to reassert their own claims to power by raising private armies. The middle and lower classes chafed at the constant tax increases and in some places organized revolts. Conflicts erupted throughout the kingdom, and rampaging soldiers devastated rural areas and disrupted commerce. Neither the nobles nor the judges of the parlements really wanted to overthrow the king; they simply wanted a greater share in power. But Louis XIV never forgot the humiliation and uncertainty that marred his childhood. Years later he recalled an incident in which a band of Parisians had invaded his bedchamber to determine whether he had fled the city, and he declared the event an affront not only to himself but also to the state. His own policies as ruler would be designed to prevent the repetition of any such revolts.

Court Culture as an Element of Absolutism

When Cardinal Mazarin died in 1661, Louis XIV decided to rule without a first minister. He described the dangers of his situation in memoirs he wrote later for his son's instruction: "Everywhere was disorder. My Court as a whole was still very far removed from the sentiments in which I trust you will find it." Typically quarrelsome, the French nobles had long exercised local authority by maintaining their own fighting forces, meting out justice on their estates, arranging jobs for underlings, and resolving their own conflicts through dueling.

Louis set out to domesticate the warrior-nobles by replacing violence with court ritual. Using a systematic policy of bestowing pensions, offices, honors, gifts, and the threat of disfavor or punishment, he made himself the center of French power and culture. The aristocracy soon vied for his favor, attended the ballets and theatricals he put on, and learned the rules of etiquette he supervised. Great nobles competed for the honor of holding his shirt when he dressed, foreign ambassadors squabbled for places near him, and royal mistresses basked in the glow of his personal favor. Louis de Rouvroy, duke of Saint-Simon (1675–1755), complained, "There was nothing he [Louis XIV] liked so much as flattery . . . the coarser and clumsier it was, the more he relished it." Madame de Lafayette described the effects on court life in her novel *The Princess of Cleves* (1678): "The Court gravitated around ambition. Nobody was tranquil or indifferent—everybody was busily trying to better his or her position by pleasing, by helping, or by hindering somebody else."

Louis XIV used every form of art—mock battles, theatrical performances, paintings, sculpture, poetry, medals, histories, even the ritual of his dinner—to enhance his personal prestige. Calling himself "the Sun King," Louis adorned his palace with statues of Apollo and emulated the style of the ancient Roman emperors. The king's officials treated the arts as a branch of government. Louis's ministers set up royal academies of dance, painting, architecture, and music and took control of the Académie Française (French Academy), which to this day decides on correct usage of the French language. A royal furniture workshop at the Gobelins tapestry works on the outskirts of Paris turned out the delicate and ornate pieces whose style bore the king's name. Louis's government also regulated the number and locations of theaters and closely censored all forms of publication.

Music and theater enjoyed special prominence. Louis commissioned operas to celebrate royal marriages, baptisms, and military victories. The king himself danced in ballets if a role seemed especially important. Playwrights presented their new plays directly to the court. Pierre Corneille and Jean-Baptiste Racine wrote tragedies set in Greece or Rome that celebrated the new aristocratic virtues that Louis aimed to inculcate: a reverence for order and self-control.

Louis glorified his image through massive public works projects as well. Military facilities, such as veterans' hospitals and fortified towns on the frontiers, represented his military might. Urban improvements, such as the reconstruction of the Louvre palace in Paris, proved his wealth. But his most ambitious project was the construction of a new palace at Versailles, twelve miles from the turbulent capital. Building began in the 1660s, and by 1685, the frenzied effort engaged 36,000 workers, not including the thousands of troops who diverted a local river to supply water for pools and fountains. Even the gardens reflected the spirit of Louis XIV's rule: their geometrical

The Palace of Versailles
This painting by Jean-Baptiste Martin from the late seventeenth century gives a good view of one section of the palace and especially the geometrically arranged gardens. (Réunion des Musées Nationaux/ Art Resource, NY.)

arrangements and clear lines showed that art and design could tame nature and that order and control defined the exercise of power. Versailles symbolized Louis's success in reining in the nobility and dominating Europe. Other monarchs eagerly mimicked French fashion and often conducted their business in French.

By the time Louis actually moved from the Louvre to Versailles in 1682, he had reigned as monarch for thirty-nine years. Fifteen thousand people crowded into the palace's apartments, including all the highest military officers, the ministers of state, and the separate households of each member of the royal family. After the death of his queen in 1683, Louis secretly married his mistress, Françoise d'Aubigné, marquise de Maintenon, and conducted most state affairs from her apartments at the palace. De Maintenon's opponents at court complained that she controlled all the appointments, but her efforts focused on her own projects, including her favorite: the founding in 1686 of a royal school for girls from impoverished noble families. She also inspired one of Louis XIV's most fateful decisions—to root out any alternatives to Roman Catholicism.

Enforcing Religious Conformity

Louis believed that he ruled by divine right. As Bishop Jacques-Benigne Bossuet (1627–1704) explained, "We have seen that kings take the place of God." Louis believed it was his duty as God's lieutenant to bring his subjects to the one true religion. He first focused on the Jansenists, Catholics whose doctrines and practices resembled some aspects of Protestantism. Following the posthumous publication of the book *Augustinus* (1640) by the Flemish theologian Cornelius Jansen (1585–1638), the Jansenists stressed the need for God's grace in achieving salvation. They emphasized the importance of original sin and insisted on an austere religious practice. Prominent among the Jansenists was Blaise Pascal (1623–1662), a mathematician of genius, who wrote his *Provincial Letters* (1656–1657) to defend Jansenism against charges of heresy. Many judges in the parlements likewise endorsed Jansenist doctrines.

Some questioned Louis's understanding of the finer points of Catholic doctrine. According to his German-born sister-in-law, Louis himself "has never read anything about religion, nor the Bible either, and just goes along believing whatever he is told." Louis rejected any teaching that gave priority to considerations of individual conscience over the demands of the official church hierarchy. He insisted on obedience to authority. Therefore, in 1660 he began enforcing various papal bulls (decrees) against Jansenism and closed down Jansenist theological centers. Jansenists were forced underground for the rest of his reign.

After many years of escalating pressure on the Calvinist Huguenots, Louis revoked the Edict of Nantes in 1685 and eliminated all of the Calvinists' rights. Louis considered the edict (1598), by which his grandfather Henry IV granted the Protestants religious freedom and a degree of political independence, a temporary measure, and he fervently hoped to reconvert the Huguenots to Catholicism. He closed their churches and schools, purged all Calvinists from official positions, and forced Calvinist ministers into exile even while refusing to let ordinary Protestants leave. Nonetheless, at least 150,000 Huguenots refused to submit and fled to England, Brandenburg-Prussia, or the Dutch Republic. Refugee Calvinists soon wrote essays and books denouncing Louis XIV's absolutism. Protestant European countries were shocked by this crackdown on religious dissent and would cite it when they went to war against Louis.

Extending State Authority at Home and Abroad

Louis XIV could not have enforced his religious policies without the services of a nationwide **bureaucracy**. The word *bureaucracy*—a network of state officials carrying out orders according to a regular and routine line of authority—comes from *bureau,* the French word for "desk," which came to mean "office," in the sense of both a physical space and a position of authority. Louis extended the bureaucratic forms his predecessors had developed, especially the use of intendants, officials who held their positions directly from the king rather than owning their offices. Louis handpicked them to represent his will against entrenched local interests such as the parlements, provincial estates, and noble governors. The intendants reduced local powers over finances and insisted on more efficient tax collection. Despite the doubling of taxes in Louis's reign, the local rebellions that had so beset the crown from the 1620s to the 1640s subsided in the face of these better-organized state forces.

Louis's success in consolidating his authority depended on hard work, an eye for detail, and an ear to the ground. In his memoirs he explained his priorities:

> to be well-informed on an infinite number of matters about which we are supposed to know nothing; to elicit from our subjects what they hide from us with the greatest care; to discover the most remote opinions of our courtiers and the most hidden interests of those who come to us with quite contrary professions [claims].

To gather all this information, Louis relied on a series of talented ministers, usually of modest origins, who gained fame, fortune, and even noble status by serving the king. Most important among them was Jean-Baptiste Colbert (1619–1683), the son of a wool merchant turned royal official. Colbert had managed Mazarin's personal finances and worked his way up under Louis XIV to become controller general, the head of royal finances, public works, and the navy.

Colbert followed the policy of **mercantilism**, which held that governments must intervene to increase national wealth by whatever means possible. Such government intervention inevitably increased the role and eventually the number of bureaucrats needed. Under Colbert, the French government established overseas trading companies, granted manufacturing monopolies, and standardized production methods for textiles, paper, and soap. A government inspection system regulated the quality of finished goods and compelled all craftsmen to organize into guilds, in which masters could supervise the work of the journeymen and apprentices. To protect French production, Colbert rescinded many internal customs fees while enacting high tariffs on foreign imports. To compete more effectively with England and the Dutch Republic, Colbert also subsidized shipbuilding, a policy that dramatically expanded the number of seaworthy vessels. Such mercantilist measures aimed to ensure France's prominence in world markets and to provide the resources needed to fight wars against its increasingly long list of enemies. Although later economists questioned the value of this state intervention in the economy, nearly every government in Europe embraced mercantilism.

Colbert's mercantilist projects extended to Canada, where in 1663 he took control of the trading company that had founded New France. He transplanted several thousand peasants from western France to the present-day province of Quebec, which France had claimed since 1608, and he sent fifteen hundred soldiers to fend off the Iroquois, who regularly raided French fur-trading convoys. Shows of French military force, including the burning of Indian villages and winter food supplies, forced the Iroquois to make peace, and from 1666 to 1680 French traders moved westward with minimal interference. In 1672, the fur trader Louis Jolliet and Jesuit missionary Jacques Marquette reached the upper Mississippi River and traveled downstream as far as Arkansas. In 1684, the French explorer Sieur de La Salle ventured all the way down to the Gulf of Mexico, claiming a vast territory for Louis XIV and calling it Louisiana after him. Louis and Colbert encouraged colonial settlement as part of their rivalry with the English and Dutch in the New World.

Colonial settlement occupied only a small portion of Louis XIV's attention, however, for his main foreign policy goal was to extend French power in Europe. In pursuing this purpose, he inevitably came up against the Spanish and Austrian Habsburgs, whose lands encircled his. To expand French power, Louis needed the biggest possible army. The ministry of war centralized the organization of French troops. Barracks built in major towns received supplies from a central distribution system. The state began to provide uniforms for the soldiers and to offer veterans some hospital care. A militia draft instituted in 1688 supplemented the army in times of war and enrolled 100,000 men. Louis's wartime army could field a force as large as that of all his enemies combined.

Louis gained new enemies as he tried to expand the territory under his rule. In 1667–1668, in the first of his major wars after assuming personal direction of French affairs, Louis defeated the Spanish armies but had to make peace when England, Sweden, and the Dutch Republic joined the war. In the Treaty of Aix-la-Chapelle in 1668, he gained control of towns on the border of the Spanish Netherlands (Map 13.1). Pamphlets sponsored by the Habsburgs accused Louis of aiming for "universal monarchy," or domination of Europe.

In 1672, Louis XIV opened hostilities against the Dutch because they stood in the way of his acquisition of more territory in the Spanish Netherlands. He declared war again on Spain in 1673. By now the Dutch had allied themselves with their former Spanish masters to hold off the French. Louis also marched his troops into territories of the Holy Roman Empire, provoking many of the German princes to join with the emperor, the Spanish, and the Dutch in an alliance against Louis, now denounced as a "Christian Turk" for his imperialist ambitions. But the French armies more than held their own. Faced with bloody yet inconclusive results on the battlefield, the parties agreed to the Treaty of Nijmegen of 1678–1679, which ceded several Flemish towns and Franche-Comté to Louis (Map 13.1, page 489). These territorial additions were costly: French government deficits soared, and increases in taxes touched off the most serious antitax revolt of Louis's reign in 1675.

Louis had no intention of standing still. Heartened by the Habsburgs' seeming weakness, he pushed eastward, seizing the city of Strasbourg in 1681 and invading the province of Lorraine in 1684. Lorraine would remain a subject of contention between France and its neighbors for nearly three centuries. In 1688, Louis attacked some of the small German cities of the Holy Roman Empire and was soon involved in a long war against a coalition made up of England, Spain, Sweden, the Dutch Republic, the Austrian emperor, and various German princes. Between 1689 and 1697, the coalition fought Louis to a stalemate. When hostilities ended in the Treaty of Rijswijk in 1697, Louis returned many of his conquests made since 1678, with

Map 13.1 Louis XIV's Acquisitions, 1668–1697
Every ruler in Europe hoped to extend his or her territorial control, and war was often the result. Louis XIV steadily encroached on the Spanish Netherlands to the north and the lands of the Holy Roman Empire to the east. Although coalitions of European powers reined in Louis's grander ambitions, he incorporated many neighboring territories into the French crown.

the exception of Strasbourg (Map 13.1). Louis never lost his taste for war, but his enemies learned how to set limits on his ambitions.

Louis was the last French ruler before Napoleon to accompany his troops to the battlefield. In later generations, as the military became more professional, French rulers left the fighting to their generals. Although Louis had managed to suppress the private armies of his noble courtiers, he constantly promoted his own military prowess in order to keep his noble officers under his sway. He had miniature battle scenes painted on his high heels and commissioned tapestries showing his military processions into cities, even those he did not take by force. He seized every occasion to assert his supremacy, insisting that other fleets salute his ships first.

War required money and men, which Louis obtained by expanding state control over finances, conscription into the army, and military supply. Thus absolutism and warfare fed each other, as the bureaucracy created new ways to raise and maintain an army and the army's success in war justified the expansion of state power. But constant warfare also eroded the state's resources. Further administrative and legal reform, the elimination of the buying and selling of offices, and the lowering of taxes—all were made impossible by the need for more money.

The playwright Corneille wrote, no doubt optimistically, "The people are very happy when they die for their kings." What is certain is that the wars touched many peasant and urban families. The people who lived on the routes leading to the battlefields had to house and feed soldiers; only nobles were exempt from this requirement. Everyone, moreover, paid the higher taxes that were necessary to support the army. By the end of Louis's reign, one in six Frenchmen had served in the military.

REVIEW How "absolute" was the power of Louis XIV?

Absolutism in Central and Eastern Europe

Central and eastern European rulers saw in Louis XIV a powerful model of absolutist state building. Yet they did not blindly emulate the Sun King, in part because they confronted conditions peculiar to their regions. The ruler of Brandenburg-Prussia had to rebuild lands ravaged by the Thirty Years' War and unite far-flung territories. The Austrian Habsburgs needed to govern a mosaic of ethnic and religious groups while fighting off the Ottoman Turks. The Russian tsars wanted to extend their power over a large but relatively impoverished empire. The great exception to absolutism in eastern Europe was Poland-Lithuania, where a long crisis virtually destroyed central authority and sucked much of eastern Europe into its turbulent wake.

Brandenburg-Prussia and Sweden: Militaristic Absolutism

Brandenburg-Prussia began as a puny state on the Elbe River, but it would have a remarkable future. In the nineteenth century, it would unify the disparate German states into modern-day Germany. The ruler of Brandenburg was an elector, one of the seven German princes entitled to select the Holy Roman Emperor. Since the sixteenth century, the ruler of Brandenburg had also controlled the duchy of East Prussia; after 1618, the state was called Brandenburg-Prussia. Despite meager resources, Frederick William of Hohenzollern, the Great Elector of Brandenburg-Prussia (r. 1640–1688), succeeded in welding his scattered lands into an absolutist state.

Pressured first by the necessities of fighting the Thirty Years' War and then by the demands of reconstruction, Frederick William determined to force his territories' estates (representative institutions) to grant him a dependable income. The Great Elector struck a deal with the Junkers (nobles) of each land: in exchange for allowing him to collect higher taxes to support his growing army, he gave them complete control over the peasants. The tactic worked. By the end of his reign the estates met only on ceremonial occasions.

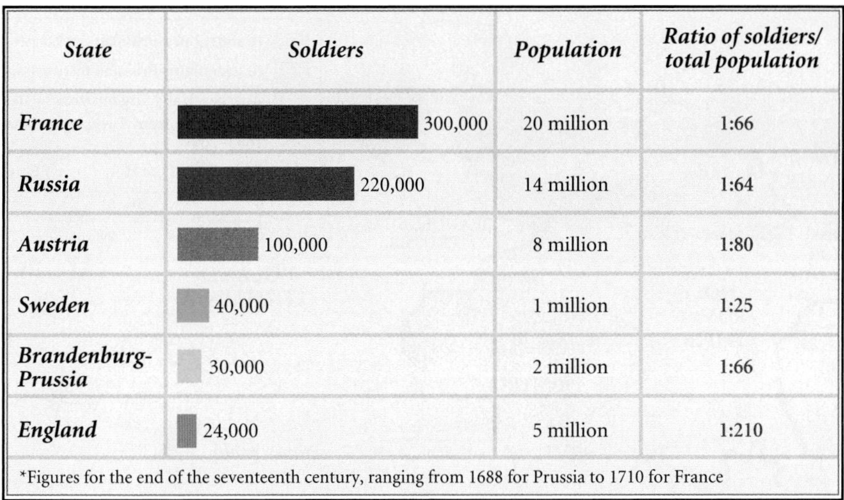

State	Soldiers	Population	Ratio of soldiers/ total population
France	300,000	20 million	1:66
Russia	220,000	14 million	1:64
Austria	100,000	8 million	1:80
Sweden	40,000	1 million	1:25
Brandenburg-Prussia	30,000	2 million	1:66
England	24,000	5 million	1:210

*Figures for the end of the seventeenth century, ranging from 1688 for Prussia to 1710 for France

Taking Measure The Seventeenth-Century Army
The figures in this chart are only approximate, but they tell an important story. What conclusions can we draw about the relative weight of the military in the different European states? Why would England's army have been so much smaller than the other states'? Is the absolute or the relative size of the military the more important indicator?

Supplied with a steady income, Frederick William could devote his attention to military and bureaucratic consolidation. Over forty years he expanded his army from eight thousand to thirty thousand men (see "Taking Measure"). The army mirrored the rigid domination of nobles over peasants that characterized Brandenburg-Prussian society: peasants filled the ranks, and Junkers became officers. Nobles also took positions as bureaucratic officials, but military needs always had priority. The Great Elector named special war commissars to take charge not only of military affairs but also of tax collection. To hasten military dispatches, he also established one of Europe's first state postal systems.

As a Calvinist ruler, Frederick William disdained the ostentation of the French court, even while following the absolutist model of centralizing state power. He boldly rebuffed Louis XIV by welcoming twenty thousand French Huguenot refugees after Louis's revocation of the Edict of Nantes. In pursuing policies that promoted state power, Frederick William adroitly switched sides in Louis's wars and would stop at almost nothing to crush resistance at home. In 1701, his son Frederick I (r. 1688–1713) persuaded Holy Roman Emperor Leopold I to grant him the title "king in Prussia." Prussia had arrived as an important power (Map 13.2).

Across the Baltic, Sweden also stood out as an example of absolutist consolidation. In the Thirty Years' War, King Gustavus Adolphus's superb generalship and highly trained army had made Sweden the supreme power of northern Europe. The huge but sparsely populated state included not only most of present-day Sweden but also Finland, Estonia, half of Latvia, and much of the Baltic coastline of modern Poland

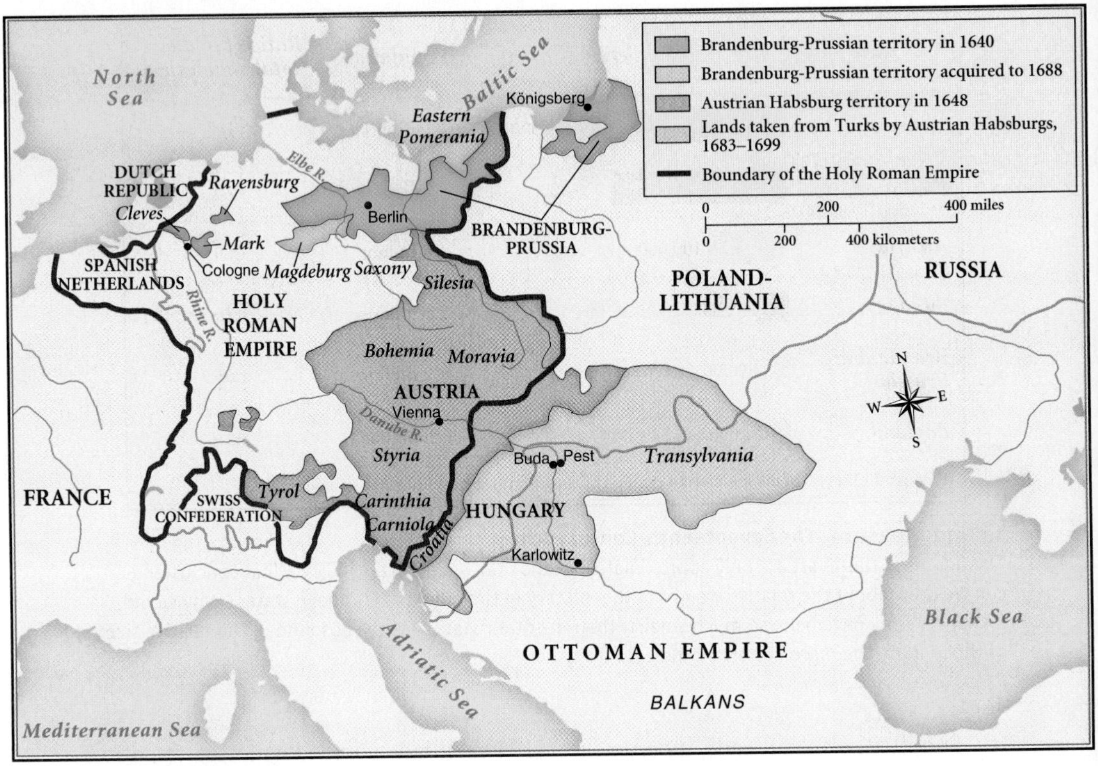

Map 13.2 State Building in Central and Eastern Europe, 1648–1699
The Austrian Habsburgs had long contested the Ottoman Turks for dominance of eastern Europe, and by 1699 they had pushed the Turks out of Hungary. In central Europe, the Austrian Habsburgs confronted the growing power of Brandenburg-Prussia, which had emerged from relative obscurity after the Thirty Years' War to begin an aggressive program of expanding its military and its territorial base. As emperor of the Holy Roman Empire, the Austrian Habsburg ruler governed a huge expanse of territory, but the emperor's control was in fact only partial because of guarantees of local autonomy.

and Germany. The Baltic, in short, was a Swedish lake. After Gustavus Adolphus died, his daughter Queen Christina (r. 1632–1654) conceded much authority to the estates. Absorbed by religion and philosophy, Christina eventually abdicated and converted to Catholicism. Her successors temporarily made Sweden an absolute monarchy.

Absolutism in Sweden (as in neighboring Denmark-Norway) took the form of the estates standing aside while the king led the army on lucrative foreign campaigns. The aristocracy went along because it staffed the bureaucracy and reaped war profits. Though intrigued by French culture, Sweden also gleamed with national pride. In 1668, the nobility demanded the introduction of a distinctive national costume: should Swedes, they asked, "who are so glorious and renowned a nation . . . let ourselves be led by the nose by a parcel of French dancing-masters"? Sweden spent the forty years after 1654 continuously warring with its neighbors. By the 1690s, war expenses began to outrun the small Swedish population's ability to pay, threatening the continuation of absolutism.

An Uneasy Balance: Austrian Habsburgs and Ottoman Turks

Holy Roman Emperor Leopold I (r. 1658–1705) ruled over a variety of territories of different ethnicities, languages, and religions, yet in ways similar to his French and Prussian counterparts, he gradually consolidated his power. Like all the Holy Roman emperors since 1438, Leopold was an Austrian Habsburg. He was simultaneously duke of Upper and Lower Silesia, count of Tyrol, archduke of Upper and Lower Austria, king of Bohemia, king of Hungary and Croatia, and ruler of Styria and Moravia (Map 13.2, page 492). Some of these territories were provinces in the Holy Roman Empire; others were simply ruled from Vienna as Habsburg family holdings.

Leopold needed to build up his armies and state authority in order to defend the Holy Roman Empire's international position, which had been weakened by the Thirty Years' War, and to push back the Ottoman Turks, who steadily encroached from the southeast. The emperor and his closest officials took control over recruiting, provisioning, and strategic planning and worked to replace the mercenaries hired during the Thirty Years' War with a permanent standing army that promoted professional discipline. To pay for the army and to staff his growing bureaucracy, Leopold had to gain the support of local aristocrats and chip away at the powers of the provincial institutions. Intent on replacing Bohemian nobles who had supported the 1618 revolt against Austrian authority, the Habsburgs promoted a new nobility made up of Czechs, Germans, Italians, Spaniards, and even Irish, who used German as their common tongue, professed Catholicism, and loyally served the Austrian dynasty. Bohemia became a virtual Austrian colony. "You have utterly destroyed our home, our ancient kingdom," lamented a Czech Jesuit in 1670, addressing Leopold. "Of smiling towns you have made straggling villages." Austrian censors prohibited publication of this protest for over a century.

In addition to holding Louis XIV in check on his western frontiers, Leopold confronted the ever-present challenge of the Ottoman Turks to his east. In 1683, the Turks once again pushed all the way to the gates of Vienna and laid siege to the Austrian capital. After reaching this high-water mark, however, Turkish power ebbed. With the help of Polish cavalry, the Austrians finally broke the siege and turned the tide in a major counteroffensive. By the Treaty of Karlowitz of 1699, the Ottoman Turks surrendered almost all of Hungary to the Austrians (Map 13.2, page 492).

Hungary's "liberation" from the Turks came at a high price. The fighting laid waste vast stretches of Hungary's central plain, and the population may have declined as much as 65 percent since 1600. To repopulate the land, the Austrians settled large communities of foreigners: Romanians, Croats, Serbs, and Germans. Magyar (Hungarian) speakers became a minority, and the seeds were sown for the poisonous nationality conflicts that would take place in nineteenth- and twentieth-century Hungary, Romania, and Yugoslavia.

The Siege of Vienna, 1683 This detail from a painting by Franz Geffels shows the camp of the Ottoman Turks. The Turkish armies surrounded Vienna on July 14, 1683. Jan Sobieski led an army of Poles that joined with Austrian and German forces to beat back the Turks on September 12. (© The Art Archive/ Corbis.)

Once the Turks had been beaten back, Austrian rule over Hungary tightened. In 1687, the Habsburg dynasty's hereditary right to the Hungarian crown was acknowledged by the Hungarian diet, a parliament revived by Leopold in 1681 to gain the support of Hungarian nobles. The diet was dominated by nobles who had amassed huge holdings in the liberated territories. They formed the core of a pro-Habsburg Hungarian aristocracy that would buttress the dynasty until it fell in 1918. As the Turks retreated from Hungary, Leopold systematically rebuilt churches, monasteries, roadside shrines, and monuments in the flamboyant Austrian baroque style.

The Ottoman Turks also pursued state consolidation, but in a very different fashion from the Europeans. The Ottoman state extended its authority through a combination of settlement and military control. Hundreds of thousands of Turkish families moved with Turkish soldiers into the Balkan peninsula in the 1400s and 1500s. As locals converted to Islam, administration passed gradually into their hands. In the Ottoman homeland of Anatolia, the sultans, the Ottoman rulers, were often challenged by mutinous army officers. Despite frequent palace coups and assassinations, the Ottoman state survived by hiring restive peasants as mercenaries and by playing bureaucratic elites off one another. This constantly shifting social and political system explains how the coup-ridden Ottoman state could appear "weak" in Western eyes and still pose a massive military threat on Europe's southeastern borders. In the end, the Ottoman state lasted much longer than Louis XIV's absolute monarchy.

Russia: Foundations of Bureaucratic Absolutism

Seventeenth-century Russia seemed a world apart from the Europe of Louis XIV. Straddling Europe and Asia, it stretched across Siberia to the Pacific Ocean. Western visitors either sneered or shuddered at the "barbarism" of Russian life, and Russians reciprocated by nursing deep suspicions of everything foreign. But under the surface, Russia was evolving along paths much like the rest of absolutist Europe; the tsars increased their power by surmounting internal disorder and coming to an accommodation with noble landlords.

When Tsar Alexei (r. 1645–1676) tried to extend state authority by imposing new administrative structures and taxes in 1648, Moscow and other cities erupted in bloody rioting. The government immediately doused the fire. In 1649, Alexei convoked the Assembly of the Land (consisting of noble delegates from the provinces) to consult on a sweeping law code to organize Russian society in a strict social hierarchy that would last for nearly two centuries. The code of 1649 assigned all subjects to a hereditary class according to their current occupation or state needs. Slaves and free peasants were merged into a serf class. As serfs they could not change occupations or move; they were tightly tied to the soil and to their noble masters. To prevent tax evasion, the code also forbade townspeople to move from the community where they resided. Nobles owed absolute obedience to the tsar and were required to serve in the army, but in return no other group could own estates worked by serfs. Serfs became the chattel of their lords, who could sell them like horses or land. Their conditions of life differed little from those of the slaves on the plantations in the Americas.

Some peasants resisted enserfment. In 1667, Stenka Razin led a huge rebellion in southern Russia that promised liberation from "the traitors and bloodsuckers of the peasant communes"—the great noble landowners, local governors, and Moscow courtiers. Razin was a Cossack, the name given to bandit gangs consisting of runaway serfs and poor nobles in southern Russia and Ukraine. Captured four years later by the tsar's army, Razin was dismembered, his head and limbs publicly displayed and his body thrown to the dogs. Thousands of his followers also suffered grisly deaths, but his memory lived on in folk songs and legends. Landlords successfully petitioned for the abolition of the statute of limitations on runaway serfs and for harsh penalties against those who harbored runaways. The increase in Russian state authority went hand in hand with the enforcement of serfdom.

To extend his power and emulate his western rivals, Tsar Alexei wanted a bigger army, exclusive control over state policy, and a greater say in religious matters. The size of the army increased dramatically from 35,000 in the 1630s to 220,000 by the end of the century (see "Taking Measure," page 491). The Assembly of the Land, once an important source of noble consultation, never met again after 1653. In 1666, the Russian Orthodox church reaffirmed the tsar's role as God's direct representative on earth and took action against a religious group called the Old Believers, who rejected church efforts to bring Russian worship in line with Byzantine tradition. Whole communities of Old Believers starved or burned themselves to death rather than submit. Religious schism opened a gulf between the Russian people and the crown.

Stenka Razin in Captivity
After leading a revolt of thousands of serfs, peasants, and members of non-Russian tribes of the middle and lower Volga region, Razin was captured by Russian forces and led off to Moscow, where he was executed in 1671. He has been the subject of songs, legends, and poems ever since. (RIA Novosti.)

The tsar's emulation of western rivals extended to culture, too. Alexei set up the first Western-style theater in the Kremlin, and his daughter Sophia translated French plays. Nobles and ordinary citizens commissioned portraits of themselves instead of buying only religious icons. The most adventurous nobles began to wear German-style clothing. A long struggle over Western influence had begun.

Poland-Lithuania Overwhelmed

Unlike the other eastern European powers, Poland-Lithuania did not follow the absolutist model. Decades of war weakened the monarchy and made the great nobles into practically autonomous warlords. They used the parliament and demands for constitutionalism to stymie monarchical power. The result was a precipitous slide into political disarray and weakness.

In 1648, Ukrainian Cossack warriors revolted against the king of Poland-Lithuania, inaugurating two decades of tumult known as the Deluge. In 1654, the Cossacks offered Ukraine to Russian rule, provoking a Russo-Polish war that ended in 1667 when the tsar annexed eastern Ukraine and Kiev. Sweden, Brandenburg-Prussia, and Transylvania sent armies to seize territory, too. As much as a third of the Polish population eventually perished in the fighting. The once prosperous Jewish and Protestant minorities suffered great losses: some 56,000 Jews were killed by either the Cossacks, Polish peasants, or Russian troops. One rabbi wrote, "We were slaughtered each day, in a more agonizing way than cattle: they are butchered quickly, while we were being executed slowly." Surviving Jews moved from towns to shtetls (Jewish villages), where they could survive only by petty trading, moneylending, tax gathering, and tavern leasing—activities that fanned peasant anti-Semitism. Desperate for protection amid the war, most Protestants backed the violently anti-Catholic Swedes, and the victorious Catholic majority branded them as traitors, forcing some Protestants to seek refuge as far away as the Dutch Republic and England. In Poland-Lithuania, once an outpost of religious toleration, it came to be assumed that a good Pole was a Catholic.

The commonwealth revived briefly when Jan Sobieski (r. 1674–1696) was elected king. He gained a reputation throughout Europe when he led 25,000 Polish cavalrymen into battle in the siege of Vienna in 1683. His cavalry helped rout the Turks and turned the tide against the Ottomans. Married to a politically shrewd French princess, Sobieski openly admired Louis XIV's France. Despite his efforts to rebuild the monarchy, he could not halt Poland-Lithuania's decline into powerlessness.

Elsewhere the ravages of war had created opportunities for kings to increase their power, but in Poland-Lithuania the great nobles gained all the advantage. They dominated the Sejm (parliament), and to maintain an equilibrium among themselves, they each wielded an absolute veto power. This "free veto" constitutional system soon deadlocked parliamentary government. The monarchy lost its room to maneuver, and with it much of its remaining power. An appalled Croat visitor in 1658 commented, "Among the Poles there is no order in the state. . . . Everybody who is stronger thinks to have the right to oppress the weaker, just as the wolves and bears are free to capture and kill cattle. . . . Such abominable depravity is called by the Poles 'aristocratic freedom.'" The Polish version of constitutionalism fatally weakened the state and made it prey to its neighbors.

REVIEW Why did absolutism succeed everywhere in eastern Europe except Poland-Lithuania?

Constitutionalism in England

In the second half of the seventeenth century, western and eastern Europe began to move in different directions. In general, the farther east one traveled, the more absolutist the style of government (with the exception of Poland-Lithuania) and the greater the gulf between landlord and peasant. In eastern Europe, nobles lorded over their serfs but owed almost slavish obedience in turn to their rulers. In western Europe, even in absolutist France, serfdom had almost entirely disappeared, and nobles and rulers alike faced greater challenges to their control. The greatest challenges of all would come in England.

This outcome might seem surprising, for the English monarchs enjoyed many advantages compared with their continental rivals: they needed less money for their armies because they had stayed out of the Thirty Years' War, and their island kingdom was in theory easier to rule because they governed a relatively homogeneous population only one-fourth the size of France's with few regional institutions to block the ruler's will. Yet the English rulers failed in their efforts to install absolutist policies. The English revolutions of 1642–1660 and 1688–1689 overturned two kings, confirmed the constitutional powers of an elected parliament, and laid the foundation for the idea that government must guarantee certain rights under the law.

England Turned Upside Down, 1642–1660

Disputes about the right to levy taxes and the nature of authority in the Church of England had long troubled the relationship between the English crown and Parliament. For over a hundred years, wealthy English landowners had been accustomed to participating in government through Parliament and expected to be consulted on royal policy. Although England had no one constitutional document, customary procedures and a variety of laws, judicial decisions, charters, and petitions granted by the king regulated relations between king and Parliament. When Charles I tried to assert his authority over Parliament, a civil war broke out. It set in motion an unpredictable chain of events, which included an extraordinary ferment of religious and political ideas. Some historians view the English civil war of 1642–1646 as the last great war of religion because it pitted Puritans against those trying to push the Anglican church toward Catholicism, but it should be considered the first modern revolution because it gave birth to democratic political and religious movements.

Charles I (r. 1625–1649) inherited the problems that had been left by his father, James I, and James's predecessor, Elizabeth I. Elizabeth had defended the crown's right to regulate religion, but neither she nor James definitively reined in the Puritans. In addition, James antagonized Parliament by selling monopolies and titles to raise money and by relying increasingly on the advice of his favorite courtier, George Villiers, rumored to be his lover. Charles consequently faced an increasingly aggressive Parliament when he inherited the throne. In 1628, Parliament forced Charles to agree to the Petition of Right, by which he promised not to levy taxes without its consent. Charles hoped to avoid further interference with his plans by simply refusing to call Parliament into session between 1629 and 1640.

Religious tensions brought conflicts over the king's authority to a head. The Puritans had long agitated for the removal of any vestiges of Catholicism, but Charles, married to a French Catholic, moved in the opposite direction. With Charles's encouragement, the archbishop of Canterbury, William Laud (1573–1645), imposed increasingly elaborate ceremonies on the Anglican church. Angered by these moves toward "popery," the Puritans poured forth vituperative pamphlets and sermons. In response Laud hauled them before the feared Court of Star Chamber, a special court consisting of handpicked members of the king's council. The Court of Star Chamber came to stand for royal tyranny and religious persecution because it rode roughshod over the regular judicial process and imposed its own penalties. The court ordered harsh sentences for Laud's Puritan critics; they were whipped, pilloried, and branded and even had their ears cut off and their noses split. When Laud tried to apply his policies to Scotland, however, they backfired completely. The stubborn Presbyterian Scots rioted against the imposition of bishops and a prayer book modeled on the Anglican Book of Common Prayer. In 1640 the Scots invaded the north of England and defeated Charles's army. To raise money, Charles called Parliament into session and unwittingly opened the door to a constitutional and religious crisis.

Reformers in the House of Commons (the lower house of Parliament) seized the opportunity to undo what they saw as the growing royal tyranny of the 1630s. Parliament removed Laud from office, ordered the execution of an unpopular royal commander, abolished the Court of Star Chamber, repealed recently levied taxes, and provided for a parliamentary assembly at least once every three years, thus establishing a constitutional check on royal authority. Moderate reformers expected to stop there and resisted Puritan pressure to abolish bishops and eliminate the Anglican prayer book. But their hand was forced in January 1642, when Charles and his soldiers invaded Parliament and tried unsuccessfully to arrest those leaders who had moved to curb his power. Faced with mounting opposition within London, Charles withdrew from the city and prepared to fight.

The ensuing civil war between king and Parliament lasted four years (1642–1646) and divided the country. The king's army of royalists, known as Cavaliers, enjoyed the most support in northern and western England. The parliamentary forces, called Roundheads because they cut their hair short, had their stronghold in the southeast, including London. Although Puritans dominated on the parliamentary side, they were divided about the proper form of church government: the Presbyterians wanted a Calvinist church with some central authority, whereas the Independents favored entirely autonomous congregations free from other church government (hence the term *congregationalism,* often associated with the Independents). Putting aside their differences for the sake of military victory, the Puritans united under an obscure member of the House of Commons, the country gentleman Oliver Cromwell (1599–1658). Cromwell was one of the generals of the New Model Army, so called because it was a disciplined national force rather than a hodgepodge of local militias. The New Model Army defeated the Cavaliers at the battle of Naseby in 1645. Charles fled to Scotland but was turned over by the Scots in 1647.

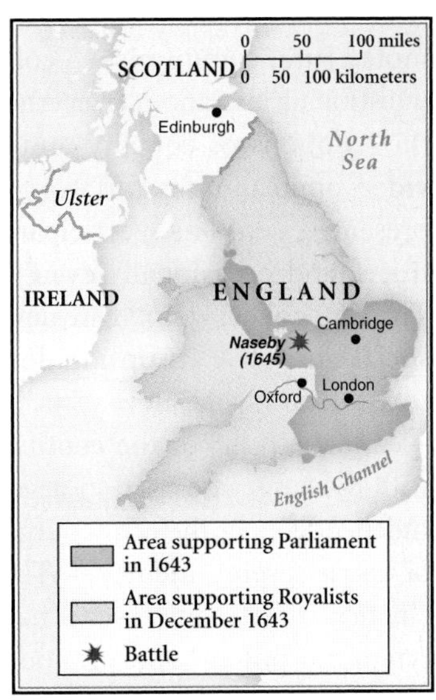

England during the Civil War, 1642–1646

Although the civil war between king and Parliament had ended in victory for Parliament, divisions within the Puritan ranks now came to the fore: the Presbyterians dominated Parliament, but the Independents controlled the army. The disputes between elites drew lower-class groups into the debate. When Parliament tried to disband the New Model Army in 1647, disgruntled soldiers protested. Called Levellers because of their insistence on leveling social differences, the soldiers took on their officers in a series of debates about the nature of political authority. The Levellers demanded that Parliament meet annually, that members be paid so as to allow common people to participate, and that all male heads of households be allowed to vote. Their ideal of political participation excluded servants, the propertyless, and women but offered access to artisans, shopkeepers, and modest farmers. Cromwell and other army leaders rejected the Levellers' demands as threatening to property owners. Cromwell insisted, "You have no other way to deal with these men but to break them in pieces. . . . If you do not break them they will break you."

Just as political differences between Presbyterians and Independents helped spark new political movements, so too did their conflicts over church organization foster the emergence of new religious doctrines. The new sects had in common only their emphasis on the "inner light" of individual religious inspiration and a disdain for hierarchical authority. Their emphasis on equality before God and greater participation in church governance appealed to the middle and lower classes. The Baptists, for example, insisted on adult baptism because they believed that Christians should choose their own church and that every child should not automatically become a member of the Church of England. Quaker men pointedly refused to take off their hats as a sign of respect to men in authority. Manifesting their religious experience by trembling, or "quaking," the Quakers believed that anyone, man or woman, inspired by a direct experience of God could preach.

Parliamentary leaders feared that the new sects would overturn the whole social hierarchy. Rumors abounded, for example, of naked Quakers running through the streets waiting for a "sign." Some sects did advocate sweeping change. Diggers promoted rural communism—collective ownership of all property. Seekers and Ranters questioned just about everything. A few men advocated free love. In keeping with their notions of equality and individual inspiration, many of the new sects provided opportunities for women to become preachers and prophets. Women also presented petitions, participated prominently in street demonstrations, distributed tracts, and occasionally even dressed as men, wearing swords and joining armies. The outspoken women in new sects like the Quakers underscored the threat of a social order turned upside down. These developments convinced the political elite that tolerating the new sects would lead to skepticism, anarchy, and debauchery.

At the heart of the continuing political struggle was the question of what to do with the king, who tried to negotiate with the Presbyterians in Parliament. In late 1648, Independents in the army purged the Presbyterians from Parliament, leaving a "rump" of about seventy members. This Rump Parliament then created a high court to try Charles I. The court found him guilty of attempting to establish "an unlimited and tyrannical power" and pronounced a death sentence. On January 30, 1649, Charles was beheaded before an enormous crowd, which reportedly groaned as one when the axe fell. Although many had objected to Charles's autocratic rule, few had wanted him killed. For royalists, Charles immediately became a martyr, and reports of miracles, such as the curing of blindness by the touch of a handkerchief soaked in his blood, soon circulated. In 1650, the dead king's son Charles (the future Charles II) allied with Scottish royalists, but Cromwell's forces routed them. Charles escaped to France.

Execution of Charles I
This print of the execution of the English king Charles I on January 30, 1649, appeared on the first page of the fictitious confessions of his executioner, Richard Brandon, who supposedly claimed to feel pains in his own neck from the moment he cut off Charles's head. (© British Library, London, UK/The Bridgeman Art Library.)

The Rump Parliament abolished the monarchy and the House of Lords (the upper house of Parliament). It set up a republic with Cromwell as head of the Council of State. Cromwell did not tolerate dissent from his policies. He saw the hand of God in events and himself as God's agent. When plans for mutiny within the army were discovered, Cromwell had the perpetrators executed. Although Cromwell allowed the various Puritan sects to worship rather freely and permitted Jews with needed skills to return to England for the first time since the thirteenth century, Catholics could not worship publicly, nor could Anglicans use the Book of Common Prayer. The elites, many of whom were still Anglicans, were troubled by Cromwell's religious policies but pleased to see some social order reestablished.

The new regime aimed to extend state power just as Charles I had before. Cromwell laid the foundation for a Great Britain made up of England, Wales, Ireland, and Scotland by reconquering Scotland and subduing Ireland. Anti-English rebels in Ireland had seized the occasion of troubles between king and Parliament to revolt in 1641. When Cromwell's position was secured in 1649, he went to Ireland with a large force and easily defeated the rebels, massacring whole garrisons and their priests. He encouraged expropriating the lands of the Irish "barbarous wretches," and Scottish immigrants resettled the northern county of Ulster. This seventeenth-century English conquest left a legacy of bitterness that the Irish even today call "the curse of Cromwell." In 1651, Parliament turned its attention overseas, putting mercantilist ideas into practice in the first Navigation Act, which allowed imports only if they were carried on English ships or came directly from the producers of goods. The Navigation Act was aimed at the Dutch, who dominated world trade; Cromwell tried to carry the policy further by waging naval war on the Dutch from 1652 to 1654.

At home, however, Cromwell faced growing resistance. His wars required a budget twice the size of Charles I's, and his increases in property taxes and customs duties alienated landowners and merchants. In 1653, when the Rump Parliament considered disbanding the army, Cromwell abolished Parliament in a military coup and made himself Lord Protector. His regime came to be known as the Protectorate. Cromwell silenced his critics by banning newspapers and using networks of spies and mail readers to keep tabs on his enemies. Cromwell's death in 1658 revived the prospect of civil war and political chaos. In 1660, a newly elected, staunchly Anglican Parliament invited Charles II, the son of the executed king, to return from exile. The period between the regicide of Charles I and the restoration of Charles II came to be known as the Interregnum (literally, "between reigns").

The Restoration and the "Glorious Revolution" of 1688

The traditional monarchical form of government was reinstated in 1660, restoring the king to full partnership with Parliament. Charles II (r. 1660–1685) promised to extend religious toleration, especially to Catholics, with whom he sympathized. Yet in the first years of his reign more than a thousand Puritan ministers lost their positions, and after 1664, attending a service other than one conforming with the Anglican prayer book was illegal. Natural disasters also marred the early years of the restoration of the monarchy. The plague stalked London's rat-infested streets in May 1665 and claimed more than thirty thousand victims by September. Then in 1666, the Great Fire swept the city, causing cataclysmic destruction. The crown now had a city as well as a monarchy to rebuild.

The restoration of monarchy made some in Parliament fear that the English government would come to resemble French absolutism. This fear was not unfounded. In 1670, Charles II made a secret agreement, soon leaked, with Louis XIV in which he promised to announce his conversion to Catholicism in exchange for money for a war against the Dutch. Charles never proclaimed himself a Catholic, but in his Declaration of Indulgence (1673) he did suspend all laws against Catholics and Protestant dissenters. Parliament refused to continue funding the Dutch war unless Charles rescinded his Declaration of Indulgence. Asserting its authority further, Parliament passed the Test Act in 1673, requiring all government officials to profess allegiance to the Church of England and in effect disavow Catholic doctrine. Then in 1678, Parliament precipitated the so-called Exclusion Crisis by explicitly denying the throne to a Roman Catholic. This action was aimed at the king's brother and heir, James, an open convert to Catholicism. Charles refused to allow it to become law.

The dynastic crisis over the succession of a Catholic gave rise to two distinct factions in Parliament: the Tories, who supported a strong, hereditary monarchy

Great Fire of London, 1666

This painting shows the three-day fire at its height. The writer John Evelyn described the scene in his diary: "All the sky was of a fiery aspect, like the top of a burning oven, and the light seen above 40 miles round about for many nights. God grant mine eyes may never behold the like, who now saw above 10,000 houses all in one flame; the noise and cracking and thunder of people, the fall of towers, houses, and churches, was like an hideous storm." Everyone in London at the time felt overwhelmed by the catastrophe, and many attributed it to God's punishment for the upheavals of the 1640s and 1650s. (Museum of London.)

and the restored ceremony of the Anglican church, and the Whigs, who advocated parliamentary supremacy and toleration for Protestant dissenters such as Presbyterians. The Tories favored James's succession despite his Catholicism, whereas the Whigs opposed a Catholic monarch. The loose moral atmosphere of Charles's court also offended some Whigs, who complained tongue in cheek that Charles was father of his country in much too literal a fashion (he had fathered more than one child by his mistresses but had produced no legitimate heir).

Upon Charles's death, James succeeded to the throne as James II (r. 1685–1688). James pursued pro-Catholic and absolutist policies even more aggressively than his brother. When a male heir—who would take precedence over James's two adult Protestant daughters and be reared a Catholic—was born, Tories and Whigs banded together. They invited the Dutch ruler William, prince of Orange and the husband of James's older daughter, Mary, to invade England. James fled to France, Parliament declared that he had abdicated, and hardly any blood was shed. Parliament offered the throne jointly to William (r. 1689–1702) and Mary (r. 1689–1694) on the condition that they accept a bill of rights guaranteeing Parliament's full partnership in a constitutional government.

In the Bill of Rights (1689), William and Mary agreed not to raise a standing army or to levy taxes without Parliament's consent. They also agreed to call meetings of Parliament at least every three years, to guarantee free elections to parliamentary seats, and to abide by Parliament's decisions and not suspend duly passed laws. The agreement gave England's constitutional government a written, legal basis by formally recognizing Parliament as a self-contained, independent body that shared power with the rulers. Victorious supporters of the coup declared it the **Glorious Revolution**. Constitutionalism had triumphed over absolutism in England.

The propertied classes who controlled Parliament prevented any resurgence of the popular turmoil of the 1640s. The Toleration Act of 1689 granted all Protestants freedom of worship, though non-Anglicans were still excluded from the universities; Catholics got no rights but were often left alone to worship privately. When the Catholics in Ireland rose to defend James II, William and Mary's troops brutally suppressed them. With the Whigs in power and the Tories in opposition, wealthy landowners now controlled political life throughout the realm. Differences between the factions had become minor; the Tories simply enjoyed less access to the king's patronage.

REVIEW What differences over religion and politics caused the conflict between king and Parliament in England?

Other Outposts of Constitutionalism

When William and Mary came to the throne in England in 1689, the Dutch and English put aside the rivalries that had brought them to war against each other in 1652–1654, 1665–1667, and 1672–1674. Under William, the Dutch Republic and England together led the coalition that blocked Louis XIV's efforts to dominate continental Europe. The two states had much in common: oriented toward commerce, especially overseas, they were the successful exceptions to absolutism in Europe. Also among the few outposts of constitutionalism in the seventeenth century were the English North American colonies, which developed representative government while the English were preoccupied with their revolutions at home. Constitutionalism was not the only factor shaping this Atlantic world; as constitutionalism developed in the colonies, so too did the enslavement of black Africans as a new labor force.

The Dutch Republic

When the Dutch Republic gained formal independence from Spain in 1648, it had already established a decentralized, constitutional state. Rich merchants called regents effectively controlled the internal affairs of each province and through the Estates General (an assembly made up of deputies from each province) named the *stadholder*, the executive officer responsible for defense and for representing the state at all ceremonial occasions. They almost always chose one of the princes of the house of Orange, but the prince of Orange resembled a president more than a king.

The decentralized state encouraged and protected trade, and the Dutch Republic soon became Europe's financial capital. The Bank of Amsterdam offered interest rates less than half those available in England and France. Praised for their industriousness, thrift, and cleanliness—and maligned as greedy, dull "butterboxes"—the Dutch dominated overseas commerce with their shipping (Map 13.3). They imported products from all over the world: spices, tea, and silk from Asia; sugar and tobacco from

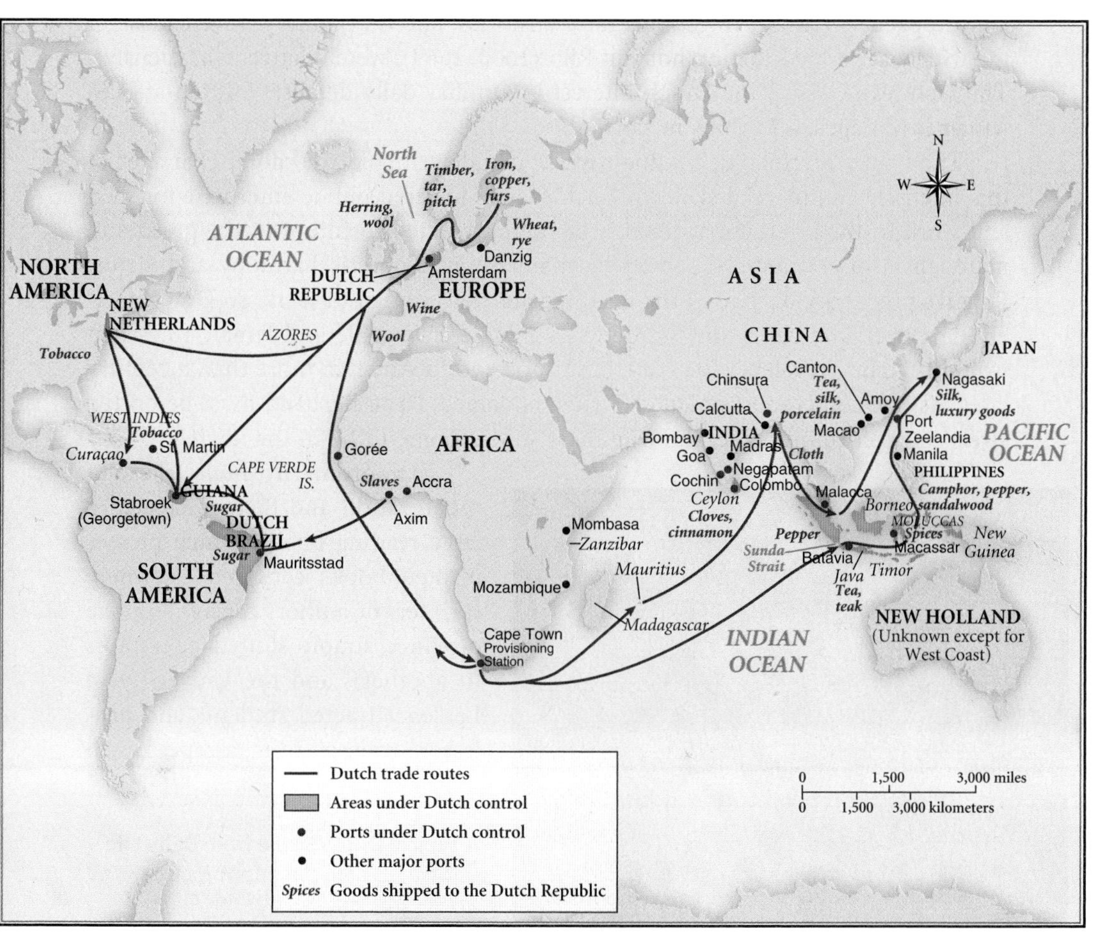

Map 13.3 Dutch Commerce in the Seventeenth Century
Even before gaining formal independence from Spain in 1648, the Dutch had begun to compete with the Spanish and Portuguese all over the world. In 1602, a group of merchants established the Dutch East India Company, which soon offered investors an annual rate of return of 35 percent on the trade in spices with countries located on the Indian Ocean. Global commerce gave the Dutch the highest standard of living in Europe and soon attracted the envy of the French and English. **For more help analyzing this map, see the map activity for this chapter in the Online Study Guide at** bedfordstmartins.com/huntconcise.

the Americas; wool from England and Spain; timber and furs from Scandinavia; grain from eastern Europe. A widely reprinted history of Amsterdam that appeared in 1662 described the city as "risen through the hand of God to the peak of prosperity and greatness. . . . The whole world stands amazed at its riches."

The Dutch rapidly became the most prosperous and best-educated people in Europe. Middle-class people supported the visual arts, especially painting, to an unprecedented degree. In the town of Delft, with a population of thirty thousand, for example, two-thirds of the households owned paintings. Whereas in other countries, kings, nobles, and churches bought art, Dutch buyers were merchants, artisans, and shopkeepers. Engravings, illustrated histories, and oil paintings, even those of the widely acclaimed Rembrandt van Rijn (1606–1669), were relatively inexpensive. The pictures reflected the Dutch interest in familiar daily details: children at play, winter landscapes, and ships in port.

The family household, not the royal court, determined the moral character of this intensely commercial society. Dutch society fostered public enterprise for men and work in the home for women, who were expected to filter out the greed and materialism of commercial society by maintaining domestic harmony and virtue. Relative prosperity decreased the need for married women to work, so Dutch society developed the clear contrast between middle-class male and female roles that would become prevalent elsewhere in Europe and in America more than a century later. As one contemporary Dutch writer explained, "The husband must be on the street to practice his trade; the wife must stay at home to be in the kitchen."

Extraordinarily high levels of urbanization and literacy created a large reading public. Dutch presses printed books censored elsewhere (printers or authors censored in one province simply shifted operations to another), and the University of Leiden attracted students and professors from all over Europe. Dutch

A Typical Dutch Scene from Daily Life
Jan Steen painted *The Baker Arent Oostwaard and His Wife* in 1658. Steen ran a brewery and tavern in addition to painting, and he was known for his interest in the details of daily life. Dutch artists popularized this kind of "genre" painting, which showed ordinary people at work and play. **For more help analyzing this image, see the visual activity for this chapter in the Online Study Guide at** bedfordstmartins.com/huntconcise. (Rijksmuseum, Amsterdam.)

tolerance extended to the works of Benedict Spinoza (1633–1677), a Jewish philosopher and biblical scholar who was expelled by his synagogue for alleged atheism but was left alone by the Dutch authorities. Spinoza strove to reconcile religion with science and mathematics, but his work scandalized many Christians and Jews because he seemed to equate God and nature. Like nature, Spinoza's God followed unchangeable laws and could not be influenced by human actions, prayers, or faith.

Dutch learning, painting, and commerce all enjoyed wide renown in the seventeenth century, but this luster proved hard to maintain. The Dutch lived in a world of international rivalries in which strong central authority gave their enemies an advantage. Though inconclusive, the naval wars with England drained the state's revenues. Even more dangerous were the land wars with France, which continued into the eighteenth century. The Dutch survived these challenges but increasingly depended on alliances with other powers, such as England. By the end of the seventeenth century, the regent elite had become more exclusive, more preoccupied with ostentation, less tolerant of deviations from strict Calvinism, and more concerned with imitating French styles than with encouraging their own.

Freedom and Slavery in the New World

The French and English also increasingly overshadowed the Dutch in the New World colonies. While the Dutch concentrated on shipping, including the slave trade, the French and English established settler colonies that would eventually provide fabulous revenues to the home countries. Many European governments encouraged private companies to vie for their share of the slave trade, and slavery began to take clear institutional form in the New World in this period. While whites found in the colonies greater political and religious freedom than in Europe, they subjected black Africans to the most degrading forms of bondage.

After the Spanish and Portuguese had shown that African slaves could be transported and forced to labor in South and Central America, the English and French endeavored to set up similar labor systems in their new Caribbean island colonies. White planters with large tracts of land bought African slaves to work fields of sugarcane, and as they gradually built up their holdings, the planters displaced most of the original white settlers, who moved to mainland North American colonies. After 1661, when Barbados instituted a slave code that stripped all Africans of rights under English law, slavery became codified as an inherited status that applied only to blacks. The result was a society of extremes: the very wealthy whites—about 7 percent of the population in Barbados—and the enslaved, powerless black majority. The English brought little of their religious or constitutional practices to the Caribbean. Other Caribbean colonies followed a similar pattern of development. Louis XIV promulgated a "black code" in 1685 to regulate the legal status of slaves in the French colonies. Although one of his aims was to prevent non-Catholics from owning slaves in the French colonies, the code had much the same effect as the English codes on the slaves themselves: they had virtually no legal rights.

The highest church and government authorities in Catholic and Protestant countries alike condoned the gradually expanding slave trade. The governments of England, France, Spain, Portugal, the Dutch Republic, and Denmark all encouraged private companies to traffic in black Africans. The Dutch West India Company was the most successful of them in this period. In the early 1600s, about 9,000 Africans were exported from Africa to the New World every year; by 1700, this figure had increased to 25,000 annually. Historians advance several different reasons for the increase in the slave trade: some claim that improvements in muskets made European slavers more formidable; others cite the rising price of slaves, which made their sale more attractive to Africans; still others focus on factors internal to Africa, such as the increasing size of African armies and their use of muskets in fighting and capturing other Africans for sale as slaves. Whatever the reason, the way had been prepared for the development of an Atlantic economy based on slavery.

Virtually left to themselves during the upheavals in England, the fledgling English colonies in North America developed representative government on their own. Almost every colony had a governor and a two-house legislature. The colonial legislatures constantly sought to increase their power and resisted the efforts of Charles II and James II to reaffirm royal control. William and Mary reluctantly allowed emerging colonial elites more control over local affairs. The social and political elite among the settlers hoped to impose an English social hierarchy dominated by rich landowners. Ordinary immigrants to the colonies, however, took advantage of plentiful land to carve out their own farms using white servants and, later in some colonies, African slaves.

For native Americans, the expanding European presence meant something else altogether. They faced death through unfamiliar diseases and warfare and the accelerating loss of their homelands. Unlike white settlers, native Americans believed that land was a divine gift provided for their collective use and not subject to individual ownership. As a result, Europeans' claims that they owned exclusive land rights caused frequent skirmishes. In 1675–1676, for instance, three tribes allied under Metacomet (called King Philip by the English) threatened the survival of New England settlers, who savagely repulsed the attacks and sold their captives as slaves. Whites portrayed native Americans as conspiring villains and sneaky heathens, akin to Africans in their savagery.

REVIEW How could outposts of constitutionalism coexist with slavery?

The Search for Order in Elite and Popular Culture

While freedom and slavery simultaneously took root in the New World, the conflict between absolutist and constitutional forms of government in Europe was giving rise to profound new thinking about the foundations of the political order. Concerns about order were not limited to politics. Poetry, painting, and architecture reflected those preoccupations, too. As European states, both absolutist and constitutional, expanded their powers, elites worked to distinguish themselves from the lower classes. They developed new codes of correct behavior for themselves and tried to teach order and discipline to their social inferiors.

Social Contract Theory: Hobbes and Locke

Two figures stood out prominently in the debates over the foundations of political authority: Thomas Hobbes and John Locke. Their writings helped shape the modern subject of political science. Hobbes justified absolute authority; Locke provided the rationale for constitutionalism. Yet both argued that all authority came not from divine right but from a social contract between citizens.

Thomas Hobbes (1588–1679) was a royalist who sat out the English civil war of the 1640s in France, where he tutored the future king Charles II. Returning to England in 1651, he published his masterpiece, *Leviathan,* in which he argued for unlimited authority in a ruler. Absolute authority could be vested in either a king or a parliament; it had to be absolute, he insisted, in order to overcome the defects of human nature. Believing that people are essentially self-centered and driven by the "right to self-preservation," Hobbes made his case by referring to science, not religion. To Hobbes, human life in a state of nature—that is, any situation without firm authority—was "solitary, poor, nasty, brutish, and short." He believed that the desire for power and natural greed would inevitably lead to unfettered competition. Only the assurance of social order could make people secure enough to act according to law; consequently, giving up personal liberty, he maintained, was the price of collective security. Rulers derived their power, he concluded, from a contract by which people gave up their natural rights to an absolute authority that guaranteed their rights in society.

Hobbes's notion of rule by an absolute authority left no room for political dissent or nonconformity, and it infuriated both royalists and supporters of Parliament. He enraged royalists by arguing that authority came not from divine right but from the social contract between citizens. Parliamentary supporters resisted Hobbes's claim that rulers must possess absolute authority to prevent the greater evil of anarchy; they believed that a constitution should guarantee shared power between king and parliament and protect individual liberties. Like Machiavelli before him, Hobbes became associated with a cynical, pessimistic view of human nature, and future political theorists often began their arguments by refuting Hobbes.

Rejecting both Hobbes and the more traditional royalist defenses of absolute authority, John Locke (1632–1704) used the notion of a social contract to provide a foundation for constitutionalism. Locke experienced political life firsthand as the physician, secretary, and intellectual companion of the earl of Shaftesbury, a leading English Whig. In 1683, Locke fled with Shaftesbury to the Dutch Republic when Charles II clamped down on those conspiring to prevent his Catholic brother from succeeding him. There Locke continued work on his *Two Treatises of Government,* which, when published in 1690, served to justify the Glorious Revolution of 1688. Locke's position was thoroughly anti-absolutist. He denied the divine right of kings and ridiculed the common royalist idea that political power in the state mirrored the father's authority in the family. Like Hobbes, he posited a state of nature that applied to all people. Unlike Hobbes, he thought people were reasonable and the state of nature peaceful.

Locke insisted that government's only purpose was to protect life, liberty, and property, a notion that linked economic and political freedom. Ultimate authority rested in the will of a majority of men who owned property, and government should be limited to its basic purpose of protection. A ruler who failed to uphold his part of the social contract between the ruler and the populace could be justifiably resisted, an idea that would become crucial for the leaders of the American Revolution a century later. For England's landowners, however, Locke helped validate a revolution that consolidated their interests and ensured their privileges in the social hierarchy.

Locke defended his optimistic view of human nature in the immensely influential *Essay concerning Human Understanding* (1690). He denied the existence of any innate ideas and asserted instead that each human is born with a mind that is a tabula rasa (blank slate). Everything humans know, he claimed, comes from sensory experience, not from anything inherent in human nature. Locke's views promoted the belief that "all men are created equal," a belief that challenged absolutist forms of rule and ultimately raised questions about women's roles as well. Not surprisingly, Locke devoted considerable energy to rethinking educational practices; he believed that education crucially shaped the human personality by channeling all sensory experience. Although he himself owned shares in the Royal African Company and justified slavery, Locke's writings were later used by abolitionists in their campaign against slavery.

Freedom and Order in the Arts and Sciences

Hobbes and Locke were not alone in wrestling with the conflicts between desires for greater freedom and the need for reassuring order. The French mathematician Blaise Pascal vividly captured the fear of chaos in his *Pensées* (*Thoughts*) of 1660: "I look on all sides, and I see only darkness everywhere. Nature presents to me nothing which is not a matter of doubt and concern. . . . It is incomprehensible that God should exist, and incomprehensible that He should not exist." Poets, artists, and scientists all tried to make sense of the individual's place within what Pascal called "the eternal silence of these infinite spaces."

The English Puritan poet John Milton (1608–1674) responded to the challenge by giving priority to individual liberty. In 1643, in the midst of the civil war between king and Parliament, he published writings in favor of divorce. When Parliament enacted a censorship law aimed at such literature, Milton countered in 1644 with one of the first defenses of freedom of the press, *Areopagitica* (*Tribunal of Opinion*). Forced into retirement after the restoration of the monarchy, Milton published in 1667 his epic poem *Paradise Lost.* He used Adam and Eve's Fall to meditate on human freedom and the tragedies of rebellion. Although Milton wanted to "justify the ways of God to man," his Satan, the proud angel who challenges God, is so compelling as to be heroic. Individuals must learn the limits of their freedom, Milton seems to say, and yet the

Gian Lorenzo Bernini, *Ecstasy of St. Teresa of Ávila*
This ultimate statement of baroque sculpture captures all the drama and even sensationalism of a mystical religious faith. Bernini based the figures in this piece, created around 1650, on a vision reported by St. Teresa in which she saw an angel: "In his hands I saw a great golden spear, and at the iron tip there appeared to be a point of fire. This he plunged into my heart several times so that it penetrated my entrails. When he pulled it out I felt that he took them with it, and left me utterly consumed by the great love of God." (Scala/Art Resource, NY.)

desire for liberty remains essential to their nature as humans, creating at times a tragic discord.

The dominant artistic styles on the continent, the baroque and the classical, both submerged the individual in a grander design, emphasizing the majesty of authority. The baroque style proved to be especially suitable for public displays of faith and power that overawed individual beholders. The combination of religious and political purposes in baroque art is best exemplified in the architecture and sculpture of Gian Lorenzo Bernini (1598–1680), the papacy's official artist. His architectural masterpiece was the gigantic square facing St. Peter's Basilica in Rome (1656–1671). His use of freestanding colonnades and a huge open space is meant to impress the individual observer with the power of the popes and the Catholic religion.

Bernini sculpted tombs and statues for the popes and private patrons. In 1665, Louis XIV hired Bernini to plan the rebuilding of the Louvre palace in Paris but then rejected his ideas as incompatible with French tastes. Although France was a Catholic country, French painters, sculptors, and architects, like their patron Louis XIV, preferred the standards of **classicism** to those of the baroque. French artists developed classicism to be a national style, distinct from the baroque style that was closely associated with France's enemies, the Austrian and Spanish Habsburgs. As its name suggests, classicism reflected the ideals of the art of antiquity; geometric shapes, order, and harmony of lines took precedence over the sensuous, exuberant, and emotional forms of the baroque. Rather than being overshadowed by the sheer power of emotional display, in classicism the individual could be found at the intersection of converging, symmetrical, straight lines. These influences were apparent in the work

French Classicism

This painting by Nicolas Poussin, *Discovery of Achilles on Skyros* (1649–1650), shows the French interest in classical themes and ideals. In the Greek story, Thetis dresses her son Achilles as a young woman and hides him on the island of Skyros so that he will not have to fight in the Trojan War. When a chest of treasures is offered to the women, Achilles reveals himself (he is the figure on the far right) because he cannot resist the sword. In telling the story, Poussin emphasizes harmony and almost a sedateness of composition, avoiding the exuberance and emotionalism of the baroque style. (Photograph © 2011 Museum of Fine Arts, Boston.)

of the leading French painters of the period, Nicolas Poussin (1594–1665) and Claude Lorrain (1600–1682), both of whom worked in Rome and tried to re-create classical Roman values in their mythological scenes and Roman landscapes.

Art might also serve the interests of science. One of the most skilled illustrators of insects and flowers was Maria Sibylla Merian (1646–1717), a German-born painter-scholar whose engravings were widely celebrated for their brilliant realism and microscopic clarity. Merian sought her own version of freedom by separating from her husband and joining a sect called the Labadists (after its French founder, Jean de Labadie), whose members did not believe in formal marriage ties and established a colony in the northern Dutch province of Friesland. After moving there with her daughters, Merian went with missionaries from the sect to the Dutch colony of Surinam in South America and painted watercolors of the exotic flowers, birds, and insects she found in the jungle around the cocoa and sugarcane plantations. In the seventeenth century, many women became known for their still lifes and especially their paintings of flowers. Paintings by the Dutch artist Rachel Ruysch, for example, fetched higher prices than works by Rembrandt.

Because of their exclusion from most universities, women only rarely participated in the new scientific discoveries. In 1667, nonetheless, the English Royal Society invited Margaret Cavendish—a writer of poems, essays, letters, and philosophical treatises—to attend a meeting to watch the exhibition of experiments. She attacked the use of telescopes and microscopes because she detected in the new experimentalism a mechanistic view of the world that exalted masculine prowess and challenged the Christian belief in free will. She nonetheless urged the formal education of women, complaining that "we are kept like birds in cages to hop up and down in our houses." She insisted, "Many of our Sex may have as much wit, and be capable of Learning as well as men."

Scientists needed freedom to publish their results, as Galileo had discovered, yet they also required support in order to carry out their work. As the scientific revolution of Galileo, Kepler, and Newton steadily gained new adherents, rulers seized upon the potential for enhancing their prestige and glory. Various German princes funded the work of Gottfried Wilhelm Leibniz (1646–1716), one of the inventors, along with Newton, of calculus. A lawyer, diplomat, and scholar who wrote about metaphysics, logic, and history, Leibniz, like Milton, ultimately wanted to explain the ways of God to humans. His most controversial view was that we live in the best of all possible worlds because it was created by a perfect God. Leibniz did not intend to expound a mindless optimism. He thought of God as like a mathematician who aims to solve problems in the simplest and most elegant fashion. Many modern scientific principles, such as the conservation of energy, followed from Leibniz's view. Leibniz also helped establish scientific societies in the German states. Government involvement in science was greatest in France, where it became an arm of mercantilist policy. In 1666, Jean-Baptiste Colbert founded the Royal Academy of Sciences, which supplied fifteen scientists with government stipends.

Women and Manners

Philosophers, poets, and painters all imaginatively explored the place of the individual within a larger whole, but real-life individuals had to learn to navigate their own social worlds. Manners—the learning of individual self-discipline—were essential skills of social navigation, and women usually took the lead in teaching them. Under the tutelage of their mothers and wives, nobles learned to hide all that was crass and to maintain a fine sense of social distinction. In some ways, aristocratic men were expected to act more like women. Just as women had long been expected to please men, now aristocratic men had to please their monarch or patron by displaying proper manners and conversing with elegance and wit. Men as well as women had to master the art of pleasing, which included a facility with foreign languages (especially French), skill in dance, a taste for fine music, and attention to dress.

As part of the evolution of new aristocratic ideals, nobles learned to disdain all that was lowly. The upper classes began to reject popular festivals and fairs in favor of private theaters, where seats were relatively expensive and behavior was formal. Clowns and buffoons now seemed vulgar; the last king of England to keep a court fool was Charles I. The greatest French playwright of the seventeenth century, Molière (the pen name of Jean-Baptiste Poquelin, 1622–1673), wrote sparkling comedies of manners that revealed much about the new aristocratic behavior. Molière's play *The*

Middle-Class Gentleman, first performed at the royal court in 1670, revolves around the yearning of a rich, middle-class Frenchman, Monsieur Jourdain, to learn to act like a *gentilhomme* (meaning both "gentleman" and "nobleman" in French). By making fun of Jourdain's outlandish aspirations, the play seems to have been an attempt to reassure the nobles at court: only true nobles by blood could hope to act like nobles. But the play also shows how the middle classes were learning to emulate the nobility: if one could learn to *act* nobly through self-discipline, could not anyone with some education and money pass himself off as noble?

As Molière's play demonstrates, new attention to manners trickled down from the court to the middle class. A French treatise on manners from 1672 explained:

> If everyone is eating from the same dish, you should take care not to put your hand into it before those of higher rank have done so. . . . Formerly one was permitted . . . to dip one's bread into the sauce, provided only that one had not already bitten it. Nowadays that would be a kind of rusticity. Formerly one was allowed to take from one's mouth what one could not eat and drop it on the floor, provided it was done skillfully. Now that would be very disgusting.

The key words "rusticity" and "disgusting" reveal the association of unacceptable social behavior with the peasantry, dirt, and repulsion. Courtly manners often permeated the upper reaches of society by means of the salon, an informal gathering held regularly in private homes and presided over by a socially eminent woman. In 1661, one French author claimed to have identified 251 Parisian women as hostesses of salons. Although the French government occasionally worried that these gatherings might be seditious, the three main topics of conversation were love, literature, and philosophy. Hostesses often worked hard to encourage the careers of budding authors. Before publishing a manuscript, many authors would read their compositions to a salon gathering. Corneille, Racine, and even Bishop Bossuet sought female approval for their writings.

Women who wrote on their own faced many obstacles. Marie-Madeleine Pioche de la Vergne, known as Madame de Lafayette, wrote several short novels that were published anonymously because it was considered inappropriate for aristocratic women to appear in print. After the publication of *The Princess of Cleves* in 1678, she denied having written it. Hannah Wooley, the English author of many books on domestic conduct, published under the name of her first husband. Women were known for writing wonderful letters, many of which circulated in handwritten form; hardly any appeared in print during the authors' lifetimes. In the 1650s, despite these limitations, French women began to turn out best sellers in a new type of literature, the novel. Their success prompted the philosopher Pierre Bayle to remark in 1697 that "our best French novels for a long time have been written by women."

The new importance of women in the world of manners and letters did not sit well with everyone. Although the French writer François Poulain de la Barre (1647–1723), in a series of works published in the 1670s, used the new science to assert the equality of women's minds, most men resisted the idea. Clergymen, lawyers, scholars, and playwrights attacked women's growing public influence. Women, they complained, were corrupting forces and needed restraint. Women were accused of raising "the banner of prostitution in the salons, in the promenades, and in the streets." Molière wrote plays denouncing women's pretension to judge literary merit. English playwrights derided learned women by creating characters with names such as Lady Knowall, Lady Meanwell, and Mrs. Lovewit. A real-life target of the English playwrights was Aphra Behn (1640–1689), one of the first professional woman authors, who supported herself as a journalist and also wrote plays and poetry. Her short novel *Oroonoko* (1688) tells the story of an African prince mistakenly sold into slavery. The story was so successful that it was adapted by playwrights and performed repeatedly in England and France for the next hundred years. Behn responded to her critics by arguing that there was "no reason why women should not write as well as men."

Reforming Popular Culture

The illiterate peasants who made up most of Europe's population had little or no knowledge of political theory, philosophy, or novels, no matter who authored them. Their culture had three main elements: the skills needed to work at farming or in a trade; popular forms of entertainment such as village fairs and dances; and their religion, which shaped every aspect of life and death. In the seventeenth century the division between elite and popular culture widened as elites insisted on their difference from the lower orders and pushed forward the ongoing effort to instill religious and social discipline in their social inferiors.

Building upon campaigns against popular "paganism" that began during the sixteenth-century Protestant and Catholic reform movements, Protestant and Catholic churches alike pushed hard to change popular religious practices. Puritans in England tried to root out maypole dances, Sunday village fairs, gambling, taverns, and bawdy ballads because they interfered with sober observance of the Sabbath. In Lutheran Norway, pastors denounced a widespread belief in the miracle-working powers of St. Olaf. The word *superstition* previously meant "false religion" (Protestantism was a superstition for Catholics, Catholicism for Protestants). In the seventeenth century, it took on its modern meaning of irrational fears, beliefs, and practices, which anyone educated or refined would avoid. *Superstition* became synonymous with popular or ignorant beliefs.

The Catholic campaign against superstitious practices found a ready ally in Louis XIV. While he reformed the nobles at court through etiquette and manners, Catholic bishops in the French provinces trained parish priests to reform their flocks by using catechisms in local dialects and insisting that parishioners attend Mass. The church faced a formidable challenge. One bishop in France complained in 1671, "Can you believe that there are in this diocese entire villages where no one has even heard of Jesus Christ?" In some places, believers sacrificed animals to the Virgin Mary, prayed to the new moon, and worshipped at the sources of streams as in pre-Christian times.

Like its Protestant counterpart, the Catholic campaign against ignorance and superstition helped extend state power. Clergy, officials, and local police worked together to limit carnival celebrations (festivities before the beginning of Lent that often had a riotous character), to regulate pilgrimages to shrines, and to replace

Corpus Christi Procession in Peru
The Catholic campaign against paganism extended to Spanish possessions in the New World. This painting shows a Catholic procession by Incas that took place in the late 1670s in Cuzco, Peru. The Inca in front is wearing his native dress; he is followed by a float and religious figures carrying traditional Catholic imagery. (Museo del Arzobispo, Cuzco, Peru.)

"indecent" images of saints with more restrained and decorous ones. In Catholicism, the cult of the Virgin Mary and devotions closely connected with Jesus, such as the Holy Sacrament and the Sacred Heart, took precedence over the celebration of more popular saints who seemed to have pagan origins or were credited with unverified miracles. Reformers everywhere tried to limit the number of feast days on the grounds that they encouraged lewd behavior.

The campaign for more disciplined religious practices helped generate a new attitude toward the poor. Poverty previously had been closely linked with charity and virtue in Christianity: it was a Christian duty to give alms to the poor, and Jesus and many of the saints had purposely chosen lives of poverty. In the sixteenth and seventeenth centuries, the upper classes, the church, and the state increasingly regarded the poor as dangerous, deceitful, and lacking in character. "Criminal laziness is the source of all their vices," wrote a Jesuit expert on the poor. The courts had previously expelled beggars from cities; now local leaders, both Catholic and Protestant, tried to reform their character. In the sixteenth century, local and state officials began to levy taxes for more organized poor relief; after the mid-seventeenth century officials began to transform hospitals into houses of confinement for beggars. In Catholic France, upper-class women's religious associations, known as confraternities, set up asylums that confined prostitutes (by arrest if necessary) and rehabilitated them. Confraternities also founded hospices where orphans learned order and respect. Such groups advocated harsh discipline as the cure for poverty.

Although hard times had increased the numbers of poor people and the rates of violent crime as well, the most important changes were attitudinal. The elites wanted to separate the very poor from society either to change them or to keep them from contaminating others. Hospitals became holding pens for society's unwanted

Mapping the West Europe at the End of the Seventeenth Century
Size was not necessarily an advantage in the late 1600s. Poland-Lithuania, a large country on the map, had been fatally weakened by internal conflicts. In the next century it would disappear entirely. While the Ottoman Empire still controlled an extensive territory, outside of Anatolia its rule depended on intermediaries. The Austrian Habsburgs had pushed the Turks out of Hungary and back into the Balkans. The tiny Dutch Republic, meanwhile, had become very rich through international commerce and was the envy of far larger nations.

members, where the poor joined the disabled, the incurably diseased, and the insane. The founding of hospitals demonstrates the connection between these attitudes and state building. In 1676, Louis XIV ordered every French city to establish a hospital, and his government took charge of their finances. Other rulers soon followed the same path.

REVIEW In what ways did elite and popular culture become more separate during the second half of the seventeenth century?

Conclusion

The search for order in the wake of religious warfare and political upheaval took place on various levels, from the reform of the disorderly poor to the establishment of more regular bureaucratic routines in government. The biggest factor shaping the search for order was the growth of state power. Whether absolutist or constitutionalist in form, seventeenth-century states all aimed to penetrate more deeply into the lives of their subjects. They wanted more men for their armed forces, higher taxes to support their projects, and more control over foreign trade, religious dissent, and society's unwanted.

Some tearing had begun to appear, however, in the seamless fabric of state power. In England, the Dutch Republic, and the English North American colonies, property owners successfully demanded constitutional guarantees of their right to participate in government. In the eighteenth century, moreover, new levels of economic growth and the appearance of new social groups would exert pressures on the European state system. The success of seventeenth-century rulers created the political and economic conditions in which their critics would flourish.

CHAPTER REVIEW QUESTIONS

1. What are the most important differences between absolutism and constitutionalism as political systems?
2. Why was the search for order a major theme in science, politics, and the arts during the second half of the seventeenth century?

For practice quizzes and other study tools, see the Online Study Guide at bedfordstmartins.com/huntconcise.

For primary-source material from this period, see Chapter 16 of *Sources of The Making of the West*, Third Edition.

TIMELINE

1640 · 1650 · 1660

1642–1646 Civil war between King Charles I and Parliament in England

1648 Thirty Years' War ends; the Fronde revolt challenges royal authority in France; Ukrainian Cossack warriors rebel against the king of Poland-Lithuania

1649 Execution of Charles I of England; new Russian legal code enacted

1651 Thomas Hobbes publishes *Leviathan*

1660 Monarchy restored in England

1661 Slave code set up in Barbados

1667 Louis XIV begins the first of many wars that continue throughout his reign

Suggested References

Recent studies have insisted that absolutism could never be entirely absolute because the king depended on collaboration to enforce his policies. Some of the best sources for Louis XIV's reign are the letters written by important noblewomen.

Barkey, Karen. *The Ottoman Route to State Centralization.* 1994.

*Beik, William. *Louis XIV and Absolutism: A Brief Study with Documents.* 2000.

Brook, Timothy. *Vermeer's Hat: The Seventeenth Century and the Dawn of the Global World.* 2008.

Cowart, Georgia. *The Triumph of Pleasure: Louis XIV and the Politics of Spectacle.* 2008.

Cromwell, Oliver: http://www.olivercromwell.org/

Davis, Natalie Zemon. *Women on the Margins: Three Seventeenth-Century Lives.* 1995.

*Forster, Elborg, trans. *A Woman's Life in the Court of the Sun King: Elisabeth Charlotte, Duchesse d'Orléans.* 1984.

France in America (site of the Library of Congress on French colonies in North America): http://international.loc.gov/intldl/fiahtml/fiatheme.html#track1

Hill, Christopher. *The World Turned Upside Down: Radical Ideas during the English Revolution.* 1972.

Kotilaine, Jarmo, and Marshall Poe, eds. *Modernizing Muscovy: Reform and Social Change in Seventeenth-Century Russia.* 2004.

*Pincus, Steven C. A. *England's Glorious Revolution, 1688–1689: A Brief History with Documents.* 2006.

Versailles: http://www.chateauversailles.fr

Wilkinson, Richard. *Louis XIV.* 2007.

■ **1670** Molière's play *The Middle-Class Gentleman* first performed at the French court

■ **1678** Marie-Madeleine Pioche de la Vergne (Madame de Lafayette) anonymously publishes *The Princess of Cleves*

■ **1683** Austrian Habsburgs break the Turkish siege of Vienna

■ **1685** Louis XIV revokes toleration for French Protestants granted by the Edict of Nantes

■ **1688** Parliament forces James II to abdicate and invites the daughter of James II, Mary, and her husband, William of Orange, to take the English throne in the "Glorious Revolution"

■ **1690** John Locke publishes *Two Treatises of Government* and *Essay concerning Human Understanding*

1670 | 1680 | 1690

14

The Atlantic System and Its Consequences

1690–1740

JOHANN SEBASTIAN BACH (1685–1750), composer of mighty organ fugues and church cantatas, was not above amusing his Leipzig audiences, many of them university students. In 1732 he produced a cantata about a young woman in love with coffee. Her old-fashioned father rages that he won't find her a husband unless she gives up the fad. She agrees, secretly vowing to admit no suitor who will not promise in the marriage contract to let her brew coffee whenever she wants. Bach offers this conclusion:

London Coffeehouse
This gouache (a variant on watercolor painting) from about 1725 depicts a scene from a London coffeehouse located in the courtyard of the Royal Exchange (merchants' bank). Middle-class men, wearing wigs, read newspapers, drink coffee, smoke pipes, and discuss the news of the day. The coffeehouse draws them out of their homes into the new public sphere. *(© British Museum, London, England/The Bridgeman Art Library.)*

The cat won't give up its mouse,
Girls stay faithful coffee-sisters
Mother loves her coffee habit,
Grandma sips it gladly too—
Why then shout at the daughters?

Bach's era might well be called the age of coffee. European travelers at the end of the sixteenth century had noticed Middle Eastern people drinking a "black drink," *kavah*. Few Europeans sampled it at first, and the Arab monopoly on its production kept prices high. This changed around 1700 when the Dutch East India Company introduced coffee plants to Java and other Indonesian islands. Coffee production then spread to the French Caribbean, where African slaves provided the plantation labor. In Europe, imported coffee spurred the development of a new kind of meeting place: London's first coffeehouse opened in 1652, and the idea spread quickly to other European cities. Coffeehouses became gathering places for men to drink, read newspapers, and talk politics. Even Isaac Newton had his favorite coffeehouse. As a London newspaper commented in 1737, "There's scarce an Alley in City and Suburbs but has a Coffeehouse in it, which may be called the School of Public Spirit, where every Man over Daily and Weekly Journals, a Mug, or a Dram . . . devotes himself to that glorious one, his Country."

European consumption of coffee, tea, chocolate, and other novelties increased dramatically as European nations forged worldwide economic links. At the center of this new world economy was the **Atlantic system**, which bound together western Europe, Africa, and the Americas. Europeans bought slaves in western Africa, transported and sold them in their colonies in North and South America and the Caribbean, bought commodities such as coffee and sugar produced by the new colonial **plantations**, and then sold the goods in European ports for refining and reshipment. This Atlantic system first took clear shape in the early eighteenth century; it was the hub of European expansion all over the world.

Coffee drinking was one example among many of the new social and cultural patterns that took root between 1690 and 1740. Improvements in agricultural production at home reinforced the effects of trade overseas; Europeans now had more disposable income for "extras," and they spent their money not only in the new coffeehouses and cafés that sprang up all over Europe but also on newspapers, musical concerts, paintings, and novels. A new middle-class public began to make its presence felt in every domain of culture and social life, creating a new public sphere that would ultimately transform the nature of politics on both sides of the Atlantic.

Although the rise of the Atlantic system gave Europe new prominence in the global context, European rulers still focused most of their political, diplomatic, and military energies on their rivalries within Europe. A coalition of countries succeeded in containing French aggression, and a more balanced diplomatic system emerged. In eastern Europe, Prussia and Austria had to contend with the rising power of Russia under Peter the Great. In western Europe, both Spain and the Dutch Republic declined in influence but continued to vie with Britain and France for colonial spoils in the Atlantic. The more evenly matched competition among the great powers encouraged the development of diplomatic skills and drew attention to public health as a way of encouraging population growth.

In the aftermath of Louis XIV's revocation of the Edict of Nantes in 1685, a new intellectual movement known as the **Enlightenment** began to germinate. French Protestant refugees began to publish works critical of absolutism in politics and religion. Increased prosperity, the growth of a middle-class public, and the decline in warfare after Louis XIV's death in 1715 all fostered the development of this new critical spirit. Fed by the popularization of science and the growing interest in travel literature, the Enlightenment encouraged greater skepticism about religious and state authority. Building on the growth of the new public sphere, eventually the movement would question almost every aspect of social and political life in Europe. The Enlightenment began in western Europe in those countries—Britain, France, and the Dutch Republic—most affected by the new Atlantic system. It, too, was a product of the age of coffee.

CHAPTER FOCUS QUESTION What were the most important consequences of the growth of the Atlantic system?

The Atlantic System and the World Economy

European ships had been circling the globe since the early 1500s, and European colonization had dramatically altered the landscape and populations of the Americas, yet only in the 1700s did Europe draw most of the rest of the world into its economic orbit. Western European trading nations sent ships loaded with goods to buy slaves from local rulers on the western coast of Africa; transported the slaves to the colonies in North and South America and the Caribbean and sold them to the owners of plantations producing coffee, sugar, cotton, and tobacco; and bought the raw commodities produced in the colonies and shipped them back to Europe, where they were refined or processed and then sold to other parts of Europe and the world. This Atlantic system and the growth of international trade helped create a new consumer society.

Slavery and the Atlantic System

Spain and Portugal had dominated Atlantic trade in the sixteenth and seventeenth centuries, but in the eighteenth century European trade in the Atlantic rapidly expanded and became more systematically interconnected (Map 14.1). By 1650, Portugal had already sent 200,000 African slaves to Brazil to work on the new sugar plantations (large tracts of lands farmed by slave labor). Realizing that plantations producing staples for Europeans could bring fabulous wealth, the European powers grew less interested in the dwindling trade in precious metals and more eager to colonize. Large-scale planters of sugar, tobacco, and coffee displaced small farmers who relied on one or two servants. Planters and their plantations won out because slave labor was cheap and therefore able to produce mass quantities of commodities at low prices.

State-chartered private companies from Portugal, Spain, France, Britain, the Dutch Republic, Prussia, and even Denmark exploited the 3,500-mile coastline of West Africa for slaves. Before 1675, most blacks taken from Africa had been sent to Brazil or Spanish America on Portuguese ships, but by 1725 more than 60 percent of African slaves landed in the Caribbean (Figure 14.1), and more and more of them were carried on British or French ships. All in all, 90 percent of the slaves were transported by Portuguese, British, or French ships. After 1700, the plantation economy also began to expand on the North American mainland. The numbers stagger the imagination. More than 11 million Africans were transported to the Americas before the slave trade began to wind down after 1850. Some 1.4 million died during the passage across the ocean. Many traders gained spectacular wealth, but companies did not always make profits. The English Royal African Company, for example, delivered 100,000 slaves to the Caribbean and imported 30,000 tons of sugar to Britain, yet lost money after the few profitable years following its founding in 1672.

The balance of white and black populations in the New World colonies was determined by the staples produced. New England merchants and farmers bought few slaves because they did not own plantations. Blacks—both slave and free—made

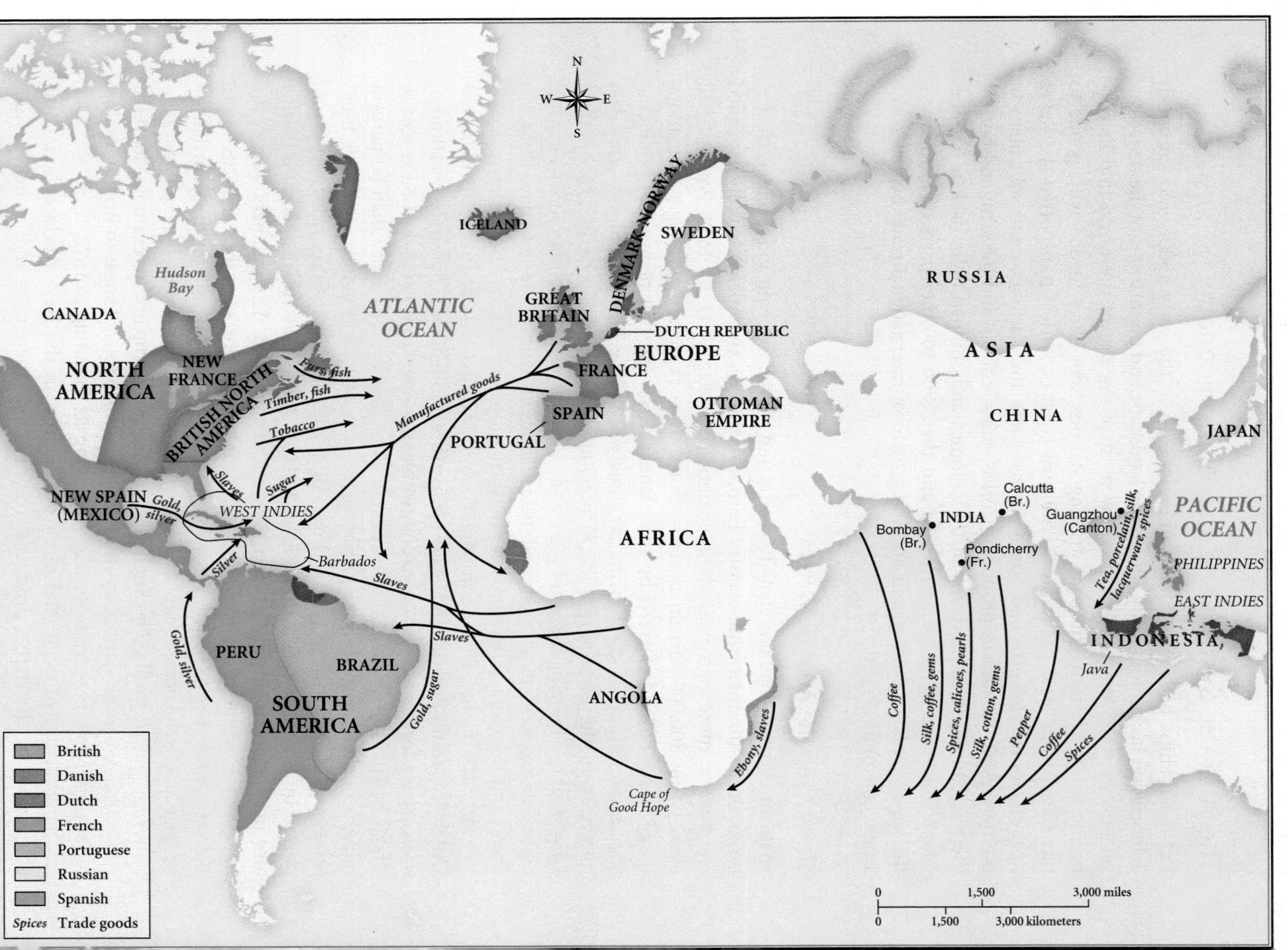

CANADA
Hudson Bay
NORTH AMERICA
NEW FRANCE
BRITISH NORTH AMERICA
NEW SPAIN (MEXICO)
Gold, silver
Furs, fish
Timber, fish
Tobacco
Slaves
Sugar
WEST INDIES
Barbados
Silver
Gold, silver
PERU
BRAZIL
SOUTH AMERICA
Gold, sugar
Slaves
Slaves
ATLANTIC OCEAN
Manufactured goods
ICELAND
GREAT BRITAIN
DENMARK-NORWAY
SWEDEN
DUTCH REPUBLIC
EUROPE
FRANCE
SPAIN
PORTUGAL
OTTOMAN EMPIRE
AFRICA
ANGOLA
Cape of Good Hope
Ebony, slaves
RUSSIA
ASIA
CHINA
JAPAN
INDIA
Calcutta (Br.)
Bombay (Br.)
Pondicherry (Fr.)
Guangzhou (Canton)
Tea, porcelain, silk, lacquerware, spices
PACIFIC OCEAN
PHILIPPINES
EAST INDIES
INDONESIA
Java
Coffee
Silk, coffee, gems
Spices, calicoes, pearls
Silk, cotton, gems
Pepper
Coffee
Spices
British
Danish
Dutch
French
Portuguese
Russian
Spanish
Spices Trade goods
0 1,500 3,000 miles
0 1,500 3,000 kilometers

Map 14.1 European Trade Patterns, c. 1740
By 1740, the European powers had colonized much of North and South America and incorporated their American colonies into a worldwide system of commerce centered on the slave trade and plantation production of staple crops. Europeans still sought spices and luxury goods in China and the East Indies, but outside of Java, few Europeans had settled permanently in these areas. How did control over colonies determine dominance in this period? **For more help analyzing this map, see the map activity for this chapter in the Online Study Guide at** bedfordstmartins.com/huntconcise.

up only 3 percent of the population in eighteenth-century New England, compared with 60 percent in South Carolina. On the whole, the British North American colonies contained a higher proportion of African Americans from 1730 to 1765 than at any other time in American history. The imbalance of whites and blacks was even more extreme in the Caribbean. In the early 1700s, the British sugar islands had a population of about 150,000 people, only 30,000 of them Europeans. The remaining 80 percent were African slaves, as most indigenous people died fighting Europeans or the diseases they brought.

Enslaved women and men suffered terribly. Most had been sold to European traders by Africans from the west coast who acquired them through warfare or kidnapping. The vast majority were between fourteen and thirty-five years old. Before they were crammed onto ships for the three-month transatlantic trip, their heads were shaved, they were stripped naked, and some were branded with red-hot irons. Men and women were separated. Men were shackled with leg irons. Sailors and officers raped the women whenever they wished and beat those who refused their

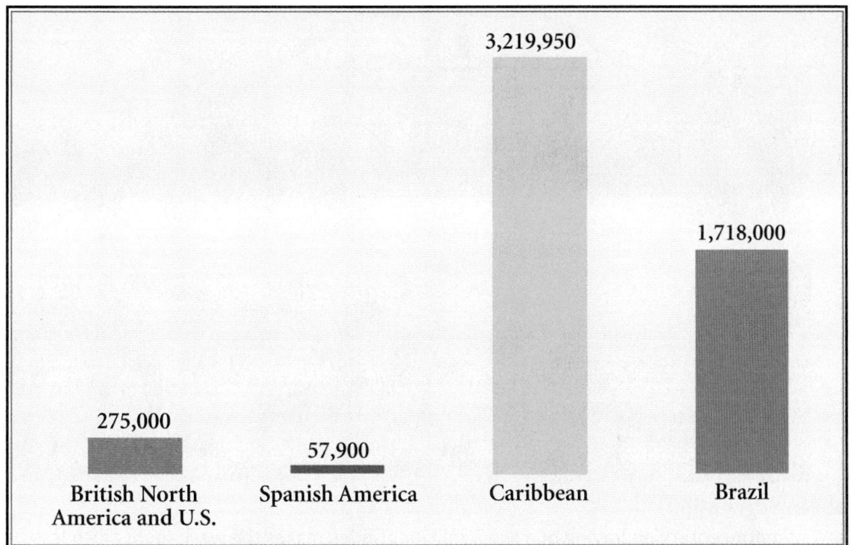

Figure 14.1 African Slaves Imported into American Territories, 1701–1800
During the eighteenth century, planters in the newly established Caribbean colonies imported millions of African slaves to work the new plantations. The vast majority of African slaves transported to the Americas ended up either in the Caribbean or in Brazil.

advances. In the cramped and appalling conditions aboard ship, as many as one-fourth of the slaves died in transit.

Once they landed, slaves were forced into degrading and oppressive conditions. As soon as masters bought slaves, they gave them new names, often only first names, and in some colonies branded them as personal property. Slaves had no social identities of their own; they were expected to learn their master's language and to do any job assigned. Slaves worked fifteen- to seventeen-hour days and were fed only enough to keep them on their feet. Brazilian slaves consumed more calories than the poorest Brazilians do today, but that hardly made them well fed. The death rate among slaves was high, especially in Brazil, where quick shifts in the weather, lack of clothing, and squalid living conditions made them susceptible to a variety of deadly illnesses.

Not surprisingly, despite the threat of torture or death on recapture, slaves sometimes ran away. In Brazil, runaways hid in *quilombos* (hideouts) in the forests or backcountry. When the quilombo of Palmares was discovered and destroyed in 1695, it had thirty thousand fugitives, who had formed their own social organization complete with elected kings and councils of elders. Outright revolt was uncommon,

Caribbean Sugar Mill

This seventeenth-century engraving of a sugar mill, or grinder, makes the work seem much less difficult than it was in practice. Slaves cut the sugarcane and then hauled it from the fields to the mill, where it was crushed. Many slaves lost fingers or hands in the process. The slaves then collected the juice (bottom center) and carried it to the boilers (bottom left and right). The sap was poured into molds and dried. The bricks of raw sugar were then exported to Europe for refining. (The Granger Collection, NY.)

especially before the nineteenth century, but other forms of resistance included stealing food, breaking tools, and feigning illness or stupidity. Slaveholders' fears about conspiracy and revolt lurked beneath the surface of every slave-based society. In 1710, the royal governor of Virginia reminded the colonial legislature of the need for unceasing vigilance: "We are not to Depend on Either Their Stupidity, or that Babel of Languages among 'em; freedom Wears a Cap which Can Without a Tongue, Call Togather all Those who Long to Shake off the fetters of Slavery." Masters defended whipping and other forms of physical punishment as essential to maintaining discipline. Laws called for the castration of a slave who struck a white person.

Plantation owners often left their colonial possessions in the care of agents and collected the revenue to live as wealthy landowners back home, where they built opulent mansions and gained influence in local and national politics. William Beckford, for example, was sent from Jamaica to England to attend school as a young boy. When he inherited sugar plantations and shipping companies from his father and older brother, he moved the headquarters of the family business to London in the 1730s to be close to the government and financial markets. His holdings formed the single most powerful economic interest in Jamaica, but he preferred to live in England, where he could collect art for his many luxurious homes, hold political office (he served as lord mayor of London and in Parliament), and even lend money to the government.

The slave trade permanently altered consumption patterns for ordinary people. Sugar had been prescribed as medicine before the end of the sixteenth century, but the development of plantations in Brazil and the Caribbean made it a standard food item. By 1700, the British sent home fifty million pounds of sugar a year, a figure that doubled by 1730. During the French Revolution of the 1790s, sugar shortages would become a cause for rioting in Paris. Equally pervasive was the spread of tobacco. By the 1720s, Britain imported two hundred shiploads of tobacco from Virginia and Maryland every year, and men of every country and class smoked pipes or took snuff.

The traffic in slaves disturbed many Europeans. As a government memorandum to the Spanish king explained in 1610, "Modern theologians in published books commonly report on, and condemn as unjust, the acts of enslavement which take place in provinces of this Royal Empire." Between 1667 and 1671, the French Dominican monk Father Du Tertre published three volumes in which he denounced the mistreatment of slaves in the French colonies.

In the 1700s, however, slaveholders began to justify their actions by demeaning the mental and spiritual qualities of enslaved Africans. White Europeans and colonists sometimes described black slaves as animal-like, akin to apes. A leading New England Puritan asserted this about black slaves: "Indeed their *Stupidity* is a *Discouragement.* It may seem, unto as little purpose, to *Teach,* as to *wash an Aethiopian* [Ethiopian]." One of the great paradoxes of this time was that talk of liberty and self-evident rights, especially prevalent in Britain and its North American colonies, coexisted with the belief that some people were meant to be slaves. Although Christians believed in principle in a kind of spiritual equality between blacks and whites, the churches often defended or at least did not oppose the inequities of slavery.

World Trade and Settlement

The Atlantic system helped extend European trade relations across the globe. The textiles that British shippers exchanged for slaves on the west coast of Africa, for example, were manufactured in India and exported by the British East India Company, a government-chartered joint-stock company that ended up virtually ruling India. As much as one-quarter of the British exports to Africa in the eighteenth century were actually reexports from India. To expand its trade in the rest of the world, Europeans seized territories and tried to establish permanent settlements. The eighteenth-century extension of European power prepared the way for western global domination in the nineteenth and twentieth centuries.

In contrast to the sparsely inhabited trading outposts in Asia and Africa, the colonies in the Americas bulged with settlers. The British North American colonies, for example, contained about 1.5 million nonnative (that is, white settler and black slave) residents by 1750. While the Spanish competed with the Portuguese for control of South America, the French competed with the British for control of North America. Spanish and British settlers came to blows over the boundary between the British colonies and Florida, which was held by Spain.

Local economies shaped colonial social relations. Men in French trapper communities in Canada, for example, had little in common with the men and women of the plantation societies in Barbados or Brazil. Racial attitudes also differed from place to place. The Spanish and Portuguese tolerated intermarriage with the native populations in both America and Asia. Sexual contact, both inside and outside marriage, fostered greater racial variety in the Spanish and Portuguese colonies than in the French and British territories (though mixed-race people could be found everywhere). By 1800, **mestizos**, children of Spanish men and Indian women, accounted for more than a quarter of the population in the Spanish colonies, and many of them aspired to join the local elite. Greater racial diversity seems not to have improved the treatment of slaves, however, which was probably harshest in Portuguese Brazil.

Where intermarriage between colonizers and natives was common, conversion to Christianity proved most successful. Although the Indians maintained many of their native religious beliefs, the majority of Indians in the Spanish colonies had come to consider themselves Catholics by 1700. Indian carpenters and artisans in the villages produced innumerable altars, retables (painted panels), and sculpted images to adorn their local churches, and individual families put up domestic shrines. Yet the clergy remained overwhelmingly Spanish: the church hierarchy concluded that the Indians' humility and innocence made them unsuitable for the priesthood.

In the early years of American colonization, many more men than women emigrated from Europe. At the end of the seventeenth century, the gender imbalance began to decline but remained substantial. Two and a half times as many men as women were among the immigrants leaving Liverpool, England, between 1697 and 1707, for example. Women who emigrated as indentured servants ran great risks: if they did not die of disease during the voyage, they might end up giving birth to illegitimate children (the fate of at least one in five servant women) or being virtually sold into marriage.

The uncertainties of life in the American colonies provided new opportunities for European women and men willing to live outside the law, however. In the 1500s and 1600s, the English and Dutch governments had routinely authorized pirates to prey on the shipping of their rivals, the Spanish and Portuguese. Then, in the late 1600s, English, French, and Dutch bands made up of deserters and crews from wrecked vessels began to form their own associations of pirates, especially in the Caribbean. Called **buccaneers** from their custom of curing strips of beef, called *boucan* by the native Caribs of the islands, the pirates governed themselves and preyed on everyone's shipping without regard to national origin. After 1700, the colonial governments tried to stamp out piracy. As one English judge argued in 1705, "A pirate is in perpetual war with every individual and every state. . . . They are worse than ravenous beasts."

White settlements in Africa and Asia remained small and almost insignificant, except for their long-term potential. Europeans had little contact with East Africa and almost none with Africa's vast interior. A few Portuguese trading posts in Angola and Dutch farms on the Cape of Good Hope provided the only toeholds for future expansion. In China, the emperors had welcomed Catholic missionaries at court in the seventeenth century, but the priests' credibility diminished as they squabbled among themselves and associated with European merchants, whom the Chinese considered pirates. "The barbarians [Europeans] are like wild beasts," one Chinese official concluded. In 1720, only one thousand Europeans resided in Guangzhou (Canton), the sole place where foreigners could legally trade for spices, tea, and silk (Map 14.1, page 524).

Europeans exercised more influence in India and Java, in the East Indies. Dutch coffee production in Java and nearby islands increased phenomenally in the early 1700s, and many Dutch settled there to oversee production and trade. In India, Dutch, British, French, Portuguese, and Danish companies competed for spices, cotton, and silk. By the 1740s the British and French had become the leading rivals in India, just as they were in North America. Both countries extended their power as India's Muslim rulers lost control to local Hindu princes, rebellious Sikhs, invading Persians, and their own provincial governors. A few thousand Europeans lived in India, though many thousands more soldiers were stationed there to protect them. The staple of trade with India in the early 1700s was calico—lightweight, brightly colored cotton cloth that caught on as a fashion in Europe.

Europeans who visited India were especially struck by what they viewed as exotic religious practices. In a book published in 1696 of his travels to western India, an Anglican minister described fakirs (religious ascetics), "some of whom show their devotion by a shameless appearance, and walking naked." Such writings increased European interest in the outside world, but they also fed a European sense of superiority that helped excuse violent forms of colonial domination.

India Cottons and Trade with the East
This colored cotton cloth (now faded with age) was painted and embroidered in Madras, in southern India, in the late 1600s. The male figure with the mustache may be a European, but the female figures are clearly Asian. Europeans, especially the British, discovered that they could make big profits on the export of Indian cotton cloth to Europe. They also traded Indian cotton in Africa for slaves and sold large quantities in the colonies. (V&A Images/Victoria and Albert Museum, London.)

The Birth of a Consumer Society

Worldwide colonization produced new supplies of goods, from coffee to calico, and population growth in Europe fueled demand for them. Beginning first in Britain, then in France and the Italian states, and finally in eastern Europe, population surged, growing by about 20 percent between 1700 and 1750. The gap between a fast-growing northwestern Europe and a more stagnant southern and central Europe now diminished as regions that had lost population during the seventeenth-century downturn recovered. Cities in particular grew. Between 1600 and 1750, London's population more than tripled, and Paris's more than doubled.

Although contemporaries could not have realized it then, this was the start of the modern "population explosion." It appears that a decline in the death rate, rather than a rise in the birthrate, explains the turnaround. Three main factors contributed to this decline in the death rate: better weather and hence more bountiful harvests, improved agricultural techniques, and the plague's disappearance after 1720.

By the early eighteenth century, the effects of economic expansion and population growth brought about a **consumer revolution**. The British East India Company began to import into Britain huge quantities of calico. British imports of tobacco doubled between 1672 and 1700. At Nantes, the center of the French sugar trade, imports quadrupled between 1698 and 1733. Tea, chocolate, and coffee became virtual necessities. In the 1670s, only a trickle of tea reached London, but by 1720 the East India Company sent 9 million pounds to England—a figure that rose to 37 million pounds by 1750. In 1700, England had two thousand coffeehouses; by 1740, every English country town had at least two. Paris got its first cafés at the end of the seventeenth century; Berlin opened its first coffeehouse in 1714; Bach's Leipzig boasted eight coffeehouses by 1725.

The birth of consumer society did not go unnoticed by eyewitnesses. In the English economic literature of the 1690s, writers began to express a new view of humans as consuming animals with boundless appetites. Such opinions gained a wide audience with the appearance of Bernard Mandeville's poem *Fable of the Bees* (1705), which argued that private vices might have public benefits. Mandeville insisted that pride, self-interest, and the desire for material goods (all Christian vices) in fact promoted economic prosperity: "every part was full of Vice, Yet the whole mass a Paradise." Many authors attacked the new doctrine of consumerism, and the French government banned the poem's publication. But Mandeville had captured the essence of the emerging market for consumption.

REVIEW How is consumerism related to slavery?

New Social and Cultural Patterns

The impact of the Atlantic system and world trade was most apparent in the cities, where people had more money for consumer goods and more opportunities to participate in new public activities. But rural changes also had significant long-term influence, as a revolution in agricultural techniques made it possible to feed more and more people with a smaller agricultural workforce. As population increased, more people moved to the cities, where they found themselves caught up in innovative urban customs such as attending musical concerts and reading novels. Along with a general increase in literacy, these activities helped create a new public sphere ready to respond to new styles and new ideas. Social and cultural changes were not uniform across Europe, however; as usual, people's experiences varied depending on whether they lived in wealth or poverty, in urban or rural areas, or in eastern or western Europe.

The Agricultural Revolution

Although Britain, France, and the Dutch Republic shared the enthusiasm for consumer goods, Britain's domestic market grew most quickly. In Britain, as agricultural output increased 43 percent over the course of the 1700s, the population increased by 70 percent. The British imported grain to feed the growing population, but they also benefited from the development of techniques that together constituted an

agricultural revolution. No new machinery propelled this revolution—just more aggressive attitudes toward investment and management. The Dutch and Flemish had pioneered many of these techniques in the 1600s, but the British took them further.

Four major changes occurred in British agriculture that eventually spread to other countries. First, farmers increased the amount of land under cultivation by draining wetlands and by growing crops on previously uncultivated common lands (acreage maintained by the community for grazing). Second, farmers who could afford to do so consolidated smaller, scattered plots into larger, more efficient units. Third, livestock raising became more closely linked to crop growing, and the yields of each increased. (See "Taking Measure.") For centuries, most farmers had rotated their fields in and out of production to replenish the soil. Now farmers planted carefully chosen fodder crops such as clover and turnips that added nutrients to the soil, thereby eliminating the need to leave a field fallow (unplanted) every two or three years. With more fodder available, farmers could raise more livestock, which in turn produced more manure to fertilize grain fields. Fourth, selective breeding of animals combined with the increase in fodder to improve the quality and size of herds. New crops had only a slight impact. Potatoes, for example, were introduced

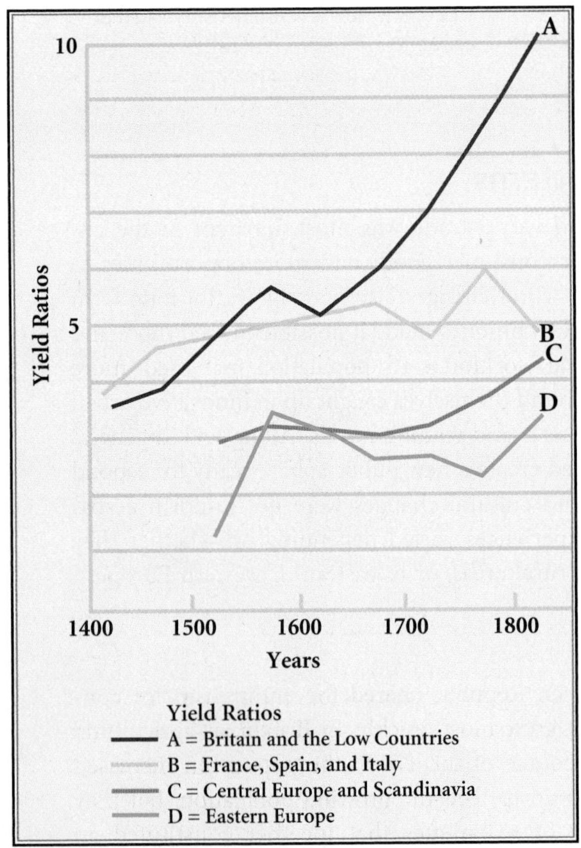

Taking Measure Relationship of Crop Harvested to Seed Used, 1400–1800
The impact and even the timing of the agricultural revolution can be seen in this figure, based on yield ratios (the number of grains produced for each seed planted). Britain, the Dutch Republic, and the Austrian Netherlands all experienced huge increases in crop yields after 1700. Other European regions lagged behind right into the 1800s. What are the economic and social consequences of having a higher crop yield?

to Europe from South America in the 1500s, but because people feared they might cause leprosy, tuberculosis, or fevers, they were not grown in quantity until the late 1700s. By the 1730s and 1740s, agricultural output had increased dramatically, and prices for food had fallen because of these interconnected innovations.

Changes in agricultural practices did not benefit all landowners equally. The biggest British landowners consolidated their holdings in the "enclosure movement." They put pressure on small farmers and villagers to sell their land or give up their common lands. The big landlords then fenced off ("enclosed") their property. Because enclosure eliminated community grazing rights, it frequently sparked a struggle between the big landlords and villagers, and in Britain it normally required an act of Parliament. Such acts became increasingly common in the second half of the eighteenth century, and by the century's end six million acres of common lands had been enclosed and developed. "Improvers" produced more food more efficiently and thus supported a growing population.

Contrary to the fears of contemporaries, small farmers and cottagers (those with little or no property) were not forced off the land all at once. But most villagers could not afford the litigation involved in resisting enclosure, and small landholders consequently had to sell out to landlords or farmers with larger plots. Landlords with large holdings leased their estates to tenant farmers at constantly increasing rents, and tenant farmers in turn employed cottagers as salaried agricultural workers. In this way the English peasantry largely disappeared, replaced by a more hierarchical society of big landlords, enterprising tenant farmers, and poor agricultural laborers.

The new agricultural techniques spread slowly from Britain and the Low Countries (the Dutch Republic and the Austrian Netherlands) to the rest of western Europe. Outside a few pockets in northern France and the western German states, however, subsistence agriculture (producing just enough to get by rather than surpluses for the market) continued to dominate farming in western Europe and Scandinavia. In southwestern Germany, for example, 80 percent of the peasants produced no surplus because their plots were too small. Unlike the populations of the highly urbanized Low Countries (where half the people lived in towns and cities), most Europeans, western and eastern, eked out an existence in the countryside.

In eastern Europe, the condition of peasants worsened in the areas where landlords tried hardest to improve their yields. To produce more for the Baltic grain market, aristocratic landholders in Prussia, Poland, and parts of Russia drained wetlands, cultivated moors, and built dikes. They also forced peasants off lands the peasants worked for themselves, increased compulsory labor services (the critical element in serfdom), and began to manage their estates directly. Some eastern landowners grew fabulously wealthy. The Potocki family in the Polish Ukraine, for example, owned three million acres of land and had 130,000 serfs. In parts of Poland and Russia, the serfs hardly differed from slaves in status, and their "masters" ran their huge estates much like American plantations.

Social Life in the Cities

Because of emigration from the countryside, cities grew in population and consequently exercised more influence on culture and social life. Between 1650 and 1750, cities with at least 10,000 inhabitants increased in population by 44 percent. From the eighteenth century onward, urban growth would be continuous. Along with the general growth of cities, an important south-to-north shift occurred in the pattern of urbanization. Around 1500, half of the people in cities of at least 10,000 residents could be found in the Italian states, Spain, or Portugal; by 1700, the urbanization of northwestern and southern Europe was roughly equal. Eastern Europe, despite the huge cities of Istanbul and Moscow, was still less urban than western Europe. London was by far the most populous European city, with 675,000 inhabitants in 1750; Berlin had 90,000 people, Warsaw only 23,000.

Many landowners kept a residence in town, so the separation between rural and city life was not as extreme as might be imagined, at least not for the very rich. At the top of the ladder in the big cities were the landed nobles. Some of them filled their lives only with conspicuous consumption of fine food, extravagant clothing, coaches, books, and opera; others held key political, administrative, or judicial offices. However they spent their time, these rich families employed thousands of artisans, shopkeepers, and domestic servants. Many English peers (the highest-ranking nobles) had thirty or forty servants at each of their homes.

The middle classes of officials, merchants, professionals, and landowners occupied the next rung down on the social ladder. London's population, for example, included about twenty thousand middle-class families (constituting, at most, one-sixth of the city's population). In this period, the middle classes began to develop distinctive ways of life that set them apart from both the rich noble landowners and the lower classes. Unlike the rich nobles, the middle classes lived primarily in the cities and towns, even if they owned small country estates. They ate more moderately than nobles but much better than peasants or laborers. For breakfast, the British middle classes ate toast and rolls and, after 1700, drank tea. Dinner, served midday, consisted of roasted or boiled beef, mutton, poultry, or pork, and vegetables. Supper was a light meal of bread and cheese with cake or pie. Beer was the main drink in London, and many families brewed their own. Even children drank beer because of the lack of fresh water.

In contrast to the gigantic and sprawling countryseats of the richest English peers, middle-class houses in town had about seven rooms, including four or five bedrooms and one or two living rooms, still many more than the homes of poor agricultural workers. New household items reflected society's increasing wealth and its exposure to colonial imports. By 1700, the middle classes of London typically had several mirrors, a coffeepot and coffee mill, numerous pictures and ornaments, a china collection, and several clocks. Life for the middle classes on the European continent was quite similar, though wine replaced beer in France.

Below the middle classes came the artisans and shopkeepers (most of whom were organized in professional guilds), then the journeymen, apprentices, servants, and laborers. At the bottom of the social scale were the unemployed poor, who survived on intermittent work and charity. Women married to artisans and shopkeepers often kept the accounts, supervised employees, and ran the household. Every home from the middle classes to the upper classes employed servants; artisans and shopkeepers frequently hired them, too. Women from poorer families usually worked as domestic servants until they married. Four out of five domestic servants in the city were female. In large cities such as London, the servant population grew faster than the population of the city as a whole.

Social status in the cities was readily visible. Wide, spacious streets graced rich districts; the houses had gardens, and the air was relatively fresh. In poor districts, the streets were narrow, dirty, dark, humid, and smelly, and the houses were damp and crowded. The poorest people were homeless, sleeping under bridges or in abandoned homes. A Neapolitan prince described his homeless neighbors as "lying like filthy animals, with no distinction of age or sex." In some districts, rich and poor lived in the same buildings; the poor clambered up to shabby, cramped apartments on the top floors.

Like shelter, clothing was a reliable social indicator. The poorest workingwomen in Paris wore woolen skirts and blouses of dark colors over petticoats, bodice, and corset. They also donned caps of various sorts, cotton stockings, and shoes (probably their only pair). Workingmen dressed even more drably. Many occupations could be recognized by their dress: no one could confuse lawyers in their dark robes with masons or butchers in their special aprons, for example. People higher on

Vauxhall Gardens, London

This hand-colored print from the mid-1700s shows the newly refurbished gardens near the Thames River. Prosperous families show off their brightly colored clothes and listen to a public concert by the orchestra seated just above them. These activities helped form a more self-conscious public.

(© Bibliothèque des Arts Décoratifs, Paris, France/The Bridgeman Art Library.)

the social ladder were more likely to sport a variety of fabrics, colors, and unusual designs in their clothing and to own many different outfits. Social status was not an abstract idea; it permeated every detail of daily life.

Public Hygiene and Health Care

The growth of cities created new challenges for public hygiene. Cities were notoriously unhealthy because excrement (animal and human) and garbage accumulated where people lived densely packed together. Paris seemed to a visitor "so detestable that it is impossible to remain there" because of the smell. Even the facade of the Louvre palace was soiled by the contents of night commodes that servants routinely dumped out of windows every morning. Only the wealthy could escape walking in mucky streets, by hiring men to carry them in sedan chairs or drive them in coaches.

After investigating specific cities, medical geographers urged government campaigns to improve public sanitation. Everywhere, environmentalists gathered and analyzed data on climate, disease, and population, searching for correlations to help direct policy. As a result of these efforts, local governments undertook such measures as draining low-lying areas, burying refuse, and cleaning wells, all of which eventually helped lower the death rates from epidemic diseases.

Hospitals and medical care underwent lasting transformations. Founded originally as charities concerned foremost with the moral worthiness of the poor, hospitals gradually evolved into medical institutions that defined patients by their diseases. The process of diagnosis changed as physicians began to use specialized Latin terms for illnesses. The gap between medical experts and their patients increased, as physicians now also relied on postmortem dissections in the hospital to gain better knowledge, a practice most patients' families resented. Press reports of body snatching and grave robbing by surgeons and their apprentices outraged the public well into the 1800s.

Despite the change in hospitals, individual health care remained something of a free-for-all in which physicians competed with bloodletters, itinerant venereal disease doctors, bonesetters, druggists, midwives, and "cunning women," who specialized in home remedies. The medical profession, with nationwide organizations and licensing, had not yet emerged, and no clear line separated trained physicians from quacks. Physicians often followed popular prescriptions for illnesses because they had nothing better to offer. Patients were as likely to die of diseases caught in the hospital as to be cured there. Antiseptics were nearly unknown.

The various "medical opinions" about childbirth highlight the confusion people faced. Midwives delivered most babies, though they sometimes encountered criticism even from within their own ranks. One consulting midwife complained that ordinary midwives in Bristol, England, made women in labor drink a mixture of leek juice and their husbands' urine. By the 1730s, female midwives faced competition from male midwives, who were known for using instruments such as forceps to pull babies out of the birth canal. Women rarely sought a physician's help in giving birth, however; they preferred the advice and assistance of trusted local midwives. In any case, trained physicians were few in number and almost nonexistent outside cities.

Hardly any infectious diseases could be cured, though inoculation against smallpox spread from the Middle East to Europe in the early eighteenth century, thanks largely to the efforts of Lady Mary Wortley Montagu, who learned about the technique while living in Constantinople. After 1750, physicians developed successful procedures for wide-scale vaccination, although even then many people resisted the idea of inoculating themselves with a disease. Other diseases spread quickly in the unsanitary conditions of urban life. Ordinary people washed or changed clothes rarely, lived in overcrowded housing with poor ventilation, and got their water from contaminated sources, such as refuse-filled rivers.

Until the mid-1700s, most people considered bathing dangerous. Public bathhouses had disappeared from cities in the sixteenth and seventeenth centuries because they seemed a source of disorderly behavior and epidemic illness. In the eighteenth century, even private bathing came into disfavor because people feared the effects of contact with water. Fewer than one in ten newly built private mansions in Paris had baths. Bathing was hazardous, physicians insisted, because it opened the body to disease. One manners manual of 1736 admonished, "It is correct to clean the face every morning by using a white cloth to cleanse it. It is less good to wash with water, because it renders the face susceptible to cold in winter and sun in summer." The upper classes associated cleanliness not with baths but with frequently changed linens, powdered hair, and perfume, which was thought to strengthen the body and refresh the brain by counteracting corrupt and foul air.

The New Public Sphere

Cities may have been unhealthy, but they promoted the development of a new public sphere that rested in the first instance on the spread of literacy. City people were more literate than peasants. Protestant countries appear to have been more successful at promoting education and literacy than Catholic countries, perhaps because of the Protestant emphasis on Bible reading. Widespread popular literacy was first achieved in the Protestant areas of Switzerland and in Presbyterian Scotland, and rates were also very high in the New England colonies and the Scandinavian countries. In France, literacy doubled in the eighteenth century thanks to the spread of parish schools, but still only one in two men and one in four women could read and write. Despite the efforts of some Protestant German states to encourage primary education, primary schooling remained woefully inadequate almost everywhere in Europe: few schools existed, teachers received low wages, and no country had yet established a national system of control or supervision.

Despite the deficiencies of primary education, a new literate public arose, especially among the middle classes of the cities. More books and periodicals were published than ever before. England and the Dutch Republic led the way in this powerful outpouring of printed words. The trend began in the 1690s and gradually accelerated. In 1695, the English government allowed the licensing system through which it controlled publications to lapse, and new newspapers and magazines appeared almost immediately. The first London daily newspaper came out in 1702, and in

1709 Joseph Addison and Richard Steele published the first literary magazine, the *Spectator*. They devoted their magazine to the cultural improvement of the increasingly influential middle class. By the 1720s, twenty-four provincial newspapers were published in England. In the London coffeehouses, an edition of a single newspaper might reach ten thousand male readers. Women did their reading at home.

Newspapers on the continent lagged behind and often consisted mainly of advertising with little critical commentary. France, for example, had no daily paper until 1777. The new literate public did not just read newspapers; its members now pursued an interest in painting, attended concerts, and besieged booksellers in search of popular novels. Because increased trade and prosperity put money into the hands of the growing middle classes, the new public sphere began to compete with the churches, rulers, and courtiers as chief patrons of new work. As the public for the arts expanded, printed commentary on them emerged, setting the stage for the appearance of political and social criticism. New artistic tastes thus had effects far beyond the realm of the arts.

Developments in painting reflected the tastes of the new public. The **rococo** style challenged the hold of the baroque and classical schools, especially in France. Like the baroque, the rococo emphasized irregularity and asymmetry, movement and curvature, but it did so on a much smaller, subtler scale. Many rococo paintings depicted scenes of intimate sensuality rather than the monumental, emotional grandeur favored by classical and baroque painters. Personal portraits and pastoral paintings took the place of heroic landscapes and large ceremonial canvases. Rococo

Rococo Painting
This painting by the Venetian artist Rosalba Carriera (1675–1757) is titled *Africa*. The young black girl wearing a turban represents the African continent. Carriera was known for her use of pastels. In 1720, she journeyed to Paris, where she became an associate of Antoine Watteau and helped inaugurate the rococo style in painting. Why might the artist have chosen to paint an African girl? **For more help analyzing this image, see the visual activity for this chapter in the Online Study Guide at bedfordstmartins.com/huntconcise.** (Gemäldegalerie Alte Meister, Staatliche Kunstsammlungen Dresden.)

paintings adorned homes as well as palaces and served as a form of interior decoration rather than as a statement of piety. Its decorative quality made rococo art an ideal complement to newly discovered materials such as stucco and porcelain, especially the porcelain vases now imported from China.

Rococo was an invented word (from the French word *rocaille,* meaning "shellwork") and originally a derogatory label meaning "frivolous decoration." But the great French rococo painters, such as Antoine Watteau (1684–1721) and François Boucher (1703–1770), were much more than mere decorators. Although both emphasized the erotic in their depictions, Watteau captured the melancholy side of a passing aristocratic style of life, and Boucher painted middle-class people at home during their daily activities. Both painters thereby contributed to the emergence of new sensibilities in art that increasingly attracted a middle-class public.

Music as well as art grew in popularity. The first public music concerts were performed in England in the 1670s, becoming much more regular and frequent in the 1690s. City concert halls typically seated about two hundred, but the relatively high price of tickets limited attendance to the better-off. Music clubs provided entertainment in smaller towns and villages. In continental Europe, Frankfurt organized the first regular public concerts in 1712; Hamburg and Paris began holding them within a few years. Opera continued to spread in the eighteenth century; Venice had sixteen public opera houses by 1700, and Covent Garden opera house opened in London in 1732.

The growth of a public that appreciated and supported music had much the same effect as the extension of the reading public: like authors, composers could now begin to liberate themselves from court patronage and work for a paying audience. This development took time to solidify, however, and court or church patrons still commissioned much eighteenth-century music. Bach, a German Lutheran, wrote his *St. Matthew Passion* for Good Friday services in 1729 while he was organist and choirmaster for the leading church in Leipzig. He composed secular works (like the "Coffee Cantata" quoted at the beginning of this chapter) for the public and a variety of private patrons.

The composer George Frederick Handel (1685–1759) was among the first to grasp the new directions in music. He began his career playing second violin in the Hamburg opera orchestra and then moved to Britain in 1710, where he eventually turned to composing oratorios, a form he introduced in Britain. The oratorio combined the drama of opera with the majesty of religious and ceremonial music and featured the chorus over the soloists. Handel's most famous oratorio, *Messiah* (1741), reflects his personal, deeply felt piety but also his willingness to combine musical materials into a dramatic form that captured the enthusiasm of the new public. In 1740, a poem published in the *Gentleman's Magazine* exulted, "His art so modulates the sounds in all, / Our passions, as he pleases, rise and fall." Music had become an integral part of the new public sphere.

But nothing captured the imagination of the new public more than the novel, the literary genre whose very name underscored the eighteenth-century taste for novelty. Over three hundred French novels appeared between 1700 and 1730. During this unprecedented explosion, the novel took on its modern form and became more concerned with individual psychology and social description than with the picaresque adventures popular earlier (such as Cervantes's *Don Quixote*). The novel's popularity was closely tied to the expansion of the reading public, and novels were available in serial form in periodicals or from the many booksellers who popped up to serve the new market.

Women figured prominently in novels as characters, and women writers abounded. The English novel *Love in Excess* (1719) quickly reached a sixth printing, and its author, Eliza Haywood (1693?–1756), earned her living turning out a stream of novels with titles such as *Persecuted Virtue, Constancy Rewarded,* and *The History of Miss Betsy Thoughtless*—all showing a concern for the proper place of women as models of virtue in a changing world. Haywood had first worked as an actress when her husband deserted her and her two children, but she soon turned to writing plays and novels. In the 1740s, she began publishing a magazine, the *Female Spectator,* which argued in favor of higher education for women.

Haywood's male counterpart was Daniel Defoe (1660?–1731), a merchant's son who had a diverse and colorful career as a manufacturer, political spy, novelist, and social commentator. Defoe's novel about a shipwrecked sailor, *Robinson Crusoe* (1719), portrayed the new values of the time: to survive, Crusoe had to meet every challenge with fearless entrepreneurial ingenuity. He had to be ready for the unexpected and be able to improvise in every situation. He was, in short, the model for the new man in an expanding economy. Crusoe's patronizing attitude toward the black man Friday now draws much critical attention, but his discovery of Friday shows how the fate of blacks and whites had become intertwined in the new colonial environment.

Religious Revivals

Despite the novel's growing popularity, religious books and pamphlets still sold in huge numbers, and most Europeans remained devout, even as their religions were changing. In this period, a Protestant revival known as **Pietism** rocked the complacency of the established churches in the German Lutheran states, the Dutch Republic, and Scandinavia. Pietists believed in a mystical religion of the heart; they wanted a more deeply emotional, even ecstatic religion. They urged intense Bible study, which in turn promoted popular education and contributed to the increase in literacy. Many Pietists attended catechism instruction every day and also went to morning and evening prayer meetings in addition to regular Sunday services.

Catholicism also had its versions of religious revival. A Frenchwoman, Jeanne Marie Guyon (1648–1717), attracted many noblewomen and a few leading clergymen to her own Catholic brand of Pietism, known as Quietism. Claiming miraculous visions and astounding prophecies, she urged a mystical union with God through prayer and simple devotion. Despite papal condemnation and intense controversy within Catholic circles in France, Guyon had followers all over Europe.

Even more influential were the Jansenists, who gained many new adherents to their austere form of Catholicism despite Louis XIV's harassment and repeated condemnation by the papacy (see page 486). Under the pressure of religious and political persecution, Jansenism took a revivalist turn in the 1720s. At the funeral of a Jansenist priest in Paris in 1727, the crowd that flocked to the grave claimed to witness a series of miraculous healings. Within a few years, a cult formed around the priest's tomb, and clandestine Jansenist presses reported new miracles to the reading public. When the French government tried to suppress the cult, one enraged wit placed a sign at the tomb that read, "By order of the king, God is forbidden to work miracles here." Some believers fell into frenzied convulsions, claiming to be inspired by the Holy Spirit through the intercession of the dead priest. After midcentury, Jansenism became even more politically active as its adherents joined in opposition to crown policies on religion.

REVIEW What were the social and political consequences of the agricultural revolution?

Consolidation of the European State System

The spread of Pietism and Jansenism reflected the emergence of a middle-class public that now participated in every new development, including religion. The middle classes could pursue these interests because the European state system gradually stabilized. Warfare settled three main issues between 1690 and 1740: a coalition of powers held Louis XIV's France in check on the continent; Great Britain emerged from the wars against Louis as the preeminent maritime power; and Russia defeated Sweden in the contest for supremacy in the Baltic. After Louis XIV's death in 1715, Europe enjoyed the fruits of a more balanced diplomatic system, in which warfare became less frequent and less widespread. States could then spend their resources establishing and expanding control over their own populations, both at home and in their colonies.

French Ambitions Thwarted

Lying on his deathbed in 1715, the seventy-six-year-old Louis XIV watched helplessly as his accomplishments continued to unravel. Not only had his plans for territorial expansion been thwarted, but his incessant wars had exhausted the treasury, despite new taxes. In 1689, Louis's rival, William III, prince of Orange and king of England and Scotland (r. 1689–1702), had set out to forge a European alliance that eventually included Britain, the Dutch Republic, Sweden, Austria, and Spain. The allies fought Louis to a stalemate in the War of the League of Augsburg, sometimes called the Nine Years' War (1689–1697), and when hostilities resumed four years later, they finally put an end to Louis's expansionist ambitions.

The War of the Spanish Succession (1701–1713) broke out when the mentally and physically feeble Charles II (r. 1665–1700) of Spain died without a direct heir. The Spanish succession could not help but be a burning issue. Even though Spanish power had declined steadily since Spain's golden age in the sixteenth century, Spain still had extensive territories in Italy and the Netherlands and colonies overseas. Before Charles died, he named Louis XIV's second grandson, Philip, duke of Anjou, as his heir, but the Austrian emperor Leopold I refused to accept Charles's deathbed will. In the ensuing war, the French lost several major battles and had to accept disadvantageous terms in the Peace of Utrecht of 1713–1714 (Map 14.2). Although Philip was recognized as king of Spain, he had to renounce any future claim to the French crown, thus barring unification of the two kingdoms. Spain surrendered its territories in Italy and the Netherlands to the Austrians and Gibraltar to the British; France ceded possessions in North America (Newfoundland, the Hudson Bay area, and most of Nova Scotia) to Britain. France no longer threatened to dominate European power politics.

At home, Louis's policy of absolutism had fomented bitter hostility. Nobles fiercely resented his promotions of commoners to high office. The duke of Saint-Simon complained that "falseness, servility, admiring glances, combined with a dependent and cringing attitude, above all, an appearance of being nothing without him, were the only ways of pleasing him." On his deathbed, Louis XIV gave his blessing and some sound advice to his five-year-old great-grandson and successor, Louis XV (r. 1715–1774): "My child, you are about to become a great King. Do not imitate my love of building nor my liking for war."

After being named regent, the duke of Orléans (1674–1723), nephew of the dead king, revived some of the parlements' powers and tried to give leading nobles a greater say in political affairs. Financial problems plagued the regency as they would beset all succeeding French regimes in the eighteenth century. In 1719, the regent appointed the Scottish financier John Law to the top financial position of controller general. Law founded a trading company for North America and a state bank that issued paper money and stock (without them, trade depended on the available supply of gold and silver). The bank was supposed to offer lower interest rates to the state, thus cutting the cost of financing the government's debts. The value of the stock rose rapidly in a frenzy of speculation, only to crash a few months later. With it vanished any hope of establishing a state bank or issuing paper money for nearly a century.

France finally achieved a measure of financial stability under the leadership of Cardinal Hercule de Fleury (1653–1743), the most powerful member of the government after the death of the regent. Fleury aimed to avoid adventure abroad and keep social peace at home; he balanced the budget and carried out a large project for road and canal construction. Colonial trade boomed. Peace and the acceptance of limits on territorial expansion inaugurated a century of French prosperity.

British Rise and Dutch Decline

The English and Dutch had formed a coalition against Louis XIV under their joint ruler, William III, who was simultaneously stadholder of the Dutch Republic and, with his English wife, Mary (d. 1694), ruler of England, Wales, Scotland, and Ireland. After William's death in 1702, the English and Dutch went their separate ways. Dutch imperial power declined, even though Dutch merchants still controlled a substantial

Map 14.2 Europe, c. 1715

Although Louis XIV succeeded in putting his grandson Philip on the Spanish throne, France emerged from the War of the Spanish Succession considerably weakened. France ceded large territories in Canada to Britain, which also gained key Mediterranean outposts from Spain as well as a monopoly on providing slaves to the Spanish colonies. Spanish losses were catastrophic: Philip had to renounce any future claim to the French crown and give up considerable territory in the Netherlands and Italy to the Austrians.

portion of world trade. English relations with Scotland and Ireland were complicated by the problem of succession: William and Mary had no children. To ensure a Protestant succession, Parliament ruled that Mary's sister, Anne, would succeed William and Mary and that the Protestant house of Hanover in Germany would succeed Anne if she had no surviving heirs. Catholics were excluded. When Queen Anne (r. 1702–1714) died leaving no children, the elector of Hanover, a Protestant great-grandson of James I, consequently became King George I (r. 1714–1727). The house of Hanover—renamed the house of Windsor during World War I in response to anti-German sentiment—still occupies the British throne.

Support from the Scots and Irish for this solution did not come easily because many in Scotland and Ireland supported the claims to the throne of the deposed Catholic king, James II, and, after his death in 1701, his son James Edward. Out of fear of this Jacobitism (from the Latin *Jacobus,* "James"), Scottish Protestant leaders agreed to the Act of Union of 1707, which abolished the Scottish Parliament and affirmed the Scots' recognition of the Protestant Hanoverian succession. The Scots agreed to obey the Parliament of Great Britain, which would include Scottish members in the House of Commons and the House of Lords. A Jacobite rebellion in Scotland in 1715, aiming to restore the Stuart line, was suppressed (Map 14.2, page 543). The threat of Jacobitism nonetheless continued into the 1740s.

The Irish, 90 percent of whom were Catholic, proved even more difficult to subdue. When James II went to Ireland in 1689 to raise a Catholic rebellion against the new monarchs of England, William III responded by taking command of the joint English and Dutch forces and defeating James's Irish supporters. James fled to France, and the Catholics in Ireland faced yet more confiscation and legal restrictions. By 1700, Irish Catholics, who in 1640 had owned 60 percent of the land in Ireland, owned just 14 percent. The Protestant-controlled Irish Parliament passed a series of laws limiting the rights of the Catholic majority: Catholics could not bear arms, send their children abroad for education, establish Catholic schools at home, or marry Protestants. Catholics could not sit in Parliament, nor could they vote for its members unless they took an oath renouncing Catholic doctrine. These and a host of other laws reduced Catholic Ireland to the status of a colony. One British official commented in 1745, "The poor people of Ireland are used worse than negroes." Most of the Irish were peasants who lived in primitive housing and subsisted on a meager diet that included no meat.

The Parliament of Great Britain was soon dominated by the Whigs. In Britain's constitutional system, the monarch ruled with Parliament. The crown chose the ministers, directed policy, and supervised administration, while Parliament raised revenue, passed laws, and represented the interests of the people to the crown. The powers of Parliament were reaffirmed by the Triennial Act of 1694, which provided that Parliament must meet at least once every three years (this was extended to seven years in 1716, after the Whigs had established their ascendancy). Only 200,000 propertied men could vote, out of a population of more than five million people, and not surprisingly, most members of Parliament came from the landed gentry. In fact, a few hundred families controlled all the important political offices.

George I and George II (r. 1727–1760) relied on one man, Sir Robert Walpole (1676–1745), to help them manage their relations with Parliament. From his position as first lord of the treasury, Walpole made himself into first, or "prime," minister, leading the House of Commons from 1721 to 1742. Although appointed initially by the king, Walpole established an enduring pattern of parliamentary government in which a prime minister from the leading party guides legislation through the House of Commons. Walpole also built a vast patronage machine that dispensed government jobs to win support for the crown's policies. Walpole's successors relied more and more on the patronage system and eventually alienated not only the Tories but also the middle classes in London and even the North American colonists.

The partisan division between the Whigs, who had supported the Hanoverian succession and the rights of dissenting Protestants, and the Tories, who had backed the Stuart line and the Anglican church, did not hamper Great Britain's pursuit of economic, military, and colonial power. In this period, Britain became a great power on the world stage by virtue of its navy and its ability to finance major military involvement in the wars against Louis XIV. The founding in 1694 of the Bank of England—which, unlike the French bank, endured—enabled the government to raise money at low interest for foreign wars. By the 1740s, the government could borrow more than four times what it could in the 1690s.

Sir Robert Walpole at a Cabinet Meeting
Sir Robert Walpole and George II developed the institution of the cabinet, which brought together the important heads of government departments. Walpole's cabinet was the ancestor of modern cabinets in Great Britain and the United States. How might discussions in the new coffeehouses (shown in the illustration on page 520) have influenced the kinds of decisions made by Walpole and his cabinet? (The Fotomas Index, U.K./The Bridgeman Art Library.)

By contrast, the Dutch Republic, one of the richest and most influential states of the seventeenth century, saw its power eclipsed in the eighteenth. When William of Orange (William III of England) died in 1702, he left no heirs, and for forty-five years the Dutch lived without a stadholder. The merchant ruling class of some two thousand families dominated the Dutch Republic more than ever, but they presided over a country that counted for less in international power politics. In some areas, Dutch decline was only relative. The Dutch population was not growing as fast as populations elsewhere, for example, and the Dutch share of the Baltic trade decreased from 50 percent in 1720 to less than 30 percent by the 1770s. After 1720, the Baltic countries—Prussia, Russia, Denmark, and Sweden—began to ban imports of manufactured goods to protect their own industries, and Dutch trade in particular suffered. The output of Leiden textiles dropped to one-third its 1700 level by 1740. Shipbuilding, paper manufacturing, tobacco processing, salt refining, and pottery production all dwindled as well. The biggest exception to the downward trend was trade with the New World, which increased with escalating demands for sugar and tobacco. The Dutch shifted their interest away from great-power rivalries toward those areas of international trade and finance where they could establish an enduring presence.

Russia's Emergence as a European Power

The commerce and shipbuilding of the Dutch and English so impressed the Russian tsar Peter I (r. 1689–1725) that he traveled incognito to their shipyards in 1697 to learn their methods firsthand. Known to history as Peter the Great, he dragged Russia kicking and screaming all the way to great-power status. Although he came to the throne while still a minor (on the eve of his tenth birthday), grew up under the threat of a palace coup, and enjoyed little formal education, his accomplishments soon matched his seven-foot-tall stature. Peter transformed public life in Russia and established an absolutist state on the Western model. His **Westernization** efforts ignited an enduring controversy: did Peter set Russia on a course of inevitable Westernization required to compete with the West, or did he forever and fatally disrupt Russia's natural evolution into a distinctive Slavic society?

Peter reorganized government and finance on Western models and, like other absolute rulers, strengthened his army. With ruthless recruiting methods, which included branding a cross on every recruit's left hand to prevent desertion, he forged an army of 200,000 men and equipped it with modern weapons. He created schools for artillery, engineering, and military medicine and built the first navy in Russian history. Not surprisingly, taxes tripled.

The tsar allowed nothing to stand in his way. He did not hesitate to use torture and executed thousands. He allowed a special regiment of guards unprecedented power to expedite cases against those suspected of rebellion, espionage, pretensions to the throne, or just "unseemly utterances against him." Opposition to his policies reached into his own family. When his only son, Alexei, allied himself with Peter's critics, the young man was thrown into prison, where he mysteriously died.

Peter the Great
In this painting by Gottfried Danhauer (1680–1733/7), the Russian tsar appears against the backdrop of his most famous battle, Poltava. The angel holds a laurel wreath, a symbol of victory, over his head. (© Tretyakov Gallery, Moscow, Russia/The Bridgeman Art Library.)

To control the often restive nobility, Peter insisted that all noblemen engage in state service. The Table of Ranks (1722) classified them into military, administrative, and court categories, a codification of social and legal relationships in Russia that would last for nearly two centuries. All social and material advantages now depended on serving the crown. Because the nobles lacked a secure independent status, Peter could command them to a degree that was unimaginable in western Europe. State service was not only compulsory but also permanent. Moreover, the male children of those in service had to be registered by the age of ten and begin serving at fifteen. To increase his authority over the Russian Orthodox church, Peter allowed the office of patriarch (supreme head) to remain vacant, and in 1721 he replaced it with the Holy Synod, a bureaucracy of laymen under his supervision. To many Russians, Peter was the Antichrist incarnate.

With the goal of Westernizing Russian culture, Peter set up the first greenhouses, laboratories, and technical schools and founded the Russian Academy of Sciences. He ordered translations of Western classics and hired a German theater company to perform the French plays of Molière. He replaced the traditional Russian calendar with the Western one,* introduced Arabic numerals, and in 1703 brought out the first public newspaper. He ordered his officials and the nobles to shave their beards and dress in Western fashion, and he even issued precise regulations about the suitable style of jacket, boots, and cap (generally French or German). He published a book on manners for young noblemen and experimented with dentistry on his courtiers.

Peter built a new capital city, named St. Petersburg after him. It symbolized Russia opening to the West. Construction began in 1703 in a Baltic province that had been recently conquered from Sweden. By the end of 1709, forty thousand recruits a year

*Peter introduced the Julian calendar, then still used in Protestant but not Catholic countries. Later in the eighteenth century, Protestant Europe abandoned the Julian for the Gregorian calendar. Not until 1918 was the Julian calendar abolished in Russia, at which point it had fallen thirteen days behind Europe's Gregorian calendar.

found themselves assigned to the projects there. Peter ordered skilled workers to move to the new city and commanded all landowners possessing more than forty serf households to build houses there. In the 1720s, a German minister described the city "as a wonder of the world, considering its magnificent palaces . . . and the short time that was employed in the building of it." By 1710, the permanent population of St. Petersburg reached eight thousand. At Peter's death in 1725, it had forty thousand residents.

As a new city far from the Russian heartland around Moscow, St. Petersburg represented a decisive break with Russia's past. Peter widened that gap by every means possible. At his new capital, he tried to improve the traditionally denigrated, secluded status of women by ordering them to dress in European styles and appear publicly at his dinners for diplomatic representatives. Imitating French manners, he decreed that women attend his new social salons of officials, officers, and merchants for conversation and dancing. A foreigner headed every one of Peter's new technical and vocational schools, and for its first eight years the new Academy of Sciences included no Russians. Every ministry was assigned a foreign adviser. Upper-class Russians learned French or German, which they often spoke even at home. Such changes affected only the very top of Russian society, however. The mass of the population had no contact with the new ideas and ended up paying for the innovations either in ruinous new taxation or by building St. Petersburg, a project that cost the lives of thousands of workers. Serfs remained tied to the land, completely dominated by their noble lords.

Despite all his achievements, Peter could not ensure his succession. In the thirty-seven years after his death in 1725, Russia endured six different rulers, including a boy of twelve, an infant, and an imbecile. Recurrent palace coups weakened the monarchy and enabled the nobility to loosen Peter's rigid code of state service. In the process, the status of the serfs only worsened. They ceased to be counted as legal subjects; the criminal code of 1754 listed them as property. They not only were bought and sold like cattle but also had become legally indistinguishable from them. Westernization had not yet touched their lives.

Changes in the Balance of Power in the East

Peter the Great's success in building up state power changed the balance of power in eastern Europe. Overcoming initial military setbacks, Russia eventually defeated Sweden and took its place as the leading power in the Baltic region. Russia could then turn its attention to eastern Europe, where it competed with Austria and Prussia. Formerly mighty Poland-Lithuania became the playground for great-power rivalries.

Sweden had dominated the Baltic region since the Thirty Years' War and did not easily give up its preeminence. In 1700, when Peter the Great formed an anti-Swedish coalition with Denmark, Saxony, and Poland, Sweden's Charles XII (r. 1697–1718) stood up to the test. Still in his teens at the beginning of the Great Northern War, Charles first defeated Denmark, then destroyed the new Russian army, and quickly marched into Poland and Saxony. After defeating the Poles and occupying Saxony, Charles invaded Russia. Here Peter's rebuilt army finally defeated him at the battle of Poltava (1709).

The Russian victory resounded everywhere. The Russian ambassador to Vienna reported, "It is commonly said that the tsar will be formidable to all Europe, that he will be a kind of northern Turk." Prussia and other German states joined the anti-Swedish alliance, and when Charles XII died in battle in 1718, the Great Northern War finally came to an end. By the terms of the Treaty of Nystad (1721), Sweden ceded its eastern Baltic provinces—Livonia, Estonia, Ingria, and southern Karelia—to Russia. Sweden also lost territories on the north German coast to Prussia and the other allied German states (Map 14.3). An aristocratic reaction against Charles XII's incessant demands for war supplies swept away Sweden's absolutist regime, essentially removing Sweden from great-power competition.

Prussia had to make the most of every military opportunity, as it did in the Great Northern War, because it was much smaller in size and population than Russia, Austria, or France. King Frederick William I (r. 1713–1740) doubled the size of the Prussian army; though much smaller than the armies of his rivals, it was the best trained and most up-to-date force in Europe. By 1740, Prussia had Europe's highest proportion of men at arms (1 of every 28 people, versus 1 in 157 in France and 1 in 64 in Russia) and the highest proportion of nobles in the military (1 in 7 noblemen, as compared with 1 in 33 in France and 1 in 50 in Russia).

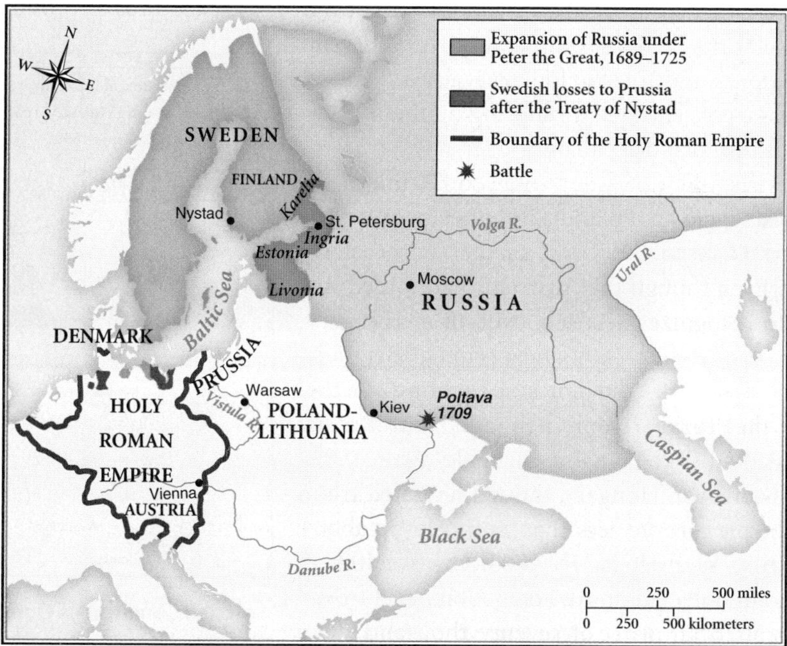

Map 14.3 Russia and Sweden after the Great Northern War, 1721
After the Great Northern War, Russia supplanted Sweden as the major power in the north. Although Russia had a much larger population from which to draw its armies, Sweden made the most of its advantages and gave way only after a great military struggle.

The army so dominated life in Prussia that the country earned the description "a large army with a small state attached." So obsessed was Frederick William with his soldiers that the five-foot-five-inch-tall king formed a regiment of "giants," the Grenadiers, composed exclusively of men over six feet tall. Royal agents scoured Europe trying to find such men and sometimes kidnapped them right off the street. Frederick William, "the Sergeant King," was one of the first rulers to wear a military uniform as his everyday dress. He subordinated the entire domestic administration to the army's needs. He also installed a system for recruiting soldiers by local district quotas. He financed the army growth by subjecting all the provinces to an excise tax on food, drink, and manufactured goods and by increasing rents on crown lands. Prussia was now poised to become one of the major players on the continent of Europe.

During the War of the Polish Succession (1733–1735), Prussia stood on the sidelines, content to watch the bigger powers fight each other. The war showed how the balance of power had changed since the heyday of Louis XIV: France had to maneuver within a complex great-power system that now included Russia, and Poland-Lithuania no longer controlled its own destiny. When the king of Poland-Lithuania died in 1733, France, Spain, and Sardinia went to war against Austria and Russia, each side supporting rival claimants to the Polish throne. After Russia drove the French candidate out of Poland-Lithuania, France agreed to accept the Austrian candidate. In exchange, Austria gave the province of Lorraine to the French candidate, the father-in-law of Louis XV, with the promise that the province would pass to France on his death. France and Britain went back to pursuing their colonial rivalries. Prussia and Russia concentrated on shoring up their influence within Poland-Lithuania.

Austrian Conquest of Hungary, 1657–1730

Austria did not want to become mired in a long struggle in Poland-Lithuania because its armies still faced the Turks on its southeastern border. Even though the Austrians had forced the Turks to recognize their rule over all of Hungary and Transylvania in 1699 and occupied Belgrade in 1717, the Turks did not stop fighting. In the 1730s, the Turks retook Belgrade, and Russia now claimed a role in the struggle against the Turks. Moreover, Hungary, though liberated from Turkish rule, proved less than enthusiastic about submitting to Austria. In 1703, the wealthiest Hungarian noble landlord, Ferenc Rákóczi (1676–1735), raised an army of seventy thousand men who fought for "God, Fatherland, and Liberty" until 1711. They forced the Austrians to recognize local Hungarian institutions, grant amnesty, and restore confiscated estates in exchange for confirming hereditary Austrian rule.

The Power of Diplomacy and the Importance of Numbers

No single power emerged from the wars of the first half of the eighteenth century clearly superior to the others, and the idea of maintaining a balance of power guided both military and diplomatic maneuvering. The Peace of Utrecht had explicitly declared that such a balance was crucial to maintaining peace in Europe, and in 1720 a British pamphleteer wrote, "There is not, I believe, any doctrine in the law of nations, of more certain truth . . . than this of the balance of power." It was the universal law of gravitation of European politics. This system of equilibrium often rested on military force, such as the leagues formed against Louis XIV or the coalition against Sweden. All states counted on diplomacy, however, to resolve issues even after fighting had begun.

To meet the new demands placed on it, the diplomatic service, like the military and financial bureaucracies before it, had to develop regular procedures. The French set a pattern of diplomatic service that the other European states soon imitated. By 1685, France had embassies in all the important capitals. Nobles of ancient families served as ambassadors to Rome, Madrid, Vienna, and London, whereas royal officials were chosen for Switzerland, the Dutch Republic, and Venice. Most held their appointments for at least three or four years, and all went off with elaborate written instructions that included explicit statements of policy as well as full accounts of the political conditions of the country to which they were posted. The ambassador selected and paid for his own staff. This practice could make the journey to a new post very cumbersome, because the staff might be as large as eighty people, and they brought along all their own furniture, pictures, silverware, and tapestries. It took one French ambassador ten weeks to get from Paris to Stockholm.

By the early 1700s, French writings on diplomatic methods were read everywhere. François de Callières's manual *On the Manner of Negotiating with Sovereigns* (1716) insisted that sound diplomacy was based on the creation of confidence, rather than deception: "The secret of negotiation is to harmonize the real interests of the parties concerned." Callières believed that the diplomatic service had to be professional—that young attachés should be chosen for their skills, not their family connections. These sensible views did not prevent the development of a dual system of diplomacy, in which rulers issued secret instructions that often negated the official ones sent by their own foreign offices. Secret diplomacy had some advantages because it allowed rulers to break with past alliances, but it also led to confusion and, sometimes, scandal, for the rulers often employed unreliable adventurers as their confidential agents. Still, the diplomatic system in the early eighteenth century proved successful enough to ensure a continuation of the principles of the Peace of Westphalia (1648): in the midst of every crisis and war, the great powers would convene and hammer out a written agreement detailing the requirements for peace.

Adroit diplomacy could smooth the road toward peace, but success in war still depended on sheer numbers—of men and muskets. Because each state's strength depended largely on the size of its army, the growth and health of the population increasingly entered into government calculations. The publication in 1690 of the

Englishman William Petty's *Political Arithmetick* quickened the interest of government officials everywhere. Petty offered statistical estimates of human capital—that is, of population and wages—to determine England's national wealth. In 1727, Frederick William I of Prussia founded two university chairs to encourage population studies, and textbooks and handbooks advocated state intervention to improve the population's health and welfare.

REVIEW What were the consequences of the stabilization of the balance of power in Europe at the start of the eighteenth century?

The Birth of the Enlightenment

Economic expansion, the emergence of a new consumer society, and the stabilization of the European state system all generated optimism about the future. The intellectual corollary was the Enlightenment, a term used later in the eighteenth century to describe the loosely knit group of writers and scholars who believed that human beings could apply a critical, reasoning spirit to every problem they encountered in the world. The new secular, scientific, and critical attitude first emerged in the 1690s, scrutinizing everything from the absolutism of Louis XIV to the traditional role of women in society. After 1740, criticism took a more systematic turn as writers provided new theories for the organization of society and politics, but even by the 1720s and 1730s, established authorities realized they faced a new set of challenges.

The Popularization of Science and the Challenges to Religion

The writers of the Enlightenment glorified the geniuses of the new science and championed the scientific method as the solution for all social problems. One of the most influential popularizations was the French writer Bernard de Fontenelle's *Conversations on the Plurality of Worlds* (1686). Presented as a dialogue between an aristocratic woman and a man of the world, the book made the Copernican, sun-centered view of the universe available to the literate public. By 1700, mathematics and science had become fashionable pastimes in high society, and the public flocked to lectures explaining scientific discoveries. Journals complained that scientific learning had become the passport to female affection: "There were two young ladies in Paris whose heads had been so turned by this branch of learning that one of them declined to listen to a proposal of marriage unless the candidate for her hand undertook to learn how to make telescopes." Such writings poked fun at women with intellectual interests, but they also demonstrated that women now participated in discussions of science.

Interest in science spread in literate circles because it offered a model for all forms of knowledge. As the prestige of science increased, some developed a skeptical attitude toward attempts to enforce religious conformity. A French Huguenot refugee from Louis XIV's persecutions, Pierre Bayle (1647–1706), launched an internationally influential campaign against religious intolerance from his safe haven in the Dutch Republic. His *News from the Republic of Letters* (first published

A Budding Scientist
In this engraving, *Astrologia,* by the Dutch artist Jacob Gole (c. 1660–1723), an upper-class woman looks through a telescope to do her own astronomical investigations. Women were not allowed to attend university classes in any European country, yet the Italian Laura Bassi (1711–1778) still managed to become a professor of physics at the University of Bologna. Because many astronomical observatories were set up in private homes rather than public buildings or universities, wives and daughters of scientists could make observations and even publish their own findings. (Bibliothèque nationale de France.)

in 1684) bitterly criticized the policies of Louis XIV and was quickly banned in Paris and condemned in Rome. After attacking Louis XIV's anti-Protestant policies, Bayle took a more general stand in favor of religious toleration. No state in Europe officially offered complete tolerance, though the Dutch Republic came closest with its tacit acceptance of Catholics, dissident Protestant groups, and open Jewish communities. In 1697, Bayle published the *Historical and Critical Dictionary,* which cited all the errors and delusions that he could find in past and present writers of all religions. Even religion must meet the test of reasonableness: "Any particular dogma, whatever it may be, whether it is advanced on the authority of the Scriptures, or whatever else may be its origins, is to be regarded as false if it clashes with the clear and definite conclusions of the natural understanding [reason]." Although Bayle claimed to be a believer himself, his insistence on rational investigation seemed to challenge the authority of faith. As one critic complained, "It is notorious that the works of M. Bayle have unsettled a large number of readers, and cast doubt on some of the most widely accepted principles of morality and religion." Bayle asserted, for example, that atheists might possess moral codes as effective as those of the devout. Bayle's *Dictionary* became a model of critical thought in the West.

Other scholars challenged the authority of the Bible by subjecting it to historical criticism. Discoveries in geology in the early eighteenth century showed that marine fossils dated immensely farther back than the biblical flood. Investigations of miracles, comets, and oracles, like the growing literature against belief in witchcraft, urged the use of reason to combat superstition and prejudice. Comets, for example, should not be considered evil omens just because such a belief had been passed on from earlier generations. Defenders of church and state published books warning of the dangers of the new skepticism. The spokesman for Louis XIV's absolutism, Bishop Bossuet, warned that "reason is the guide of their choice, but reason only brings them face to face with vague conjectures and baffling perplexities." Human beings, the traditionalists held, were simply incapable of subjecting everything to reason, especially in the realm of religion.

State authorities found religious skepticism particularly unsettling because it threatened to undermine state power, too. The extensive literature of criticism was not limited to France, but much of it was published in French, and the French government took the lead in suppressing the more outspoken works. Forbidden books were then often published in the Dutch Republic, Britain, or Switzerland and smuggled back across the border to a public whose appetite was only whetted by censorship.

The most influential writer of the early Enlightenment was a Frenchman born into the upper middle class, François-Marie Arouet, known by his pen name, Voltaire (1694–1778). In his early years, Voltaire suffered arrest, imprisonment, and exile, but he eventually achieved wealth and acclaim. His tangles with church and state began in the early 1730s, when he published his *Letters concerning the English Nation* (the English version appeared in 1733), in which he devoted several chapters to Newton and Locke and used the virtues of the British as a way to attack Catholic bigotry and government rigidity in France. Impressed by British toleration of religious dissent (at least among Protestants),Voltaire spent two years in exile in Britain when the French state responded to his book with yet another order for his arrest.

Voltaire also popularized Newton's scientific discoveries in his *Elements of the Philosophy of Newton* (1738). The French state and many European theologians considered Newtonianism threatening because it glorified the human mind and seemed to reduce God to an abstract, external, rationalistic force. So sensational was the success of Voltaire's book on Newton that a hostile Jesuit reported, "The great Newton was, it is said, buried in the abyss, in the shop of the first publisher who dared to print him. . . . M. de Voltaire finally appeared, and at once Newton is understood or is in the process of being understood; all Paris resounds with Newton, all Paris stammers Newton, all Paris studies and learns Newton." The success was international, too. Before long, Voltaire was elected a fellow of the Royal Society in London and in Edinburgh, as well as to twenty other scientific academies. Voltaire's fame continued to grow, reaching truly astounding proportions in the 1750s and 1760s (see Chapter 15).

Travel Literature and the Challenge to Custom and Tradition

Just as scientific method could be used to question religious and even state authority, a more general skepticism also emerged from the expanding knowledge about the world outside of Europe. During the seventeenth and eighteenth centuries, accounts of travel to exotic places dramatically increased as travel writers used the contrast between their home societies and other cultures to criticize the customs of European society.

In their travels to the new colonies, visitors sought something resembling "the state of nature"—that is, ways of life that preceded sophisticated social and political organization—although they often misinterpreted different forms of society and politics as having no organization at all. Travelers to the Americas found "noble savages" (native peoples) who appeared to live in conditions of great freedom and equality; they were "naturally good" and "happy" without taxes, lawsuits, or much organized government. In China, in contrast, travelers found a people who enjoyed prosperity and an ancient civilization. Christian missionaries made little headway in China, and visitors had to admit that China's religious systems had flourished for four or five thousand years with no input from Europe or from Christianity. The basic lesson of travel literature in the 1700s, then, was that customs varied: justice, freedom, property, good government, religion, and morality all were relative to the place. One critic complained that travel encouraged free thinking and the destruction of religion: "Some complete their demoralization by extensive travel, and lose whatever shreds of religion remained to them. Every day they see a new religion, new customs, new rites."

Travel literature turned explicitly political in Montesquieu's *Persian Letters* (1721). Charles-Louis de Secondat, baron of Montesquieu (1689–1755), the son of an eminent judicial family, was a high-ranking judge in a French court. He published *Persian Letters* anonymously in the Dutch Republic, and the book went into ten printings in just one year—a best seller for the times. In the book, Montesquieu tells the story of two Persians, Rica and Usbek, who leave their country "for love of knowledge" and travel to Europe. They visit France in the last years of Louis XIV's reign, writing of the king: "He has a minister who is only eighteen years old, and a mistress of eighty. . . . Although he avoids the bustle of towns, and is rarely seen in company, his one concern, from morning till night, is to get himself talked about." Other passages ridicule the pope. Beneath the satire, however, is a serious investigation into the foundation of good government and morality. Montesquieu chose Persians for his travelers because they came from what was widely considered the most despotic of all governments, in which rulers had life-and-death powers over their subjects. In the book, the Persians constantly compare France to Persia, suggesting that the French monarchy itself might verge on despotism.

The paradox of a judge publishing an anonymous work attacking the regime that employed him demonstrates the complications of the intellectual scene in this period. Montesquieu's anonymity did not last long, and soon Parisian society lionized him. In the late 1720s, he sold his judgeship and traveled extensively in Europe, including an eighteen-month stay in Britain. In 1748, he published a widely influential work on comparative government, *The Spirit of Laws*. The Vatican soon listed both *Persian Letters* and *The Spirit of Laws* in its index of forbidden books.

Raising the Woman Question

Many of the letters exchanged in *Persian Letters* focus on women, marriage, and the family because Montesquieu considered the position of women a sure indicator of the nature of government and morality. Although he was not a feminist, his depiction of Roxana, the favorite wife in Usbek's harem, struck a chord with many readers. Roxana revolts against the authority of Usbek's eunuchs and writes a final letter to her husband announcing her impending suicide: "I may have lived in servitude, but I have always been free, I have amended your laws according to the laws of nature, and my mind has always remained independent." Women writers used the same language of tyranny and freedom to argue for concrete changes in their status.

The most systematic of these women writers was the English author Mary Astell (1666–1731), the daughter of a businessman and herself a supporter of the Tory party and the Anglican religious establishment. In 1694, she published *A Serious Proposal to the Ladies,* in which she advocated founding a private women's college to remedy women's lack of education. Addressing women, she asked, "How can you be content to be in the World like Tulips in a Garden, to make a fine *shew* [show] and be good for nothing?" Astell argued for intellectual training based on Descartes's principles, in which reason, debate, and careful consideration of the issues took priority over custom or tradition. Her book was an immediate success: five printings appeared by 1701. In later works, such as *Reflections upon Marriage* (1706), Astell criticized the relationship between the sexes within marriage: "If Absolute Sovereignty be not necessary in a State, how comes it to be so in a family? . . . *If all Men are born free,* how is it that all Women are born slaves?" Her critics accused her of promoting subversive ideas and of contradicting the Scriptures.

The influence of such views should not be overestimated. Most male writers unequivocally stuck to the traditional view of women, which held that women were less capable of reasoning than men and therefore did not need systematic education. Such opinions often rested on biological suppositions. The long-dominant Aristotelian view of reproduction held that only the male seed carried spirit and individuality. At the beginning of the eighteenth century, however, scientists began to undermine this belief. More physicians and surgeons began to champion the doctrine of ovism—that the female egg was essential in making new humans. During the decades that followed, male Enlightenment writers would continue to debate women's nature and appropriate social roles.

REVIEW What were the main issues in the early decades of the Enlightenment?

Conclusion

Europeans crossed a major threshold in the first half of the eighteenth century. They moved silently but nonetheless momentously from an economy governed by scarcity and the threat of famine to one of ever increasing growth and the prospect of continuing improvement. Expansion of colonies overseas and economic development

Mapping the West Europe in 1740
By 1740 Europe had achieved a kind of diplomatic equilibrium in which no one power predominated. But the relative balance should not deflect attention from important underlying changes. Spain, the Dutch Republic, Poland-Lithuania, and Sweden had all declined in power and influence, while Great Britain, Russia, Prussia, and Austria had solidified their positions, each in a different way. France's ambitions had been thwarted, but the combination of a large army and rich overseas possessions made France a major player for a long time to come.

at home created greater wealth, longer life spans, and higher expectations for the future. In these better times for many, a spirit of optimism prevailed. People could now spend money on newspapers, novels, and travel literature as well as on coffee, tea, and cotton cloth. Participants in the growing public sphere avidly followed the latest trends in religious debates, art, and music. Everyone did not share equally in the benefits: slaves toiled in abjection in the Americas; serfs in eastern Europe found themselves ever more closely bound to their noble lords; and rural folk almost everywhere tasted few fruits of consumer society.

Politics, too, changed as population and production increased and cities grew. Experts urged government intervention to improve public health, and states found it in their interest to settle many international disputes by diplomacy, which itself became more regular and routine. The consolidation of the European state system allowed a tide of criticism and new thinking about society to swell in Great Britain and France and begin to spill throughout Europe. Ultimately, the combination of the Atlantic system and the Enlightenment would give rise to a series of Atlantic revolutions.

CHAPTER REVIEW QUESTIONS

1. How did the rise of slavery and the plantation system change European politics and society?
2. Why did the Enlightenment begin just at the moment that the Atlantic system took shape?

For practice quizzes and other study tools, see the Online Study Guide at bedfordstmartins.com/huntconcise.

For primary-source material from this period, see Chapter 17 of *Sources of The Making of the West*, Third Edition.

TIMELINE

1690 | 1700 | 1710

- **1690s** Beginning of the rapid development of plantations in the Caribbean
- **1694** Bank of England established; Mary Astell's *A Serious Proposal to the Ladies* argues for the founding of a private women's college
- **1697** Pierre Bayle publishes the *Historical and Critical Dictionary*, detailing errors of religious writers
- **1699** Turks forced to recognize Habsburg rule over Hungary and Transylvania
- **1703** Peter the Great of Russia begins the construction of St. Petersburg and founds the first Russian newspaper
- **1709** Joseph Addison and Richard Steele publish the first edition of the *Spectator* in England
- **1713–1714** Peace of Utrecht, following the War of the Spanish Succession (1701–1713)
- **1714** Elector of Hanover becomes King George I of England
- **1715** Death of Louis XIV

Suggested References

A new Web site on the slave trade offers the most up-to-date information about the workings of the Atlantic system. The definitive study of the early Enlightenment is the book by Hazard, but many others have contributed biographies of individual figures or studies of women writers.

Bach's Leipzig, 1725–1750: http://www.baroquemusic.org/bachleipzig.html

Black, Jeremy. *European Warfare in a Global Context, 1660–1815.* 2007.

Blackburn, Robin. *The Making of New World Slavery: From the Baroque to the Modern, 1492–1800.* 1997.

Brewer, John. *The Sinews of Power: War, Money, and the English State, 1688–1783.* 1990.

Cracraft, James. *The Revolution of Peter the Great.* 2003.

Handel's Messiah: The New Interactive Edition (CD-ROM). 1997.

Hazard, Paul. *The European Mind: The Critical Years, 1680–1715.* 1990.

*Hill, Bridget. *The First English Feminist: Reflections upon Marriage and Other Writings by Mary Astell.* 1986.

Hunt, Margaret R. *The Middling Sort: Commerce, Gender, and the Family in England, 1680–1780.* 1996.

*Jacob, Margaret C. *The Enlightenment: A Brief History with Selected Readings.* 2000.

Pearson, Roger. *Voltaire Almighty: A Life in Pursuit of Freedom.* 2005.

Slave trade: http://www.slavevoyages.org/tast/index.faces

War of the Spanish Succession: http://www.spanishsuccession.nl/

- **1719** Daniel Defoe publishes *Robinson Crusoe*
- **1720** Last outbreak of bubonic plague in western Europe
- **1721** Treaty of Nystad; Montesquieu publishes *Persian Letters* anonymously in the Dutch Republic; Robert Walpole becomes the first prime minister of Great Britain
- **1733** Voltaire's *Letters concerning the English Nation* attacks French intolerance and narrow-mindedness
- **1733–1735** War of the Polish Succession
- **1741** George Frederick Handel composes *Messiah*

1720 | 1730 | 1740

15 The Promise of Enlightenment

1740–1789

IN THE SUMMER OF 1766, Empress Catherine II ("the Great") of Russia wrote to Voltaire, one of the leaders of the Enlightenment:

> It is a way of immortalizing oneself to be the advocate of humanity, the defender of oppressed innocence. . . . You have entered into combat against the enemies of mankind: superstition, fanaticism, ignorance, quibbling, evil judges, and the powers that rest in their hands. Great virtues and qualities are needed to surmount these obstacles. You have shown that you have them: you have triumphed.

Catherine the Great
In this portrait by the Danish painter Vigilius Eriksen, the Russian empress Catherine the Great is shown on horseback (c. 1762), much like any male ruler of the time. Born Sophia Augusta Frederika of Anhalt-Zerbst in 1729, Catherine was the daughter of a minor German prince. When she married the future tsar Peter III in 1745, she promptly learned Russian and adopted Russian Orthodoxy. Peter, physically and mentally frail, proved no match for her. In 1762, she staged a coup against him and took his place when he was killed. *(Erich Lessing/Art Resource, NY.)*

Over a fifteen-year period Catherine corresponded regularly with Voltaire, a writer who at home in France found himself in constant conflict with church and state authorities. Her admiring letter shows how influential Enlightenment ideals had become by the middle of the eighteenth century.

Catherine's letter aptly summed up Enlightenment principles: progress for humanity could be achieved only by rooting out the wrongs left by superstition, religious fanaticism, ignorance, and outmoded forms of justice. Enlightenment writers used every means at their disposal—from encyclopedias to novels to personal interaction with rulers—to argue for reform. Everything had to be examined in the clear light of reason, and anything that did not promote the improvement of humanity was to be jettisoned. As a result, Enlightenment writers attacked the legal use of torture to extract confessions, favored the spread of education to eliminate ignorance, supported religious toleration, and criticized censorship by state or church. The book trade and new places for urban socializing, such as coffeehouses and Masonic lodges (social clubs organized around the rituals of masons' guilds), spread these ideas within a new elite of middle- and upper-class men and women.

Rulers pursued Enlightenment reforms that they believed might enhance state power, but they feared changes that might unleash popular discontent. For example, Catherine aimed to bring Western culture and reforms to Russia, but when faced with a massive uprising of the serfs, she not only suppressed the revolt but also increased the nobles' power over their serfs. All reform-minded rulers faced similar potential challenges to their authority.

Even though the movement for reform had its limits, governments now needed to respond to a new force: public opinion. Rulers wanted to portray themselves as modern, open to change, and responsive to the segment of the public that was reading newspapers and closely following political developments. Enlightenment writers appealed to public opinion, but they still looked to rulers to effect reform. Writers such as Voltaire expressed little interest in the future of peasants or lower classes; they favored neither revolution nor political upheaval. Yet their ideas paved the way for something much more radical and unexpected. The American Declaration of Independence in 1776 showed how lofty Enlightenment goals could be translated into democratic political practice. After 1789, democracy would come to Europe as well.

CHAPTER FOCUS QUESTION What was the influence of Enlightenment ideals on public opinion and on European rulers?

The Enlightenment at Its Height

The Enlightenment emerged as an intellectual movement before 1740 but reached its peak only in the second half of the eighteenth century. The writers of the Enlightenment called themselves **philosophes** (French for "philosophers"), but that term is somewhat misleading. Whereas philosophers generally concern themselves with theoretical questions (for example, "What is truth?"), the philosophes were public intellectuals dedicated to solving the real problems of the world. They wrote on subjects ranging from current affairs to art criticism, and they wrote in every conceivable format. The Swiss philosophe Jean-Jacques Rousseau, for example, wrote a political tract, a treatise on education, a constitution for Poland, an analysis of the effects of the theater on public morals, a best-selling novel, an opera, and a notorious autobiography.

The philosophes wrote for an educated public of readers who snatched up every Enlightenment book they could find at their local booksellers, even when rulers or churches tried to forbid publication. Between 1740 and 1789, the Enlightenment acquired its name and, despite heated conflicts between the philosophes and state and religious authorities, gained support in the highest reaches of government.

The Men and Women of the Republic of Letters

Although *philosophe* is a French word, the Enlightenment was distinctly cosmopolitan; philosophes could be found from Philadelphia to Moscow. The philosophes considered themselves part of a grand "republic of letters" that transcended national political boundaries. They were not republicans in the usual sense—that is, people who supported representative government and opposed monarchy. What united them were the ideals of reason, reform, and freedom. In 1784, the German philosopher Immanuel Kant summed up the program of the Enlightenment in two Latin words: *sapere aude,* "dare to know"—have the courage to think for yourself.

The philosophes used reason to attack superstition, bigotry, and religious intolerance, which they considered the chief obstacles to free thought and social reform. "Once fanaticism has corrupted a mind," Voltaire proclaimed, "the malady is almost incurable. . . . The only remedy for this epidemic malady is the philosophical spirit." Enlightenment writers did not necessarily oppose organized religion, but they strenuously objected to religious intolerance. They believed that the systematic application of reason could do what religious belief could not: improve the human condition by pointing to needed reforms. Reason meant critical, informed, scientific thinking about social issues and problems. Many Enlightenment writers collaborated on a new multivolume *Encyclopedia,* published between 1751 and 1772, that

Bookbinding

In this plate from the *Encyclopedia*, the various stages in bookbinding are laid out from left to right. Binding was not included in the sale of books; owners had to order leather bindings from a special shop. The man at (a) is pounding the pages to be bound on a marble block. The woman at (b) is stitching the pages with a special frame. The worker at (c) cuts the pages, and at (d) the volumes are pressed to prevent warping. In what ways is this illustration representative of the aims of the *Encyclopedia*?

aimed to gather together knowledge about science, religion, industry, and society. The chief editor of the *Encyclopedia,* Denis Diderot (1713–1784), explained the goal: "All things must be examined, debated, investigated without exception and without regard for anyone's feelings."

The philosophes believed that the spread of knowledge would encourage reform in every aspect of life, from the grain trade to the penal system. The philosophes wanted freedom of the press and freedom of religion, which they considered "natural rights" guaranteed by "natural law." In their view, progress depended on these freedoms. As Voltaire asserted, "I quite understand that the fanatics of one sect slaughter the enthusiasts of another sect . . . [but] that Descartes should have been forced to flee to Holland to escape the fury of the ignorant . . . these things are a nation's eternal shame."

Most philosophes, like Voltaire, came from the upper classes, yet Rousseau's father was a modest watchmaker in Geneva, and Diderot was the son of a cutlery maker. The French noblewoman Émilie du Châtelet (1706–1749) was one of the rare female philosophes. She wrote extensively about the mathematics and physics of Leibniz and Newton. (Her lover Voltaire learned much of his science from her.) Few of the leading writers held university positions, except those who were German or Scottish. Universities in France were dominated by the clergy and unreceptive to Enlightenment ideas.

Enlightenment ideas developed instead through personal contacts; through letters that were hand-copied, circulated, and sometimes published; through informal readings of manuscripts; and through letters to the editor and book reviews in periodicals. **Salons**—informal gatherings usually sponsored by middle-class or aristocratic women—gave intellectual life an anchor outside the royal court and the church-controlled universities. Best known was the Parisian salon of Madame Marie-Thérèse Geoffrin (1699–1777), a wealthy middle-class widow who had been raised by her grandmother and married off at fourteen to a much older man. She brought together the most exciting thinkers and artists of the time; her social gatherings provided a forum for new ideas and an opportunity to establish new intellectual contacts. In the salon, the philosophes could discuss ideas they might hesitate to put into print and thus test public opinion and even push it in new directions. Madame Geoffrin corresponded extensively with influential people across Europe, including Catherine the Great. One Italian visitor commented, "There is no way to make Naples resemble Paris unless we find a woman to guide us, organize us, *Geoffrinize* us."

Women's salons helped galvanize intellectual life and reform movements all over Europe. Wealthy Jewish women created nine of the fourteen salons in Berlin at the end of the eighteenth century, and in Warsaw Princess Zofia Czartoryska gathered around her the reform leaders of Poland-Lithuania. Middle-class women in London used their salons to raise money to publish women's writings. Salons could be tied closely to the circles of power: in France, for example, Louis XV's mistress, Jeanne-Antoinette Poisson, first made her reputation as hostess of a salon frequented by Voltaire and Montesquieu. When she became Louis XV's mistress in 1745, she gained the title Marquise de Pompadour and turned her attention to influencing artistic styles by patronizing architects and painters.

Conflicts with Church and State

Madame Geoffrin did not approve of discussions that attacked the Catholic church, but elsewhere voices against organized religion could be heard. Criticisms of religion required daring because the church, whatever its denomination, wielded enormous power in society, and most influential people considered religion an essential foundation of good society and government. Defying such opinion, the Scottish philosopher David Hume (1711–1776) boldly argued in *The Natural History of Religion* (1755) that belief in God rested on superstition and fear rather than on reason.

Before the scientific revolution, nearly every European believed in God. After Newton, however, and despite Newton's own deep religiosity, people could conceive of the universe as an eternally existing, self-perpetuating machine in which God's intervention was unnecessary. In short, such people could become either **atheists**, who did not believe in any kind of God, or **deists**, who believed in God but gave him no active role in earthly affairs. For the first time, writers claimed the label *atheist* and disputed the common view that atheism led inevitably to immorality.

Deists continued to believe in a benevolent, all-knowing God who had designed the universe and set it in motion. But deists usually rejected the idea that God directly intercedes in the functioning of the universe, and they often criticized the churches for their dogmatic intolerance of dissenters. Voltaire was a deist, and in his popular *Philosophical Dictionary* (1764) he attacked most of the claims of organized Christianity, both Catholic and Protestant. Christianity, he argued, had been the prime source of fanaticism and brutality among humans. Throughout his life, Voltaire's motto was *Écrasez l'infâme*—"Crush the infamous thing" (the "thing" being bigotry and intolerance). French authorities publicly burned his *Philosophical Dictionary.*

Criticism of religious intolerance involved more than simply attacking the churches. Critics also had to confront the states to which churches were closely tied. In 1761, a judicial case in Toulouse provoked throughout France an outcry that Voltaire soon joined. When the son of a local Calvinist was found hanged (he probably committed suicide), authorities accused his father, Jean Calas, of murdering him to prevent his conversion to Catholicism. (Since Louis XIV's revocation of the Edict of Nantes in 1685, it had been illegal to practice Calvinism publicly in France.) The all-Catholic parlement of Toulouse tried to extract the names of accomplices through torture—using a rope to pull up Calas's arm while weighting down his feet and then by pouring pitchers of water down his throat (now known as "water boarding")—and then executed him by breaking every bone in his body. Voltaire launched a successful crusade to rehabilitate Jean Calas's good name and to restore the family's properties, which had been confiscated after his death. Voltaire's efforts eventually helped bring about the extension of civil rights to French Protestants and encouraged campaigns to abolish the legal use of torture.

Critics also assailed state and church support for European colonization and slavery. One of the most popular books of the time was the *Philosophical and Political History of European Colonies and Commerce in the Two Indies,* published in 1770 by Abbé Guillaume Raynal (1713–1796), a French Catholic clergyman. Raynal and his collaborators described in excruciating detail the destruction of native populations by Europeans and denounced the slave trade. Raynal was forced into exile, and his work was banned by both the Catholic church and the French government, but the Enlightenment belief in natural rights led many others to denounce slavery. An article in the new *Encyclopedia* proclaimed, "There is not a single one of these hapless souls . . . who does not have the right to be declared free . . . since neither his ruler nor his father nor anyone else had the right to dispose of his freedom." Some Enlightenment thinkers, however, took a more ambiguous or even negative view. Hume judged blacks to be "naturally inferior to . . . whites," concluding, "There never was a civilized nation of any other complexion than white."

Enlightenment critics of church and state advocated reform, not revolution. Although Voltaire, for example, lived near the French-Swiss border in case he had to flee arrest, he made a fortune from financial speculations, wrote a glowing history called *The Age of Louis XIV* (1751), and lived to be celebrated in his last years as a national hero even by many former foes. Other philosophes also lived respectably, believing that published criticism, rather than violent action, would bring about necessary reforms. As Diderot said, "We will speak against senseless laws until they are reformed; and, while we wait, we will abide by them." Those few who lived long enough to see the French Revolution in 1789 resisted its radical turn, for the philosophes generally regarded the lower classes—"the people"—as ignorant, violent, and prone to superstition, hence in need of leadership from above. They pinned their hopes on educated elites and enlightened rulers.

Despite the philosophes' preference for reform, in the long run their books often had a revolutionary impact. For example, Montesquieu's widely reprinted *Spirit of the Laws* (1748) warned against the dangers of despotism, opposed the divine right of kings, and favored constitutional government. In his somewhat rosy view, Great Britain was "the one nation in the world which has political liberty as the direct object of its constitution." His analysis of British constitutionalism inspired French critics of absolutism and would greatly influence the American revolutionaries.

The Individual and Society

In previous centuries, questions of theological doctrine and church organization had been the main focus of intellectual and even political interest. The Enlightenment writers shifted attention away from religious questions toward the secular study of society and the individual's role in it. In this way, the Enlightenment advanced the secularization of European political life that had begun after the Wars of Religion of the sixteenth and seventeenth centuries. At the same time, it laid the foundations for the social sciences of the modern era.

Just as Newton had used his reason to penetrate the laws of nature, so too the philosophes hoped to use reason to discern the laws of social life. But they did not necessarily agree about the conclusions to be drawn. Among the many different approaches were two that proved enduringly influential, those of the Scottish philosopher Adam Smith and the Swiss writer Jean-Jacques Rousseau. Smith provided a theory of modern capitalist society and devoted much of his energy to defending free markets as offering the best way to maximize individual efforts. The modern discipline of economics took shape around the questions raised by Smith. Rousseau set out the principles of a more communitarian philosophy, one that emphasized the needs of the community over those of the individual. His work led both toward democracy and toward communism and continues to inspire heated debate in political science and sociology. A closer look at these two thinkers will demonstrate the breadth and depth of Enlightenment thought.

Adam Smith (1723–1790) optimistically believed that individual interests naturally harmonized with those of the whole society. To explain how this natural harmonization worked, he published *An Inquiry into the Nature and Causes of the Wealth of Nations* in 1776. Smith insisted that individual self-interest, even greed, was quite compatible with society's best interest: the market served as an "invisible hand" ensuring that individual interests would be synchronized with those of the whole society. "By pursuing his own interest," the merchant "frequently promotes that of the society more effectually than when he really intends to promote it."

Smith rejected the prevailing mercantilist views that the general welfare would be served by accumulating national wealth through agriculture or the hoarding of gold and silver. Instead, he argued that the division of labor in manufacturing would increase productivity and generate more wealth for society and well-being for the individual. To maximize the effects of market forces and the division of labor, Smith endorsed a concept called **laissez-faire** (that is, "to leave alone") to free the economy from government intervention and control. He insisted that governments eliminate all restrictions on the sale of land, remove restraints on the grain trade, and abandon duties on imports. He believed that free international trade would stimulate production everywhere and thus ensure the growth of national wealth. He argued:

> The natural effort of every individual to better his own condition, when suffered to exert itself with freedom and security, is so powerful a principle, that it is alone, and without any assistance, not only capable of carrying the society to wealth and prosperity, but of surmounting a hundred impertinent obstructions with which the folly of human laws too often encumbers its operations.

Governments should restrict themselves to providing "security"—that is, national defense, internal order and a secure framework for market activity, and public works.

Much more pessimistic about the relation between individual self-interest and the good of society was Jean-Jacques Rousseau (1712–1778). In Rousseau's view, society itself threatened natural rights or freedoms: "Man is born free, and everywhere he is in chains." Rousseau first gained fame by writing a prizewinning essay in 1749 in which he argued that the revival of science and the arts had corrupted social morals, not improved them. This startling conclusion seemed to oppose some of the Enlightenment's most cherished beliefs. Rather than improving society, he claimed, science and art raised artificial barriers between people and their natural state. Rousseau's works extolled the simplicity of rural life over urban society. Although he participated in the salons, Rousseau always felt ill at ease in high society, and he periodically withdrew to live in solitude far from Paris. Paradoxically, his "solitude" was often paid for by wealthy upper-class patrons, who lodged him on their estates, even as his writings decried the upper-class privilege that made his efforts possible.

Rousseau explored the tension between the individual and society in various ways, including his widely influential work on education, *Émile* (1762), in which a boy develops practical skills and independent thinking under the guidance of his

Jean-Jacques Rousseau
This eighteenth-century engraving of Rousseau shows him in his favorite place, outside in nature, where he walked, read, and, in this case, collected plants. Rousseau claimed that he came to his most important insights while taking long walks, and in *Émile* he underlines the importance of physical activity for children. (© Private Collection/The Bridgeman Art Library.)

tutor. In *The Social Contract* (1762), Rousseau proposed a political solution to the tension between the individual and society. Whereas earlier he had argued that society corrupted the individual by taking him out of nature, in this work Rousseau insisted that individual moral freedom could be achieved only by learning to subject one's individual interests to "the general will"—that is, to the good of the community. Individuals did this by entering into a social contract, not with their rulers but with one another. If everyone followed the general will, then all individuals would be equally free and equally moral because they lived under a law to which they had all consented.

These arguments threatened the legitimacy of eighteenth-century governments. Rousseau derived his social contract from human nature, not from history, tradition, or the Bible. He implied that people would be most free and moral under a republican form of government with direct democracy, and his abstract model included no reference to differences in social status. He roundly condemned slavery: "To decide that the son of a slave is born a slave is to decide that he is not born a man." Not surprisingly, authorities in both Geneva and Paris banned *The Social Contract* for undermining political authority. Rousseau's works would become a kind of political bible for the French revolutionaries of 1789, and his attacks on private property would inspire the communists of the nineteenth century such as Karl Marx. Rousseau's rather mystical concept of the general will remains controversial. The "greatest good of all," according to Rousseau, was liberty and equality, but he also insisted that the individual could be "forced to be free" by the terms of the social contract. He provided no legal protections for individual rights. In other words, Rousseau's particular version of democracy did not guarantee the individual freedoms so important to Adam Smith.

Spreading the Enlightenment

The Enlightenment flourished in places where the new public sphere provided an eager audience for ideas of constitutionalism and reform. Where constitutionalism and the guarantee of individual freedoms were most advanced, as in Great Britain and the Dutch Republic, the movement had less of an edge because there was, in a sense, less need for it. Scottish and English writers concentrated on economics, philosophy, and history rather than politics or social relations. Dutch printers made money publishing the books that were forbidden in France. In British North America, Enlightenment ideas helped stiffen growing colonial resistance to British rule after 1763. In places with small middle classes, such as Spain, the Italian states, and Russia, governments successfully suppressed writings they did not like. Italian philosophes, such as the Milanese penal reformer Cesare Beccaria (1738–1794), got moral support from their French counterparts in the face of stern censorship at home.

The hot spot of the Enlightenment was France. French writers published the most daring critiques of church and state and suffered the most intense harassment and persecution. Voltaire, Diderot, and Rousseau all faced arrest, exile, or even imprisonment. The Catholic church and royal authorities routinely forbade the publication of their books, and the police arrested publishers who ignored their warnings. Yet the French monarchy was far from the most autocratic in Europe, and Voltaire, Diderot, and Rousseau all were revered as cultural heroes. France seems to have been curiously caught in the middle during the Enlightenment: with fewer constitutional guarantees of individual freedom than Great Britain, it still enjoyed much higher levels of prosperity and cultural development than most other European countries. In short, French elites had reason to complain, the means to make their complaints known, and a government torn between the desires to censor dissident ideas and to appear open to modernity and progress.

The government in France controlled publishing—all books had to get official permission—but not as tightly as in Spain, where the Catholic Inquisition made up its own list of banned books, or in Russia, where Catherine the Great allowed no opposition. In the 1760s and 1770s, a growing flood of works printed abroad poured into France and circulated underground. In the Dutch Republic and Swiss cities, private companies made fortunes smuggling illegal books into France over mountain passes and back roads. Foreign printers provided secret catalogs of their offerings and sold their products through booksellers who were willing to market forbidden texts for a high price—among them not only philosophical treatises of the Enlightenment but also pornographic works and pamphlets (some by Diderot) lampooning the Catholic clergy and leading members of the royal court.

Whereas the French philosophes often took a violently anticlerical and combative tone, their German counterparts avoided direct political confrontations with authorities. Gotthold Lessing (1729–1781) complained in 1769 that Prussia was still "the most slavish society in Europe" in its lack of freedom to criticize government policies. As a playwright, literary critic, and philosopher, Lessing promoted religious toleration of Jews and spiritual emancipation of Germans from foreign, especially French, models of culture, which still dominated. Lessing also introduced the German Jewish writer Moses Mendelssohn (1729–1786) into Berlin salon society. Mendelssohn labored to build bridges between German and Jewish culture by arguing that Judaism was a rational and undogmatic religion. He believed persecution and discrimination against the Jews would end as reason triumphed.

Reason was also the chief focus of the most influential German thinker of the Enlightenment, Immanuel Kant (1724–1804). A university professor who lectured on everything from economics to astronomy, Kant wrote one of the most important works in the history of Western philosophy, *The Critique of Pure Reason* (1781). He admired Adam Smith and especially Rousseau, whose portrait he displayed proudly in his lodgings. Just as Smith founded modern economics and Rousseau modern political theory, Kant in *The Critique of Pure Reason* set the foundations for modern philosophy. In this complex book, Kant established the doctrine of *idealism,* the belief that true understanding can come only from examining the ways in which ideas are formed in the mind. Ideas are shaped, Kant argued, not just by sensory information (a position central to *empiricism,* a philosophy based on John Locke's writings) but also by the operation on that information of mental categories such as space and time. In Kant's philosophy, these "categories of understanding" were neither sensory nor supernatural; they were entirely ideal and abstract and located in the human mind. For Kant the supreme philosophical questions—Does God exist? Is personal immortality possible? Do humans have free will?—were unanswerable by reason alone. But like Rousseau, Kant insisted that people could achieve true moral freedom only by living in society and obeying its laws.

The Limits of Reason: Roots of Romanticism and Religious Revival

In reaction to what some saw as the Enlightenment's excessive reliance on the authority of human reason, a new artistic movement called **romanticism** took root. Although it would not fully flower until the early nineteenth century, romanticism traced its emphasis on individual genius, deep emotion, and the joys of nature to thinkers like Rousseau who had scolded the philosophes for ignoring those aspects of life that escaped and even conflicted with the power of reason. Rousseau's autobiographical *Confessions,* published posthumously in 1782, caused an immediate sensation because it revealed so much about his inner emotional life, including his sexual longings and his almost paranoid distrust of other Enlightenment figures.

The appeal to feelings and emotions also increased interest in the occult. In the 1780s, a charismatic Austrian physician turned "experimenter," Franz Mesmer, awed crowds of aristocrats and middle-class admirers with his demonstrations in Paris of "animal magnetism." He passed a weak electrical current through tubs filled with water or iron filings, around which groups of his disciples sat, holding hands; with this process of "mesmerism" he claimed to cure their ailments. (The word *mesmerize,* meaning "hypnotize" or "hold spellbound," is derived from Mesmer's name.)

A novel by the German writer Johann Wolfgang von Goethe (1749–1832) captured the early romantic spirit with its glorification of emotion. *The Sorrows of Young Werther* (1774) tells of a passionate youth who reveres nature and rural life and is unhappy in love. When the woman he loves marries someone else, he falls into deep melancholy and eventually kills himself. Reason cannot save him. The book spurred a veritable Werther craze: there were Werther costumes, Werther engravings and embroidery, Werther medallions, and a perfume called Eau de Werther. Tragically, there were even a few imitations of Werther's suicide. The young Napoleon Bonaparte, who was to build an empire for France, claimed to have read Goethe's novel seven times.

Religious revivals underlined the limits of reason in a different way. Much of the Protestant world experienced an "awakening" in the 1740s. In the German states, Pietist groups founded new communities, and in the British North American colonies, revivalist Protestant preachers drew thousands of fervent believers in a movement called the Great Awakening. In North America, bitter conflicts between revivalists and their opponents in the established churches prompted the leaders on both sides to set up new colleges to support their beliefs. These included Princeton, Columbia, Brown, and Dartmouth, all founded between 1746 and 1769.

George Whitefield
One of the most prominent preachers of the Great Awakening in the British North American colonies was the English Methodist George Whitefield, painted here by John Wollaston in 1742. Whitefield visited the North American colonies seven times, sometimes for long periods, and drew tens of thousands of people to his dramatic and emotional open-air sermons. (National Portrait Gallery, London.)

Revivalism also stirred eastern European Jews at about the same time. Israel ben Eliezer (1698–1760) laid the foundation for Hasidism in the 1740s and 1750s. He traveled the Polish countryside offering miraculous cures and became known as the Ba'al Shem Tov (meaning "Master of the Good Name") because he used divine names to effect healing and bring believers into closer personal contact with God. He emphasized mystical contemplation of the divine, rather than study of Jewish law, and his followers, the **Hasidim** (Hebrew for "most pious" Jews), often expressed their devotion through music, dance, and fervent prayer. Their practices soon spread all over Poland-Lithuania.

Most of the waves of Protestant revivalism ebbed after the 1750s, but in Great Britain the movement known as **Methodism** continued to grow. John Wesley (1703–1791), the Oxford-educated son of an Anglican cleric, founded Methodism, a term evoked by Wesley's insistence on strict self-discipline and a methodical approach to religious study and observance. In 1738, Wesley began preaching a new brand of Anglicanism, with some similarities to Calvinism, that emphasized an intense personal experience of salvation and a life of thrift, abstinence, and hard work. Traveling all over the British Isles, Wesley would mount a table or a box to speak to the ordinary people of the village or town. He slept in his followers' homes and treated their illnesses with various remedies, including small electric shocks for nervous diseases. (Wesley eagerly followed Benjamin Franklin's experiments with electricity.)

In fifty years, Wesley preached forty thousand sermons, an average of fifteen a week. When the Anglican authorities refused to let him preach in the churches, Wesley began to ordain his own clergy. Nevertheless, during Wesley's lifetime the Methodist leadership remained politically conservative. Wesley himself denounced political agitation in the 1770s because, he said, it threatened to make Great Britain "a field of blood" ruled by "King Mob."

REVIEW Why was France the center of the Enlightenment, and in what ways was it surprising that the philosophes and new ideas flourished there?

Society and Culture in an Age of Enlightenment

Religious revivals and the first stirrings of romanticism show that all intellectual currents did not flow in the same channel. Similarly, some social and cultural developments manifested the influence of Enlightenment ideas, but others did not. The traditional leaders of European societies—the nobles—responded to Enlightenment ideals in contradictory fashion: many simply reasserted their privileges and resisted the influence of the Enlightenment, but an important minority embraced change and actively participated in reform efforts. The expanding middle classes saw in the Enlightenment a chance to make their claim for joining society's governing elite. They bought Enlightenment books, joined Masonic lodges, and patronized new styles in art, music, and literature. The lower classes were more affected by economic growth. Continuing population increases contributed to a rise in prices for basic goods. At the same time, peasants had to face rising rents, which created resentment of upper-class privileges.

The Nobility's Reassertion of Privilege

Nobles made up about 3 percent of the European population, but their numbers and way of life varied greatly from country to country. At least 10 percent of the population in Poland and 7 to 8 percent in Spain was noble, in contrast to only 2 percent in Russia and between 1 and 2 percent in the rest of western Europe. Many Polish and Spanish nobles lived in poverty; a title did not guarantee wealth. The wealthiest European nobles luxuriated in almost unimaginable opulence. Many of the English peers, for example, owned more than ten thousand acres of land (the average western European peasant owned about five acres), invested widely in government bonds and trading companies, kept several country residences with scores of servants as well as houses in London, and occasionally even had their own private orchestras, libraries of expensive books, greenhouses for exotic plants, kennels of pedigree dogs, and collections of antiques, firearms, and scientific instruments.

In the face of the commercialization of agriculture and the inflation of prices, European aristocrats converted their remaining legal rights (called *seigneurial dues*, from the French *seigneur*, for "lord") into money payments and used them to support an increasingly expensive lifestyle. Peasants felt the squeeze as a result. French peasants, for instance, paid a wide range of dues to their landlords—including payments to grind grain at the lord's mill, bake bread in his oven, and press grapes in his winepress—and various inheritance taxes on the land. In addition, peasants had to work on the public roads without compensation for a specified number of days every year. They also paid taxes to the government on salt, an essential preservative, and on the value of their land; customs duties if they sold produce or wine in town; and the tithe on their grain (one-tenth of the crop) to the church.

In Britain, the landed gentry could not claim these same onerous dues from their tenants, but they fiercely defended their exclusive right to hunt game. The game laws kept the poor from eating meat and helped protect the social status of the rich. The gentry enforced the game laws themselves by hiring gamekeepers who hunted down poachers and even set traps for them in the forests. According to the law, anyone who poached deer or rabbits while armed or disguised could be sentenced to death. After 1760, the number of arrests for breaking the game laws increased dramatically. In most other countries, too, hunting was the special right of the nobility and a cause of deep popular resentment.

Even though Enlightenment writers sharply criticized nobles' insistence on special privileges, most aristocrats maintained their marks of distinction. The male court nobility continued to sport swords, plumed hats, makeup, and powdered hair; middle-class men wore simpler and more somber clothing. Aristocrats had their own seats in church and their own quarters in the universities. Frederick II ("the Great") of Prussia (r. 1740–1786) made sure that nobles dominated both the army officer corps and the civil bureaucracy. Catherine II of Russia (r. 1762–1796) granted the nobility vast tracts of land, the exclusive right to own serfs, and exemption from personal taxes and corporal punishment. Her Charter of the Nobility of 1785 codified these privileges in exchange for nobles' political subservience to the state. In many countries, including Spain and France, the law prohibited aristocrats from engaging directly in retail trade. In Austria, Spain, the Italian states, Poland-Lithuania, and Russia, most nobles consequently cared little about Enlightenment ideas; they did not read the books of the philosophes and feared reforms that might challenge their dominance of rural society.

In France, Britain, and the western German states, however, the nobility proved more open to the new ideas. Among those who personally corresponded with Rousseau, for example, half were nobles, as were 20 percent of the 160 contributors to the *Encyclopedia.* It had not escaped their notice that Rousseau had denounced inequality. In his view, it was "manifestly contrary to the law of nature . . . that a handful of people should gorge themselves with superfluities while the hungry multitude goes in want of necessities."

The Middle Class and the Making of a New Elite

The Enlightenment offered middle-class people an intellectual and cultural route to social improvement. The term *middle class* referred to the middle position on the social ladder; middle-class families did not have legal titles like the nobility above them but did not work with their hands like the peasants, artisans, or workers below them. Most middle-class people lived in towns or cities and earned their living in the professions—as doctors, lawyers, or lower-level officials—or through investment in land, trade, or manufacturing. In the eighteenth century, the ranks of the middle class—also known as the bourgeoisie (after *bourgeois*, the French word for "city dweller")—grew steadily in western Europe as a result of economic expansion. In France, for example, the overall population grew by about one-third in the 1700s, but the bourgeoisie nearly tripled in size. Although middle-class people had many reasons to resent the nobles, they also aspired to be like them.

Nobles and middle-class professionals mingled in Enlightenment salons and joined the new Masonic lodges and local learned societies. The members of Masonic lodges were known as **Freemasons** because that was the term given to apprentice masons when they were deemed "free" to practice as masters of their guild. The Freemasons quickly lost any connection to guild life, however; they held secret rituals and meetings devoted to philanthropy and the discussion of new ideas. Although not explicitly political in aim, the lodges encouraged equality among members, and both aristocrats and middle-class men could join. Members wrote constitutions for their lodges and elected their own officers, thus promoting a direct experience of constitutional government.

Freemasonry arose in Great Britain and spread eastward: the first French and Italian lodges opened in 1726; Frederick II of Prussia founded a lodge in 1740; and after 1750, Freemasonry spread in Poland, Russia, and British North America. In France, women set up their own Masonic lodges. Despite the papacy's condemnation of Freemasonry in 1738 as subversive of religious and civil authority, lodges continued to multiply throughout the eighteenth century because they offered a place for socializing outside of the traditional channels and a way of declaring one's interest in the Enlightenment and reform. In short, Freemasonry offered a kind of secular religion. After 1789 and the outbreak of the French Revolution, conservatives would blame the lodges for every kind of political upheaval, but in the 1700s many high-ranking nobles became active members and saw no conflict with their privileged status.

Shared tastes in travel, architecture, and the arts helped strengthen the links between nobles and members of the middle class. "Grand tours" of Europe often led upper-class youths to the recently discovered Roman ruins at Pompeii and Herculaneum in Italy. The excavations aroused enthusiasm for the neoclassical style in architecture and painting, which began pushing aside the rococo and the long dominant baroque. Urban residences, government buildings, furniture, fabrics, wallpaper, and even pottery soon reflected the neoclassical emphasis on purity and clarity of forms. The English potter Josiah Wedgwood (1730–1795) almost single-handedly created a mass market for domestic crockery by appealing to middle-class desires to emulate the rich and royal. His designs of special tea sets for the British queen, for Catherine the Great of Russia, and for leading aristocrats allowed him to advertise his wares as fashionable. By 1767, he claimed that his Queensware pottery

Neoclassical Style
In this Georgian interior of Syon House on the outskirts of London, various neoclassical motifs are readily apparent: Greek columns, Greek-style statuary on top of the columns, and Roman-style mosaics in the floor. The Scottish architect Robert Adam created this room for the duke of Northumberland in the 1760s. Adam had spent four years in Italy and returned to London in 1758 to decorate homes in the "Adam style," meaning the neoclassical manner. (© The Fotomas Index, U.K./ The Bridgeman Art Library.)

had "spread over the whole Globe," and indeed by then his pottery was being marketed in France, Russia, Venice, the Ottoman Empire, and British North America.

This period also supported artistic styles other than neoclassicism. Frederick II of Prussia built himself a palace in the earlier rococo style; gave it a French name, Sans-souci (meaning "worry-free"); and filled it with paintings and sculptures by the French masters of the rococo. The new emphasis on emotion and family life was reflected in a growing taste for moralistic family scenes in painting. The paintings of Jean-Baptiste Greuze (1725–1805), much praised by Diderot, depicted ordinary families at moments of domestic crisis. Such subjects appealed in particular to the middle-class public, which now attended the official painting exhibitions in France that were held regularly every other year after 1737.

Although wealthy nobles still patronized Europe's leading musicians, music too began to reflect the broadening of the elite, and the spread of Enlightenment ideals as classical forms replaced the baroque style. Complex polyphony gave way to melody, which made music more accessible to the ordinary listener. The first subscription concerts open to the public took place in London in the 1670s and in Frankfurt in 1712, and the German city of Leipzig opened the first public orchestra hall in 1781. The public concert gradually displaced the private recital, and a new attitude toward "the classics" developed: for the first time in the 1770s and 1780s, concert groups began to play older music rather than simply playing the latest commissioned works. This laid the foundation for what we still call classical music today—that is, a repertory of the greatest music of the eighteenth and early nineteenth centuries. Because composers now created works that would be performed over and over again as part of a classical repertory, rather than occasional pieces for

Jean-Baptiste Greuze, *Broken Eggs* (1756)
Greuze made his reputation as a painter of moralistic family scenes. In this one, an old woman (perhaps the mother) confronts the lover of a young girl and points to the eggs that have fallen out of a basket. The broken eggs are a symbol of lost virginity. Denis Diderot praised Greuze's work as "morality in paint," but the paintings often had an erotic subtext. (© Francis G. Mayer/Corbis.)

the court or noble patrons, they deliberately attempted to write lasting works. As a result, the major composers began to produce fewer symphonies: the Austrian composer Franz Joseph Haydn (1732–1809) wrote more than one hundred symphonies, but his successor Ludwig van Beethoven (1770–1827) would create only nine.

The two supreme masters of the new musical style of the eighteenth century show that the transition from noble patronage to classical concerts was far from complete. The Austrians Haydn and Wolfgang Amadeus Mozart (1756–1791) both wrote for noble patrons, but by the early 1800s their compositions had been incorporated into the canon of concert classics all over Europe. Incredibly prolific, both excelled in combining lightness, clarity, and profound emotion. Both also wrote numerous Italian operas, a genre whose popularity continued to grow: in the 1780s, the Papal States alone boasted forty opera houses. Haydn spent most of his career working for a Hungarian noble family, the Eszterházys. Asked why he had written no string quintets (at which Mozart excelled), he responded simply, "No one has ordered any."

Interest in reading, like attending public concerts, took hold of the middle classes. Shaped by coffeehouses, Masonic lodges, and public concerts more than by formal schooling, the new reading public fueled a frenzied increase in publication. By the end of the eighteenth century, six times as many books were being published in the German states, for instance, as at the beginning of the century. One Parisian author commented that "people are certainly reading ten times as much in Paris as they did a hundred years ago." Provincial towns in Britain, France, the Dutch Republic, and the German states published their own newspapers; by 1780, thirty-seven English towns had local newspapers. Newspapers advertised arithmetic, dancing, and drawing lessons—and potions to induce abortions and cures for venereal disease. Lending libraries multiplied, and in England especially, even small villages housed book clubs. Women benefited as much as men from the spread of print. As one Englishman observed, "By far the greatest part of ladies now have a taste for books."

The novel had become a respectable and influential genre. Among the most widely read novels were those of the English printer and writer Samuel Richardson (1689–1761). In *Clarissa Harlowe* (1747–1748), a long novel in eight volumes, Richardson tells the story of a young woman from a heartless upper-class family who is torn between her family's choice of a repulsive suitor and her attraction to Lovelace, an aristocratic rake. Although she runs off with Lovelace to escape her family, she resists his advances; after being drugged and raped by Lovelace—despite the frantic pleas of readers of the first volumes to spare her—Clarissa dies of what can only be called a broken heart. One woman complained to Richardson, "I verily believe I have shed a pint of tears, and my heart is still bursting." Richardson claimed that he wrote *Clarissa Harlowe* as a kind of manual of virtuous female conduct, yet critics nonetheless worried that novels undermined morals with their portrayals of lowlife characters, the seductions of virtuous women, and other examples of immoral behavior.

Although he himself grew up reading novels with his father, Rousseau discouraged novel reading in *Émile.* Still, he helped change attitudes in the new elite toward children by offering an educational approach for gently drawing the best out of children rather than repressing their natural curiosity and love of learning. Paintings now showed individual children playing at their favorite activities rather than formally posed with their families. Books about and for children became popular. *The Newtonian System of the Universe Digested for Young Minds,* by "Tom Telescope," was published in Britain in 1761 and reprinted many times. Toys, jigsaw puzzles, and clothing designed for children all appeared for the first time in the 1700s. At the same time, however, the Enlightenment's emphasis on reason, self-control, and childhood innocence made parents increasingly anxious about their children's sexuality. Moralists and physicians wrote books about the evils of masturbation, "proving" that it led to physical and mental degeneration and even madness. One English writer linked masturbation to debility of body and of mind; infertility; epilepsy; loss of memory, sight, and hearing; distortions of the eyes, mouth, and face; a pale, sallow, and bluish complexion; wasting of the limbs; idiotism; and death itself. While the Enlightenment thus encouraged excessive concern about children being left to their own devices, it nevertheless taught the middle and upper classes to value their children and to expect their improvement through education.

Life on the Margins

Even more than worrying about their children, the upper and middle classes worried about the increasing numbers of poor people. Although booming foreign trade—French colonial trade, for example, increased tenfold in the 1700s—fueled a dramatic economic expansion, the results did not necessarily trickle all the way down the social scale. The population of Europe grew by nearly 30 percent, with especially striking gains in England, Ireland, Prussia, and Hungary. Even though food production increased, shortages and crises still occurred periodically. Prices went up in many countries after the 1730s and continued to rise gradually until the early nineteenth century; wages in many trades rose as well, though less quickly than prices. Peasants who produced surpluses to sell in local markets and shopkeepers and artisans who could increase their sales to meet growing demand prospered. But those at the bottom of the social ladder—day laborers in the cities and peasants with smallholdings—lived on the edge of dire poverty, and when they lost their land or work, they either migrated to the cities or wandered the roads in search of food and work. In France alone, 200,000 workers left their homes every year in search of seasonal employment elsewhere. At least 10 percent of Europe's urban population depended on some form of charity.

The growing numbers of poor people overwhelmed local governments and created fears about rising crime. In some countries, officials sent beggars and vagabonds to workhouses. The expenses for running these overcrowded institutions increased 60 percent in England between 1760 and 1785. After 1740, most German towns began to set up workhouses that were part workshop, part hospital, and part prison. Such institutions also appeared for the first time in Boston, New York, and Philadelphia. To supplement the inadequate system of religious charity, offices for the poor, public workshops, and workhouse-hospitals, the French government created *dépôts de mendicité,* or "beggar houses," in 1767. The government sent people to these new workhouses to labor in manufacturing, but most were too weak or sick to work, and 20 percent of them died within a few months of incarceration.

Those who were able to work or keep their land fared better. An increase in literacy, especially in the cities, allowed some lower-class people to participate in new tastes and ideas. One French observer insisted, "These days, you see a waiting-maid in her backroom, a lackey in an ante-room reading pamphlets. People can read in almost all classes of society." In France, however, only 50 percent of men and 27 percent of women could read and write in the 1780s (although that was twice the rate of a century earlier). Literacy rates were higher in England and the Dutch Republic, much lower in eastern Europe. About one in four Parisians owned books, but the lower classes overwhelmingly read religious books, as they had in the past.

Whereas the new elite might attend salons, concerts, or art exhibitions, peasants enjoyed their traditional forms of popular entertainment, such as fairs and festivals, and the urban lower classes relaxed in cabarets and taverns. Sometimes pleasures were cruel. In Britain, bullbaiting, bearbaiting, dogfighting, and cockfighting were all common forms of entertainment that provided opportunities for organized gambling. Even "gentle" sports frequented by the upper classes had their violent side, showing that the upper classes had not become so different as they sometimes thought. Cricket matches, whose rules were first laid down in 1744, were often accompanied by brawls among fans (not unlike soccer matches today, though on a much smaller scale). Many British enjoyed what one observer called a "battle royal with sticks, pebbles and hog's dung."

As population increased and villagers began to move to cities to better their prospects, sexual behavior changed, too. The rates of births out of wedlock soared, from less than 5 percent of all births in the seventeenth century to nearly 20 percent at the end of the eighteenth. Historians have disagreed about the causes and meaning of this change. Some detect in this pattern a sign of sexual liberation and the beginnings of a modern sexual revolution: as women moved out of the control of their families, they began to seek their own sexual fulfillment. Others view this change more bleakly, as a story of seduction and betrayal: family and community pressure had once forced a man to marry a woman pregnant with his child, but now a man could abandon a pregnant lover by simply moving away.

Increased mobility brought freedom for some women, but it also aggravated the vulnerability of those newly arrived in cities from the countryside. Desperation, not reason, often ruled their choices. Women who came to the city as domestic servants had little recourse against masters or fellow servants who seduced or raped them. The result was a startling rise in abandoned babies. Most European cities established foundling hospitals to care for abandoned children in the 1700s, but infant and child mortality was 50 percent higher in such institutions than for children brought up at home. For women of this era who wanted to terminate a pregnancy, the options were limited and usually handled in secrecy. Some women tried herbs, laxatives, or crude surgical means of abortion; a few, usually servants who would lose their jobs if their employers discovered they had borne a child, resorted to infanticide. Reformers criticized the harshness of laws against infanticide, but they showed no mercy for "sodomites" (as male homosexuals were called), who in some places, in particular the Dutch Republic, were systematically persecuted and imprisoned or even executed. Male homosexuals attracted the attention of authorities because they had begun to develop networks and special meeting places. The stereotype of the effeminate, exclusively homosexual male seems to have appeared for the first time in the eighteenth century, perhaps as part of a growing emphasis on separate roles for men and women.

REVIEW What were the major differences in the impact of the Enlightenment on nobles, the middle classes, and the lower classes?

State Power in an Era of Reform

Rulers turned to Enlightenment-inspired reforms to improve life for their subjects and gain commercial or military advantage over rival states. Historians label many of the sovereigns of this time **enlightened despots** or enlightened absolutists, for they aimed to promote Enlightenment reforms without giving up their absolutist powers. Catherine the Great's admiring relationship with Voltaire showed how even the most absolutist rulers championed reform when it suited their own goals. Foremost among those goals was the expansion of a ruler's territory.

War and Diplomacy

Europeans no longer fought devastating wars over religion that killed hundreds of thousands of civilians; instead, professional armies and navies battled for control of overseas empires and for dominance on the European continent. Rulers continued to expand their armies; the Prussian army, for example, nearly tripled in size between 1740 and 1789. Widespread use of flintlock muskets required deployment in long lines, usually three men deep, with each line in turn loading and firing on command. Military strategy became cautious and calculating, but this did not prevent the outbreak of hostilities. The instability of the European balance of power resulted in two major wars, a diplomatic reversal of alliances, and the partition of Poland-Lithuania among Russia, Austria, and Prussia.

The War of the Austrian Succession (1740–1748) broke out when Holy Roman Emperor Charles VI died in 1740 without a male heir. Most European rulers recognized the emperor's chosen heiress, his daughter Maria Theresa, because Charles's Pragmatic Sanction of 1713 had given women the right to inherit the Habsburg crown lands. The new king of Prussia, Frederick II, who had just succeeded his father a few months earlier in 1740, saw his chance to grab territory and immediately invaded the rich Austrian province of Silesia. France joined Prussia in an attempt to further humiliate its traditional enemy Austria, and Great Britain allied with Austria to prevent the French from taking the Austrian Netherlands (Map 15.1). French and British colonials in North America soon fought each other all along their boundaries, enlisting native American auxiliaries. Britain tried but failed to isolate the French Caribbean colonies during the war, and hostilities broke out in India, too. Maria Theresa (r. 1740–1780) survived only by conceding Silesia to Prussia in order to split the Prussians off from France. The Peace of Aix-la-Chapelle of 1748 recognized Maria Theresa as the heiress to the Austrian lands, and her husband, Francis I, became Holy Roman Emperor, thus reasserting the integrity of the Austrian Empire.

In 1756, a major reversal of alliances reshaped relations among the great powers. Prussia and Great Britain signed a defensive alliance, prompting Austria to overlook two centuries of hostility and ally with France. Austrian and French willingness to put aside their long-standing dynastic rivalry in favor of more immediate strategic

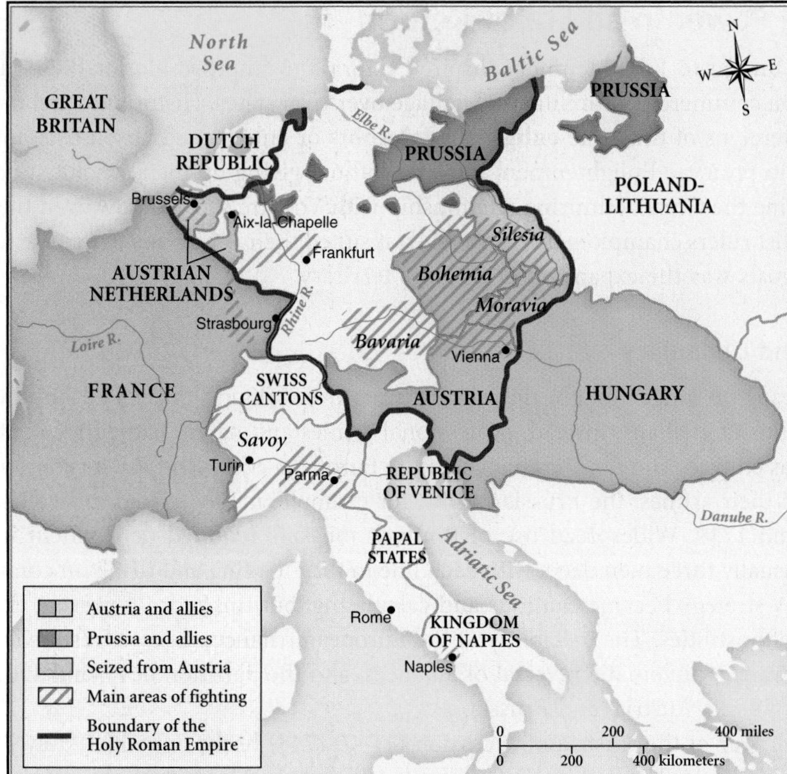

Map 15.1 The War of the Austrian Succession, 1740–1748
The accession of a twenty-three-year-old woman, Maria Theresa, to the Austrian throne gave the new king of Prussia, Frederick II, an opportunity to invade the province of Silesia. France joined on Prussia's side, Great Britain on Austria's. In 1745, the French defeated the British in the Austrian Netherlands and helped instigate a Jacobite uprising in Scotland. The rebellion failed, and British attacks on French overseas shipping forced the French to negotiate. The peace treaties guaranteed Frederick's conquest of Silesia, which soon became the wealthiest province of Prussia. France came to terms with Great Britain to protect its overseas possessions; Austria had to accept the peace settlement after a formal public protest.

interests prompted some to call this a "diplomatic revolution." Russia and Sweden soon joined the Franco-Austrian alliance. When Frederick II invaded Saxony, an ally of Austria, with his bigger and better-disciplined army, the long-simmering hostilities between Great Britain and France over colonial boundaries flared into a general war that became known as the Seven Years' War (1756–1763).

Fighting soon raged around the world (Map 15.2). The French and British battled on land and sea in North America (where the conflict was called the French and Indian War), the West Indies, and India. The two coalitions also fought each other in central Europe. At first, in 1757, Frederick the Great surprised Europe with a spectacular victory at Rossbach in Saxony over a much larger Franco-Austrian army. But in time, Russian and Austrian armies encircled his troops. Frederick despaired: "I believe all is lost. I will not survive the ruin of my country." A fluke of history saved him. Empress Elizabeth of Russia (r. 1741–1762) died and was succeeded by the mentally unstable Peter III, a fanatical admirer of Frederick and things Prussian. Peter withdrew Russia from the war. (He was soon mysteriously murdered, probably at the instigation of his wife, Catherine the Great.) In separate peace treaties with Russia and Austria, Frederick kept all his territory, including Silesia.

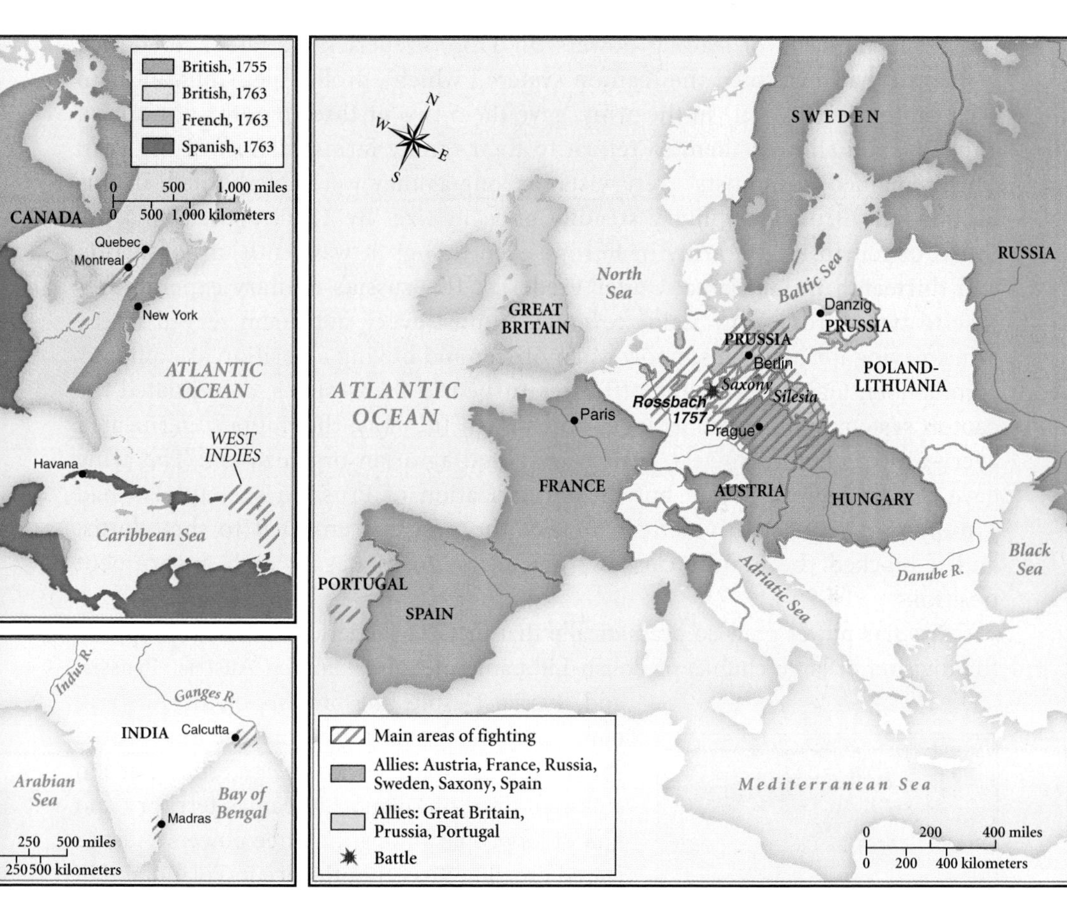

Map 15.2 The Seven Years' War, 1756–1763
In what might justly be called the first worldwide war, the French and British fought each other in Europe, the West Indies, North America, and India. Skirmishing in North America helped precipitate the war, which became more general when Austria, France, and Russia allied to check Prussian influence in central Europe. The treaty between Austria and Prussia simply restored the status quo in Europe, but the changes overseas were much more dramatic. Britain gained control over Canada and India but gave back to France the West Indian islands of Guadeloupe and Martinique. Britain was now the dominant power of the seas. **For more help analyzing this map, see the map activity for this chapter in the Online Study Guide at** bedfordstmartins.com/huntconcise.

The Anglo-French overseas conflicts ended more decisively than the continental land wars. British naval superiority, fully achieved only in the 1750s, enabled Great Britain to rout the French in North America, India, and the West Indies. In the Treaty of Paris of 1763, France ceded Canada to Great Britain and agreed to remove its armies from India, in exchange for keeping its rich West Indian islands. Eagerness to avenge this defeat would motivate France to support the British North American colonists in their War of Independence just fifteen years later.

Although Prussia suffered great losses in the Seven Years' War—some 160,000 Prussian soldiers died either in action or of disease—the army helped vault Prussia to the rank of leading powers. In 1733, Frederick II's father, Frederick William I, had instituted the "canton system," which enrolled peasant youths in each canton (or district) in the army, gave them two or three months of training annually, and allowed them to return to their family farms the rest of the year. They remained "cantonists" (reservists) as long as they were able-bodied. In this fashion, the Prussian military steadily grew in size. By 1740, Prussia had the third- or fourth-largest army in Europe even though it was tenth in population and thirteenth in land area. Under Frederick II, Prussia's military expenditures rose to two-thirds of the state's revenue. Almost every nobleman served in the army, paying for his own support as an officer and buying a position as company commander. Once retired, the officers returned to their estates, coordinated the canton system, and served as local officials. In this way, the military permeated every aspect of rural society, fusing army and agrarian organization. The army gave the state great power, but the militarization of Prussian society also had a profoundly conservative effect: it kept the peasants enserfed to their lords, and it blocked the middle classes from access to estates or high government positions.

Prussia's power grew so dramatically that in 1772 Frederick the Great proposed the division of large chunks of Polish-Lithuanian territory among Austria, Prussia, and Russia. Despite the protests of the Austrian empress Maria Theresa that the partition would spread "a stain over my whole reign," she agreed to split one-third of Poland-Lithuania's territory and half of its people among the three powers. Austria feared growing Russian influence in Poland and in the Balkans, where Russia had been successfully battling the Ottoman Empire. Conflicts among Catholics, Protestants, and Orthodox Christians in Poland were used to justify this cynical move. Russia took over most of Lithuania, effectively ending the large but weak Polish-Lithuanian commonwealth.

The First Partition of Poland, 1772

Dividing Poland, 1772
In this contemporary depiction, Catherine the Great, Joseph II, and Frederick II point on the map to the portion of Poland-Lithuania each plans to take. The artist makes it clear that Poland's fate rested in the hands of neighboring rulers, not its own people. Can you infer the sentiments of the artist from the content of this engraving? (Mansell/Time Life Pictures/Getty Images.)

State-Sponsored Reform

In the aftermath of the Seven Years' War, all the belligerents faced pressing needs for more money to fund their growing armies, to organize navies to wage overseas conflicts, and to counter the impact of inflation. To make tax increases more palatable to public opinion, rulers appointed reform-minded ministers and gave them a mandate to modernize government. As one adviser to Joseph II of Austria (r. 1780–1790) put it, "A properly constituted state must be exactly analogous to a machine . . . and the ruler must be the foreman, the mainspring . . . which sets everything else in motion." Such reforms always threatened the interests of traditional groups, however, and the spread of Enlightenment ideas aroused sometimes unpredictable desires for more change.

Legal reform, both of the judicial system and of the often disorganized and irregular law codes, was central to the work of many reform-minded monarchs. Although Frederick II favored all things French in culture—he insisted on speaking French in his court and prided himself on his personal friendship with Voltaire—he made Prussian justice the envy of Europe. His institution of a uniform civil justice system created the most consistently administered laws and efficient judiciary of the time. Joseph II also ordered the compilation of a unified law code, a project that required many years for completion. Catherine II of Russia began such an undertaking even more ambitiously. In 1767, she called together a legislative commission of 564 deputies and asked them to consider a long document called the *Instruction,* which represented her hopes for legal reform based on the ideas of Montesquieu and the Italian writer Cesare Beccaria. Montesquieu had insisted that any punishment should fit the crime; he also criticized the use of torture and brutal corporal punishment. In his influential book *On Crimes and Punishments* (1764), Beccaria argued that laws should be printed for everyone to read and administered in rational procedures, that torture should be abolished as inhumane, and that the accused should be presumed innocent until proven guilty. Despite much discussion and hundreds of petitions and documents about local problems, little came of Catherine's commission because the monarch herself—despite her regard for Voltaire and his fellow philosophes—proved ultimately unwilling to see through far-reaching legal reform.

Rulers everywhere wanted more control over church affairs, and they used Enlightenment criticisms of the organized churches to get their way. In Catholic countries, many government officials resented the influence of the Jesuits, the major Catholic teaching order. The Jesuits trained the Catholic intellectual elite, ran a worldwide missionary network, enjoyed close ties to the papacy, and amassed great wealth. Critics mounted campaigns against the Jesuits in many countries, and by the early 1770s the Society of Jesus had been dissolved in Portugal, France, and Spain. In 1773, Pope Clement XIV (r. 1769–1774) agreed under pressure to disband the order, an edict that held until a reinvigorated papacy restored the society in 1814. Joseph II of Austria not only applauded the suppression of the Jesuits but also required Austrian bishops to swear fidelity and submission to him. Under Joseph, the Austrian state supervised seminaries, reorganized diocesan boundaries, abolished contemplative monastic orders, and confiscated their property to pay for education and poor relief.

Enlightened absolutists also tried to gain greater state authority over education, even while extending education to the lower classes. Joseph II launched the most ambitious educational reforms of the period. In 1774, once the Jesuits had been disbanded, the General School Ordinance in Austria ordered state subsidies for local schools, which the state would regulate. By 1789, one-quarter of the school-age children attended school. In Prussia, the school code of 1763 required all children between the ages of five and thirteen to attend school. Although not enforced uniformly, the Prussian law demonstrated Frederick II's belief that modernization depended on education. Catherine II of Russia also tried to expand elementary education—and the education of women in particular—and founded engineering schools.

No ruler pushed the principle of religious toleration as far as Joseph II of Austria, who became Holy Roman Emperor and co-regent with his mother, Maria Theresa, in 1765 and then ruled alone after 1780. In 1781, he granted freedom of religious worship to Protestants, Orthodox Christians, and Jews. For the first time, these groups were allowed to own property, build schools, enter the professions, and hold political and military offices. The efforts of other rulers to extend religious toleration proved more limited. Louis XVI signed an edict in 1787 restoring French Protestants' civil rights—but still they could not hold political office. Great Britain continued to deny Catholics freedom of open worship and the right to sit in Parliament. Most European states limited the rights and opportunities available to Jews. In Russia, only wealthy Jews could hold municipal office, and in the Papal States, the pope encouraged forced baptism. The leading philosophes opposed the persecution of Jews in theory but often treated them with undisguised contempt. Diderot's comment was all too typical: Jews, he said, bore "all the defects peculiar to an ignorant and superstitious nation."

Limits of Reform

When enlightened absolutist leaders introduced reforms, they often faced resistance from groups threatened by the proposed changes. The most contentious area of reform was agricultural policy. Whereas Frederick II and Catherine II reinforced the authority of nobles over their serfs, Joseph II tried to remove the burdens of serfdom in the Habsburg lands. In 1781, he abolished the personal aspects of serfdom: serfs could now move freely, enter trades, or marry without their lords' permission. Joseph abolished the tithe to the church, shifted more of the tax burden to the nobility, and converted peasants' labor services into cash payments.

The Austrian nobility furiously resisted these far-reaching reforms. When Joseph died in 1790, his brother Leopold II had to revoke most reforms to appease the nobles. On his deathbed, Joseph recognized the futility of many of his efforts; as his epitaph he suggested, "Here lies Joseph II, who was unfortunate in all his enterprises." Prussia's Frederick II, like Joseph, encouraged such agricultural innovations as planting potatoes and turnips (new crops that could help feed a growing population), experimenting with cattle breeding, draining swamplands, and clearing forests. But Prussia's noble landlords, the Junkers, continued to expand their estates at the expense of poorer peasants, and Frederick did nothing to ameliorate serfdom except on his own domains.

Reforming ministers also tried to stimulate agricultural improvement in France. Unlike most other western European countries, France still had about 100,000 serfs; though their burdens weighed less heavily than those in eastern Europe, serfdom did not entirely disappear until 1789. A group of economists called the **physiocrats** urged the French government to deregulate the grain trade and make the tax system more equitable to encourage agricultural productivity. In the interest of establishing a free market, they also insisted that urban guilds be abolished because they prevented free entry into the trades. Their proposed reforms applied the Enlightenment emphasis on individual liberties to the economy; Adam Smith took up many of the physiocrats' ideas in his writing in favor of free markets. The French government heeded some of this advice and gave up its system of price controls on grain in 1763, but it had to reverse this decision in 1770 when grain shortages caused a famine.

French reform efforts did not end there. To break the power of the parlements (the thirteen high courts of law that had led the way in opposing royal efforts to increase and equalize taxation), Louis XV appointed a reform-minded chancellor who in 1770 replaced the parlements with courts in which the judges no longer owned their offices and thus could not sell them or pass them on as an inheritance. Justice would then be more impartial. Nevertheless, the judges of the displaced parlements aroused widespread opposition to what they portrayed as tyrannical royal policy. The furor calmed down only when Louis XV died in 1774 and his successor, Louis XVI (r. 1774–1792), yielded to aristocratic demands and restored the old parlements. Louis XV died one of the most despised kings in French history, resented both for his high-handed reforms and for his private vices. Underground pamphlets lampooned him, describing his final mistress, Madame du Barry, as a prostitute who pandered to the elderly king's well-known taste for young girls. This often pornographic literature linked despotism to the supposedly excessive influence of women at court.

Louis XVI tried to carry out part of the program suggested by the physiocrats, and he chose one of their disciples, Jacques Turgot (1727–1781), as his chief minister. Turgot pushed through several edicts that again freed the grain trade, suppressed many guilds, converted the peasants' forced labor on roads into a money tax payable by all landowners, and reduced court expenses. He also began making plans to introduce a system of elected local assemblies, which would have made government much more representative. Faced with broad-based resistance led by the parlements and his own courtiers, as well as with riots against rising grain prices, Louis XVI dismissed Turgot, and one of the last possibilities to overhaul France's monarchy collapsed.

The failure of reform in France paradoxically reflected the power of Enlightenment ideas; everyone now endorsed Enlightenment ideals but used them for different ends. The nobles in the parlements blocked the French monarchy's reform efforts using the very same Enlightenment language spoken by the crown's ministers. But unlike Austria, the other great power that faced persistent aristocratic resistance to reform, France had a large middle-class public that was increasingly frustrated by the failure to institute social change, a failure that ultimately helped undermine the monarchy itself. Where Frederick II, Catherine II, and even Joseph II used reform to bolster the efficiency of absolutist government, attempts at change in France backfired. French kings found that their ambitious programs for reform succeeded only in arousing unrealistic hopes.

REVIEW What prompted enlightened absolutists to undertake reforms in the second half of the eighteenth century?

Rebellions against State Power

Although traditional forms of popular discontent had not disappeared, Enlightenment ideals and reforms changed the rules of the game in politics. Governments had become accountable for their actions to a much wider public sphere than ever before. In Britain and France, ordinary people rioted when they perceived government as failing to protect them against food shortages. The growth of informed public opinion had its most dramatic consequences in the North American colonies, where a struggle over the British Parliament's right to tax turned into a full-scale war for independence. The American War of Independence showed that once put into practice, Enlightenment ideals could have revolutionary implications.

Food Riots and Peasant Uprisings

Population growth, inflation, and the extension of the market system put added pressure on the already beleaguered poorest classes of people. Seventeenth-century peasants and townspeople had rioted to protest new taxes. In the last half of the eighteenth century, the food supply became the focus of political and social conflict. Poor people living in the villages and towns believed it was the government's responsibility to ensure that they had enough food, and many governments did stockpile grain to make up for the occasional bad harvest. At the same time, in keeping with Adam Smith's and the French physiocrats' free-market proposals, governments wanted to allow grain prices to rise with market demand, because higher profits would motivate producers to increase the supply of food.

Free trade in grain meant selling to the highest bidder even if that bidder was a foreign merchant. In the short run, in times of scarcity, big landowners and farmers could make huge profits by selling grain outside their hometowns or villages. This practice enraged poor farmers, agricultural workers, and city wageworkers, who could not afford the higher prices. Lacking the political means to affect policy, they could enforce their desire for old-fashioned price regulation only by rioting. Most did not pillage or steal grain, but rather forced the sale of grain or flour at a "just" price and blocked the shipment of grain out of their villages to other markets. Women often led these "popular price fixings," as they were called in France, in desperate attempts to protect the food supply for their children.

Such food riots occurred regularly in Britain and France in the second half of the eighteenth century. One of the most turbulent was the so-called Flour War in France in 1775. Turgot's deregulation of the grain trade in 1774 caused prices to rise in several provincial cities. Rioting spread from there to the Paris region, where villagers attacked grain convoys heading to the capital city. Local officials often ordered merchants and bakers to sell at the price the rioters demanded, only to find themselves arrested by the central government for overriding free trade. The government brought in troops to restore order and introduced the death penalty for rioting.

Frustrations with serfdom and hopes for a miraculous transformation provoked the Pugachev rebellion in Russia beginning in 1773. An army deserter from the southeast frontier region, Emelian Pugachev (1742–1775) claimed to be Tsar Peter III, the dead husband of Catherine II. Pugachev's appearance seemed to confirm peasant hopes for a "redeemer tsar" who would save the people from oppression. He rallied around him Cossacks like himself who resented the loss of their old

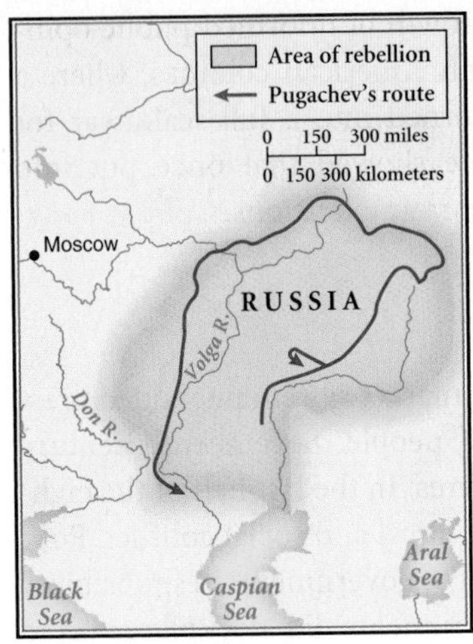

The Pugachev Rebellion, 1773

tribal independence. Now increasingly enserfed or forced to pay taxes and endure army service, these nomadic bands joined with other serfs, rebellious mineworkers, and Muslim minorities. Catherine dispatched a large army to squelch the uprising, but Pugachev eluded them, and the fighting spread. Nearly three million people eventually participated, making this the largest single rebellion in the history of tsarist Russia.

When Pugachev urged the peasants to attack the nobility and seize their estates, hundreds of noble families perished. Foreign newspapers called it "the revolution in southern Russia" and offered fantastic stories about Pugachev's life history. Finally, the army captured the rebel leader and brought him in an iron cage to Moscow, where he was tortured and executed. In the aftermath, Catherine tightened the nobles' control over their serfs and harshly punished those who dared to criticize serfdom.

A Cossack
Emelian Pugachev and many of his followers were Cossacks, Ukrainians who set up nomadic communities of horsemen to resist outside control, whether from the Turks, Poles, or Russians. This eighteenth-century engraving captures the common view of Cossacks as horsemen always ready for battle but with a fondness for music, too. **For more help analyzing this image, see the visual activity for this chapter in the Online Study Guide at** bedfordstmartins.com/huntconcise.

Public Opinion and Political Opposition

Peasant uprisings might briefly shake even a powerful monarchy, but the rise of public opinion as a force independent of court society caused more enduring changes in European politics. Across much of Europe and in the North American colonies, demands for broader political participation reflected Enlightenment notions about individual rights. Aristocratic bodies such as the French parlements, which had no legislative role like that of the British Parliament, insisted that the monarch consult them on the nation's affairs, and the new educated elite wanted more influence, too. Newspapers began to cover daily political affairs, and the public learned the basics of political life, despite the strict limits on political participation in most countries.

Monarchs turned to public opinion to seek support against aristocratic groups that opposed reform. Gustavus III of Sweden (r. 1771–1792) called himself "the first citizen of a free people" and promised to deliver the country from "insufferable aristocratic despotism." Shortly after coming to the throne, Gustavus proclaimed a new constitution that divided power between the king and the legislature, abolished the use of torture in the judicial process, and ensured some freedom of the press.

In France, both the parlements and the monarch appealed to the public through the printed word. The crown hired writers to make its case; the magistrates of the parlements wrote their own rejoinders. French-language newspapers published in the Dutch Republic provided many people in France with detailed accounts of political news and also gave voice to pro-parlement positions. One of the new French-language newspapers printed inside France, *Le Journal des Dames (The Ladies' Journal),* was published by women and mixed short stories and reviews of books and plays with demands for more women's rights.

The Wilkes affair in Great Britain showed that public opinion could be mobilized to challenge a government. In 1763, during the reign of George III (r. 1760–1820), John Wilkes, a member of Parliament, attacked the government in his newspaper, *North Briton,* and sued the crown when he was arrested. He won his release as well as damages. When he was reelected, Parliament denied him his seat, not once but three times.

The Wilkes episode soon escalated into a major campaign against the corruption and social exclusiveness of Parliament, complaints the Levellers had first raised during the English revolutions of the late 1640s. Newspapers, magazines, pamphlets, handbills, and cheap editions of Wilkes's collected works all helped promote his cause. Those who could not vote demonstrated for Wilkes. In one incident, eleven people died when soldiers broke up a huge gathering of his supporters. The slogan "Wilkes and Liberty" appeared on walls all over London. Middle-class voters formed the Society of Supporters of the Bill of Rights, which circulated petitions for Wilkes; they gained the backing of about one-fourth of all the voters. The more determined Wilkesites proposed sweeping reforms of Parliament, including more frequent elections, more representation for the counties, the elimination of "rotten boroughs" (election districts so small that they could be controlled by one big patron), and restrictions of pensions used by the crown to gain support. These demands would be at the heart of agitation for parliamentary reform in Britain for decades to come.

Popular demonstrations did not always support reforms. In 1780, the Gordon riots devastated London. They were named after the fanatical anti-Catholic crusader Lord George Gordon, who helped organize huge marches and petition campaigns against a bill the House of Commons passed to grant limited toleration to Catholics. The demonstrations culminated in a seven-day riot that left fifty buildings destroyed and three hundred people dead. Despite the continuing limitation on voting rights in Great Britain, British politicians were learning that they could ignore public opinion only at their peril.

Political opposition also took artistic forms, particularly in countries where governments restricted organized political activity. A striking example of a play with a political message was *The Marriage of Figaro* (1784) by Pierre-Augustin Caron de Beaumarchais (1732–1799), a watchmaker, a judge, a gunrunner in the American War of Independence, and a French spy in Britain. *The Marriage of Figaro* was first a hit at court, when Queen Marie-Antoinette had it read for her friends. But when her husband, Louis XVI, read it, he forbade its production on the grounds that "this man mocks at everything that should be respected in government." When finally performed publicly, the play caused a sensation. The chief character, Figaro, is a clever servant who gets the better of his noble employer. When speaking of the count, he cries, "What have you done to deserve so many rewards? You went to the trouble of being born, and nothing more." Two years later, Mozart based an equally famous but somewhat tamer opera on Beaumarchais's story.

Revolution in North America

Oppositional forms of public opinion came to a head in Great Britain's North American colonies, where the result was American independence and the establishment of a republican constitution that stood in stark contrast to most European regimes. The successful revolution was the only blow to Britain's increasing dominance in world affairs in the eighteenth century, and as such it was another aspect of the power rivalries existing at that time. Yet many Europeans saw the American War of Independence, or the American Revolution (1775–1783), as a triumph for Enlightenment ideas. As one German writer exclaimed in 1777, an American victory would give "greater scope to the Enlightenment, new keenness to the thinking of peoples and new life to the spirit of liberty."

The American revolutionary leaders had been influenced by a common Atlantic civilization; they participated in the Enlightenment and shared political ideas with the opposition Whigs in Britain. Supporters demonstrated for Wilkes in South Carolina and Boston, and the South Carolina legislature donated a substantial sum to the Society of Supporters of the Bill of Rights. In the 1760s and

1770s, both British and American opposition leaders became convinced that the British government was growing increasingly corrupt and despotic. British radicals wanted to reform Parliament so the voices of a broader, more representative segment of the population would be heard. The colonies had no representatives in Parliament, and the colonists claimed that "no taxation without representation" should be allowed. Indeed, they denied that Parliament had any jurisdiction over the colonies, insisting that the king govern them through colonial legislatures and recognize their traditional British liberties. The failure of the "Wilkes and Liberty" campaign to produce concrete results convinced many Americans that Parliament was hopelessly tainted and that they would have to stand up for their rights as British subjects.

The British colonies remained loyal to the crown until Parliament's encroachment on their autonomy, and the elimination of the French threat at the end of the Seven Years' War transformed colonial attitudes. Unconsciously perhaps, the colonies had begun to form a separate nation. Their economies generally flourished in the eighteenth century, and between 1750 and 1776 their population almost doubled. More slaves were imported during that quarter-century than at any other time in American history. With the British clamoring for lower taxes and the colonists paying only a fraction of the tax rate levied on the Britons at home, Parliament passed new taxes, including the Stamp Act in 1765, which required a special tax stamp on all legal documents and publications. After violent rioting in the colonies, the tax was repealed, but in 1773 a new Tea Act revived colonial resistance, which culminated in the so-called Boston Tea Party of 1773. Colonists dressed as Indians boarded British ships and dumped the imported tea (by this time an enormously popular beverage) into Boston's harbor. The British government tried to clamp down on the unrest, but British troops in the colonies soon found themselves fighting locally organized militias.

Political opposition in the American colonies turned belligerent when Britain threatened to use force to maintain control. In 1774, the First Continental Congress convened, composed of delegates from all the colonies, and unsuccessfully petitioned the crown for redress. The next year the Second Continental Congress organized an army with George Washington in command. After actual fighting had begun, in 1776, the congress proclaimed the Declaration of Independence. An eloquent statement of the American cause written principally by Thomas Jefferson, a delegate from Virginia, the Declaration of Independence was couched in the language of universal human rights, which enlightened Europeans could be expected to understand. George III denounced the American "traitors and rebels." But European newspapers enthusiastically reported on every American response to "the cruel acts of oppression they have been made to suffer." Two years after the Declaration was issued, France boosted the American cause by entering on the colonists' side in 1778. Spain, too, saw an opportunity to check the growing power of Britain, though without actually endorsing American independence out of fear of the response of its Latin American colonies. Spain declared war on Britain in 1779. The following year, Britain declared war on the Dutch Republic in retaliation for Dutch support of the rebels. The worldwide conflict that resulted was more than Britain could handle. The American colonies achieved their independence in the peace treaty of 1783.

The newly independent states still faced the challenge of republican self-government. The Articles of Confederation, drawn up in 1777 as a provisional constitution, proved weak because they gave the central government few powers. In 1787, a constitutional convention met in Philadelphia to draft a new constitution. It established a two-house legislature, an indirectly elected president, and an independent judiciary. The Constitution's preamble insisted explicitly, for the first time in history, that government derived its power solely from the people and did not depend on divine right or on the tradition of royalty or aristocracy. The new educated elite of the eighteenth century had now created a government based on a "social contract" among male, property-owning, white citizens. It was by no means a complete democracy, and women and slaves were excluded from political participation. But the new government represented a radical departure from European models. In 1791, the Bill of Rights, outlining the essential rights (such as freedom of speech) that the government could never overturn, was appended to the Constitution. Although slavery continued in the American republic, the new emphasis on rights helped fuel a movement for its abolition in both Britain and the United States.

Interest in the new republic was greatest in France. The U.S. Constitution and various state constitutions were published in French with commentary by leading thinkers. Even more important in the long run were the effects of the American war. Dutch losses to Great Britain aroused a widespread movement for political reform in the Dutch Republic, and debts incurred by France in supporting the American colonies would soon force the French monarchy to the edge of bankruptcy and then to revolution. Ultimately, the entire European system of royal rule would be challenged.

REVIEW Why did public opinion become a new factor in politics in the second half of the eighteenth century?

Conclusion

The American Revolution was the most profound practical result of the general European movement known as the Enlightenment. When Thomas Jefferson looked back many years later on the Declaration of Independence, he said he hoped it would be "the signal of arousing men to burst the chains under which monkish ignorance and superstition had persuaded them to bind themselves."

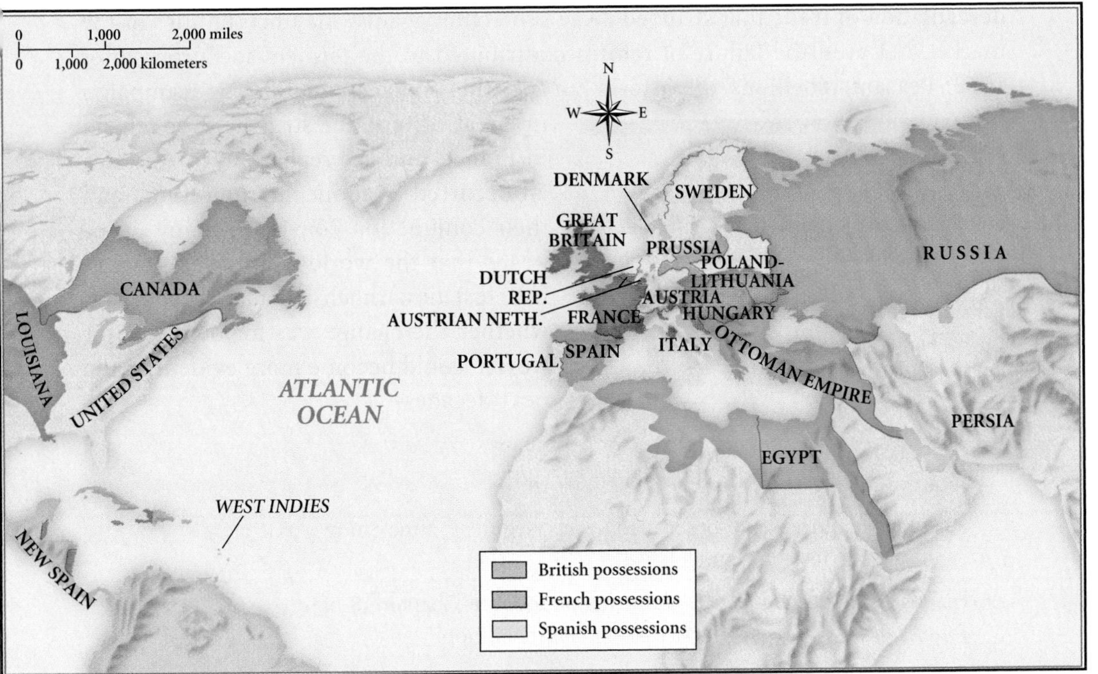

Mapping the West Europe and the World, c. 1780
Although Great Britain lost control over its North American colonies, which became the new United States, European influence on the rest of the world grew dramatically in the eighteenth century. The slave trade linked European ports to African slave-trading outposts and to plantations in the Caribbean, South America, and North America. The European countries on the Atlantic Ocean benefited most from this trade. Yet almost all of Africa, China, and Japan and large parts of India still resisted European incursion, and the Ottoman Empire, with its massive territories, still presented Europe with a formidable military challenge.

What began as a cosmopolitan movement of a few intellectuals in the first half of the eighteenth century reached a relatively wide audience among the educated elite of men and women. The spirit of reform swept from the salons and coffeehouses into the halls of government. Reasoned, scientific inquiry into the causes of social misery and laws defending individual rights and freedoms gained adherents everywhere.

For most Europeans, however, Enlightenment remained a promise rather than a reality. Rulers such as Catherine the Great had every intention of retaining their full, often unchecked, powers, even as they corresponded with leading philosophes, announced support for their causes, and entertained them at their courts. Moreover, would-be reformers often found themselves thwarted by the resistance of nobles, by the priorities rulers gave to waging wars, or by popular resistance to deregulation of trade that stripped away protection against the uncertainties of the market. Yet even the failure of reform contributed to the ferment in Europe after 1770. Peasant rebellions in eastern Europe, the "Wilkes and Liberty" campaign in Great Britain, the struggle over reform in France, and the revolution in America all occurred at about the same time, and their conjunction convinced many Europeans that the world was in fact changing. Just how much it had changed, and whether the change was for better or for worse, would become more evident in the next decades.

CHAPTER REVIEW QUESTIONS

1. Why would rulers feel ambivalent about the Enlightenment, supporting reform on the one hand, while clamping down on political dissent on the other?
2. Which major developments in the second half of the eighteenth century ran counter to the influence of the Enlightenment?

For practice quizzes and other study tools, see the Online Study Guide at bedfordstmartins.com/huntconcise.

For primary-source material from this period, see Chapter 18 of *Sources of* THE MAKING OF THE WEST, Third Edition.

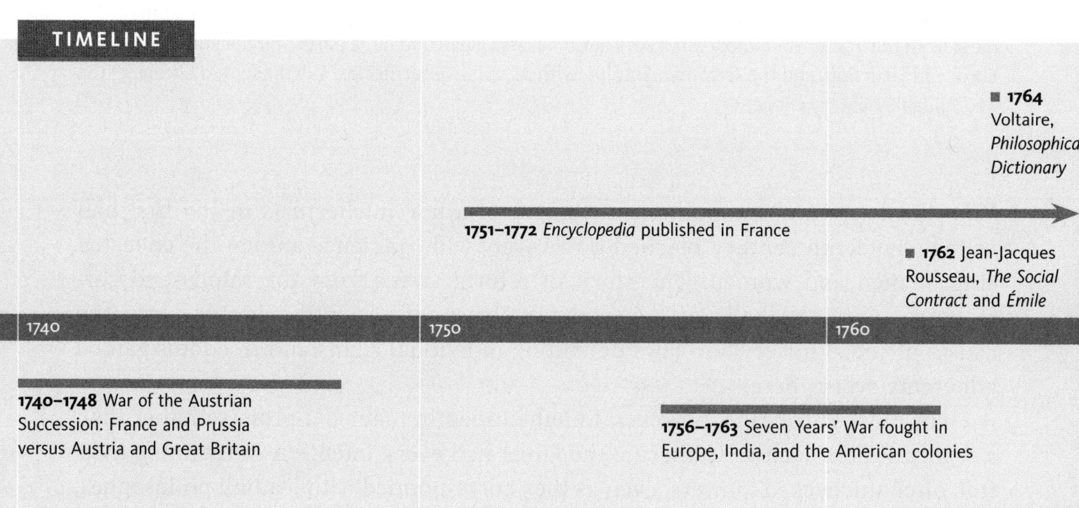

Suggested References

The interpretive study by Gay remains useful, but the Kors volumes offer the most up-to-date views on the Enlightenment. As the autobiography of Equiano (Allison) shows, the influence of new ideas spread far and wide.

*Allison, Robert J., ed. *The Interesting Narrative of the Life of Olaudah Equiano*. 2006.

Beales, Derek. *Enlightenment and Reform in Eighteenth-Century Europe*. 2005.

Cash, Arthur H. *John Wilkes: The Scandalous Father of Civil Liberty*. 2006.

Catherine the Great: http://russia.nypl.org/level4.html

Gay, Peter. *The Enlightenment: An Interpretation*. 2 vols. 1966, 1969.

Hull, Isabel V. *Sexuality, State, and Civil Society in Germany, 1700–1815*. 1996.

Kors, Alan Charles, ed. *Encyclopedia of the Enlightenment*. 4 vols. 2003.

Lessing, Gotthold Ephraim. *Nathan the Wise*. Ed. Ronald Schechter. 2004.

McMahon, Darrin M. *Enemies of the Enlightenment: The French Counter-Enlightenment and the Making of Modernity*. 2001.

Mozart Project: http://www.mozartproject.org

*Rakove, Jack N. *Declaring Rights: A Brief History with Documents*. 1998.

Seven Years' War: http://www.historyworld.net/wrldhis/PlainTextHistories.asp?historyid=aa66

Thompson, E. P. *Whigs and Hunters: The Origin of the Black Act*. 1975.

Venturi, Franco. *The End of the Old Regime in Europe, 1768–1776: The First Crisis*. Trans. R. Burr Litchfield. 1989.

*Voltaire. *Candide*. Ed. and trans. Daniel Gordon. 1999.

Voltaire Foundation: http://www.voltaire.ox.ac.uk

1770 | 1780 | 1790

- **1770** Louis XV of France fails to break the power of the French law courts
- **1772** First partition of Poland
- **1773** Pugachev rebellion of Russian peasants
- **1775** Flour War in France
- **1776** American Declaration of Independence from Great Britain; Adam Smith, *The Wealth of Nations*
- **1780** Joseph II of Austria assumes sole power and undertakes wide-reaching reform; Gordon (anti-Catholic) riots in London
- **1781** Immanuel Kant, *The Critique of Pure Reason;* Leipzig opens first public orchestra hall
- **1785** Catherine the Great's Charter of the Nobility grants nobles exclusive control over their serfs in exchange for subservience to the state
- **1787** Delegates from the states draft a new U.S. Constitution

16

The French Revolution and Napoleon

1789–1815

On October 5, 1789, a crowd of several thousand women marched in a drenching rain twelve miles from the center of Paris to Versailles. They demanded the king's help in securing more grain for the hungry and his reassurance that he did not intend to resist the emerging revolutionary movement. Joined by thousands of men who came from Paris to reinforce them, they broke into the royal family's private apartments the next morning. To prevent further bloodshed—two of the royal bodyguards had already been killed and their heads paraded on pikes—the king agreed to move his family and his government back to Paris. A dramatic procession guarded by thousands of ordinary men and women made its slow way back to the city. The people's proud display of cannons and pikes underlined the fundamental transformation that was occurring. The women's march to Versailles had forced the king of France to respond to their grievances. The French monarchy was in danger, and if such a powerful and long-lasting institution could come under fire, could any monarch of Europe rest easy?

Women's March to Versailles
Thousands of prints broadcast the events of the French Revolution to the public in France and elsewhere. They varied from fine art engravings signed by the artists to anonymous simple woodblock prints. This colored etching shows a crowd of armed women marching to Versailles on October 5, 1789, to confront the king. The sight of armed women frightened many observers and demonstrated that the Revolution was not only a men's affair. *(The Granger Collection, NY.)*

The French Revolution first grabbed the attention of the entire world because it seemed to promise universal human rights, constitutional government, and broad-based political participation. In the words of its most famous slogan, it pledged "Liberty, Equality, and Fraternity" for all. The revolutionaries did not stop with the establishment of constitutional monarchy, however: they abolished nobility, executed the king and queen, established a republic for the first time in French history, and gave the vote to almost all adult men. At the same time, the Revolution inaugurated a new cycle of violence and intimidation. When the revolutionaries encountered resistance to their programs, they set up a government of terror to compel obedience. Some historians therefore see in the French Revolution the origins of modern totalitarianism—that is, governments that try to control every aspect of life, including daily activities, while limiting all forms of political dissent.

The Revolution might have remained a strictly French affair if war had not involved the rest of Europe. After 1792, huge French republican armies, fueled by patriotic nationalism, marched across Europe. These campaigns promised Europeans liberation from traditional monarchies, but in the end they delivered old-fashioned conquest and annexation benefiting France. Nevertheless, French victories spread revolutionary ideas far and wide, from the colonies in the Caribbean, where the first successful slave revolt established the republic of Haiti, to Poland and Egypt.

The army's success ultimately undermined the republic and made possible the rise of Napoleon Bonaparte, a remarkable young general from the French-controlled island of Corsica, who brought France more wars, more conquests, and a form of military dictatorship. By 1812, Emperor Napoleon I ruled over an empire greater than any Europe had seen since Roman times. Eventually, resistance to the French armies and the ever-mounting costs of military glory toppled him, but not before he had established himself as an almost mythic figure. The French Revolution produced many surprises; Napoleon Bonaparte was the most astonishing of them.

CHAPTER FOCUS QUESTION Did Napoleon represent the continuation or end of the French Revolution?

The Revolution of Rights and Reason

France was not the only country experiencing upheaval. Between 1787 and 1789, revolts in the name of liberty also broke out in the Dutch Republic, the Austrian Netherlands (present-day Belgium and Luxembourg), and Poland. At the same time, the newly independent United States of America prepared a new federal constitution. Historians have sometimes referred to these revolts as the "Atlantic revolutions" because so many protest movements arose in countries on both sides of the North Atlantic in the late 1700s. Internal divisions and external interference doomed the Dutch, Belgian, and Polish revolts: the Prussians invaded the Dutch Republic and restored the stadholder, the Austrian emperor Leopold II reinstated Austrian authority in Belgium, and Catherine the Great engineered the failure of the new Polish constitution of 1791. Not only was France the richest, most powerful, and most populous state in western Europe, but its revolution lasted longer, brought about more startling changes, and caused more violence. It shaped European politics for generations afterward.

Origins of the French Revolution, 1787–1789

On the surface the French monarchy in the late 1780s seemed as strong as ever. After suffering humiliation at the hands of the British in the Seven Years' War (1756–1763), the French had regained international prestige by supporting the victorious

Americans. Success came at a high price, however. About half of the French national budget went to paying interest on the debt that had accumulated over the years of involvement in the American War of Independence. In contrast to Great Britain, which had a national bank to help raise loans for the government, the French government lived off relatively short-term, high-interest loans from private sources, including Swiss banks, government annuities, and advances from tax collectors. For years the French government had been trying unsuccessfully to modernize the tax system to make it more equitable. The peasants bore the greatest burden of taxes and resented the exemptions enjoyed by the nobles and clergy. Private contractors collected many taxes and pocketed a large share of the proceeds. With the growing support of public opinion, the bond and annuity holders from the middle and upper classes now demanded a clearer system of fiscal accountability.

Faced with budget shortfalls and growing criticism of Queen Marie-Antoinette's personal spending, Louis XVI (r. 1774–1792) tried every available avenue to raise funds. In 1787, he submitted proposals for reform to the Assembly of Notables, a group of handpicked nobles, clergymen, and officials. When this group refused to cooperate, the king presented his plan for a more uniform land tax to his old rival, the parlement of Paris. When it too refused, he ordered the parlement judges into exile in the provinces. Overnight, the judges (members of the nobility because of the offices they held) became popular heroes for resisting the king's "tyranny"; in reality, however, the judges, like the notables, wanted reform only on their own terms. Louis finally gave in to demands that he call a meeting of the **Estates General**, which had last met 175 years before.

The calling of the Estates General electrified public opinion. Who would determine the fate of the nation? There were three estates, or orders, in the Estates General. The deputies in the First Estate represented some 100,000 clergy of the Catholic church, which owned about 10 percent of the land and collected its own taxes (the tithe) on peasants. The deputies of the Second Estate represented the nobility, about 400,000 men and women who owned about 25 percent of the land and collected seigneurial dues and rents from their peasant tenants. The deputies of the Third Estate represented everyone else, at least 95 percent of the nation. In 1614, at the last meeting of the Estates General, each order had voted separately, and either the clergy or the nobility could therefore veto any decision of the Third Estate. Before the elections to the Estates General in 1789, the king agreed to double the number of deputies for the Third Estate (making them equal in number to the other two combined), but he left it to the Estates General to decide whether the estates would continue to vote separately by order rather than by individual head. Voting by order would conserve the traditional powers of the clergy and nobility; voting by head would give the Third Estate an advantage because many clergymen and even some nobles sympathized with the Third Estate.

In this excited political climate, the state's censorship apparatus broke down. Pamphleteers by the hundreds denounced the traditional privileges of the nobility and clergy and called for voting by head rather than by order. In the winter and

The Third Estate Awakens

This print, produced after the fall of the Bastille (notice the two heads raised on pikes outside the prison), shows a clergyman (First Estate) and a nobleman (Second Estate) alarmed by the awakening of the commoner (Third Estate). The Third Estate breaks the chains of oppression and arms itself to battle for its rights. In what ways does this print draw attention to the social conflicts that lay behind the political struggles in the Estates General? **For more help analyzing this image, see the visual activity for this chapter in the Online Study Guide at** bedfordstmartins.com/huntconcise. (Réunion des Musées Nationaux/Art Resource, NY.)

spring of 1789, thousands of men (and a few women by proxy) held meetings to elect deputies and write down their grievances. The effect was immediate. Although educated men dominated the meetings at the regional level, the humblest peasants also voted in their villages and burst forth with complaints, especially about taxes. As one villager lamented, "The last crust of bread has been taken from us." The grievance lists demanded fairer distribution of taxes, constitutional recognition of rights, revision of the law codes, and a variety of other reforms. The meetings and the compiling of grievances raised expectations that the Estates General would help the king to solve all the nation's ills.

These new hopes soared just at the moment France experienced a dangerous food shortage. Bad weather damaged the harvest of 1788, causing bread prices to rise in many places in the spring and summer of 1789 and threatening starvation for the poorest people. A serious slump in textile production had been causing massive unemployment since 1786. Hundreds of thousands of textile workers were out of work and hungry, adding another volatile element to an already tense situation.

When some twelve hundred deputies journeyed to the king's palace of Versailles for the opening of the Estates General in May 1789, many readers avidly followed the developments in newspapers that sprouted up overnight. Although most nobles insisted on voting by order, the deputies of the Third Estate refused to proceed on that basis. After six weeks of stalemate, on June 17, 1789, the deputies of the Third Estate took unilateral action and declared themselves and whoever would join them the National Assembly, in which each deputy would vote as an individual. Two days later, the clergy voted by a narrow margin to join them. Barred from their meeting hall on June 20, the deputies met on a nearby tennis court and swore an oath not to disband until they had given France a constitution that reflected their newly declared authority. This "tennis court oath" expressed the determination of the Third Estate to carry through a constitutional revolution.

At first Louis appeared to agree to the new representative assembly, but he also ordered thousands of soldiers to march to Paris. The deputies who supported the new National Assembly feared a plot by the king and high-ranking nobles to arrest them and disperse the Assembly. "Everyone is convinced that the approach of the troops covers some violent design," one deputy wrote home. Their fears were confirmed when on July 11 the king fired Jacques Necker, his finance minister and the one high-ranking official regarded as sympathetic to the deputies' cause.

The furious reaction in Paris to Necker's dismissal and the threat of military force changed the course of the French Revolution. When the news spread, the common people in Paris began to arm themselves and attack places where either grain or arms were thought to be stored (Map 16.1). A deputy in Versailles reported home: "Today all of the evils overwhelm France, and we are between despotism, carnage, and famine." On July 14, 1789, an armed crowd marched on the Bastille, the fortified prison that symbolized royal authority. After a chaotic battle in which one hundred armed citizens died, the prison officials surrendered. The angry crowd shot and stabbed the governor of the prison and flaunted his head on a pike.

The fall of the Bastille (an event now commemorated as a French national holiday) set an important precedent. The common people showed themselves willing to intervene violently at a crucial political moment. All over France, food riots turned into local revolts. Local governments were forced out of power and replaced by committees of "patriots" loyal to the revolutionary cause. The patriots relied on newly formed National Guard units composed of civilians. One of their first duties was to calm the peasants in the countryside, who feared that the beggars and vagrants crowding the roads might be part of an aristocratic plot to starve the people by burning crops or barns. In some places, the **Great Fear** (the term used by historians to describe this rural panic) turned into peasant attacks on aristocrats or on seigneurial records of peasants' dues kept in the lord's château. The king's

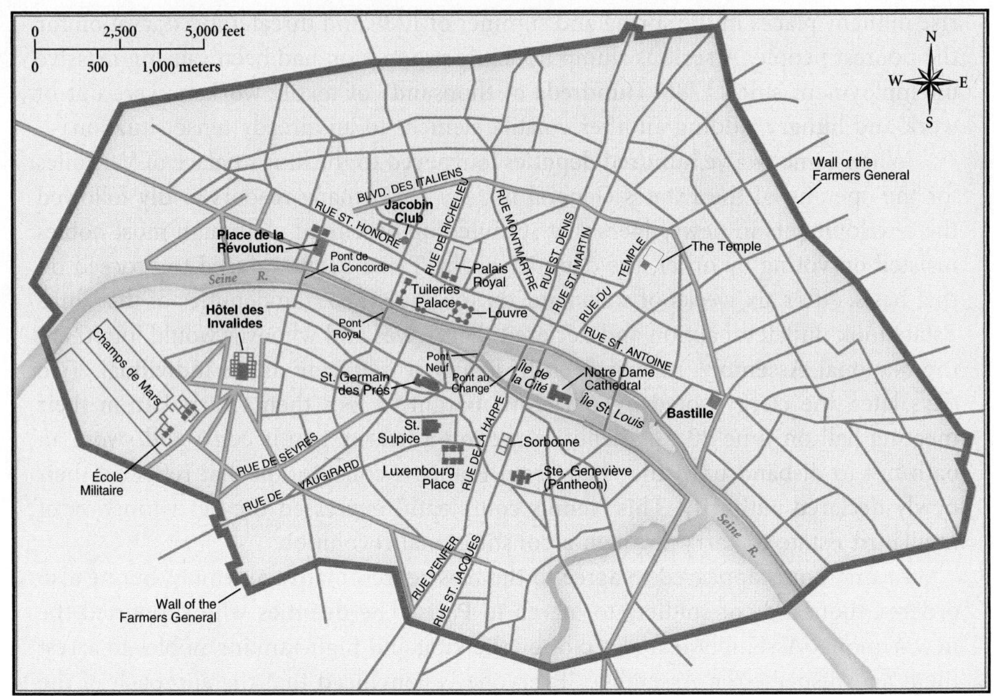

Map 16.1 Revolutionary Paris, 1789
The French Revolution began with the fall of the Bastille on July 14, 1789. The huge fortified prison was located in a working-class neighborhood on the eastern side of the city. Before attacking the Bastille, crowds had torn down many of the customs booths located in the wall of the Farmers General (the private company in charge of tax collection) and had taken the weapons stored in the Hôtel des Invalides, a veterans' hospital on the western side of the city where the upper classes lived. During the Revolution, executions took place on the Place de la Révolution, now called the Place de la Concorde.

government began to crumble. One of Louis XVI's brothers and many other leading aristocrats fled into exile. In Paris, the Marquis de Lafayette, a hero of the American War of Independence and a noble deputy in the National Assembly, became commander of the new National Guard. The Revolution thus had its first heroes, its first victims, and its first enemies.

From Monarchy to Republic

Until July 1789, the French Revolution followed a course much like that of the protest movements in the Low Countries. Unlike the Dutch and Belgian uprisings, however, the French Revolution did not come to a quick end. The French revolutionaries first tried to establish a constitutional monarchy based on the Enlightenment principles of human rights and rational government. This effort failed when the king attempted to raise a counterrevolutionary army. When war broke out in 1792, new tensions culminated in a second revolution on August 10, 1792,

Fall of the Bastille
The Bastille prison is shown here in all its imposing grandeur. The moment depicted is that of the surrender of the fortress's governor, Bernard René de Launay. Because so many of the besieging citizens had been killed (only one of the defenders died), popular anger ran high, and de Launay was to be the sacrificial victim. As the hastily formed citizens' guard marched him off to city hall, huge crowds taunted and spat at him. When he lashed out at one of the men nearest him, he was stabbed, shot, and then beheaded. The head was displayed as a trophy on a pike held high above the crowd. Royal authority had been successfully challenged and even humiliated. (The Granger Collection, NY.)

that deposed the king and established a republic in which all power rested in an elected legislature.

Before drafting a new constitution, the deputies of the National Assembly had to confront growing violence in the countryside, as the Great Fear sparked peasant attacks on their lords' castles and records. In response to peasant unrest, on the night of August 4, 1789, noble deputies announced their willingness to give up their tax exemptions and seigneurial dues. By the end of the night, amid wild enthusiasm, dozens of deputies had come to the podium to relinquish the tax exemptions of their own professional groups, towns, or provinces. The National Assembly decreed the abolition of what it called "the feudal regime"—that is, it freed the few remaining serfs and eliminated all special privileges in matters of taxation, including all seigneurial dues on the land (a few days later, the deputies insisted on financial compensation for some of these dues, but most peasants refused to pay). The peasants had achieved their goals. The Assembly also mandated equality of opportunity in access to official posts. Talent, rather than birth, was to be the key to success. Enlightenment principles were beginning to become law.

Three weeks later, the deputies drew up the **Declaration of the Rights of Man and of the Citizen** as a preamble to the constitution. In words reminiscent of the American Declaration of Independence, whose principal author, Thomas Jefferson, was in Paris at the time, it proclaimed, "Men are born and remain free and equal in rights." The Declaration granted freedom of religion, freedom of the press, equality of taxation, and equality before the law. By pronouncing all "men" free and equal, the Declaration immediately created new dilemmas. Did women have equal rights with men? What about free blacks in the colonies? How could slavery be justified if all men were born free? Did religious toleration of Protestants and Jews include equal political rights? Women never received the right to vote during the French Revolution, though Protestant and Jewish men did. Women were theoretically citizens under civil law but without the right to full political participation.

Some women did not accept their exclusion, viewing it as a betrayal of the promised new order. In addition to joining demonstrations, such as the march to Versailles in October 1789 described at the beginning of this chapter, women wrote petitions, published tracts, and organized political clubs to demand more participation. In her Declaration of the Rights of Women of 1791, Olympe de Gouges (1748–1793) played on the language of the official Declaration to make the point that women should also be included. In Article I, she announced, "Woman is born free and lives equal to man in her rights." Unresponsive to such calls for women's equality, the National Assembly gave voting rights only to white men who paid a minimum level of taxation. The constitution defined them as the "active citizens"; all others were "passive."

Despite these limitations, France became a constitutional monarchy, in which the king served simply as the leading state functionary. A one-house legislature was responsible for making laws. The king could hold up the enactment of laws but could not veto them absolutely. The nobles not only lost their tax exemptions, but on June 19, 1790, the Assembly abolished all titles of nobility. The deputies replaced the old administrative divisions of the provinces with a national system of eighty-three regional departments (*départements*) with identical administrative and legal structures. All officials were elected; no offices could be bought and sold. The deputies also abolished the old taxes and replaced them with new ones that were supposed to be uniformly levied. The National Assembly had difficulty collecting taxes, however, because many people had expected a substantial cut in the tax rate. The new administrative system survived, nonetheless, and these departments are still the basic units of the French state today.

When the deputies turned to reforming the Catholic church, they created enduring conflicts. Motivated partly by the ongoing financial crisis, the Assembly confiscated all the church's property and promised to pay clerical salaries in return. The Civil Constitution of the Clergy passed in July 1790 set pay scales for the clergy and provided that the voters elect their own parish priests and bishops just as they elected other officials. Impounded church property served as a guarantee for the new paper money, called assignats, issued by the government. The government began to sell the church lands to the highest bidders in state auctions. The sales increased the landholdings of wealthy city dwellers and prosperous peasants but cut the ground out from under the assignats. Convinced that monastic life encouraged idleness and a decline in the nation's population, the deputies also outlawed any future monastic vows and encouraged monks and nuns to return to private life on state pensions.

Faced with resistance to these changes, the National Assembly in November 1790 required all clergy to swear an oath of loyalty to the Civil Constitution of the Clergy. Pope Pius VI in Rome condemned the constitution, and half of the French clergy refused to take the oath. The oath of allegiance permanently divided the Catholic population, which had to choose between loyalty to the old church and commitment to the Revolution with its "constitutional" church. The revolutionary government passed laws against the clergy who refused to take the oath, forcing some into exile and executing others as traitors. Riots and demonstrations led by women confronted many of the oath-taking priests who showed up to replace those who refused.

Louis XVI deeply resented the new limits on his powers and in particular the changes imposed on the Catholic church. On June 20, 1791, the royal family escaped in disguise from the Tuileries palace in Paris and fled to the eastern border of France, where they hoped to gain support from the Austrian emperor Leopold II (r. 1790–1792), the brother of Marie-Antoinette. The plans went awry when a postmaster recognized the king from his portrait on the new French money, and the royal family was arrested at Varennes, forty miles from the border with the Austrian Netherlands. The National Assembly tried to depict this incident as a kidnapping, but the "flight to Varennes" touched off demonstrations in Paris against the royal family, whom some now regarded as traitors. Cartoons depicting the royal family as animals being returned "to the stable" circulated among the public.

The constitution finally completed in 1791 provided for the immediate election of the new Legislative Assembly. The status of the king might have remained uncertain if war had not intervened, but by early 1792 everyone seemed intent on war with Austria. Louis and Marie-Antoinette hoped that war would lead to the definitive defeat of the Revolution, whereas the deputies in the new Assembly who favored a republic believed that war would reveal the king's treachery and lead to his downfall. On April 20, 1792, Louis declared war on Austria. Prussia immediately entered on the Austrian side. Thousands of French aristocrats, including two-thirds of the army officer corps, had already emigrated, including both the king's brothers, and they were gathering along France's eastern border in expectation of joining Leopold's counterrevolutionary army.

When fighting broke out in 1792, all the powers expected a brief and relatively contained war. Instead, it would continue despite brief interruptions for the next twenty-three years. War had an immediate radicalizing effect on French politics. When the French armies proved woefully unprepared for battle, the authority of the Legislative Assembly came under fire. In June 1792, an angry crowd invaded the hall of the Assembly in Paris and threatened the royal family. When the Prussians crossed the border and advanced on Paris, the Prussian commander, the duke of Brunswick, issued a manifesto announcing that Paris would be destroyed if the royal family suffered any violence.

The ordinary people of Paris did not passively await their fate. Known as **sans-culottes** (without breeches)—because men who worked with their hands wore long trousers rather than the knee breeches of the upper classes—they had followed every twist and turn in revolutionary fortunes. Political clubs had multiplied since the founding in 1789 of the first and most influential of them, the **Jacobin Club**, named after the former monastery in Paris where the club first met. Every local district in Paris had its club, where men and women listened to the news of the day and discussed their opinions. Faced with the threat of military retaliation and frustrated with the inaction of the Legislative Assembly, the sans-culottes organized an insurrection on August 10, 1792, and attacked the Tuileries palace, where the king resided. The Legislative Assembly ordered new elections, this time by universal male suffrage (no wealth qualifications as in the constitution of 1791), for a National Convention that would write a new constitution.

Before the National Convention could meet, violence exploded again in early September 1792 when the Prussians approached Paris. Hastily gathered mobs stormed the overflowing prisons to seek out traitors who might help the enemy. In an atmosphere of near hysteria, eleven hundred inmates were killed, including many innocent people. The princess of Lamballe, one of the queen's favorites, was hacked to pieces, and her mutilated body was displayed beneath the windows where the royal family was kept under guard. These "September massacres" showed the dark side of popular revolution, in which the common people demanded instant revenge on supposed enemies and conspirators.

The Execution of Louis XVI

When it met, the National Convention abolished the monarchy and, on September 22, 1792, established the first republic in French history. The republic would answer only to the people, not to any royal authority. The new government faced a dire situation. It was supposed to write a new constitution for the republic while fighting a war with external enemies and confronting increasing resistance at home. The Revolution had divided the population: for some, it had not gone far enough toward providing food, land, and retribution against enemies; for others, it had gone too far by dismantling the church and the monarchy. The French people had never known any government other than monarchy. Only half the population could read and write at even a basic level. In this situation, symbolic actions became very important. Any public sign of monarchy was at risk, and revolutionaries soon pulled down statues of kings and burned reminders of the former regime.

The fate of Louis XVI and the future direction of the republic divided the deputies elected to the National Convention. Most of the deputies were middle-class lawyers and professionals who had developed their ardent republican beliefs in the national network of Jacobin Clubs. After the fall of the monarchy in August 1792, however, the Jacobins divided into two factions: the Girondins and the Montagnards. The Girondins (named after a department in southwestern France, the Gironde, which provided some of its leading orators) resented the growing power of Parisian militants and tried to appeal to the departments outside Paris. The Montagnards (French for "men of the mountain," so called because they sat in the highest seats) were closely allied with the Paris militants and willing to enact the extreme measures urged on them by the sans-culottes.

The first showdown between the Girondins and the Montagnards occurred during the trial of the king in December 1792. Although the Girondins agreed that the king was guilty of treason, many of them argued for clemency, exile, or a popular referendum on his fate. After a long and bitter debate, the deputies voted by a very narrow majority to execute the king. Louis XVI went to the guillotine on January 21, 1793, sharing the fate of Charles I of England in 1649. "We have just convinced ourselves that a king is only a man," wrote one newspaper, "and that no man is above the law." The Girondins lasted only a few months longer. On June 2, 1793, twenty-nine Girondin deputies were arrested after militants in Paris organized an armed demonstration against them and invaded the National Convention. Dissent, even among republicans, could now prove fatal.

The Execution of King Louis XVI
Louis XVI was executed by order of the National Convention on January 21, 1793. In this print, the executioner shows the severed head to the National Guard arranged in orderly silence around the scaffold. (Mary Evans Picture Library.)

European elites reacted with horror to the execution of Louis XVI. The British government suppressed the many corresponding societies made up of democrats and reformers who had established links with the Paris Jacobins and charged some of their leaders with sedition. Ireland posed even greater problems to the British government because Catholics and Presbyterians, both excluded from the vote, joined together in the Society of United Irishmen in 1791. In the United States, opinion fiercely divided on the virtues of the French Revolution. In Sweden, when Gustavus III (r. 1771–1792) was assassinated by a nobleman, the king's son and heir, Gustavus IV (r. 1792–1809), believed that the French Jacobins had sanctioned the killing. Spain's royal government suppressed all news from France, fearing that it might ignite the spirit of revolt. This fear was not misplaced; even in Russia, for instance, 278 outbreaks of peasant unrest occurred between 1796 and 1798. One Russian landlord complained, "This is the self-same . . . spirit of insubordination and independence, which has spread through all Europe."

REVIEW Why did the French Revolution not stop with the installation of a constitutional monarchy?

The British Reaction to the French Revolution
In this caricature, James Gillray satirizes the French version of liberty. Gillray produced thousands of political caricatures. How would you interpret the message of this print? (© Copyright The Trustees of The British Museum.)

Terror and Resistance

The execution of the king and the arrest of the Girondins did not end the new regime's problems. The continuing war required ever more men and money, and the introduction of a national draft provoked massive resistance in some parts of France. The new republic's armies fought not only in Europe and within France but also in the Caribbean, where a major slave uprising threatened French control. In response to growing pressures, the National Convention set up a highly centralized government designed to provide food, direct the war effort, and punish counterrevolutionaries. Thus began the **Terror**, in which the guillotine became the most terrifying instrument of a government that suppressed almost every form of dissent. The leader of this government, Maximilien Robespierre (1758–1794), aimed to create a "Republic of Virtue," in which the government would teach, or force, citizens to become virtuous republicans through a massive program of political reeducation. These policies only increased divisions, which ultimately led to Robespierre's fall from power and to a dismantling of government by terror.

The Guillotine
Before 1789, only nobles were decapitated if condemned to death; commoners were usually hanged. J. I. Guillotin, a professor of anatomy and a deputy for the Third Estate in the National Assembly, first proposed equalization of the death penalty. He also suggested that a mechanical device be constructed for decapitation, leading to the instrument's association with his name. The Assembly decreed decapitation as the death penalty in June 1791. Another physician, A. Louis, actually invented the guillotine. Its use began in April 1792 and did not end until 1981, when the French government abolished the death penalty. Although it was invented to make death equal and painless, the guillotine disturbed many observers; its mechanical operation and efficiency—the executioner merely pulled up the blade by a cord and then released it—seemed somehow inhumane. Nonetheless, the guillotine fascinated as much as it repelled. Reproduced in miniature, painted on snuffboxes and china, worn as jewelry, and even serving as a toy, the guillotine became part of popular culture, celebrated as the people's avenger by supporters of the Revolution and vilified as the preeminent symbol of the Terror by opponents. (Réunion des Musées Nationaux/Art Resource, NY.)

Robespierre, War, and Slavery

Setting the course for government and the war increasingly fell to the twelve-member Committee of Public Safety, set up by the Convention on April 6, 1793. When Robespierre, one of the Montagnards, was elected to the committee three months later, he became in effect its guiding spirit and the chief spokesman of the Revolution. A lawyer from northern France known as "the incorruptible" for his stern honesty and fierce dedication to democratic ideals, Robespierre remains one of the most controversial figures in world history because of his association with the Terror. In September 1793, another demonstration organized by Parisian militants demanded that the Convention "put Terror on the agenda." Although he originally opposed the death penalty and the war (he also opposed slavery), Robespierre took the lead in implementing emergency measures, including death for those, such as the Girondins, who opposed the committee's policies. At the same time, he maneuvered to clamp down on popular demonstrations.

Like many other educated eighteenth-century men, Robespierre read the classics of republicanism, from the ancient Roman writers Tacitus and Plutarch to the Enlightenment thinkers Montesquieu and Rousseau. But he took them a step further. He spoke eloquently about "the theory of revolutionary government" as "the war of liberty against its enemies." He defended the people's right to democratic government, while in practice he supported many measures that restricted their liberties. He personally favored a free-market economy, as did almost all middle-class deputies, but in this time of crisis he was willing to enact price controls and requisitioning. The Convention had organized paramilitary bands called "revolutionary armies" to hunt down hoarders and political suspects, and on September 29, 1793, it established the General Maximum on wages and the prices of thirty-nine essential commodities. In a speech to the Convention, Robespierre explained the necessity of a government by terror: "The first maxim of your policies must be to lead the people by reason and the people's enemies by terror. . . . Without virtue, terror is deadly; without terror, virtue is impotent." *Terror* was not an idle term; it seemed to imply that the goal of democracy justified what we now call totalitarian means—that is, the suppression of all dissent.

The Committee of Public Safety did everything possible to ensure its control. It sent deputies out "on mission" to purge unreliable officials and organize the war effort. In the first universal draft of men in history, every unmarried man and childless widower between the ages of eighteen and twenty-five was declared eligible for conscription. Revolutionary tribunals set up in Paris and provincial centers tried political suspects. In October 1793, the Revolutionary Tribunal in Paris convicted Marie-Antoinette of treason and sent her to the guillotine. The Girondin leaders were also guillotined, as was Olympe de Gouges. The government confiscated all the property of convicted traitors.

The government won its greatest success on the battlefield. As of April 1793, France faced war with Austria, Prussia, Great Britain, Spain, Sardinia, and the Dutch

Republic—all fearful of the impact of revolutionary ideals on their own populations. To face this daunting coalition of forces, the French republic tapped a new and potent source of power—nationalist pride—in decrees mobilizing young and old alike: "The young men will go to battle; married men will forge arms and transport provisions; women will make tents and clothing and serve in hospitals; children will make bandages." Forges were set up in the parks and gardens of Paris to produce thousands of guns, and citizens everywhere helped collect saltpeter, a rock salt used to make gunpowder.

The powers allied against France squandered their best chance for victory in 1793, when the French army verged on chaos because of the emigration of noble officers and the problems of integrating new draftees. At that moment, Prussia, Russia, and Austria were preoccupied once again with Poland. Catherine the Great abolished Poland's constitution of 1791 and joined with Prussia in gobbling up generous new slices of Polish territory in the second partition of 1793 (Map 16.2). When Tadeusz Kościuszko (1746–1817), an officer who had been a foreign volunteer in the War of American Independence, tried to lead a nationalist uprising, Catherine's army struck again. This time, Russia, Prussia, and Austria wiped Poland completely off the map in the third partition of 1795. "The Polish question" would plague international relations for more than a century, as Polish rebels flocked to any international upheaval that might undo the partitions.

While Russia, Prussia, and Austria feasted on Poland, France regrouped and by the end of 1793 had amassed through the new national draft a huge fighting force of 700,000 men. The French first stopped the advance of the allied powers and then moved into the territories of its enemies, aiming to carry the gospel of

Map 16.2 The Second and Third Partitions of Poland, 1793 and 1795
In 1793, Prussia took over territory that included 1.1 million Poles, while Russia gained 3 million new inhabitants. Austria gave up any claims to Poland in exchange for help from Russia and Prussia in acquiring Bavaria. In the final division of 1795, Prussia absorbed an additional 900,000 Polish subjects, including those in Warsaw; Austria incorporated 1 million Poles and the city of Cracow; Russia gained another 2 million Poles. The three powers determined never to use the term *Kingdom of Poland* again. How had Poland fallen prey to the other powers?

revolution and republicanism to the rest of Europe. The French army proved less successful in the faraway Caribbean colonies, in part because the armed forces in place were small and in part because the British navy controlled the seas. Twice the size in land area of the neighboring British colonies, the French Caribbean colonies also produced nearly twice as much revenue in exports. The slave population had doubled in the French colonies in the twenty years before 1789. St. Domingue (present-day Haiti) was the most important French colony. Occupying the western half of the island of Hispaniola, it was inhabited in 1789 by approximately 465,000 slaves, 30,000 whites, and 28,000 free people of color, whose primary job was to apprehend runaway slaves and ensure plantation security.

Despite the efforts of a Paris club called the Friends of Blacks, most French revolutionaries did not consider slavery a pressing problem in 1789. As one deputy explained, "This regime [in the colonies] is oppressive, but it gives a livelihood to several million Frenchmen. This regime is barbarous but a still greater barbarity will result if you interfere with it without the necessary knowledge." In August 1791, slaves in northern St. Domingue organized a large-scale revolt. To restore authority over the slaves, the Legislative Assembly in Paris granted civil and political rights to the free people of color. This action infuriated white planters and merchants, and in 1793 they signed an agreement with Great Britain, now France's enemy in war, declaring British sovereignty over St. Domingue. To complicate matters further, Spain, which controlled the rest of the island and had entered on Great Britain's side in the war with France, offered freedom to individual slave rebels who joined the Spanish army as long as they agreed to maintain the slave regime for other blacks.

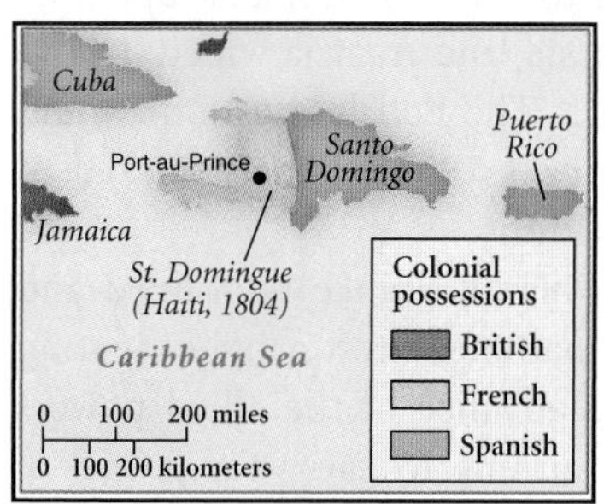

St. Domingue on the Eve of the Revolt, 1791

The few thousand French republican troops on St. Domingue were outnumbered, and to prevent complete military disaster, the French commissioner freed all the slaves in his jurisdiction in August 1793 without permission from the government in Paris. In February 1794, the National Convention formally abolished slavery and granted full rights to all black men in France's colonies. These actions had the desired effect. One of the ablest black generals allied with the Spanish, the ex-slave François Dominique Toussaint L'Ouverture (1743–1803), changed sides and committed his troops to the French. The French eventually appointed Toussaint governor of St. Domingue as a reward for his efforts.

The Republic of Virtue, 1793–1794

Even while war raged in Europe and the Caribbean, Robespierre and the Committee of Public Safety encouraged efforts to win hearts and minds to the republic back home. Songs—especially the new national anthem, "La Marseillaise" (named after the soldiers from the city of Marseille who first sang it)—placards, posters, pamphlets, books, engravings, paintings, sculpture, even everyday crockery, chamber pots, and playing cards conveyed republican slogans and symbols. Foremost among them was the figure of Liberty (an early version of the Statue of Liberty now in New York harbor), which appeared on coins and bills, on letterheads and seals, in engravings and paintings, and as statues in festivals. Hundreds of new plays were produced, and old classics were revised. To encourage the production of patriotic and republican works, the government sponsored state competitions for artists to "awaken the public spirit and make clear how atrocious and ridiculous were the enemies of liberty and of the Republic."

At the center of this elaborate cultural campaign were revolutionary festivals that first emerged in 1789 with the spontaneous planting of liberty trees in villages and towns. The Festival of Federation on July 14, 1790, marked the first anniversary of the fall of the Bastille. Under the Convention, the well-known

Representing Liberty
Liberty was always represented by a female figure because in French the noun is gendered feminine (*la liberté*). This painting, *La Liberté*, by a woman, Jeanne-Louise (Nanine) Vallain, from 1793–1794, captures the usual attributes of liberty: she is soberly seated, wearing a Roman-style toga and holding a pike with a Roman liberty cap on top. Her Roman appearance signals that she is not a contemporary Frenchwoman but rather the representation of an abstract quality. The fact that she holds an instrument of battle suggests that women might have been active participants. The Statue of Liberty in New York harbor, given to the United States by the French, is a late-nineteenth-century version of the same figure, but without any suggestion of battle. (Musée de la Révolution Française, Vizille. On loan from the Musée du Louvre. Inv. MRFD1986-4. Oil on cloth.)

painter Jacques-Louis David (1748–1825), who was a deputy and an associate of Robespierre, took over festival planning. David aimed to destroy the mystique of monarchy and to make the republic sacred. His Festival of Unity on August 10, 1793, for example, celebrated the first anniversary of the overthrow of the monarchy. In front of the statue of Liberty built for the occasion, a bonfire consumed the crowns and scepters of royalty, while a cloud of three thousand white doves rose into the sky.

Some hoped the festival system would replace the Catholic church altogether. They initiated a campaign of **de-Christianization** that included closing churches (Protestant as well as Catholic), selling many church buildings to the highest bidder, and trying to force even those clergy who had taken the oath of loyalty to abandon their clerical vocations and marry. Great churches became storehouses for arms or grain, or their stones were sold off to contractors. The medieval statues of kings on the facade of Notre Dame cathedral were beheaded. Church bells were dismantled and church treasures melted down for government use. In the ultimate step in de-Christianization, extremists tried to establish a cult of reason to supplant Christianity. The Committee of Public Safety halted the de-Christianization campaign because the deputies feared it would turn rural, devout populations against the republic.

In principle, the best way to ensure the future of the republic was through the education of the young. The Convention voted to make primary schooling free and compulsory for both boys and girls. It took control of education away from the Catholic church and tried to set up a system of state schools at the primary and secondary levels, but it lacked trained teachers to replace those the Catholic religious orders provided. As a result, opportunities for learning how to read and write may have diminished. In 1799, only one-fifth as many boys enrolled in the state secondary schools as had studied in church schools ten years earlier.

Although many of the ambitious republican programs failed, almost all aspects of daily life became politicized, even colors. The tricolor—the combination of red, white, and blue that was to become the flag of France—was devised in July 1789, and by 1793 everyone had to wear a cockade (a badge made of ribbons) with the colors. Using formal forms of speech—*vous* for "you" or the title *monsieur* or *madame*—might identify someone as an aristocrat; true patriots used the informal *tu* and *citoyen* or *citoyenne* (citizen) instead. Some people changed their names or gave their children new names. Biblical and saints' names, such as Jean, Pierre, Joseph, or Marie, gave way to names recalling heroes of the ancient Roman republic (Brutus, Gracchus, Cornelia), revolutionary heroes, or flowers and plants. Such changes symbolized adherence to the republic and to Enlightenment ideals rather than to Catholicism.

Even the measures of time and space were revolutionized. In October 1793, the Convention introduced a new calendar to replace the Christian one. Year I dated from the beginning of the republic on September 22, 1792. Twelve months of exactly thirty days each received new names derived from nature—for example,

Pluviôse (roughly equivalent to February) recalled the rain (*la pluie*) of late winter. Instead of seven-day weeks, ten-day *décades* provided only one day of rest every ten days and pointedly eliminated the Sunday of the Christian calendar. The five days left at the end of the calendar year were devoted to special festivals called *sans-culottides*. The calendar remained in force for twelve years despite continuing resistance to it. More enduring was the new metric system based on units of ten that was invented to replace the hundreds of local variations in weights and measures. Other countries in Europe and throughout the world eventually adopted the metric system.

Successive revolutionary legislatures also changed the rules of family life. The state took responsibility for all family matters away from the Catholic church. Birth, death, and marriage registration now happened at city hall, not the parish church. Marriage became a civil contract and as such could be broken. The new divorce law of September 1792 was the most far-reaching in Europe: a couple could divorce by mutual consent or for reasons such as insanity, abandonment, battering, or criminal conviction. Thousands of men and women took advantage of the law to dissolve unhappy marriages, even though the pope had condemned the measure. (In 1816, the government revoked the right to divorce.) In one of its most influential actions, the National Convention passed a series of laws that created equal inheritance among all children in a family, including girls. A father's right to favor one child, especially the oldest male, was considered aristocratic and hence antirepublican.

Resisting the Revolution

By intruding into religion, culture, and daily life, the republic inevitably provoked resistance. Shouting curses against the republic, uprooting liberty trees, carrying statues of the Virgin Mary in a procession, hiding a priest who would not take the loyalty oath, singing a royalist song—all these actions expressed discontent with the new symbols, rituals, and policies. Many women, in particular, suffered from the hard conditions of life that persisted in this time of war, and they had their own ways of dissenting. Long breadlines in the cities exhausted the patience of women, and police spies reported their constant grumbling, which occasionally turned into spontaneous demonstrations or riots over high prices or food shortages. Other forms of resistance were more individual. One young woman, Charlotte Corday, assassinated the outspoken deputy Jean-Paul Marat in July 1793. Corday fervently supported the Girondins, and she considered it her patriotic duty to kill the Montagnard deputy who, in the columns of his paper *The Friend of the People*, had constantly demanded more heads and more blood.

Organized resistance broke out in many parts of France. The arrest of the Girondin deputies in June 1793 sparked in several departments insurrections that if coordinated might have threatened the central government in Paris. But the army promptly dispatched the rebels. After the government retook the city of Lyon, one of the centers of the revolt, the deputy "on mission" there ordered sixteen hundred houses demolished. Special courts sentenced almost two thousand people to death. The name of the city was changed to Ville Affranchie (Liberated Town).

In the Vendée region of western France, resistance turned into full-scale civil war. Between March and December 1793, peasants, artisans, and weavers joined under noble leadership to form the Catholic and Royal Army. One rebel group explained its motives: "They [the republicans] have killed our king, chased away our priests, sold the goods of our church, eaten everything we have and now they want to take our bodies [in the draft]." The uprising took two different forms: in the Vendée itself, a counterrevolutionary army organized to fight the republic; in nearby Brittany, resistance took the form of guerrilla bands, which united to attack a target and then quickly melted into the countryside. Great Britain provided money and underground contacts for these attacks.

For several months in 1793, the Vendée rebels stormed the largest towns in the region. Both sides committed atrocities. At the small town of Machecoul, for example, the rebels massacred more than a hundred republicans, including administrators and National Guard members; many were tied together, shoved into freshly dug graves, and shot. By the fall, however, republican soldiers had turned back the rebels. A republican general wrote to the Committee of Public Safety claiming, "There is no more Vendée, citizens, it has perished under our free sword along with its women and children. . . . Following the orders that you gave me I have crushed children under the feet of horses, massacred women who at least . . . will engender no more brigands." "Infernal columns" of republican troops marched through the region to restore control, military courts ordered thousands executed, and republican soldiers massacred thousands of others. In one especially gruesome incident, the deputy Jean-Baptiste Carrier supervised the drowning of some two thousand Vendée rebels, including a number of priests. Barges loaded with prisoners were floated onto the Loire River near Nantes and then sunk. Controversy still rages about the rebellion's death toll. Estimates of rebel deaths alone range from about 20,000 to 250,000 and higher. Many thousands of republican soldiers and civilians also lost their lives. Even the low estimates reveal the carnage of this catastrophic confrontation between the republic and its opponents.

The Fall of Robespierre and the End of the Terror, 1794–1799

In the atmosphere of fear of conspiracy that these outbreaks fueled, Robespierre tried simultaneously to exert the Convention's control over popular political activities and to weed out opposition among the deputies. The Convention cracked down on popular clubs and societies in the fall of 1793. First to be suppressed were women's political clubs. Founded in early 1793, the Society of Revolutionary Republican Women played a very active part in sans-culottes politics. The society urged harsher measures against the republic's enemies and insisted that women have a voice in politics even if they did not have the vote. The Convention abolished women's political clubs in order to limit agitation in the streets. The deputies called on biological arguments about natural differences between the sexes to bolster their case. As one argued, "Women are ill suited for elevated thoughts and serious meditations."

In the spring of 1794, the Committee of Public Safety moved against its critics in Paris and among deputies in the Convention. Most of those critics were once Montagnards themselves. First, a handful of men labeled "ultrarevolutionaries"—in fact a motley collection of local Parisian politicians—were arrested and executed. Next came the other side, the "indulgents," so called because they favored moderation of the Terror. Included among them was the popular deputy Georges-Jacques Danton (1759–1794), once a member of the Committee of Public Safety and a friend of Robespierre despite the striking contrast in their personalities. Danton was the Revolution's most flamboyant orator and, unlike Robespierre, was a high-living, high-spending, excitable politician. At every turning point in national politics, his booming voice had swayed opinion in the National Convention. Now, under government pressure, the Revolutionary Tribunal convicted him and his friends of treason and sentenced them to death.

With the arrest and execution of these leaders in Paris, the prophecies of doom for the Revolution seemed about to be realized. "The Revolution," as one of the Girondin victims of 1793 had remarked, "was devouring its own children." Even after the major threats to the committee's power had been eliminated, the Terror continued and in some cases worsened. A law passed in June 1794 denied the accused the right of legal counsel, reduced the number of jurors necessary for conviction, and allowed only two judgments: acquittal or death. The category of political crimes expanded to include "slandering patriotism" and "seeking to inspire discouragement." Ordinary people risked the guillotine if they expressed any discontent. The rate of executions in Paris rose from five a day in the spring of 1794 to twenty-six a day in the summer. The political atmosphere darkened even though the military situation improved. At the end of June, French armies decisively defeated the main Austrian army and advanced through the Austrian Netherlands to Brussels and Antwerp. The emergency measures for fighting the war were working, yet Robespierre and his inner circle had made so many enemies that they could not afford to loosen the grip of the Terror.

The Terror hardly touched many parts of France, but overall the experience was undeniably traumatic. Across the country, the official Terror cost the lives of at least 40,000 French people, most of them living in the regions of major insurrections or near the borders with foreign enemies, where suspicion of collaboration ran high. As many as 300,000 people—one out of every fifty French people—went to prison as suspects between March 1793 and August 1794. The toll for the aristocracy and the clergy was especially high. Many leading nobles perished under the guillotine, and thousands emigrated. Thirty thousand to forty thousand clergy who refused to take the oath of allegiance emigrated, at least two thousand (including many nuns) were executed, and thousands were imprisoned. Clergy were singled out in particular in the civil war zones: 135 priests were massacred at Lyon in November 1793, and 83 were shot in one day during the Vendée revolt. Yet many victims of the Terror were peasants or ordinary working people.

The final crisis of the Terror came in July 1794. Conflicts within the Committee of Public Safety and the National Convention left Robespierre isolated. On July 27, 1794 (9 Thermidor, Year II, according to the revolutionary calendar), Robespierre appeared before the Convention with yet another list of deputies to be arrested. Many feared they would be named, and they shouted him down and ordered him arrested along with his followers on the committee, the president of the Revolutionary Tribunal in Paris, and the commander of the Parisian National Guard. An armed uprising led by the Paris city government failed to save Robespierre when most of the National Guard took the side of the Convention. Robespierre tried to kill himself with a pistol but only broke his jaw. The next day, he and scores of followers went to the guillotine.

The men who led the attack on Robespierre in Thermidor (July 1794) did not intend to reverse all his policies, but that happened nonetheless because of a violent backlash known as the **Thermidorian Reaction**. Newspapers attacked the Robespierrists as "tigers thirsting for human blood." The new government released hundreds of suspects and arranged a temporary truce in the Vendée. It purged Jacobins from local bodies and replaced them with their opponents. It arrested some of the most notorious "terrorists" in the National Convention and put them to death. Within the year, the new leaders abolished the Revolutionary Tribunal and closed the Jacobin Club in Paris. Popular demonstrations met severe repression. In southeastern France, in particular, the "White Terror" replaced the Jacobins' "Red Terror." Former officials and local Jacobin leaders were harassed, beaten, and often murdered by paramilitary bands that had tacit support from the new authorities. Those who remained in the National Convention prepared yet another constitution in 1795, setting up a two-house legislature and an executive body—the Directory—headed by five directors.

Between 1795 and 1799, the Directory government maintained itself by alternately purging royalists and Jacobins who did well in the yearly elections of deputies. While politically weak at home, the government continued the Convention's largely successful war effort abroad. In 1794 the reconstituted French army invaded the Austrian Netherlands, which France then annexed. In 1795 the French swarmed into the Dutch Republic, abolished the office of stadholder, and—with the revolutionary penchant for renaming—created the new Batavian Republic, a satellite of France. The Cisalpine Republic (northern Italy), Helvetic Republic (Switzerland), and Roman Republic soon followed. Ironically, however, these triumphs would ultimately bring to power the man who would dismantle the republic itself.

REVIEW What factors can explain the Terror? To what extent was it simply a response to a national emergency or a reflection of deeper problems with the French Revolution?

The Rise and Fall of Napoleon Bonaparte

The story of the rise of Napoleon Bonaparte (1769–1821) is one of the most remarkable in Western history. It would have seemed astonishing in 1795 that the twenty-six-year-old son of a Corsican noble would within four years become the supreme ruler of France and one of the greatest military leaders in world history. In 1795, he was a penniless artillery officer, only recently released from prison as a presumed Robespierrist. Continuing warfare, the upheavals caused in the rest of Europe by the impact of the French Revolution, and political divisions within the republican leadership gave Bonaparte the opportunity to change the course of history. Yet because his power rested on his military prowess, in the end he could not survive defeat on the battlefield.

Creating an Authoritarian State

The Directory regime never succeeded in establishing a firm center that could appeal to a majority of voters. In Paris bands of young dandies picked fights with known Jacobins and disrupted theater performances with loud antirevolutionary songs. All over France, people banded together and petitioned to reopen churches closed during the Terror. If necessary, they broke into a church to hold services with a priest who had been in hiding or with a lay schoolteacher who was willing to say Mass. Amid increasing political instability, generals like Bonaparte became practically independent, and the troops felt greater loyalty to their units and generals than to the republic. Military victories made the army a parallel and rival force to the state.

Thanks to some early military successes and links to Parisian politicians, Bonaparte was named commander of the French army in Italy in 1796. His astounding success in the Italian campaigns of 1796–1797 launched his meteoric career. With an army of fewer than fifty thousand men, he defeated the Piedmontese and the Austrians. He molded the army into his personal force by paying the soldiers in cash taken as tribute from the newly conquered territories. He mollified the Directory government by sending home wagonloads of Italian masterpieces, which were added to Parisian museum collections (most are still there) after being paraded in victory festivals.

In 1798, the Directory set aside its plans to invade England, gave Bonaparte command of the army raised for that purpose, and sent him across the Mediterranean Sea to Egypt, away from the Parisian centers of power. The French had encouraged the Irish to time a rebellion to coincide with their planned invasion, and when the French went elsewhere, the British mercilessly repressed the revolt. Thirty thousand people were killed. Twice as many regular British troops (seventy thousand) as fought in any of the major continental battles against Napoleon were required to put down the Irish rebellion.

The Directory government hoped that French occupation of Egypt would strike a blow at British trade by cutting the route to India and thus compensate France for its losses there years before. Bonaparte took France's leading scientists with him on the expedition, and his soldiers discovered a slab of black basalt dating

Napoleon as Military Hero

In this painting from 1800–1801, *Napoleon Crossing the Alps at St. Bernard,* Jacques-Louis David reminds the French of Napoleon's heroic military exploits. Napoleon is a picture of calm and composure, while his horse shows the fright and energy of the moment. David painted this propagandistic image shortly after one of his former students went to the guillotine on a trumped-up charge of plotting to assassinate the new French leader. The former organizer of republican festivals during the Terror, David became a kind of court painter for the new regime. (Réunion des Musées Nationaux/Art Resource, NY.)

from 196 B.C.E. written in both hieroglyphic and Greek. Called the Rosetta stone after a nearby town, it enabled scholars to finally decipher the hieroglyphs used by the ancient Egyptians. Once the army disembarked in Egypt, however, the British admiral Horatio Nelson destroyed the French fleet while it was anchored in Aboukir Bay. With his army pinned down after its initial successes, Napoleon slipped out of Egypt and made his way secretly across the Mediterranean to southern France.

In October 1799, Bonaparte arrived in Paris at just the right moment. Resistance to the Directory was growing, and many government leaders wanted to revise the constitution of 1795. Disillusioned members of the government saw in Bonaparte's return an occasion to overturn the constitution. On November 9, 1799 (18 Brumaire, Year VIII, by the revolutionary calendar), the conspirators within the Directory government persuaded the legislature to move out of Paris to avoid an alleged Jacobin plot. But when Bonaparte stomped into the meeting hall the next day and demanded changes in the constitution, he was greeted with cries of "Down with the dictator." His quick-thinking brother Lucien, president of the Council of Five Hundred (the lower house), saved Bonaparte's coup by summoning troops guarding the hall and claiming that the deputies had tried to assassinate the popular general. The soldiers ejected the deputies, and a hastily assembled legislature voted to abolish the Directory and establish a new three-man executive called the consulate.

The deputies of the legislature who engineered the coup d'état of 18 Brumaire picked Bonaparte as one of three provisional consuls because he was a famous general. But under the new constitution of 1799, he was named **First Consul**, a title revived from the ancient Roman republic, with the right to pick the Council of State, which drew up all laws. Millions had abstained from voting on the new constitution, which eliminated direct elections for deputies and granted no independent powers to the three houses of the legislature. Bonaparte and his advisers chose the legislature's members out of a small pool of "notables." Inside France, political apathy had overtaken the original enthusiasm for revolutionary ideals. Bonaparte's coup appeared to be just the latest in a long line of upheavals in revolutionary France. Within the year, however, Bonaparte had set France on a new course toward an authoritarian state.

Bonaparte's most urgent task was to reconcile to his regime Catholics who had been alienated by revolutionary policies. Though nominally Catholic, Napoleon held no deep religious convictions. "How can there be order in the state without religion?" he asked cynically. "When a man is dying of hunger beside another who is stuffing himself, he cannot accept this difference if there is not an authority who tells him: 'God wishes it so.'" In 1801, a concordat with Pope Pius VII (r. 1800–1823) ended a decade of church-state conflict. The pope validated all sales of church lands, and Catholicism was officially recognized as the religion of "the great majority of French citizens." (The state continued to pay the salaries of clergymen, both Catholic and Protestant.) The pope thus brought the huge French Catholic population back into the fold, and Napoleon gained the pope's support for his regime.

Napoleon centralized state power more effectively than kings or revolutionaries had before him. He personally appointed prefects to directly supervise local affairs in every department. He created the Bank of France to facilitate government borrowing and relied on gold and silver coinage rather than paper money. He severely limited political expression, refusing to allow those who opposed him to meet in clubs or influence elections. A decree reduced the number of newspapers in Paris from seventy-three to thirteen (and then finally to four), and the newspapers that remained became government mouthpieces. Government censors had to approve all operas and plays, and they banned "offensive" artistic works even more frequently than their royal predecessors. The minister of police, Joseph Fouché, a leading figure in the Terror, kept political dissidents under constant surveillance. When a bomb attack on Napoleon's carriage failed in 1800, Fouché suppressed evidence of a royalist plot and instead arrested hundreds of former Jacobins. More than one hundred of them were deported and seven hundred imprisoned.

The one place that escaped Napoleon's grasp was St. Domingue. The vicious fighting and flight of whites during the slave revolt had left the island's economy in ruins. In 1800 the plantations produced one-fifth of what they had in 1789. In 1802 Napoleon sent French armies to regain control of St. Domingue and reimpose slavery. They arrested Toussaint and transported him to France, where he died in prison. His arrest prompted the English romantic poet William Wordsworth (1770–1850) to write of him:

> There's not a breathing of the common wind
> That will forget thee; thou hast great allies;
> Thy friends are exultations, agonies,
> And love, and man's unconquerable mind.

Toussaint became a hero to abolitionists everywhere, a potent symbol of black struggles to win freedom. The remaining black generals defeated Napoleon's armies, which had been weakened by yellow fever, and in 1804 proclaimed the Republic of Haiti.

France itself proved more pliable. In 1802, Napoleon set up a referendum to approve him as First Consul for life, and then in 1804, with the pope's blessing, he crowned himself Emperor Napoleon I. Like the kings who preceded him, Napoleon cultivated personal symbolism. His face and name adorned coins, engravings, histories, paintings, and public monuments. His favorite painters embellished his legend by depicting him as a warrior-hero of mythic proportions. Believing that "what is big is always beautiful," Napoleon embarked on ostentatious building projects that would outshine even those of Louis XIV. Government-commissioned architects built the Arc de Triomphe, the Stock Exchange, fountains, and even slaughterhouses. In his imperial court, Napoleon staged his entrances carefully to maximize his personal presence: his wife and courtiers were dressed in regal finery, and he was announced with great pomp—but he usually arrived dressed in a simple military uniform with no medals.

Toussaint L'Ouverture
The leader of the St. Domingue slave uprising appears in his general's uniform, sword in hand. This portrait appeared in one of the earliest histories of the revolt, Marcus Rainsford's *Historical Account of the Black Empire of Hayti* (London, 1805). Toussaint, a former slave who educated himself, fascinated many of his contemporaries in Europe as well as the New World by turning a chaotic slave rebellion into an organized and ultimately successful independence movement. (North Wind Picture Archives.)

Napoleon also worked hard at establishing his reputation as an efficient administrator with broad intellectual interests. He met frequently with scientists, jurists, and artists, and stories abounded of his unflagging energy. To assist him, Napoleon relied on men who had served with him in the army. His chief of staff, Alexandre Berthier, for example, became minister of war, and the chemist Claude Berthollet, who had organized the scientific part of the expedition to Egypt, became vice president of the Senate in 1804. Napoleon's bureaucracy was based on a patron-client relationship, with Napoleon as the ultimate patron. Some of Napoleon's closest associates married into his family.

The New Paternalism

"Authority," declared Napoleon's adviser Abbé Emmanuel-Joseph Sieyès, "must come from above and confidence from below." Napoleon applied this basic military model to all of French society. Combining aristocratic and revolutionary values in a new social hierarchy that rewarded merit and talent, Napoleon used the Senate to dispense his patronage and personally chose as senators the nation's most illustrious generals, ministers, prefects, scientists, rich men, and former nobles. In 1802, he took a step toward creating a new nobility by founding the Legion of Honor, 95 percent of whose members in 1814 were military men. In 1808, Napoleon introduced a complete hierarchy of noble titles, ranging from princes down to barons and chevaliers. Titles could be inherited, but all Napoleonic nobles served the state in one way or

Napoleon's Coronation as Emperor
In *The Coronation of Napoleon and Josephine* (1805–1807), Jacques-Louis David shows Napoleon crowning his wife at the ceremony in 1804. Napoleon orchestrated the entire event and took the only active role in it. Pope Pius VII gave his blessing to the ceremony (he can be seen seated behind Napoleon), but Napoleon crowned himself. What is the significance of Napoleon crowning himself? (Erich Lessing/ Art Resource, NY.)

another. To go along with their new titles, Napoleon gave his favorite generals huge fortunes, often in the form of estates in the conquered territories.

Napoleon's own family reaped the greatest benefits. He made his older brother, Joseph, ruler of the newly established kingdom of Naples in 1806; the same year he installed his younger brother Louis as king of Holland. He proclaimed his twenty-three-year-old stepson Eugène de Beauharnais viceroy of Italy in 1805 and established his sister Caroline and brother-in-law General Murat as king and queen of Naples in 1808, when he moved Joseph to the throne of Spain. Napoleon wanted to establish an imperial succession, but he lacked an heir. In thirteen years of marriage, his wife, Josephine, had borne no children, so in 1809 he divorced her and in 1810 married the eighteen-year-old Princess Marie-Louise of Austria. The next year she gave birth to a son, to whom Napoleon immediately gave the title "king of Rome."

Napoleon believed that authority in the family and the workplace had to be reestablished in the same way that he had reasserted the authority of the state. The critical element in his vision of paternalism was the new **Civil Code** of 1804. Napoleon succeeded where previous governments had failed in unifying and standardizing France's local law codes. Called the Napoleonic Code as a way of further exalting his image, it defined and ensured property rights, guaranteed religious liberty, and provided equal legal treatment for all adult males. At the same time, however, the code sharply curtailed women's rights. The law obligated a husband to support his wife, but he alone controlled any property held in common. A wife could not sue in court, sell or mortgage her own property, or contract a debt without her husband's consent. Divorce was still possible, but a wife could petition for divorce only if her husband brought his mistress to live in the family home. In contrast, a wife convicted of adultery could be imprisoned for up to two years. The code's framers saw these discrepancies as a way to reinforce the family and make women responsible for private virtue, while leaving public decisions to men. The French code was imitated in many European and Latin American countries and in the French colony of Louisiana, where it had a similar negative effect on women's rights. Not until 1965 did French wives gain legal status equal to that of their husbands.

The Civil Code also reinforced a father's control over his children, which revolutionary legislation had limited. For example, children under age sixteen who refused to follow their fathers' commands could be sent to prison for up to a month with no hearing of any sort. At the same time, the code required fathers to provide for their children's welfare. Napoleon himself encouraged the foundation of private charities to help indigent mothers, and one of his decrees made it easier for women to abandon their children anonymously to a government foundling hospital. Napoleon hoped such measures would discourage abortion and infanticide, especially among the poorest classes in the fast-growing urban areas. The new paternalism extended to relations between employers and employees. The state required all workers to carry a work card attesting to their good conduct, and it prohibited all workers' organizations.

Napoleon continued the central government's patronage of science and intellectual life but once again put his own distinctive paternalist stamp on these activities. He closely monitored the research institutes established during the Revolution, sometimes intervening personally to achieve political conformity. Napoleon aimed to modernize French society through science, but he could not tolerate criticism. He considered most writers useless or dangerous, "good for nothing under any government." Some of the most talented French writers of the time had to live in exile. The best known of them was Germaine de Staël (1766–1817). When explaining his desire to banish her, Napoleon exclaimed, "She is a machine in motion who stirs up the salons." While exiled in the German states, Madame de Staël wrote a novel, *Corinne* (1807), whose heroine is a brilliant woman thwarted by a patriarchal system, and *On Germany* (1810), an account of the important new literary currents east of the Rhine. Her books were banned in France.

Despite Napoleon's accommodation with the pope, many royalists and Catholics still criticized him as an impious usurper. François-René de Chateaubriand

Germaine de Staël
One of the most fascinating intellectuals of her time, Anne-Louise Germaine de Staël seemed to irritate Napoleon more than any other person did. The daughter of Louis XVI's finance minister, Jacques Necker, and the wife of a Swedish diplomat, Madame de Staël frequently criticized Napoleon's regime. She published best-selling novels and influential literary criticism, and whenever allowed to reside in Paris, she encouraged the intellectual and political dissidents from Napoleon's regime. (Réunion des Musées Nationaux/Art Resource, NY.)

(1768–1848) admired Napoleon as "the strong man who has saved us from the abyss," but he preferred monarchy. In his view, Napoleon had not properly understood the need to defend Christian values against the Enlightenment's excessive reliance on reason. Chateaubriand wrote his *Genius of Christianity* (1802) to draw attention to the power and mystery of faith. He warned, "It is to the vanity of knowledge that we owe almost all our misfortunes. . . . The learned ages have always been followed by ages of destruction."

"Europe Was at My Feet": Napoleon's Military Conquests

Building on innovations introduced by the republican governments before him, Napoleon revolutionized the art of war with tactics and strategies based on a highly mobile army. Napoleon attributed his military success "three-quarters to morale" and the rest to leadership and superiority of numbers at the point of attack. Conscription provided the large numbers: 1.3 million men ages twenty to twenty-four were drafted between 1800 and 1812, another million in 1813–1814. Military service was both a patriotic duty and a means of social mobility. The men who rose through the ranks to become officers were young, ambitious, and accustomed to the new ways of war. Consequently, the French army had higher morale than the armies of other powers, most of which rejected conscription as too democratic and continued to restrict their officer corps to the nobility. Only in 1813–1814 did French morale plummet, as the military tide turned against Napoleon.

When Napoleon came to power in 1799, desertion was rampant, and the generals competed with one another for predominance. Napoleon united all the armies into one Grand Army under his personal command. By 1812, he commanded 700,000 troops. In any given battle, between 70,000 and 180,000 men, not all of them French, fought for France. Napoleon inspired almost fanatical loyalty. A brilliant strategist who carefully studied the demands of war, he outmaneuvered nearly all his opponents. He gathered the largest possible army for one great and decisive battle and then followed with a relentless pursuit to break enemy morale altogether. He fought alongside his soldiers in some sixty battles and had nineteen horses shot out from under him. One opponent said that Napoleon's presence alone was worth 50,000 men.

One of Napoleon's greatest advantages was the lack of coordination among his enemies. Britain dominated the seas but did not want to field huge land armies. The French republic had already established satellite regimes in the Netherlands and Italy, which served as a buffer against the big powers to the east—Austria, Prussia, and Russia. By maneuvering diplomatically and militarily, Napoleon could usually take these on one by one. After reorganizing the French armies in 1799, for example, Napoleon won striking victories against the Austrians at Marengo and Hohenlinden in 1800, forcing them to agree to peace terms. Once the Austrians had withdrawn, Britain agreed to the Treaty of Amiens in 1802, effectively ending hostilities in Europe for a time. Napoleon considered the peace with Great Britain merely a truce, however, and it lasted only until 1803. When the attempt to retake St. Domingue failed, Napoleon abandoned his plans to extend his empire to the Western Hemisphere and sold the Louisiana Territory to the United States in 1803.

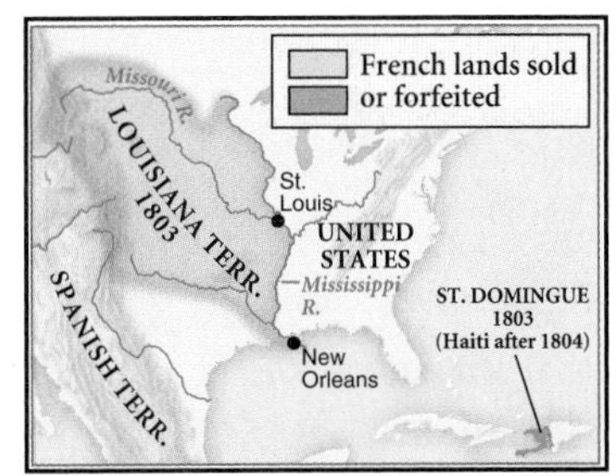

France's Retreat from America

When war resumed in Europe, the British navy once more proved its superiority by defeating the French and their Spanish allies in a huge naval battle at Trafalgar off the Spanish coast in 1805. France lost many ships; the British lost no vessels, but their renowned admiral Lord Horatio Nelson died in the battle. On land, however, Napoleon remained invincible. In 1805, Austria took up arms again when Napoleon demanded that it declare neutrality in the conflict with Britain. Napoleon promptly captured 25,000 Austrian soldiers at Ulm in Bavaria in 1805. After marching on to Vienna, he again trounced the Austrians, who had been joined by their new ally, Russia. The battle of Austerlitz, often considered Napoleon's greatest victory, was fought on December 2, 1805, the first anniversary of his coronation.

After maintaining neutrality for a decade, Prussia declared war on France. In 1806, the French promptly destroyed the Prussian army at Jena and Auerstadt. In 1807, Napoleon defeated the Russians at Friedland. Personal negotiations between Napoleon and the young tsar Alexander I (r. 1801–1825) resulted in a humiliating settlement imposed on Prussia, which paid the price for temporary reconciliation between France and Russia. The Treaties of Tilsit turned Prussian lands west of the Elbe River into the kingdom of Westphalia under Napoleon's brother Jerome, and Prussia's Polish provinces became the duchy of Warsaw. Alexander recognized Napoleon's conquests in central and western Europe and promised to help him against the British in exchange for Napoleon's support against the Turks. Neither party kept the bargain. Napoleon once again had turned the divisions among his enemies in his favor.

Wherever the Grand Army conquered, Napoleon's influence soon followed. By annexing some territories and setting up others as satellite kingdoms with much-reduced autonomy, Napoleon attempted to colonize large parts of Europe. He brought the disparate German and Italian states together to rule them more effectively and to exploit their resources for his own ends. In 1806, he established the Confederation of the Rhine, which soon included almost all the German states except Austria and Prussia. The Holy Roman Emperor gave up his title, held since the thirteenth century, and became simply the emperor of Austria. Napoleon established three units in Italy: the territories directly annexed to France and the satellite kingdoms of Italy and Naples. Italy had not been so unified since the Roman Empire.

Consolidation of the German and Italian States, 1812

Napoleon forced French-style reforms on both the annexed territories, which were ruled directly from France, and the satellite kingdoms, which were usually ruled by one or another of Napoleon's relatives but with a certain autonomy. Napoleon brought in French experts to work with handpicked locals to abolish serfdom, eliminate seigneurial dues, introduce the Napoleonic Code, suppress monasteries, subordinate church to state, and extend civil rights to Jews and other religious minorities. Reactions to these innovations were mixed. Napoleon's chosen rulers often made real improvements in roads, public works, law codes, and education. Yet tax increases and ever-rising conscription quotas also fomented discontent. The annexed territories and satellite kingdoms paid half the French war expenses. Napoleon's brother Louis would not allow conscription in his kingdom of the Netherlands because the Dutch had never had compulsory military service. In 1810, Napoleon annexed the satellite kingdom because his brother had become too sympathetic to Dutch interests.

Napoleon's victories forced defeated rulers to rethink their political and cultural assumptions. After suffering a crushing military defeat in 1806, Prussian king Frederick William III (r. 1797–1840) appointed a reform commission, and on its recommendation he abolished serfdom. Peasants gained their personal independence from their noble landlords, who could no longer sell them to pay gambling debts, for example, or refuse them permission to marry. Yet the lives of the former serfs remained bleak; they were left without land, and their landlords no longer had to care for them in hard times. The king's advisers also overhauled the army to make the high command more efficient and to open the way for the appointment of middle-class officers. Prussia instituted these reforms to try to compete with the French, not to promote democracy. As one reformer wrote to Frederick William, "We must do from above what the French have done from below."

Reform received lip service in Russia. Tsar Alexander I had gained his throne after an aristocratic coup deposed and killed his autocratic and capricious father, Paul (r. 1796–1801). In the early years of his reign, the remorseful young ruler created Western-style ministries, lifted restrictions on importing foreign books, and founded six new universities. There was even talk of drafting a constitution. But none of these efforts reached beneath the surface of Russian life, and by the second decade of his reign, Alexander began to reject the Enlightenment spirit that his grandmother Catherine the Great had instilled in him.

Napoleon's Fall

Despite Napoleon's repeated successes on the battlefield, his empire ultimately failed because it was based on a contradiction: Napoleon tried to reduce almost all of Europe to the status of colonial dependents even though Europe had long consisted of independent states. His actions resulted in a great upsurge of the nationalist feeling that has dominated European politics to the present.

The one power always standing between Napoleon and total dominance of Europe was Great Britain. The British ruled the seas and financed anyone who would oppose Napoleon. In an effort to bankrupt this "nation of shopkeepers" by choking its trade, Napoleon inaugurated the **Continental System** in 1806. It prohibited all commerce between Great Britain and France as well as between Great Britain and France's dependent states and allies. After an initial decline in British exports and industrial production, the system proved impossible to enforce, and widespread smuggling brought British goods into the European market. British industrial growth resumed; calico-printing works, for example, quadrupled their production. The temporary protection from British competition could not make up for French losses in the port cities, whose trade with the Caribbean colonies had been disrupted by war and Haitian independence.

Smuggling British goods was only one way of opposing the French. Resistance to French demands for money or for draftees eventually prompted that patriotic defense of the nation known as nationalism. In southern Italy, opposition led to the formation of a network of secret societies, called the *carbonari* (charcoal burners), which got its name from the practice of marking each new member's forehead with a charcoal mark. Throughout the nineteenth century, the carbonari played a leading role in Italian nationalism. In the German states, intellectuals wrote passionate defenses of the virtues of the German nation and of the superiority of German literature. A thriving press, the multiplication of Masonic lodges and literary clubs, and a resurgence of intellectual life in the German universities all eventually connected with anti-French nationalism.

No nations bucked under Napoleon's reins more than Portugal and Spain. In 1807, Napoleon sent 100,000 troops through Spain to invade Portugal, forcing the royal family to flee to the Portuguese colony of Brazil. But fighting continued, aided by a British army. When Napoleon got his brother Joseph named king of Spain in place of the senile Charles IV (r. 1788–1808), the Spanish clergy and nobles raised bands of peasants to fight the French occupiers. The peasants hated French requisitioning of their food supplies; Spanish nobles feared revolutionary reforms. The Spanish Catholic church spread anti-French propaganda that equated Napoleon with heresy. As the former archbishop of Seville wrote to the archbishop of Granada in 1808, "You realize that we must not recognize as king a free-mason, heretic, Lutheran, as are all the Bonapartes and the French nation." Even Napoleon's taking personal command of French forces failed to quell the Spanish. Germaine de Staël commented that Napoleon "never understood that a war might be a crusade. . . . He never reckoned with the one power that no arms could overcome—the enthusiasm of a whole people."

Despite opposition, Napoleon controlled more territory by 1812 than any European ruler had since Roman times (see "Mapping the West," page 635). Only two major European states remained fully independent—Great Britain and Russia—but once allied they would successfully challenge his dominion and draw many other states to their side. Britain sent aid to the Portuguese and Spanish rebels, while Russia once again prepared for war. Tsar Alexander I made peace with the Ottoman Turks and allied himself with Great Britain and Sweden. In 1812, Napoleon invaded Russia with 250,000 horses and 600,000 men, including contingents of Italians, Poles, Swiss, Dutch, and Germans. This daring move proved to be his undoing.

Napoleon followed his usual strategy of trying to strike quickly, but the Russian generals avoided confrontation and retreated eastward, destroying anything that might be useful to the invaders. In September, on the road to Moscow, Napoleon finally engaged the main Russian force in the gigantic battle of Borodino. French casualties were 30,000 men, including 47 generals; the Russians lost 45,000. Once again the Russians retreated, leaving Moscow undefended. Napoleon entered the deserted city, but the victory turned hollow when the departing Russians set the wooden city on fire. Within a week, three-fourths of it had burned to the ground. Alexander refused to negotiate, and French morale plunged with worsening problems of supply. Weeks of constant marching in the dirt and heat had worn down the foot soldiers, who were dying of disease or deserting in large numbers.

In October, Napoleon began his retreat; in November came the cold. Napoleon himself reported that on November 14 the temperature fell to 24 degrees Fahrenheit. A German soldier in the Grand Army described trying to cook fistfuls of raw bran with snow to make something like bread. For him the retreat was "the indescribable horror of all possible plagues." Within a week, the Grand Army lost 30,000 horses and had to abandon most of its artillery and food supplies. Russian forces harassed the retreating army, now more pathetic than grand. By December, only 100,000 troops remained, one-sixth the original number, and the retreat had turned into a rout: the Russians had captured 200,000 soldiers, including 48 generals and 3,000 other officers.

Napoleon had made a classic military mistake that would be repeated by Adolf Hitler in World War II: fighting a war on two distant fronts simultaneously. The Spanish war tied up 250,000 French troops and forced Napoleon to bully Prussia and Austria into supplying soldiers of dubious loyalty for the Moscow campaign. They deserted at the first opportunity. The fighting in Spain and Portugal also worsened the already substantial logistical and communications problems involved in marching to Moscow.

Napoleon's humiliation might have been temporary if the British and Russians had not successfully organized a coalition to complete the job. Napoleon still had resources at his command; by the spring of 1813 he had replenished his army with another 250,000 men. With British financial support, Russian, Austrian, Prussian, and Swedish armies met the French outside Leipzig in October 1813 and defeated Napoleon in the Battle of the Nations. One by one, Napoleon's German allies deserted him to join the German nationalist "war of liberation." The Confederation of the Rhine dissolved, and the Dutch revolted and restored the prince of Orange. Joseph Bonaparte fled Spain, and a combined Spanish-Portuguese army under British command invaded France. In only a few months, the allied powers crossed the Rhine and marched toward Paris. In March 1814, the French Senate deposed Napoleon, who abdicated when his remaining generals refused to fight. Napoleon went into exile on the island of Elba off the Italian coast. His wife, Marie-Louise, refused to accompany him. The allies restored to the throne Louis XVIII (r. 1814–1824), the brother of Louis XVI (whose son was known as Louis XVII even though he died in prison in 1795 without ever ruling).

Napoleon had one last chance to regain power. Lacking a solid base of support, Louis XVIII tried to steer a middle course by granting a charter that established a British-style monarchy with a two-house legislature and guaranteed civil rights. But he was caught between returning émigré nobles who demanded a complete restoration of their lands and powers and those who had supported either the republic or Napoleon during the previous twenty-five years. Sensing an opportunity, Napoleon escaped from Elba in early 1815 and, landing in southern France, attracted cheering crowds and former soldiers to his side. The period known as the Hundred Days (the length of time between his escape and his final defeat) had begun. Louis XVIII fled across the border, waiting for help from France's enemies.

Napoleon quickly moved his reconstituted army into present-day Belgium. At first it seemed that he might succeed in separately fighting the two armies arrayed against him—a Prussian army and a joint force of Belgian, Dutch, German, and British troops led by Sir Arthur Wellesley (1769–1852), the duke of Wellington. But the Prussians evaded him and joined with Wellington at Waterloo. Completely routed, Napoleon had no choice but to abdicate again. This time the victorious allies banished him permanently to the remote island of St. Helena, far off the coast of West Africa, where he died in 1821 at the age of fifty-two.

REVIEW Why was Napoleon able to gain control over so much of Europe?

Conclusion

The cost of Napoleon's rule was high: 750,000 French soldiers and 400,000 others from annexed and satellite states died fighting for the French between 1800 and 1815. The losses among those attempting to stop Napoleon were at least as high, but no military figure since Alexander the Great in the fourth century B.C.E. had made such an impact on world history. Napoleon's plans for a united Europe, his insistence on spreading the legal reforms of the French Revolution, his model of an authoritarian state, and even his inadvertent awakening of national sentiment set the agenda for European history in the modern era.

The revolutionary cataclysm permanently altered the political landscape of Europe. The French executed their king as a traitor and set up Europe's first republic with universal male suffrage and a written guarantee of "the rights of man." Ordinary people marched in demonstrations, met in clubs, and in the case of men, voted in national elections for the first time. They got their first taste of democracy. But the ideals of universal education, religious toleration, and democratic participation could not prevent the institution of new forms of government terror to persecute, imprison, and kill dissidents. The French revolutionary experiment thus led to democracy *and* to a kind of totalitarianism. The French used the new spirit of national pride to inspire a huge citizen army, but the army conquered other peoples and gave a leading general the chance to take power for himself. Napoleon in turn created yet another new form of rule with a long history in the modern era: a police state in which the generals played a leading political role. Napoleon suppressed all other meaningful political participation and offered in its place law and order and modernization from above. Like many other authoritarian rulers after him, however, Napoleon could not maintain his position once he lost in battle.

Mapping the West Europe under Napoleonic Domination, 1812
In 1812, Napoleon had at least nominal control of almost all of western Europe. Even before he made his fatal mistake of invading Russia, however, his authority had been undermined in Spain and seriously weakened in the Italian and German states. His efforts to extend French power sparked resistance almost everywhere. As Napoleon insisted on French domination, local people began to think of themselves as Italian, German, or Dutch. Thus, Napoleon inadvertently laid the foundations for the nineteenth-century spread of nationalism. **For more help analyzing this map, see the map activity for this chapter in the Online Study Guide at** bedfordstmartins.com/huntconcise.

As events unfolded between 1789 and 1815, the French Revolution became *the* model of modern revolution and in the process set the enduring patterns of all modern politics. Republicanism, democracy, terrorism, nationalism, and military dictatorship all took their modern forms during the French Revolution. Even the terms *left* and *right* got their political meaning in this period: "the left" was a reference to deputies who favored extensive change and sat together in seats to the speaker's left in 1789; deputies who preferred a more cautious and conservative stance sat as a group to the speaker's right. The breathtaking succession of regimes in France between 1789 and 1815 inevitably raised disturbing questions about the relationship between rapid political change and violence. Do all revolutions in the name of democracy inevitably degenerate into wars of conquest or terror? Is a regime democratic if it does not allow poor men, women, or blacks to vote? Is a militaristic, authoritarian style of government the only answer to divisive political conflicts in a time of war? The French Revolution and its aftermath—the era of Napoleon—raised these questions and many more.

CHAPTER REVIEW QUESTIONS

1. Why did the other rulers of Europe find the French Revolution so threatening?
2. What was the long-term significance of Napoleon for Europe?

For practice quizzes and other study tools, see the Online Study Guide at bedfordstmartins.com/huntconcise.

For primary-source material from this period, see Chapters 19 and 20 of *Sources of The Making of the West,* Third Edition.

TIMELINE

1785 | 1795 | 1805 | 1815

- **1789** French Revolution begins
- **1791** Slave revolt in St. Domingue (Haiti)
- **1792** Start of war between France and the rest of Europe; second revolution of August 10 overthrows French monarchy
- **1793** Second partition of Poland by Prussia and Russia; Louis XVI of France executed for treason
- **1794** France annexes the Austrian Netherlands; abolition of slavery in French colonies; Robespierre falls, ending the Terror
- **1795** Third (final) partition of Poland
- **1799** Napoleon Bonaparte comes to power in a coup
- **1801** Napoleon signs a concordat with the pope
- **1804** Napoleon crowns himself emperor of France and issues the Civil Code
- **1805** British naval forces defeat the French at the battle of Trafalgar; Napoleon wins his greatest victory at the battle of Austerlitz
- **1810** Germaine de Staël publishes *On Germany*
- **1812** Napoleon invades Russia
- **1815** Napoleon defeated at Waterloo and exiled to island of St. Helena, where he dies in 1821

Suggested References

The most influential book on the meaning of the French Revolution is still the classic study by Tocqueville, who insisted that the Revolution continued the process of state centralization undertaken by the monarchy. Recent works on Napoleon show how powerfully his armies affected every European state.

Andress, David. *The Terror: The Merciless War for Freedom in Revolutionary France.* 2006.

Beaucour, Fernand Emile, Yves Laissus, and Chantal Orgogozo. *The Discovery of Egypt.* Trans. Bambi Ballard. 1990.

Bell, David A. *The First Total War: Napoleon's Europe and the Birth of Warfare as We Know It.* 2007.

*Blaufarb, Rafe. *Napoleon: A Symbol for an Age; A Brief History with Documents.* 2008.

Censer, Jack R., and Lynn Hunt. *Liberty, Equality, Fraternity: Exploring the French Revolution* (includes CD-ROM of images and music). 2001. See also the accompanying Web site: http://www.chnm.gmu.edu/revolution

Cole, Juan. *Napoléon's Egypt: Invading the Middle East.* 2007.

*Dubois, Laurent, and John D. Garrigus. *Slave Revolution in the Caribbean, 1789–1804: A Brief History with Documents.* 2006.

Englund, Steven. *Napoleon: A Political Life.* 2004.

Furet, François. *Interpreting the French Revolution.* Trans. Elborg Forster. 1981.

Godineau, Dominique. *The Women of Paris and Their French Revolution.* Trans. Katherine Streip. 1998.

*Hunt, Lynn, ed. *The French Revolution and Human Rights: A Brief Documentary History.* 1996.

*Levy, Darline Gay, Harriet Branson Applewhite, and Mary Durham Johnson, eds. *Women in Revolutionary Paris, 1789–1795.* 1979.

Napoleon Foundation: http://www.napoleon.org

Palmer, R. R. *The Age of the Democratic Revolution: A Political History of Europe and America, 1760–1800.* Vol. 2, *The Struggle.* 1964.

Tocqueville, Alexis de. *The Old Regime and the French Revolution.* Trans. Stuart Gilbert. 1955. Originally published 1856.

17

Industrialization and Social Ferment

1815–1850

IN 1830, THE LIVERPOOL AND MANCHESTER RAILWAY LINE opened in England to the cheers of crowds and the congratulations of government officials, including the duke of Wellington, the hero of Waterloo and now prime minister. The thirty-mile-long line required an act of Parliament and cost the private company formed to build it some £800,000, twice the original estimate. The sum was enormous; by contrast, the engine man earned only £54 a year. In the excitement of the opening, some of the dignitaries gathered on a parallel track. Another engine, George Stephenson's *Rocket*, approached at high speed—the engine could go as fast as twenty-seven miles per hour. Most of the gentlemen scattered to safety, but former cabinet minister William Huskisson fell and was hit. He died within a few hours, the first official casualty of the newfangled railroad.

The New Railroad
This engraving by H. Pyall from 1831 shows the entrance of the Liverpool and Manchester Railway Line at Edge Hill in Liverpool. The engine seems quaint to us now, but at the time it impressed everyone with its size and speed. Even upper-class men and women flocked to see the new engine in operation. Railroads immediately became the symbol of the industrial age, as well as its driving force. *(Getty Images.)*

Dramatic and expensive, railroads were the most striking symbol of the new industrial age. Industrialization and its by-product rapid urban growth fundamentally altered political conflicts, social relations, cultural concerns, and even the landscape itself. So great were these changes that they are collectively labeled the Industrial Revolution. Although this revolution did not take place in a single decade like the French Revolution, the introduction of steam-driven machinery, large factories, and a new working class transformed life in the Western world. Peasants and workers streamed into the cities. The population of London grew by 130,000 people in the 1830s alone; Berlin more than doubled between 1819 and 1849; and Paris expanded by 120,000 just between 1841 and 1846. To many observers, overcrowding, disease, prostitution, crime, and drinking all seemed to be on the increase as a result.

Although Europeans longed for peace and stability in the aftermath of the Napoleonic whirlwind, they lived in a world that was deeply unsettled by two parallel revolutions: the French Revolution and the Industrial Revolution. Social and political ferment prompted the development of a whole spectrum of ideologies to explain the meaning of the changes taking place. **Ideology**, a word coined during the French Revolution, refers to a coherent set of beliefs about the way a society's social and political order should be organized. Conservatism, nationalism, liberalism, socialism, and communism each offered their adherents a doctrine that explained social change and advocated a political program to confront it.

The claims of the new ideologies, the revolutionary legacy, and the new problems created by industrialization and urbanization all posed pressing challenges to rulers. After the Congress of Vienna (1814–1815) settled the boundaries of post-Napoleonic Europe and established conservatism as a kind of official ideology on the continent, restored monarchs tried to limit challenges to their rule. Despite their efforts, political revolts broke out sporadically in the 1820s and again in 1830. Most of these revolts failed, except in Latin America and Greece, where new nations emerged. Demands for social and political change came to a head in 1848, when the rapid transformation of European society provided the combustible material for a new set of revolutionary outbreaks more consuming than any since 1789.

CHAPTER FOCUS QUESTION How did the Industrial Revolution create new social and political conflicts?

The Industrial Revolution

French and British writers of the 1820s introduced the term *Industrial Revolution* to capture the drama of contemporary economic change and to draw a parallel with the French Revolution. But unlike the French upheaval, the Industrial Revolution did not have definite dates that marked its beginning or end. From their first appearance in Great Britain in the second half of the eighteenth century, steam-driven machines, large factories, and a new working class spread fitfully across Europe and eventually to the rest of the world. In the first half of the nineteenth century, many Europeans began to take notice of the acceleration of **industrialization** and urbanization and often complained of the consequences.

Roots of Industrialization

British inventors had been steadily perfecting and adapting steam engines for five decades before George Stephenson built his *Rocket*. A key breakthrough took place in 1776, when James Watt adapted the existing model to make a more efficient steam engine for pumping water from coal mines and for driving machinery in textile factories. Since coal fired the steam engines that drove the new textile machines, innovations tended to reinforce each other. This kind of synergy built on previous changes in the textile industry. In 1733, the Englishman John Kay had patented the flying shuttle, which weavers operated by pulling a cord that drove the shuttle to either side of the loom, enabling them to "throw" yarn across the loom rather than draw it back and forth by hand. When the flying shuttle came into widespread use in the 1760s, weavers began producing cloth more quickly than spinners could produce thread. The resulting shortage of spun thread propelled the invention of machines to speed the process of spinning. The spinning jenny and water frame, a power-driven spinning machine, were introduced in the 1760s. In the following decades, water frames replaced thousands of women spinners working at home by hand. Using the engines produced by Watt and his partner, Matthew Boulton, Edmund Cartwright designed a mechanized loom in the 1780s, which when perfected could be run by a small boy and yield fifteen times the output of a skilled adult weaver working a handloom. By the end of the century, all the new power machinery was assembled in large factories that hired semiskilled men, women, and children to replace skilled weavers.

Several factors interacted to make England the first site of the Industrial Revolution. Because population increased by more than 50 percent in England in the second half of the eighteenth century, manufacturers had an incentive to produce more and cheaper cotton cloth. England had a good supply of private investment capital from overseas trade and commercial profits, ready access to raw cotton from the plantations of its Caribbean colonies and the southern United States, and the necessary natural resources at home, such as coal and iron. Good opportunities for social mobility and relative political stability in the eighteenth century provided an environment that fostered the pragmatism of the English and Scottish inventors who designed the machinery. These early industrialists shared a culture of informal scientific education through learned societies and popular lectures (one of the prominent forms of the Enlightenment in Britain). Manufacturers proved eager to introduce steam-driven machinery to increase output and gradually established factories to house the new machines and concentrate the labor of their workers. The agricultural revolution of the eighteenth century had enabled England to produce food more efficiently, freeing some agricultural workers to move to the new manufacturing centers. Cotton textile production skyrocketed.

Elsewhere in Europe, textile manufacturing—long a linchpin in the European economy—expanded in the eighteenth century even without the introduction of new machines and factories. Textile production increased because of the spread of the "putting-out" or "domestic" system. Under the putting-out system, manufacturers supplied the raw materials, such as woolen or cotton fibers, to families working at home. The mother and children washed the fibers and carded and combed them. Then the mother and older daughters spun them into thread. The father, assisted by the children, wove the cloth. The cloth was then "finished" (bleached, dyed, smoothed, and so on) under the supervision of the manufacturer in a large workshop, located either in town or in the countryside. This system had existed in the textile industry for hundreds of years, but in the eighteenth century it grew dramatically, and it included not only textiles but also the manufacture of products such as glassware, baskets, nails, and guns. The spread of the domestic system of manufacturing is sometimes called proto-industrialization to signify that the process helped pave the way for the full-scale Industrial Revolution. Because of this expansion, ordinary people began to wear underclothes and nightclothes, both rare in the past. White, red, blue, yellow, green, and even pastel shades of cotton now replaced the black, gray, or brown of traditional woolen clothing.

Engines of Change

Steam-driven engines took on a dramatic new form in the 1820s, when the English engineer George Stephenson perfected an engine to pull wagons along iron tracks. The idea of a railroad was not new: iron tracks had been used since the seventeenth century to haul coal from mines in wagons pulled by horses. Railroads, however, developed only after Stephenson's invention of a steam-powered locomotive. In the 1830s, railroad building became a new industry throughout Europe (see "Taking Measure"). Belgium, newly independent in 1830, opened the first continental railroad in 1835 with state bonds backed by British capital. Railroads grew spectacularly in the United States in the 1830s and 1840s as well, and the British also began to

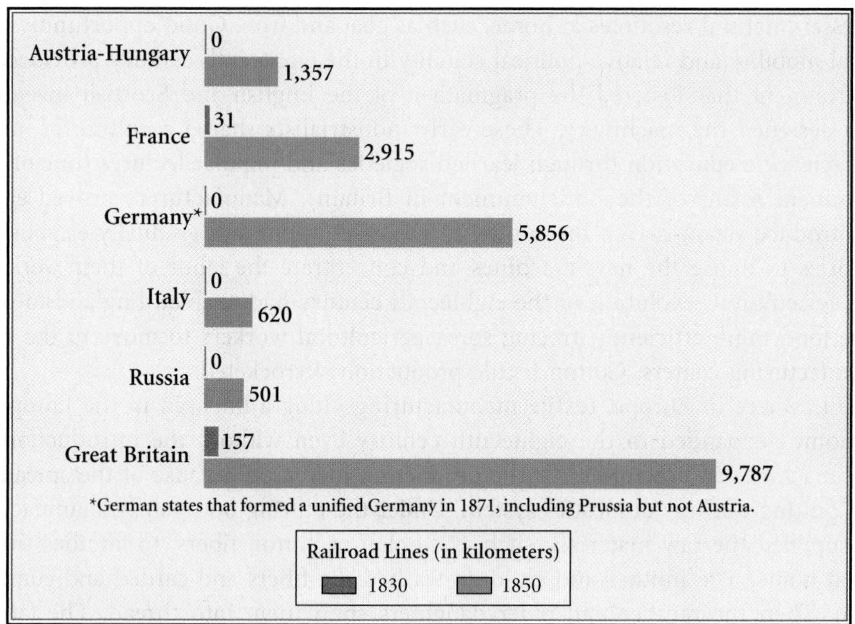

Taking Measure Railroad Lines, 1830–1850
Great Britain quickly extended its lead in building railroads. The extension of commerce and, before long, the ability to wage war would depend on the development of effective rail networks. These statistics might be taken as predicting a realignment of power within Europe after 1850. What do the numbers say about the relative positions of Germany (the German states, including Prussia but excluding Austria), Austria-Hungary, and France?

build railroads in India. In all, the world had 23,500 miles of track by midcentury, the vast majority of them in Europe.

Railroad building spurred both industrial development and state power (see "Mapping the West," page 679). Placed on the new tracks, steam-driven carriages could transport people and goods to the cities and link coal and iron deposits to the new factories. Governments everywhere participated in the construction of railroads, which depended on private and state funds to pay for the massive amounts of iron, coal, heavy machinery, and human labor required to build and run them. One-third of all investment in the German states in the 1840s went into railroads. Some people expected social and political change to follow. One German entrepreneur confidently predicted, "The locomotive is the hearse which will carry absolutism and feudalism to the graveyard." But the most obvious effects could be seen in the demand for iron products. Until the 1840s, cotton had led industrial production, but afterward iron and coal began to count more and more.

Steam-powered engines made Great Britain the world leader in manufacturing. By midcentury, more than half of Britain's national income came from manufacturing and trade. The number of steamboats in Britain increased from two in 1812 to six hundred in 1840. Between 1840 and 1850, steam power doubled in Britain and increased even more rapidly elsewhere in Europe, as those adopting British inventions strove to catch up. Although Britain consciously tried to protect its industrial supremacy, thousands of British engineers defied laws against the export of machinery or the emigration of artisans. The best known of them, John Cockerill, set up a machine works in Belgium that was soon selling its products as far east as Poland and Russia. Cockerill claimed to know about every innovation within ten days of its appearance in Britain.

Only slowly, thanks to such pirating of British methods and to new technical schools, did most continental European countries begin closing the gap. Belgium became the fastest-growing industrial power on the continent. Between 1830 and 1844, the number of steam engines in Belgium quadrupled, and Belgians exported seven times as many steam engines as they imported. Even so, by 1850 continental Europe still lagged almost twenty years behind Great Britain in industrial development.

Formation of the Working Class

Steam-driven machines first brought workers together in factories in the textile industry. By 1830, more than one million people in Britain depended on the cotton industry for employment, and cotton cloth constituted 50 percent of the country's exports. The rapid expansion of the British textile industry had as its colonial corollary the destruction of the hand-manufacture of textiles in India. The British put high import duties on Indian cloth entering Britain and kept such duties very low for British cloth entering India. The figures are dramatic: in 1813, the Indian city of Calcutta exported to England £2 million of cotton cloth; by 1830, Calcutta was importing from England £2 million of cotton cloth. When Britain abolished slavery in its Caribbean colonies in 1833, British manufacturers began to buy raw cotton in the southern United States, where slavery still flourished.

Factories drew workers from the urban population surge, which had begun in the eighteenth century and now accelerated. The population of such new industrial cities as Manchester and Leeds increased 40 percent in the 1820s alone. Historians long thought that factory workers came from the countryside, pushed off the land by the field enclosures of the 1700s. But recent studies have shown that the number of agricultural laborers actually increased during industrialization in Britain, suggesting that a growing birthrate created a larger population and fed workers into the new factory system. A system of employment that resembled family labor on farms or in putting-out, or cottage, industries also developed in the new factories. Entire families came to toil for a single wage, although family members performed different tasks. Workdays of twelve to seventeen hours were typical, even for children, and the work was grueling.

As urban factories grew, their workers gradually came to constitute a new socioeconomic class with a distinctive culture and traditions. Like *middle class,* the term *working class* came into use for the first time in the early nineteenth century. It referred to the laborers in the new factories. In the past, workers had labored in isolated trades: water and wood carrying, gardening, laundry, and building. In contrast, factories brought people together with machines, under close supervision by their employers.

Factory Work
This 1836 depiction of the mechanized spinning of cotton in England captures the dangers of child labor: the child (lower right) is sweeping even while the machine works. The print does not portray the churning noise and swirling dust of the workplace, but it does show how machines could produce thread much more efficiently than individuals working on their own. Do you think the artist aimed to provide a positive or a negative picture of factory work? (Mary Evans Picture Library.)

Workers soon developed a sense of common interests and organized societies for mutual help and political reform. From these would come the first labor unions.

In 1811 and 1812, bands of handloom weavers, fearing their displacement by machines, wrecked factory machinery and burned mills in the Midlands, Yorkshire, and Lancashire. To restore order and protect industry, the British government sent in an army of twelve thousand regular soldiers and made machine wrecking punishable by death. The rioters were called Luddites, after the fictitious figure Ned Ludd, whose signature appeared on their manifestos. (The term is still used to describe those who resist new technology.)

Other British workers focused their organizing efforts on reforming Parliament, whose members were chosen in elections dominated by the landowning elite. One reformer complained that the members of the House of Commons were nothing but "toad-eaters, gamblers, public plunderers, and hirelings." Reform clubs held large open-air meetings, and ordinary people eagerly bought cheap newspapers that clamored for change. In August 1819, sixty thousand people attended an illegal meeting held in St. Peter's Fields in Manchester. When the local authorities sent the cavalry to arrest the speaker, panic resulted. Eleven people were killed and many hundreds were injured in what was soon labeled the Peterloo massacre (combining St. Peter's with Waterloo, the battle that had ended Napoleon's reign only four years before). An alarmed government passed the Six Acts, which forbade large political meetings and restricted press criticism, suppressing the reform movement for a decade.

Despite increasing industrial growth, factory workers remained a minority everywhere. In the 1840s, factories in England employed only 5 percent of the workers, in France 3 percent, and in Prussia 2 percent. Most workers, both men and women, continued to toil at home in cottage industries. In the 1840s, for example, two-thirds of the manufacturing workers in Prussia and Saxony labored at home for contractors or merchants who supplied raw materials and then sold the finished goods. Some peasants kept their options open by combining factory work with agricultural labor. They worked in agriculture during the spring and summer and in manufacturing in the fall and winter. Unstable industrial wages made such arrangements essential. Some new industries idled periodically: for example, iron forges stopped for several months when the water level in streams dropped, and blast furnaces shut down for repairs several weeks every year. In hard times, factory owners simply closed their doors until demand for their goods improved.

Even though factories employed only a small percentage of the population, they attracted much attention because they created both unheard-of riches and new forms of poverty. "From this filthy sewer pure gold flows," wrote the French aristocrat Alexis de Tocqueville after visiting Manchester in the 1830s. "Here humanity attains its most complete development and its most brutish, here civilization works its miracles and civilized man is turned almost into a savage." Studies by physicians set the life expectancy of workers in Manchester at just seventeen years in 1840 (partly because of high rates of infant mortality), compared to the average life span of forty years throughout England. Visitors invariably complained about the smoke and soot. One American visitor to Britain in the late 1840s described how "in the manufacturing town, the fine soot or *blacks* darken the day, give white sheep the color of black sheep, discolor the human saliva, contaminate the air, poison many plants, and corrode monuments and buildings."

Authorities worried in particular about the effects on families. A doctor in the Prussian town of Breslau (population 111,000 in 1850), for example, reported that in working-class districts "several persons live in one room in a single bed, or perhaps a whole family, and use the room for all domestic duties, so that the air gets vitiated [polluted]. . . . Their diet consists largely of bread and potatoes." In Great Britain, the Factory Act of 1833 outlawed the employment of children under the age of nine in textile mills. It also limited the workdays of children ages nine to thirteen to nine hours a day and those ages thirteen to eighteen to twelve hours. Adults worked even longer hours. When investigating commissions showed that women and young children, sometimes under age six, were hauling coal trucks through low, cramped passageways in coal mines, Parliament passed the Mines Act of 1842 prohibiting the employment of women and girls underground. In 1847, the Central Short Time Committee, one of Britain's many social reform organizations, successfully pressured Parliament to limit the workday of women and children to ten hours. Countries in continental Europe followed Britain's lead, but since most did not insist on government inspection, enforcement was lax.

The advance of industrialization in eastern Europe was slow, in large part because serfdom still survived there, hindering labor mobility and tying up investment capital. As long as peasants were legally tied to the land as serfs, they could not migrate to the new factory towns, and landlords felt little incentive to invest their income in manufacturing. The problem was worst in Russia, where industrialization had hardly begun and would not take off until the end of the nineteenth century. Nevertheless, even in Russia signs of industrialization could be detected: raw cotton imports (a sign of a growing textile industry) increased sevenfold between 1831 and 1848, and the number of factories doubled, along with the size of the industrial workforce.

Urbanization and Its Consequences

Industrial development spurred urban growth wherever factories were located in or near cities, yet cities grew even with little industry. Here, too, Great Britain led the way: half the population of England and Wales lived in towns by 1850, while in France and the German states the urban population was only about a quarter of the total. In the 1830s and 1840s, many European cities ballooned. Massive rural emigration, rather than births to women already living in cities, accounted for this remarkable increase. Europe's population grew by nearly 100 percent between 1800 and 1850, yet agricultural yields increased by only 30 to 50 percent. City life and new factories beckoned those faced with hunger and poverty, including emigrants from other lands: thousands of Irish emigrated to English cities, Italians went to French cities, and Poles flocked to German cities. Since the construction of new housing could not keep up with population growth, overcrowding was inevitable. In 1847 in

St. Giles, the Irish quarter of London, 461 people lived in just twelve houses. Men, women, and children huddled together on piles of filthy, rotting straw or potato peels because they had no money for fuel to keep warm.

Severe crowding worsened already dire sanitation conditions. Residents dumped refuse into streets or courtyards, and human excrement collected in cesspools under apartment houses. At midcentury, London's approximately 250,000 cesspools were emptied only once or twice a year. Water was scarce and had to be fetched daily from nearby fountains. Despite the diversion of water from provincial rivers to Paris and a tripling of the number of public fountains, Parisians had enough water for only two baths annually per person (the upper classes enjoyed more baths, the lower classes fewer). In London, private companies that supplied water turned on pumps in the poorer sections for only a few hours three days a week. In rapidly growing British industrial cities such as Manchester, one-third of the houses contained no latrines. Human waste ended up in the rivers that supplied the cities' drinking water. The horses that provided transportation inside the cities left droppings everywhere, and city dwellers often kept chickens, ducks, goats, pigs, geese, and even cattle, as well as dogs and cats, in their houses. The result was, as one observer noted, a "universal atmosphere of filth and stink."

Such conditions made cities prime breeding grounds for disease. In 1830–1832 and again in 1847–1851, devastating outbreaks of **cholera** swept across Asia and Europe, touching the United States as well in 1849–1850. Today we know that a waterborne bacterium causes cholera, but at the time no one understood the disease and everyone feared it. The usually fatal illness induced violent vomiting and diarrhea and left the skin blue. While cholera particularly ravaged the crowded, filthy neighborhoods of rapidly growing cities, it also claimed many rural and some well-to-do victims. In Paris, 18,000 people died in the 1832 epidemic and 20,000 in that of 1849; in London, 7,000 died in each epidemic; and in Russia, the epidemics were catastrophic, claiming 250,000 victims in 1831–1832 and 1 million in 1847–1851.

Rumors and panic followed in the wakes of epidemics such as cholera. In Paris in April 1832, a crowd of workers attacked a central hospital, believing the doctors were poisoning the poor and using cholera as a hoax to cover up the conspiracy. Eastern European peasants burned estates and killed physicians and officials. Though devastating, cholera did not kill as many people as tuberculosis, Europe's deadliest disease. Tuberculosis took its victims one by one, however, and therefore had less impact on social relations.

Reformers believed that overcrowding among the poor led not only to disease but also to sexual promiscuity, illegitimacy, and crime. A physician visiting Lille, France, in 1835 wrote of "individuals of both sexes and of very different ages lying together, most of them without nightshirts and repulsively dirty. . . . The reader will complete the picture." Officials collected statistics on illegitimacy that seemed to bear out these fears: one-quarter to one-half of the babies born in the big European cities in the 1830s and 1840s were illegitimate, and alarmed medical men wrote about thousands of infanticides. Between 1815 and the mid-1830s in France, 33,000 babies were abandoned at foundling hospitals every year. Middle-class observers linked sexual disorder with drinking and crime. Beer halls and pubs dotted the urban landscape. One London street boasted of twenty-three pubs in three hundred yards. Police officials estimated that London had 70,000 thieves and 80,000 prostitutes. A Swiss pastor warned of the consequences of lower-class poverty: "Their hearts seethe with hatred of the well-to-do; their eyes lust for a share of the wealth about them; their mouths speak unblushingly of a coming day of retribution."

Reforming the Social Order

Government reports, medical accounts, and fictionalized depictions prompted reformers to organize to help the poor. Charitable impulses often went hand in hand with attempts to impose order and discipline on lower-class families deemed to be lacking in both. Although women's professional opportunities were severely limited, they took a prominent role in charitable and reform work. Catholic religious orders, which by 1850 enrolled many more women than men, ran schools, hospitals, leper colonies, insane asylums, and old-age homes. New Catholic orders, especially for women, were established, and Catholic missionary activity overseas increased.

Protestant women in Great Britain and the United States established Bible, missionary, and female reform societies by the hundreds. Many societies dedicated themselves to reforming prostitutes and castigating their male clients. Others promoted missionary activity in other parts of the world. In the British colony of India, Protestant missionaries argued for the reform of Hindu customs. *Sati*—the burning of widows on the funeral pyres of their husbands—was abolished by the British administration of India in 1829. Protestant and Catholic missionary activity would become an arm of European imperialism and cultural influence in the nineteenth century.

Religiously motivated reformers first had to overcome the perceived indifference of the working classes. Less than 10 percent of the workers in cities attended religious services. To combat such indifference, British religious groups launched the Sunday school movement, which reached its zenith in the 1840s. By 1851, more than half of all working-class children between the ages of five and fifteen were attending Sunday schools, which taught children how to read at a time when few working-class children could go to school during the week. Many Sunday schools were run by Methodists, who followed the teachings of John Wesley (1703–1791). The Methodists, or Wesleyans, gradually separated from the Church of England and in the early decades of the nineteenth century attracted thousands of members in huge revival meetings that lasted for days. Shopkeepers, artisans, agricultural laborers, miners, and workers in cottage industries, both male and female, flocked to the new denomination.

Social reformers elsewhere also saw education as one of the main prospects for uplifting the poor and the working class. In 1833, the French government passed an education law that required every town to maintain a primary school, pay a teacher, and provide free education to poor boys. The law's author, François Guizot, explained the government's attitude: "Ignorance renders the masses turbulent and ferocious."

Girls' schools were optional. By the late 1830s, 60 percent of children attended primary school in France, still less than in Protestant Prussia, where 75 percent of children went to school. Popular education remained woefully undeveloped in most of eastern Europe. Peasants were specifically excluded from the few primary schools in Russia.

Catholics and Protestants alike promoted the **temperance movement** to fight the "pestilence of hard liquor." The first temperance societies had appeared in the United States as early as 1813, and by 1835 the American Temperance Society claimed 1.5 million members. Temperance advocates saw drunkenness as a sign of moral weakness and a threat to the social order. One German temperance advocate insisted, "One need not be a prophet to know that all efforts to combat the widespread and rapidly spreading pauperism will be unsuccessful as long as the common man fails to realize that the principal source of his degradation and misery is his fondness of drink." Yet temperance societies also attracted working-class people who shared the desire for respectability.

Organizations such as the Society for the Prevention of Cruelty to Animals tried to eliminate popular blood sports such as cockfighting and bearbaiting. Their members believed that such entertainments encouraged violent behavior outside the arena. By the end of the 1830s, bullbaiting had been abandoned in Great Britain. "This useful animal," rejoiced one reformer in 1839, "is no longer tortured amidst the exulting yells of those who are a disgrace to our common form and nature." Other blood sports died out more slowly, and efforts in other countries generally lagged behind those of the British.

When private charities failed to meet the needs of the poor, governments often intervened. Great Britain sought to control the costs of public welfare by passing a new poor law in 1834, called by its critics the "Starvation Act." The law required that all able-bodied persons receiving relief be placed in workhouses, with husbands separated from wives and parents from children. Workhouse life was designed to be as unpleasant as possible so that poor people would move on to regions of higher employment. British women from all social classes organized anti–poor law societies to protest the separation of mothers from their children in the workhouses.

Many women viewed charitable work as the extension of their domestic roles: they promoted virtuous behavior and morality and thus improved society. Yet women's social reform activities concealed a paradox. According to the set of beliefs that historians call the doctrine or ideology of **domesticity**, women should live their lives entirely within the domestic sphere; they should devote themselves to the home, not public activities. The English poet Alfred, Lord Tennyson, captured this view in a popular poem published in 1847: "Man for the field and woman for the hearth; / Man for the sword and for the needle she. . . . All else confusion." Many believed that maintaining proper and distinct roles for men and women was critically important to maintaining social order in general.

Most women had little hope of economic independence. The notion of a separate, domestic sphere for women prevented them from pursuing higher education, work in professional careers, or participation in politics through voting or holding office—all activities deemed appropriate only to men. Laws everywhere codified the subordination of women. Many countries followed the model of Napoleon's Civil Code, which classified married women as legal incompetents along with children, the insane, and criminals.

Distinctions between men and women were most noticeable in the privileged classes. Whereas boys attended secondary schools, most middle- and upper-class girls still received their education at home or in church schools, where they were taught to be religious, obedient, and accomplished in music and languages. As men's fashions turned practical—long trousers and short jackets of solid, often dark colors; no makeup (previously common for aristocratic men); and simply cut hair rather than wigs—women continued to dress for decorative effect, now with tightly corseted waists that emphasized the differences between female and male bodies. Middle- and upper-class women had long hair that required hours of brushing and pinning up, and they wore long, cumbersome skirts. Advice books written by women detailed the tasks that such women undertook in the home: maintaining household accounts, supervising servants, and organizing social events.

Scientists reinforced stereotypes. Once considered sexually insatiable, women were now described as incapacitated by menstruation and largely uninterested in sex, an attitude that many equated with moral superiority. Thus was born the "Victorian" woman, a figment of the largely male medical imagination. Physicians and scholars considered women mentally inferior. In 1839, Auguste Comte, an influential early French sociologist, wrote, "As for any functions of government, the radical inaptitude of the female sex is there yet more marked . . . and limited to the guidance of the mere family."

Novels by women often revealed the bleaker side of women's situations. *Jane Eyre* (1847), a novel by the English writer Charlotte Brontë, describes the difficult life of an orphaned girl who becomes a governess, the only occupation open to most single middle-class women. Although she is in an economically weak position, Jane Eyre refuses to achieve respectability and security through marriage, the usual option for women. The French novelist George Sand (Amandine-Aurore Dupin, 1804–1876) took her social criticism a step further. She announced her independence in the 1830s by dressing like a man and smoking cigars. Like many other women writers of the time, she published her work under a male pseudonym while creating female characters who prevail in difficult circumstances through romantic love and moral idealism. Sand's novel *Indiana* (1832), about an unhappily married woman, was read all over Europe. Her notoriety made the term *George-Sandism* a common expression of disdain for independent women.

Whether by women or men, novels proved to be the art form best suited to portraying the new society and its social ills. Thanks to increased literacy, the spread of reading rooms and lending libraries, and serialization in newspapers and journals, novels reached a large reading public and helped shape public awareness. Unlike the fiction of the eighteenth century, which had focused on individual personalities, the great novels of the 1830s and 1840s specialized in the description of social life in all its varieties. Manufacturers, financiers, starving students, workers, bureaucrats, prostitutes, underworld figures, thieves, and aristocratic men and women filled the pages of works

George Sand
In this lithograph by Alcide Lorentz (1842), George Sand is shown in one of her notorious masculine costumes. Sand published numerous works, including novels, plays, essays, travel writing, and an autobiography. She actively participated in the revolution of 1848 in France, writing pamphlets in support of the new republic. (The Granger Collection, NY.)

by popular writers such as Honoré de Balzac and Charles Dickens. Pushing himself to exhaustion and a premature death to get out of debt, the French writer Balzac (1799–1850) cranked out ninety-five novels and many short stories.

The English author Charles Dickens (1812–1870) worked with a similar frenetic energy and for much the same reasons. When his father was imprisoned for debt in 1824, the young Dickens took a job in a shoe-polish factory. After working briefly as a political journalist, he began publishing novels, many of which drew attention to the poverty and misery produced by industrialization and urbanization. In *The Old Curiosity Shop* (1841), for example, he depicts the Black Country, the manufacturing region west and northwest of Birmingham, as a "cheerless region" and a "mournful place," in which tall chimneys "made foul the melancholy air." In addition to publishing such enduring favorites as *Oliver Twist* (1838) and *A Christmas Carol* (1843), he set up a home for homeless women and personally ran it for twelve years. For Dickens, the ability to portray the problems of the poor went hand in hand with a personal commitment to reform.

REVIEW Why were cities seen as dangerous places?

New Ideologies

Although reform organizations grew rapidly in the 1830s and 1840s, many Europeans found them insufficient to answer the questions raised by industrialization and urbanization. How did the new social order differ from the earlier one, which was less urban and less driven by commercial concerns? Who should control this new order? Should governments try to moderate or accelerate the pace of change? New ideologies such as liberalism and socialism offered competing answers to these questions and provided the platform for new political movements. This was an era of "isms"—conservatism, liberalism, socialism, nationalism, and romanticism.

Conservatism

The French Revolution and Napoleonic domination of Europe had shown contemporaries that government could be changed overnight, that the old hierarchies could be overthrown in the name of reason, and that even Christianity could be written off or at least profoundly altered with the stroke of a pen. The potential for rapid change raised many questions about the proper sources of authority. Kings and churches could be restored and former revolutionaries locked up or silenced, but the old order no longer commanded automatic obedience. The old order was now merely *old,* no longer "natural" and "timeless." It had been ousted once and therefore might fall again. People insisted on having reasons to believe in their "restored" governments. The political doctrine that justified the restoration was **conservatism.**

Conservatives benefited from the disillusionment that permeated Europe after 1815. In the eyes of most Europeans, Napoleon had become a tyrant who ruled in his own interests. Conservatives believed it was crucial to analyze the roots of such tyranny so that established authorities could use their knowledge of history to prevent its recurrence. They saw a logical progression in recent history: the Enlightenment based on reason led to the French Revolution, with its bloody guillotine and horrifying Terror, which in turn spawned the authoritarian and militaristic Napoleon. Conservative intellectuals therefore either rejected Enlightenment principles or at least subjected them to scrutiny and skepticism.

The most influential spokesman of conservatism was Edmund Burke (1729–1799), the British critic of the French Revolution. He argued that the revolutionaries erred in thinking they could construct an entirely new government based on reason. Government, Burke said, had to be rooted in long experience, which evolved over generations. All change must be gradual and must respect national and historical traditions.

Like Burke, later conservatives believed that religious and other major traditions were an essential foundation for any society. Conservatives blamed the French Revolution's attack on religion on the skepticism and anticlericalism of such Enlightenment thinkers as Voltaire, and they defended both hereditary monarchy and the authority of the church, whether Catholic or Protestant. Only the church, the state, and the family, rather than the individualistic "rights of man," could provide an enduring social order. Faith, history, and tradition must fill the vacuum left by the failures of reason and excessive belief in individual rights. Across Europe, these views were taken up and elaborated by government advisers, professors, and writers.

Liberalism

The adherents of **liberalism** defined themselves in opposition to conservatives on one end of the political spectrum and revolutionaries on the other. Nineteenth-century liberals should not be confused with those of the present day. In the nineteenth century, liberals emphasized constitutionalism and free trade above all else. They generally applauded the social and economic changes produced by the Industrial Revolution, while opposing the violence and excessive state power promoted by the French Revolution. The leaders of the rapidly expanding middle class, composed of manufacturers, merchants, and professionals, favored liberalism.

The foremost exponent of early-nineteenth-century liberalism was the English philosopher and jurist Jeremy Bentham (1748–1832). He called his brand of liberalism "utilitarianism" because he held that the best policy is the one that produces "the greatest good for the greatest number" and is thus the most useful, or utilitarian. Bentham's criticisms spared no institution; he railed against the injustices of the British parliamentary process, the abuses of the prisons and the penal code, and the educational system.

Bentham and many other liberals joined the abolitionist movement, which intensified between the 1790s and 1820s. Agitation by groups such as the London Society for Effecting the Abolition of the Slave Trade succeeded in gaining a first victory in 1807 when the British House of Lords voted to abolish the slave trade. The abolitionists' efforts finally bore fruit in 1833 when Britain abolished slavery in all its colonies.

British liberals pushed for two major reforms in addition to the abolition of slavery: expansion of the electorate to give representation to a broader segment of the middle class and repeal of the **Corn Laws**, or tariffs on foreign grain. They gained their first goal in the Reform Bill of 1832. When the Tories in Parliament resisted the proposed extension of the right to vote, liberals and their supporters organized mass demonstrations. The Reform Bill passed after the king threatened to create enough new peers to obtain its passage in the House of Lords. Although the number of male voters increased by about 50 percent, only one in five Britons could now vote, and voting still depended on holding property. Nevertheless, the bill gave representation to new cities in the industrial north for the first time and set a precedent for further widening suffrage.

When landholders in the House of Commons thwarted efforts to lower grain tariffs, two Manchester cotton manufacturers set up the Anti–Corn Law League. The league denounced the landlords as "blood-sucking vampires" and attracted working-class backing by promising lower food prices. The league established local branches, published newspapers and the journal *The Economist* (founded in 1843 and now one of the world's most influential periodicals), and campaigned in elections. The league eventually won the support of the Tory prime minister Sir Robert Peel, whose government repealed the Corn Laws in 1846.

Liberalism had less appeal in continental Europe, except in France, because industrial growth was slower and the middle classes smaller than in Britain. French liberals agitated for greater freedom of the press and a broadening of the vote. The flamboyant Hungarian nationalist Lajos Kossuth (1802–1894) grabbed every opportunity to publicize American democracy and British political liberalism, all in a fervent nationalist spirit. Considered subversive ideas in Russia, Western liberal writings, as well as all books about the United States, were banned by Tsar Nicholas I (r. 1825–1855). He sent nearly ten thousand people a year into exile in Siberia as punishment for their political activities.

Socialism and the Early Labor Movement

Socialism took up where liberalism left off. Socialists believed that the liberties advocated by liberals benefited only the middle class—the owners of factories and businesses—not the workers. They sought to reorganize society totally rather than to reform it piecemeal through political measures. Many were utopians who believed that ideal communities are based on cooperation rather than competition. Like Thomas More, whose book *Utopia* (1516) gave the movement its name, the utopian socialists believed that society would benefit all its members only if private property ceased to exist.

Socialists criticized the new industrial order for dividing society into two classes: the new middle class, or capitalists, who owned the wealth; and the working class, their downtrodden and impoverished employees. Such divisions tore the social fabric, and as their name suggests, the socialists aimed to restore harmony and cooperation through social reorganization. Three early socialists helped instigate the movement: Robert Owen, Claude Henri de Saint-Simon, and Charles Fourier.

Robert Owen (1771–1858) founded British socialism. A successful Welsh-born manufacturer, Owen bought a cotton mill in New Lanark, Scotland, in 1800 and began to set up a model factory town, where workers labored only ten hours a day (instead of seventeen, as was common). He moved to the United States in the 1820s to establish a community in Indiana named New Harmony. The experiment collapsed after three years, a victim of internal squabbling. Nonetheless, Owen's experiments and writings inspired the movement for producer cooperatives (businesses owned and controlled by their workers), consumer cooperatives (stores in which consumers owned shares), and a national trade union.

Claude Henri de Saint-Simon (1760–1825) and Charles Fourier (1772–1837) were Owen's contemporaries in France. Saint-Simon was a noble who had served as an officer in the American War of Independence and lost a fortune speculating in national property during the French Revolution. Fourier traveled as a salesman for a Lyon cloth merchant. Both shared Owen's alarm about the effects of industrialization on social relations. Saint-Simon coined the terms *industrialism* and *industrialist* to define the new economic order and its chief organizers. He believed that work, the central element in the new society, should be controlled not by politicians but by scientists, engineers, artists, and industrialists. To correct the abuses of the new industrial order, Fourier urged the establishment of communities that were part garden city and part agricultural commune; all jobs would be rotated to maximize happiness. The emancipation of women was essential to Fourier's vision of a harmonious community: "The extension of the privileges of women is the fundamental cause of all social progress."

Women participated actively in the socialist movements of the day, even though socialist men often shared the widespread prejudice against women's political activism. In Great Britain, many women joined the Owenites and helped form cooperative societies and unions. They defended women's working-class organizations against the complaints of men in the new societies and trade unions. As one woman wrote, "Do not say the unions are only for men. . . . 'Tis a wrong impression, forced on our minds to keep us slaves!" As women became more active, Owenites agitated for women's rights, marriage reform, and popular education. In 1832, Saint-Simonian women founded a feminist newspaper in France, *The Free Woman.* Some followers of Saint-Simon's brand of socialism developed a quasi-religious cult with elaborate rituals and a "he-pope" and "she-pope," or ruling father and mother. They lived and worked together in cooperative arrangements and scandalized some by advocating free love.

The French activist Flora Tristan (1801–1844) devoted herself to reconciling the interests of male and female workers. She had seen the "frightful reality" of London's poverty and made a reputation reporting on British working conditions. Tristan published a stream of books and pamphlets urging male workers to address women's unequal status, arguing that "the emancipation of male workers is *impossible* so long as women remain in a degraded state." She advocated the Universal Union of Men and Women Workers.

Even though most male socialists ignored Tristan's plea for women's participation, like her they worked to found working-class associations. French socialist Pierre-Joseph Proudhon (1809–1865) urged workers to form producers' associations so that they could control the work process and eliminate profits made by capitalists. His 1840 book *What Is Property?* argues that property is theft: labor alone is productive, and rent, interest, and profit are unjust.

After 1840, some socialists began to call themselves **communists**, emphasizing their desire to replace private property with communal, collective ownership. The two most influential communists were Karl Marx (1818–1883) and Friedrich Engels (1820–1895), both sons of prosperous German-Jewish families that had converted to Christianity. Marx studied philosophy at the University of Berlin, edited a liberal newspaper until the Prussian government suppressed it, and then left for Paris, where he met Engels. While working in the offices of his wealthy family's cotton manufacturing interests in Manchester, England, Engels had been shocked into writing *The Condition of the Working Class in England in 1844* (1845), a sympathetic depiction of industrial workers' dismal lives. In Paris, where German and eastern European intellectuals could pursue their political interests more freely than at home, Marx and Engels organized the Communist League, in whose name they published *The Communist Manifesto* (1848). It eventually became the touchstone of Marxist and communist revolution all over the world.

Limited as was the influence of Marx and Engels in the 1840s, they had already begun their lifework of scientifically understanding the "laws" of capitalism and fostering revolutionary organizations. Their principles and analysis of history were in place: communists, the *Manifesto* declared, must aim for "the downfall of the bourgeoisie [capitalist class] and the ascendancy of the proletariat [working class], the abolition of the old society based on class conflicts and the foundation of a new society without classes and without private property." Marx and Engels embraced industrialization because they believed it would eventually bring on the proletarian revolution and lead inevitably to the abolition of exploitation, private property, and class society.

Socialism accompanied, and in some places incited, an upsurge in working-class organization in western Europe. In 1824, the British government repealed laws prohibiting labor unions, though it maintained restrictions on strikes. Other European rulers forbade unions. Artisans and skilled workers in France formed mutual aid societies that provided insurance, death benefits, and education. In eastern and central Europe, socialism and labor organization—like liberalism—had less impact than in western Europe. Cooperative societies and workers' newspapers did not appear in the German states until 1848. Working-class organization, even in limited form, struck fear in the hearts of many in the upper classes. A British newspaper exclaimed in 1834, "The trade unions are, we have no doubt, the most dangerous institutions that were ever permitted to take root."

Nationalism

Nationalists could be liberals, socialists, or even conservatives. In the nineteenth century, **nationalism** began as a radical or revolutionary movement and then evolved in a more conservative direction over time. Nationalism holds that all peoples derive their identities from their nations, which are defined by common language, shared cultural traditions, and sometimes religion. When such "nations" do not coincide with state boundaries, as they often did not in the nineteenth and twentieth centuries, nationalism can produce violence and warfare as different national groups compete for control over territory.

The French showed the power of national feeling in their revolutionary and Napoleonic wars, but they also provoked nationalism in the people they conquered. Once Napoleon and his satellite rulers departed, nationalist sentiment turned against other outside rulers—the Ottoman Turks in the Balkans, the Russians in Poland, and the Austrians in Italy. Intellectuals took the lead in demanding unity and freedom for their peoples. They collected folktales, poems, and histories and prepared grammars and dictionaries of their native languages (Map 17.1). Students, middle-class professionals, and army officers formed secret societies to promote national independence and constitutional reform.

Nationalist aspirations were especially explosive for the Austrian Empire, which included a variety of peoples united only by their enforced allegiance to the Habsburg emperor. The empire included three main national groups: the Germans, who made up one-fourth of the population; the Magyars of Hungary (which included Transylvania and Croatia); and the Slavs, who together formed the largest group in the population but were divided into different nationalities such as Poles, Czechs, Croats, and Serbs. The empire also included Italians in Lombardy and Venetia and Romanians in Transylvania. The Austrian government under the Habsburg emperor Francis I (r. 1792–1835) tried to keep nationalist impulses in check with the help of a secret police force set up on the Napoleonic model.

Students in some German states established nationalist student societies, or *Burschenschaften.* In 1817, they held a mass rally at which they burned books they did not like, including Napoleon's Civil Code. One of their leaders, Friedrich Ludwig

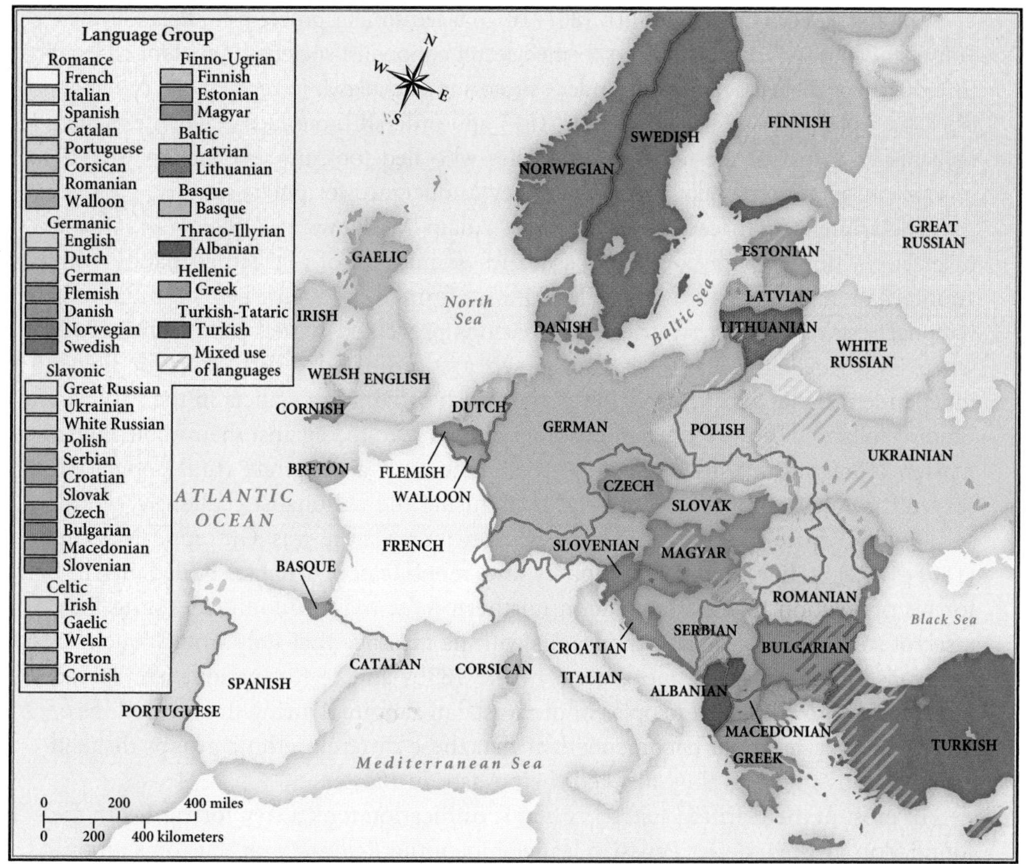

Map 17.1 Languages of Nineteenth-Century Europe
Even this detailed map of linguistic diversity understates the number of different languages and dialects spoken in Europe. In Italy, for example, few Italians spoke Italian as their first language. Instead, they spoke local dialects such as Piedmontese or Ligurian, and some might have spoken better French than Italian if they came from the regions bordering France. How does the map underline the inherent contradictions of nationalism in Europe? What were the consequences of linguistic diversity within national borders? Keep in mind that even in Spain, France, and Great Britain, linguistic diversity continued right up to the beginning of the 1900s.

Jahn, spouted such xenophobic (antiforeign) slogans as "If you let your daughter learn French, you might just as well train her to become a whore." The Austrian government, led by its chief minister, Prince Klemens von Metternich (1773–1859), was convinced that the Burschenschaften in the German states and the carbonari in Italy were linked in an international conspiracy. In 1820, when a student assassinated the playwright August Kotzebue because he ridiculed the student movement, Metternich convinced the leaders of the biggest German states to pass the Karlsbad Decrees dissolving the student societies and more strictly censoring the press. No evidence of a conspiracy was found, but Metternich's efforts to nip dissent in the bud worked.

The Russian tsar Alexander I (r. 1801–1825) faced similar problems in Poland, when Polish students and military officers formed secret nationalist societies to plot for change. In 1830, they rebelled against Alexander's successor, Nicholas I. In reprisal, the tsar abolished the Polish constitution granted in 1815 and ordered thousands of Poles executed or banished. Most of the ten thousand Poles who fled took up residence in western European capitals, especially Paris, where they campaigned for public support.

Their intellectual leader was the poet Adam Mickiewicz (1798–1855), whose mystical writings portrayed the Polish exiles as martyrs of a crucified nation with an international Christian mission. Mickiewicz formed the Polish Legion to fight for national restoration, but rivalries and divisions prevented united action until 1846, when Polish exiles in Paris tried to launch a coordinated insurrection for Polish independence. Plans for an uprising in the Polish province of Galicia in the Austrian Empire collapsed, however, when peasants instead revolted against their noble Polish masters. Slaughtering some two thousand aristocrats, a desperate rural population served the Austrian government's end by defusing the nationalist challenge.

One of those most touched by Mickiewicz's vision was Giuseppe Mazzini (1805–1872), a fiery Italian nationalist and republican journalist. Exiled in 1831 for his opposition to Austrian rule in northern Italy, Mazzini founded Young Italy, a secret society that attracted thousands with its message that Italy would touch off a European revolutionary movement. In the 1830s and 1840s, nationalism spread among the many different peoples of the Austrian Empire. During the revolutions of 1848, however, it would become evident that these different ethnic groups disliked each other as much as they disliked their Austrian masters.

In most of the German states, economic unification took a step forward with the foundation in 1834, under Prussian leadership, of the *Zollverein,* or "customs union." Economist Friedrich List argued that the elimination of tariffs within the borders of the union would promote industrialization and cooperation and enable the union to compete with the rest of Europe. German nationalists sought a government uniting German-speaking peoples, but they could not agree on its boundaries. Austria was not part of the Zollverein. Would the unified German state include both Prussia and the Austrian Empire? If it included Austria, what about the non-German territories of the Austrian Empire? And could the powerful and conservative kingdom of Prussia coexist in a unified German state with other, more liberal but smaller states? These questions would vex German history for decades to come.

In Russia, nationalism took the form of opposition to Western ideas. Russian nationalists, or Slavophiles (lovers of the Slavs), opposed the "Westernizers," who wanted Russia to follow Western models of industrial development and constitutional government. The Slavophiles favored maintaining rural traditions infused by the values of the Russian Orthodox church. Only a return to Russia's basic historical principles, they argued, could protect the country against the corrosion of rationalism and materialism. Slavophiles sometimes criticized the regime, however, because they believed the state exerted too much power over the church. The conflict between Slavophiles and Westernizers continues to shape Russian cultural and intellectual life to the present day.

Nationalism also played a significant role in Ireland. The Irish had struggled for centuries against English occupation, but Irish nationalists developed strong organizations only in the 1840s. In 1842, a group of writers founded the Young Ireland movement that aimed to recover Irish history and preserve the Gaelic language (spoken by at least one-third of the peasantry). Daniel O'Connell (1775–1847), a Catholic lawyer and landowner who sat in the British House of Commons, hoped to force the British Parliament to repeal the Act of Union of 1801, which had made Ireland part of Great Britain. In 1843, London newspapers reported "monster meetings" that drew crowds of as many as 300,000 people in support of repeal of the union. In response, the British government arrested O'Connell and convicted him of conspiracy. More radical leaders, who preached insurrection against the English, replaced him.

Romanticism

More an artistic movement than a true ideology, romanticism glorified nature, emotion, genius, and imagination. It proclaimed these as correctives to the Enlightenment and to classicism in the arts, challenging the reliance on reason, symmetry, and cool, geometric spaces. Classicism idealized models from Roman history; romanticism turned to folklore and medieval legends. Classicism celebrated orderly, crisp lines; romantics sought out all that was wild, fevered, and disorderly. Chief among the romantic arts were poetry, painting, and music, which captured the deep-seated emotion characteristic of romantic expression. George Gordon, Lord Byron (1788–1824), explained his aims in writing poetry:

> For what is Poesy but to create
> From overfeeling, Good and Ill, and aim
> At an external life beyond our fate,
> And be the new Prometheus of new man.

Prometheus was the mythological figure who brought fire from the Greek gods to human beings. Byron did not seek the new Prometheus among the men of industry; he sought him within his own "overfeeling," his own intense emotions.

Romantic poetry elevated the wonders of nature almost to the supernatural. Nature, wrote the English poet William Wordsworth (1770–1850), "to me was all in all." It allowed him to sing "the still, sad music of humanity." Like many poets of his time, Wordsworth greeted the French Revolution with joy. In his poem "French Revolution" (1809), he remembered his early enthusiasm: "Bliss was it in that dawn to be alive." But gradually he became disenchanted with the revolutionary experiment and celebrated British nationalism instead. In 1816, he published a poem to commemorate the "intrepid sons of Albion [England]" who had died at the battle of Waterloo.

Romanticism in painting often expressed anxiety about the coming industrial order while idealizing nature. These concerns came together in an emphasis on the natural landscape. The German romantic painter Caspar David Friedrich (1774–1840) depicted scenes—often in the mountains, far from any factory—that captured the romantic

Caspar David Friedrich, *Wanderer above the Sea of Fog* (1818)
Friedrich, a German romantic painter, captured many of the themes most dear to romanticism: melancholy, isolation, and individual communion with nature. He painted trees reaching for the sky and mountains stretching into the distance. Nature to him seemed awesome, powerful, and overshadowing of human perspectives. The French sculptor David d'Angers said of Friedrich, "Here is a man who has discovered the tragedy of landscape." (© Hamburger Kunsthalle, Hamburg/The Bridgeman Art Library.)

fascination with the sublime power of nature. Friedrich hated the new modern world and considered industrialization a disaster. The English painter Joseph M. W. Turner (1775–1851) depicted his vision of nature in mysterious, misty seascapes, anticipating later artists by blurring the outlines of objects. The French painter Eugène Delacroix (1798–1863) chose contemporary as well as medieval scenes of great turbulence to emphasize light and color and to break away from what he saw as "the servile copies repeated *ad nauseam* in academies of art." Critics denounced the new techniques as "painting with a drunken broom." To broaden his experience of light and color, Delacroix traveled in the 1830s to North Africa and painted many exotic scenes in Morocco and Algeria.

Architects of the period sought to recapture a preindustrial world. When the British Houses of Parliament were rebuilt after they burned down in 1834, the architect Sir Charles Barry constructed them in a Gothic style reminiscent of the Middle Ages. This medievalism was taken even further by A. W. N. Pugin, who prepared the Gothic details for the Houses of Parliament. In his polemical book *Contrasts* (1836), Pugin denounced modern conditions and compared them unfavorably with those in the 1400s. To underline his view, Pugin wore medieval clothes at home.

The towering presence of the German composer Ludwig van Beethoven (1770–1827) in early-nineteenth-century music helped establish the direction for musical romanticism. His music, according to one leading German romantic, "sets in motion the lever of fear, of awe, of horror, of suffering, and awakens just that infinite longing which is the essence of Romanticism." Beethoven's symphonies conveyed the impression of growth, a metaphor for the organic process with an emphasis on the natural that was dear to the romantics. For example, his Sixth Symphony, the *Pastoral* (1808), used a variety of instruments to represent sounds heard in the country. Some of his work was explicitly political. His Ninth Symphony (1824), for example, employed a chorus to sing the German poet Friedrich Schiller's verses in praise of universal human solidarity.

If any common political thread linked the romantics, it was support for nationalist aspirations, especially through the search for the historical origins of national identity. The Polish composer and pianist Frédéric Chopin (1810–1849) became a powerful champion for the cause of his native land with music that incorporated Polish folk rhythms and melodies. Lord Byron died fighting for Greek independence. The career of the writer Sir Walter Scott (1771–1832) exemplifies the romantic obsession with history and national identity. He published Scottish ballads that he heard as a child, but after achieving immediate success with his poetry, he switched to historical novels, a genre that he helped create. *Rob Roy* (1817), for example, tells of Scottish resistance to the English in the early eighteenth century. Scott used novels to bring history to life for readers all over Europe. One contemporary critic claimed that "there is more history in the novels of Walter Scott than in half of the historians."

REVIEW Why did ideologies have such a powerful appeal in the 1830s and 1840s?

Restoration, Revolt, and Revolution

When Napoleon went off to his permanent exile on St. Helena, those allied against him breathed a collective sigh of relief. Revolution, it seemed, had finally been defeated. Even as Napoleon had made his last desperate bid for power, his enemies were meeting in the Congress of Vienna (1814–1815) to decide the fate of post-revolutionary Europe. Many of Europe's monarchs hoped to nullify revolutionary and Napoleonic reforms and "restore" their old regimes. Revolts in the 1820s and especially in 1830 weakened the Vienna settlement, and then a massive series of uprisings in 1848 threatened to demolish it altogether.

The Congress of Vienna and Restoration Europe

The Congress of Vienna produced a new equilibrium that relied on cooperation among the major powers while guaranteeing the status of smaller states. Besides redrawing the boundaries of France and determining who would rule each nation, the congress had to decide the fate of Napoleon's duchy of Warsaw, the German province of Saxony, the Netherlands, the states once part of the Confederation of the Rhine, and various Italian territories. All had either changed hands or been created during the wars. These issues were resolved by face-to-face negotiations among representatives of the five major powers: Austria, Russia, Prussia, Britain, and France.

The Congress of Vienna
An unknown French engraver caricatured the efforts of the diplomats at the Congress of Vienna, complaining that they used the occasion to divide up Europe. What elements in this engraving make it a caricature? (Copyright © Wien Museum.)

With its aim to arrange a long-lasting, negotiated peace endorsed by all parties—both winners and losers—it also established a new framework for international relations based on periodic meetings, or congresses, between the major powers. This congress system, or "concert of Europe," helped prevent another major war until the 1850s, and no conflict comparable to the Napoleonic wars would occur until 1914.

Austria's Metternich took the lead in negotiations. Although his penchant for womanizing made him a security risk in the eyes of the British Foreign Office (he even had an affair with Napoleon's younger sister), he worked with the British prime minister Robert Castlereagh (1769–1822) to ensure a moderate agreement that would check French aggression yet maintain France's great-power status. Metternich and Castlereagh believed that France must remain a major player so that no one European power might dominate the others. In this way, France could help Austria and Britain counter the ambitions of Prussia and Russia.

When the French army failed to oppose Napoleon's return to power in the Hundred Days, the allies took away all territory conquered by France since 1790 and required France to pay an indemnity and support an army of occupation until it was paid. The goal of the congress was to achieve postwar stability by establishing secure states with guaranteed borders (Map 17.2). Where possible, the congress simply restored traditional rulers, as in Spain and the Italian states. The great powers decided to turn Napoleon's duchy of Warsaw into a new Polish kingdom but made

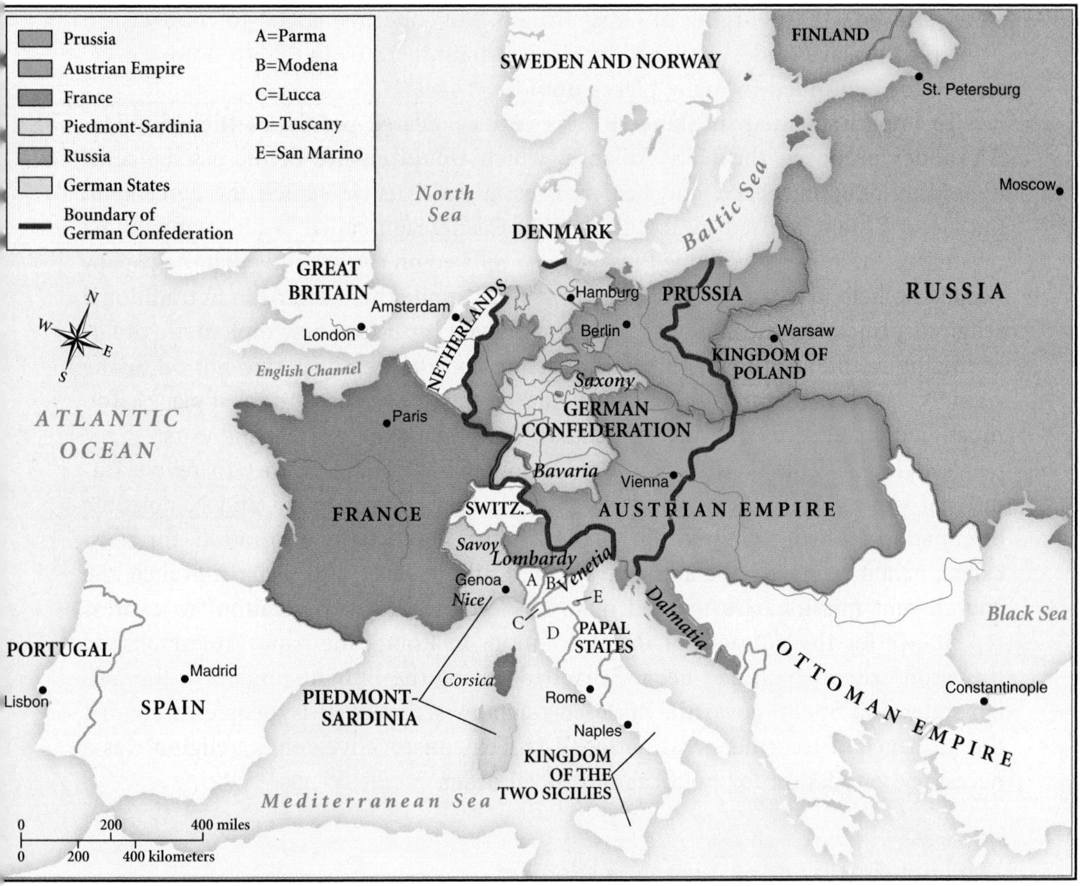

Map 17.2 Europe after the Congress of Vienna, 1815
The Congress of Vienna forced France to return to its 1789 borders. The Austrian Netherlands and the Dutch Republic were united in a new kingdom of the Netherlands; the German states were joined in the German Confederation, which built on Napoleon's Confederation of the Rhine; and Napoleon's duchy of Warsaw became the kingdom of Poland, with the tsar of Russia as king.

the tsar of Russia its king. (Poland would not regain its independence until 1918.) The former Dutch Republic and the Austrian Netherlands, both annexed to France in the preceding years, now united as the new kingdom of the Netherlands under the restored stadholder. Prussia gained territory in Saxony and on the left bank of the Rhine to compensate for its losses in Poland. To make up for its losses in Poland and Saxony, Austria reclaimed the Italian provinces of Lombardy and Venetia and the Dalmatian coast. Austria now presided over the German Confederation, which replaced the defunct Holy Roman Empire and also included Prussia.

The lesser powers were not forgotten. The kingdom of Piedmont-Sardinia took Genoa, Nice, and part of Savoy. Sweden obtained Norway from Denmark but had to accept Russia's conquest of Finland. Finally, various international trade issues were resolved. At the urging of Great Britain, the congress agreed to condemn in principle the slave trade, abolished by Great Britain in 1807. In reality, however, the slave trade continued in many places until the 1840s.

To impart spiritual substance to this very calculated political settlement, Tsar Alexander proposed the Holy Alliance, which would ensure divine assistance in upholding religion, peace, and justice. Prussia and Austria signed the agreement, but Great Britain refused to accede to what Castlereagh called "a piece of sublime mysticism and nonsense." Pope Pius VII also refused on the grounds that the papacy needed no help in interpreting Christian truth. Despite the reassertion of traditional religious principles, the congress had in fact given birth to a new diplomatic order: in the future, the legitimacy of states depended on the treaty system, not on divine right. It was clear that traditional rule could not just be restored in most places. Too much had changed during the French Revolution and the Napoleonic wars.

Religion did play a significant role, nonetheless, in the effort to revive traditional values. Many Europeans felt that the French Revolution and Napoleonic domination had undermined the religious fabric of society. Restoration, for most rulers, meant renewing the authority of the Catholic church as well. In France, the church sent missionaries to hold open-air "ceremonies of reparation" to express repentance for the outrages of the Revolution. In Rome, the papacy reestablished the Jesuit order, which had been disbanded during the Enlightenment. In the Italian states and Spain, governments used religious societies of laypeople to combat the influence of reformers and nationalists. For conservative rulers, religion was a necessary foundation for political and social order.

The First Cracks in the Vienna Settlement

Attempts to restore traditional rule soon provoked resistance. After Ferdinand VII regained the Spanish crown in 1814, he had foreign books and newspapers confiscated at the frontier and allowed the publication of only two newspapers. In 1820, disgruntled soldiers demanded that Ferdinand proclaim his adherence to the constitution of 1812, which he had abolished in 1814. Ferdinand stalled for time, and in 1823 a French army invaded with the consent of the other Vienna powers to support him. His government then tortured and executed hundreds of rebels; thousands were imprisoned or forced into exile. Nothing was spared to crush dissent.

Hearing of the Spanish uprising, rebellious soldiers in the kingdom of Naples joined forces with the carbonari and demanded a constitution. But when a new parliament met, it broke down over internal disagreements. The promise of reform sparked rebellion in the northern Italian kingdom of Piedmont-Sardinia, where rebels urged Charles Albert, the young heir to the Piedmont throne, to fight the Austrians for Italian unification. He vacillated, and in 1821, after the rulers of Austria, Prussia, and Russia met and agreed on intervention, the Austrians defeated the rebels in Naples and Piedmont (Map 17.2, page 663). Despite the opposition of

Great Britain, which condemned the "indiscriminate" suppression of revolutionary movements, Metternich convinced the other powers to agree to his muffling of the Italian opposition to Austrian rule.

Aspirations for constitutional government surfaced in Russia when Alexander I died in 1825. On the December day that the troops assembled in St. Petersburg to take an oath of loyalty to Alexander's brother Nicholas as the new tsar, rebel officers insisted that the crown belonged to another brother, Constantine, whom they hoped would be more favorable to constitutional reform. Constantine, though next in the line of succession after Alexander, had refused the crown. The soldiers nonetheless raised the cry "Long live Constantine; long live the Constitution." Soldiers loyal to Nicholas easily suppressed the outnumbered Decembrists (so called after the month of their uprising). For the next thirty years, Nicholas I used a new political police force to spy on potential opponents and stamp out rebelliousness.

The Ottoman Turks faced growing nationalist challenges in the Balkans, but the European powers feared that supporting them would encourage a rebellious spirit at home. The Serbs nonetheless revolted against Turkish rule and won virtual independence by 1817. An uprising by Greek peasants sparked a wave of mutual atrocities in 1821 and 1822. In retaliation for the killing of many Turks, the Ottoman authorities hanged the Greek patriarch (head of the Greek Orthodox church), and in the areas they still controlled, the Turks pillaged churches, massacred thousands of men, and sold the women into slavery.

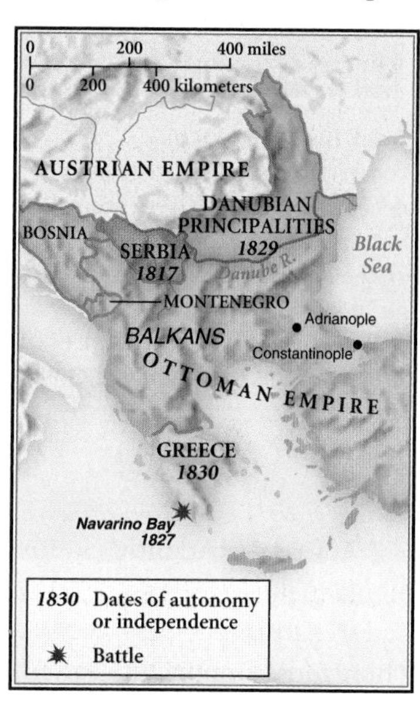

Nationalistic Movements in the Balkans, 1815–1830

Western opinion turned against the Turks; Greece, after all, was the home of Western civilization. While the great powers negotiated, Greeks and pro-Greece committees around the world sent food and military supplies; a few enthusiastic European and American volunteers even joined the Greeks. The Greeks held on until the great powers were willing to intervene. In 1827, a combined force of British, French, and Russian ships destroyed the Turkish fleet at Navarino Bay, and in 1828 Russia declared war on the Turks and advanced close to Istanbul. The Treaty of Adrianople (1829) gave Russia a protectorate over the Danubian principalities (now part of Romania) and provided for a conference among representatives of Britain, Russia, and France, all of whom had broken with Austria in support of the Greeks. In 1830, Greece was declared an independent kingdom under the guarantee of the three powers. Nationalism, with the support of European public opinion, had opened a hole in Metternich's system.

Greek Independence
From 1836 to 1839, the Greek painter Panagiotis Zographos worked with his two sons on a series of scenes depicting the Greek struggle for independence from the Turks. The response was so favorable that one Greek general ordered lithographic reproductions for popular distribution. Nationalistic feeling could thus be encouraged even among those who were not directly touched by the struggle. Here the Turkish sultan Mehmet the Conqueror, exulting over the fall of Constantinople in 1453, views a row of Greeks under the yoke, a sign of submission. **For more help analyzing this image, see the visual activity for this chapter in the Online Study Guide at bedfordstmartins.com/huntconcise.** (The Visual Connection.)

Across the Atlantic, national revolts also succeeded after a series of bloody wars of independence. Taking advantage of the upheavals in Spain and Portugal that had begun under Napoleon, restive colonists from Mexico to Argentina rebelled. Their most important leader was Simón Bolívar (1783–1830), the son of a slave owner, who was educated in Europe on the works of Voltaire and Rousseau. With help from newly independent Haiti and in exchange for agreeing to abolish slavery, Bolívar liberated the lands of northern South America (Venezuela, Colombia, Ecuador, Panama, and eventually Peru and Bolivia) from Spanish rule (Map 17.3). Although Bolívar fancied himself a Latin American Napoleon, he had to acquiesce to the formation of a series of independent republics between 1821 and 1823, even in Bolivia, which is named after him. At the same time, Brazil (then still a monarchy) separated from Portugal. The United States recognized the new states, and in 1823 President James Monroe (1758–1831) announced his Monroe Doctrine, closing the Americas to European intervention—a prohibition that depended on

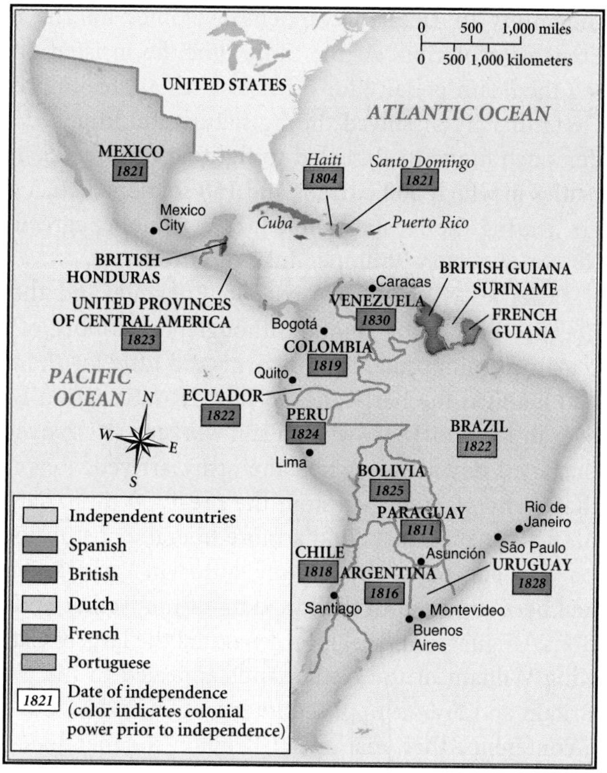

Map 17.3 Latin American Independence, 1804–1830
Napoleon's occupation of Spain and Portugal seriously weakened the hold of those countries on their Latin American colonies. Despite the restoration of the Spanish and Portuguese rulers in 1814, most of their colonies successfully broke away in a wave of rebellions between 1811 and 1830. **For more help analyzing this map, see the map activity for this chapter in the Online Study Guide at** bedfordstmartins.com/huntconcise.

British naval power and British willingness to declare neutrality. The Vienna powers were able to maintain their settlement only in areas where they could intervene militarily.

The Revolutions of 1830

Although the restored Bourbon monarchy in France worked in concert with the other great powers to maintain the Vienna settlement, at home it had to confront the legacy of twenty-five years of upheaval. Louis XVIII (r. 1814–1824) tried to ensure a measure of continuity by maintaining Napoleon's Civil Code and confirming the rights of ownership to church lands sold during the revolutionary period. He created a parliament composed of the Chamber of Peers, nominated by the king, and the Chamber of Deputies, elected by highly restricted suffrage (fewer than 100,000 voters in a population of 30 million). The Ultras (ultraroyalists) pushed for a more complete repudiation of the revolutionary past, including the abolition of divorce. When an assassin killed Louis XVIII's nephew in 1820, the Ultras demanded even more extreme measures.

The Ultras got the ear of the king when Charles X (r. 1824–1830), the younger brother of Louis XVIII, succeeded to the throne. He pushed through the Law of

Indemnity in 1825 to compensate nobles for the loss of their lands during the French Revolution. At the same time, he insisted on the Law of Sacrilege, imposing the death penalty for offenses such as stealing religious objects from churches. He ultimately dissolved the legislature and imposed strict censorship. Spontaneous demonstrations in Paris led to fighting on July 26, 1830. After three days of street battles in which 500 citizens and 150 soldiers died, a group of moderate liberal leaders, fearing the reestablishment of a republic, agreed to offer the crown to Charles X's cousin Louis-Philippe, duke of Orléans.

Charles X went into exile in England, and the new king extended political liberties and voting rights. Although the number of voting men nearly doubled, it remained minuscule. Such reforms did little for the poor and working classes, who had manned the barricades in July. Dissatisfaction with the 1830 settlement boiled over in Lyon in 1831, when a silk workers' strike over wages turned into a rebellion that died down only when the army arrived. Revolution had broken the hold of those who wanted to restore the pre-1789 monarchy and nobility, but it had gone no further than installing a more liberal, constitutional monarchy.

The success of the July revolution in Paris ignited the Belgians, whose country had been annexed to the kingdom of the Netherlands in 1815. Differences in traditions, language, and religion separated the largely Catholic Belgians from the Dutch. King William of the Netherlands appealed to the great powers for help, but Great Britain and France opposed intervention and invited Russia, Austria, and Prussia to a conference that guaranteed Belgium independence in exchange for its neutrality in international affairs. Belgian neutrality would remain a cornerstone of European diplomacy for a century.

European Influence Overseas

When the new Latin American republics abolished slavery in the 1820s and 1830s, they helped put slavery back on the European agenda. Despite British efforts to end the European slave trade, more than 3 million slaves were transported to the Americas between 1801 and 1850, and slavery still continued even in the British colonies. As many as 350,000 British women signed one major petition to Parliament demanding the abolition of slavery in the British colonies. Parliament finally agreed in 1833. In France, the new government of Louis-Philippe took strong measures against clandestine slave traffic, virtually ending French participation in the slave trade during the 1830s. Slavery was abolished in the remaining French Caribbean colonies in 1848.

Slavery did not disappear immediately just because the major European powers had given it up. Although the transatlantic trade in slaves dwindled away after 1850, human bondage continued unabated in Brazil, Cuba (still a Spanish colony), and the United States. Some American reformers supported abolition, but it remained a minority movement. Like serfdom in Russia, slavery in the Americas involved a quagmire of economic, political, and moral problems that worsened over time.

As Europeans turned their interest away from the plantation colonies of the Caribbean toward colonies in Asia and Africa, they developed new forms of colonial rule. Colonialism became **imperialism**—a term first coined in the mid-nineteenth century. Colonialism most often led to the establishment of settler colonies, direct rule by Europeans, slave labor from Africa, and the wholesale destruction of indigenous peoples. In contrast, imperialism usually meant more indirect forms of economic exploitation and political rule. Europeans still aimed to derive economic profit from their colonies, but now they also wanted to reform colonial peoples in their own image.

In the 1830s and 1840s, France and Britain continued to extend their influence across the globe. Using the pretext of an insult to its envoy, France invaded the North African country of Algeria in 1830 and after a long military campaign established political control over most of the region in the next two decades. By 1850, more than seventy thousand French, Italian, and Maltese colonists had settled in Algeria, often confiscating the lands of native peoples. Eventually France would not only incorporate Algeria into France but also try to assimilate its native population to French culture. France also imposed a protectorate government over the South Pacific island of Tahiti.

Although the British granted Canada greater self-determination in 1839, they extended their dominion elsewhere by annexing Singapore (1819), an island off the Malay peninsula, and New Zealand (1840). They also increased their control in India through the administration of the East India Company, a private group of merchants chartered by the British crown. The British educated a native elite to take over much of the day-to-day business of administering the country and used native soldiers to augment their military control. By 1850, only one in six soldiers serving Britain in India was European.

The East India Company also tried to establish a regular trade with China in **opium**, a drug long known for its medicinal uses but increasingly bought in China as a recreational drug. Bypassing the efforts of the Chinese government to ban the import of opium, British traders smuggled opium grown in India into China and, by bribing local officials, built up a flourishing market. When in 1839 the Chinese authorities expelled British merchants from southern China, Britain retaliated by bombarding Chinese coastal cities, beginning the First Opium War. In 1842, it dictated to a defeated China the Treaty of Nanking, by which the British forced the opening of four more Chinese ports to Europeans, took sovereignty over the island of Hong Kong, received a substantial war indemnity, and were assured of a continuation of the opium trade. The complaints of religious groups in Britain fell on deaf ears.

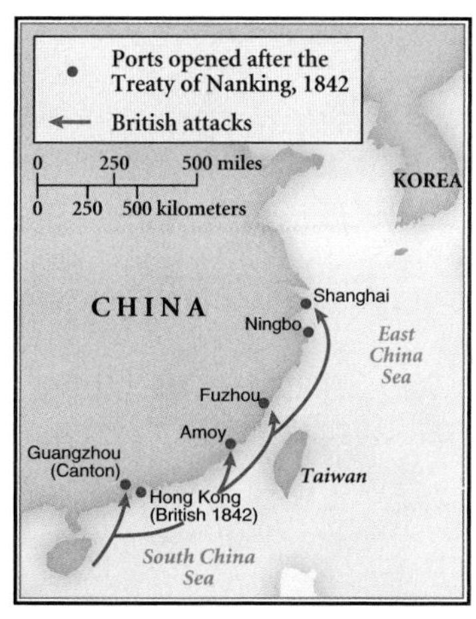

The First Opium War, 1839–1842

The Revolutions of 1848

Imperialist ventures abroad continued even as the revolutionary legacy revived again in Europe in 1848. As in 1789, food shortages and constitutional crises fueled the rebellion, but now class tensions and nationalist impulses sparked outbreaks in capitals across Europe. Crop failures in many countries threatened the food supply, and food prices shot skyward. In the best of times, urban workers paid 50 percent of their income for a diet consisting largely of bread or potatoes; now even those foods were beyond workers' means. Overpopulation hastened famine in some places, especially Ireland, where an airborne blight destroyed the potato crop in 1846, 1848, and 1851. Out of a population of eight million, as many as one million people died of starvation and disease. Corpses lay unburied on the sides of roads, and whole families were found dead in their cottages, half-eaten by dogs. Hundreds of thousands emigrated to England, the United States, and Canada.

High food prices also drove down the demand for manufactured goods, resulting in increased unemployment. Industrial workers' wages had been rising—in the German states, for example, wages rose an average of 5.5 percent in the 1830s and 10.5 percent in the 1840s—but the cost of living rose about 16 percent each decade, canceling out wage increases. Seasonal work and regular unemployment were already the norm when the crisis of the late 1840s intensified the uncertainties of urban life. "The most miserable class that ever sneaked its way into history" is how Friedrich Engels described underemployed and starving workers in 1847.

The Irish Famine
Contemporary engravings such as this one from 1847 drew attention to the plight of Irish peasants when a blight infected potato plants, destroying Ireland's single most important staple crop. In this illustration, a girl turns up the ground looking for potatoes, while a starving boy looks dazed. The artist reported seeing six dead bodies nearby. (The Granger Collection, NY.)

The specter of hunger tarnished the image of established rulers and amplified voices critical of them. Louis-Philippe's government had blocked all moves for electoral reform, and in February 1848, a campaign for reform sponsored by the liberal opposition turned into a revolution. At first the police and the army dispersed the demonstrators who took to the streets on February 22, 1848. The next day, however, forty or fifty people died when panicky soldiers opened fire on the crowd. On February 24, faced with fifteen hundred barricades and a furious populace, Louis-Philippe abdicated and fled to England. A hastily formed provisional government declared France a republic once again.

Revolutions of 1848

1848	
February	Revolution in Paris; proclamation of a republic
March	Insurrections in Vienna, German cities, Milan, and Venice; autonomy movement in Hungary; Charles Albert of Piedmont-Sardinia declares war on Austrian Empire
May	Frankfurt parliament opens
June	Austrian army crushes revolutionary movement in Prague; June Days end in defeat of workers in Paris
July	Austrians defeat Charles Albert and Italian forces
November	Insurrection drives the pope out of Rome
December	Francis Joseph becomes Austrian emperor; Louis-Napoleon elected president of France
1849	
February	Rome declared a republic
April	Frederick William of Prussia rejects crown of united Germany offered by Frankfurt parliament
July	Roman republic overthrown by French intervention
August	Russian and Austrian armies combine to defeat Hungarian forces

The new republican government issued liberal reforms—an end to the death penalty for political crimes, the abolition of slavery in the colonies, and freedom of the press—and agreed to introduce universal adult male suffrage despite misgivings about political participation by peasants and unemployed workers. To address the gnawing problem of unemployment, the government allowed Paris officials to organize a system of "national workshops" to provide those out of jobs with construction work. When women protested their exclusion, the city set up a few workshops for women workers, albeit with wages lower than men's. To meet a mounting deficit, the provisional government then levied a 45 percent surtax on property taxes, alienating peasants and landowners.

The establishment of the republic politicized many segments of the population. Scores of newspapers and political clubs revived grassroots democratic fervor; meeting in concert halls, theaters, and government auditoriums, clubs became a regular attraction for the citizenry. Women also formed clubs, published women's newspapers, and demanded representation in national politics. Street-corner activism alarmed middle-class liberals and conservatives. To maintain control, the republican government paid some unemployed youths to join a mobile guard with its own uniforms and barracks. Tension between the government and the workers in the national workshops rose; class warfare loomed like a thunderstorm on the horizon.

Faced with rising radicalism in Paris and other big cities, the voters elected a largely conservative National Assembly in April 1848, which immediately appointed a five-man executive committee to run the government and deliberately excluded known supporters of workers' rights. Suspicious of all demands for rapid change, the deputies dismissed a petition to restore divorce and voted down woman suffrage, 899 to 1. When the numbers enrolled in the national workshops in Paris rocketed from a predicted 10,000 to 110,000, the government ordered the workshops closed to new workers, and on June 21 it directed that those already enrolled move to the provinces or join the army.

The workers of Paris responded to these measures on June 23 by taking to the streets in the tens of thousands. In the June Days, as the following week came to be called, the government summoned the army, the National Guard, and the newly recruited mobile guard to fight the workers. Provincial volunteers came to help put down the workers, who had been depicted as lazy ruffians intent on destroying order and property. One observer breathed a sigh of relief: "The Red Republic [red being associated with demands for socialism] is lost forever; all France has joined against it. The National Guard, citizens, and peasants from the remotest parts of the country have come pouring in." The republic's army crushed the protesters; more than 10,000 were killed or injured, 12,000 were arrested, and 4,000 eventually were convicted and deported.

When the National Assembly adopted a new constitution calling for a presidential election in which all adult men could vote, the electorate chose Louis-Napoleon Bonaparte, nephew of the dead emperor. Bonaparte got more than 5.5 million votes out of some 7.4 million cast. He had lived most of his life outside France, and the leaders of the republic expected him to follow their tune. In uncertain times, the Bonaparte name promised something to everyone. Even many workers supported him because he had no connection with the blood-drenched June Days.

In reality, Bonaparte's election spelled the end of the Second Republic, just as his uncle had dismantled the first one, established in 1792. In 1852, on the forty-eighth anniversary of Napoleon I's coronation as emperor, Louis-Napoleon declared himself Emperor Napoleon III (r. 1852–1870). (Napoleon I's son died and never became Napoleon II, but Napoleon III wanted to create a sense of legitimacy and so used the Roman numeral III.) Political division and class conflict had proved fatal to the Second Republic. Although the revolution of 1848 never had a period of terror like that in 1793–1794, it nonetheless ended in a similar fashion, with an authoritarian government that played monarchists and republicans off against each other.

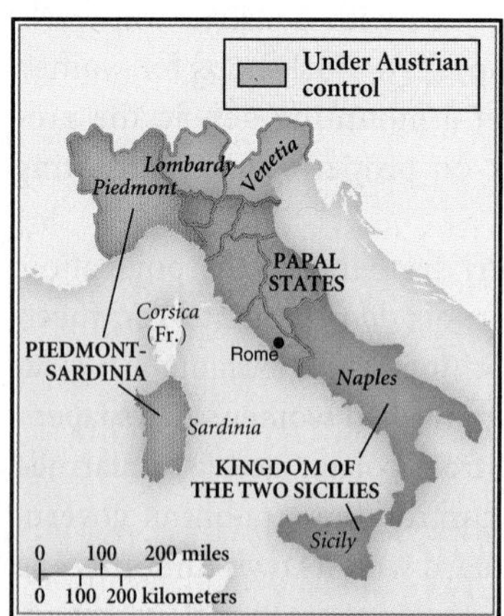

The Divisions of Italy, 1848

The Parisian uprising galvanized Italian nationalists. Armed demonstrators took on the Austrians in Milan and actually drove them out of Venice. Peasants in the south occupied their landowners' estates, while across central Italy the poor and unemployed rose up against local rulers. But class tensions and regional differences still stood in the way of Italian national unity. Some nationalists favored a loose federation; others wanted a monarchy under Charles Albert of Piedmont-Sardinia; still others urged rule by the pope. A few shared Mazzini's Young Italy movement vision of a republic with a strong central government. Many leaders of national unification spoke Italian only as a second language; most Italians spoke regional dialects.

As king of the most powerful Italian state, Charles Albert played a central role. After some hesitation caused by fears of French intervention, he led a military campaign against Austria. It failed, partly because of dissension over goals and tactics among the nationalists. Although Austrian troops defeated Charles Albert in the north in the summer of 1848, democratic and nationalist forces prevailed at first in the south. In the fall, the insurgents drove the pope from the city, and in February 1849 they declared Rome a republic. For the next few months republican leaders, such as Mazzini and Giuseppe Garibaldi (1807–1882), congregated in Rome to organize the new republic. These efforts faltered in July when foreign powers intervened. The new president of republican France, Louis-Napoleon Bonaparte, sent an expeditionary force to secure the papal throne for Pius IX (r. 1846–1878). Mazzini and Garibaldi fled. Although revolution had been defeated in Italy, the memory of the Roman republic and the commitment to unification remained, and they would soon emerge again with new force.

News of the revolution in Paris also provoked popular demonstrations in the German states. "My heart beat with joy. The monarchy had fallen. Only a little blood had been shed for such a high stake, and the great watchwords Liberty, Equality, Fraternity were again inscribed on the banner of the movement." So responded one Frankfurt woman to Louis-Philippe's overthrow. The Prussian army's efforts to clear the square in front of Berlin's royal palace on March 18, 1848, provoked panic and street fighting around hastily assembled barricades. The next day the crowd paraded wagons loaded with dead bodies under King Frederick William IV's window, forcing him to salute the victims killed by his own army. In a state of near collapse, the king promised to call an assembly to draft a constitution and adopted the German nationalist flag of black, red, and gold.

The goal of German unification soon took precedence over social reform or constitutional changes within the separate states. In March and April 1848, most of the German states agreed to elect delegates to a federal parliament at Frankfurt that would attempt to unite Germany. Local princes and even the more powerful kings of Prussia and Bavaria seemed to totter. In Bavaria, students marched to "La Marseillaise" and called for a republic. Yet the revolutionaries' weaknesses soon became apparent. The eight hundred delegates to the Frankfurt parliament had little practical political experience: "a group of old women," one socialist called them; a "Professors Parliament" was the common sneer. These delegates had no access to an army, and they dreaded the demands of the lower classes for social reforms.

Unemployed artisans and workers smashed machines; peasants burned landlords' records and occasionally attacked Jewish moneylenders; women established clubs and newspapers to demand their emancipation from "perfumed slavery." The advantage lay with the princes, who retained legal authority and control over the armed forces. The most powerful German states, Prussia and Austria, expected to determine whether and how Germany should unite. While the Frankfurt parliament laboriously prepared a liberal constitution for a united Germany—one that denied self-determination to Czechs, Poles, and Danes within its proposed German borders—the Prussian king Frederick William IV (r. 1840–1860) recovered his confidence. First his army crushed the revolution in Berlin in the fall of 1848. Prussian troops then intervened to help other local rulers put down the last wave of democratic and nationalist insurrections in the spring. In April 1849, when the Frankfurt parliament finally concluded its work, offering the emperorship of a constitutional, federal Germany to the king of Prussia, Frederick William contemptuously refused this "crown from the gutter."

Events followed a similar course in the Austrian Empire. Just as Italians were driving the Austrians out of their lands in northern Italy and Magyar nationalists were demanding political autonomy for Hungary, on March 13, 1848, a student-led demonstration for political reform in Vienna turned into rioting, looting, and machine breaking. Metternich resigned, escaping to England in disguise. The Austrian emperor Ferdinand I (r. 1835–1848) promised a constitution, an elected parliament, and the end of censorship. Beleaguered authorities in Vienna could not refuse Magyar demands for home rule, and the Hungarian nationalist Lajos Kossuth became a minister in the new Hungarian government.

Ethnic, political, and social conflicts divided the revolutionaries. The Magyars were the largest ethnic group in Hungary but still did not make up 50 percent of the population, which included Romanians, Slovaks, Croats, and Slovenes, who preferred Austrian rule to domination by local Magyars. The new Hungarian government alienated the other nationalities when it imposed the Magyar language on them. Fears of peasant insurrection prompted the Magyar nationalists around Kossuth to abolish serfdom, but this measure alienated the largest noble landowners. In Prague, Czech nationalists convened a Slav congress as a counter to the Germans' Frankfurt parliament and called for a reorganization of the Austrian Empire that would recognize the rights of ethnic minorities. Such assertiveness by non-German peoples provoked German nationalists to protest on behalf of German-speaking people in areas with a Czech or Magyar majority.

The Austrian government slowly took advantage of these divisions. To quell peasant discontent and appease liberal reformers, it abolished all remaining peasant obligations to the nobility in March 1848. Rejoicing country folk soon lost interest in the revolution. Military force finally broke up the revolutionary movements. The first blow fell in Prague in June 1848. General Prince Alfred von Windischgrätz, the military governor, bombarded the city into submission when a demonstration led to violence (including the shooting death of his wife, watching from a window). After another uprising in Vienna a few months later, Windischgrätz marched 70,000 soldiers into the capital and set up direct military rule. In December, the Austrian monarchy came back to life when the eighteen-year-old Francis Joseph (r. 1848–1916), unencumbered by promises extracted by the revolutionaries from his now feeble uncle Ferdinand, assumed the imperial crown after intervention by leading court officials. In the spring of 1849, General Count Joseph Radetzky defeated the last Italian challenges to Austrian power in northern Italy, and his army moved east, joining with Croats and Serbs to take on the Hungarian rebels. In August, the Austrian army teamed up with Tsar Nicholas I, who marched into Hungary with more than 300,000 Russian troops. Hungary was put under brutal martial law. Kossuth sought refuge in the United States. Social conflicts and ethnic divisions weakened the revolutionary movements from the inside and gave the Austrian government the opening it needed to restore its position.

The Aftermath of 1848

The revolutionaries of 1848 failed to achieve most of their goals, but their efforts left a profound mark on the political and social landscape. Between 1848 and 1851, the French served a kind of republican apprenticeship that prepared the population for another, more lasting republic after 1870. No French government could henceforth rule without extensive popular consultation. In Italy, the failure of unification did not stop the spread of nationalist ideas and the rooting of demands for democratic participation. In the German states, the revolutionaries of 1848 turned nationalism from an academic idea into a popular movement. The very idea of the Frankfurt parliament and the insistence on brandishing a German national flag at demonstrations showed that German nationalism had become a practical reality. The initiation of artisans, workers, and journeymen into democratic clubs increased political awareness in the lower classes and helped prepare them for broader political participation. Almost every German state had a constitution and a parliament after 1850. The spectacular failures of 1848 thus hid some important successes.

The absence of revolution in 1848 was just as significant as its presence. No revolution occurred in Great Britain, the Netherlands, or Belgium, the three places where industrialization and urbanization had developed most rapidly. In Great Britain, the prospects for revolution actually seemed quite good. Many British workers joined in **Chartism**, a movement that aimed to transform Britain into a democracy. In 1838, political radicals had drawn up the People's Charter, which demanded universal manhood suffrage, vote by secret ballot, equal electoral districts, annual elections, and the elimination of property qualifications for and the payment of stipends to members of Parliament. Chartists denounced their opponents as seeking "to keep the people in social slavery and political degradation." Many women took part by founding female political unions, setting up Chartist Sunday schools, organizing boycotts of unsympathetic shopkeepers, and joining Chartist temperance associations. Nevertheless, the People's Charter refrained from calling for woman suffrage because the movement's leaders feared that doing so would alienate potential supporters.

The Chartists organized a massive campaign during 1838 and 1839, with large public meetings, fiery speeches, and torchlight parades. Presented with petitions for the People's Charter signed by more than a million people, the House of Commons refused to act. In response to this rebuff from middle-class liberals, the Chartists

The Revolution of 1848 in Eastern Europe
This painting by an unknown artist shows Ana Ipatescu leading a group of Romanian revolutionaries in Transylvania in opposition to Russian rule. In April 1848, local landowners began to organize meetings. Paris-educated nationalists spearheaded the movement, which demanded the end of Russian control and various legal and political reforms. By August, the movement had split between those who wanted independence only and those who were pushing for the end of serfdom and for universal manhood suffrage. In response, the Russians invaded Moldavia, and the Turks moved into Walachia. By October, the uprising was over. Russia and Turkey agreed to control the provinces jointly. (The Art Archive.)

allied themselves in the 1840s with working-class strike movements in the manufacturing districts and associated with various European revolutionary movements.

Inspired by the outbreak of nearly simultaneous revolutions in 1848, the Chartists mounted several gigantic demonstrations to force Parliament into granting all adult males the vote. But Parliament refused and no uprising occurred, in part because the government had already proved its responsiveness. The middle classes in Britain had been co-opted into the established order by the Reform Bill of 1832, and the working classes had won parliamentary regulation of children's and women's work.

The other notable exception to revolution among the great powers was Russia, where Tsar Nicholas I maintained a tight grip through police surveillance and censorship. The Russian schools, limited to the upper classes, taught Nicholas's three most cherished principles: autocracy (the unlimited power of the tsar), orthodoxy (obedience to the church in religion and morality), and nationality (devotion to Russian traditions). These provided no space for political dissent. Social conditions also fostered political passivity: serfdom continued in force, and the slow rate of industrial and urban growth created little discontent.

For all the differences between countries, some developments touched them all. European states continued to expand their bureaucracies. For example, in 1750 the Russian government employed approximately 10,500 functionaries; a century later it needed almost 114,000. New government agencies such as the British urban police forces (10,000 strong in the 1840s) intruded increasingly in ordinary people's lives. States wanted to take children out of the fields and factories where they worked with their families and educate them. And in some German cities, the police reported people who cleared snow off their roofs after the permitted hour or smoked in the streets, reflecting the expansion of government powers.

Although much had changed, the aristocracy remained the dominant power in most places. As army officers, aristocrats put down revolutionary forces. As landlords, they continued to dominate the rural scene and control parliamentary bodies. They also held many official positions in the state bureaucracies. One Italian princess explained, "There are doubtless men capable of leading the nation . . . but their names are unknown to the people, whereas those of noble families . . . are in every memory." Aristocrats kept their authority by adapting to change: they entered the bureaucracy and professions, turned their estates into moneymaking enterprises, and learned how to invest shrewdly.

The reassertion of conservative rule hardened gender definitions. Women everywhere had participated in the revolutions, especially in the Italian states, where they had joined armies in the tens of thousands and applied household skills to making bandages, clothing, and food. Schoolgirls in Prague had thrown desks and chairs out windows and helped build students' barricades. Many women in Paris had supported the new republic and seized the occasion of greater political openness to demand women's rights, only to experience isolation as their claims were denied by most republican men. Men in the revolutions of 1848 almost always defined universal suffrage as a male right. When workingmen gained the vote and women did not, the notion of separate spheres penetrated even into working-class life: political participation became one more way to distinguish masculinity from femininity. As conservatives returned to power, all signs of women's political activism disappeared. The French feminist movement, the most advanced in Europe, fell apart after the June Days, when the increasingly conservative republican government forbade women to form political clubs and arrested and imprisoned two of the most outspoken women leaders for their socialist activities.

In May 1851, Europe's most important female monarch presided over a midcentury celebration of peace and industrial growth that helped dampen the still smoldering fires of revolutionary passion. Queen Victoria (r. 1837–1901), who herself promoted the notion of domesticity as women's sphere, opened the international Exhibition of the Works of Industry of All Nations in London on May 1. A monument of modern iron and glass architecture had been constructed to house the display; the building

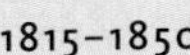

The Crystal Palace, 1851
George Baxter's lithograph shows the exterior of the main building for the Exhibition of the Works of Industry of All Nations in London. It was designed by Sir Joseph Paxton to gigantic dimensions: 1,848 feet long, 456 feet wide, and 135 feet high—772,784 square feet of ground-floor area covering no less than 18 acres. (© Maidstone Museum and Art Gallery, Kent, England/The Bridgeman Art Library.)

was more than a third of a mile long and so tall that it was erected over the trees of its Hyde Park site. Soon people referred to it as the Crystal Palace; its nine hundred tons of glass created an aura of fantasy, and the abundant goods from all nations inspired satisfaction and pride. One German visitor described it as "this miracle which has so suddenly appeared to dazzle the inhabitants of our globe." In the place of revolutionary fervor, the Crystal Palace offered a government-sponsored spectacle of what industry, hard work, and technological imagination could produce.

REVIEW Why did the revolutions of 1848 fail?

Conclusion

Many of the six million people who visited the Crystal Palace display traveled there on railroads and wore the cheaper cotton clothing produced by workers in mechanized textile factories. They had not forgotten the threat of disease, fears of overpopulation, and lingering popular resentments. The revolutions of 1848, in particular, had brought to the surface the profound tensions within a European society in transition toward industrialization and modernization. Industrialization and urbanization continued; workers developed more extensive organizations; and liberals, conservatives, and socialists fought over the pace of reform.

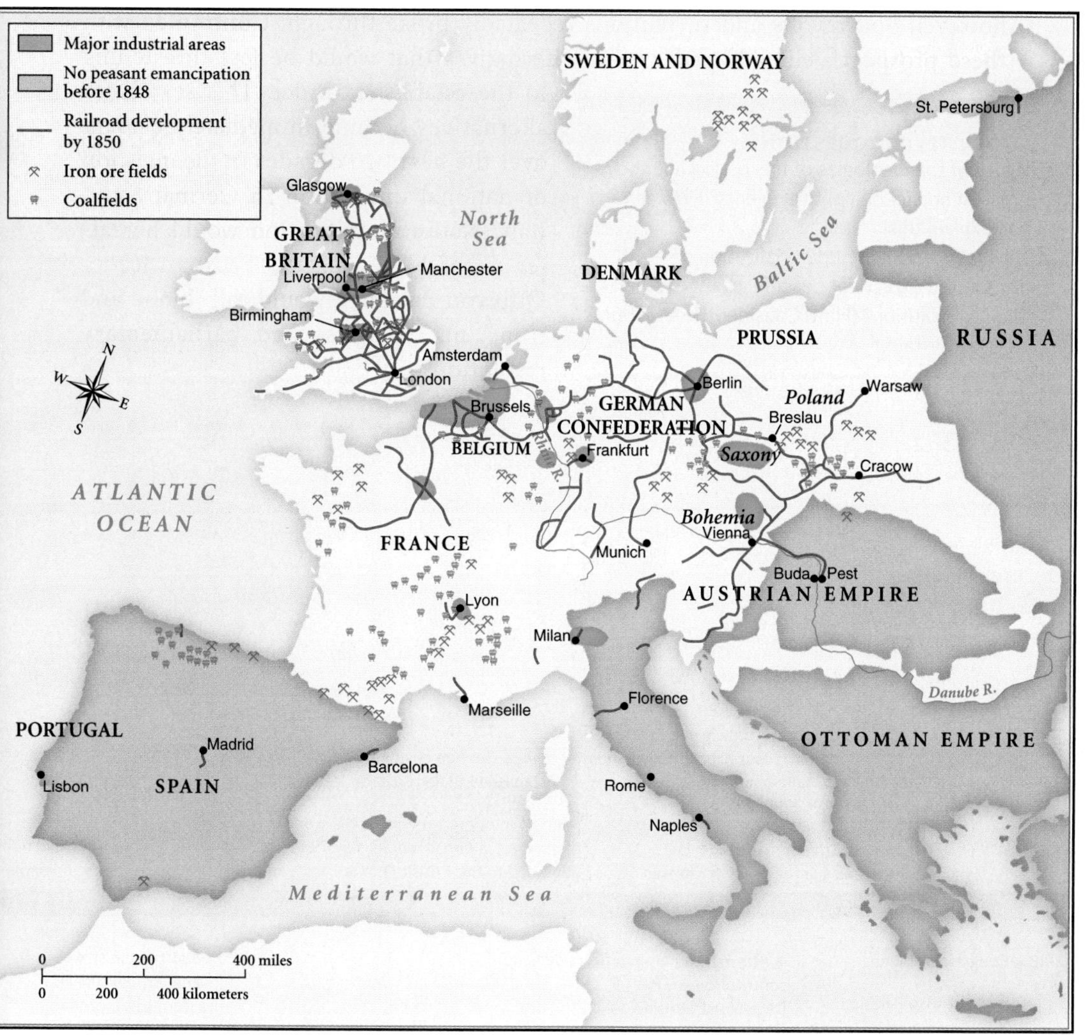

Mapping the West Industrialization in Europe, c. 1850
Industrialization first spread across northern Europe in a band that included Great Britain, northern France and the region around Lyon, Belgium, the northern German states, the region around Milan in northern Italy, and Bohemia. Much of Scandinavia and southern and eastern Europe did not participate in this first phase of industrial development. Although railroads were not the only factor in promoting industrialization, the map makes clear the interrelationship between railroad building and the development of new industrial sites of coal mining and textile production.

The Congress of Vienna had sought to clamp a lid on the various forces that threatened political and social order, and for some time the major powers succeeded in holding back demands for change. Nationalist aspirations, desires for constitutional rights, and calls for social reform proved impossible to contain, however, and revolts and revolutions repeatedly broke through. Confronted with these prospects, elites hoped to find alternatives that would be less threatening to the established order. This search for alternatives became immediately evident over the next two decades in the question of national unification in Germany and Italy. National unification would hereafter depend on what the Prussian leader Otto von Bismarck would call "blood and iron," not speeches and parliamentary resolutions.

CHAPTER REVIEW QUESTIONS

1. Which of the ideologies of this period had the greatest impact on political events? How can you explain this?
2. In what ways might industrialization be considered a force for peaceful change rather than a revolution? (Hint: Consider the situation in Great Britain.)

TIMELINE

1815 | 1827 | 1839 | 1851

- **1814–1815** Congress of Vienna
- **1819** Peterloo massacre in Manchester, England
- **1820** Revolt of liberal army officers against the Spanish crown; Karlsbad Decrees abolish German student societies and tighten press censorship
- **1824** Ludwig van Beethoven composes his Ninth Symphony
- **1825** Russian army officers demand constitutional reform in the Decembrist uprising
- **1830** Liverpool and Manchester Railway Line opens in England; Greece gains independence from Ottoman Turks; France invades and begins conquest of Algeria; rebels overthrow Charles X of France and install Louis-Philippe; cholera epidemic begins in Europe
- **1831** Belgium becomes an independent country
- **1832** British Parliament passes the Reform Bill
- **1833** Factory Act regulates the work of children in Great Britain; slavery abolished in the British Empire
- **1834** German customs union (*Zollverein*) established under Prussian leadership
- **1839** First Opium War between Britain and China begins
- **1846** Famine strikes Ireland; Britain repeals the Corn Laws; peasant insurrection in the Austrian province of Galicia
- **1847** Charlotte Brontë, *Jane Eyre*
- **1848** Last great wave of Chartist demonstrations in Britain; Karl Marx and Friedrich Engels, *The Communist Manifesto;* revolutions of 1848 throughout Europe; slavery abolished in French colonies; serfdom ended in Austrian Empire
- **1851** Crystal Palace exhibition in London

For practice quizzes and other study tools, see the Online Study Guide at bedfordstmartins.com/huntconcise.

For primary-source material from this period, see Chapters 20 and 21 of *Sources of The Making of the West*, Third Edition.

Suggested References

The spread of industrialization has elicited much more historical interest than the process of urbanization because the analysis of industrialization occupied a central role in Marxism. The Web site Gallica, produced by the National Library of France, offers a wealth of imagery and information on French cultural history.

Davidoff, Leonore, and Catherine Hall. *Family Fortunes: Men and Women of the English Middle Class, 1780–1850*. 1987.

Dickens Project: http://humwww.ucsc.edu/dickens

Gallica: Images and Texts from Nineteenth-Century French-Speaking Culture: http://gallica.bnf.fr

Hobsbawm, E. J. *The Age of Revolution, 1789–1848*. 1996.

Johnson, Paul. *The Birth of the Modern: World Society, 1815–1830*. 1991.

Kahan, Alan S. *Liberalism in Nineteenth-Century Europe: The Political Culture of Limited Suffrage*. 2003.

Kramer, Lloyd S. *Nationalism: Political Cultures in Europe and America, 1775–1865*. 1998.

Laven, David, and Lucy Riall, eds. *Napoleon's Legacy: Problems of Government in Restoration Europe*. 2000.

*Marx, Karl, and Frederick Engels. *The Communist Manifesto: With Related Documents*. Ed. John E. Toews. 1999.

McLean, Stuart. *The Event and Its Terrors: Ireland, Famine, Modernity*. 2004.

Mokyr, Joel. *The Enlightened Economy: An Economic History of Britain, 1700–1850*. 2009.

Murray, Christopher John, ed. *Encyclopedia of the Romantic Era, 1760–1850*. 2004.

*Pollard, S., and C. Holmes. *Documents of European Economic History*. Vol. 1, *The Process of Industrialization, 1750–1870*. 1968.

Romantic Chronology: http://english.ucsb.edu:591/rchrono

Sperber, Jonathan. *The European Revolutions, 1848–1851*. 2d ed. 2005.

Thompson, E. P. *The Making of the English Working Class*. 1964.

VENEZIA
TEATRO LA FENICE
IN OCCASIONE DEL
CONGRESSO GEOGRAFICO INTERNAZIONALE
IMPRESA CESARE TREVISAN
DALL'11 AL 22 SETTEMBRE SI DARANNO 7 RAPPRESENTAZIONI DELLA GRANDIOSA OPERA-BALLO
AIDA
MUSICA DEL COMM.re GIUSEPPE VERDI
ESEGUITA DAI SEGUENTI ARTISTI
PRIME DONNE
EMMA TUROLLA — GIUSEPPINA PASQUA
PRIMO TENORE
GIOVANNI SANI
PRIMO BARITONO
COMM.re GOTTARDO ALDIGHIERI
PRIMI BASSI
ENRICO SERBOLINI + FRANCESCO PANARI
MAESTRO DIRETTORE D'ORCHESTRA
CAV.re FRANCO FACCIO
ALTRO MAESTRO
RAFAELE BRACÂLE
TENORE COMPRIMARIO
GIUSEPPE CINQUANTA
M.o ISTRUTTORE DEI CORI
LORENZO POLI
SUGGERITORE
ANTONIO RENIER
COREOGRAFO
RINALDO ROSSI
Direttore
RINALDO ROSSI
Direttore delle masse
GAETANO ARCHINTI
Pittore Scenografo
CESARE RECANATINI
LUIGI CAPRARA
L. ZAMPERONI
CROCE e FIGLIO
ANTONIO TREVISAN
Parrucchiere
G. GASPEROTTO
R. MAVEROFFER
Biglietto d'ingresso alla platea e palchi (in sere ordinarie) L. 5.—
detto al loggione (id) . 2.—
Poltrona a bracciuoli, oltre l'ingresso . 10.—
Posti riservati in platea (scanni in velluto) . 5.—
Posti riservati in Galleria (Loggione) . 1.50
Abbonamento per le sette rappresent.ni (compresa quella di gala) . 25.—
detto limitato a N.° 40 Poltrone . 50.—
detto ai posti riservati (scanni) . 25.—
Le suddette 7 rappresentazioni
sono finora stabilite nelle sere
del 11-13-15-17-18-20-22
Settembre
Proprietà dello spartito
Tito di Gio. Ricordi
Venezia 1 Agosto 1881

18

Constructing the Nation-State

c. 1850–1880

IN 1859, THE NAME "VERDI" suddenly appeared scrawled on walls across the disunited cities of the Italian peninsula. The graffiti seemed to celebrate the composer Giuseppe Verdi, whose operas thrilled crowds of Europeans. Verdi was a particular hero among Italians, however, for his stories of downtrodden groups struggling against tyrannical government seemed to refer specifically to them. As his operatic choruses thundered out calls to rebellion in the name of the nation, Italian audiences were sure that Verdi meant for them to throw off Austrian and papal rule and unite in a reborn Roman Empire. Yet the graffiti was doubly political, a call to arms in the days before mass media. For VERDI also formed an acronym for *V*ittorio *E*mmanuele *R*e ("king") *d'I*talia, and in 1859 it summoned Italians to unite immediately under Victor Emmanuel II, king of Piedmont-Sardinia—the one leader with a nationalist, modernizing profile. The graffiti was good publicity, for the very next year Italy united as a result of warfare and hard bargaining by political realists.

***Aïda* Poster**
Aïda (1871), Giuseppe Verdi's opera of human passion and state power, became a staple of Western culture. As the opera played across Europe, it brought Europeans into a common cultural orbit. Written to celebrate the opening of the Suez Canal, *Aïda* also celebrated Europe's better access to Asian resources provided by the new waterway. As the poster shows, the opera ushered in another wave of Egyptomania—the craze for Egyptian styles and objects. *(Madeline Grimoldi.)*

After the failed revolutions of 1848, European statesmen and the politically conscious public increasingly rejected the politics of idealism in favor of **Realpolitik**—a politics of tough-minded realism aimed at strengthening the state and tightening social order. Realpolitikers disliked the romanticism and high-minded ideas of the revolutionaries. Instead they put their faith in power politics, a strong national economy, and the use of violence to attain their goals. Two particularly skilled practitioners of Realpolitik, the Italian Camillo di Cavour and the Prussian Otto von Bismarck, succeeded in unifying Italy and Germany, respectively, not by consensus but by war and diplomacy. Most leading figures of these decades, enmeshed like Verdi's operatic heroes in power politics, strengthened their states by harnessing the forces of nationalism and liberalism.

Making modern nation-states and empires during these momentous decades was complicated. Continued economic development was crucial, and entrepreneurs produced a host of new inventions, new procedures, and new ways of doing business. A growing sense of national identity and common purpose was forged by both culture and government policy. As productivity and wealth increased, governments took vigorous steps to improve their rapidly growing cities, monitor public health, and promote national loyalty. State support for cultural developments ranging from public schools to opera productions helped establish a common fund of knowledge and even shared political beliefs. Authoritarian leaders such as Bismarck and the new French emperor Napoleon III believed that a better quality of life would not only calm revolutionary impulses and build state power but also quiet political opponents.

Culture built a sense of belonging. Reading novels, attending operas and art exhibitions, and visiting the newly fashionable world's fairs created a greater sense not only of being French or German or British but also of being European. Cultural works increasingly rejected romanticism, featuring instead realistic aspects of daily life. Artists painted nudes in shockingly blunt ways, eliminating dreamy poses. Russian author Leo Tolstoy depicted the bleak life of soldiers in the Crimean War, which erupted in 1853 between the Russian and Ottoman empires, while his countryman Fyodor Dostoevsky wrote of criminals and murders in urban neighborhoods. **Realism** in the arts paralleled that in politics.

Realpolitik focused on outcomes in building strong nations with far less concern for the costs to ordinary people. Strengthening nation-states involved global expansion and stamping out resistance to it. At home, governments uprooted neighborhoods in favor of constructing public buildings, roads, and parks. The process of nation building was often brutal, bringing foreign wars, arrests, and even civil war—all the centerpieces of many Verdi operas. In 1871, an uprising of Parisians challenged the central government's violent intrusion into everyday life. The powerful Western state did not spring up spontaneously during these years. Instead, its growth depended on shrewd policy, deliberate warfare, and new inroads into the lives of people around the world. Realpolitik relied on all of these factors, as well as on a modern climate of opinion that valued realism and hard facts.

CHAPTER FOCUS QUESTION How did the creation and strengthening of nation-states change European politics, society, and culture in the mid-nineteenth century?

The End of the Concert of Europe

The revolutions of 1848 had weakened the concert of Europe, driving out its architect, Klemens von Metternich, and allowing the forces of nationalism to flourish. It became more difficult for countries to control their competing ambitions and act together. In addition, the dreaded revival of Bonapartism in the person of Napoleon III (Louis-Napoleon, the nephew of Napoleon I) added to European instability as

France reasserted itself. One of Napoleon's direct targets was Russia, formerly a mainstay of the concert of Europe. To limit Russia's and Austria's grip on power, France helped engineer the Crimean War of 1853–1856, which reduced these two states' authority over Europe as a whole.

Napoleon III and the Quest for French Glory

Louis-Napoleon Bonaparte encouraged the resurgence of French grandeur and the cult of his famous uncle as part of nation building. "There are certain men who are born to serve as a means for the march of the human race," he wrote. "I consider myself to be one of these." Louis-Napoleon used political coups to rise from president of the Second Republic to emperor. Arresting opponents in towns and cities, he declared himself Emperor Napoleon III (r. 1852–1870) and proclaimed the Second Empire on December 2, 1852—the anniversary of Napoleon I's own ascension to power.

Napoleon III acted as Europe's schoolmaster, showing its leaders how to combine economic liberalism and nationalism with authoritarian rule. Cafés where men might discuss politics were closed, and a rubber-stamp legislature, the Corps législatif, made representative government a charade. Imperial style replaced republican simplicity. Napoleon's opulent court dazzled the public, and the emperor cultivated a masculine image of strength and majesty by wearing a military uniform (like his namesake) and conspicuously maintaining mistresses. Napoleon's wife, Empress

Napoleon III and Eugénie Receive the Siamese Ambassadors
At a splendid gathering of their court, Emperor Napoleon III, Empress Eugénie, and their son and heir greet ambassadors from Siam, whose exoticism and servility before the French imperial family are the centerpiece of this depiction. Amid the grandeur of the Napoleonic dynasty, the West towers above the East. (Bridgeman-Giraudon/Art Resource, NY.)

Eugénie, followed middle-class norms by serving as a devoted mother to her only son and supporting many volunteer charities. The authoritarian, apparently old-fashioned order imposed by Napoleon satisfied many in the countryside that the radicalism of 1848 was under control.

Yet Napoleon III simultaneously pushed for a modern economy, and he promoted industrial growth, public works programs, and jobs, which lured the middle and working classes away from radical politics. The magnificent rebuilding of Paris made France prosper. Empress Eugénie wore lavish gowns, encouraging French silk production and keeping Paris at the center of the lucrative fashion trade. The regime also reached a free-trade agreement with Britain and backed an innovative investment bank, the Crédit Mobilier. Such new institutions led the way in financing railroad expansion, and railway mileage increased fivefold during Napoleon's reign. During the economic downturn of the late 1850s, he wooed support by allowing working-class organizations to exist and introducing features of democratic government. Although some historians have judged Napoleon III to be devious because of these abrupt changes, he made practical responses to economic change.

On the international scene, Napoleon III's main goals were to overcome the containment of France imposed by the Congress of Vienna and to acquire international glory like a true Bonaparte. To realign European politics in France's favor, Napoleon pitted France first against Russia in the Crimean War, then against Austria in the War of Italian Unification (1860–1861), and finally against Prussia in the Franco-Prussian War (1870–1871). Beyond Europe, Napoleon's army continued to enforce French rule in Algeria and Southeast Asia and tried to install Habsburg emperor Francis Joseph's brother Maximilian as ruler of Mexico and ultimately of all Central America (a plan that displayed French weakness in 1867 when Mexican forces executed Maximilian). Napoleon's foreign policy transformed relations among the great powers by causing a breakdown in the international system of peaceful diplomacy established at the Congress of Vienna. While his encouragement of projects like the Suez Canal to connect the Mediterranean and the Red Sea proved visionary, his push for worldwide influence eventually destroyed him. The French overthrew him after Prussia easily defeated his army in 1870.

The Crimean War, 1853–1856: Turning Point in European Affairs

Napoleon first flexed his diplomatic muscles in the Crimean War, which began as a conflict between the Russian and Ottoman empires. Russia continued to build state power by expanding further into Asia and the Middle East. In particular, Tsar Nicholas I eyed territory in the Ottoman Empire, fast becoming known as "the sick man of Europe" because of its declining political authority. Napoleon III encouraged Nicholas to be more aggressive, and in October 1853 war erupted between the two eastern empires (Map 18.1).

The Crimean War drew in other states and undid Europe's balance of power as set in the Congress of Vienna. Napoleon III convinced Austria to remain neutral

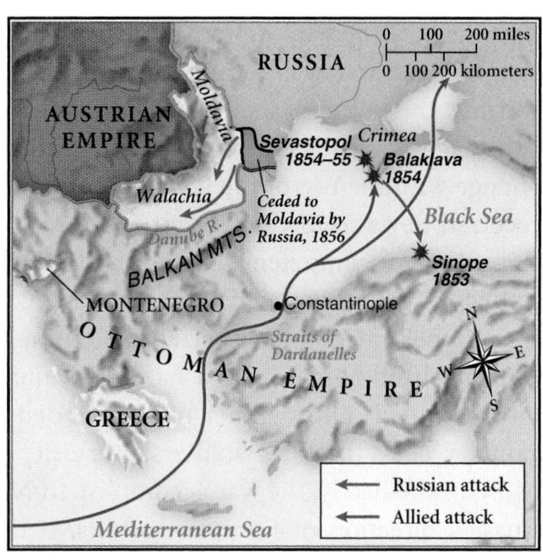

Map 18.1 The Crimean War, 1853–1856 The most destructive war in Europe between the Napoleonic wars and World War I, this conflict drew attention to the competing ambitions around territories of the declining Ottoman Empire. Importantly for state building in these decades, it fractured the alliance of conservative forces from the Congress of Vienna, allowing Italy and Germany to come into being as unified states and permitting Napoleon III to pursue his ambitions for France. **For more help analyzing this map, see the map activity for this chapter in the Online Study Guide at** bedfordstmartins.com/huntconcise.

during the war, thus fracturing the conservative Russian-Austrian coalition that had checked French ambitions since 1815. The Austrian government was concerned that defeat of the Ottomans would bring Russian expansion into the Balkans. To protect their Mediterranean routes to Asia, the British prodded the Ottomans to stand up to Russia, but in the fall of 1853, the Russians blasted the wooden Turkish ships to bits at the Ottoman port of Sinope on the Black Sea. In 1854, France and Great Britain, enemies in war for more than a century, declared war on Russia to defend the Ottoman Empire's sovereignty and territories. Their own interests, however, were their main motivation.

Faced with attacking the massive Russian Empire, the allies settled for limited military goals focused on capturing the Russian naval base at Sevastopol, on the Black Sea in the Crimea. Even so, the Crimean War was spectacularly bloody. British and French troops landed in the Crimea in September 1854 and waged a long siege of Sevastopol, which fell after a year of savage and costly combat. Generals on both sides demonstrated their incompetence, and governments failed to provide combatants with even minimal supplies, sanitation, or medical care. The war claimed a massive toll. A million men died, more than two-thirds from disease and starvation.

In the midst of this unfolding catastrophe, Alexander II (r. 1855–1881) ascended the Russian throne after the death of his father, Nicholas I, in 1855. With casualties mounting, the new tsar asked for peace. As a result of the Peace of Paris, signed in March 1856, Russia lost the right to base its navy in the Black Sea or in the Straits of Dardanelles (the strait between Europe and Asia Minor), which were declared neutral waters. Moldavia and Walachia (which soon merged to form Romania) became autonomous Turkish provinces under the victors' protection.

Some historians have called the Crimean War one of the most senseless conflicts in modern history, because competing claims in southeastern Europe could have been settled by diplomacy had it not been for Napoleon III's driving ambition. Yet the war was full of consequence. New technologies were introduced into warfare: the railroad, shell-firing cannons, breech-loading rifles, and steam-powered ships. The relationship of the home front to the battlefront was beginning to change with the use of the telegraph and increased press coverage. Home audiences received news from the Crimea more rapidly and in more detail than ever before. Reports of incompetence, poor sanitation, and the huge death toll outraged the public, inspiring some civilians, such as Florence Nightingale, to head for the front lines to help. Nightingale seized the moment to escape the confines of middle-class domesticity by organizing a battlefield nursing service to care for the British sick and wounded. Through her tough-minded organization of nursing units, she made sanitary conditions for soldiers a priority and pioneered nursing as a profession. More immediately, the war accomplished Napoleon III's goal of ending Austria's and Russia's direction of European affairs. It thus undermined their ability to control European politics and thereby contain the forces of liberalism and nationalism.

The Spirit of Reform in Russia

Defeat in the Crimean War forced Russia on the path of long-overdue reform. Hundreds of peasant insurrections had erupted during the decade before the war. Serf defiance ranged from malingering while at forced labor to boycotting vodka in protest of the heavy tax on it. "Our own and neighboring households were gripped with fear," one aristocrat reported, because everyone expected a massive serf uprising. The Russian economy stagnated compared with western Europe. Old-fashioned farming techniques depleted the soil and led to food shortages, and the nobility was often contemptuous of ordinary people. Works of art, such as novelist Ivan Turgenev's sympathetic portrayals of serfs and depictions of openly brutal masters in *A Hunter's Sketches* (1852), contributed to the spirit of reform. A Russian translation of Harriet Beecher Stowe's antislavery novel *Uncle Tom's Cabin* (1852) also hit home. When Russia lost the Crimean War, the educated public, including some government officials, found the poor performance of serf armies a disgrace and the system of serf labor a liability.

Confronted with the need for change, Alexander acted. Educated and widely traveled, he ushered in what came to be known as the age of Great Reforms, granting Russians new rights from above as a way of preventing violent action from below. The most dramatic reform was the emancipation of almost fifty million serfs beginning in 1861. By the terms of emancipation, communities of former serfs, headed by male village elders, received grants of land. Each community, called a **mir**, had full power to allocate this land among individuals and to direct their economic activity. Thus, although emancipation partially laid the groundwork for a modern labor force in Russia, communal landowning and decision making prevented the free movement of country people who could otherwise have become an industrial labor force. More burdensome to them, peasants were not given land

Emancipation of the Russian Serfs

This trading card was used as a marketing gimmick by businesspeople hoping to push their new products—in this case, canned meat. They were given away by the thousands in stores and traded just as baseball cards are today. Historical scenes were popular subjects for the cards. This one shows the emancipation of the serfs in Russia, which was a major event to people across Europe. Note that the caption is in French, the language used by many in Europe's upper classes, including those in Russia, who would have consumed this product. The emancipation is presented as a wholly beneficial act with no drawbacks, such as the immense debt imposed on former serfs. (Mary Evans Picture Library.)

along with their personal freedom; they were forced to "redeem" the land they farmed by accepting long-term government loans, which in turn reimbursed the big landowners. The best land remained in the hands of the nobility, and most peasants ended up actually owning less land than they had farmed as serfs. These conditions, especially the huge burden of debt and regulations, slowed Russian agricultural development for decades. Even so, idealistic reformers believed the emancipation of the serfs produced miraculous results. As one reformer put it, "The people are without any exaggeration transfigured from head to foot. . . . The look, the walk, the speech, everything is changed."

The state also reformed local administration, the judiciary, and the military. The government set up zemstvos—regional councils through which aristocrats could direct neglected local matters such as education and public health. Aristocratic control ensured that zemstvos would remain conservative but also offer some balance to the authoritarian central government. Simultaneously, judicial reform gave all Russians, even former serfs, access to modern civil courts, rather than leaving them at the mercy of a landowner's version of justice. The Western principle of equality of all persons before the law, regardless of social rank, was introduced in Russia for the first time. Military reform followed in 1874, when the government replaced the twenty-five-year period of service with a six-year term and focused on educating Russian troops in an effort to match the efficiency of soldiers elsewhere in western Europe.

Alexander's reforms helped landowners be more effective in the market, just as enclosures and emancipation had done much earlier in western Europe. At the same time, the changes diminished the privileges of the nobility, leaving their authority weakened and sparking family conflict. "An epidemic seemed to seize upon [noble] children . . . an epidemic of fleeing from the parental roof," one observer noted. Rejecting aristocratic leisure, youthful rebels from the upper classes valued practical activity and sometimes identified with peasants and workers. Some formed communes where they hoped to do humble manual labor; others turned to higher education, especially the sciences. Daughters of the nobility rebelled by cutting their hair short, wearing black, and escaping from home through phony marriages so they could study in western European universities. This rejection of traditional norms led Turgenev to label radical youths *nihilists* (from the Latin for "nothing"), a term that meant a lack of belief in any values whatsoever. In fact, they represented the defiant spirit growing in Russian society.

Reform also inspired resistance among the more than one hundred minority nationalities in the Russian Empire. Aristocratic and upper-class Poles staged an uprising in 1863, but Alexander II's army regained control of the Russian section of Poland by 1864. The government then intensified repression and **Russification**—a tactic meant to reduce the threat of future rebellions by minorities within the empire by forcing them to adopt the Russian language and culture. In this era of the Great Reforms, the tsarist regime only partially succeeded in developing the administrative, economic, and civic institutions of the nation-state. The tsar and his inner circle tightly controlled the government, allowing few to share power. In imperial Russia, autocracy and the continued abuse of many in the population slowed the development of the sense of citizenship forming elsewhere in the West, while it increased the urge to revolt.

REVIEW What were the main results of the Crimean War?

War and Nation Building

Dynamic leaders in the German and Italian states used the opportunity offered by the weakened concert of Europe to unify their countries through warfare. When national disunity threatened, the United States also waged a bloody civil war to maintain its integrity, which opened the way for dynamic economic growth. Historians sometimes treat the rise of powerful nation-states such as Italy, Germany, and the United States as part of an inevitable process, but millions of individuals, especially those living in rural areas, maintained a local sense of identity even as nation building was taking place and national sentiment was on the rise.

Cavour, Garibaldi, and the Process of Italian Unification

Despite the failed revolutions of 1848 in the Italian states, hope for national unification, or Risorgimento (rebirth), remained strong, aided by diplomatic instability across Europe. This time the kingdom of Piedmont-Sardinia, in the economically modernizing north of Italy, drove the unification process. The kingdom rallied to the operas of Verdi, but its nation-building efforts depended on the construction of railroads and a modern army, along with military help from France.

The architect of the new Italy was the pragmatic Camillo di Cavour (1810–1861), prime minister of the kingdom of Piedmont-Sardinia from 1852 until his death. A rebel in his youth, the young Cavour had conducted agricultural experiments on his aristocratic father's land. He organized steamship companies, played the stock market, and inhaled the spirit of modernization during his travels to Paris and London. As prime minister, he pushed the development of a healthy Piedmontese economy, a modern army, and a liberal political climate as the foundation of Piedmont-Sardinia's claim to lead the unification process (Map 18.2).

To unify Italy, however, Piedmont-Sardinia would have to confront Austria, which governed the provinces of Lombardy and Venetia and exerted a strong influence over most of the peninsula. Cavour turned for help to Napoleon III, who in the summer of 1858 promised French assistance in exchange for the city of Nice and the region of Savoy. Napoleon additionally expected that France rather than Austria would influence the peninsula thereafter. Sure of French help, Cavour provoked the Austrians into invading northern Italy in April 1859. The cause of Piedmont-Sardinia's monarchy now became the cause of nationalist Italians everywhere, even those who had supported romantic republicanism in 1848. Using the newly built Piedmontese railroad to move troops, the French and Piedmontese armies achieved rapid victories. Suddenly fearing the growth of Piedmont as a potential competing force, Napoleon independently signed a peace treaty with Austria that gave Lombardy but not Venetia to Piedmont-Sardinia. The rest of Italy remained disunited, and Cavour's nationalist ambitions were not yet realized.

Napoleon's plans for the controlled liberation of Lombardy and Venetia and a partitioned peninsula were derailed as support for Piedmont continued to swell across Italy. Ousting their rulers, citizens of states in the center of Italy (except Rome, which French troops occupied) elected to join Piedmont. In May 1860, Giuseppe Garibaldi (1807–1882), a committed republican and veteran of the revolutions of 1848, set sail from Genoa with a thousand red-shirted volunteers (many of them teenage boys) to liberate Sicily, where peasant revolts against landlords and the corrupt government were under way. In the autumn of 1860, the army of King Victor Emmanuel of Piedmont-Sardinia and "Garibaldi's Thousand" joined forces in Naples (Map 18.2, page 692). Although some of Garibaldi's supporters still clamored for social reform and a republic, he threw his support to the king. In 1861, the kingdom of Italy was proclaimed, with Victor Emmanuel as ruler (r. 1861–1878).

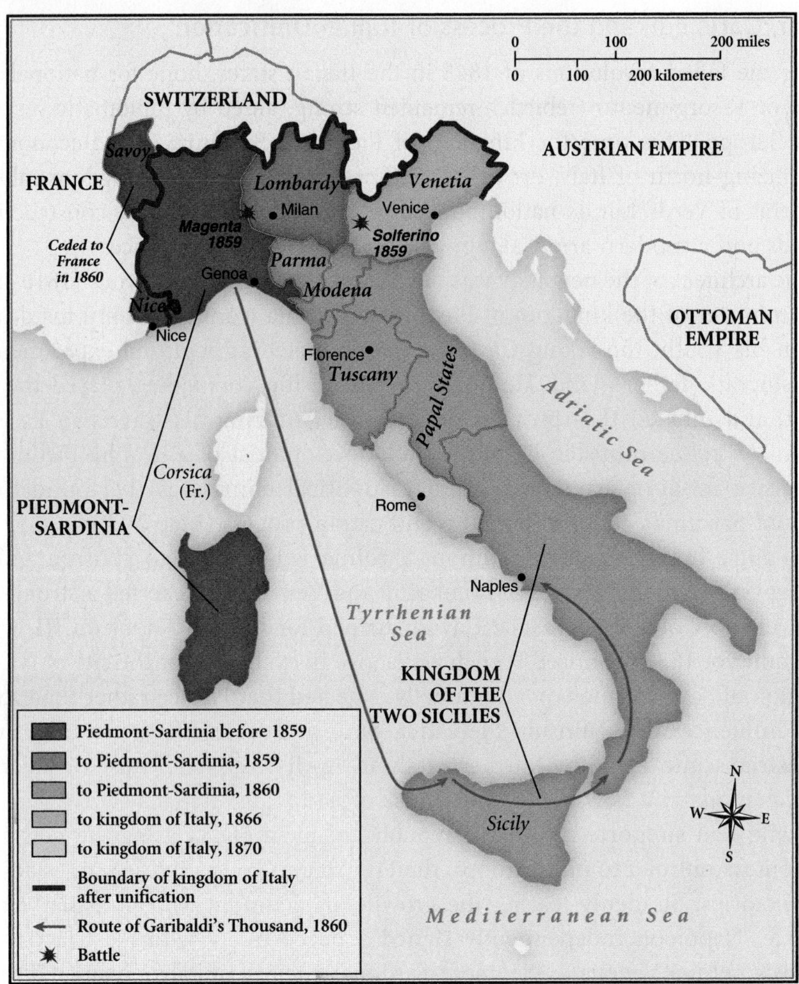

Map 18.2 Unification of Italy, 1859–1870
The many states of the Italian peninsula had different languages, ways of life, and economic interests. In the north, the kingdom of Piedmont-Sardinia had much to gain from a unified market and a more extensive labor pool. Although the armies of King Victor Emmanuel and Garibaldi unified these states into a single country, it would take decades to construct a culturally, socially, and economically connected nation.

Exhausted by a decade of overwork, Cavour died within months of leading the unification, leaving lesser men to organize the new Italy. Consensus among Italy's elected leaders was hard to achieve once the war was over, and admirers of Cavour, such as Verdi (who had been made a senator), quit the quarrelsome political scene. The wealthy commercial north and impoverished agricultural south remained at odds over basic policies (as they do even today). Finally, Venetia and Rome, under Austrian and French control, respectively, remained outside Italy's borders. Amid

Seamstresses of the Red Shirts
Sewing uniforms and making battle flags, European women like these Italian volunteers saw themselves as contributors to the nation. Donating their domestic skills and raising the next generation of citizens to be patriotic, many nineteenth-century women participated in nation building as "republican mothers." (akg-images/Electa.)

these strains, the legend of an Italian struggle for freedom symbolized by the figure of Garibaldi and his Red Shirts became a powerful unifying force even though it sentimentalized the Realpolitik that had made unification possible. Many citizens of the new country took pride in the Italian nation based on this and other national myths.

Bismarck and the Realpolitik of German Unification

The most momentous act of nation building for the future of Europe was the creation of a united Germany in 1871. This, too, was the product of Realpolitik, undertaken once the concert of Europe was smashed and the champions of the status quo were defeated. Employing the old military order to wage war, yet with the support of economic modernizers who saw the benefits of a single national market, the Prussian state brought a vast array of cities and kingdoms under its control within just one decade. From then on, Germany prospered, continuing to consolidate its economic and political might. By the end of the century, it would be the foremost continental power.

The architect of a unified Germany was Otto von Bismarck (1815–1898). Bismarck came from a traditional Junker (Prussian landed nobility) family on his father's side; his mother's family included high-ranking bureaucrats of the middle class. At university, the young Bismarck had gambled and womanized, interested only in one academic course, on the economic foundations of politics. After failing in the civil service, he worked to modernize operations on his landholdings while leading an otherwise rowdy life. His marriage to a sober Lutheran woman gave him new purpose. In the 1850s, his diplomatic service to the Prussian state made him increasingly angry about the Habsburg grip on German affairs. Establishing Prussia as a respected and dominant power became his cause.

In 1862, William I (king of Prussia, r. 1861–1888; German emperor, r. 1871–1888) appointed Bismarck prime minister in hopes that he would crush the growing power of the liberals in the Prussian parliament. The liberals, representing the prosperous professional and business classes, had gained parliamentary strength at the expense of conservative landowners during the decades of industrial expansion. Indeed, the liberals' wealth was crucial to Prussia's growing power. Desiring Prussia to be like western Europe, Prussian liberals advocated the extension of political rights and increased civilian control of the military. By contrast, William, along with members of the traditional Prussian elite such as Bismarck, rejected the western European model. Bismarck simply rammed through programs to build the army and thwart civilian control. "Germany looks not to Prussia's liberalism, but to its power," he proclaimed. "The great questions of the day will not be settled by speeches and majority decisions—that was the great mistake of 1848 and 1849—but by iron and blood."

After his triumph over the parliament, Bismarck led Prussia into a series of wars—against Denmark in 1864, Austria in 1866, and France in 1870. Using war as a political tactic, he kept the disunited German states from choosing Austrian leadership and instead united them around Prussia. Bismarck drew Austria into a joint war with Prussia against a rebellious Denmark in 1864 over Denmark's proposed incorporation of the provinces of Schleswig and Holstein, with their partially German populations. Their joint victory resulted in an agreement that Prussia would administer Schleswig and Austria would oversee Holstein. Such an arrangement stretched Austria's geographic interests far from its central European base.

Austria proved weaker than Prussia, as the Habsburgs lagged in economic development and suffered from a swelling national debt and the discontent of its many national minorities. Bismarck, however, so encouraged Habsburg pretensions of grandeur and influence that Austria disputed the administration of Schleswig and Holstein and, in the summer of 1866, confidently declared war on Prussia, with the support of most of the German Confederation. Within seven weeks, the modernized Prussian army, using railroads and fast breech-loading rifles against the outdated Austrian military, won decisively. The masterful victory allowed Bismarck to drive Austria from the German Confederation and create the North German Confederation, led by Prussia (Map 18.3).

To bring the remaining German states into Prussia's orbit, Bismarck next moved to entrap France in a war. During the Austro-Prussian War, Bismarck had suggested to Napoleon III that his neutrality would bring France territory, thus heating up nationalist sentiments in both France and Germany. The atmosphere became even more charged when Spain proposed a minor Prussian prince to fill its vacant throne. This candidacy threatened France with Prussian rulers on two of its borders. Bismarck used the occasion to stir up nationalist feelings in Prussia and France by editing a diplomatic communication (known as the Ems telegram) to make it look as if the king of Prussia had insulted France over the succession issue. His release of the revised version to journalists inflamed the French public into demanding

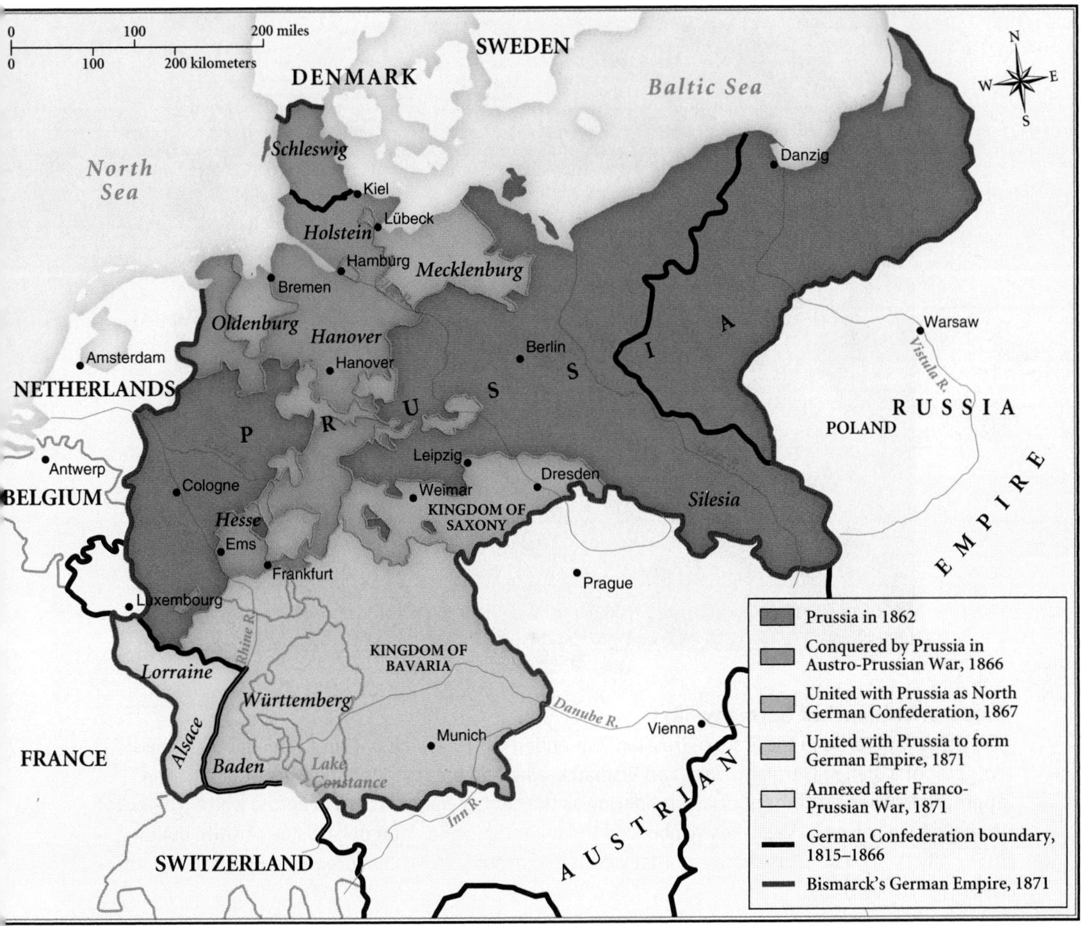

Map 18.3 Unification of Germany, 1862–1871
In a complex series of diplomatic maneuvers, Otto von Bismarck welded disunited kingdoms and small states into a major continental power independent of the other dominant German dynasty, the Habsburgs. Prussia's use of force unified Germany politically, and almost immediately that unity unleashed the new nation's economic potential. An aristocratic and agrarian elite remained firmly in power, but a rapidly growing working class would soon become a political force to be reckoned with.

war against Prussia. The French parliament gladly declared war on July 19, 1870, setting in motion the alliances Prussia had created with the other German states. The Prussians captured Napoleon III with his army on September 2, 1870, and the Second Empire fell two days later.

With Prussian forces still besieging Paris, in January 1871 in the Hall of Mirrors at Versailles, King William of Prussia was proclaimed the kaiser (or emperor) of a new, imperial Germany. By the terms of the peace signed in May 1871, France lost the rich industrial provinces of Alsace and Lorraine to

Emperor William I of Germany, 1871
The defeat of France in the Franco-Prussian War ended with the king of Prussia being proclaimed emperor of a unified Germany. Otto von Bismarck, who had orchestrated the wars of unification, appropriately appears in this artistic rendering as the central figure attired in heroic white. The event in the French palace of Versailles symbolized the militaristic and antagonistic side of state building, especially the Franco-German rivalry that would disastrously motivate European politics in the future. (akg-images, London.)

Germany and paid a multibillion-franc indemnity. Without French protection for the papacy, Rome became part of Italy. Germany was now poised to dominate continental politics.

Prussian military might served as the foundation for German state building, and a complex constitution ensured the continued political dominance of the aristocracy and monarchy despite the growing wealth of the business classes. The kaiser, who remained Prussia's king, controlled the military and appointed Bismarck to the powerful position of imperial chancellor. The Reichstag, an assembly elected by universal male suffrage, ratified all budgets. Bismarck accorded constitutional rights such as suffrage in the belief that the masses would uphold the monarchy out of their fear of modernizing businessmen, whom Bismarck opposed as a source of "liberal power." He balanced this move with an electoral system in Prussia in which votes from the upper classes counted more than votes from the lower classes. He had little to fear from liberals, however. Dizzy with German military success, they came to support the blend of economic progress, constitutionalism, and militaristic nationalism that Bismarck represented.

Francis Joseph and the Creation of the Austro-Hungarian Monarchy

The Austrian monarchy took a different approach to nation building, proving that there was no one model for the modern nation-state. Just as the Crimean War left Russia searching for solutions to its social and political problems, so the confrontation with Cavour and Bismarck left the Habsburg Empire struggling to keep its standing in a rapidly changing Europe. The Habsburg Empire emerged from the revolutions of 1848 renewed by the ascension of Francis Joseph (r. 1848–1916), who favored absolutist rule. A tireless worker, Francis Joseph enhanced his authority through stiff, formal court ceremonies, playing to people's fascination with the lavish trappings of royalty. Although the emperor stubbornly resisted change, official standards of honesty and efficiency improved, and the government promoted local education. The German language was used by the administration and taught by the schools, but the government respected the rights of national minorities such as Czechs and Poles to receive education and to communicate with officials in their native tongues. Above all, the government abolished most internal customs barriers, boosted railway construction, and attracted foreign capital. The capital city, Vienna, underwent extensive rebuilding, and people found jobs as industrialization progressed, if unevenly.

In the fast-moving nineteenth century, the emperor could not match Bismarck in modern nation building; too much of the old regime remained as a roadblock. The Catholic church had nearly a free hand in education and in civil institutions such as marriage, and wealthy businessmen lacked influence in such important policy matters as taxation and finance. After Prussia's victory over Francis Joseph's armies in 1866, the most disaffected but wealthiest part of the empire, Hungary, became the key to stability, even to the empire's existence. The leaders of the Hungarian agrarian elites forced the emperor to accept a **dual monarchy**—that is, Magyar home rule over the Hungarian kingdom. This agreement restored the Hungarian parliament and gave it control of internal policy (including the right to decide how to treat Hungary's national minorities). Although the Habsburg emperor Francis Joseph was crowned king of Hungary and Austro-Hungarian foreign policy was coordinated from Vienna, the Hungarians mostly ruled themselves after 1867 and hammered out common policies such as tariffs in negotiations with Vienna. These negotiations were mostly bitter, weakening the process of nation building.

The Austro-Hungarian Monarchy, 1867

A second weakness in the dual monarchy was that it was designed specifically to address Hungarian demands. In doing so, it strengthened the voices of Czechs, Slovaks, and at least half a dozen other national groups in the Habsburg Empire wanting the same kind of self-rule. The Czechs, who helped the empire advance industrially, failed to gain Hungarian-style liberties. More menacing, some of the dissatisfied ethnic groups turned to **Pan-Slavism**—the transnational unity of all ethnic Slavs—and looked beyond the borders of Austria-Hungary to Russia, the largest Slavic country, to achieve this. With so many competing ethnicities, the Austro-Hungarian monarchy remained a dynastic, or princely, state in which people were ultimately loyal to the Habsburg dynasty but had difficulty relating to one another as members of a single nation.

Political Stability through Gradual Reform in Great Britain

In contrast to the turmoil in continental Europe, Britain appeared the model of liberal progress. By the 1850s, the monarchy symbolized domestic tranquillity and stability. Unlike their predecessors, Queen Victoria (r. 1837–1901) and her husband, Prince Albert, were considered models of middle-class virtue. Britain's parliamentary system steadily brought more men into the political process. Economic prosperity fortified peaceful political reform, except in Ireland, where suffering and failure to achieve justice continued. An evolving but focused party system helped in decision making. The Tory Party changed into the Conservatives, many of whose policies favored the aristocracy. Nonetheless, the Conservatives still went along with the liberal consensus in support of economic development and representative government. Skilled politician William Gladstone, who would serve four terms as prime minister, helped the Whigs and several other political groups become the Liberals. In 1867, the Conservatives, led by Benjamin Disraeli, passed the Second Reform Bill, which made a million more men eligible to vote.

Political parties supported reforms because citizens now formed pressure groups to influence national policies. The Law Amendment Society and the Social Science Association, for example, lobbied for laws to improve social conditions. Women's groups advocated the Matrimonial Causes Act of 1857, which facilitated divorce, and the Married Women's Property Act of 1870, which allowed married women to own property and keep the wages they earned. Plush royal ceremonies helped critics, activists, and, more important, different social classes bond as one people. Whereas previous monarchs' sexual scandals had caused riots, the monarchy of Queen Victoria and Prince Albert, with its newly invented celebrations of royal marriages, anniversaries, and births, drew respectful crowds. Promoting the monarchy in this way was so successful that the term *Victorian* came to symbolize almost the entire century and could refer to anything from manners to political institutions. Yet Britain's politicians were as devoted to Realpolitik as were those in Germany, Italy, or France, endorsing violence to expand their overseas empire and control Ireland. The violence was far beyond the view of most British people, however, allowing them to imagine their nation as peaceful, advanced, and united.

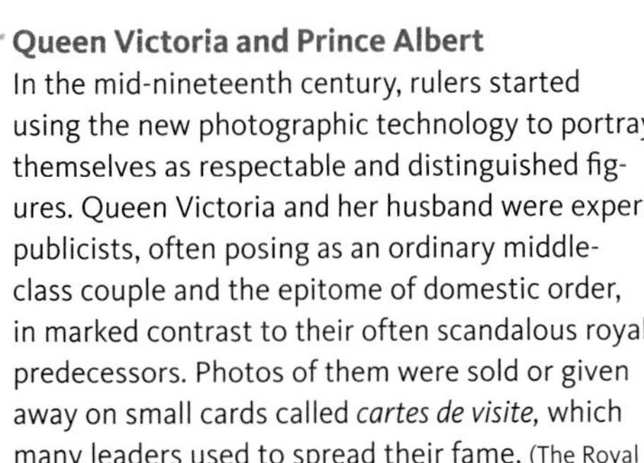

Queen Victoria and Prince Albert
In the mid-nineteenth century, rulers started using the new photographic technology to portray themselves as respectable and distinguished figures. Queen Victoria and her husband were expert publicists, often posing as an ordinary middle-class couple and the epitome of domestic order, in marked contrast to their often scandalous royal predecessors. Photos of them were sold or given away on small cards called *cartes de visite,* which many leaders used to spread their fame. (The Royal Collection © 2009 Her Majesty Queen Elizabeth II.)

Civil War and Nation Building in the United States and Canada

In North America, increasing nationalism and powerful economic growth characterized the nation-building experience. The United States experienced the midcentury as a period of unprecedented and destructive upheaval born of nation building. It had a far more democratic political culture than existed in Europe, including almost universal white male suffrage, a rowdy independent press, and mass political parties, all of which upheld the view that sovereignty came from the people.

The United States continued to expand its territory to the west (Map 18.4). In 1848, victory in a war with Mexico almost doubled the size of the country. Texas was officially annexed, and large portions of California and the Southwest extended the borders of the United States into former Mexican land. Politicians and ordinary citizens alike favored removing the native Indian peoples from these western lands. Complicating matters, however, was the question of whether the U.S. West would be settled by free white farmers or whether southern slaveholders could bring in their slaves. The issue polarized the country. In the North, the new Republican Party emerged to demand "free soil, free labor, free men," although few Republicans endorsed the abolitionists' demand to end slavery.

With the 1860 election of Republican Abraham Lincoln to the presidency, most of the slaveholding states of the South seceded to form the Confederate States of

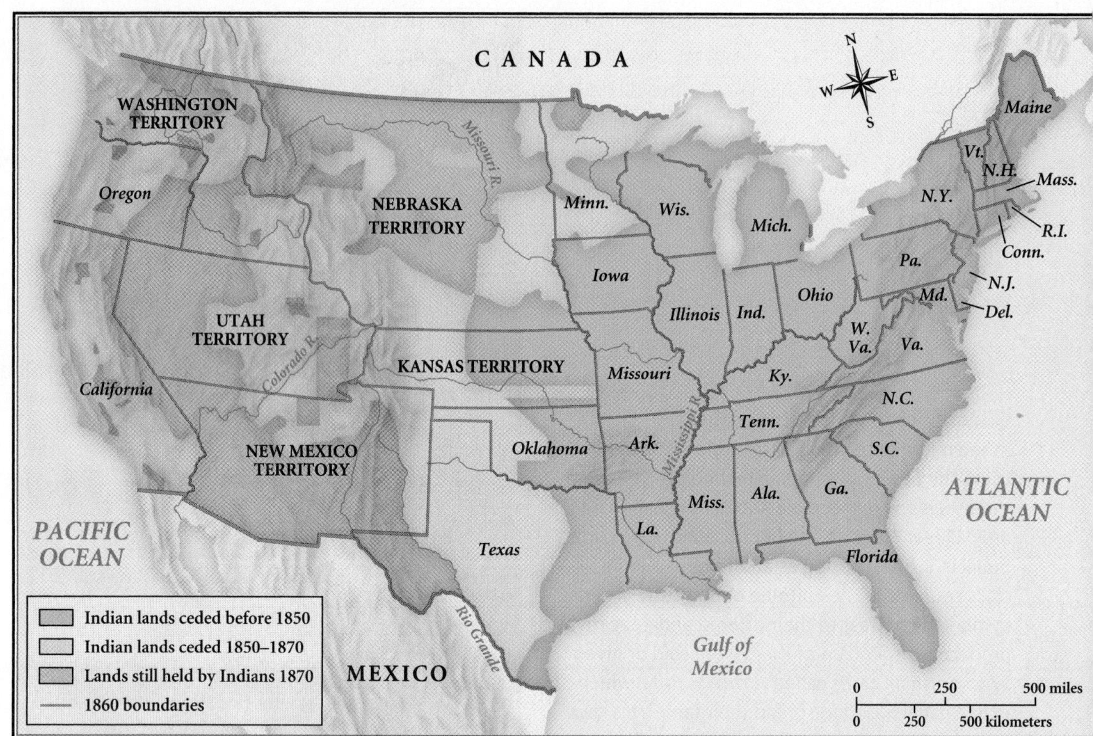

Map 18.4 U.S. Expansion, 1850–1870
Like Russia, the United States expanded into adjacent regions to create a continental nation-state, conquering indigenous peoples and taking over their territories. The United States' treatment of those whose lands it took was different from that of Russia, however. Native American peoples were herded into small, confined spaces called reservations so that settlers could take for themselves thousands of square miles for farming and other enterprises. Gradually, some native Americans acquired the right to vote, and the U.S. government granted full citizenship to all native Americans in 1925.

America. Under Lincoln's leadership, the North fought a civil war against the South to restore the Union. Lincoln did not initially aim to abolish slavery, but in January 1863 his Emancipation Proclamation came into force as a wartime measure, officially freeing all the slaves in the Confederate states and turning the war into a fight not only for the Union but also for liberation from slavery. After the summer of 1863, the superior industrial strength and military might of the North overpowered and physically destroyed much of the South. In April 1865, the North won even as a Confederate sympathizer assassinated Lincoln. Constitutional amendments ended slavery and promised political rights for African American men.

Northerners welcomed their victory as the triumph of American values, but racism remained entrenched throughout the United States. By 1871, southern whites began regaining control of state politics, often by organized violence. The end of northern occupation of the South in 1877 put on hold the promise of rights for blacks for nearly a century. Nonetheless, in ending slavery, the Union victory opened the way to a more coherent national government and economic advancement beyond the old Atlantic system based on slave plantation production.

The North's triumph also had profound effects elsewhere in North America. For one thing, it allowed the reunited United States to help defeat Napoleon III in Mexico in 1867. The United States also eyed the annexation of Canada in retribution for Britain's bias toward the Confederacy (due to British dependence on southern cotton). To head off this threat, the British government allowed Canadians to form a united, self-governing dominion. According dominion status answered Canadians' appeals for home rule, lessened domestic opposition to Britain's control of Canada, and advanced the cause of Canadian national unity.

REVIEW What varying roles did warfare play in nineteenth-century nation building?

Industry and Nation Building

Behind the growing power of European states lay the dramatic development of economic and technological power. Industry turned out an unbelievable array of new products, and the wages of many workers increased. Beginning in 1873, however, downturns in business threatened both businesspeople and the working class. Businesspeople sought remedies in new managerial techniques and a revolutionary marketing institution—the department store. Governments played their part by changing business law and supporting the drive for global profits. The steady advance of industry, global trade, and the consumer economy further transformed people's daily lives.

Industrial Innovation

Industrial, technological, and commercial innovation abounded in nineteenth-century Europe to back the ambitions of the nation-state. New products ranging from the bicycle, typewriter, and telephone to the internal combustion engine were striking proof of industrial progress. Alongside independent tinkerers and inventor-manufacturers were sophisticated engineers—for example, Karl Benz of Germany and Armand Peugeot of France—who invented revolutionary technologies such as the gasoline engine. Electricity began to provide the power to light everything from private drawing rooms to government office buildings. To fuel growth, the leading industrial nations mined and produced massive quantities of coal, iron, and steel during the 1870s and 1880s. The production of iron increased from 11 million to 23 million tons. Steel output in the industrial nations grew just as impressively, increasing from 500,000 to 11 million tons in the 1870s and 1880s. Manufacturers used the metal to build the more than 100,000 locomotives that pulled trains during these years—trains that transported 2 billion people annually.

Historians used to contrast a "second" Industrial Revolution, with its concentration on heavy industrial products, with the "first" Industrial Revolution of the eighteenth and early nineteenth centuries, in which innovations in textile making and the use of steam energy predominated. But many historians now believe this distinction applies mainly to Britain. In countries where industrialization came later, the two stages occurred simultaneously. Numerous textile mills were installed on the European continent later than in Britain, for instance, at the same time that blast furnaces were being constructed. Industrialization led to the decline of cottage production in traditional crafts like weaving. Domestic production, or "outwork," persisted in garment making, metalwork, and "finishing trades" such as porcelain painting and button polishing. Urban families painted tin soldiers, wrapped chocolate, and made cheese boxes. Factory owners liked to employ outworkers because the low piece rates forced them to work extremely long days. A German seamstress at her new home sewing machine reported that she "pedaled at a stretch from six o'clock in the morning until midnight. . . . At four o'clock I got up and did the housework and prepared meals." This coexistence of home and factory enterprise has continued through all the changes in manufacturing to the present day.

Industrial innovations also changed agriculture. Chemical fertilizers boosted crop yields, and reapers and threshers mechanized harvesting. In the 1870s, Sweden produced a cream separator, the first step toward mechanizing dairy farming. Wire fencing and barbed wire replaced wooden fencing and stone walls, both of which were labor-intensive to create. Refrigeration, developed during this period, allowed fruits, vegetables, and meat to be transported long distances without spoiling, thus diversifying and increasing the urban food supply. Tin from colonial trade facilitated large-scale commercial canning, which made many foods available year-round to people in cities.

During these decades, Britain's rate of industrial growth slowed as its entrepreneurs remained wedded to older, successful technologies. Two countries began surpassing Britain in technical education, innovation, and industrial development: Germany and the United States. Profiting from the acquisition of resource-rich Alsace and Lorraine after the Franco-Prussian War, German businesses invested in research and began to mass-produce goods that other countries had originally manufactured. Germany also spent as much money on education as on its military in the 1870s and 1880s. This investment resulted in highly skilled engineers and technical workers, whose productivity enabled Germany's electrical and chemical engineering capabilities to soar. The United States began an intensive exploitation of its vast natural resources, including coal, ore, gold, and oil. Whereas German accomplishments rested more on state promotion of industrial efforts, innovative entrepreneurs, such as Andrew Carnegie in iron and steel and John D. Rockefeller in oil, drove U.S. growth. Most other countries trailed the three leaders in the pervasiveness of industry.

French industry grew steadily, but French businesses remained smaller than those in Germany and the United States. Although France had some huge mining, textile, and metallurgical establishments, many French businessmen retired early to imitate the still enviable aristocratic way of life. Industrial development in Spain, Austria-Hungary, and Italy was primarily a local phenomenon. Austria-Hungary had densely industrialized areas around Vienna and in Styria and Bohemia, but the rest of the country remained tied to traditional, unmechanized agriculture. The Italian government spent more on building Rome into a grand capital than it invested in economic growth. A mere 1.4 percent of Italy's 1872 budget went to education and science, compared with 10.8 percent in Germany. The commercial use of electricity helped Scandinavians, who were poor in coal and ore, to industrialize in the last third of the nineteenth century and become leaders in the use of hydroelectric power. Russia's industrialization was slowed by the terms of the emancipation of the serfs, but it was fostered by the new railroad lines and the development of metallurgy and mining late in the nineteenth century.

Facing Economic Crisis

Economic conditions were far from rosy throughout the 1870s and 1880s despite industrial innovation. In 1873, prosperity abruptly gave way to a severe economic depression, followed by almost three decades of economic fluctuations featuring sharp downturns. People of all classes lost their jobs or businesses or faced long stretches of unemployment or bankruptcy. Because economic ties bound industrialized western Europe to international markets, recession affected the economies of such diverse regions as Australia, South Africa, California, Newfoundland, and the West Indies.

By the 1870s, as industry gained in influence, industrial and financial setbacks—not agricultural ones, as in the past—were sending the economy into a long tailspin. Businesspeople faced real problems. First, the start-up costs of new enterprises skyrocketed. Textile mills had required relatively modest amounts of capital in comparison with factories producing steel and iron. Industrialization had become what modern economists call *capital-intensive* rather than *labor-intensive*: industrial growth required the purchase of expensive machinery, not merely the hiring of more workers. Second, the distribution and consumption of goods were inadequate to sustain industrial growth, in part because businessmen kept wages so low despite rising productivity that workers could afford little besides food. Industrialists had made their fortunes by emphasizing production, not consumption. The series of slumps refocused entrepreneurial efforts on building sales.

Governments took steps to address the economic crisis. New laws established the limited liability corporation, which protected businesspeople from personal responsibility for a firm's debts and thus encouraged investment. Before limited liability, owners were personally responsible for the debts of a bankrupt business. In one case in England, a former partner who failed to have his name removed from a legal document after leaving the business remained responsible to creditors when the company went bankrupt. He lost everything he owned except a watch and the equivalent of $100. By reducing personal risk, limited liability made investors more confident about financing businesses. Public financing in stocks also helped raise vast amounts of new capital. Early stock exchanges had dealt mainly in government bonds and in government-sponsored enterprises such as railroads. By the end of the century, stock markets traded heavily in industrial corporate stock, thus raising money from a larger pool of private capital than before.

Another way businesses met the crisis was to band together in cartels and trusts to control prices and competition. Cartels were organizations of industries powerful enough to set prices; they flourished particularly in the German chemical, iron, coal, and electric industries. A single German coal cartel founded in the 1890s eventually dominated more than 95 percent of coal production in Germany. Trusts appeared first in the United States. In 1882, John D. Rockefeller created the Standard Oil Trust by acquiring stock from many different oil companies and placing it under the direction of trustees. The trustees then controlled so much of the companies' stock that they could set prices for the entire industry and even dictate to the railroads the rates for transporting the oil. While praising competition and free trade, the directors of cartels and trusts were actually limiting the free market. Soon governments began to do the same by imposing import tariffs.

Much of Europe had adopted free trade after midcentury, but during the recessions of the 1870s, the resulting huge trade deficits caused when imports exceed exports had soured many Europeans on the concept. A country with a trade deficit had less capital available to invest internally. Fewer jobs were created, and the chances of social unrest increased. Farmers in many European countries were hurt when improvements in transportation made it possible to import perishable foods, such as cheaper grain from the United States and Ukraine. With broad popular support, governments approved tariffs throughout these decades to prevent competition from foreign goods.

A Revolution in Business Practices

Industrialists also tried to minimize the damage of economic downturns by revolutionizing the everyday operations of their businesses. A generation earlier, a factory owner was directly involved in every aspect of his business and often learned to run the firm through trial and error. In the late 1800s, industrialists began to hire managers to run their increasingly complex day-to-day operations. Managers who specialized in sales and distribution, finance, or the purchase of raw materials made decisions in their areas of expertise. Other managers dealt with the factory floor, determining skill levels for each task. Managers used the concept of skill (based on the old craft traditions) to segment or divide the labor force according to levels of skill and thus levels of pay. The trend toward breaking down and separating work processes into discrete tasks advanced with the management revolution. For example, builders came to employ excavators, scaffolders, and haulers to do the "dirty work," hiring fewer highly paid carpenters. At the same time, skill levels were often arbitrary. When women were assigned certain tasks, for instance, those tasks were said to require less skill. Thus when women ran weaving machines in some mills, the job was considered an unskilled job worth lower pay; when men performed the same job in other mills, it was considered a higher-skilled job.

The rise of management led to the emergence of a white-collar service sector of office workers such as secretaries, file clerks, and typists to guide the flow of business information. Banks, railroads, insurance companies, and government-run telegraph and telephone companies all needed armies of white-collar employees. Workers with mathematical skills and literacy acquired in the new public primary schools staffed this service sector, which also provided clean work for educated, middle-class women. Whether to support themselves or to help pay the growing cost of raising and educating children, unmarried and an increasing number of married women of the respectable middle class took jobs despite the relatively new ideology of domesticity for women. Employers, as one put it, found in the new women workers a "quickness of eye and ear, and the delicacy of touch" essential to office work. By hiring women for newly created clerical jobs, business and government contributed further to a dual labor market in which certain categories of jobs were predominantly male and others were overwhelmingly female. White-collar work gradually became the domain of cheap female labor. In the absence of competition, businesses in the service sector boosted their profits by paying women low wages—much less than they would have had to pay men for the same work.

Finally, the rise of consumer capitalism magnified the scale of consumption, just as industrial capitalism had revolutionized the scale of production. The principal institution of this change was the department store. Founded after midcentury in large cities, department stores gathered such an impressive variety of goods in one place that consumers popularly called them "marble palaces" or "the eighth wonder of the world." Created by daring entrepreneurs, department stores eventually replaced the single-item stores that people entered knowing clearly what they wanted to purchase. Instead, these modern palaces stimulated consumer whims and desires with lavish displays spilling over railings and counters in glorious disarray. Shoppers no longer bargained rationally over prices; now they reacted to sales, a new marketing technique that could incite a buying frenzy. Because most men lacked the time for shopping expeditions, department stores appealed mostly to women, who came out of their domestic sphere into a new public role. Attractive salesgirls, another variety of service workers, were hired to inspire customers to buy. Glossy mail-order catalogs brought to rural households both necessities and exotic items from the faraway dream world of the city.

REVIEW What were the major economic changes in the West between 1850 and 1880?

Interior of Au Coin de la Rue (c. 1870)
This Parisian department store, not the grandest or first of its kind, shows the typical cascade of goods displayed on railings and balconies. The abundance of textiles and carpets sparked shoppers' imaginations, inciting them to let go of thrift and wander wherever their fancy took them, among many counters and displays, until they had overspent. (© Stefano Bianchetti/Corbis.)

Nation Building through Social Order

Government officials and reformers worked to establish social unity and order in an attempt to make political unity stronger. With an array of new improvements and policies, they also hoped to offset the violent changes of the nation-building process. Population rose dramatically and cities grew crowded as the nineteenth century progressed, leading officials across Europe to attend to public health and safety. Many liberal theorists advocated a laissez-faire government that left social and economic life largely to private enterprise. Nevertheless, confident in the benefits of European institutions in general, bureaucrats and reformers paid more attention to citizens' lives and, with the help of missionaries and explorers, spread European power and policies to the farthest reaches of the globe. Some of these efforts met violent resistance both within Europe and outside it.

Ordering Cities and the Countryside

European cities became the backdrop for displays of state power and national solidarity; thus efforts to improve sanitation, control disease, and beautify the landscape redounded to the state's credit. In 1857, Francis Joseph ordered the destruction of the old Viennese city walls and replaced them with boulevards lined with major public buildings such as an opera house and government offices. Such buildings showed off national wealth and power, and the broad boulevards allowed crowds to observe royal pageantry. These wider roads were also easier for troops to navigate than the twisted, narrow medieval streets that in 1848 had concealed insurrectionists in cities such as Vienna and Paris—an advantage that convinced some otherwise reluctant officials to approve the expense. Impressive parks and public gardens showed the state's control over nature, helped order people's leisure time, and inspired respect for the nation-state's achievements.

One effect of renovated cities was to highlight class differences. Construction first required destruction: buildings and entire neighborhoods of housing for the poor disappeared, and thousands of city dwellers were dislocated. The boulevards often served as boundaries marking rich and poor sections of the city. In Paris, the process of urban change was called **Haussmannization**, named for the prefect Georges-Eugène Haussmann, who implemented a grand design that included

Museums and Nation Building
The Kunsthistorisches Museum (Museum of Fine Arts) in Vienna was part of a huge rebuilding project that beautified the city with wide boulevards and grand public buildings. Art museums such as the one shown here represented the cultural wealth of the state and allowed citizens to take pride in this wealth while they routinely strolled the streets to view it.
(ullstein—imagebroker.net.)

eighty-five miles of new city streets, many lined with showy dwellings for the wealthy. The size and spaciousness of the many new banks and insurance companies built in London, one architect believed, "help[ed] the impression of stability," thus creating social order. The civic pride resulting from urban rebuilding would replace rebelliousness.

Yet amid redevelopment and beautification, serious problems loomed. Repeated epidemics of diseases such as cholera mowed down city dwellers and gave the strong impression of social decay. Poor sanitation allowed typhoid bacteria to spread through sewage and into water supplies, infecting rich and poor alike. In 1861, Britain's Prince Albert died of typhus, commonly known as a "filth disease." Unregulated urban slaughterhouses and tanneries; heaps of animal excrement in chicken coops, pigsties, and stables; human waste alongside buildings; and garbage everywhere facilitated the spread of disease. The stench of cities alone made sanitation a top priority.

Scientific research, increasingly undertaken in public universities and hospitals, provided the means to promote public health and control disease. France's Louis Pasteur, whose three young daughters had died of typhus, advanced the germ theory of disease. Seeking a method to prevent wine from spoiling, Pasteur began his work in the mid-1850s by studying fermentation. He found that the growth of living organisms caused fermentation, and he suggested that certain organisms—bacteria and parasites—might be responsible for human and animal diseases. Pasteur demonstrated that heating foods such as wine and milk to a certain temperature, a process soon known as pasteurization, killed these organisms and made food safe. English surgeon Joseph Lister applied the germ theory to medicine. He connected Pasteur's theory of bacteria to infection and developed antiseptics for treating wounds and preventing puerperal fever, a condition that was caused by the dirty hands of physicians and midwives and that killed innumerable women after childbirth.

Governments undertook projects to improve sewer and other sanitary systems, including the straightening of rivers to eliminate marshes and other stagnant pools of water that could breed disease. Citizens often prized such improvements as signs of national superiority. In Paris, sewage flowed into newly built underground, watertight collectors. In addition, Haussmann piped in water from uncontaminated sources in the countryside to provide each household with a secure supply. Such ventures were imitated throughout Europe: the Russian Empire's port city Riga (now in Latvia), for example, organized its first water company in 1863. To prevent devastating floods and the persistence of disease-ridden marshlands, governments rerouted and straightened rivers such as the Rhine and built canals. Alongside such grand projects were those affecting the details of everyday life. When public toilets for men became a feature of modern cities, for instance, women petitioned governments for similar facilities. On the lookout for disease and sanitary dangers, the average person became more aware of smells and the foul air that had been an accepted part of daily life for thousands of years. To show that they were becoming more "civilized," the middle and lower-middle classes bathed more regularly, mirroring in their own lives the quest of governments for order.

Expanding the Reach of Bureaucracy

Improved sanitation meant a more active role for the state, and bureaucracies expanded in these years to direct nation building and the drive for social order. The nation-state required citizens to follow a growing catalog of regulations as government authority reached further into the realm of everyday life. The censuses that Britain, France, and the United States had begun early in the nineteenth century became routine in most other countries as well. Censuses provided the state with personal details of citizens' lives, such as age, occupation, marital status, residential patterns, and fertility. Governments used these data for a variety of endeavors, ranging from setting quotas for military conscription to predicting needs for new prisons. Reformers like Florence Nightingale, who gathered statistics to support sanitary reform, believed that such quantitative information made government less susceptible to corruption and inefficiency. In 1860, Sweden introduced the income tax, which opened an area of private life—one's earnings from work or investment—to government scrutiny.

To bring about their vision of social order, many governments also expanded their regulation and investigation of prostitution. Venereal disease, especially syphilis, was common and, like typhus, infected individuals and whole families. Officials blamed prostitutes, not their clients, for its spread. The police picked up suspect women, who were examined for syphilis and incarcerated for treatment. As states began monitoring prostitution and other social matters such as public health and housing, they had to add departments and agencies. In 1867, Hungary's bureaucracy handled fewer than 250,000 individual cases, ranging from health to poverty issues; twenty years later, it handled more than a million.

Schooling and Professionalizing Society

An emphasis on knowledge and objective standards changed the professions and raised their status. Growing numbers of middle-class doctors, lawyers, managers, and journalists employed solid information in their work. The middle classes argued that civil service jobs should be awarded according to talent and skill rather than automatically going to those of aristocratic birth or with political connections. In Britain, a civil service law passed in 1870 required competitive examinations to ensure competency in government posts—a system long used in China. Governments began to allow professional people to influence state policy and determine rules for admission to "the professions." Such legislation had both positive and negative effects: groups could set high standards, but some otherwise qualified people were prohibited from working because they lacked the established credentials. The medical profession, for example, gained the authority to license physicians, but it tried to block experienced midwives from attending childbirths. Science became the province of the trained specialist rather than the experienced amateur.

Nation building required major improvements in the education of all citizens, professional or not. "We have made Italy," one Italian official announced. "Now we have to make Italians." Education was one way of bringing citizens to hold common beliefs and values. Bureaucrats and professionals called for radical changes in the curriculum and faculty of schools—from kindergarten to university—to make the general population more fit for citizenship and more useful in furthering economic progress. Expansion of the electorate and lower-class activism prompted one British aristocrat to say of the common people, whom he feared as they gained influence, "We must now educate our masters!" Governments thus introduced compulsory schooling to reduce illiteracy, at a level of more than 65 percent in Italy and Spain in the 1870s and even higher in eastern Europe (see "Taking Measure"). As ordinary people were allowed to vote, books taught them about the responsibilities of citizenship and provided the practical knowledge they needed to participate in an industrial society.

Education reform was not easy. At midcentury, religious authorities supervised schools and charged tuition, making primary education an option chosen only by prosperous or religious parents. After the 1850s, national politicians felt that their states could not afford masses of ignorant citizens, whose backwardness one French official blamed on parish priests. In 1861, an English commission on education concluded that instead of the Bible, "the knowledge most important to a labouring man is that of the causes which regulate the amount of his wages, the hours of his work, the regularity of his employment, and the prices of what he consumes." Replacing religion was a challenge for the increasingly knowledge-based nation.

Enforcing school attendance was another. Although the Netherlands, Sweden, and Switzerland had functioning primary school systems before midcentury, many parents in these and other countries resisted sending their children to school. Farm families depended on children to perform chores and believed that work in the

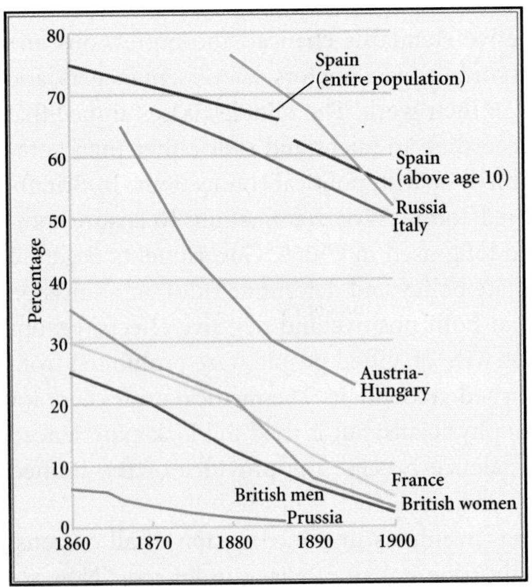

Taking Measure The Decline of Illiteracy, 1850–1900
The development of mass politics and the consolidation of the nation-state depended on building a cohesive group of citizens concerned with the progress of the nation. Increasing literacy was thus a national undertaking that varied throughout Europe, ranging from the low levels of illiteracy in Prussia to the high levels in Austria-Hungary and Russia. Even in regions of high levels of illiteracy, however, governments successfully got people reading.

fields or the household provided the best education. Urban homemakers needed their children to fetch water, dispose of waste, tend the younger children, and scavenge for household necessities such as stale bread from bakers. Yet some of the poor joined a craze for learning, which made traveling lecturers, public forums, reading groups, and debating societies popular among the middle and working classes.

Secondary and university education also expanded, yet remained even more of a luxury. In authoritarian countries such as Russia, advanced education, including education in science and technology, was often suspect because it empowered the young with information and taught them to think for themselves. Reformers pushed for more advanced and more complex courses for young women as part of nation building. In France and Russia, for example, government leaders themselves saw that "public education has had in view only half the population—the male sex," as the Russian minister of education wrote to Tsar Alexander II in 1856. They started secondary- and university-level courses for women as part of their programs to make women more interesting wives and better mothers and to control the modernization of society. In Britain, the founders of two women's colleges, Girton (1869) and Newnham (1871) at Cambridge University, believed that exacting standards in women's higher education would provide an example of a modern curriculum and also raise the low standards of scholarship prevalent in the men's colleges of Cambridge and Oxford at the time. Nonetheless, higher education for women remained controversial, as many people felt that knowledge of religion, sewing, and deportment was adequate for women.

Education also opened professional doors to women, who came to attend universities—in particular medical schools—in Zurich and Paris in the 1860s. Despite the complaint that their practice of medicine would weaken the system of separate spheres, women doctors thought they would bring feminine values to health care and also get better results, because their women patients would be more open with them than with male doctors. The need for knowledgeable citizens also offered opportunities for large numbers of women to enter teaching, a field once dominated by men. Hundreds of women founded nurseries, kindergartens, and primary schools based on the Enlightenment idea that learning starts at an early age. In Italy, women founded schools as a way to expand knowledge and teach civics lessons, thus providing a service to the nation. Yet many men opposed the idea of women teaching. "I shudder at philosophic women," wrote one German critic of female kindergarten teachers. Seen as radical because it brought middle-class women out of the home, the cause of early childhood education, or the "kindergarten movement," was as controversial as other education reforms.

Spreading National Power and Order beyond the West

In an age of nation building and industrial development, colonies took on new importance because they were seen to add to the power of the nation-state. This benefit led Great Britain, France, and Russia to expand their political control and rule colonies directly rather than through trading companies. Sometimes they offered social and cultural services such as schools. For instance, in the 1850s and 1860s Russian officials promoted the expansion of Russia's borders to gain control over nomadic tribes in central and eastern Asia. The Russian government then instituted educational and religious programs, such as instruction in the Russian language and in the beliefs of the Orthodox church, as a means to strengthen social order.

Great Britain, the era's mightiest imperial power, made a dramatic change of course toward political rule abroad as part of nation building during these decades. Before the 1850s, British liberals desired commercial gain from colonies, but believing in laissez-faire, they kept government involvement in colonial affairs minimal. In India, the East India Company worked across the subcontinent on Britain's behalf, and many regional rulers awarded the company commercial advantages. Since the eighteenth century, the East India Company had gained control over various kingdoms on the Indian subcontinent and had built railroads throughout the countryside to make commerce and revenue collecting more efficient. As commerce with Britain grew, many Indian merchants became wealthy. Other local men enlisted in the British-run Indian army, which became one of the largest standing armies in the world.

European expansion, including Britain's, was contested around the world, and in 1857 Indian troops, both Muslim and Hindu, violently rebelled when a rumor spread that Britain would force them to use ammunition cartridges greased with cow and pig fat, which violated the Hindu ban on beef and the Muslim prohibition of pork. This was not their main grievance, though. The soldiers, more generally angered at widening British control, stormed and conquered the old Mughal capital of Delhi and declared the independence of the Indian nation—an uprising that became known as the Indian Rebellion of 1857.

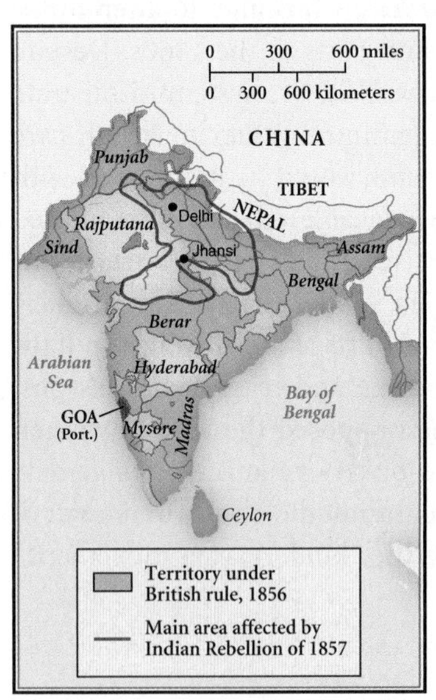

Indian Resistance, 1857

Simultaneously, civil rebellions erupted among leaders who were being displaced and the general populace who backed them against "the tyranny and oppression of the infidel and treacherous English." The rani (queen) Lakshmibai, widow of the ruler of the state of Jhansi in central India, led a separate military revolt when the East India Company tried to take over her lands after her husband died. As the British brutally crushed the rebels, Indian nationalism was born. Victorious, the British government took direct control of India in 1858, and the British Parliament declared Queen Victoria the empress of India in 1876.

A system of rule emerged in which close to half a million Indians governed a region the British called India under the supervision of a few thousand British men. Indians also collected taxes and distributed patronage. Colonial rule meant both outright oppression and more subtle intervention in everyday life. British production of cheap goods forced the impoverishment of such artisans as Indian handloom weavers, who had once dominated international markets. The British aimed to divert colonial populations into the production of cheap raw materials such as wheat, cotton, and jute to supply their industries. Nonetheless, some Indians benefited from improved sanitation and medicine and chose to accept British arguments against Indian customs such as infanticide, child marriage, and *sati*—a widow's self-immolation on her husband's funeral pyre. Others found Europe's scientific values attractive and, ironically, also came to appreciate that British rule brought a kind of unity to the many separate princedoms, thus laying the foundation for Indian nationalism.

French political expansion was similarly complex. The French government pushed to control Cochin China (modern southern Vietnam) in the 1860s. But missionaries in the area, ambitious French naval officers stationed in Asia, and even some local peoples pulled the French government further into the region. Like the British, the French brought improvements, such as the Mekong Delta project that increased the amount of cultivated land and spurred rapid growth of the food supply. Sanitation and public health programs proved a mixed blessing, because they led to population growth that strained other resources. Furthermore, landowners and French imperialists siphoned off most of the profits from economic improvement. The French also undertook a cultural mission to transform cities such as Saigon with tree-lined boulevards and other signs of Western urban life as they were doing in France itself. French literature, theater, and art diverted not only colonial officials but also upper-class Indochinese.

In this age of Realpolitik, the Crimean War had shown the great powers that the Mediterranean basin was crucial to expansion. Napoleon III, remembering his uncle's campaign in Egypt, took an interest in building the Suez Canal, which would dramatically shorten the route to Asia. The canal was completed in 1869, and as "canal fever" spread, Verdi composed the opera *Aïda* (set in ancient Egypt) in celebration. Great Britain and France were especially eager to do business with Egypt, where the combined value of imports and exports had jumped from 3.5 million Egyptian pounds in 1838 to 21 million in 1880 (and would grow to 60 million in 1913). European financial investment in the region also rose, first in ventures such as the Suez Canal in the 1860s and then in the laying of thousands of miles of railroad tracks and the creation of telegraph systems. Improvement-minded rulers in Asia and Africa paid dearly in 12 percent interest rates on loans for such projects. The completion of harbors, dams, canals, and railroads increased the Middle East's desirability as a market for European exports and as an intermediate stop on the way to trade with Asia. Having invested in the Suez Canal and in other commercial development, the British and French soon took over the Egyptian treasury to secure their own financial investments, and after invading Egypt in 1882, the British effectively took over the government, despite heated parliamentary opposition at home. Britain reshaped the Egyptian economy from a system based on multiple crops that maintained the country's self-sufficiency to one that emphasized the production of a few crops—mainly cotton, raw silk, wheat, and rice—that were especially useful to Europe. Local landowners and moneylenders also profited from these agricultural changes, while the bulk of the rural population barely eked out an existence.

The rest of the Mediterranean felt the heightened presence of the European powers. Driving deep into North Africa, the French army occupied all of Algeria by 1870, when the number of European immigrants to that region reached one-quarter million. French rule in Algeria as elsewhere brought profits to those dealing in European goods. Local leaders made money building railroads and government buildings and sometimes sent their children to European-style schools. Many local peoples, however, resisted the invasions and died from European-spread diseases. By 1872, the native population in Algeria had declined by more than 20 percent from five years earlier. As a further guarantee of their Mediterranean claims, the French occupied neighboring Tunisia in 1881. Western businessmen flooded the region with cheap goods, driving artisans from their trades and into low-paid work on railroads or in tobacco factories. Instead of basing wage rates on gender (as they did at home), Europeans used ethnicity and religion to segment the workforce, paying Muslims less than Christians and Arabs less than other ethnic groups.

The vastness of China allowed it to escape complete takeover, but traders and missionaries from European countries, carrying their message of Christian salvation, made inroads for the Western powers. Missionaries directed the Christian message to a population of 430 million, which had nearly doubled since the last century. Defeat in the Opium Wars caused an economic slump and helped generate the mass opposition movement known as the Taiping (Heavenly Kingdom). Headed by a leader who claimed to be the brother of Jesus, the movement attracted millions of followers who wanted an end to the ruling Qing dynasty, the expulsion of foreigners, more equal treatment of women, and land reform. By the mid-1850s, the Taiping controlled half of China. The threatened Qing regime promised the British and French greater influence in exchange for aid in defeating the Taiping. More than 20 million Chinese died in the resulting civil war (compared with 600,000 dead in the U.S. Civil War). When peace finally came in 1864, Western governments controlled much of the Chinese customs service and had almost unlimited access to the country.

Japan alone was able to escape European domination but not its influence. Through Dutch traders at Nagasaki, the Japanese had become keenly aware of the industrial, military, and commercial innovations of European society. In 1854, when the Japanese agreed to open the country to foreign trade, contacts with Europe had already given the Japanese a healthy appetite for Western knowledge and goods, including its superior weaponry. In 1867, reformers overthrew a government that resisted change, and in 1868 they enacted the **Meiji Restoration**. The word *Meiji* pointed to the "enlightened rule" of the new emperor whom the reformers had installed. Its goal was to combine "Western science and Eastern values" as a way of "making new"—hence, a combination of restoration and innovation. The new regime established Japan as a modern, technologically powerful state free from Western control.

Contesting the Nation-State at Home

Europeans did not simply sit by as the growing nation-state disrupted their lives. A better-informed working class protested the upheavals in everyday life caused when cities were ripped apart for improvement and when the growth of factories destroyed people's livelihoods. Workers' organizations slowly reemerged after their repression in the 1850s, and new theories arose to explain the growing power of the nation-state and the spread of industry on which the state depended. Increasingly educated by public schools, urban workers frequented cafés and pubs to hear news and discuss economic and political changes.

Many of the most outspoken labor activists were artisans, struggling to survive in the new industrializing climate. They were attracted either by the ideas of political theorist and former printer Pierre-Joseph Proudhon or by anarchist thought. In the 1840s, Proudhon proclaimed, "Property is theft," suggesting that ownership robbed workers of their rightful share of the earth's benefits. He opposed the centralized state and proposed that society be organized instead around natural groupings of men (but not women, who should work in seclusion at home for their husbands' comfort) in artisans' workshops. These workshops and a central bank crediting each worker for his labor would replace government and would lead to a "mutualist" social organization. **Anarchism** maintained that the existence of the state was the root of social injustice. According to the Russian nobleman and anarchist leader Mikhail Bakunin, the slightest infringement on freedom, especially by the central state and its laws, was unacceptable. Anarchists thus advocated the destruction of all state power, an increasingly attractive platform in this age of the expanding nation-state.

Political theorist and labor organizer Karl Marx opposed both mutualism and anarchism. These doctrines, he insisted, were wrongheaded, lacking the sound, scientific basis of his own theory, subsequently called **Marxism**. Marx's analysis, explained most notably in his book *Das Kapital* (*Capital*), adopted the liberal idea, dating back to John Locke in the seventeenth century, that human existence was defined by the requirement to work as a way of fulfilling basic needs such as food and shelter. Published between 1867 and 1894, *Das Kapital* was based on mathematical calculations of production and profit that would justify Realpolitik for the working classes. Marx held that the fundamental organization of any society, including its politics and culture, derived from the relationships arising from work or production. This idea, known as materialism, meant that the foundation of a society rested on class relationships—such as those between slave and master, serf and nobleman, or worker and capitalist. Marx called the class relationships that developed around work the "mode of production"—for instance, slavery, feudalism, or capitalism. He rejected the liberal focus on individual rights and emphasized instead the unequal class relations caused by those who had taken from the workers control of the means of production—that is, the capital, land, or factories—necessary to fulfill basic human needs.

Marx, like the politicians around him, took a tough-minded and realistic look at society as a whole. When a wave of strikes erupted in the late 1860s—in France alone, forty thousand workers participated in strikes in 1869, followed by more than eighty-five thousand in 1870—Marx saw struggle, not the warmhearted cooperation proposed by Proudhon or the utopian socialists (see page 654), as the means for bringing about change. Workers' awareness of their oppression would produce class consciousness among those in the same predicament and ultimately lead them to revolt against their exploiters—the capitalists, or bourgeoisie. Capitalism would be overthrown by these workers—the proletariat—bringing about a socialist society.

Marx saw the uprisings in France as the Franco-Prussian War ended in 1871 as a sign that his predictions were coming true. As the Prussians laid siege to Paris in 1870–1871, causing death and starvation in the bitter cold, the besieged Parisians rose up and demanded new republican liberties, new systems of work, and a more balanced distribution of power between the central government and the localities. To counter what they saw as the despotism of the centralized government, they declared themselves a self-governing commune on March 28, 1871. One issue behind the unrest was the nation-state's takeover of city life. As urban renovation displaced tens of thousands of workers from their homes in the heart of the city, homelessness and chaos embittered many Parisians against the state. Other French municipalities declared themselves communes as well, in an attempt to form a decentralized nation of independent, confederated units run by local citizens, not bureaucrats.

In the Paris Commune's two months of existence, its forty-member council, National Guard, and many other improvised offices found themselves at cross-purposes. Trying to maintain "communal" instead of "national" values, Parisians quickly developed a wide array of political clubs, local ceremonies, and self-managed, cooperative workshops. Women workers, for example, banded together to make National Guard uniforms on a cooperative rather than a profit-making basis. Beyond liberal political equality, the Commune proposed to liberate the worker and ensure "the absolute equality of women laborers." Thus a *commune* in contrast to a *republic* was meant to bring about social revolution. Communards, however, often disagreed about how specifically to change society. Mutualism, feminism, international socialism, and anarchism were but a few of the proposed avenues to social justice.

In the meantime, the provisional government that succeeded the defeated Napoleon III struck back to reinstitute national order. On May 21, 1871, the army

Woman Incendiary
The Paris Commune galvanized women activists, many of whom hoped to reform social conditions. After the fall of the Commune, women Communards were denigrated as half-clothed degenerates, using gender disorder to highlight the disorderliness of the Commune's resistance to the state. (© Bibliothèque nationale, Paris, France/The Bridgeman Art Library.)

entered Paris. In a week of fighting, both Communards and the army set the city ablaze (the Communards did so to slow the progress of government troops), and both sides executed hostages. Ultimately, however, the well-supplied French national army won. In the wake of victory, the army shot tens of thousands of citizens found on the streets. Parisian insurgents, one citizen commented, "deserved no better judge than a soldier's bullet." The Communards had fatally promoted a kind of antistate in an age of growing national power, and soon a different interpretation of the Paris Commune emerged: it was the work of the *pétroleuse,* or "woman incendiary"—a case of women running mad, crowding the streets in frenzy and fury. Within a year, writers were blaming the burning of Paris on women—"shameless slatterns, half-naked women, who kindled courage and breathed life into arson." Revolutionary men later became heroes in the history books, but women in political situations were characterized as "sinister females, sweating, their clothing undone, [who] passed from man to man."

The Franco-Prussian War, the Paris Commune, and the civil war were all horrendous blows from which France struggled to recover. The keys to restoring order in France after 1871 were instilling family values, fortifying religion, and claiming that the Commune had resulted from the collapsed boundaries between the male political sphere and the female domestic sphere. Karl Marx disagreed: he analyzed the Commune as a class struggle of workers attacking capitalist interests, which were protected by the centralized state. In the struggle against the Commune, the nation-state once again showed its strengthening muscle.

REVIEW How did nation-states expand their reach, and what resistance did they face?

The Culture of Social Order

Artists and writers of the mid-nineteenth century had reactions to the expanding nation-state as complex as those of people in Europe and around the world. In one way, artists took a remarkable turn by adopting a realistic style in cultural works in the 1850s to 1870s that paralleled Realpolitik. After 1848, many artists and writers expressed anger about political repression and economic growth. They saw daily life as filled with commercial values and organized by mindless officials. Unlike the romantics of the first half of the century, artists of the second half often had trouble seeing ordinary people as heroic. "How tired I am of the ignoble workman, the inept bourgeois, the stupid peasant, and the odious priest," wrote French novelist Gustave Flaubert. Rejecting romanticism, he described ordinary people in a new style called realism. Intellectuals proposed theories called **positivism** and Darwinism, which also took a cold, hard look at society. It was a stark realism similar to that which statesmen applied to politics.

The Arts Confront Social Reality

Culture helped the cause of national unity. The reading public devoured biographies of political leaders, past and present, and credited daring heroes with creating the triumphant nation-state. As literacy spread, readers of all classes responded to the mid-nineteenth-century novel and to an increasing number of artistic, scientific, and natural history exhibitions sponsored by the nation-state. While reading the same novels or attending exhibitions, citizens were schooled to appreciate the artistic style called realism and, more generally, to embrace their shared national heritage.

A well-financed press and commercially minded publishers produced an age of best sellers out of the craving for realism—or true-to-life portrayals of society without romantic or idealistic overtones. The novels of Charles Dickens appeared in serial form in newspapers, and each installment attracted buyers eager for the latest plot twist. His characters, drawn from contemporary English society, included starving orphans, grasping lawyers, and ruthless opportunists. *Hard Times* (1854) depicts the grinding poverty and ill health of workers alongside the heartlessness of businessmen. Novelist George Eliot (the pseudonym of Mary Ann Evans) deeply probed private, "real-life" dilemmas in works such as *The Mill on the Floss* (1860) and *Middlemarch* (1871–1872). Describing rural society, high and low, Eliot allowed Britons to see one another's predicaments, wherever they lived. She knew the pain of ordinary life from her own experience: she was a social outcast because she lived with a married man; despite her fame, she was not received in polite society. These popular novels showed a hard reality and thus helped form a shared culture among people in distant parts of a nation much as state institutions did.

French writers also scorned dreams of political utopias and ideal beauty. Gustave Flaubert's *Madame Bovary* (1857) tells the story of a bored doctor's wife whose life is filled with romantic fantasies. She has one love affair after another and becomes so hopelessly indebted buying gifts for her lovers that she commits suicide. *Madame Bovary* scandalized French society for its frank picture of women's sexuality but attracted a wide readership. Poet Charles-Pierre Baudelaire wrote explicitly about sex; in *Les Fleurs du mal*

(*Flowers of Evil,* 1857), he expressed sexual passion and described drug- and wine-induced fantasies. French authorities brought charges against both Flaubert and Baudelaire for these violations of social convention. At issue was social and artistic order. "Art without rules is no longer art," the prosecutor maintained, as both were found guilty.

During the era of the Great Reforms, Russian writers debated whether western European values were harming Russian culture. Rather than dividing the nation, this discussion about Russian culture united people around a national issue. Adopting one viewpoint, Ivan Turgenev created a powerful novel of Russian life, *Fathers and Sons* (1862), a story of nihilistic children rejecting not only parental authority but also their parents' spiritual values in favor of science and facts. Expressing another point of view, Fyodor Dostoevsky in *The Possessed* (1871–1872) and other works showed the dark, ridiculous, and neurotic side of nihilists, thus holding up Turgenev as a softheaded romantic. Dostoevsky's highly intelligent characters in *Crime and Punishment* (1866) are often personally tormented and condemned to lead absurd, even criminal lives. He used these antiheroes to emphasize spirituality and traditional Russian values, but he gave his works a "realistic" spin by planting such values in ordinary, often seedy people.

Visual artists had a different relationship to their governments than did writers, yet many also depicted society in harsh terms. Artists usually depended on government support rather than sales to thousands of readers. Leaders such as Britain's Prince Albert purchased works for official collections and for themselves. Having artwork chosen for display at government-sponsored exhibitions was another way for artists to gain prominence and earn a living. Officially appointed juries selected works of art to be exhibited and then chose prizewinners from among them. Hundreds of thousands of people from all classes attended these exhibitions.

After 1848, artists began rejecting romantic conventions idealizing ordinary folk and grand historic events. Instead, painters like French artist Gustave Courbet portrayed weary laborers at backbreaking work because, as he stated, an artist should "never permit sentiment to overthrow logic." Édouard Manet broke with romantic conventions of the nude. His *Olympia* (1865) depicts a white courtesan lying on her bed, attended by a black woman. This disregard for the classical traditions of showing women in dreamy poses or mythical settings was too much for the critics; one called *Olympia* "a sort of female gorilla." Shocking at first, graphic portrayals that shattered comforting illusions were a feature of realism.

Artistic realism faced a challenge from photography—a challenge that found its response in the 1860s to 1890s in a new style called **impressionism**. Manet coined the term to reflect artists' attempts to capture a single moment by focusing on the ever-changing light and color found in everyday vision. Using splotches and dots, impressionists moved away from the precise realism of earlier painters. Claude Monet, for example, was fascinated by the way light transformed an object, and he often portrayed the same place—a bridge or a railroad station—at different times of day. Dutch-born painter Vincent Van Gogh used vibrant colors in great swirls to capture sunflowers and the starry night sky. Such distortions of reality made the impressionists' visual style seem outrageous to those accustomed to realism, but others enthusiastically greeted impressionism's luminous quality as more real than realism. Industry contributed to the

Gustave Courbet, *Wrestlers* (1850) Courbet painted his dirty, grunting wrestlers in the realist style, which rejected the dreamy romanticism of revolutionary Europe. These muscular men sum up the resort to physical struggle during these state-building decades and convey the art world's recognition that Realpolitik had taken over the governance of society. (© Museum of Fine Arts, Budapest, Hungary/ The Bridgeman Art Library.)

new style, as factories produced paint from chemicals rather than plants in a wider, more intense spectrum of colors.

In both composition and style, impressionists borrowed heavily from Asian art, knowledge of which rapidly spread in Europe as the West extended its reach. The concept of the fleetingness of situations came from a centuries-old Japanese concept called *mono no aware* (sensitivity to the fleetingness of life). The color, line, and delicacy of Japanese art (which many impressionists collected) is evident in Monet's later paintings of water lilies, his studies of wisteria, and even his re-creation of a Japanese garden at his home in France. Similarly, American artist Mary Cassatt used the two-dimensionality of Japanese art in her work. Some of the characters in her paintings, though European, look Japanese. Van Gogh sometimes filled the background of portraits with copies of intensely colored Japanese prints.

Artists also commented on the changing economic scene, especially the fact that a growing segment of service workers did less physical work and had more energy for leisure. French painter Georges Seurat, for example, depicted the newly created parks with their walking paths and Sunday bicyclists; white-collar workers carrying books or newspapers paraded in their store-bought clothing. Degas focused on portraying women—from ballet dancers to laundrywomen—in various states of exertion and fatigue. Van Gogh, avoiding the intense colors he typically used for the countryside, depicted the gray outskirts of cities, where industries were often located and where the desperately poor lived.

Unlike most of the visual arts, opera was commercially profitable, accessible to most classes of society, and thus an effective means of reaching the public. Verdi used musical theater to contrast noble ideals with the deadly effects of power, and the lure of passion with the need for social order. The German composer Richard Wagner, the most musically innovative composer of this era, hoped to revolutionize opera by combining music and drama to arouse the audience's fear, awe, and engagement. A gigantic cycle of four operas, *The Ring of the Nibelung* (1854–1874), reshaped ancient German myths into a modern, nightmarish allegory of a world doomed by its obsessive pursuit of money and power and redeemable only through unselfish love. Another of his operas, *The Mastersingers of Nuremberg* (1867), was a nationalistic tribute to German culture, and like the arts elsewhere, it helped unite individuals into a public with a shared, if debated, cultural experience.

Religion and Secular Order

The expansion of state power set the stage for clashes over the role of organized religion in the nation-state. Should religion have the same hold on government and public life as in the past, thus competing with loyalty to the nation? In the 1850s, many politicians supported religious institutions and attended religious services because they were another source of order. Simultaneously, some nation builders, intellectuals, and economic liberals rejected the competing worldview and authority of established churches, particularly Roman Catholicism. Bismarck was one of these. Believing that the church slowed the development of nationalist sentiment, he mounted a full-blown *Kulturkampf* (culture war) against Catholic influence in 1872. Mercilessly attacking the church, the German government expelled the Jesuits in 1872, increased state power over the clergy in Prussia in 1873, and introduced obligatory civil marriage in 1875. Bismarck, however, overestimated his ability to manipulate politics, for both conservatives and Catholics objected to religious repression in the name of state building.

The Catholic church felt assaulted by a growing rationalism that was supposed to replace religious faith and by the state building in Italy and Germany that competed for people's traditional loyalty. In addition, nation building had resulted in the extension of liberal rights to Jews, whom many Christians considered enemies. Attacking reform and changing values, Pope Pius IX (r. 1846–1878) issued *The Syllabus of Errors* (1864), and in 1870 the First Vatican Council approved the dogma of papal infallibility. This teaching proclaimed that the pope spoke divinely revealed truth on issues of morality and faith. Eight years later, a new pope, Leo XIII (r. 1878–1903), began the process of reconciliation with modern politics by encouraging up-to-date scholarship in Catholic institutes and universities and by accepting aspects of democracy. Leo's ideas marked a dramatic turn, ending the Kulturkampf and calming worried Catholics across Europe.

Religious doctrine continued to have powerful popular appeal, but the place of organized religion in society was changing. Church attendance declined among workers and artisans, but many people in the upper and middle classes and most of the peasantry remained faithful. The Orthodox church of Russia and eastern Europe, with its Pan-Slavic appeal, fostered nationalism among Serbs and became a rallying point. Women's spirituality intensified, and Roman Catholic and Russian Orthodox religious orders of women increased in size and number. Men, by contrast, were falling away from religious devotion. In 1858, an outburst of popular religious fervor, especially among women, followed a young peasant girl's visions of the Virgin Mary at Lourdes in southern France. Bernadette Soubirous said that Mary told her to drink from the ground, at which point a spring appeared. Crowds besieged the area to be cured of ailments by the waters of Lourdes. In 1867, less than ten years later, a railroad line was laid to Lourdes to enable millions of pilgrims to visit the shrine on church-organized trips. The Catholic church thus showed that it was up-to-date, willing to use modern means such as railroads and medical verification of miraculous cures to make Lourdes itself the center of a brisk commercial as well as religious culture.

At nearly the same time as Bernadette's vision, the English naturalist Charles Darwin published *On the Origin of Species* (1859), which challenged the Judeo-Christian worldview that humanity was the creation of God. Darwin argued that life had taken shape over countless millions of years before humans existed and that human life was the result of this slow development, called evolution. Instead of believing that God had miraculously brought the universe and all life into being in six days as described in the Bible, Darwin held that human life had developed from lower forms through a battle for survival, and through the selection of sexual partners, more-evolved individuals passed their natural strength to the next generation. In a perpetual challenge to meet the forces of nature, Darwin suggested, some species die out, and those with better-adapted characteristics survive. A highly respectable Victorian gentleman, Darwin announced that the Bible gave a "manifestly false history of the world." Darwin's theories also undermined certain liberal, secular beliefs. The Enlightenment,

Darwin Ridiculed, c. 1860
Charles Darwin's theories claimed that humans had evolved from animal species and rejected the long-standing explanation of a divine human origin. His scientific ideas so diverged from people's beliefs that cartoonists made fun of both the respectable Darwin and his theory. Despite the controversy, evolution withstood the test of further scientific study. **For more help analyzing this image, see the visual activity for this chapter in the Online Study Guide at bedfordstmartins.com/huntconcise.** (Hulton Archive/Getty Images.)

for example, had glorified nature as tranquil and noble and viewed human beings as essentially rational. The theory of **natural selection**, in which the fittest survive, suggested that human society is one in which combative individuals and groups constantly fight one another.

Darwin's findings and other innovative biological research placed religious views under attack. Working with pea plants in his monastery garden in the 1860s, Gregor Mendel determined the principles of heredity, from which the science of genetics later developed. Investigation into the female reproductive cycle led other scientists to discover the principle of spontaneous ovulation—the automatic release of the egg by the ovary whether sexual intercourse took place or not. This discovery caused theorists to conclude that men had aggressive and strong sexual drives because reproduction depended on their sexual arousal. In contrast, the spontaneous and regular release of the egg independent of emotions indicated that women were passive and lacked sexual feeling.

Darwin added to this social commentary. The legal, political, and economic privilege of white European men in the nineteenth century, he maintained, was natural because they were more highly evolved than white women or people of color. Despite his belief in a common ancestor for people of all races, Darwin held that people of color, or "lower races," were far behind whites in intelligence and civilization. As for women, "the chief distinction in the intellectual powers of the two sexes," Darwin declared, "is shewn by man's attaining to a higher eminence in whatever he takes up." The school of Social Darwinism developed its own version of evolutionary theory to lobby for racist, sexist, and nationalist policies. Social Darwinist arguments were influential in the years to come.

From Natural Science to Social Science

Darwin's thought motivated the search for alternatives to the idea that the social order was created by God. French social philosopher Auguste Comte developed positivism—a theory claiming that the careful study of facts would generate accurate and useful, or "positive," laws of society. Comte's *System of Positive Politics, or Treatise on Sociology* (1851) proposed that social scientists construct knowledge of the political order as they would construct understanding of the natural world—that is, through observation and objective study. This idea inspired people to believe they could solve the problems resulting from economic and social change. To accomplish this goal, tough-minded reformers founded study groups and scientifically oriented associations to dig up social facts such as statistics on poverty or the conditions of working-class life. Comte encouraged women's participation in reform because he saw "womanly" compassion and scientific public policy to be equally important to producing social harmony. Positivism led not only to women's increased public activism but also to the growth of the social sciences.

The celebrated English philosopher John Stuart Mill used Comte's theories to promote widespread reform and mass education. In his political essay *On Liberty*

(1859), Mill argued for the improvement of society generally, but he also expressed concern that "superior" people not be brought down or confined by the will of the masses. Influenced by his wife, Harriet Taylor Mill, he advocated rights for women and introduced a woman suffrage bill into the House of Commons after her death. The bill's defeat prompted Mill to publish *The Subjection of Women* (1869), which presented the family as maintaining an older kind of order lacking modern concepts of rights and freedom. Mill exposed women's cheerful obedience in marriage as a sham. To make women appear "not a forced slave, but a willing one," he said, they were trained not to value their own talent and independence but to embrace "submission." Critiquing the century's basic beliefs about men's and women's roles, *The Subjection of Women* became an internationally celebrated argument for the rights of women.

The progressive side of Mill's social thought was soon lost in a flood of Social Darwinist theories and became one among several visions of social order—all of them claiming to be scientific and thus true. The theories of Mill, Comte, Darwin, and others influenced later national debates over policy in the West. Inspired by the social sciences, policymaking came to rely on statistics and fact gathering to produce realistic, hardheaded appraisals for the purpose of building strong, unified nations.

REVIEW What were the results of applying the scientific method to social thought?

Conclusion

Throughout modern history, the development of nation-states and the economic prosperity on which they depended has been neither inevitable nor uniform nor peaceful. This was especially true in the nineteenth century, when ambitious politicians and determined bureaucrats used a variety of methods to transform very different countries into effective nation-states. Nation building was most dramatic in Germany and Italy, where states unified through military force and where people of opposing political opinions ultimately agreed that national unity should be the primary goal. Compelled by military defeat to shake off centuries of tradition, the Austrian and Russian monarchs instituted reforms as a way of keeping their systems in place. The Habsburg Empire became a dual monarchy that raised the level of disunity. Reforms in Russia left the authoritarian monarchy intact but partially transformed the social order.

After decades of romantic fervor, realism in politics and the industrial economy became a much-celebrated principle, which spread to cultural matters as well. Proponents of realism such as Darwin and Marx developed theories disturbing to those who maintained an Enlightenment faith in social and political harmony. Realist novels and artworks jarred polite society and, like the operas of Verdi, portrayed dilemmas of the times. Growing government administrations set policies that were meant to bring order but often brought disorder and resistance, including the Taiping uprising, the Indian Rebellion, and the Paris Commune—all of

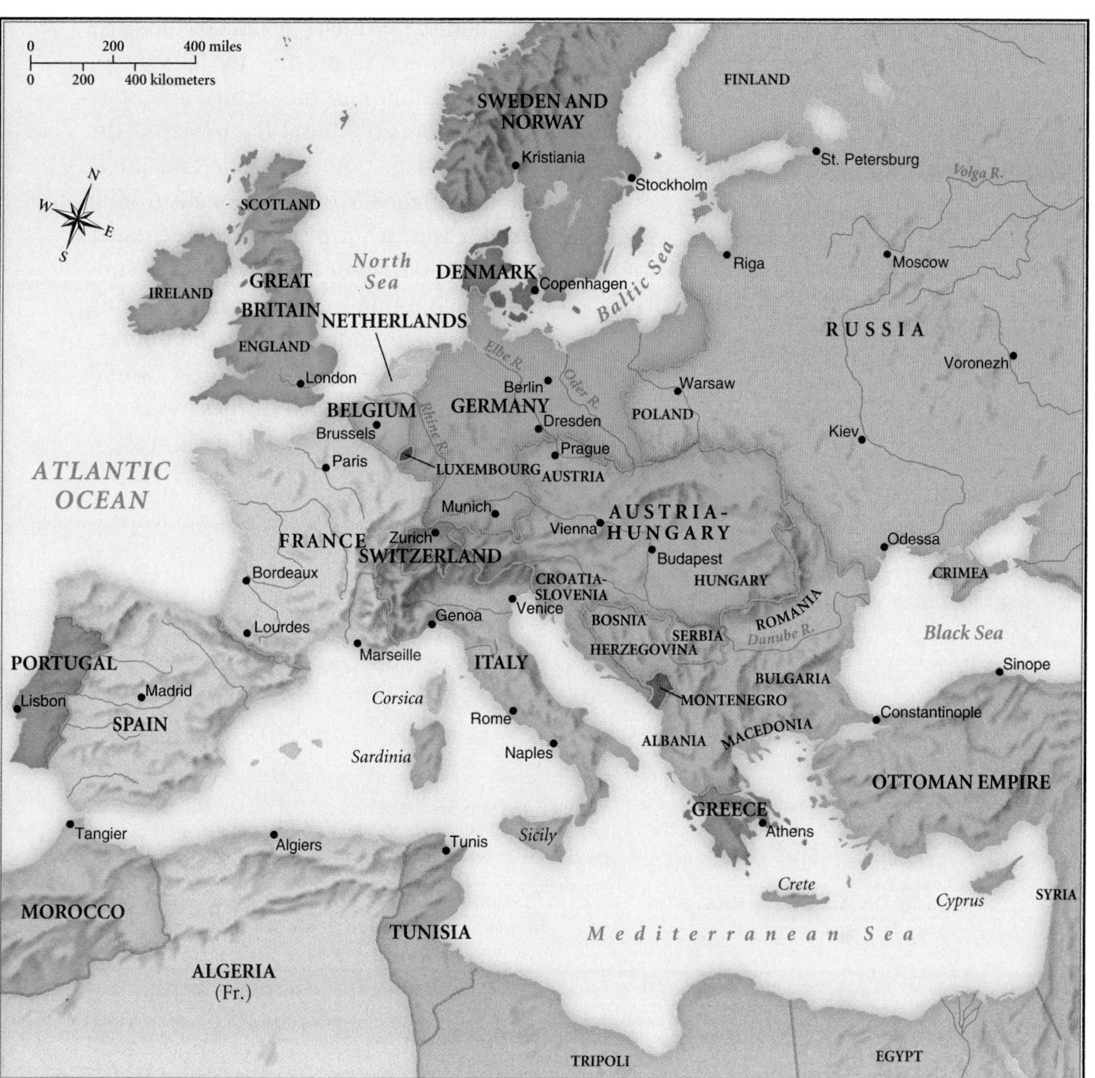

Mapping the West Europe and the Mediterranean, c. 1880
European nation-states consolidated their power by building unified state structures and by developing the means to foster social and cultural integration of the diverse peoples within their borders. They also were rapidly expanding outside their boundaries, extending the economic and political reach of the nation-state. North Africa and the Middle East—parts of the declining Ottoman Empire—had particular appeal to Europeans because of their natural resources and their potential for further European settlement. They also provided a gateway to the rest of the world.

them challenging European nation building. When the ordinary people of the Paris Commune rose up to protest the loss of French power and prestige in the Franco-Prussian War, they also defied the trend toward economic modernity and state building. Their actions raised difficult questions. How far should the power of the state extend in both domestic and international affairs? Would nationalism be a force for war or for peace? As these issues ripened, the next decades would see continued economic advancement, growing competition for global power, and unprecedented changes that ultimately would lead to a major war. All of these were the result of successes in nation building.

CHAPTER REVIEW QUESTIONS

1. Some would call the decades between 1850 and 1880 a period of order, while others would call it a period of disorder. Which characterization would you choose and why?
2. What ingredients contribute to the "realism" historians see in the events and actions of this period?

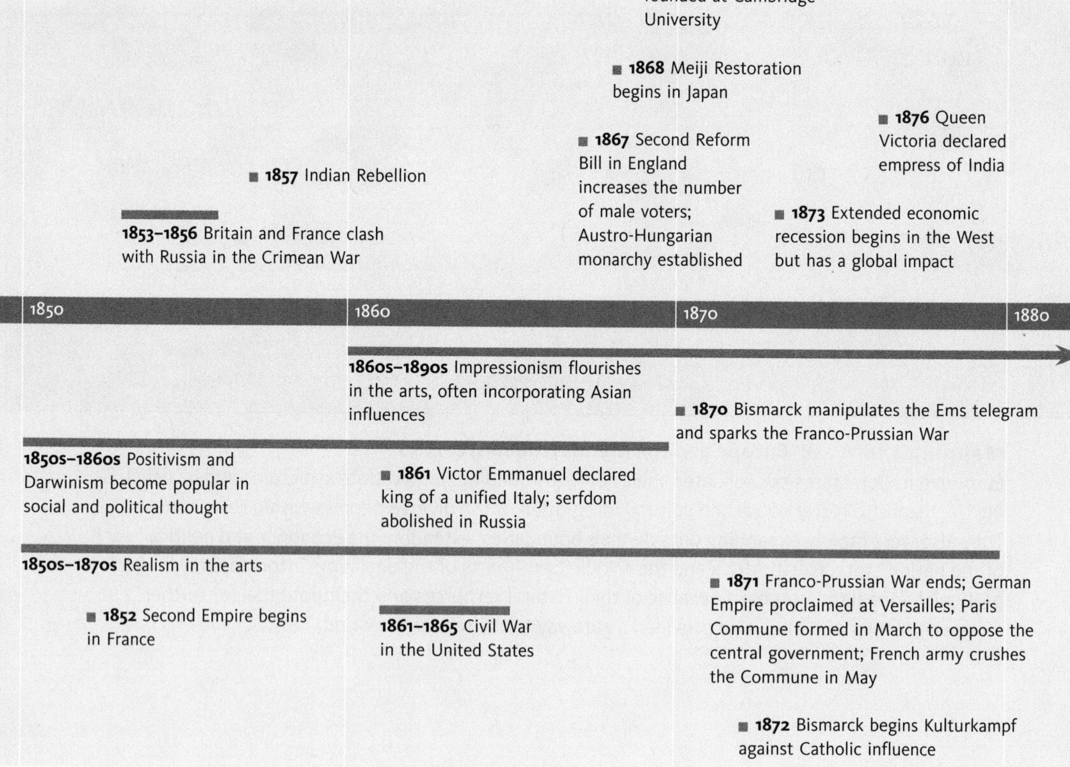

For practice quizzes and other study tools, see the Online Study Guide at bedfordstmartins.com/huntconcise.

For primary-source material from this period, see Chapters 22 and 23 of *Sources of The Making of the West,* Third Edition.

Suggested References

Nation building has produced a varied literature ranging from studies of royalty as unifying figures to histories of the arts and industry. Bayly's book puts the development of the Western nation-state into a world history perspective.

Bayly, C. A. *The Birth of the Modern World, 1780–1914: Global Connections and Comparisons.* 2004.

Blackbourn, David. *The Conquest of Nature: Water, Landscape, and the Making of Modern Germany.* 2006.

*Darwin, Charles. *Autobiography.* 1969.

Eichner, Carolyn. *Surmounting the Barricades: Women in the Paris Commune.* 2004.

Eley, Geoff. *Forging Democracy: A History of the Left in Europe, 1850–2000.* 2002.

Faust, Drew Gilpin. *This Republic of Suffering: Death and the American Civil War.* 2008.

Gross, Michael B. *The War against Catholicism: Liberalism and the Anti-Catholic Imagination in Nineteenth-Century Germany.* 2005.

Homans, Margaret. *Royal Representations: Queen Victoria and British Culture, 1837–1876.* 1998.

Kaufman, Suzanne. *Consuming Visions: Mass Culture and the Lourdes Shrine.* 2005.

King, Jeremy. *Budweisers into Czechs and Germans: A Local History of Bohemian Politics, 1848–1948.* 2002.

Papayanis, Nicholas. *Planning Paris before Haussmann.* 2004.

Rappaport, Erika. *Shopping for Pleasure: Women in the Making of London's West End.* 2000.

Rappaport, Helen. *No Place for Ladies: The Untold Story of Women in the Crimean War.* 2007.

Roy, Tapti. *The Raj of the Rani.* 2007.

*Seacole, Mary. *Wonderful Adventures of Mrs. Seacole in Many Lands.* 1857.

Stites, Richard. *Serfdom, Society, and the Arts in Imperial Russia.* 2005.

Victorian Web: http://www.victorianweb.org

19

Empire, Modernity, and the Road to War

c. 1880–1914

IN THE FIRST DECADE of the twentieth century, a wealthy young Russian man traveled from one country to another to find relief from a common ailment of the time called neurasthenia. Its symptoms included fatigue, lack of interest in life, depression, and sometimes physical sickness. In 1910, the young man encountered Sigmund Freud, a Viennese doctor whose unconventional treatment—eventually called **psychoanalysis** took the form of conversations about the patient's dreams, sexual experiences, and everyday life. Over the course of four years, Freud uncovered his patient's deeply hidden fear of castration disguised as a fear of wolves—thus the name "Wolf-Man," by which he is known to us. Freud worked his cure, as the Wolf-Man himself put it, "by bringing repressed ideas into consciousness."

Edvard Munch, *The Scream* (1893)
In some of his paintings, Norwegian artist Edvard Munch captured the spirit of the turn of the century using delightful pastel colors to convey the leisured life of people strolling in the countryside. But modern life at this time also had its tortured side, which Munch was equally capable of portraying. *The Scream* is seen as emblematic of the torments of modernity as the individual turns inward, driven by neuroses, self-destructive impulses, and even madness. While some people, like the two figures in the background, could react calmly to whatever modern life had to offer, others, like the screamer, agonized over every turn of events. It can also be suggested that the screamer, like Europe, was traveling the road to World War I. *(Scala/Art Resource, NY. © 2010 The Munch Museum/The Munch-Ellingsen Group/Artists Rights Society [ARS], NY.)*

The Wolf-Man could be said to represent his time. Born into a family that owned vast estates, he reflected the growing prosperity of Europeans, though on a grander scale than most. Countless individuals were troubled, even mentally disturbed like the Wolf-Man, and suicide was not uncommon. The Wolf-Man's own sister and father died from intentional drug overdoses. At the turn of the century, Europeans raised questions about family life, gender relationships, empire, religion, and the consequences of technology. Every sign of imperial wealth brought on a sense of Europe's decline. British writer H. G. Wells saw in this era "humanity upon the wane . . . the sunset of mankind." Gloom filled the pages of many a book and upset the lives of individuals like the Wolf-Man.

Conflict rattled the world as a growing number of powers, including Japan, fought their way into even more territories and took political control. As the race for worldwide empire continued—most notably in Africa—colonized peoples developed liberation movements to become independent, like their oppressors. While the great powers fought to dominate people around the world, the competition for empire fueled an arms race that threatened to turn Europe, the "most civilized" continent in the world according to its leaders, into a savage battleground. In domestic politics, militant nationalism fueled anti-Semitism and ethnic hatred. Women suffragists along with politically disadvantaged groups such as the Slavs and Irish demanded full rights, even as political assassinations and public brutality swept away the liberal values of tolerance and rights.

Those were just some of the conflicts associated with **modernity**—a term often used to describe the faster pace of life, the rise of mass politics, and the decline of a rural social order that were so visible in the West from the late nineteenth century on. The word *modernity* also refers to the celebrated "modern" art, music, science, and philosophy of this period. Although many people today admire the brilliant qualities of the modern arts, some people at the time were offended, even outraged, by the new styles and sounds. Freud's theory that sexual drives exist even in the youngest children shocked early-twentieth-century people. Middle-class faith in artistic and scientific progress was tested, and just as the Wolf-Man was finishing his treatment in June 1914, all the tensions that had been building nationally and internationally were coming to a head. The Wolf-Man rejoiced at the end of June 1914 that "he could now leave Vienna a healthy man." Yet the political, social, and diplomatic friction of the past few decades was about to erupt into World War I—one of the most horrific wars the world has ever seen.

CHAPTER FOCUS QUESTION How did developments in social and intellectual life, imperial expansion, and politics at the turn of the twentieth century produce instability and set the backdrop for war?

The Challenge of Empire

Imperialism surged in the last third of the nineteenth century and increasingly caused conflict in the early twentieth century. Colonies provided investments and crucial markets for some businesses, and heated rivalry among nations fueled competition for territory in Africa and Asia. The imperialism of these decades is called "new" because of the rush to rule more territories directly rather than just control trade with them. But the situation was complicated and the distribution of benefits uneven. Late in the century, for example, French colonies bought 65 percent of France's exports of soap, and imperialism provided huge numbers of jobs to people in European port cities. Yet Europeans did not benefit uniformly from the search for new markets, which often proved more costly than profitable. Whether they benefited or not, taxpayers in all parts of a nation paid for colonial armies, increasingly costly weaponry, and colonial administrators. Although imperialism was supposed to advance peaceful "civilization," this wave of "new imperialism" actually intensified international tensions. In securing India's borders, for example, the British faced Russian expansion in Afghanistan and China. Generating conflict around the world, imperial competition even made areas of Europe, such as the Balkans, more volatile than ever as states struggled for control of disputed territory.

Motives for imperialism were complex. Goals such as fostering national might and Christianizing peoples often proved difficult to achieve. Governments worried that imperialism—because of its expense and the constant possibility of war—might weaken rather than strengthen them. The French statesman Jules Ferry argued that France "must keep its role as the soldier of civilization." But it was unclear whether imperialists should emphasize soldiering—that is, conquest and conflict—or the goal of exporting culture and religion. Hoping to Christianize colonized peoples, European missionaries ventured to newly occupied areas of Africa and Asia. A woman missionary working among the Tibetans reflected a common view when she remarked that the native peoples were "going down, down into hell, and there is no one but me . . . to witness for Jesus amongst them." Europeans were confident of their religious and cultural superiority and thus fought their way into distant countries, undermining age-old civilizations.

The Scramble for Africa

After the British takeover of the Egyptian government in the 1880s, European commerce with sub-Saharan Africa turned into political rule, as one territory after another fell to European military force. Europeans' principal objective was obtaining Africa's raw materials, such as palm oil, cotton, diamonds, cocoa, and rubber. Additionally, Britain wanted the southern and eastern coasts of Africa secure for stopover ports on the route to Asia. The British, French, Belgians, Portuguese, Italians, and Germans competed to dominate peoples, land, and resources—"the magnificent cake of Africa," as King Leopold II of Belgium put it (Map 19.1). Driven by insatiable greed, Leopold claimed the Congo region of central Africa (Map 19.2, page 734), competing with France for that territory and inflicting on local Africans unparalleled acts of cruelty. German chancellor Otto von Bismarck, who saw colonies mostly as political bargaining chips, established German control over Cameroon and a section of East Africa. Faced with competition, the British poured millions of pounds into conquering the continent "from Cairo to Cape Town," as the slogan went, and the French cemented their hold on large portions of West Africa.

The scramble for Africa escalated tensions in Europe, prompting Bismarck to call a conference of European nations at Berlin. The fourteen nations at the conference, held in a series of meetings in 1884 and 1885, decided that their settlements along the African coast guaranteed their rights to the interior territory as well. This

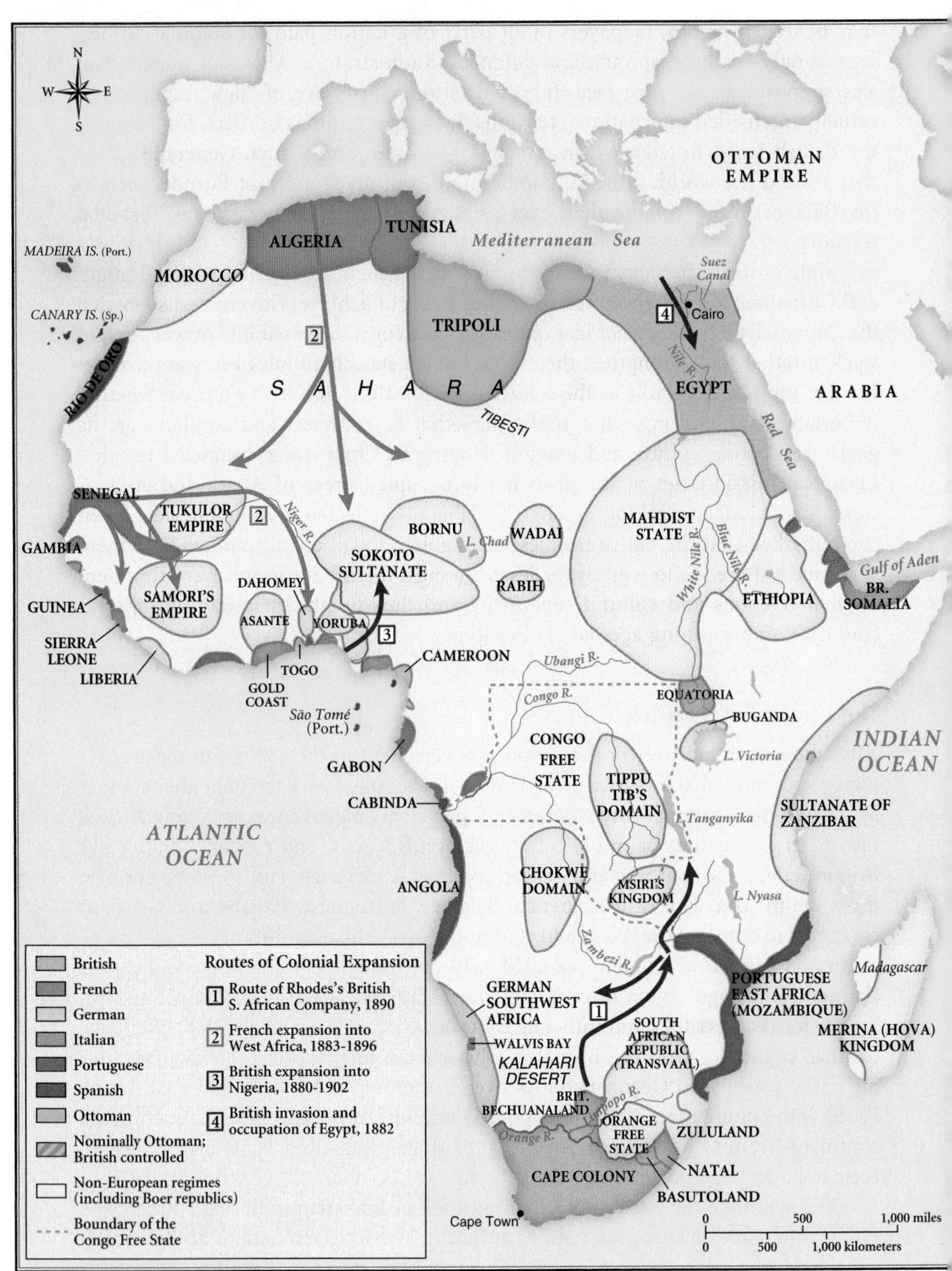
OTTOMAN EMPIRE
ALGERIA
TUNISIA
Mediterranean Sea
MADEIRA IS. (Port.)
MOROCCO
CANARY IS. (Sp.)
RIO DE ORO
TRIPOLI
Suez Canal
Cairo
Nile R.
EGYPT
ARABIA
S A H A R A
TIBESTI
Red Sea
SENEGAL
TUKULOR EMPIRE
Niger R.
BORNU
L. Chad
WADAI
MAHDIST STATE
GAMBIA
SOKOTO SULTANATE
White Nile R.
Blue Nile R.
Gulf of Aden
BR. SOMALIA
GUINEA
SAMORI'S EMPIRE
DAHOMEY
RABIH
ETHIOPIA
ASANTE
YORUBA
SIERRA LEONE
LIBERIA
TOGO
GOLD COAST
CAMEROON
Ubangi R.
Congo R.
EQUATORIA
BUGANDA
São Tomé (Port.)
CONGO FREE STATE
TIPPU TIB'S DOMAIN
L. Victoria
INDIAN OCEAN
GABON
CABINDA
L. Tanganyika
SULTANATE OF ZANZIBAR
ATLANTIC OCEAN
ANGOLA
CHOKWE DOMAIN
MSIRI'S KINGDOM
L. Nyasa
Zambezi R.
Madagascar
GERMAN SOUTHWEST AFRICA
PORTUGUESE EAST AFRICA (MOZAMBIQUE)
SOUTH AFRICAN REPUBLIC (TRANSVAAL)
MERINA (HOVA) KINGDOM
WALVIS BAY
KALAHARI DESERT
BRIT. BECHUANALAND
Limpopo R.
ORANGE FREE STATE
ZULULAND
Orange R.
CAPE COLONY
NATAL
BASUTOLAND
Cape Town
British
French
German
Italian
Portuguese
Spanish
Ottoman
Nominally Ottoman; British controlled
Non-European regimes (including Boer republics)
Boundary of the Congo Free State
Routes of Colonial Expansion
1 Route of Rhodes's British S. African Company, 1890
2 French expansion into West Africa, 1883-1896
3 British expansion into Nigeria, 1880-1902
4 British invasion and occupation of Egypt, 1882
0 500 1,000 miles
0 500 1,000 kilometers

agreement led to the strictly linear dissection of the continent; geographers and diplomats cut across local boundaries of African culture and ethnic life (Map 19.2). The Berlin conference also banned the sale of alcohol and controlled the sale of arms to native peoples. The Berlin settlement was supposed to reduce bloodshed and to calm growing concerns about European ambitions in Africa, but the greedy Europeans continued to plunder the continent and terrorize its people. The popular appetite for news of imperialist ventures grew, too.

Industrial technology provided the powerful guns, railroads, steamships, and medicines that made Western penetration of all the continents possible. The gunboats that forced the Chinese to open their borders to opium in the 1830s played a part in forcing African ethnic groups to give up their independence. Quinine and guns were also an important factor in African conquest. Before the development of medicinal quinine in the 1840s and 1850s, the deadly tropical disease malaria decimated many European groups setting out for exploration or military conquest, giving Africa the nickname "the White Man's Grave." Treating malaria with quinine, extracted from cinchona bark from the Andes, radically cut death rates among missionaries, traders, and soldiers.

While quinine saved lives, the technology to take lives advanced with improvements to the breech-loading rifle and the development of the machine gun between 1862 and the 1880s. Europeans took advantage of these developments, while also carrying on a brisk trade selling inferior guns to Africans along the coast. As a result of this trade, as well as the fact that peoples in the interior still used bows and arrows, Muslim slave traders and European Christians alike were able to crush African resistance with their superior firepower. "The whites did not seize their enemy as we do by the body, but thundered from afar," claimed one local African resister. "Death raged everywhere."

This destructive capacity had a great effect in southern Africa, where farmers of European descent and immigrant prospectors, rather than military personnel, battled African peoples for control of the frontier regions of the Transvaal, Natal, Orange Free State, and Cape Colony (Map 19.1, page 732). The Dutch had moved into the area in the seventeenth century, but the British had gained control by 1815. Thereafter, descendants of the Dutch, called Boers (Dutch for "farmers"), were joined by British immigrants in seizing farmland and mineral resources from the natives. British businessman and politician Cecil Rhodes, sent to South Africa for his health just as diamonds were being discovered in 1870, cornered the diamond

Map 19.1 Africa, c. 1890

The scramble for Africa entailed an expansion of European trading practices, which until approximately 1880 generally were limited to the coastline. The effort to conquer, penetrate economically, and rule the interior would result in a map of the continent that made sense only to the imperial powers (Map 19.2, page 734). This map divided ethnic groups and created colonial entities that had nothing to do with Africans' sense of geography, patterns of settlement, or political organization.

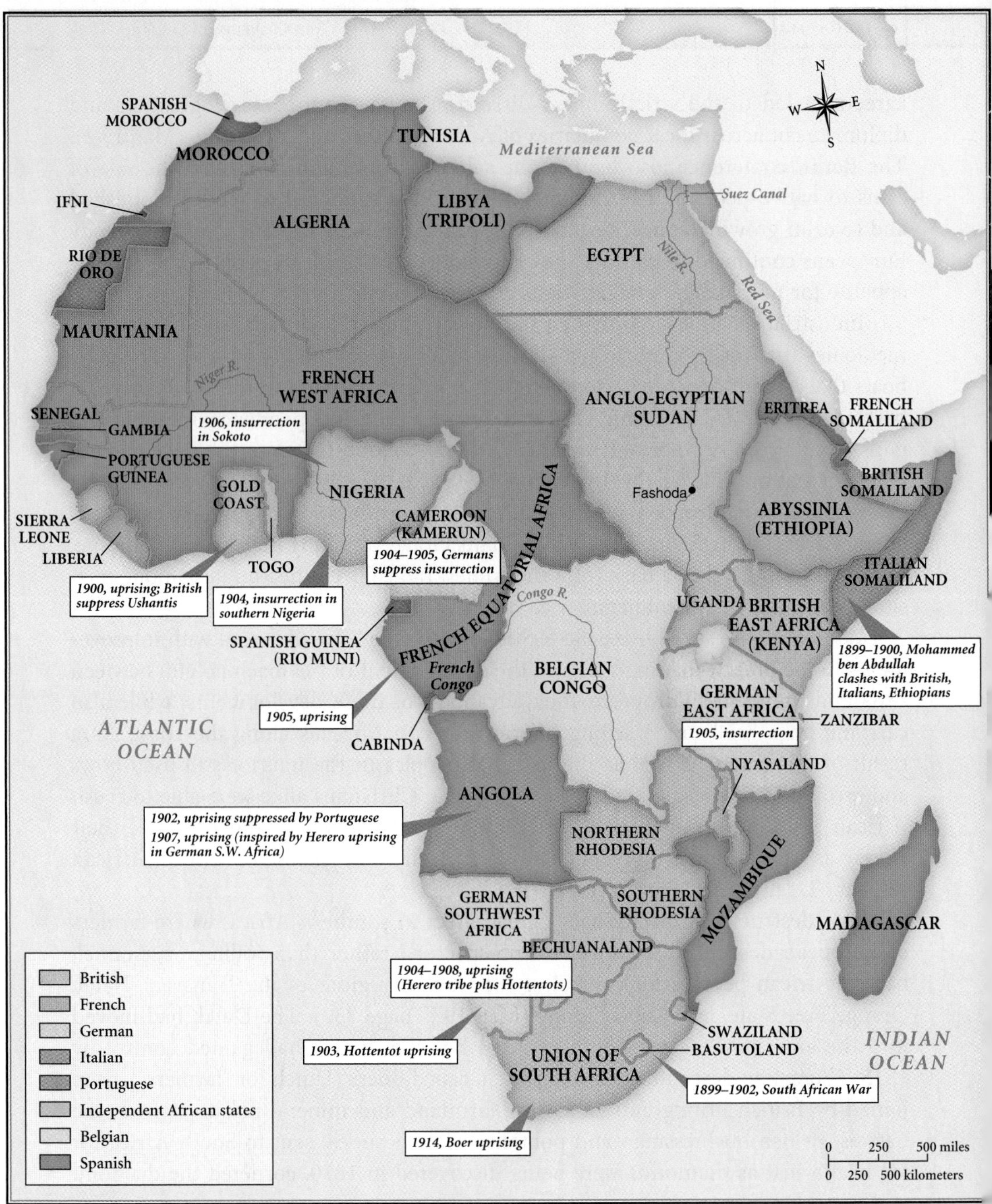

Map 19.2 Africa in 1914

Uprisings intensified in Africa in the early twentieth century as Europeans tried to consolidate their rule through bureaucratization and military action and to extract more wealth from the continent. While the Europeans were putting down rebellions against their rule, a pan-African movement arose, attempting to unite Africans as one people. As in Asia and the Middle East, the more the colonial powers tried to impose their will, the greater the political forces that took shape against them.

market, moved into gold mining, and claimed a huge amount of African territory with the help of the British government. His ambition for Britain and for himself was boundless. "I contend that we are the finest race in the world," he explained, "and that the more of the world we inhabit the better it is."

Social Darwinism justified the treatment of Africans. While Europeans credited China and India with a scientific and artistic heritage, Africans were seen as valuable only for their manual labor, despite their many accomplishments in other areas such as dyeing fabrics, building roads, and designing architecture. By confiscating Africans' land, Europeans forced native people to work for them to earn a living and pay the taxes they imposed. Subsistence agriculture, often performed by women and slaves, declined in favor of mining and farming cash crops. Standards of living dropped for Africans who lost their land without realizing the Europeans were claiming permanent ownership.

Tensions among whites escalated, too, when in 1896 the British experienced a bloody defeat after Rhodes directed his right-hand man, Dr. Leander Jameson, to lead a raid into the Transvaal. The goal was to stir up enough trouble between the Boers and the more recent immigrants from Britain that the British would be justified in taking over the Transvaal and Orange Free State, which the Boers controlled. The Boers, however, easily routed the raiders, striking a blow at British imperial pride. The British did not accept this loss. From 1899 to 1902, they fought the South African War, also called the Boer War, in the Transvaal and Orange Free State. Britain finally won that conflict in 1902 and annexed the disputed area, but the cost of the war—in money, destruction, and loss of life—horrified many Britons and caused them to see imperialism as a burden.

Imperial Newcomers

The bloodiness of the South African War was not the only challenge to the sense that this new imperialism was Europe's destiny. Europeans' confident approach to imperialism was also weakened by the rise of Japan as a power after the Meiji Restoration of 1868. Japan escaped the "new" European imperialism by rapidly transforming itself into a modern industrial nation with its own imperial agenda. "All classes high and low shall unite in vigorously promoting the economy and welfare of the nation," the new regime pronounced. The Japanese embraced knowledge from other countries, and in the 1870s deputations traveled to Europe and the United States to study technological and industrial developments. Western dress became the rule at the imperial court, and when a fire destroyed Tokyo in 1872, a European directed the rebuilding of the city in Western architectural style.

The new Japanese government, led by some of the old samurai, or warrior elite, crushed massive rebellions against modernization. It also merged older samurai traditions, such as spiritual discipline and the drive to excel, with a technologically

Modernization in Japan
Like the West, Japan bustled with commerce and industry thanks to improved and expanding transportation. Railroads, ships, and a range of new inventions such as the rickshaw speeded goods and individuals within cities, across the country, and ultimately to new, foreign destinations. The Japanese traveled widely to learn about ongoing technological innovation. (Rue des Archives/The Granger Collection, NY.)

modern military and sponsorship of trade. The state stimulated economic development by building railroads and shipyards, establishing financial institutions, and encouraging heavy industries such as mining and shipping. In Japan, unlike the rest of Asia, Western-style accomplishments became a patriotic goal.

Like its Western models, Japan started intervening elsewhere in Asia, ultimately provoking war with its powerful neighbors China and Russia. In 1894 the Japanese defeated the Chinese in the brief Sino-Japanese War, which in 1895 ended China's domination of Korea. Japan's imperial ambitions next clashed with those of the European powers. Pushing into eastern Asia, the Russians had built the Trans-Siberian Railroad through Manchuria, sent millions of Russian settlers eastward, and sponsored anti-Japanese groups in Korea. In 1904 Japan attacked tsarist forces at Port Arthur (Map 19.3). The Russian military proved inept in the ensuing yearlong Russo-Japanese War. In an astonishing display of poor leadership, Russia's Baltic Fleet sailed halfway around the globe, only to be destroyed in the battle of Tsushima Strait (1905). Opening an era of Japanese domination in East Asian politics, the victory was the first by a non-European nation over a European great power in the modern age. As one British general observed of the Russian defeat, "I have today seen the most stupendous spectacle it is possible for the mortal brain to conceive—Asia advancing, Europe falling back." Japan went on to annex Korea in 1910 and to target other areas for colonization.

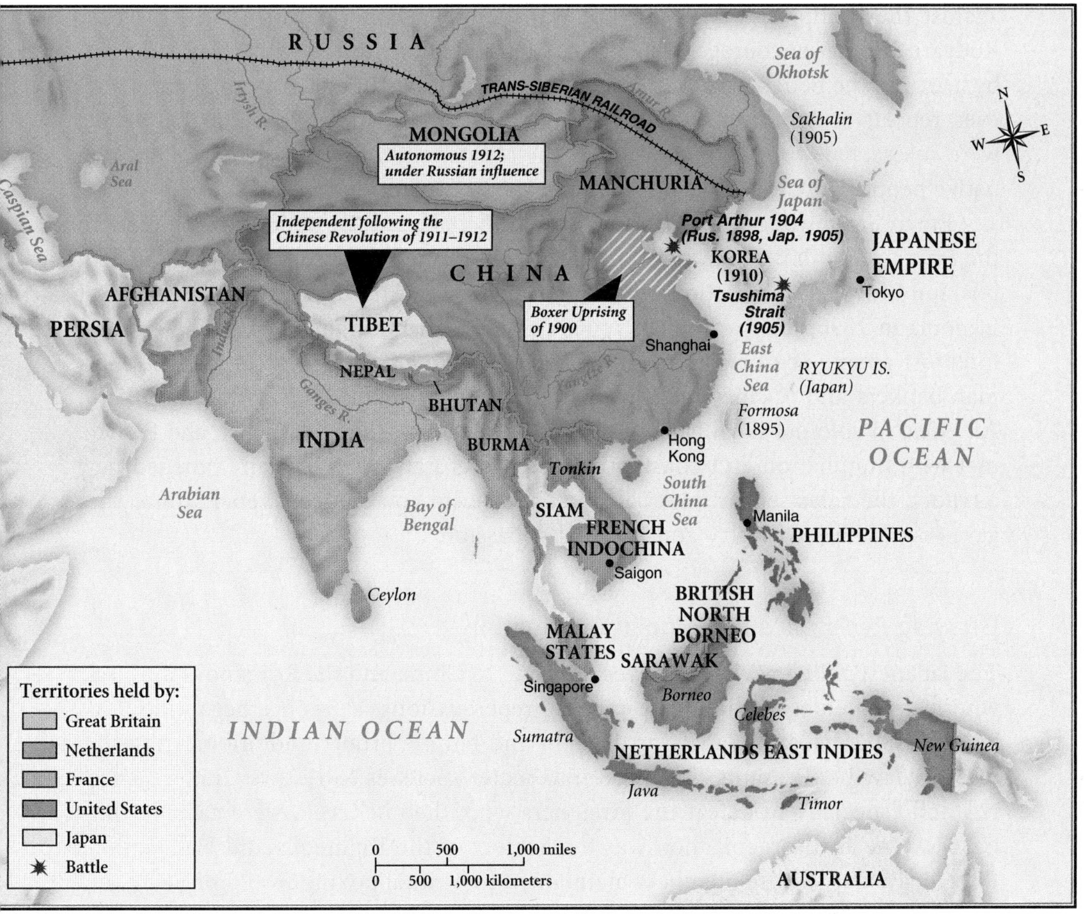

Map 19.3 Imperialism in Asia, 1894–1914
Most of the modernizing states converged on Asia. The established imperialists came to blows in East Asia as they struggled for influence in China and encountered a formidable new rival—Japan. Simultaneously, liberation movements like that of the Boxers in China were taking shape, committed to throwing off restraints imposed by foreign powers. In 1911, Sun Yat-Sen overthrew the Qing dynasty and set the country on a different course. **For more help analyzing this map, see the map activity for this chapter in the Online Study Guide at** bedfordstmartins.com/huntconcise.

There were other troublesome newcomers to the imperial table. Almost simultaneously, Spain lost Cuba, Puerto Rico, and the Philippines following its defeat by the United States in the Spanish-American War of 1898. Urged on by the expansionist-minded Theodore Roosevelt, then assistant secretary of the navy, and a fiery press, the United States went to war against Spain, claiming it was doing so to help the independence movements in Cuba and the Philippines. Instead of allowing the independence that victory promised, the United States then waged a bloody war against the Philippines who did not want another imperial ruler. British writer Rudyard Kipling encouraged the United States to "take up the white man's burden" by bringing the benefits of Western civilization to those liberated from Spain. However, reports of American brutality in the Philippines, where some 200,000 people were massacred, further disillusioned the Western public, who liked to imagine native peoples joyously welcoming the bearers of "civilization."

Emerging European powers had an emotional stake in obtaining colonies. In the early twentieth century, Italian public figures aimed to restore Italy to its ancient position of world domination by conquering Africa. After a disastrous war against Ethiopia in 1896, Italy won a costly victory over the Ottomans in Libya. Germany, foremost among the new competitors for empire, met with some success, as German bankers and businessmen prospered across Asia, the Middle East, and Latin America. In colonial skirmishes, however, the Germans, like the British and French, met with humiliation and constant problems. As Italy and Germany pursued new territory, the rules set for imperialism at the Berlin conference a generation earlier gave way to heated rivalry and nationalist passion.

Growing Resistance to Colonial Domination

The Japanese military victories over the Qing in China and the Romanovs in Russia within a single decade had wide-ranging repercussions. Uprisings began in China after its 1895 defeat by Japan, as drought and famine brought additional suffering to everyday life. Peasants organized into secret societies to restore Chinese integrity and especially to defeat the foreigners who, they believed, were causing their misery. One such organization was the Society of the Righteous and Harmonious Fists, or Boxers, whose members maintained that ritual boxing would protect them from a variety of evils, including bullets. Encouraged by the Qing government and desperate because of spreading famine, the Boxers rebelled in 1900, killing missionaries and Chinese Christians. The forces of eight colonial powers put down the Boxer Uprising and required the Chinese to pay a huge indemnity in addition to forcing a wider foreign military occupation. The Boxer Uprising thoroughly discredited the Qing dynasty and led to its overthrow by a group of revolutionaries in 1911, which declared China a republic the next year. The group's leader, Sun Yat-Sen, who had been educated in Hawaii and Japan, combined Western concepts and traditional Chinese values, including correctness in behavior between governors and the governed and modern economic reform. Sun's stirring leadership and changes brought about by the revolution threatened Western channels of trade and domination.

Meanwhile, opposition to control by outsiders was spreading in India. In 1885, the Indian elite founded the Indian National Congress, which challenged Britain's right to rule, but the Japanese victory over Russia stimulated Indian politicians to take a more radical course. The anti-British Hindu leader B. G. Tilak preached noncooperation: "We shall not give them assistance to collect revenue and keep

The Foreign Pig Is Put to Death
The Boxers sought to fortify the Chinese government against powerful threats to China's survival. As in this image from the uprising, they used brightly colored placards to spread information about their goals and their successes to build support among the Chinese population. The Boxers felt that the presence of foreigners had caused a series of disasters, including the abandonment of traditional Chinese religion, the flow of wealth from the country, and natural disasters such as famine that seemed to be taking place with greater frequency. This depiction shows the Boxers' harsh judgment of foreigners and their Chinese allies: they are pigs to be killed. **For more help analyzing this image, see the visual activity for this chapter in the Online Study Guide at** bedfordstmartins.com/huntconcise.
(© The Bridgeman Art Library.)

peace. We shall not assist them in fighting beyond the frontiers or outside India with Indian blood and money." Tilak promoted Hindu customs, asserted their distinctiveness from British ways, and inspired violent rebellion in his followers. This brand of nationalism broke with the earlier form based on assimilating to British culture and promoting gradual change. Trying to repress Tilak, the British sponsored a rival nationalist group, the Muslim League, in an attempt to divide Muslim nationalists from Hindus in the Congress. Britain hoped to maintain power by appeasing the upper and middle classes with concessions of partial representation and voting based on ownership of property. But Britain's hold on India was weakening.

Revolutionary nationalism was also undermining the Ottoman Empire, which for centuries had controlled much of the Mediterranean. Rebellions plagued Ottoman rule, and the Ottoman state itself lost its effectiveness. Sultan Abdul Hamid II tried to revitalize the multiethnic empire by using Islam to counteract the rising nationalism of the Serbs, Bulgarians, and Macedonians, just as the Habsburgs used Catholicism in Austria-Hungary. Instead, he unintentionally provoked Turkish nationalism in Constantinople itself. Turkish nationalists rejected the sultan's pan-Islamic platform and built their movement on the uniqueness of their culture, history, and language, as many European ethnic groups were doing. They hoped to change the word *Turk* from one of derision to one of pride and purged their language of Arabic and Persian words. Additionally, Japan's victory over Russia electrified these nationalists with the vision of a modern Turkey becoming "the Japan of the Middle East." In 1908, a group called the Young Turks took control of the government in Constantinople.

The Young Turks' triumph motivated other ethnic and nationalist groups in the Middle East and the Balkans to demand self-rule as well. But in order not to lose control over the extensive Ottoman territories, the Young Turks brutally tried to suppress the uprisings in Egypt, Syria, and the Balkans that their own success had encouraged. The nationalist rebellions became part of the tumult shaping international relations in the decade before World War I, upsetting the Europeans' vision of stable domination over the rest of the world.

REVIEW What changes occurred in Europe's relationships with the rest of the world between the early nineteenth and the early twentieth centuries?

Modern Life in an Age of Empire

As empire made the world an interconnected, industry-driven marketplace, it transformed everyday culture and society. Success in manufacturing and foreign ventures created millionaires, and consumers in the West could purchase goods that poured in from around the world. Many Europeans grew healthier, partly because of an improved diet and partly because of the efforts of reformers who sponsored government programs aimed at promoting the fitness they saw as necessary for citizens of imperial powers. Opportunities for mobility arose as Europeans modernized global communication with steamships and intercontinental railroads. Working people's experience of the internationalizing force of imperialism was different from that of the middle class. Increasingly from the mid-nineteenth century on, millions facing political or economic insecurity migrated from country to city and back and, as frequently, left their homelands for the United States, Canada, Australia, Argentina, Brazil, and Siberia.

While European power grew, the accepted social order in the home weakened. Western ideals of a comfortable family life flourished because of Europe's improved standard of living, but a falling birthrate, a rising divorce rate, and growing activism for marriage reform provoked intense debate about values. Although still widely condemned, homosexuality became acknowledged as a way of life and the topic of politics. Middle-class women took jobs and became active in public life to such an extent that some feared the disappearance of distinct gender roles. Debate over changing gender roles and private life contributed to rising social tensions.

Life in the "Best Circles"

Profits from empire and industrial expansion enlarged the ranks of the upper class, or "best circles," so called because of their members' wealth, education, and social status. People in the best circles came from the aristocracy, which retained much of its power, but increasingly aristocrats had to share their position with new millionaires from the upper middle class. In fact, the very distinction between aristocrat and bourgeois became blurred, as monarchs gratefully bestowed aristocratic titles on wealthy businesspeople for their contributions to the nation. Moreover, poorer aristocrats were only too willing to offer their children in marriage into the families of the newly rich. Such arrangements brought much-needed money to old established families and the glamour of an aristocratic title to upstarts. Thus Jeanette Jerome, daughter of a wealthy New York financier, married Britain's Lord Randolph Churchill (their son Winston later became Britain's prime minister). Millionaires without official connections to the aristocracy abandoned the thrifty ways of a century earlier in order to build palatial villas and engage in flashy displays of wealth. To justify their success, the wealthy quoted Social Darwinist principles that their prosperity resulted from their natural superiority over the poor.

Upper-class men bonded around hunting, a favorite leisure-time activity, which was reshaped by imperial contact. For centuries, aristocrats had pursued fox and bird hunting locally; now big-game hunting in Asia and Africa became the rage. European hunters forced native Africans, who traditionally depended on hunting for income or food and for group unity, to work as guides, porters, and domestics on hunts. Mastering foreign activities like big-game hunting, Europeans brought exotic specimens back to Europe for zoological exhibits and natural history museums, all of which flourished during this period as signs that they could master not only territory but culture as well.

People in the best circles saw themselves as an imperial elite, and upper-class women devoted themselves to maintaining rigid standards of social conduct. Members of the upper class did their best to exclude inferiors by controlling their children's social lives, especially by preventing girls' sexual activity and relationships with the lower classes. Upper-class men had liaisons with working-class women, because a double standard judged promiscuity normal for men and immoral for women. Few upper-class men thought of marrying these women, though. Parents still arranged many marriages directly, and "visiting days" brought eligible young people together to help ensure correct matrimonial decisions.

Instead of working for pay, upper-class women devoted themselves to having children, directing staffs of servants, and maintaining standards of social conduct. Furnishings in fashionable homes displayed imperial treasures such as Oriental carpets, bamboo furniture, and Chinese porcelains. With the importation of azaleas, rhododendrons, and other plants from around the world, lavish flower gardens replaced parks and lawns. Being an active consumer of fashionable clothing was also a time-consuming activity for women. In contrast to men's plain garments, upper-class women's clothing was elaborate, ornate, and dramatic, featuring constricting

Tiger Hunting in the Punjab Big-game hunting became the imperial sport of choice, as shown in this colorful Indian painting. European and American hunters adopted the sport from local Asians and Africans, who had previously depended on the hunt for their livelihood. Now these Asians and Africans served the Western amateurs, many of whom were in wretched physical shape and inexperienced in hunting big game. Nonetheless, Western manliness was coming to depend on such feats, as imperialists saw those who continued the old aristocratic foxhunt as effeminate. Some Western women enjoyed hunting, too. As a chivalrous gesture, men would let women issue the coup de grace, or death shot, should a tiger materialize during the hunt. (V & A Images, London/Art Resource, NY.)

corsets, long voluminous skirts, bustles, and low-cut necklines for evening wear. Women took their roles seriously by keeping detailed accounts of their expenditures and monitoring their children's religious and intellectual development. In addition, they tried to offset the drabness of industrial life with art and music. One Hungarian observer wrote, "The piano mania has become almost an epidemic in Budapest as well as Vienna." Some upper-class women also engaged in religious and philanthropic activities to aid lower-class women and children.

Although middle-class professionals could sometimes mingle with people at the apex of society, especially in charity work, their lives remained more modest. They usually employed at least one servant, which created the illusion of leisure for middle-class women, who in fact worked hard to maintain their homes. Professional men working at home did so from the best-appointed room. Middle-class domesticity substituted cleanliness and polish for upper-class conspicuous consumption.

The middle classes pointed to their hard work, along with their bathing with soap, as a sign of their racial superiority over colonized peoples, who actually labored to produce the raw materials for goods such as soap.

The "Best Circles" Transformed

Despite the well-being of the middle and upper classes, urgent concerns over population, marriage, and sexuality were hotly discussed from the 1880s on. The staggering population increases of the eighteenth century continued through the nineteenth century (see "Taking Measure"), and rural people crowded into cities. Germany increased in size from 41 million people in 1871 to 64 million in 1910; tiny Denmark grew from 1.7 million in 1870 to 2.7 million in 1911. Improvements in sanitation and public health that extended longevity and reduced infant mortality contributed to the growth. To cope with their bulging populations, Berlin, Budapest, and Moscow were torn down and rebuilt, following the earlier lead of Vienna and Paris. The German government reconstructed Berlin with new roadways and mass-transport systems as the capital's population grew to more than four million. Rebuilding was not confined to the most powerful states, however. Balkan cities such as Sofia, Belgrade, and Bucharest gained tree-lined boulevards, public buildings, and improved sanitation.

While the absolute size of the population was rising in the West, the birthrate (measured in births per thousand people) was actually falling. The birthrate had been decreasing in France since the eighteenth century; other European countries began experiencing a decline late in the nineteenth century. The Swedish birthrate dropped

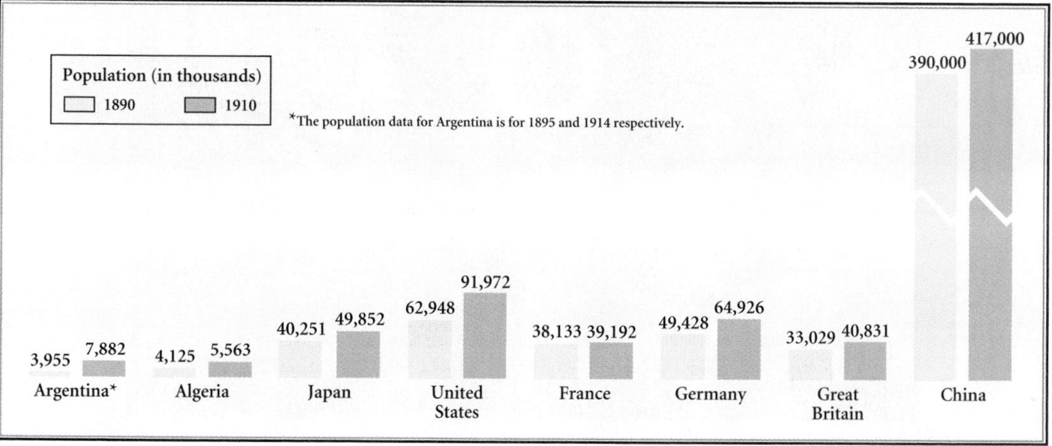

Taking Measure Population Growth Worldwide, 1890–1910
Countries in the West underwent a demographic revolution in these decades as birthrates declined sharply. Nevertheless, population soared in many countries because of improved health and immigration. Exceptions were China and other regions suffering the effects of imperialism, as well as France, where growth stagnated because the French had drastically curtailed reproduction early in the nineteenth century.

from 35 births per thousand people in 1859 to 24 per thousand in 1911. Even populous Germany went from 40 births per thousand in 1875 to 27 per thousand in 1913.

Industrialization and urbanization helped bring about this change. Farm families needed fewer hands because agricultural machinery was taking the place of human laborers, causing individual couples to practice birth control to limit family size. The use of new birth-control practices spread through cities to villages, cutting Europe's birthrate dramatically—a trend that would encompass most of the globe by the end of the twentieth century. In cities, pamphlets and advice books supplied information about coitus interruptus—the withdrawal method of preventing pregnancy. Industrial technology also played a role in curtailing reproduction: condoms, improved after the vulcanization of rubber in the 1840s, proved fairly reliable in preventing conception. In the 1880s, Aletta Jacobs, a Dutch physician, opened the first birth-control clinic, which specialized in promoting the new, German-invented diaphragm. Abortions were not uncommon.

The wider use of birth control stirred controversy. Critics accused middle-class women, whose fertility was falling most rapidly, of holding a "birth strike." Anglican bishops condemned birth control as "demoralizing to character and hostile to national welfare." Politicians worried about a crisis in masculinity that would put military strength at risk. In the United States, Theodore Roosevelt, who

A Large Czech Family
This photograph of a rural family in Czechoslovakia shows the differences that were coming to distinguish urban from rural people. Although even a farm family, especially in eastern Europe, might proudly display technology such as a new phonograph, it might not practice family limitation, which was gradually reducing the size of urban households. In eastern Europe, several generations often lived together, especially in rural areas. How many generations do you see in this image? (© Scheufler Collection/Corbis.)

became president in 1901, blamed middle-class women's selfishness for the population decline, calling it "one of the most unpleasant and unwholesome features of modern life." The quality of those who were giving birth worried activists. If the best circles had fewer children, politicians asked, what would society look like when peopled mostly by the "worst" classes? Racism and nationalism grew. The decline in fertility, one German nationalist warned, would fill the country with "alien peoples, above all Slavs and probably East European Jews as well." The political climate grew heated around the population question.

Reformers thought that improving conditions within marriage would raise the quality of children born. Many educated Europeans believed in eugenics—a set of ideas about the importance of producing "superior" people through selective breeding and of preventing the disabled and those from other ethnicities and races from polluting one's nation. As a famed Italian criminologist put it, people from "lower" groups were not humans but "orangutans." Eugenicists wanted increased fertility for "the fittest" and sterilization, or at least limited fertility, for "degenerates." Women of the better classes, reformers felt, would have more children if the disadvantages of marriage were removed and wives gained the legal right to their own wages and property. To this end, Sweden made men's and women's control over property equal in marriage and allowed women to work without their husbands' permission. Other countries legalized divorce. Reformers believed that divorce would allow unhappy couples to separate and undertake new, more loving—and thus more fertile—marriages.

The conditions of women's lives varied throughout Europe. For example, a greater number of legal reforms occurred in western Europe; however, women could get university degrees in Austrian universities long before they could at Oxford or Cambridge. In much of rural eastern Europe, the father's power over the extended family remained almost absolute. According to a survey of family life in eastern Europe in the early 1900s, fathers married off their children so young that 25 percent of women in their early forties had been pregnant more than ten times. Yet reform of everyday customs did occur, as community control gave way to individual practice in some places. For instance, in some Balkan villages, a kind of extended-family system called the *zadruga,* in which several nuclear families shared a common great house, survived from earlier times. By the turn of the century, individual couples had developed a degree of privacy by building one-room sleeping dwellings surrounding the great house. In addition, among the middle and upper classes of eastern Europe, many grown children were coming to believe they had the right to select a marriage partner, not just accept the spouse their parents chose for them.

The spread of empire and rapid social change set the stage for even bolder behaviors among some middle-class women. Adventurous women traveled the globe to promote Christianity, earn money, or obtain knowledge of other cultures. The increasing availability of white-collar jobs for educated women meant that more of them could afford to adopt an independent way of life. The so-called **new woman** dressed more practically with fewer petticoats and looser corsets, biked through

Sydney Grundy, *The New Woman* (1900)
By the opening of the twentieth century, the "new woman" had become a much-discussed phenomenon. Artists painted portraits of this independent creature, while playwrights such as Henrik Ibsen depicted her ambition to throw off the wifely role—or at least to shape that role more to her own personality. The new woman was also well educated: she had been to university or was working as a journalist or in a profession such as law or medicine. (© Private Collection/The Stapleton Collection/The Bridgeman Art Library.)

city streets and down country lanes, lived apart from her family in a women's club or apartment, and supported herself financially. Italian educator Maria Montessori, for example, went to medical school and secretly gave birth to an illegitimate child. Not surprisingly the growing number of women living on their own led to criticism. The "new woman," German philosopher Friedrich Nietzsche wrote, had led to the "uglification of Europe."

Sexual identity also fueled debate. A popular book in the new field of "sexology," which discussed sex scientifically, was *Sexual Inversion* (1894) by Havelock Ellis. Ellis, a British medical doctor, proposed a new personality type—the homosexual—identifiable by such traits as effeminate behavior and interest in the arts in males and physical passion for members of their own sex in both males and females. Homosexuals joined the discussion, calling for recognition that they composed a natural "third sex" and were not just people behaving sinfully. Some maintained that homosexuals were members of an "intermediate" sex, possessing both male and female qualities, and were thus of a higher order.

The issue became explosive when in the spring of 1895, Irish playwright Oscar Wilde was sentenced to two years in prison for indecency—a charge that referred to his sexual affairs with young men. After Wilde's conviction, the press went wild. "Open the windows! Let in the fresh air!" one newspaper rejoiced at the conviction. Between 1907 and 1909, German newspapers broadcast the courts-martial of men in Kaiser William II's closest circle who were condemned for homosexuality and transvestitism. Amid growing concern over population and family values, the government assured the public that William's own family life "provides the entire country with a fine model." Heterosexuality thus took on patriotic overtones: the accused homosexual elite in Germany was said by journalists to "emasculate our courageous master race." Despite their less-than-tolerant outcomes, these cases paved the way for growing sexual openness in the next generations and made sexual issues regular weapons in politics.

Working People's Strategies

For centuries, working people had migrated from countryside to city and from country to country to make a living. By the end of the nineteenth century, empire and economic change were spurring millions more to emigrate (Figure 19.1). Older port cities of Europe, such as Riga, Marseille, and Hamburg, offered jobs in global trade; new colonies provided land, jobs for soldiers and administrators, and the possibility of unheard-of wealth in diamonds, gold, and other natural resources.

Europeans left their homes for a variety of reasons. In parts of Europe, the land simply could not support so rapidly expanding a population. Sicilians by the hundreds of thousands left the eroded soil of their island to find work in the industrial cities of North and South America. Between 1840 and 1920, one-third of all European emigrants came from the British Isles, especially Ireland, first because of the potato famine and then because landlords drove them from their farms to get higher rents from newcomers. Between 1886 and 1900, half a million Swedes, out of a population of 4.75 million, quit their country. Millions of rural Jews, especially in

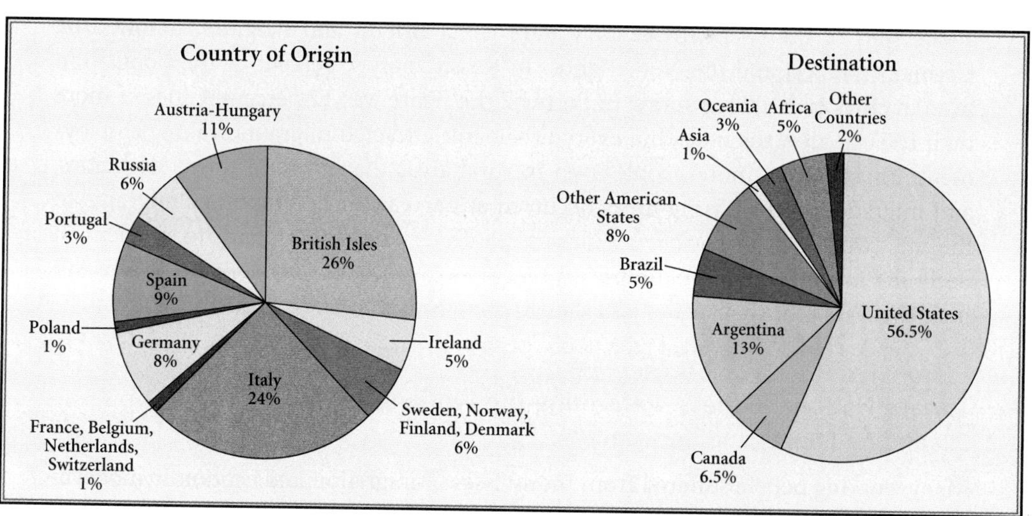

Figure 19.1 European Emigration, 1881–1910
The suffering caused by economic change and political persecution motivated people from almost every European country to leave their homes for greater security elsewhere. North America attracted nearly two-thirds of these migrants, many of whom had heard reports of vast quantities of available land in Canada and the United States. Both countries were known for following the rule of law and for economic opportunity in urban as well as rural areas.

eastern Europe, left their villages for economic reasons, but Russian Jews also fled as vicious mobs attacked their communities, even murdering some of them. These ritualized attacks, called pogroms, were scenes of horror.

As news of opportunity abroad reached Europe, migrants headed to North and South America, Australia, and New Zealand. The railroad and steamship made journeys across Europe and then across the ocean more affordable and faster, although most migrants traveled in steerage, with no comforts. Once established elsewhere, migrants frequently sent money back home and thus remained part of the family economy. Nationalist commentators in Slovakia, Poland, Hungary, and other parts of eastern and central Europe bemoaned the loss of ethnic vigor, but peasants themselves welcomed the arrival of "magic dollars" from their relatives. Migrants appreciated the chance to begin anew without the deprivation and social constraints of the Old World. One settler in the United States was relieved to escape the skimpy peasant meal of rye bread and herring. "God save us from . . . all that is Swedish," he wrote home sourly.

Migration out of Europe often meant the end of the old ways of life. Workers had to learn new languages and compete for jobs in unfamiliar cities, where they formed the cheapest labor pool. Women who worked in the home, however, tended to keep to themselves, preserving traditional ways. More isolated, they might never learn the new language or abandon their peasant dress. Their husbands and children were more likely to leave the past behind, as they faced the challenges of a new world.

Internal migration from rural areas to European cities—more common than international migration—accelerated urbanization. The most urbanized countries at the start of the twentieth century were Great Britain and Belgium, followed by Germany, France, and the Netherlands. In Russia, only 7 percent of the population lived in cities of 10,000 or more; in Portugal the figure was 12 percent. Cities of more than 100,000 grew the most, but every urban area attracted migrants seeking employment. Nevertheless, more people lived in rural areas than lived in towns and cities, and migration back to rural areas occurred at harvest time. Temporary migrants to the cities worked as masons, horse-drawn cab drivers, or factory hands to supplement declining income from agriculture. To maintain their status as independent artisans, hand-weavers sent their wives and daughters to towns to work in factories.

Toward National Fitness: Reforming the Working Class, Expanding Sports and Leisure

Many working people suffered from the stresses of migration and economic modernization, and in an age of Social Darwinist concerns about national fitness, middle- and upper-class reformers worked to address these problems. Settlement houses, clinics, and maternal and child wellness societies seemed to spring up overnight in cities. Young men and women, often from universities, eagerly took up residence in poor neighborhoods to study and help the people there. Belief in the scientific approach to solving social problems, as well as compassion for the poor, led them to seek the causes of social ills and their solutions. The Fabian Society in London, an organization established in 1884, undertook studies to determine the course of socialist reform based on planning rather than revolution. The Fabians helped found the Labour Party in 1893 to make social improvement a political cause. Religious fervor also shaped reform efforts. Some Protestants and Catholics across Europe countered growing secularization with increased missionary efforts among the urban poor at home. The Catholic church in Hungary, for example, channeled some of its efforts away from its traditional constituency in villages and toward ministering to workers in cities.

To make the poor more fit in a competitive world, philanthropists and government agencies intervened more and more in the lives of working-class families. They sponsored health clinics and milk centers to provide good medical care and food for children, and they instructed mothers in child care, including breast-feeding—an important way, reformers maintained, to promote infant health. Some schools distributed free lunches, medicine, and clothing, and some health care professionals began to spread birth-control information in the belief that small families were more likely to survive the rigors of urban life. Other reformers believed that the sexual exploitation of women would increase if the likelihood of pregnancy were overcome so easily. Government officials and charity workers, considering themselves the creators of "wise social legislation," believed they had the right to enter working-class apartments whenever they wanted. Such interfering pressured poor, overworked mothers to adopt middle-class norms for their children—such as providing them with "respectable" shoes and clothing, which they could not afford.

Fearing that women were not producing healthy enough children and were stealing jobs from men, reformers pushed for "protective" legislation. Such legislation barred women across Europe from night work and "dangerous" jobs (such as florist), allegedly for health reasons, even though medical statistics demonstrated that women became sick on the job less often than men. The new laws made the task of earning a living harder by blocking women's access to well-paid work.

Officials also promoted competitive sports and healthy leisure-time activities to build national fitness and provide some relief from the stresses of daily life. As nations competed for territory and economic markets, team sports arose, eventually replacing village games. Soccer, rugby, and cricket drew mass followings and helped integrate migrants, as well as people from the lower and upper classes, into a common national culture. Large audiences drawn from all classes backed their favorite teams, and competitive sports began to be seen as valuable promoters of national strength and spirit. Newspapers reported the results of all sorts of new contests, including the Tour de France bicycle race, sponsored by tire makers who wanted to prove the superiority of their products. Team sports further differentiated male and female spheres and thus promoted a social order based on distinctions between the sexes. Some team sports for women emerged—soccer, field hockey, and rowing—but women generally were encouraged to engage in individual sports. "Riding improves the temper, the spirits and the appetite," wrote one sportswoman; others practiced yoga. Rejecting the idea of women's natural frailty, reformers introduced

Anglo-Indian Polo Team
Team sports underwent rapid development during the imperial years, as spectators rooted for the success of their sports teams in the same spirit they rooted for their armies abroad. Some educators believed that team sports formed the male character, making men more effective soldiers. In cricket, soccer, and other sports, city challenged city, nation challenged nation, and race challenged race. Although mixed-race teams were generally unusual, they were more common in polo, because the British learned the sport from the Indians. (Hulton Archive/Getty Images.)

exercise and gymnastics into schools for girls, often with the idea that they would strengthen young women for motherhood and thus help build the nation-state.

The middle classes saw leisure pursuits such as mountain climbing as building mental and physical skills. Working-class people adopted middle-class habits by joining clubs for bicycling, touring, and hiking. Laborers and their families also sought the benefits of fresh air and exercise by visiting the beach, taking the train into the countryside, and enjoying day trips on river steamships. Clubs that sponsored trips often had names such as "The Patriots" or "The Nationals," again associating physical fitness with national strength. The new emphasis on healthy recreation gave people a greater sense of individual freedom and power and thereby fostered a sense of citizenship based less on constitutions and rights than on an individual nation's exercise of raw power. A farmer's son in the 1890s boasted that with a bicycle, "I was king of the road, since I was faster than a horse."

Sciences of the Modern Self

Scientists and Social Darwinists found cause for alarm not only in the condition of the working class but also in modern society's complaints about fatigue and irritability. Such illnesses originated in the "nerves," they reasoned, which were overstimulated by the pace and demands of urban living. A rash of books in the 1890s discussed the blossoming of nervous illnesses, such as that suffered by the Wolf-Man and his family. The most widely translated of them, *Degeneration,* written by Hungarian-born physician Max Nordau, saw increasingly bizarre modern art, male lethargy, and female hysteria as symptoms of a general downturn in the human species. The Social Darwinist prescription for curing such mental decline was imperial adventure, renewed virility, and increased childbearing.

Some researchers attempted to quantify and classify mental characteristics. Scientific study of the origins of criminal traits created the field of criminology. French psychologist Alfred Binet designed intelligence tests that he claimed could measure the capacity of the human mind more accurately than schoolteachers could. In Russia, physiologist Ivan Pavlov proposed that conditioning mental reflexes—that is, causing a subject to associate a desired response with a previously unrelated stimulus—could modify behavior. His experiments, especially his success in changing the behavior of a dog, formed the basis of modern psychology.

Sigmund Freud (1856–1939) devised an approach to treating modern anxieties that, he claimed, avoided traditional moralizing about human behavior. He became convinced that individuals were far from rational. Dreams, he explained in *The Interpretation of Dreams* (1900), reveal an unseen, repressed part of the personality—the "unconscious"—where all sorts of desires are more or less hidden. Freud also believed that the human psyche is made up of three competing parts: the *ego,* the part that is most in touch with reality; the *id* (or libido), the part that governs instincts and sexual energy; and the *superego,* the part that serves as the conscience. Like Darwin's ideas, Freud's notions challenged the widespread liberal belief, dating from the Enlightenment, in a rational self that peacefully acts in its own best interest.

Freud shocked many of his contemporaries by insisting that all children have a sexual drive from the moment of birth. He believed that many sexual impulses have to be rigorously repressed for the individual to attain maturity and for society to remain civilized. Attaining one's adult sexual identity is always a painful process, he maintained, because it depends on repressing infantile urges, which include bisexuality and incest. Thus the Wolf-Man's nightmare of white wolves outside his window symbolized his unresolved sexual fears and feelings. Freud also claimed that certain aspects of gender roles—such as motherhood—are "normal" and that throughout their lives, women in general achieve far less than men do, becoming neurotic when they strive to excel. At the same time, he believed that adult gender identity results not from anatomy alone (motherhood is not the only way to be female) but from the inescapable mental processing of life experiences as well. He thus made gender more complicated than simple biology would suggest. Finally, Freud's psychoanalytic theory maintained that girls and women have powerful sexual feelings, an assertion that broke with ideas of women's passionlessness.

The influence of psychoanalysis was complex and widespread. Two mainstays of psychoanalysis—free association of ideas and interpretation of dreams—derived from African and Asian influences on Freud's thought. The "talking cure," as it was quickly

Freud's Office in London
Sigmund Freud's therapy room, where his patients experienced the "talking cure," was filled with imperial "trophies" such as Oriental rugs and African art. Freud himself was fascinated by shamanism, trances, and other non-Western medical practices, as well as by drug-induced mental states. Freud fled to England in 1938 to escape the Nazis. (Mary Evans Picture Library/Sigmund Freud copyrights.)

labeled, gave rise to a general acceptance of talking out one's problems. As psychoanalysis became an accepted means of recovering mental health, terms such as *neurosis, unconscious,* and *libido* came into widespread use and could apply to anyone, not just the mentally ill. On the one hand, Freud was a meticulous scientist, examining symptoms, urging attention to the most minute evidence from everyday life, and demanding that sexual life be regarded with a rational rather than a religious eye. On the other hand, he was pessimistic: he abandoned the optimism of Enlightenment science and instead theorized that humans were motivated by irrational drives toward death and destruction and that these drives shaped society's collective mentality. Freud would later interpret the devastation of World War I as proof of his bleak theories.

REVIEW What social changes were transforming Europe at the start of the twentieth century?

Modernity and the Revolt in Ideas

Toward the beginning of the twentieth century, intellectuals and artists so completely rejected long-standing beliefs and established artistic forms that they ushered in a new era. In science the theories of Albert Einstein and other researchers established shocking new truths in physics. Artists and musicians who produced deliberately outrageous works were, like Freud, heavily influenced by advances in science and the progress of empire. Their blending of the scientific and the irrational, and of forms from the West and non-West, helped launch the disorienting revolution in ideas and creative expression that we now identify collectively as **modernism**.

The Challenge to Positivism

Late in the nineteenth century, many philosophers and social thinkers suddenly rejected the century-old belief that using scientific methods would uncover enduring social laws. This belief, called positivism, had emphasized the permanent nature of fundamental laws and had motivated reformers' attempts to perfect legislation based on studies of society. Challenging positivism, some critics declared that because human experience is ever changing, there are no constant or enduring social laws. German political theorist Max Weber maintained that the sheer number of factors involved in policymaking would often make a decisive action by bureaucrats impossible. In times of crisis, a charismatic leader might take power because of his ability to act simply on intuition. These turn-of-the-century thinkers, called relativists and pragmatists, influenced thinking about society throughout the twentieth century.

The most radical among the scholars was the German philosopher Friedrich Nietzsche (1844–1900), who early in his career distinguished between the "Apollonian," or rational, side of human existence and the "Dionysian" side, with its expression of more primal urges. Nietzsche believed that people generally prefer rational, Apollonian explanations of life because the powerful Dionysian sense of death and love, as found in Greek tragedy, is too disturbing. He maintained that all assertions of scientific fact and theory are mere illusions, that knowledge of nature is only a mathematical, linguistic, or artistic representation. Truth, Nietzsche insisted, thus exists only in the representation itself, for humans can never experience unfiltered knowledge of nature or reality. This aspect of Nietzsche's philosophy powerfully questioned scientific certainty.

Much of Nietzsche's writing took the form of aphorisms—short, disconnected statements of truth or opinion—rather than the long, sustained argument common to traditional Western philosophy. Nietzsche used aphorisms to give the impression that his ideas were a single individual's unique perspective, not universal truths that thinkers since the Enlightenment had claimed were attainable. Nietzsche was convinced that late-nineteenth-century Europe was witnessing the decline of dogmatic truths such as those found in religion. Thus, he announced, "God is dead, we have killed him." Far from arousing dread, the death of God, according to Nietzsche, would give birth to a joyful quest for new "poetries of life" to replace worn-out religious and middle-class rules. Nietzsche believed that an uninhibited, dynamic "superman," free from traditional moralizing, would replace the rule-bound middle-class person. On his death, however, Nietzsche's sister edited his attacks on middle-class values into attacks on Jews. She revised his complicated concepts about each individual's "will to power" and the "superman" so as to appeal to nationalists, imperialists, and militarists, all of whom he actually hated.

Revolutionizing Science

While philosophers questioned the ability of traditional science to provide timeless truths, scientific inquiry itself flourished, and the sciences gained in prestige. Around the turn of the century, however, discoveries by pioneering researchers shook the foundations of traditional scientific certainty and challenged accepted knowledge about the nature of the universe. In 1896, Antoine Becquerel discovered radioactivity. He also suggested the mutability of elements by the rearrangement of their atoms. French chemist Marie Curie and her husband, Pierre Curie, isolated the elements polonium and radium, which are more radioactive than the uranium Becquerel used. From these and other discoveries, scientists concluded that atoms are not solid, as had long been believed, but are composed of subatomic particles moving about a core. In a paper published in 1900, German physicist Max Planck announced his influential quantum theorem, stating that energy is delivered in irregular packets that he later called quanta, not in a steady stream.

In this atmosphere of discovery, physicist Albert Einstein (1879–1955) proclaimed his special theory of relativity in 1905. According to this theory, space and time are not absolute categories but instead vary according to the vantage point of the observer. Only the speed of light is constant. That same year, Einstein also suggested that the solution to problems in Planck's quantum theorem lay in considering light both as little packets *and* as waves. Einstein later proposed yet another blurring of two distinct physical properties, mass and energy. He expressed this equivalence in the formulation $E = mc^2$, or energy equals mass times the square of the speed of light. In 1916, Einstein published his general theory of relativity, which connected the force, or gravity, of an object with its mass and proposed a fourth mathematical dimension to the universe. Much more lay ahead once Einstein's theories of energy were applied to technology: television, nuclear power, and, within forty years, atomic bombs.

The findings of Planck, Einstein, and others were not immediately accepted, because long-standing scientific truths were at stake. Einstein, like Planck, struggled against mainstream science and its professional institutions. As a female scientist, Marie Curie faced such resistance that even after she became the first person ever to receive a second Nobel Prize (1911), the prestigious French Academy of Science turned down her candidacy for membership, claiming that a woman could simply not have done such outstanding work. Acceptance of all these scientists' discoveries gradually came, and Max Planck institutes were established in German cities, streets across Europe were named after Marie Curie, and Einstein's name became synonymous with *genius*. These scientists achieved what historians call a paradigm shift—that is, in the face of staunch resistance, they transformed the foundations of science.

Marie Curie and Her Daughter
The recipient of two Nobel Prizes, Marie Curie traveled from Poland to western Europe to study science. Her extraordinary career made her the epitome of the "new woman." Her daughter, Irene Joliot-Curie, followed her into the field and also won a Nobel Prize. Both women died of leukemia caused by their exposure to radioactive materials. (ACJC—Fund Curie et Joliot-Curie.)

Modern Art

Conflicts between traditional values and new ideas also raged in the arts, as artists created an array of competing styles and many rejected the historic and realistic scenes still favored by powerful patrons in government and public museums. Abandoning the soft colors of impressionism as too subtle for a dynamic industrial society, a group of Parisian artists exhibiting in 1905 combined blues, greens, reds, and oranges so intensely that they were called fauves, literally "wild beasts." A leader of the short-lived fauvism, Henri Matisse soon struck out in a new direction, targeting the expanding class of white-collar workers. Matisse dreamed of "an art . . . for every mental worker, be he businessman or writer, like an appeasing influence, like a mental soother, something like a good armchair in which to rest from physical fatigue."

French artist Paul Cézanne initiated one of the most powerful and enduring trends in modern art. Cézanne used rectangular daubs of paint to portray his geometric vision of dishes, fruit, drapery, and the human body. He accentuated the lines and planes found in nature instead of presenting nature as people saw it in everyday life. Following in Cézanne's footsteps, Spanish artist Pablo Picasso developed a style called cubism. Its radical emphasis on planes and surfaces converted humans into bizarre, almost unrecognizable forms. Picasso's painting *Les Demoiselles d'Avignon* (1907) depicts the bodies of the *demoiselles,* or young ladies (prostitutes in this case), as fragmented and angular, with their faces modeled on African masks. Picasso's work showed the profound influences of African, Asian,

Pablo Picasso, *Les Demoiselles d'Avignon* (1907)
Whereas impressionists had borrowed heavily from Asian art, many artists in Picasso's time looked to Africa for inspiration. In *Les Demoiselles d'Avignon,* Picasso used the elongated, angular limbs found in African carvings, while the faces resemble African masks. He borrowed these forms even as Europeans were declaring the superiority of their civilization to that of Africa. (Digital Image © The Museum of Modern Art/Licensed by Scala/Art Resource, NY. © 2010 Estate of Pablo Picasso/Artists Rights Society [ARS], NY.)

and South American art, but his use of these features was less decorative and more brutal than Matisse's, for example. Like explorers, botanists, and foreign journalists, he was bringing knowledge of the empire into the imperial homeland.

Across Europe, artists mixed political criticism, even outrage, with the radical stylistic changes in their work. Anarchists wanted to "show the people how hideous is their actual life," and Picasso, who had spent his youth in the heart of working-class Barcelona, a hotbed of anarchist thought, aimed to reflect this goal in his art. In 1912, Picasso and the French painter Georges Braque devised a new kind of collage that incorporated bits of newspaper, string, and other useless objects. The effect was a work of art that appeared to be made of trash. The newspaper clippings Picasso included described battles and murders, suggesting that Western civilization was not as refined as it claimed to be. In eastern and central Europe, artists criticized the growing nationalism that determined official purchases of sculpture and painting. "The whole empire is littered with monuments to soldiers and monuments to Kaiser William of the same conventional type," one German artist complained. In response, groups of avant-garde artists in Vienna and Berlin created art that was critical of boastful nationalism.

Scandinavian and eastern European artists produced tormented works. Like the vision of Freud, their style of portraying inner feelings, called expressionism, broke with middle-class optimism. Norwegian painter Edvard Munch aimed "to make the emotional mood ring out again as happens on a gramophone." In his painting *The Scream* (1895), he used twisting lines and a depiction of a tortured human form to convey the horror of modern life that many artists perceived. The "Blue Rider" group of artists, including German avant-garde artist Gabriele Münter and Russian painter Wassily Kandinsky, used geometric forms and striking colors to express an inner, spiritual truth. Kandinsky is often credited with producing the first fully abstract paintings around 1909; shapes in these paintings no longer resemble actual objects but are meant to express abstract reality and deep feelings. The expressionism of Austrian painter Oskar Kokoschka was even more intense, displaying ecstasy, horror, and hallucinations. As a result, his work—like that of other expressionists and cubists before World War I—was a commercial failure in an increasingly complex marketplace that featured not only museum curators but also professional dealers—"experts" like the professionals in medicine and law.

Only one innovative style was an immediate commercial success: **art nouveau** (new art) won approval from governments, critics, and the masses. Creating everything from dishes and advertising posters to streetlamps and even entire buildings in this new style, designers manufactured beautiful things for the general public. As one French official said about the first version of art nouveau coins issued in 1895, "Soon even the most humble among us will be able to have a masterpiece in his pocket." Adapted from Asian design principles, art nouveau was meant to offset the harshness of factory and office work with images drawn from nature. The impersonality of machines was replaced by intertwined vines and flowers and the softly curving bodies of female nudes intended to soothe the viewer psychologically—an idea that contrasted directly with Picasso's artistic vision. Art nouveau was the notable exception to the public outcries over innovations in the visual arts.

The Revolt in Music and Dance

"Astonish me!" was the motto of modern dance and music, both of which shocked audiences in the concert halls of Europe. American dancer Isadora Duncan took Europe by storm at the turn of the century when, draped in a flowing garment, she danced barefoot in the first performance of modern dance. Her sophisticated style was nonetheless called primitive because it no longer followed the steps of classical ballet. Experimentation with forms of bodily expression animated the Russian Ballet's 1913 performance of *The Rite of Spring* by Igor Stravinsky, the tale of an orgiastic dance to the death performed to ensure a harvest. The dance troupe struck awkward poses and danced to rhythms intended to sound primitive. At the work's premiere in Paris, one journalist reported that "the audience began shouting its indignation. . . . Fighting actually broke out among some of the spectators." Such controversy made *The Rite of Spring* a box-office hit, although critics called its choreographer a "lunatic" and the music itself "the most discordant composition ever written."

Composers had been rebelling against Western traditions for several decades, producing music that was disturbing rather than pretty. Having heard Asian musicians at international expositions, French composer Claude Debussy transformed his style to reflect non-European musical patterns and wrote articles in praise of Asian harmonies. Italian composer Giacomo Puccini used non-Western subject matter for his opera *Madame Butterfly,* which debuted in 1904. Like the bizarre representations of reality in cubism, the works of Austrian composer Richard Strauss upset convention by using several keys simultaneously in his compositions and thus distorting familiar musical patterns. Strauss's operas *Salome* (1905) and *Elektra* (1909) reflect the modern fascination with violence and obsessive passion. A newspaper critic claimed that the notes in Strauss's dissonant music "spit and scratch and claw each other like enraged panthers."

The early orchestral work of Austrian composer Arnold Schoenberg, who also wrote cabaret music to earn a living, shocked even Strauss. In his book *Theory of Harmony* (1911), Schoenberg proposed eliminating tonality altogether; a decade later he devised a new twelve-tone scale. "I am aware of having broken through all the barriers of a dated aesthetic ideal," Schoenberg wrote of his music. But new aesthetic models distanced artists like Schoenberg from their audiences, separating high from low culture even more and ending the support of many in the upper classes, who found this music simply unpleasant. "Anarchist! Nihilist!" shouted Schoenberg's audiences, showing their distaste for modernism and using political terms to characterize the arts.

REVIEW What changes in intellectual life upset accepted cultural standards at the start of the twentieth century?

The Birth of Mass Politics

Alongside these disturbances in intellectual life, the political atmosphere heated up. On the one hand, liberal opinions led to political representation for workingmen. Networks of communication, especially the development of journalism, created a common fund of political knowledge that made mass political participation possible. On the other hand, political activists were no longer satisfied with the liberal rights sought by reformers a century earlier, and some strenuously opposed them. Militant nationalists, anti-Semites, socialists, suffragists, and others demanded changes that challenged liberal values. Traditional elites, resentful of the rising middle classes and urban people, aimed to slow constitutional processes and reverse the development of city life. Mass politics soon threatened national unity, especially in central and eastern Europe, where governments often answered reformers' demands with repression.

The Growing Power of Labor

Mass politics arose from a combination of the right to vote accorded to men across Europe before World War I and the rise of popular activism, especially among working people. In the fall of 1879, William Gladstone (1809–1898), leader of the British Liberal Party, which was then out of power, waged an experimental electoral campaign across the country. Speaking before thousands of working men and women, he advocated a way of life based on "honest, manful, humble effort" in the middle-class tradition of "hard work." Newspapers publicized his trip, further building interest in politics and helping him become prime minister. The Reform Act of 1884 doubled the British electorate to around 4.5 million men, including many urban workers and artisans, whose votes reduced traditional aristocratic influence. This move reflected the universal manhood suffrage already granted in France and Germany; much of Europe would follow suit before World War I.

Journalism helped forge a broad national community of up-to-date citizens by providing information (and misinformation) about politics and world events. The invention of mechanical typesetting and the production of newsprint from wood pulp lowered the costs of printing; the telegraph and the telephone allowed reporters to communicate news to their papers almost instantly. Once literary in content, daily newspapers now emphasized sensational news, using blaring headlines and gruesome details—particularly about murders, sexual scandals, and sagas of the empire—to sell papers. In the hustle and bustle of industrial society, one editor wrote, "you must strike your reader right between the eyes." Elites complained that the sensational press was another sign of social decay, but for up-and-coming working- and middle-class people, journalism offered another career option.

Political activism took many forms in the late nineteenth century. Housewives, who often acted in support of strikers, protested against high food prices by confiscating merchants' goods and selling them at what they considered a fair price. "There should no longer be either rich or poor," argued organized Italian peasant women. "All should have bread for themselves and for their children. We should all be equal." Women took other kinds of action, too, building working-class solidarity in neighborhoods. When landlords evicted tenants, women would gather in the streets, and as soon as the ousted families' household goods were removed from their rooms, the women would carry them back inside. Meeting on doorsteps or at fountains, laundries, pawnshops, and markets, women initiated rural newcomers into urban ways and developed class unity.

In the last third of the nineteenth century, workers also organized formal unions, which attracted the allegiance of millions. Unions demanded a say in working conditions and aimed, as one union's rule book put it, "to ensure that wages . . . always follow the rises in the price of basic commodities." After the Paris Commune, many businessmen and governments viewed striking workers as threatening, but strong unions appealed to some industrialists because the unions could make strikes more predictable (or even prevent them) and present demands more coherently.

From the 1880s on, collective action for higher pay, lower prices, and better working conditions increased. In 1888, for example, hundreds of young women who made matches in London struck to end the fining system, under which they could be penalized an entire day's wages for being a minute or two late to work. This system, the "match girls" maintained, helped companies reap profits of more than 20 percent. Newspapers and philanthropists picked up the strikers' story, helping them win their case. Soon after, London dockworkers and gasworkers went on strike to protest their working conditions. Across Europe, the number of strikes and demonstrations rose from 188 in 1888 to 289 in 1890. Fearing destructive acts, governments increasingly responded with armed force, even though most strikes were about the conditions of everyday life for workers and not political revolution.

Working-class political parties developed from unions. Craft-based unions of skilled artisans, such as carpenters and printers, were the most active and cohesive, but from the mid-1880s on, a new unionism attracted transport workers, miners, match girls, and dockworkers. These new unions were nationwide groups with salaried managers who could plan massive general strikes across the trades with common goals such as the eight-hour workday. They could thus paralyze an entire nation. Large unions in the industrialized countries of Europe, like cartels and trusts, increasingly influenced business practices. They were joined by working-class parties—the Labour Party in England, the Socialist Party in France, and the Social Democratic Parties in Sweden, Hungary, Austria, and Germany—most of which were inspired by Marxist theories. Germany was home to the largest socialist party in Europe after 1890.

Those who accepted Marx's assertion that "workingmen have no country" also founded an international movement to address workers' common interests across national boundaries. In 1889, some four hundred socialists from across Europe met in Paris to form the **Second International**, a federation of working-class organizations and political parties that replaced the First International, started by Marx before the Paris Commune. As socialists were elected to parliaments, some members of the Second International worried that their participation in government would produce helpful reform of conditions generally that would slow their ultimate goal of revolution. The preference for evolutionary tactics rather than the violent overthrow of government was known as reformism. To avoid the dangers in reformism, some socialists refused seats in government even when they were elected.

The Second International was also determined to rid the organization of anarchists, who flourished in the less industrial parts of Europe, including Russia, Italy, and Spain. In these countries, the anarchist movement got strong support from peasants, small property owners, and day laborers, for whom Marxist theories of worker-controlled factories had less appeal. In an age of tough international competition in agriculture, many rural people hoped for a life free from the control of large landowners and government. Many advocated extreme tactics, including physical violence and even murder. "We want to overthrow the government . . . with violence since it is by the use of violence that they force us to obey," wrote one Italian anarchist. In the 1880s, anarchists bombed stock exchanges, parliaments, and businesses, and by the 1890s they were assassinating heads of state—violence that members of the socialist movement believed to be counterproductive.

Workingwomen joined unions and political parties, but in much smaller numbers than men. Not able to vote in national elections, they had little reason to join political parties. Women also were usually responsible for housework in addition to their paying jobs and so had little time for meetings. In addition, their low wages barely allowed them to survive, much less pay party or union dues. Many workingmen also opposed women's presence in these organizations. Contact with women would mean "suffocation," one Russian workingman believed, and end male union members' sense of being "comrades in the revolutionary cause." The shortage of women's voices in unions and political parties paralleled women's exclusion from government; it helped make the middle-class belief in separate spheres part of a working-class ideology, too. Marxist leaders continued to maintain that injustice to women was caused by capitalism and would disappear in a socialist society. As a result, although working-class organizations wanted women's support, they did not take seriously women's concerns about issues such as lower wages and sexual harassment.

Popular community activities that intertwined politics and everyday life built worker solidarity. The gymnastic and choral societies that had once united Europeans in nationalistic fervor now served working-class goals. Songs emphasized worker freedom, progress, and eventual victory. Socialist gymnastics, bicycling, and marching societies rejected competition and prizes as middle-class preoccupations, but they valued physical fitness for helping workers in the "struggle for existence"—a reflection of the spread of Darwinian thinking to all levels of society. Workers also held festivals and gigantic parades, most notably on May 1, a centuries-old holiday that the Second International now claimed as a labor holiday. Like religious processions of an earlier time, parades fostered unity, and as a result governments frequently banned such public gatherings, calling them a public danger.

Political persecution forced some working-class groups to operate in exile. The Russian government, for instance, outlawed political parties and imprisoned activists. The foremost Russian activist, V. I. Lenin (1870–1924), who would take power during the Russian Revolution of 1917, migrated to western Europe after his release from confinement in Siberia in 1900. He earned his place among Russian Marxists there with his hard-hitting journalism and political intrigue. Lenin developed the theory that a highly disciplined socialist elite would lead a lightly industrialized Russia into socialism. At a 1903 party meeting of Russian Marxists, he maneuvered his opponents into walking out, leaving his supporters in control of the party. Thereafter, his faction was known as the Bolsheviks, from the Russian word for "majority," which they had briefly formed. Their goal was to suppress the Mensheviks, the dominant voice in Russian Marxism until Lenin outmaneuvered them. Neither of these factions, however, had as large a constituency within Russia as the Socialist Revolutionaries, whose objective was to politicize peasants rather than industrial workers as the foundation of revolution. All these groups prepared for the revolutionary moment through study, propaganda efforts, and organizing—not through the electoral politics successfully employed elsewhere in Europe.

Rights for Women and the Battle for Suffrage

Singly and in groups, women continued to agitate against their exclusion from the benefits of liberalism, such as the rights to vote and own property (including their own wages) if married. Laws in France, Austria, and Germany made women's attendance at political meetings a crime. German women focused not only on obtaining these rights but also on widening opportunities for women's education. Their activism aimed to achieve the German cultural ideal of *Bildung*—the belief that education can strengthen character and that individual development has public importance. In several countries, women continued to monitor the regulation of prostitution. Their goal was to prevent prostitutes from being imprisoned on suspicion of having syphilis when men with syphilis faced no such incarceration. Other women took up pacifism as their special cause. Many of them were inspired by Bertha von Süttner's popular book *Lay Down Your Arms* (1889), which emphasized the terror inflicted on women and families by the ravages of war.

By the 1890s, many women's rights activists decided to focus on a single issue—the right to vote—as the most effective way to correct the problems caused by male privilege. Thereafter suffragists created major organizations involving millions of activists, paid officials, and permanent offices. British suffrage leader Millicent Garrett Fawcett (1847–1929) and other women pressured members of Parliament for the vote and participated in national and international congresses on behalf of suffrage. Similarly, American suffragist Susan B. Anthony (1820–1906) traveled throughout the United States to speak at rallies, raised money to support the movement, and founded the International Woman Suffrage Association in 1904. The movement's leadership argued that despite men's promises to protect women in exchange for their inequality, the system of male chivalry had led to exploitation and abuse. "So long as the subjection of women endures, and is confirmed by law and custom, . . . women will be victimized," a leading suffragist claimed. Other activists believed that women had the values needed to counterbalance masculine qualities in the running of society. The characteristics that came from mothering were as necessary in shaping a country's destiny as were the qualities that stemmed from industry and business, they declared.

Women's rights activists were generally, though not exclusively, from the middle classes. Free from the need to earn a living, they simply had more time to be activists and to study the works of feminist theorists such as Harriet Taylor and John Stuart Mill. They attended theater productions by playwrights such as the Norwegian Henrik Ibsen, whose heroine Nora (*A Doll's House,* 1879) walks out on a loveless and oppressive marriage. Some working-class women also participated, although many saw suffrage for women as less important than their economic concerns. Textile workers in Manchester, England, however, combined calls for social and economic reform and put together a vigorous suffrage movement connecting the vote to improved working conditions.

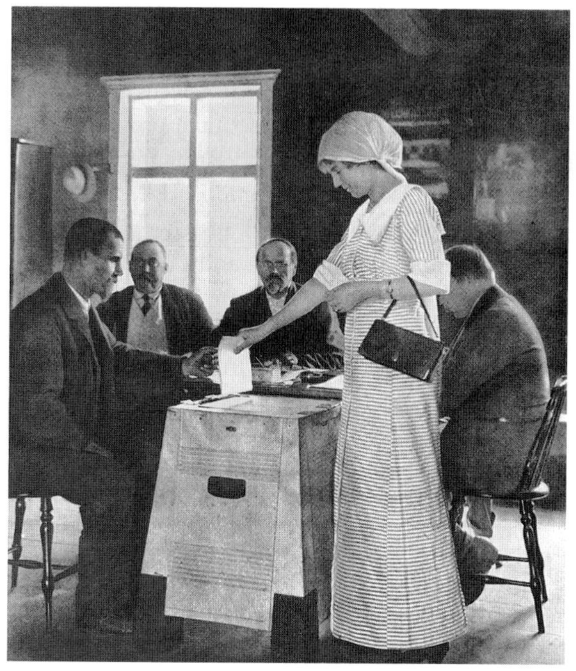

Woman Suffrage in Finland
In 1906, Finnish women became the first women in Europe to receive the vote in national elections when the Socialist Party—usually opposed to feminism as a middle-class rather than a working-class project—supported woman suffrage. The Finnish vote elated activists in the West, now linked by many international organizations, because it showed that more than a century of lobbying for reform could lead to gains. (Mary Evans Picture Library.)

In 1906, suffragists achieved their first major victory when the Finnish parliament granted women the vote. But the failure of parliaments to enact similar legislation elsewhere in Europe led some suffragists to violence. In Britain, Emmeline Pankhurst (1858–1928) and her daughters founded the Women's Social and Political Union (WSPU) in 1903 in the belief that women would accomplish nothing unless they threatened men's property. Starting in 1907, WSPU members staged parades in English cities, and in 1909 they began a campaign of violence, blowing up railroad stations, slashing works of art, and chaining themselves to the gates of Parliament. Disguising themselves as ordinary shoppers, they carried little hammers in their hand warmers to smash the plate-glass windows of department stores and shops. Parades and demonstrations made suffrage a public spectacle, provoking attacks on the marchers by outraged men. Arrested for disturbing the peace, the marchers went on hunger strikes in prison. Like striking workers, these women were willing to use confrontational tactics in order to obtain rights.

Liberalism Tested

Governments in western Europe, where liberal institutions seemed well entrenched, sought to control turn-of-the-century conflicts with practical policies that often struck at liberalism's very foundations. Some ended laissez-faire trade policies by instituting protective tariffs; others expanded social welfare programs. Both approaches were a break with the liberal idea that societies should develop freely without government interference. In 1905, the British Liberal Party won a solid majority in the House of Commons and pushed for social legislation to gain working-class support. "We are keenly in sympathy with the representatives of Labour," one Liberal politician announced. "We have too few of them in the House of Commons." The National Insurance Act of 1911 set up a program of unemployment assistance funded by new taxes on the wealthy, and Parliament eliminated the long-standing veto power of the predominantly aristocratic House of Lords.

The Irish question tested British commitment to still other liberal values: autonomy, opportunity, and individual rights. Despite the Irish receiving the secret ballot, the political climate in Ireland remained explosive because of the repressive tactics of absentee landlords, many of them English and Protestant. These landlords evicted unsuccessful and prosperous tenants alike so they could raise the rents of newcomers. In the 1890s, new groups formed to foster Irish culture as a way of challenging what they saw as Britain's continuing colonization of the country. In 1901, the circle around the modernist poet William Butler Yeats and the charismatic patriot and actress Maud Gonne founded the Irish National Theater to present Irish rather than English plays. Gonne took Irish politics into everyday life by opposing British efforts to gain support from the young. Every time an English monarch visited Ireland, he or she held special receptions for children. Gonne and other Irish volunteers sponsored competing events, handing out candies and other treats for patriotic youngsters. Promoters of an "Irish way of life" encouraged speaking Gaelic instead of English, singing Gaelic songs, and supporting Catholicism instead of Anglicanism. This cultural agenda gained political force with the founding in 1905 of Sinn Fein (We Ourselves), a group that strove for complete Irish independence. In 1913, Parliament finally approved home rule for Ireland; the outbreak of World War I prevented the legislation from taking effect, though it hardly killed Irish dreams of independence.

Italian nation builders, left with a towering debt from unification and with widespread pockets of discontent, drifted rapidly away from liberalism's moorings in solid industrial development and the rule of law. Corruption plagued Italy's constitutional monarchy, which had developed neither the secure parliamentary system of Britain nor the authoritarian monarchy of Germany to guide its growth. To forge national unity in the 1890s, Italian prime ministers used patriotic rhetoric and imperial adventure such as skirmishes in Ethiopia, culminating in the crushing defeat in 1896. Riots and strikes, followed by armed government repression, erupted in Italy, until Giovanni Giolitti, who served as prime minister for three terms between 1903 and 1914, adopted a policy known as *trasformismo* (from the Italian word for "transform"), by which he used bribes, public works programs, and other benefits to localities to influence their deputies in parliament. Political opponents called Giolitti "the Minister of the Underworld" and accused him of preferring to buy the votes of local bosses instead of spending money to develop the Italian economy. He hoped to calm unrest in the industrializing cities of Turin and Milan and in the depressed agrarian south by instituting social welfare programs and, in 1912, nearly complete manhood suffrage.

Anti-Semitism, Nationalism, and Zionism in Mass Politics

The real crisis for the liberal political values of equal citizenships and tolerance came in the two decades leading up to World War I, when many politicians used anti-Semitism and nationalism to win elections. They told voters that Jews were responsible for the difficulties of modern life and that anti-Semitism and increased patriotism would fix all of society's problems. Voters from all levels of society responded enthusiastically, agreeing that Jews were the villains and that the nation-state was the hero in the armed struggle to survive. In republics and monarchies alike, anti-Semitism and militant nationalism played key roles in mass politics by leading to the creation of a radical right committed to combating the radical left of social democracy. The new radical right shattered the older notion of nationalism as pride in constitutions, rights, and the rule of law. Liberals had hoped that voting by the masses would make politics more harmonious as parliamentary debate and compromise smoothed out class and other differences. The new politics as shaped by right-wing leaders—usually representatives of the agrarian nobility, the aristocratically controlled military, and highly placed clergy—dashed those hopes by making politics loud, emotional, and hateful.

The most notorious instance of anti-Semitism occurred in France, where the Dreyfus Affair sorely tested the principle of equal citizenship. The French Third Republic, formed after France's defeat in the Franco-Prussian War, was fragile, with the liberal alliance of businessmen, shopkeepers, professionals, and rural property owners who backed republican government opposed by the aristocracy, military, and Catholic church. The latter groups hoped that the Third Republic, like the earlier two, would be overthrown. Economic downturns and government corruption made the republic even more vulnerable, and the press stirred things up by attributing failures of almost every kind to French Jews. Despite an excellent system of primary education promoting literacy and rational thinking, the public tended to agree.

Amid rising anti-Semitism, a Jewish captain in the French army, Alfred Dreyfus, was charged with spying for Germany in 1894. Dreyfus had attended elite schools and become an officer in the French military, whose upper ranks were traditionally aristocratic, Catholic, and monarchist. The military produced manufactured evidence to gain Dreyfus's conviction and exile to the harsh fortress on Devil's Island. Even though the espionage continued after his arrest, the government stubbornly upheld his guilt. Then several newspapers received proof that the army had used false testimony and fabricated documents to convict Dreyfus. In 1898, the celebrated French novelist Émile Zola published "J'accuse" ("I Accuse") on the front page of a Paris daily, exposing how military lies and cover-ups had created the illusion of Dreyfus's guilt. The article revealed the names of the guilty parties and called for the return of a government based on honesty and the rule of law. "I have but one passion, that of Enlightenment," wrote Zola. "J'accuse" led to public riots, quarrels among families and friends, and denunciations of the army, which eroded public confidence in the republic and in French institutions. The government finally pardoned Dreyfus in 1899, dismissed the aristocratic and Catholic officers held

Public Opinion in the Dreyfus Affair: "Ah! The Dirty Beast!"
The French army used forged documents and perjured testimony to convict Captain Alfred Dreyfus of espionage. In a climate of escalating anti-Semitism, the conviction of a Jew struck many in the public as yet another narrow escape for the country. Only intense detective work by pro-Dreyfus activists and lobbying by Dreyfus's family convinced republican leaders that the system of equal rights was imperiled not by Dreyfus but by the bigotry of the army and those right-wing politicians who had trumped up the case against him. (© Musée Carnavalet/Roger Viollet/The Image Works.)

responsible, and outlawed teaching by religious orders to ensure a public school system that honored toleration and the rule of law. Nonetheless, the Dreyfus Affair made anti-Semitism a standard political tool by showing the effectiveness of hate-filled slogans in mainstream politics.

The ruling elites in Germany also used anti-Semitism to gain political support from those who feared the consequences of Germany's sudden and overwhelming industrialization. Bismarck tried to woo the working class with an array of social programs such as accident and disability insurance while out-lawing the Social Democratic Party. The agrarian elites, who controlled the highest reaches of government, lost ground as agriculture declined as a force in Germany's economy. The agrarian elites came to loathe both vibrant industry and the working class as better jobs drew rural people away from the land. As one Berlin newspaper noted, "The agrarians' hate for cities . . . blinds them to the simplest needs and the most natural demands of the urban population."

These conservatives and a growing radical right claimed that Jews, who made up less than 1 percent of the German population, were responsible for the disruption of traditional society and charged them with being the main beneficiaries of economic change. In the 1890s, nationalist and anti-Semitic pressure groups flourished, denouncing not only Jews and "new women" but also Social Democrats, whom they branded as internationalist and unpatriotic. In the 1890s, the new Agrarian League fueled the fears of small farmers by accusing Jews of causing agricultural booms and busts. Hate-filled slogans and violent expressions of nationalism, rather than rational proposals to solve problems of economic change, became regular features of political campaigns.

Politicians in Austria-Hungary, the dual monarchy, also used militant nationalism and anti-Semitism to win votes, but here the presence of many ethnic groups meant competing nationalisms and thus greater complexity in the politics of hate. Foremost among the nationalists were the Hungarians, who wanted autonomy for themselves while forcibly imposing the Magyar language and culture on all other ethnic groups within Hungary itself. This policy was called Magyarization, from the name of the dominant Hungarian ethnic group. Nationalist demands for greater Hungarian influence rested on two pieces of evidence: Budapest's importance as a thriving industrial city and the massive exportation of grain from the vast estates of the Hungarian nobility—both of which, it was claimed, saved the monarchy's finances. Yet political chaos within Hungary resulted from Magyar domination there, as Slovaks, Romanians, and Ruthenians protested horrendous labor conditions and tens of thousands of others demanded the vote. In the face of this resistance, Hungary intensified Magyarization, even decreeing that all tombstones be engraved in the Magyar language.

Principal Ethnic Groups in Austria-Hungary, c. 1900

Hungarian nationalism led other nationalists to intensify their own demands for rights in the dual monarchy. Croats, Serbs, and other Slavic groups in the south called for equality with the Hungarians. The central government allowed the Czechs more influence in the government because of growing industrial prosperity in their region. But every step favoring the Czechs provoked outrage from the traditionally dominant ethnic Germans in the region. When Austria-Hungary decreed in 1897 that government officials in the Czech region would have to speak Czech as well as German, the Germans rioted, further straining political stability.

Tensions mounted as politicians in Vienna linked the growing power of Hungarian and Czech politicians to Jews. Karl Lueger, whose newly formed Christian Social Party attracted aristocrats, Catholics, artisans, shopkeepers, and white-collar workers, had great success with this new brand of politics. In hate-filled speeches, Lueger hurled abuse at Jews and non-German groups, appealing to those people for whom modern life meant a loss of privilege and security. Lueger's ethnic nationalism and anti-Semitism threatened the multinationalism on which Austria-Hungary was based. His attacks were so effective at getting votes—he was elected mayor of Vienna in 1895—that a widening range of politicians made anti-Semitism an integral part of their election campaigns, calling Jews the "sucking vampire" of modernity and blaming them for any and all problems. Thus politics moved from parliaments to the streets, inflaming the atmosphere with racism.

Like Christians and people of other religions, Jews often differed from one another based on social class and education. Jews in many parts of Europe had responded to increasing legal tolerance by moving out of Jewish neighborhoods, intermarrying with Christians, and in some cases converting to Christianity—practices known as assimilation. Many educated Jews favored the classical culture of the German Empire over the Catholic ritual promoted by Austria-Hungary. Still, many accomplished and prosperous Jews, including Sigmund Freud, flourished amid the cosmopolitan culture of Vienna and Budapest. By contrast, less fortunate Jews, such as those in Russia and Romania, were increasingly targeted for persecution, legally disadvantaged, and forced to live in ghettos. Jews from these countries might seek refuge in the cities of central and eastern Europe or migrate to countries around the world. By 1900, Jews were prominent in cultural and economic affairs in cities across the continent and discriminated against, even victimized, in more rural areas.

Amid vast migration and continued persecution, a spirit of Jewish nationalism arose, as Jews began organizing resistance to pogroms and anti-Semitic politics, and intellectuals drew on Jewish folklore and history to establish a national identity similar to that of European nations. In the 1880s, Ukrainian physician Leon Pinsker, seeing the Jews' lack of national territory as fundamental to the persecution heaped on them, advocated the migration of Jews to Palestine—a goal known as **Zionism**. Theodor Herzl, strongly influenced by Pinsker, called not simply for migration but for the creation of a Jewish nation-state. A Hungarian-born Jew, Herzl experienced anti-Semitism firsthand as a Viennese journalist and writer in Paris during the Dreyfus Affair. With the support of poorer eastern European Jews, he succeeded in calling the first International Zionist Congress in Basel, Switzerland (1897), which endorsed settlement in Palestine and helped gain financial backing from the Rothschild banking family. By 1914, some eighty-five thousand Jews had resettled in Palestine.

Threats to the Russian Empire

Politics were equally explosive in Russia, where anti-Semitism escalated and internal affairs seemed in disarray. Russia was one of the few European countries without a constitutional government, and reform-minded Russian youths increasingly turned to revolutionary, even terrorist groups for solutions to political and social problems. Writers fueled an intense debate over Russia's future. Leo Tolstoy, author of the epic *War and Peace* (1869), opposed the revolutionaries' desire to overturn the social order, promoting the cause of spiritual regeneration instead. His novel *Anna Karenina* (1877) is the story not only of an impassioned, adulterous love affair but also of a landowner who, like Tolstoy himself, rejects modernization and idealizes the peasantry's simple values. Radicals, however, sought to change Russia by violent action rather than by spiritual uplift, and in 1881 one of them killed Tsar Alexander II in a bombing attack. Although his death failed to provoke the peasant uprising the terrorists expected, the assassination reflected Russian discontent.

Alexander III (r. 1881–1894) rejected his father's legacy of liberal reform and unleashed further repression of religious and ethnic minorities. He gave the police almost unchecked power. Intensified Russification further alienated nationalities such as the Poles and turned the once loyal German middle and upper classes of the Baltic provinces against Russian rule. But the main victims of Alexander's policies were the five million Russian Jews, confined since the eighteenth century to the Pale of Settlement, the restricted territory in which they were permitted to live. Distinctive language, dress, and isolation made them easy targets in an age when the Russian government was enforcing cultural uniformity and national identity. Government officials also encouraged people to blame Jews for heavy taxes and living costs—though the true cause was the policy of raising taxes to pay for industrialization.

When Alexander III's son Nicholas II took the throne in 1894, the empire faced mounting difficulties. Taught as a child to hate Jews, Nicholas II (r. 1894–1917) stepped up the persecutions, and many high officials eagerly endorsed anti-Semitism to gain his favor. Pogroms became a regular feature of the Easter holiday in Russia, and Nicholas increasingly limited how Jews could earn a living. Simultaneously, uprooted Russians settled much of Siberia, and the government sponsored industrialization, especially the growth of transport and manufacturing. Industrialization, however, produced urban unrest as Marxist and other activists incited workers to demand better conditions. In 1903, skilled workers led strikes in Baku, where the participation of Armenians and Tatars showed how urbanization and Russification could actually bring diverse ethnicities together to challenge—not support—the autocratic regime.

The tense situation exploded into revolution during the Russo-Japanese War. In January 1905, a crowd gathered outside the tsar's Winter Palace in St. Petersburg to try to make Nicholas aware of the brutal conditions under which they suffered. Instead of allowing the demonstration to pass, troops guarding the palace shot into the crowd, killing hundreds and wounding thousands. News of this event, referred to as Bloody Sunday, moved workers across Russia to rebel. They struck over wages, working hours, and factory conditions and demanded political representation in the government. Workers rejected the leadership of both Social Democrats and Social Revolutionaries and instead organized their own councils, called soviets. In June, sailors on the battleship *Potemkin* mutinied. In October, a massive railroad strike brought rail transportation to a halt, and the Baltic territories and Transcaucasia rebelled. In November, uprisings broke out in Moscow. Professionals, the upper

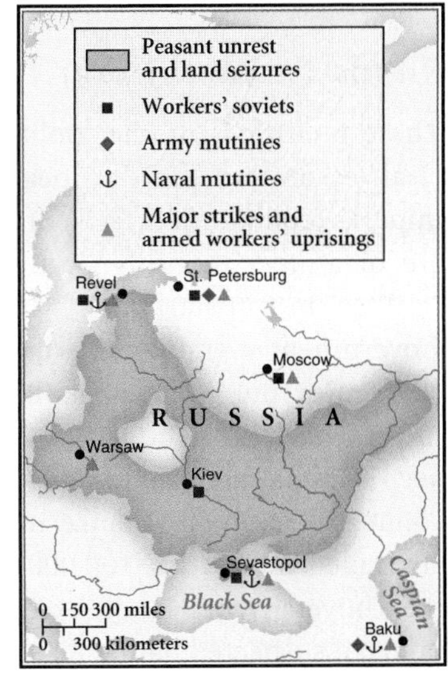

The Russian Revolution of 1905

classes, and women joined the assault on autocracy, with a series of demands including the creation of a representative legislature. They believed that the monarchy's reliance on censorship and a secret police force had relegated Russia to the ranks of the most backward nation-states.

The tsar finally yielded to the violence and created a representative body called the Duma. Although very few Russians could vote for representatives to the Duma, its mere existence, along with the new right to debate issues in public, liberalized government and allowed people to present their grievances to a more responsive body. Political parties took shape, and the Revolution of 1905 drew to a close. But people soon wondered whether anything had really changed. From 1907 to 1917, the Duma convened, but twice when the tsar disliked its recommendations, he simply sent the delegates home. Nicholas did have a successful administrator in Prime Minister Pyotr Stolypin, who tried to eliminate rural discontent by ending the mir system of communal farming, canceling the peasants' redemption payments for the land they farmed, and making loans available to peasants for the purchase of land. Although these reforms did not eradicate rural poverty, they did allow people to move to the cities in search of jobs, and they created a larger group of independent peasants. Meanwhile, another round of strikes broke out, culminating in a general strike in St. Petersburg in 1914. The imperial government and the conservative nobility still had no solution to the social turmoil, and their refusal to share power and introduce true political reform left the way open to an even greater upheaval in 1917.

REVIEW What were the major changes in political life between 1880 and 1914?

Roads to World War I

These unsettled internal politics throughout Europe kept nerves on edge, while rivalries among the European powers over empire intensified. As a result of imperial competition, one British economist wrote in 1902, "Diplomatic strains are of almost monthly occurrence between the Powers." Nationalism swelled: "militarism run stark mad" was how one U.S. official described the scene in 1914. Government spending on what people called the "arms race" stimulated European economies, but while stockpiles of arms temporarily promoted economic growth, they menaced the future. Europe was jittery, waging a growing number of wars to keep colonial peoples in line. In German East Africa, for example, colonial forces countered native resistance in 1905 with a scorched-earth policy, which eventually killed more than 100,000 Africans (Map 19.2, page 734). The French closed the University of Hanoi, executed Indochinese intellectuals, and deported thousands of suspected nationalists to maintain a tenuous grip on Indochina (Map 19.3, page 737). By 1914, a hostile international scene, militant nationalism in the Balkan states, and conflicts in domestic politics came together, driving Europeans toward mass destruction.

Competing Alliances and Clashing Ambitions

As the twentieth century opened, an alliance system first established by Bismarck to ensure the peaceful consolidation of the new German Empire and to maintain European stability was changing rapidly. Anxious about the Balkans and Russian leadership of the Slavs, Austria-Hungary had entered a defensive alliance with Germany in 1879. The **Dual Alliance**, as it was called, offered protection against Russia, which appeared to threaten Hungarian control of its Slavic peasantry. In 1882, Italy joined this partnership (called the Triple Alliance thereafter), largely because of Italy's imperial rivalries with France. Bismarck also signed the Reinsurance Treaty (1887) with Russia to check Habsburg dreams of having a free hand against this rival for Slavic loyalty. Bismarck intended these alliances to show that Germany was now a "satisfied" nation and one that would prevent further disruptive wars.

Bismarck's delicate alliance system started unraveling, however, when the blustering but deeply insecure Kaiser William II came to power in 1888. Advisers flattered the twenty-nine-year-old into thinking that Bismarck was a bother, even a rival to his own creativity. William II (r. 1888–1918) dismissed Bismarck in 1890. An ardent supporter of German nationalism, the kaiser saw Austria-Hungary as closely connected because of its German dynasty and thus let the alliance with Russia lapse, driving the Russians to form an alliance with the French. William then became "dissatisfied" with Germany's international status and inflamed rather than calmed the diplomatic atmosphere. He used the opportunity presented by the defeat of France's ally Russia in the Russo-Japanese War to contest French claims in Morocco, boldly landing his own ship in Morocco in 1905 to challenge French predominance. To resolve what became known as the First Moroccan Crisis, an international conference met in Spain in 1906. William expected Britain to side with Germany over its traditional rival France, but instead of awarding Germany Morocco, the powers supported French rule. The French and British military, faced with German aggression in Morocco, drew closer together. When the French finally took over Morocco in 1911, Germany triggered the Second Moroccan Crisis by sending a gunboat to the port of Agadir and demanding concessions from France. This time no power, not even Austria-Hungary, backed the German move.

The backdrop to William's aggressive demands was the competition for empire between France and Britain, which seemed to rule out an alliance between the two powers. Constant rivals in Africa, they had been on the brink of war in 1898, at a town in the Sudan called Fashoda (Map 19.2, page 734), when France withdrew. At that point, both nations decided it was in their own best interests to try to get along. To prevent another Fashoda, they entered into secret agreements, the first of which (1904) guaranteed British claims in Egypt and French claims in Morocco. This agreement marked the beginning of the British-French alliance called the **Entente Cordiale**. After the First Moroccan Crisis, the British and French planned for the coordination of their forces in case of war. In 1907, Britain and Russia put aside their rivalries to allow Russia to join what became the Triple Entente among

France, Britain, and Russia. Thus two opposing alliance systems were now in place. Smarting from its setbacks on the world stage, Germany reconsidered its role in continental Europe.

The Balkans, in the meantime, loomed as a site for competing ambitions on the part of the great powers and among the Balkan states themselves. Germany's bold territorial claims, along with uncertainty about alliances, unsettled Europe, particularly the Balkans. German statesmen began envisioning the creation of a **Mitteleuropa** that included central Europe, the Balkans, and Turkey under German rule. Russia, however, saw itself as the protector of the Slavs in that same region and wanted to replace the Ottomans as the major Balkan power. Meanwhile, Austria-Hungary swiftly annexed Bosnia-Herzegovina during the Young Turk revolt in 1908. This was part of its plan to control more Balkan ethnicities in order to dilute the power of any one ethnicity in the kingdom (Map 19.4).

The nineteenth century had seen the rise of nationalism and ethnicity as the basis for the development of independent nation-states in the Balkans, however, and by the early twentieth century, Balkan states, composed of several ethnicities as well as Orthodox Christians, Roman Catholics, and Muslims, sought more Ottoman and Habsburg territory and went to war to obtain it. In the First Balkan War (1912), Serbia, Bulgaria, Greece, and Montenegro joined forces to gain Macedonia and Albania from the Ottomans. The victors divided up their booty but soon turned against one another. In the Second Balkan War (1913), Serbia, Greece, and Montenegro contested Bulgarian gains in the first war. The quick victory of these allies increased Austria-Hungary's dismay at Serbia's rising power. Grievances between the Serbs and the Habsburgs, who feared that any disturbance in the Balkan balance of power would encourage ethnic rebellion at home, now seemed irreconcilable, and the angry Serbs looked to Russia for help. The situation tempted strategists on all sides to think hopefully that a quick war there—something like Bismarck's wars—could resolve this tension and uncertainty.

The Race to Arms

At the turn of the twentieth century, these and other rivalries and the drive for national greatness made constant readiness for war seem increasingly necessary. On the seas and in foreign lands, the colonial powers battled to establish control, and they developed railroad, telegraph, and telephone networks everywhere to move troops and encourage commerce. Governments began to draft ordinary citizens for periods of two to six years into large standing armies, in contrast to the smaller eighteenth-century forces that had served the more limited military goals of the time. By 1914, escalating tensions in Europe boosted the annual intake of draftees: Germany, France, and Russia called up 250,000 or more troops each year. Per capita expenditures on the military rose in all the major powers between 1890 and 1914; the proportion of national budgets devoted to defense in 1910 was lowest in Austria-Hungary at 10 percent and highest in Germany at 45 percent.

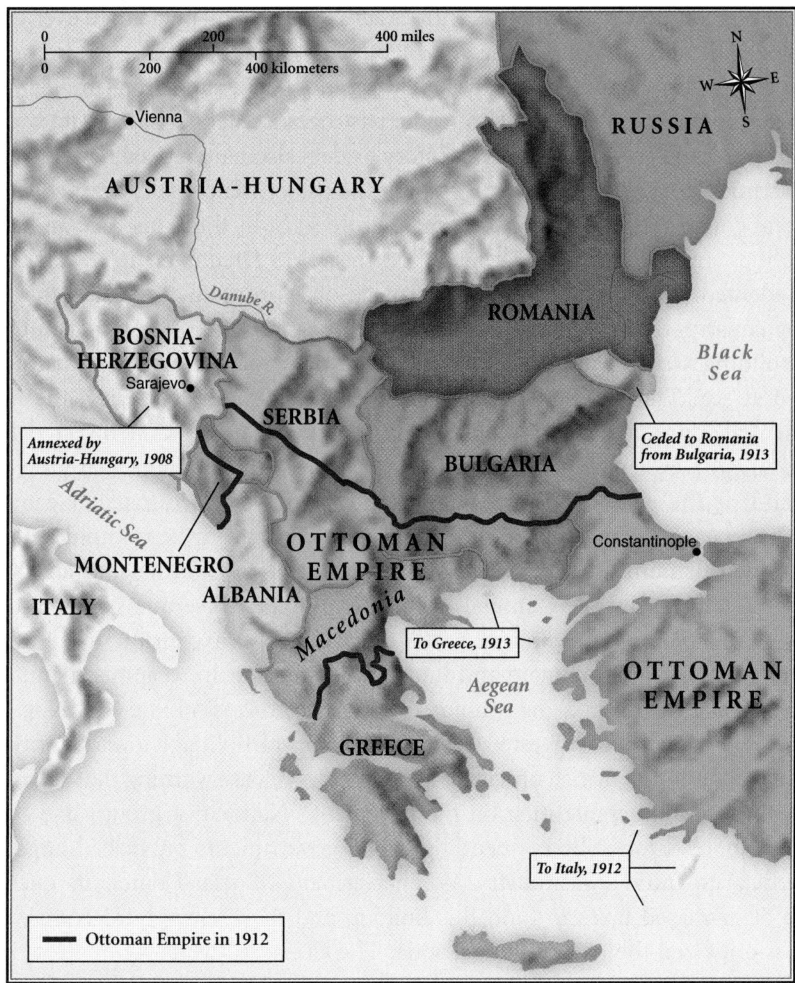

Map 19.4 The Balkans, 1908–1914
Balkan peoples—mixed in religion, ethnicity, and political views—were successful in developing and asserting their desire for independence, especially in the First Balkan War (1912), which claimed territory from the Ottoman Empire. Their increased autonomy sparked rivalries among them and continued to attract attention from the great powers. Three empires in particular—the Russian, Ottoman, and Austro-Hungarian—simultaneously sought greater influence in the region, which became a powder keg of competing ambitions.

The modernization of weaponry also transformed warfare. Swedish arms manufacturer Alfred Nobel patented dynamite and developed a kind of gunpowder that improved the accuracy of guns and reduced the amount of smoke they produced, resulting in a less clouded battlefield environment. Breakthroughs in the chemical industry led to improvements in long-range artillery, which by 1914 could fire on targets as far as six miles away. Military leaders devised strategies to protect their armies from overwhelming firepower. Munitions factories across Europe manufactured ever-growing stockpiles of howitzers, Mauser rifles, and Hotchkiss machine guns. Used in the South African and Russo-Japanese wars, these new weapons had shown that military offensives were more difficult to win than in the past because neither side could overcome such accurate and forceful firepower. Military leaders also had devised new strategies to protect armies from this firepower, including the use of trenches and barbed wire.

Naval construction also played a major role in both the arms race and nationalist politics. In 1905, the British launched the HMS *Dreadnought*, a warship with unprecedented firepower and the centerpiece of a program to update the British navy by constructing at least seven battleships per year. Germany followed British naval building step by step and made itself a force to be feared not just on land but also at sea. The German military encouraged William II to view the navy as the essential ingredient in making Germany a world power and directed him to the writings of U.S. naval theorist Alfred Thayer Mahan. Mahan's argument that command of the seas determined international power encouraged Germany to build naval bases as far away as the Pacific. The German drive to build battleships strengthened Britain's alliance with France in the Entente Cordiale, as all the powers dramatically raised their annual naval spending. The Germans announced the fleet buildup as "a peaceful policy," but like British naval expansion, it led only to a worsening international climate and intense competition in weapons manufacture.

Public relations campaigns promoted the great powers' military buildup. When critics of the arms race suggested a temporary "naval holiday" to stop British and German shipbuilding, British officials put out a news release warning that such a move "would throw innumerable men on the pavement." Nationalist groups and boosters of empire lobbied for military spending, while governments publicized large navies as beneficial to trade and industry. When Germany's Social Democrats questioned the use of increased taxes to fund this buildup and their heavy burden on workers, the press criticized the party as unpatriotic. The Conservative Party in Great Britain, eager for more battleships, made popular the slogan "We want eight and we won't wait." One military leader captured the enthusiasm for war at the time, even among the public at large. When asked in 1912 about his predictions for war and peace, he responded enthusiastically, "We shall have war. I will make it. I will win it." Everything was in place for war—alliances, stocks of armaments, war plans, mass armies, and a boiling pot of animosities and tensions—in the summer of 1914.

REVIEW What major factors made Europe set for war by 1914?

Conclusion

By 1914, Europe as a whole was ripe for a major conflict and had feverishly prepared for it, even as the Wolf-Man was completing his treatment with Freud in that summer—"a cured man," he called himself. Imperialism and the arms race had stimulated militant nationalism and brought many Europeans to favor war over peace.

Mapping the West Europe at the Outbreak of World War I, August 1914
Each of the European powers expected a swift victory when war broke out. Many were convinced that war would bring them great advantages over their rivals in trade and empire, including the chance to expand their territories. But if the powers appeared well prepared and invincible at the start of the war, relatively few would survive the conflict intact.

The rapid pace of change had helped blaze the path to war. Facing continuing violence in politics, grating new trends in the arts, and problems in society, Europeans had come to believe that war would set events back on the right course and save them from the perils of modernity. Disturbances in private life and challenges to tradition posed by new technologies and modern urban life would disappear, it was believed, in the flames of war. "Like men longing for a thunderstorm to relieve them of the summer's sultriness," wrote one Austrian official, "so the generation of 1914 believed in the relief that war might bring." Such a possibility caused many Europeans to rejoice as war approached. But instead of bringing the refreshment of summer rain, the war that erupted in the summer of 1914 opened an era of political turmoil, widespread suffering, massive human slaughter, and even greater doses of modernity.

CHAPTER REVIEW QUESTIONS

1. How did changes in society at the beginning of the twentieth century affect the development of mass politics?
2. How did cultural changes affect politics between 1880 and 1914?

For practice quizzes and other study tools, see the Online Study Guide at bedfordstmartins.com/huntconcise.

For primary-source material from this period, see Chapters 23 and 24 of *Sources of* The Making of the West, Third Edition.

Suggested References

New studies of imperialism show increasing conquest, the creation of an international economy, and the social and cultural impulses behind imperial expansion. The University of Pennsylvania's African Studies Center Web site looks at African history, politics, and culture. New forms of art and philosophy and the rise of mass politics

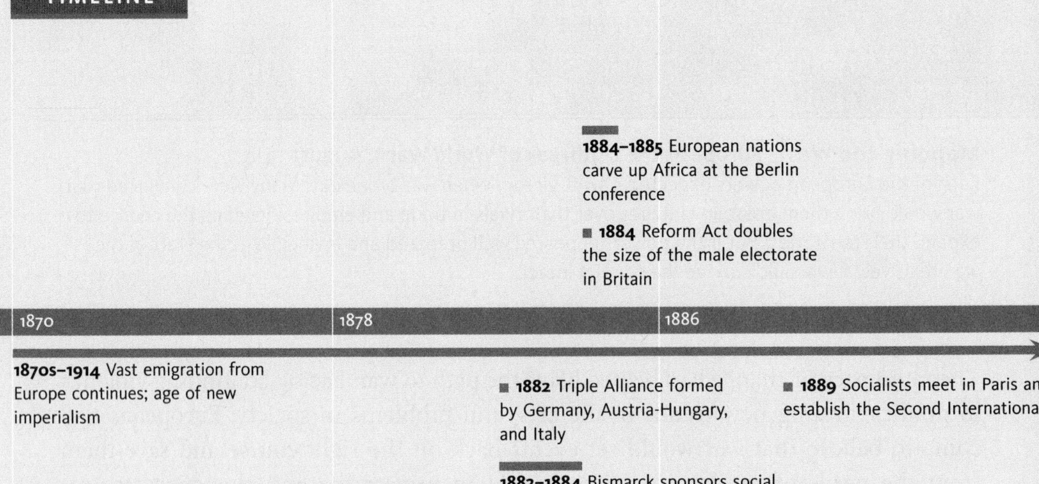

were central to the challenges Europe faced, but the question of why war broke out remains widely debated.

African Studies Center: http://www.sas.upenn.edu/African_Studies/AS.html

Cain, P. J., and A. G. Hopkins. *British Imperialism, 1688–2000*. 2002.

Childs, Peter. *Modernism*. 2008.

Davis, Mike. *Late Victorian Holocausts: El Niño Famines and the Making of the Third World*. 2001.

Hermann, David G. *The Arming of Europe and the Making of the First World War*. 1997.

Hull, Isabel. *Absolute Destruction: Military Culture and the Practices of War in Imperial Germany*. 2005.

Kaplan, Morris B. *Sodom on the Thames: Sex, Love, and Scandal in Wilde Times*. 2005.

Koven, Seth. *Slumming: Sexual and Social Politics in Victorian London*. 2004.

Marchand, Suzanne, and David Lindenfeld, eds. *Germany at the Fin de Siècle: Culture, Politics, and Ideas*. 2004.

Moch, Leslie Page. *Moving Europeans: Migration in Western Europe since 1650*. 2003.

Nineteenth- and twentieth-century philosophy: http://www.epistemelinks.com/index.asp

Reagin, Nancy. *Sweeping the German Nation: Domesticity and National Identity in Germany, 1870–1945*. 2006.

Reeder, Linda. *Widows in White: Migration and the Transformation of Rural Italian Women, Sicily, 1880–1920*. 2003.

Stanislawski, Michael. *Zionism and the Fin-de-Siècle: Cosmopolitanism and Nationalism from Nordau to Jabotinsky*. 2001.

Streets, Heather. *Martial Races: The Military, Race and Masculinity in British Imperial Culture, 1857–1914*. 2004.

Zahra, Tara. *Kidnapped Souls: National Indifference and the Battle for Children in the Bohemian Lands, 1900–1948*. 2008.

1894 | 1902 | 1910 | 1918

- **1894–1899** Dreyfus Affair lays bare anti-Semitism in France
- **1899–1902** South African War
- **1900** Sigmund Freud, *The Interpretation of Dreams*
- **1901** Irish National Theater established by the circle around Maud Gonne and William Butler Yeats
- **1903** Emmeline Pankhurst founds the Women's Social and Political Union to fight for woman suffrage in Great Britain
- **1904** French and British form the Entente Cordiale
- **1904–1905** Russo-Japanese War
- **1905** Revolution erupts in Russia; violence forces Nicholas II to establish an elected body, the Duma; Albert Einstein publishes his special theory of relativity
- **1906** Women receive the vote in Finland; international conference held in Spain to resolve the First Moroccan Crisis
- **1907** Pablo Picasso launches cubism
- **1908** Young Turks revolt against rule by the sultan in the Ottoman Empire
- **1911** Second Moroccan Crisis
- **1911–1912** Revolutionaries overthrow the Qing dynasty and declare China a republic
- **1912–1913** First and Second Balkan Wars

20

War, Revolution, and Reconstruction

1914–1929

JULES AMAR FOUND HIS TRUE VOCATION in World War I. A French expert on making industrial work more efficient, Amar switched focus after 1914. As hundreds of thousands of men returned from the battlefront missing body parts, plastic surgery and the construction of masks and other devices to hide deformities developed rapidly. Amar devised artificial limbs and appendages in these traumatic years that would allow wounded soldiers to return to everyday life by "mak[ing] up for a function lost, or greatly reduced." He designed arms that featured hooks, magnets, and other mechanisms with which the veteran could hold a cigarette, play the violin, and, most important, work with tools such as typewriters. Mangled by the weapons of modern technological warfare, the survivors of World War I would be made whole, it was thought, by technology such as Amar's.

Grieving Parents
Before World War I, the German artist Käthe Kollwitz gained her artistic reputation with woodcuts of handloom weavers, whose livelihoods were threatened by industrialization. From 1914 on, she depicted the suffering and death that swirled around her, and never with more somber force than in these two monuments to her son Peter, who died on the western front in the first months of the war. Today one can still visit his burial place in Vladslo, Belgium, to see this father and mother mourning their loss, like millions across Europe in those heartbreaking days. *(© John Parker Picture Library. © 2010 Artists Rights Society [ARS], NY/VG Bild-Kunst, Bonn.)*

Amar dealt with the human tragedy of the "Great War," so named by contemporaries because of its staggering human toll—forty million wounded or killed in battle. The Great War did not settle problems or restore social order as the European powers hoped it would. Instead, the war produced political chaos, overturning the Russian, German, Ottoman, and Austro-Hungarian empires. The crushing burden of war on the European powers accelerated the rise of the United States, while service in the war intensified the demands of colonized peoples for freedom. Many soldiers remained actively fighting long into what was supposed to be peacetime, while others had been so militarized that they longed for a life that was more like wartime.

World War I transformed society, too. A prewar feeling of doom and decline gave way to postwar cynicism. Many Westerners turned their backs on politics and attacked life with wild gaiety in the Roaring Twenties, snapping up new consumer goods, escaping their daily routines with entertainment provided by films and radio, and enjoying once forbidden personal freedoms. Others found reason for hope in the new political systems the war made possible: Soviet communism and Italian **Fascism**. Modern communication technologies such as radio gave politicians the means to promote a mass politics that, ironically, was often antidemocratic, militaristic, and eventually dictatorial.

A war that was long anticipated and even welcomed in some quarters as a remedy for modernity destabilized Europe and the world far into the following decades. From statesmen to ordinary citizens, many Europeans like Amar found themselves dealing year after year with the aftermath of the war. Some devoted their peacetime efforts to making war-ravaged society function normally; others planned to tap into the forces of militarism that the war had so glorified.

CHAPTER FOCUS QUESTION What political, social, and economic impact did World War I have during the conflict, immediately after it, and through the 1920s?

The Great War, 1914–1918

June 28, 1914, began as an ordinary day for Austria's archduke Francis Ferdinand and his wife, Sophie, as they ended a state visit to Sarajevo in Bosnia-Herzegovina. Wearing full military dress, the archduke was riding in a motorcade to bid farewell to various officials when a group of young Serbian nationalists threw bombs in an unsuccessful assassination attempt. The full danger did not register, and after a stop the archduke and his wife set out again. In the crowd was another armed nationalist, Gavrilo Princip, who for several weeks had traveled clandestinely to reach this destination, dreaming of reuniting his homeland of Bosnia-Herzegovina with Serbia. The unprotected and unsuspecting couple became Princip's victims, as he shot them both dead. Within weeks, the assassination led to all-out war. The ground had been prepared with long-standing alliances, the development of strategies for war, and the buildup of new military weapons such as heavy artillery, machine guns, and the airplane. Given recent experience, most people felt the conflict would be short and decisive. The unforeseen happened, however, and the war lasted for more than four years. It was a **total war**, mobilizing entire societies and producing the unbelievable horror that made it "great."

War Erupts

The Habsburg government saw the assassination as an opportunity to defeat Serbia once and for all. German statesmen and military leaders agreed, urging the Austrians to stand firm and repeating promises of support in case of war. Evidence showed that

Archduke Francis Ferdinand and His Wife in Sarajevo, June 1914
Archduke Francis Ferdinand, heir to the Austro-Hungarian monarchy, was a thorn in the side of many politicians because he did not want to favor Hungarian interests over other ethnic interests in his kingdom. His own family life was also unusual for royalty in those days: his wife, Sophie, and he had married for love and did not like to be apart. They were traveling together to Bosnia-Herzegovina in 1914 when they were assassinated. That event helped produce the outbreak of World War I. (Mary Evans Picture Library.)

Princip had received arms and information from Serbian officials who directed a terrorist organization from within Serbia's government. The Austrians demanded that the Serbs publicly condemn terrorism, suppress terrorist groups, and allow Habsburg officials to participate in the investigation of the crime. The ultimatum was severe. "You are setting Europe ablaze," the Russian foreign minister told the Habsburgs in light of the humiliating demands. Yet the Serbs were conciliatory, accepting all the terms except one—the participation of Austrian officials in the investigation. Kaiser William II was pleased, declaring this "a great moral success for Vienna! All reason for war is gone." His relief was premature. Confident of German backing, Austria-Hungary used Serbia's resistance to that one demand as the pretext for declaring war on July 28.

Some European statesmen tried hard to avoid war. Tsar Nicholas II and Kaiser William exchanged letters asking each other not to go to war. The British foreign secretary proposed an all-European conference, but with no success. Germany backed Austria-Hungary fully in hopes of convincing France and Britain to stay out of the war, which, German officials believed, would keep Russia from mobilizing. At the same time, however, German military leaders were determined to fight a short, preemptive war that would result in territorial gains leading to their goal of creating a Mitteleuropa. As an additional incentive, the war would allow these leaders to declare martial law in Germany and as a result justify the arrest of the leadership of the German Social Democratic Party, which threatened conservative rule.

Even as some governments were torn over what to do, the European press caught war fever. Like the press, military leaders, especially in Germany and Austria-Hungary, promoted mobilization rather than diplomacy in the last days of July. The Austrians declared war and then ordered mobilization on July 31, believing Russia would not dare intervene. But Nicholas II ordered the Russian army to mobilize in defense of Serbia—Russia's Slavic ally. Having encouraged the Austrians to attack Serbia, the German general staff mobilized on August 1.

Germany's war strategy was based on the Schlieffen Plan, named after its author, Alfred von Schlieffen, a former chief of the general staff. The plan outlined a way to combat antagonists on two fronts by concentrating on one foe at a time. First would come a rapid and concentrated German blow to the west against Russia's ally France, which would lead to France's defeat in six weeks. Accompanying that strike would be a light holding action to the east. With France beaten, German armies in the west would then be deployed against Russia, which, German war planners believed, would be slow to mobilize. The attack on France would proceed through Belgium, whose neutrality was guaranteed by the European powers. Events did not occur as the Germans hoped. The Belgian government rejected an ultimatum to allow the uncontested passage of the German army through the country, and Germany's subsequent violation of Belgium's neutrality brought Britain into the war on the side of Russia and France, which was already mobilizing in support of its ally Russia.

The Conflict Widens

World War I pitted two sets of opponents formed roughly out of the alliances developed during the previous fifty years. On one side stood the Central Powers (Austria-Hungary and Germany), which had evolved from Bismarck's Triple Alliance. On the other side stood the Allies (France, Great Britain, and Russia), which had emerged as a bloc from the Entente Cordiale between France and Great Britain and from the 1890s treaties between France and Russia. Italy, originally part of the Triple Alliance, joined the Allies in 1915. The war soon expanded globally as well. In late August 1914, Japan, eager to extend its empire into China, lined up with the Allies. In the fall, the Ottoman Empire united with the Central Powers against its traditional enemy, Russia.

Both sides fought with the same ferocious hunger for power, prestige, and prosperity that had inspired imperialism. Germany aspired to a far-flung empire to be gained by annexing Russian territory and incorporating parts of Belgium, France, and Luxembourg. Some German leaders wanted to annex Austria-Hungary as well. Austria-Hungary hoped to retain its great-power status in the face of competing nationalisms within its borders. Among the Allies, Russia wanted to reassert its status as a great power and as the protector of the Slavs by adding a reunified Poland to the Russian Empire and by taking formal leadership of other Slavic peoples. The French craved territory, especially the return of resource-rich Alsace and Lorraine, taken after the Franco-Prussian War. The British sought to cement their hold on Egypt and the Suez Canal and to secure the rest of their world empire. By the Treaty of London (1915), France and Britain promised Italy territory in Africa, Asia Minor, the Balkans, and elsewhere in return for joining the Allies.

The colonies provided massive assistance and were also battlegrounds. Some one million Africans, one million Indians, and more than one million men from the British Commonwealth served on the battlefronts. The imperial powers also conscripted uncounted numbers of colonists as forced laborers both at home and on the battlefronts. Colonial troops fought on European battlefields and also played a major role in fighting across North and sub-Saharan Africa. Relying on Arab, African, and Indian troops, the British waged a successful war on Ottoman lands in the Middle East, menacing Germany's longtime interests by taking Baghdad in 1917 and also taking Palestine, Syria, and Mesopotamia.

Unprecedented use of machinery helped determine the course of the war. In August 1914, weapons such as machine guns and fast breech-loading rifles; military vehicles such as airplanes, battleships, and submarines; and motorized transport (cars and railroads) were all at the armies' disposal. New technologies such as chlorine gas, tanks, and bombs were developed between 1914 and 1918. Countries differed, however, in their experience with and access to large quantities of these weapons. British generals knew the destructive capacity of the weapons because of their colonial wars; the Germans were far more advanced in strategy and weaponry than either the Russians or the Austrians. The war itself became a lethal testing ground, as both new and old weapons were used, often ineffectively. Many officers on both sides believed in a "cult of the offensive," which called for spirited attacks and high troop morale. Despite the availability of newer, more powerful war technology, an old-fashioned vision of warfare made many officers unwilling to abandon sabers, lances, bayonets, and cavalry charges. In the face of massive firepower, the cult of the offensive would cost millions of lives.

Battlefronts

The first months of the war crushed any hope of a quick victory. All the major armies mobilized rapidly. Guided by the Schlieffen Plan, the Germans quickly reached Luxembourg and Belgium, but the plan fell apart when the Belgians resisted, slowing the German advance and allowing British and French troops to reach the northern front after the French had mistakenly fallen for German diversionary moves on the eastern border. In September, British and French armies engaged the Germans along the Marne River in France. Neither side could defeat the other, and casualties were shocking: in the first three months of the war, more than 1.5 million men fell on the western front alone. Firepower turned what was supposed to be an offensive war of movement into a stationary standoff along a line stretching from the North Sea through Belgium and northern France to Switzerland (Map 20.1). Deep within opposing lines of trenches dug along this western front, soldiers lived a nightmarish existence.

On the eastern front, the "Russian steam-roller"—so named because of the number of men mobilized, some twelve million in all—drove far more quickly than expected into East Prussia. The Russians believed that no army could withstand their massive numbers, no matter how ill equipped and poorly trained they were. Their success was short-lived. The Germans crushed the tsar's army in East Prussia

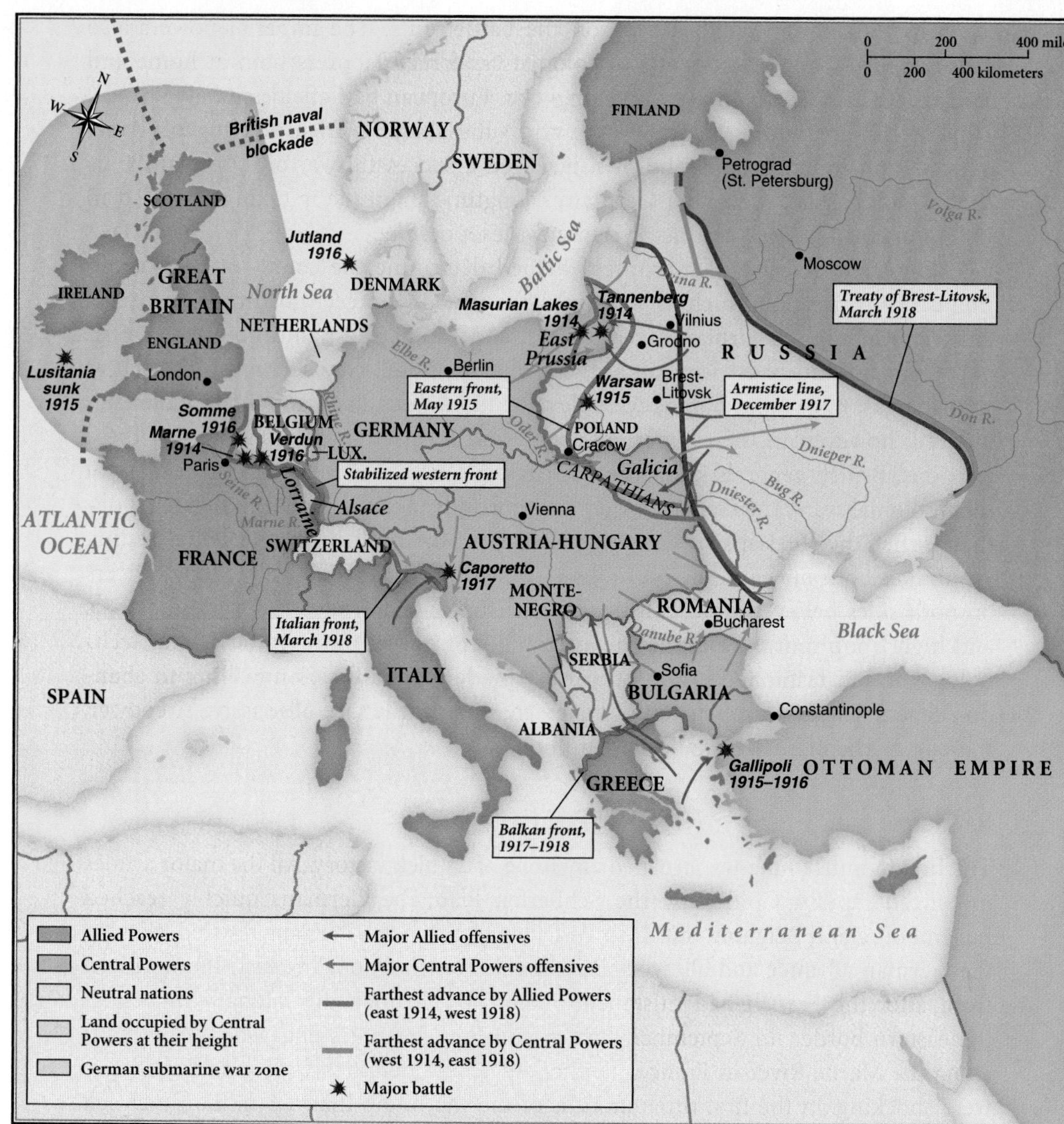

Map 20.1 The Fronts of World War I, 1914–1918

Fighting on all fronts destroyed portions of Europe's hard-won industrial and agricultural capacity. Because the western front remained relatively stationary, the devastation of land and resources in northern and eastern France was especially intense. Men engaged in trench warfare developed an intense comradeship based on their mutual suffering.

and then turned south to Galicia. Victory made heroes of military leaders Paul von Hindenburg and Erich Ludendorff. Despite victories, German triumphs in the east had failed to knock out the Russians and had also undermined the Schlieffen Plan by removing forces from the west before the western front had been won.

The war at sea proved equally indecisive. Confident of Britain's superior naval power, the Allies blockaded ports to prevent supplies from reaching Germany and Austria-Hungary. Kaiser William and his advisers planned a massive submarine, or U-boat (*Unterseeboot,* "underwater boat"), campaign against Allied and neutral shipping around Britain and France. In May 1915, German submarines sank the British passenger ship *Lusitania* and killed 1,198 people, including 124 Americans. Despite U.S. outrage, President Woodrow Wilson maintained a policy of neutrality; Germany, unwilling to provoke Wilson further, called off unrestricted submarine warfare. In May 1916, the navies of Germany and Britain finally clashed in the North Sea at Jutland. Though inconclusive, this battle demonstrated that the German fleet could not master British sea power (Map 20.1, page 784).

Ideas of a negotiated peace were discarded. "No peace before England is defeated and destroyed," the kaiser railed against his cousin King George V. "Only amidst the ruins of London will I forgive Georgy." French leaders called for a "war to the death." The general staffs on both sides continued to prepare fierce attacks several times a year. Indecisive campaigns opened with heavy artillery pounding enemy trenches and gun emplacements. Troops then responded to the order to go "over the top," scrambling out of their trenches, usually to be mowed down by machine-gun fire from defenders secure in their own trenches. On the western front, the French assaulted the Germans in the north throughout 1915 in an attempt to drive them from the industrial regions. They accomplished little, and casualties of 100,000 or more during a single campaign became commonplace. On the eastern front, Russian armies captured parts of Galicia in the spring of 1915 and lumbered toward Hungary. The Central Powers struck back in Poland later that year, bringing the front closer to Petrograd (formerly St. Petersburg), the Russian capital.

The next year was even more disastrous. To cripple French morale, the Germans launched massive assaults on the fortress at Verdun, firing as many as a million shells in a single day. Combined French and German losses totaled close to a million men. Nonetheless, the French held. Hoping to relieve their allies, the British unleashed an artillery assault on German trenches in the Somme region in June 1916. In several months of battle, 1.25 million men were killed or wounded, but the final result was a stalemate. By the end of 1916, the French had suffered more than 3.5 million casualties. To help the Allies engaged at Verdun and the Somme, the Russians struck again, driving into the Carpathian Mountains, recouping territory, and menacing the Habsburg Empire. Only the German army stopped the Russian advance.

Had military leaders thoroughly dominated the scene, historians judge, all armies would have been demolished in nonstop offensives by the end of 1915. Yet ordinary soldiers in this war were not automatons in the face of what seemed to them suicidal orders. Informal agreements among troops to avoid battles allowed some battalions to go for long stretches with hardly a casualty. Enemies facing each other across the trenches frequently ate their meals in peace even though the trenches were within a hand grenade's reach. Throughout the war, soldiers on opposing sides fraternized, playing an occasional game of soccer, shouting to each other across the battlefield, and making gestures not to fight. A British veteran of the trenches explained to a new recruit that the Germans "don't want to fight any more than we do, so there's a kind of understanding between us. Don't fire at us and we'll not fire at you." Burying enemy dead in common graves with their own fallen comrades, many ordinary soldiers came to feel more warmly toward enemies who shared the trench experience than toward uncomprehending civilians back home.

Newly forged bonds of male companionship relieved some of the misery of trench life and aided survival. Facing the danger and deprivations of the frontline experience weakened traditional class distinctions. In some cases, upper-class officers and working-class recruits became friends in that "wholly masculine way of life uncomplicated by women," as one soldier put it. Soldiers picked lice from each other's bodies and clothes, tended each other's blistered feet, and came to love each other, sometimes even passionately. This sense of community would survive the war and influence postwar politics.

Troops of colonial soldiers from Asia and Africa had different experiences. Often these soldiers were put in the front ranks where the risks were greatest. They suffered from the rigors of totally unfamiliar climates and strange food, as well as from the ruin inflicted by Western war technology. Yet like class divisions, racial barriers sometimes fell—for instance, when European soldiers took pains to alleviate the distress

War in the Trenches
Men at the front developed close friendships as they lived with daily discomfort and death and the horrors of modern technological warfare. Some of the complexities of trench warfare appear in this image showing soldiers rescuing their fallen comrades after fighting at Bagatelle in northern France. (Getty Images.)

the cold inflicted on colonial troops. The perspectives of colonial soldiers changed, too. "What miserable crowned head was able to order such horrors?" wrote one corporal from West Africa. These troops saw their "masters" completely undone and "uncivilized," for when fighting did break out, the trenches became a veritable hell of shelling and sniping, flying body parts, blinding gas, and rotting cadavers. Some soldiers became hysterical or shell-shocked; others became cynical or lost hope. "It might be me tomorrow," a young British soldier wrote to his mother in 1916. "Who cares?" Soldiers who had gone to war to escape ordinary life in industrial society learned, as one German put it, "that in the modern war . . . the triumph of the machine over the individual is carried to its most extreme form." They took this hard-won knowledge into battle, pulling their comrades back when an offensive seemed lost or too costly.

The Home Front

World War I took place off the battlefield, too. Total war meant the involvement of civilians in essential war industries manufacturing the shells and machine guns, poisonous gases, bombs and airplanes, and eventually tanks that were the backbone of technological warfare. Increased production of coffins, canes, wheelchairs, and artificial limbs (devised by the likes of Jules Amar) also was required. Because the war would have failed utterly without them, civilians had to work overtime for, believe in, and sacrifice for victory. To keep the war machine operating smoothly, governments oversaw factories, transportation systems, and resources ranging from food to coal to textiles. Before the war, such tight government control would have outraged many liberals, but now it was accepted as a necessary condition for victory.

At first, political parties put aside their differences. Many socialists and working-class people who had criticized the military buildup announced their support for the war. For decades, socialist parties had preached that "workingmen have no country" and that nationalism was an ideology meant to keep workers disunited and subjected to their employers. In August 1914, however, the socialist rank and file, along with most of the party leaders, became as patriotic as the rest of society. Feminists divided over whether to maintain their traditional condemnation of war or to support the war effort. Although many feminists actively opposed the conflict, Emmeline Pankhurst and her daughter Christabel were among those who became militant nationalists, even changing the name of their suffrage paper to *Britannia*. Parties representing the middle class dropped their distrust of socialists and the working class. In the name of victory, national leaders wanted to end political divisions of all kinds. "I no longer recognize [political] parties," William II declared on August 4, 1914. "I recognize only Germans." Ordinary people, even those who had been on the receiving end of discrimination, came to believe that a new day of unity was dawning. One rabbi proudly echoed the kaiser: "In the German fatherland there are no longer any Christians and Jews, any believers and disbelievers, there are only Germans."

Governments mobilized the home front with varying degrees of success. All countries were caught without ready replacements for the heavy losses of weapons and military equipment and soon felt the shortage of food and labor as well. War ministries set up boards to allocate labor on the home front and the battlefront and to give industrialists financial incentives to encourage productivity. The Russian bureaucracy, however, only cooperated halfheartedly with industrialists and other groups that could aid the war effort. In several countries, emergency measures allowed the drafting of both men and women for military or industrial service. Desperate for factory workers, the Germans forced Belgian citizens to move to Germany, housing them in prison camps. In rural Russia, Austria-Hungary, Bulgaria, and Serbia, youths, women, and old men struggled to sustain farms without government help.

Throughout Europe, governments passed sedition laws that made it a crime to criticize the war or official policies. To ensure civilian acceptance of longer working hours and shortages of consumer goods, governments created propaganda agencies to advertise the war as a patriotic mission to resist villainous enemies. British propagandists fabricated atrocities that the German "Huns" supposedly committed against Belgians, and German propaganda warned that French African troops would rape German women if Germany was defeated. In Russia, Nicholas II changed the German-sounding name of the capital *St. Petersburg* to the Russian *Petrograd* as another patriotic move. World War I inflicted greater danger on civilians than mind control. Maintaining that Armenians in the Ottoman Empire

War Propaganda, 1915

"Never Forget!" screams the headline of this propaganda poster depicting an assaulted woman in despair. Intended to create outrage against the Germans, the poster suggests what German passage through neutral Belgium came to be called—"the rape of Belgium." Propaganda offices for the Allies sent out reports of women attacked and children massacred as the German armies moved through Belgian territory. **For more help analyzing this image, see the visual activity for this chapter in the Online Study Guide at** bedfordstmartins.com/huntconcise. (Mary Evans Picture Library.)

were plotting against the Central Powers, the Ottomans drove those Armenians living in Turkey from their homes, forcing them into landlessness where they starved or driving them into concentration camps or on long marches during which they simply died or were murdered. The Allies also caused the deaths of civilians en masse when they created famines by blockading the Syrian provinces of the Ottoman Empire in hopes that people there would rebel or die of starvation.

Extreme persecution of civilians along with the frightening propaganda often carried in the press made a compromise peace unlikely. Nonetheless, some individuals worked to end the war. In 1915, activists in the international women's movement met in The Hague to call for peace. "We can no longer endure . . . brute force as the only solution of international disputes," declared Dutch physician Aletta Jacobs. Many of these women spent the remainder of the war meeting with statesmen to urge them to seek peace, but with little success. In Austria-Hungary, nationalist groups agitating for ethnic self-determination hampered the empire's war effort. The Czechs undertook a vigorous anti-Habsburg campaign at home and abroad, while in the Balkans, the Croats, Slovenes, and Serbs formed a committee to plan a "South Slav" state independent of Austria-Hungary or any other power. The Allies encouraged such independence movements as part of their strategy to defeat the Habsburgs.

The war upset the social order as well as the political one. In the war's early days, many women lost their jobs when luxury shops, textile factories, and other nonessential establishments closed. But governments and businesses soon recognized the amount of labor it would take to wage a technological war. As more and more men left for the trenches, many women who had lost their jobs in nonessential businesses, as well as many low-paid domestic workers, took higher-paying jobs in formerly restricted munitions and metallurgical industries. In Warsaw women drove trucks, and in London they worked as streetcar conductors. Some young women nursed the wounded near the front lines.

Women's assumption of men's jobs looked to many like a sign of social disorder. In the words of one metalworker, women were "sending men to the slaughter." Men feared that women would remain in the workforce after the war, robbing men of their breadwinner role. Many people, even some women, objected to women's loss of femininity. "The feminine in me decreased more and more, and I did not know whether to be sad or glad about this," wrote one Russian nurse about wearing rough male clothing near the battlefield. Others criticized young female munitions workers for squandering their pay on ribbons and jewelry. The heated prewar debates over the "new woman" and gender roles returned.

Although soldiers from different backgrounds often felt bonds of solidarity in the trenches, difficult wartime conditions increasingly pitted civilians against one another on the home front. Whereas workers toiled longer hours while eating less, many in the upper classes still bought fancy food and fashionable clothing on the

A New Workforce in Wartime
With men at the front, women moved into factory work, doing jobs from which they had been unofficially barred before the war, as shown in this French photograph. In addition, tens of thousands of forced laborers from the colonies were moved to Europe to replace men sent to the front. The experience of forced labor during the war and service at the front politicized colonial peoples, fortifying independence movements in the postwar period. (Roget Viollet/Getty Images.)

black market (outside the official system of rationing). Governments allowed many businesses to make high rates of profit, a policy that made the cost of living soar and contributed to social tensions. Shortages of staples such as bread, sugar, and meat grew worse; Germans called the brutal winter of 1916–1917 "the turnip winter" because turnips were often the only food available. A German roof workers' association pleaded for relief: "We can no longer go on. Our children are starving." Reviving prewar hatred, some people blamed Jews for shortages. Colonial populations suffered the most oppressive working conditions. The French forcibly transported some 100,000 Vietnamese to work in France for the war effort. Africans also faced grueling forced labor along with skyrocketing taxes and prices. Civilian suffering during the war, whether in the colonies or at home in Europe, laid the groundwork for ordinary people to take political action.

REVIEW What factors contributed to making World War I a total war?

Protest, Revolution, and War's End, 1917–1918

By 1917, the situation was becoming desperate for everyone—the military, civilians, and politicians. Discontent on the home front started shaping the course of the war. Neither patriotic slogans before the war nor propaganda during it had prepared people for wartime suffering. Across Europe civilians rebelled, soldiers mutinied, and nationalist struggles continued to plague Britain and Austria-Hungary. Soon full-fledged revolution was sweeping Europe, toppling the Russian dynasty and threatening not just war but civil war as well.

War Protests

On February 1, 1917, the German government, hard-pressed by public clamor over mounting casualties and by the military's growing control over decision making, resumed unrestricted submarine warfare. The military promised that this campaign would end the war in six months by cutting off food and military supplies being sent to Britain and thus forcing the island nation to surrender before the United States could come to its rescue. Britain responded by mining its harbors and the seas and by developing the convoy system of shipping, in which a hundred or more warships and freighters traveling together could drive off German submarines. The Germans' gamble not only failed to defeat the British but also brought the United States into the war in April 1917 after German U-boats sank several American ships.

Political opposition increased in Europe, deteriorating living conditions sparked outright revolt by civilians, and the war effort threatened to fail, causing governments to send out peace feelers. Irish nationalists attacked government buildings in Dublin on Easter Monday 1916 in an effort to gain Ireland's independence from Britain. Ill-prepared, the rebels were easily defeated, and many of them were executed. In the cities of Italy, Russia, Germany, and Austria, women rioted to get food for their families. As inflation mounted, tenants conducted rent strikes, and factory hands and white-collar workers alike walked off the job. Amid these protests, Austria-Hungary secretly asked the Allies for a negotiated peace to avoid a total collapse of the empire. In the summer of 1917, the German Reichstag made overtures to the Allies for a "peace of understanding and permanent reconciliation of peoples." In January 1918, President Woodrow Wilson issued his **Fourteen Points**, a blueprint for a nonvindictive peace settlement held out to war-weary citizens of the Central Powers. By that time, however, French soldiers were mutinying against bloody and fruitless offensives, and in Russia wartime protests turned into outright revolution. "We are living on a volcano," warned one Italian politician in the spring of 1917.

Revolution and Civil War in Russia

The volcano erupted in Russia, which of all the warring nations had sustained the greatest number of casualties—7.5 million by 1917. Slaughter on the eastern front drove hundreds of thousands of peasants into the Russian interior, spreading hunger, homelessness, and disease. In March 1917, crowds of workingwomen swarmed the streets of Petrograd demanding relief from harsh conditions. They soon fell in with protestors commemorating International Women's Day and were then joined by factory workers and other civilians. Russia's economic underdevelopment hampered the government's ability to provide basic necessities on the home front. Instead of remaining loyal to the tsar, many soldiers were bitter about the massive casualties caused by their inferior weapons and their leaders' foolhardy tactics.

The incompetence of the government and Nicholas II's stubborn resistance to change had made the war even worse in Russia than elsewhere. Unlike other heads of state, Nicholas failed to unite the bureaucracy and the people in a single-minded wartime effort. Grigori Rasputin, a combination holy man and charlatan, manipulated Nicholas and his wife, Alexandra, by claiming to control their son's hemophilia. Rasputin's disastrous influence on state matters led influential leaders to question rather than support the government. The riots erupted in March 1917, and in a week Nicholas abdicated, as the three-hundred-year-old Romanov dynasty came to an abrupt end.

Aristocratic and middle-class politicians from the old Duma formed a new administration called the **Provisional Government**. At first, hopes were high that under the Provisional Government, as one revolutionary poet put it, "our false, filthy, boring, hideous life should become a just, pure, merry, and beautiful life." To survive, the Provisional Government had to pursue the war successfully, manage internal affairs better, and set government on a firm constitutional footing to establish its credibility. However, it did not rule alone, because other political forces developed during the Revolution. Among them were **soviets**—elected councils of workers and soldiers—which competed with the government for political support. Born during the Revolution of 1905, the soviets in 1917 campaigned to end the deference society usually paid the wealthy and military officers, urged respect for workers and the poor, and temporarily gave an air of celebration to the current political upheaval. The peasants, also competing for power, began to confiscate landed estates and withhold agricultural products from the market because consumer goods, for which they would normally exchange food, were lacking. As a result, urban food shortages worsened.

In hopes of further destabilizing Russia, the Germans in April 1917 provided safe rail transportation for Lenin and other prominent Bolsheviks in exile to return to Russia through German territory. Lenin had devoted his entire existence to bringing about socialism through the force of his small band of Bolsheviks. Upon his return to Petrograd, he issued the April Theses, a radical document that called for Russia to withdraw from the war, for the soviets to seize power on behalf of workers and poor peasants, and for all private land to be nationalized. The Bolsheviks aimed to supplant the Provisional Government with the slogans "All power to the soviets" and "Peace, land, and bread."

Lenin Addressing the Second All-Russian Congress of Soviets
In the spring of 1917, the German government craftily let Lenin and other Bolsheviks travel from their exile in Switzerland back to the scene of the unfolding revolution in Russia. A committed revolutionary instead of a political reformer, Lenin used oratory and skillful maneuvering to convince many in the soviets to follow him in overthrowing the Provisional Government, taking Russia out of the war, and implementing his brand of communism. (RIA Novosti.)

Time was running out for the Provisional Government, which saw a battlefield victory as the only way to ensure its survival. On July 1, the Russian army attacked the Austrians in Galicia but was defeated once again (Map 20.1, page 784). The new prime minister, Aleksandr Kerensky, used ringing oratory to arouse patriotism, but he lacked the political skills to create an effective wartime government. In November, the Bolshevik leadership, urged on by Lenin, seized power on behalf of the soviets while simultaneously asserting its own right to form a government. In January 1918, elections for a constituent assembly failed to give the Bolsheviks a plurality, so the party used troops to take over the government completely. The Bolsheviks seized town and city administrations, and in the winter of 1918–1919, the new government, observing Marxist doctrine, abolished private property and nationalized factories in order to increase production. The Provisional Government had allowed both men and women to vote in 1917, making Russia the first great power to legalize universal suffrage. This was a hollow privilege, once the Bolsheviks limited candidates to chosen members of the Communist Party.

The Bolsheviks asked Germany for peace and agreed to the Treaty of Brest-Litovsk (March 1918), which placed vast regions of the old Russian Empire under German occupation (Map 20.2). Because the loss of millions of square miles put Petrograd at risk, the Bolsheviks relocated the capital to Moscow. They formally adopted the name Communists (taken from Marx's writings) to distinguish themselves from the socialists or Social Democrats. Lenin called the catastrophic terms of the treaty "obscene," but he accepted them not only because he had promised to bring peace to Russia but also because he believed that the rest of Europe would soon rebel against the war and overthrow the capitalist order.

A full-blown civil war now broke out in Russia, with the pro-Bolsheviks (or "Reds") facing an array of antirevolutionary forces (the "Whites"). Among the

Map 20.2 The Russian Civil War, 1917–1922
Nationalists, aristocrats, middle-class citizens, and property-owning peasants tried to combine their interests to defeat the Bolsheviks, but they failed to create an effective political consensus. The result was more suffering for ordinary people, whose agricultural products were confiscated to fight the civil war. The Western powers and Japan also sent in troops to put down this revolution that so threatened the economic and political order.

Whites, the tsarist military leadership, composed mainly of landlords and supporters of aristocratic rule, used whatever troops it could muster. Businessmen whose property had been nationalized and liberal intellectuals soon lent their support to the Whites. Many non-Russian nationalities, formerly brought into the empire through force, fought the Bolsheviks because they saw this as a chance for independence. Before World War I ended, Russia's former allies, notably the United States, Britain, France, and Japan, landed troops in the country both to block the Germans and to stop the Bolsheviks. The counterrevolutionary groups lacked a strong leader and unified goals, however. Instead, the groups competed with one another: the pro-tsarist forces, for example, alienated those wanting independent nation-state status, such as the Ukrainians, Estonians, and Lithuanians, by stressing the goal of restoring the Russian Empire. Even with the presence of Allied troops, the opponents of revolution could not defeat the Bolsheviks without a common purpose or a unified command.

The civil war shaped Russian communism. Leon Trotsky, Bolshevik commissar of war, built the highly disciplined Red Army by ending democratic procedures, such as the election of officers, which had originally attracted soldiers to Bolshevism. Lenin and Trotsky introduced the policy of war communism, whereby urban workers and troops moved through the countryside, brutally seizing grain from the peasants to feed the civil war army and workforce. The Cheka (secret police) imprisoned political opponents and black marketers and often shot them without bothering with a trial. The bureaucracy, the Cheka, and the Red Army all grew in size and strength. The result was a more authoritarian government—a development that broke with Marx's promise that revolution would bring a "withering away" of the state.

As the Bolsheviks clamped down on opposition during the bloody civil war, they organized their supporters to foster revolutionary Marxism across Europe. In March 1919, they founded the Third International, also known as the Comintern (Communist International), to replace the old Second International with a centralized organization dedicated to preaching communism. By mid-1921, the Red Army had defeated the Whites in the Crimea, the Caucasus, and the Muslim borderlands in central Asia. After ousting the Japanese from Siberia in 1922, the Bolsheviks were in charge of a state as multinational as the old Russian Empire had been (Map 20.2, page 794). Although the revolution had brought down the inept Romanovs and the privileged aristocracy, the civil war and the resulting hunger and disease took millions of lives. Meanwhile, the Bolsheviks had made brutality, which was at odds with socialist promises for a humane and flourishing society, their political style.

Ending the War, 1918

With Russia out of the war, Europe's leaders faced a new balance of military force. In the spring of 1918, the Central Powers made one final attempt to smash through the Allied lines, but the offensive ground to a bloody halt within weeks. By then, the British and French had started making limited but effective use of tanks supported by airplanes. Although the first tanks were cumbersome, their ability to withstand machine-gun fire made offensive attacks possible. In the summer of 1918, the Allies, now reinforced by the Americans, pushed back the Germans all along the western front and headed toward Germany. The German armies, suffering more than two million casualties between spring and summer, rapidly disintegrated.

By October 1918, the desperate German command had helped create a civilian government to take over on the home front. As these inexperienced politicians took power, they were also taking the blame for the defeat. Shifting the blame from the military, the generals proclaimed themselves still fully capable of winning the war. Weak-willed civilians, they claimed, had dealt the military a "stab in the back" that would force Germany's surrender. Amid this outright lying, naval officers called for a final sea battle, but the order triggered a mutiny against what sailors saw as a suicide mission. The sailors' revolt spread to workers in Berlin, Munich, and other major German cities. The uprisings led Social Democratic politicians to declare a German republic in an effort to prevent a revolution. At the end of October, the Czechs and Slovaks declared an independent state, and the Croatian parliament simultaneously announced Croatia's independence. On November 9, 1918, Kaiser William II fled as the Central Powers collapsed on all fronts. Finally, on November 11, 1918, an armistice was signed, and the guns fell silent.

In the course of four years, European civilization had been sorely tested, if not shattered. Conservative figures put the battlefield toll at ten million deaths and thirty million wounded, incapacitated, or doomed eventually to die of their wounds. In every European combatant country, industrial and agricultural production had plummeted, and much of the reduced output had been put to military use. Parts of Asia, Africa, and the Americas, which depended on European trade, felt the painful impact of Europe's decline. In 1918 and 1919, the weakened global population suffered an influenza epidemic that left as many as one hundred million more dead.

Moral questioning filled the media and private discussions alike. Soldiers returning home flooded the book market with their memoirs, trying to give meaning to their experiences. Whereas many had begun by emphasizing heroism and glory, others were cynical and bitter by war's end. They insisted that the fighting had been absolutely meaningless. Total war had drained society of resources and population and had sown the seeds of future catastrophes.

REVIEW Why did people revolt during World War I, and what turned revolt into outright revolution in Russia?

The Search for Peace in an Era of Revolution

The war was over, but revolutionary fervor now swept the continent of Europe, especially in the former empires of Germany and Austria-Hungary. Until 1921, a widespread triumph for socialism seemed plausible; many of the newly independent peoples of eastern and central Europe fervently supported socialist principles. The revolutionary mood infected workers and peasants in Germany, too. In contrast, many liberal and right-wing opponents hoped for a political order based on military authority of the kind they had relied on during the war. Faced with uprisings by radicals from both right and left, diplomats from around the world arrived in Paris in January 1919 to negotiate the terms of peace, often without recognizing the fact that the war was still going on, not only in city streets where soldiers were bringing the war home, but also in people's hearts.

Europe in Turmoil

Urban citizens and returning soldiers ignited the protest that swept Europe in 1918 and 1919. In January 1919, the red flag of socialist revolution flew from the city hall in Glasgow, Scotland, while in cities of the collapsing Austro-Hungarian monarchy, workers set up councils to direct factory production and influence politics. After the armistice, soldiers in many parts of Europe did not disband but instead formed volunteer armies, preventing a return to peacetime politics.

Germany was especially unstable, partly because of the shock of defeat. Independent socialist groups and workers' councils fought the dominant Social Democrats for control of the government, and workers and veterans took to the streets to demand food and back pay. Whereas in 1848 revolutionaries had marched to city hall or the king's residence, these protesters took over newspapers and telegraph offices to control the flow of information. One of the most radical socialist factions, the Spartacists, was led by cofounders Karl Liebknecht and Rosa Luxemburg. Unlike Lenin, the two Spartacist leaders favored political uprisings that would give workers political experience rather than simply following an all-knowing party leadership. They shared Lenin's dislike of parliamentary politics, but they argued for direct worker control of institutions.

Social Democratic leader Friedrich Ebert, who headed the new government, rejected revolution and supported the creation of a parliamentary republic to replace the monarchy. Splitting with his former socialist allies, he called on the German army and the Freikorps—a roving paramilitary band of students, demobilized soldiers, and others—to suppress the workers' councils and demonstrators. He thus appeared to endorse the idea that political differences could be settled with violence. "The enthusiasm is marvelous," wrote one young soldier. "No mercy's shown. We shoot even the wounded. . . . We were much more humane against the French in the field." Members of the Freikorps hunted down Luxemburg and Liebknecht and murdered them.

Violence continued even as a constituent assembly meeting in the city of Weimar in February 1919 approved a constitution and founded a parliamentary republic called the **Weimar Republic**. The military leadership dreamed of a restored monarchy and rebelled. "As I love Germany, so I hate the Republic," wrote one officer. Facing a military coup by Freikorps officers, Ebert called for a general strike. This action blocked a takeover by showing the lack of popular support for a military regime. In so doing, the Weimar Republic set a dangerous precedent: it relied on street violence and paramilitary groups rather than parliaments to solve political problems.

Revolutionary activism surged and was smashed. Late in the winter of 1919, leftists proclaimed "soviet republics"—governments led by workers' councils—in Bavaria and Hungary. Volunteer armies and troops soon put the soviets down. The Bolsheviks tried to establish a Marxist regime in Poland in the belief that its people wanted a workers' revolution. Instead, the Poles resisted and drove the Red Army back in 1920, while the Allied powers rushed supplies and advisers to Warsaw (Map 20.2, page 794). Though this and other revolts failed, they provided further proof that total war had let loose political and social disorder.

The Paris Peace Conference, 1919–1920

As political turmoil plagued peoples from Berlin to Moscow, the Paris Peace Conference opened in January 1919. Visions of communism spreading westward haunted the conference, but the assembled statesmen were also focused on the reconstruction of a secure Europe and the status of Germany. Leaders such as French premier Georges Clemenceau had to satisfy their angry citizens, who demanded revenge or, at the very least, money to rebuild and pay their nation's war debts. France had lost 1.3 million people—almost an entire generation of young men—as well as more than a million buildings, six thousand bridges, and thousands of miles of railroad tracks and roads. Great Britain's representative, Prime Minister David Lloyd George, had caught the mood of the British public by campaigning in 1918 with slogans such as "Hang the kaiser." The Italians arrived on the scene demanding the territory promised to them in the 1915 Treaty of London. Meanwhile, U.S. president Woodrow Wilson, head of the new world power that had helped achieve the Allied victory, had his own agenda. His Fourteen Points, on which the truce had been based, were steeped in the language of freedom and called for open diplomacy, arms reduction, and the right for nationality groups to have their own government.

The Fourteen Points did not represent the mood of the victors. Allied propaganda had made the Germans seem like inhuman monsters, and many citizens in the Allied countries demanded a harsh peace. In addition, some military experts feared that Germany was using the armistice only as an opportunity to regroup for more warfare. Indeed, the German people widely refused to admit that their army had lost the war. Eager for army support, Ebert had given returning soldiers a victors' welcome: "As you return unconquered from the field of battle, I salute you." Wilson's former allies campaigned to make him look naive and unrealistic. "Wilson bores me with his Fourteen Points," Clemenceau complained. "Why, the good Lord himself has only ten."

Nevertheless, the Fourteen Points persuaded Germans that the settlement would not be vindictive. Wilson's commitment to *settlement* as opposed to *surrender* wisely recognized that Germany was still the strongest state on the continent, and he pushed for a treaty that balanced the strengths and interests of all the European powers. Economists and other experts accompanying Wilson to Paris agreed that if Germany was dealt with harshly and humiliated, it might soon become vengeful and chaotic—a lethal combination.

After six months, the statesmen and their teams of experts produced the **Peace of Paris** (1919–1920), a cluster of individual treaties that shocked the countries that had to accept them. The treaties separated Austria from Hungary, reduced Hungary by almost two-thirds of its inhabitants and three-quarters of its territory, broke up the Ottoman Empire, and treated Germany severely (Map 20.3). They replaced the Habsburg Empire with a group of small, internally divided, and relatively weak states: Czechoslovakia, Poland, and the Kingdom of the Serbs, Croats, and Slovenes, soon renamed Yugoslavia. After a century and a half of partition, Poland was reconstructed from parts of Russia, Germany, and Austria-Hungary; one-third of its population was ethnically non-Polish. The statesmen in Paris also created the Polish Corridor, which connected Poland to the Baltic Sea and separated East Prussia from the rest of Germany. In general, the new states were politically and economically weak. Austria and Hungary were left reeling at their loss of territory and resources.

The Treaty of Versailles, the centerpiece of the Peace of Paris, dealt specifically with Germany. Under this treaty, France recovered Alsace and Lorraine, and the Allies would temporarily occupy the left, or western, bank of the Rhine River and the coal-rich Saar basin. Wilson accepted his European allies' expectations that Germany would pay substantial reparations for civilian damage during the war. The specific amount was set in 1921 at the crushing sum of 132 billion gold marks. Germany also had to reduce its army, almost eliminate its navy, stop manufacturing offensive weapons, and deliver a large amount of free coal each year to Belgium and France. Furthermore, it was forbidden to have an air force and had to give up its colonies. The average German saw in these terms an unmerited humiliation that was compounded by Article 231 of the treaty, which described Germany's "responsibility" for damage "imposed . . . by the aggression of Germany and her allies." Outraged Germans interpreted this as a "war guilt" clause, which blamed Germany for the war and allowed the victors to collect reparations from their economically developed country rather than from the ruined Austria. War guilt made Germany an outcast in the community of nations.

Besides redrawing the map of Europe, the Peace of Paris set up an organization called the **League of Nations**, whose members had a joint responsibility for maintaining peace—a principle called collective security. It was supposed to replace the divisive secrecy of prewar power politics. As part of Wilson's vision, the league would guide the world toward disarmament and arbitrate its members' disputes. The U.S. Senate, rejecting the idea of collective security, failed to ratify the peace settlement and refused to join the league. Moreover, Germany and Russia were initially excluded from the league and thus were blocked from working cooperatively with the league.

The covenant, or charter, of the League of Nations also organized the administration of the former colonies and territories of Germany and the Ottoman Empire—such as Togo, Cameroon, Syria, and Palestine—through a system of mandates (see "Mapping the West," page 821). The European powers exercised political control, or

Map 20.3 Europe and the Middle East after the Peace Settlements of 1919–1920
The political landscape of central, eastern, and east-central Europe changed dramatically as a result of the Russian Revolution and the Peace of Paris. The Ottoman, German, Russian, and Austro-Hungarian empires were either broken up into multiple small states or reduced in size. The settlement bred resentment among Germans, Austrians, and Hungarians and created a group of weak, struggling nations in the heartland of Europe. The victorious powers took over much of the oil-rich Middle East. **For more help analyzing this map, see the map activity for this chapter in the Online Study Guide at** bedfordstmartins.com/huntconcise.

mandates, over these territories, while local leaders retained limited authority. The league covenant justified the mandate system as providing governance by "advanced nations" over territories "not yet able to stand by themselves under the strenuous conditions of the modern world." The people in these territories, many of whom had served on the battlefield during the war, were enraged by the mandates and began to challenge the claims of their European masters. They had seen how savage and degraded these people who claimed to be racially superior leaders of global culture could be. "Never again will the darker people of the world occupy just the place they had before," the African American leader W. E. B. Du Bois predicted in 1918. Yet the mandate system kept imperialism alive, and like the Peace of Paris, it aroused anger and resistance.

Economic and Diplomatic Consequences of the Peace

Just as wartime conditions, including military action, continued after the armistice, so the Peace of Paris posed problems in the 1920s and beyond. Western leaders faced two related issues in the aftermath of the war: economic recovery and preserving peace. In regard to economic recovery, France, the hardest hit by the war and billions of dollars in debt to the United States, estimated that Germany owed it at least $200 billion. Britain, by contrast, had not been physically devastated and was worried instead about maintaining its empire and restoring trade with Germany, not about exacting huge reparations to rebuild. Both, however, were dependent on German funds to pay their war debts to the United States because European income from world trade had plunged during the war.

Germany claimed that the demand for reparations strained its government, which was already facing political upheaval. But Germany's economic problems had not begun with the Peace of Paris but with the kaiser's policy of not raising taxes, especially on the rich, to pay for the war, leaving the new German republic with a staggering war debt. Now this republic, an experiment in democracy, needed to win over its citizens, not anger them by hiking taxes. When Germany refused in 1921 to present a realistic payment scheme to the former Allies, the French occupied several cities in the Ruhr basin until a settlement was reached.

At odds with the powers to the west, the German government turned to eastern Europe for support. Germany reached an agreement on establishing economic ties with Russia, which was desperate for western trade, in the Treaty of Rapallo (1922). Meanwhile, Germany's relations with powers to the west continued to deteriorate. In 1923, after Germany defaulted on coal deliveries, the French and Belgians sent troops into the Ruhr, planning to use its abundant resources to recoup their wartime expenditures. Urged on by the German government, the people there fought back, shutting down production by staying home from work. The government printed trillions of marks to support the workers and to pay its own war debts, with practically worthless currency. Soon Germany was experiencing staggering inflation, which not only demoralized its citizens but also gravely threatened the international economy. At one point, a single U.S. dollar was worth 4.42 trillion marks, and wheelbarrows of money were required to buy a turnip. Negotiations to resolve this chaos resulted in the Dawes Plan (1924) and the Young Plan (1929), which reduced payments to more realistic levels and restored the German currency. In the meantime, people's savings had been wiped out, and more and more Germans were turning against their democratic government.

In addition to economic recovery, a second burning issue involved ensuring a lasting peace. Statesmen determined that peace needed disarmament, a return of Germany to the community of European nations, and security for the new countries of eastern Europe. Hard diplomatic bargaining produced two plans in Germany's favor. At the Washington Conference in 1921, the United States, Great Britain, Japan, France, and Italy agreed to reduce their numbers of battleships and to stop constructing new ones for ten years. Four years later, in 1925, the League of Nations sponsored a meeting of the great powers, including Germany, at Locarno, Switzerland. The Treaty of Locarno provided Germany with a seat in the league as of 1926. In return, Germany agreed not to violate the borders of France and Belgium and to keep the nearby Rhineland demilitarized (unfortified by troops).

To the east, statesmen feared German attempts to regain territory lost to Poland, to form a merger with Austria, or to launch aggression against the states spun off from Austria-Hungary (Map 20.3, page 800). To meet this threat, Czechoslovakia, Yugoslavia, and Romania formed the Little Entente in 1920–1921—a collective security agreement to protect themselves from Germany and Russia. Then, between 1924 and 1927, France allied itself with the Little Entente and with Poland. In 1928, sixty nations, including the major European powers, Japan, and the United States, signed the Kellogg-Briand Pact, which formally rejected international violence. The pact lacked any guarantee or mechanism for enforcement and thus resembled, as one critic put it, "an international kiss."

The publicity surrounding the international agreements during the 1920s sharply contrasted with old-style diplomacy, which had been conducted in secret and subject to little public scrutiny. The development of a system of open, collective security suggested a diplomatic revolution that would promote international peace. Yet openness in negotiations also allowed diplomats to feed the press reports designed to provoke the masses. For example, the press and politicians whipped German citizens into a nationalist fury whenever Germany's diplomats appeared to compromise, even though compromise actually helped undo the Treaty of Versailles. Right-wing journalists who hated republican government used international meetings such as the one at Locarno to fire up political hatreds and undermine the goal of collective security.

REVIEW What were the major outcomes of the postwar peacemaking process?

A Decade of Recovery: Europe in the 1920s

During the 1920s, towns and villages built their monuments to the Great War, and battlefield tourism sprang up for veterans and for families in search of a son's or father's resting place. The wartime spirit endured in words and phrases from the battlefield that became part of everyday speech. Before the war, the word *lousy* had meant "lice-infested," but English-speaking soldiers returning from the trenches now applied it to anything bad. Raincoats became *trench coats,* and military terms such as *bombarded* and *rank and file* entered civilian talk. Maimed, disfigured veterans were present everywhere, and while some received prostheses designed by Jules Amar, others without limbs were sometimes carried in baskets—hence the expression *basket case.*

Total war had generally strengthened military values and authoritarian government. Four autocratic governments—those in Germany, Austria-Hungary, Russia, and the Ottoman Empire—had collapsed as a result of the war, but whether these states would become workable democracies remained a burning question. During the war, the European economy lost many of its international markets to India, Canada, Australia, Japan, and the United States. Now worldwide economic competition with these new players also threatened European recovery. Although contemporaries referred to the 1920s as the Roaring Twenties and the Jazz Age, the sense of cultural release masked the serious problems of restoring social stability and implementing democracy. The real challenge of the 1920s was coming to terms with the grim legacy of the war.

Changes in the Political Landscape

The collapse of autocratic governments and the widespread extension of suffrage to women brought political turmoil as well as the expansion of democracy. Women's suffrage resulted in part from decades of activism, but many men in government claimed that suffrage was a "reward" for women's war efforts. In the first postwar elections, women were voted into parliaments, and the impression grew that they had also made extraordinary gains in the workplace. French men pointedly denied women the vote, however, insisting that women would use their votes to bring back the rule of kings and priests. (Only at the end of World War II did France and Italy extend suffrage to women.) The welfare state also expanded, with payments being made to veterans and to victims of workplace accidents. These

Women Gain Suffrage in the West

1906	Finland
1913	Norway
1915	Denmark, Iceland
1917	Netherlands, Russia
1918	Czechoslovakia, Great Britain (limited suffrage)
1919	Germany
1920	Austria, United States
1921	Poland
1925	Hungary (limited suffrage)
1945	Italy, France
1971	Switzerland

benefits stemmed from the belief that more evenly distributed wealth, sometimes called economic democracy, would prevent the outbreak of revolution.

The trend toward economic democracy was not easy to maintain, as the cycles of boom and bust that had characterized the late nineteenth century reemerged. A short postwar boom prompted by reconstruction and consumer spending was followed by an economic downturn that was most severe between 1920 and 1922. By the mid-1920s, many of the economic opportunities for women had disappeared, and they made up a smaller percentage of the workforce than in 1913. Veterans were especially angered by economic insecurity after their years of enduring the war's horrors, and skyrocketing unemployment resulted in more anger toward governments.

The new republics of eastern Europe were especially unprepared for hard economic times and were poorly equipped to compete in the world market. None but Czechoslovakia had a mature industrial sector, and agricultural techniques were often primitive. But more pressing problems hampered them. Vast migrations occurred as some one million people escaped the civil war in Russia and 800,000 soldiers from the defeated Whites searched for safety. Two million people fled Turkey, Greece, and Bulgaria because the postwar settlement called for the new nations to be built along "nationality" lines. One statesman called this "a great unmixing of populations." Hundreds of thousands of migrants landed in new nations with populations most closely resembling their own ethnic groups. Hungary, for example, had to receive 300,000 people of Magyar ethnicity who were no longer welcome in Romania, Czechoslovakia, or Yugoslavia. Most of these refugees lacked land or jobs. They had nothing to do "but loaf and starve," one English reporter observed of refugees in Bulgaria, and as a result conflict and chaos haunted postwar eastern Europe.

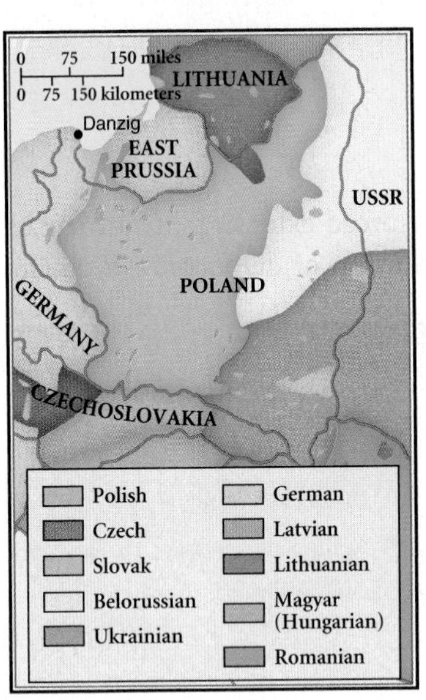

National Minorities in Postwar Poland

A reunified Poland showed how postwar turmoil could destroy the new nation's parliamentary democracy. One-third of the population consisted of Ukrainians, Belorussians, Germans, and other ethnic minorities—many of whom had grievances against the dominant Poles. Religious, dynastic, and cultural traditions also divided the Poles, who for 150 years had been split among Austria, Germany, and Russia. Polish reunification occurred without a common currency, political structure, or language. Even the railroad tracks were not a standard size. Under a new constitution that professed equal rights for all ethnicities and religions, the Sejm (parliament) tried to divide large estates among the peasantry, but declining crop prices and overpopulation made life in the countryside difficult. The economic downturn brought strikes and violence in 1922–1923. Ultimately former military leader Jozef Pilsudski responded to the disorder with a coup in 1926—a strongman solution that would become more common elsewhere in Europe and the world.

Germany was a different case, although it too received a flood of refugees from the east. Although the German economy picked up and Germany became a center of experimentation in the arts, political life remained unstable because so many people felt nostalgia for imperial glory and associated the Versailles treaty with the Weimar Republic. Extremist politicians heaped daily abuse on Weimar's parliamentary government. A wealthy newspaper and film tycoon called anyone cooperating with the parliamentary system "a moral cripple." Right-wing parties favored violence rather than consensus building, and nationalist gangs murdered democratic leaders and Jews. The Communists, feeling their muscle, jumped into street brawls too.

Support for the far right came from wealthy landowners and businessmen, white-collar workers whose standard of living had dropped during the war, and members of the lower-middle and middle classes hurt by inflation. Bands of discontented youths and veterans proliferated, among them a group called the Brown Shirts. Their leader was an ex-soldier, political newcomer, and riveting speaker named Adolf Hitler (1889–1945), a favorite among antigovernment crowds. In the wake of the Ruhr occupation of 1923, Hitler and German military leader Erich Ludendorff launched a coup from a beer hall in Munich. Government troops suppressed the Beer Hall Putsch; Hitler spent less than a year in jail, and Ludendorff was acquitted. To conservative judges, former aristocrats, and most of the prewar bureaucrats who still staffed the government, such men were national heroes.

In France and Britain, parties of the right had less effect than elsewhere because representative institutions were better established and the upper classes were not plotting to restore an authoritarian monarchy. In France, politicians from the conservative right and moderate left successively formed coalitions and rallied general support to rebuild war-torn regions and to force Germany to pay for the reconstruction. Hoping to stimulate population growth after the country's devastating loss of life, the French parliament made distributing birth-control information illegal and abortion a severely punished crime.

Britain encountered postwar boom and bust and continuing conflict in Ireland. Ramsay MacDonald, elected the first Labour prime minister, in 1924, represented the political strength of workers. Like other postwar British leaders, he had to face the fact that although Britain had the largest world empire, many of its industries were obsolete or in poor condition. A showdown came in the ailing coal industry, where prices fell and wages plummeted once the Ruhr mines reopened and began to compete with Britain again. On May 3, 1926, workers launched a nine-day general strike against wage cuts and dangerous conditions in the mines. The strike prompted unprecedented middle-class resistance. University students, homemakers, and businessmen shut down the strike by driving trains, working on docks, and replacing workers in other jobs. Citizens from many walks of life revived the wartime spirit to defeat those who appeared to them to be attacking the national economy.

In Ireland, the British government's continuing failure to allow home rule provoked bloody confrontations. In January 1919, republican leaders declared Ireland's independence from Britain and created a separate parliament. The British government refused to recognize the parliament and sent in the Black and Tans, a volunteer army of demobilized soldiers named for the color of their uniforms. Terror reigned in Ireland, as both the pro-independence forces and the Black and Tans waged guerrilla warfare, taking hostages, blowing up buildings, and even shooting into crowds at soccer matches. By 1921, public outcry forced the British to negotiate a treaty. It reversed the Irish declaration of independence and made the Irish Free State a self-governing dominion owing allegiance to the British crown. Northern Ireland, a group of six northern counties referred to as Ulster and containing a majority of Protestants, gained a separate status: it became self-governing but still had representation in the British Parliament. The settlement left bitter discontent; violence soon erupted again.

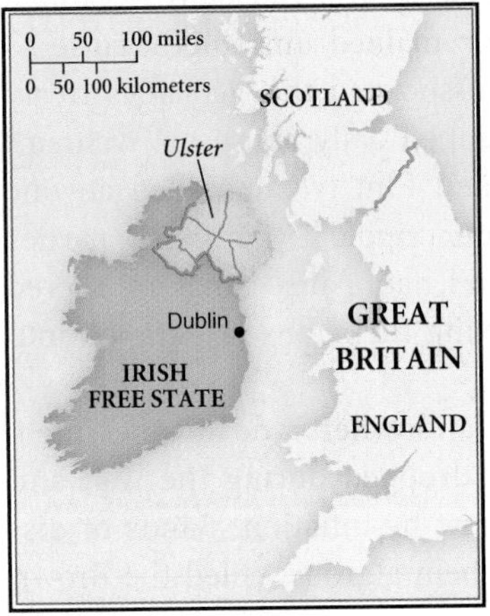

The Irish Free State and Ulster, 1921

War changed everything in the colonies, too. Colonized peoples who had fought in the war expected more rights and even independence. Indeed, European politicians and military recruiters had actually promised them the vote and other reforms in exchange for their support. These peoples' political activism, now boosted by increasing education, trade, and experience with the West, mostly met with a brutal response. British forces massacred protesters at Amritsar in India in 1919 and put down revolts against the mandate system in Egypt and Iran in the early 1920s. The Dutch jailed political leaders in Indonesia; the French punished Indochinese nationalists. For many Western governments, maintaining empires abroad was crucial to ensuring democracy at home, for any hint of declining national prestige fed antidemocratic forces.

Despite such resistance, the 1920s marked the high tide of imperialism. Britain and France, enjoying new access to Germany's colonies in Africa and the territories of the fallen Ottoman Empire in the Middle East, were at the height of their global power. No matter how battered they were by the war, all the imperial powers took advantage of the growing profitability that enterprise around the world could bring. Middle Eastern and Indonesian oil increasingly heated homes and fueled the growing numbers of automobiles, airplanes, trucks, ships, and buses. Products such as chocolate and tropical fruit became regular items in Westerners' diets, and some businessmen built fortunes by selling these products from the colonies.

Reconstructing the Economy

The war had weakened European economies and allowed newcomers and rivals—Japan, India, the United States, Australia, and Canada—to flourish in their place. At the same time, the war had forced European manufacturing to become more efficient and had expanded the demand for automotive and air transport, electrical products, and synthetic goods. The prewar pattern of mergers and cartels continued after 1918, giving rise to gigantic food-processing firms such as Nestlé in Switzerland and petroleum enterprises such as Royal Dutch Shell. Owners of these large manufacturing conglomerates wielded more financial and political power than entire small countries. By the late 1920s, Europe had overcome the wild economic swings of the immediate postwar years and was enjoying renewed economic prosperity.

Some European businesspeople recognized that the United States had become the trendsetter in economic modernization. Many made pilgrimages to the Ford Motor Company's Detroit assembly line, which by 1929 produced a Ford automobile every ten seconds. Increased productivity, founder Henry Ford pointed out, resulted in a lower cost of living and increased purchasing power for workers. Whereas France, Germany, and Britain combined had fewer than two million cars, some seventeen million cars were on U.S. streets in 1925, reinforcing Ford's point.

Scientific management also aimed to raise productivity. American efficiency expert Frederick Taylor developed methods to streamline workers' tasks and movements for maximum productivity. European industrialists adopted Taylor's methods during the war and after, but they were also influenced by European psychologists who emphasized the mental aspects of productivity and the need to balance work and leisure activities. In theory, increased productivity not only produced prosperity for all but also helped unite workers and management in a common purpose, avoiding Russian-style worker revolution. For many workers, however, the emphasis on efficiency seemed inhumane; in some workplaces, the restrictions on time and motion were so severe that workers were allowed to use the bathroom only on a fixed schedule. "When I left the factory, it followed me," wrote one worker. "In my dreams I was a machine."

The managerial sector in industry had expanded during the war and continued to do so thereafter. Workers' initiative became devalued; managers alone were seen as creative and innovative. Managers reorganized work procedures and classified workers' skills. They categorized work that required less skill as "female jobs" that deserved lower wages, thus adapting the old segmentation of the labor market to the new working conditions. With male workers' jobs increasingly threatened by laborsaving machines, unions usually agreed with management to hold down women's wages to keep women from competing with men for high-paying jobs. Like the managerial sector, union bureaucracy had ballooned during World War I to help monitor labor's part in the war. Union bureaucrats became specialists: negotiators, membership organizers, educators and propagandists, and political liaisons.

Playing a key role in political life, they could mobilize masses of people, as they demonstrated when they blocked coups against the Weimar government in the 1920s and organized the general strike in Great Britain in 1926.

Restoring Society

Postwar society met the returning millions of brutalized, incapacitated, and shell-shocked veterans with combined joy and apprehension. Civilian concerns were often valid. Tens of thousands of German, central European, and Italian soldiers refused to disband; some British veterans vandalized university classrooms and assaulted women workers. Many veterans harbored hostility toward civilians, some of whom had protested against wartime conditions instead of patriotically enduring them. The world to which the veterans returned differed from the one they had left. The war had blurred some class distinctions, giving rise to the belief that life would be fairer. Massive battlefield casualties had made it possible for commoners to become officers, suggesting greater postwar openness. British author Rudyard Kipling, whose son had been killed on the battlefield, was among those who influenced the decision that the mass graves of British soldiers killed in the war, whether rich or poor, would be marked as individual ones by identical, evenly spaced crosses in military cemeteries. Wealth, he maintained, should not allow some to "proclaim their grief above other people's grief" when all had died for the same cause.

In contrast to their expectations, however, returning veterans often had no jobs open to them, and some found that their wives and sweethearts had abandoned them. Veterans faced other changes: middle-class women did their own housework, because former servants could earn more money in factories, and greater numbers of middle-class women worked outside the home. Women of all classes cut their hair short, wore sleeker clothes, and had money of their own because of war work. Patriotic when war erupted, civilians sometimes felt estranged from returning warriors, who had inflicted so much death and had lived daily with filth, rats, and decaying animal and human flesh. Women who had served at the front had seen the soldiers' experiences firsthand and could sympathize with them. But many suffragists in Britain, for instance, who had fought for greater equality in men's and women's lives before the war now reembraced separate spheres, so fearful were they of returning veterans.

Governments tried to improve civilian life to reintegrate men into society and to reduce the appeal of communism. Politicians believed in the calming power of family life and supported social programs such as veterans' pensions, benefits for out-of-work men, and housing for veterans. The new housing—"homes for heroes," as politicians called the program—was an improvement over nineteenth-century working-class tenements. In Vienna, Frankfurt, Berlin, and Stockholm, modern housing projects provided common laundries, day-care centers, and rooms for socializing. They featured gardens, terraces, and balconies to provide a soothing,

Le Corbusier's Paris of the Future

While the war profoundly disillusioned many in the West, peace aroused utopian hopes for a better future. For modern architects like Swiss-born Le Corbusier, the "future city" and the "radiant city" would organize space, and thus life, for ordinary people. Horizontal windows, roof gardens, and plain facades were hallmarks of this new design—a dramatic break with the ornate prewar building styles. (Fondation Le Corbusier/© 2010 Artists Rights Society [ARS], NY/ADAGP, Paris/FLC.)

country atmosphere. Inside they boasted modern kitchens, indoor plumbing, central heating, and electricity.

Despite government efforts to restore family life, the war had dissolved many middle-class conventions, among them attempts to keep unmarried young men and women apart. Freer relationships and more open discussions of sex characterized the 1920s. Middle-class youths of both sexes visited jazz clubs and attended movies together. Revealing bathing suits, short skirts, and body-hugging clothing emphasized women's sexuality, seeming to invite men and women to join together and replenish the postwar population. In the long run, though, the context for sexuality remained marriage. British scientist Marie Stopes published the best seller *Married Love* in 1918, and the wildly successful *Ideal Marriage: Its Physiology and Technique* by Dutch author Theodor van de Velde appeared in 1927. Both described sex in glowing terms and offered precise information about birth control and sexual physiology. Changing ideas about sex were not limited to the middle and upper classes. One Viennese reformer described working-class marriage as "an erotic-comradely relationship of equals" rather than the economic partnership of past centuries. The flapper, a sexually liberated working woman, surpassed the dedicated housewife as representing the ordinary woman. Meanwhile, British writer D. H. Lawrence and American author Ernest Hemingway glorified men's sexual vigor in, respectively,

The Flapper
This modern working woman smoking her cigarette stood for all that had changed—or was said to have changed—in the postwar world. Women worked and had money of their own, were out in public, could vote in many countries, and were liberated from old restrictions on their sexual and other behavior. (Getty Images.)

Women in Love (1920) and *The Sun Also Rises* (1926). Mass culture's focus on heterosexuality encouraged the return to traditional social norms after the gender disorder of the prewar and war years.

As images of men and women changed, people paid more attention to bodily improvement. The increasing use of toothbrushes and toothpaste, safety and electric razors, and deodorants reflected new standards of personal hygiene and grooming. A multibillion-dollar cosmetics industry sprang up almost overnight. Women went to beauty parlors regularly to have their short hair cut, set, dyed, conditioned, straightened, or curled. They also tweezed their eyebrows, applied makeup, and even submitted to cosmetic surgery. Ordinary women "painted" their faces as formerly only prostitutes had done and competed in beauty contests that judged physical appearance. Instead of wanting to look plump and prosperous, people aimed to become thin and tanned, often through exercise and sports. Consumers' new focus on personal health coincided with industry's need for a physically fit workforce.

As prosperity returned late in the 1920s, people bought more consumer goods. Middle- and upper-class families snapped up sleek modern furniture, washing machines, and vacuum cleaners. Other modern conveniences such as electric irons and gas stoves appeared in better-off working-class households. Installment buying, popularized from the 1920s on, helped finance these purchases. Housework became more mechanized, and family intimacy increasingly depended on machines of mass communication, such as radios and phonographs, and even on automobiles. These new products not only transformed private life but also brought unforeseen changes in the public world of culture and mass politics.

REVIEW What were the major social and economic problems facing postwar Europe, and how did leaders address them?

Mass Culture and the Rise of Modern Dictators

Wartime propaganda had aimed to unite all classes against a common enemy. In the 1920s, new technology made the process of bringing diverse groups together in a single mass culture easier. The tools of mass culture—primarily radio, films, and newspapers—expanded their influence in the 1920s. Whereas some intellectuals urged elites to form an experimental avant-garde that refused to cater to "the drab mass of society," others wanted to use modern media and art to reach out to and even control the masses. The media had the potential for creating an informed citizenry and thus enhancing democracy. At the same time, it allowed authoritarian rulers and dictators such as Benito Mussolini, Joseph Stalin, and Adolf Hitler to shape political thought and behavior and to control citizens far more than earlier rulers had been able to do.

Culture for the Masses

The media had received a big boost from the war. Bulletins from the battlefront had stimulated the public's craving for news and real-life stories, and sales of nonfiction books soared. After years of deprivation, people were driven to achieve material success, and they devoured books that told them how to gain it. Henry Ford's biography, telling his story of upward mobility and technological accomplishment, became a best seller in Germany. With postwar readers pursuing practical knowledge, institutes and night schools became popular, and school systems promoted reading in geography, science, and history. Phonographs, radio, and movies also widened the scope of national culture.

In the 1920s, filmmaking changed from an experimental medium to a thriving international business in which large corporations set up theater chains and marketed films worldwide. Specialization emerged, with directors, producers, marketers, photographers, film editors, and many others subdividing the process. A "star" system turned film personalities into celebrities, promoted by professional publicity and living like royalty. Films of literary classics and political events developed people's sense of a common heritage and were often financed by governments. Bolshevik leaders backed the inventive work of director Sergei Eisenstein, whose films *Potemkin* (1925) and *Ten Days That Shook the World* (1927–1928) presented a Bolshevik view of history to Russian and international audiences.

Films incorporated familiar elements from everyday life. The piano accompaniment of silent films derived from music halls; comic characters and slapstick humor were borrowed from street or burlesque shows and from trends in postwar living. The popular comedies of the 1920s made the flapper more visible to the masses and poked fun at men's and women's inept attempts at marriage and emotional intimacy. Films played to postwar fantasies and fears. In Germany, the influential hit *The Cabinet of Doctor Caligari* (1919) depicted frightening events in an insane asylum as horrifying symbols of state power. Popular detective and cowboy films portrayed heroes who could restore wholeness to the disordered world of murder, crime, and injustice. The plight of gangsters appealed to veterans, who had seen the cheap value of life in the modern world. Charlie Chaplin, an English comedian, actor, and producer, created the character of the Little Tramp, who won international popularity as the defeated hero and the anonymous modern man, trying to preserve his dignity in a mechanized world. Films featured characters from around the world and were set in faraway deserts or mountain ranges; newsreels showed international sporting events such as boxing and cricket.

Like film, radio evolved from an experimental medium to an instrument of mass culture during the 1920s (see "Taking Measure"). Developed from Guglielmo

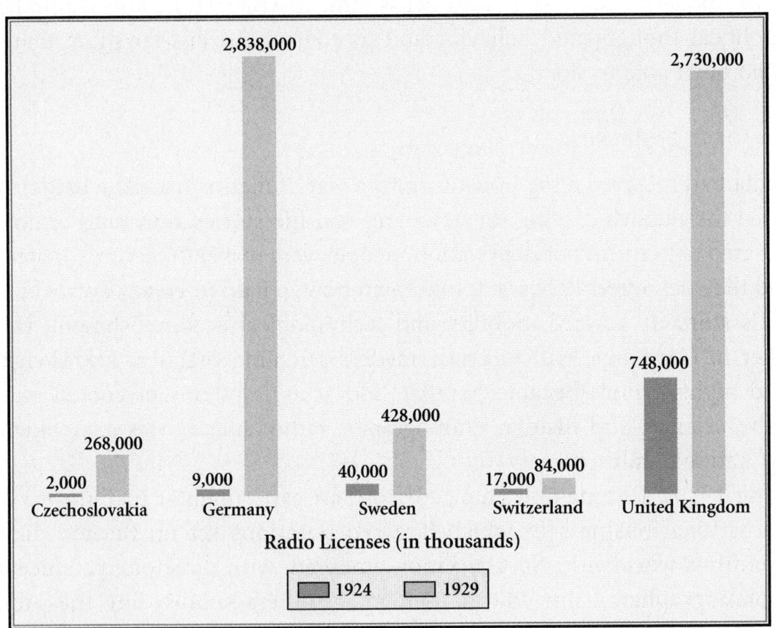

Taking Measure The Growth of Radio, 1924–1929
Radio technology, like the earlier development of printing, advanced the cultural and political unity of nation-states. Radio spread most rapidly in industrially and commercially developed societies. Governments taxed radios and, at first, provided the programming. Because of this centralized control and the paperwork it created, historians can track and compare the growth of radio in Europe and much of the rest of the world.

Marconi's wireless technology, radio broadcasts in the first half of the 1920s were heard by mass audiences in public halls (much like movie theaters) and featured orchestras and songs followed by audience discussion. The radio quickly became an affordable consumer item, and public concerts and lectures could then penetrate the individual's private living space. Disabled veterans loved radio because it allowed them to participate in public events and keep up to date, but by the 1930s radio also became downright menacing, allowing authoritarian politicians to reach the masses wherever they might be—even alone at home.

Cultural Debates over the Future

Cultural leaders in the 1920s either were obsessed with the horrendous wartime experience or, like the modernists before the war, held high hopes of creating a fresh utopian future that would have little relation to the past. Those haunted by the war produced bleak or violent visions—a common feature of postwar German art. Käthe Kollwitz, whose son died in the war, portrayed in her woodcuts bereaved parents, starving children, and other heart-wrenching, antiwar images. Others thought that Europeans needed to search for answers in far-off cultures. Seeing Europe as morally bankrupt, many turned to the spiritual richness of Asian philosophies and religions. An "Asiatic fever" seemed to grip intellectuals and artists, including English writer Virginia Woolf, who drew on ideas of reincarnation in her novel *Orlando* (1928), and Russian filmmaker Sergei Eisenstein, who modeled his new technique of juxtaposing shots (montage) on Japanese calligraphy.

Other artists used satire and contempt to express postwar rage at civilization's wartime failure. George Grosz, stunned by the war's carnage, joined Dada, an artistic and literary movement that had emerged during the war. Dadaists produced works marked by nonsense and shrieking expressions of alienation. Grosz's paintings and cartoons of maimed soldiers and brutally murdered women reflected his emotional wounds and his desire "to bellow back." In the postwar years, the modernist practice of shocking audiences intensified. Portrayals of sleazy everyday life flourished in cabarets and theaters in the 1920s and confirmed veterans' visions of civilian decadence. The art world itself became a battlefield, especially in defeated Germany, where art mirrored the Weimar Republic's contentious politics. Popular writers such as Ernst Jünger glorified life in the trenches and called for the militarization of society to restore order. Erich Maria Remarque cried out for an end to war in his controversial novel *All Quiet on the Western Front* (1928). This international best seller depicted the life shared by enemies on the battlefield, thus aiming to overcome the national hatred aroused by wartime propaganda.

Poets reflected on postwar conditions in more general terms, using styles that rejected the comforting rhymes or accessible metaphors of earlier verse. T. S. Eliot, an American-born poet who had studied Buddhism and other Asian thought and who for a time worked as a banker in Britain, portrayed postwar life as petty and futile in *The Waste Land* (1922) and "The Hollow Men" (1925). The Irish nationalist

George Grosz, *Twilight* (1922) This painting is part of Grosz's series of postwar art called Ecce Homo (Behold the Man), named after a book by Friedrich Nietzsche. The "man" to behold was the veteran, opportunistically called a "hero" by postwar politicians to get veterans' votes but in fact living a grim existence, as Grosz saw it. Surrounded by prosperous businessmen, fashionable women, and strutting military officers, the veteran was pushed to the background, gray and lonely amid the colorful peacetime society. (Bildarchiv Preussischer Kulturbesitz/Art Resource, NY/© Estate of George Grosz/Licensed by VAGA, New York, NY.)

poet William Butler Yeats joined Eliot in mourning the replacement of traditional society, with its religious and moral convictions, with a new, superficial generation dancing to jazz and engaging in promiscuous sex. Yeats's "Sailing to Byzantium" (1928) starts this way:

> That is no country for old men. The young
> In one another's arms, birds in the trees
> —Those dying generations

Both poets had an uneasy relationship with modern values and at times advocated authoritarianism rather than democracy.

The postwar arts produced many a utopian fantasy turned upside down; dystopias of life in postrevolutionary, traumatized Europe flourished. In the bizarre stories of Franz Kafka, an employee of a large insurance company in Prague, the world is a vast, impersonal machine. His novels *The Trial* (1925) and *The Castle* (1926) show the hopelessness of individuals caught in the cogs of society's relentlessly turning gears. His theme seemed to capture for civilian life the helplessness that soldiers had felt at the front. As an old social order collapsed in the face of political and technological innovation, other writers depicted the complex, sometimes nightmarish inner life of individuals.

The Irish writer James Joyce and the English writer Virginia Woolf portrayed this interior self built on memories and sensations, many of them from the war. Joyce's *Ulysses* (1922) and Woolf's *Mrs. Dalloway* (1925) illuminate the fast-moving inner lives of their characters in the course of a single day. In one of the most celebrated passages in *Ulysses,* a long interior monologue traces a woman's lifetime of erotic and emotional sensations. The technique of using a character's thoughts to propel a story was called stream of consciousness. For Woolf the war had dissolved the solid society on which absorbing stories and fascinating characters once depended. Her characters experience fragmented conversations, momentary sensations, and incomplete relationships. The character Orlando in Woolf's novel of the same name lives hundreds of years and in the course of his long life is eventually reborn as a woman.

There was another side to the postwar story—one based not on the interior thoughts of a traumatized society but on the bright promises of technology. Before the war, avant-garde artists had celebrated the new, the futuristic, the utopian. After the war, like Jules Amar crafting prostheses for shattered limbs, they were optimistic that technology could make an entire society whole. The aim of art, observed one of them, "is not to decorate our life but to organize it." German architects and artists influenced by the Bauhaus, a school of design whose name suggested a craft association, or *Bauhütte,* created streamlined office buildings and designed functional furniture, utensils, and decorative objects, many of them inspired by forms from "untainted" East Asia and Africa. Russian artists, temporarily caught up in the Communist experiment, optimistically wrote novels about cement factories and created ballets about steel.

Artists fascinated by technology and machinery were drawn to the most modern of all countries, the United States. Hollywood films, glossy advertisements, and the bustling metropolis of New York tempted careworn Europeans. They loved films and stories about the Wild West or the carefree "modern American girl." They were especially attracted to jazz, the improvisational music emanating from Harlem. Performers such as Josephine Baker and Louis Armstrong became international sensations when they toured Europe's capitals. Like jazz, the New York skyscrapers pointed to the future, not to the grim wartime past.

The Communist Utopia

Communism also promised a shining future and a modern, technological culture. As the Bolsheviks met powerful resistance, however, they became more ruthless and authoritarian. In the early 1920s, peasant bands called Green Armies revolted against the Bolshevik policy of war communism that confiscated their crops and animals. Industrial production stood at only 13 percent of prewar levels, shortages of housing affected the entire population, and millions of refugees clogged the cities and roamed the countryside. In the early spring of 1921, workers in Petrograd and sailors at the nearby naval base at Kronstadt revolted. They protested their short rations and the privileged standard of living their Bolshevik supervisors enjoyed. They called for "soviets without Communists"—that is, a worker state without elite leaders.

The Bolsheviks had many of the rebels shot, but the Kronstadt revolt pushed Lenin to institute reforms. His New Economic Policy (NEP) returned parts of the economy to the free market—a temporary retreat to capitalist methods that allowed peasants to sell their grain freely and others to trade consumer goods. Although the state still controlled large industries and banking, the NEP encouraged people to produce, sell, and even, in the words of one official, "get rich." As a result, more consumer goods and more abundant food soon became available. Although many people remained impoverished, some peasants and merchants prospered. The rise of these wealthy "NEPmen," who bought and furnished splendid homes, broke with the Marxist promise of a classless utopia.

Further protests erupted within the Communists' ranks. At the 1921 party congress, a group called the Worker Opposition objected to the party's takeover of economic control from workers' organizations and pointed out that the NEP was an agrarian program, not a proletarian one for workers. Lenin suppressed the Worker Opposition and set up procedures for purging party dissidents—a policy that would become a deadly feature of Communist rule. Bolshevik leaders also worked to make the Communist revolution a cultural reality in people's daily lives and thinking. Party leaders invaded the countryside, setting up classes in a variety of political and social subjects, and volunteers struggled to increase the literacy rate, which had been only 40 percent on the eve of World War I. To facilitate social equality between men and women, which was part of the Marxist vision of the future, the state made birth control, abortion, and divorce readily available. The commissar for public welfare, Aleksandra Kollontai, promoted birth-control education, day-care programs for children of working parents, and equality between women and men.

The bureaucracy swelled to bring modern culture to every corner of life, and *hygiene* and *efficiency* became watchwords, as they were in the rest of Europe. Agencies such as the Zhenotdel (Women's Bureau) sought to teach women about their rights under communism and about sanitary housekeeping. Efficiency experts aimed to replace tsarist backwardness with technological modernity based on American techniques. The short-lived government agency Proletkult tried to develop proletarian culture through undertakings such as workers' universities and a workers' theater. Russian artists experimented with blending high art and technology in mass culture. Poet Vladimir Mayakovsky wrote verse praising his Communist passport and essays promoting brushing one's teeth, while composers punctuated their music with the sound of train or factory whistles.

As with war communism, many resisted the reshaping of everyday life and culture. As Zhenotdel workers moved into the countryside, for example, they attempted to teach women to behave as men's equals. Peasant families, still strongly patriarchal, resisted. In Islamic regions of central Asia, incorporated from the old Russian Empire into the new Communist one, Bolsheviks urged Muslim women to remove their veils and change their way of life, but fervent Muslims often attacked both Zhenotdel workers and women who followed their advice.

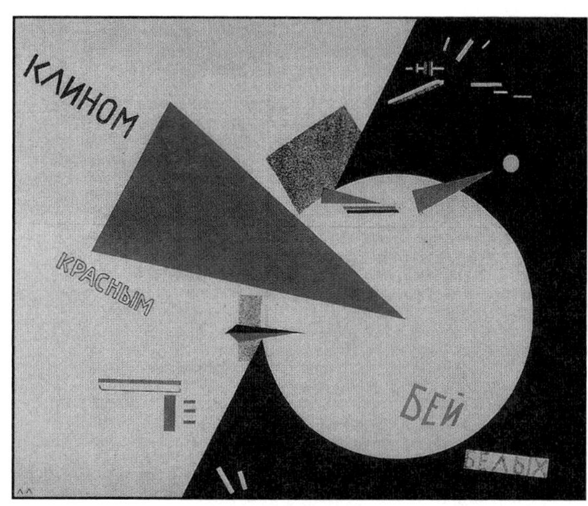

El Lissitzky, *Beat the Whites with the Red Wedge* (1919)
Russian artist El Lissitzky traveled Europe to bring news of Communist experimentation in all areas of life, including the arts. In particular, Lissitzky, like other avant-garde artists, was taken with the new physics, reflected in the use of geometric forms. Abstract art was also political. In this 1919 painting, the "red" wedge uses the force described in the laws of physics to defeat the greater counterrevolutionary power of the "whites." (David King Collection, London. © 2010 Artists Rights Society [ARS], NY/VG Bild-Kunst, Bonn.)

Lenin suffered a debilitating stroke in the spring of 1922. Amid ongoing cultural experimentation and factional fighting, the architect of the Bolshevik Revolution died in January 1924. The party congress declared the day of his death a permanent holiday, changed the name of Petrograd to Leningrad, and elevated the deceased leader to a secular god. After Lenin's death, no one was allowed to criticize anything associated with his name, a situation that opened the way for abuses of power by later Communist leaders.

Joseph Stalin (1879–1953), who served in the powerful position of general secretary of the Communist Party, was the chief mourner at Lenin's funeral, using the occasion to hand out good jobs and other patronage. He advertised his role in joining Russian and non-Russian regions into the Union of Soviet Socialist Republics (USSR) in 1923 as an example of his leadership skills, though he had used his dealings with thousands of local party officials to distribute favors in exchange for their support. Already concerned with Stalin's growing influence and ruthlessness, Lenin in his last will and testament had asked that "the comrades find a way to remove Stalin." Stalin, however, discredited his chief rival, Leon Trotsky, and prevented Lenin's will from being publicized. Simultaneously, Stalin organized the Lenin cult, which included the public display of Lenin's embalmed corpse (still on view today). Bringing in several hundred thousand new party members who owed their positions in government and industry to him, Stalin had achieved virtually complete control of the USSR by 1929.

Fascism on the March in Italy

In Italy, the war remained alive in the rise to power of Benito Mussolini (1883–1945), who, like the Bolsheviks, promised an efficient utopia. Italians raged when the Allies at Paris had refused to honor the territorial promises of the Treaty of London.

Mussolini and the Black Shirts
For movements like Fascism in Italy, the best society was one controlled by militarized politicians who killed their critics and political opponents. Fascism saw parliamentary democracies as effeminate and doomed in the modern world, which would need dictators and obedient warriors to make it strong, efficient, and machinelike. Thus, in the name of promoting state power, Mussolini gained adherents both within and outside of Italy. (Farabolafoto.)

Peasants and workers protested their economic plight, made worse by the slump of the early 1920s. Since the late nineteenth century, many Europeans had come to blame parliaments for their troubles, so Italians were responsive when Mussolini, a socialist journalist who turned politically to the right, built a personal army (the Black Shirts) of veterans and the unemployed to overturn parliamentary government. In 1922, his supporters, known as the Fascists, started the **march on Rome**, forcing the king to make the dynamic Mussolini prime minister.

The Fascist movement grew because of poverty and wounded national pride. The Black Shirts attracted many young men who felt cheated of glory by the Allies, as well as veterans who missed the vigor of military life in the Great War. The fasces, an ancient Roman symbol depicting a bundle of sticks wrapped around an ax with the blade exposed, served as the movement's emblem; it represented both unity and force to Mussolini's supporters. Unlike Marxism, Fascism scoffed at coherent ideology. "Fascism is not a church," Mussolini announced upon taking power in 1922. "It is more like a training ground." Fascism was defined by deeds, including its promotion of male violence and its attacks on the "antinationalist" socialist movement and parliamentary rule.

Mussolini secured his power by criminalizing any criticism of the state and by using violence against opponents in parliament. Fascist bands wrecked socialist offices, attacked striking workers, used the tactic of forcing castor oil (which causes diarrhea) down the throats of socialists, and even murdered political opponents. Yet this brutality and the sight of the Black Shirts marching through the streets like disciplined soldiers signaled to many Italians that their country was orderly and modern. Large landowners and businessmen approved Fascist attacks on strikers and supported the movement financially. Their generous funding allowed Mussolini to build a large staff by hiring the unemployed and thus advance the belief that the Fascists could rescue the economy when no one else could.

Like a wartime leader, Mussolini used mass propaganda to build support for a kind of military campaign to remake Italy. Peasant men huddled around radios to hear him call for a "battle of wheat" to enhance farm productivity. Peasant women, responding to his praise of maternal duty, adored him for appearing to value womanhood. In the cities, the government launched avant-garde architecture projects and used public relations promoters to advertise its achievements. The modern city became a stage set for Fascist spectacles, as broad avenues were built for Fascist parades, captured by newsreel cameras and broadcast by radio. Mussolini claimed that he made the trains run on time, and this triumph of modern technology raised people's hopes that he could restore order—even if it was military order.

Mussolini added a strong dose of traditional values and prejudices to his rule. Although he was an atheist, he recognized the power of Catholicism in Italian life. In 1929, the Lateran Agreement between the Italian government and the church made the Vatican an independent state under papal sovereignty. The government recognized the Catholic church's right to determine marriage and family policy and supported its role in education. In return, the church ended its criticism of Fascist tactics. Mussolini also introduced a "corporate" state that denied individual political rights in favor of duty to the state, as in wartime. Corporatist decrees in 1926 outlawed labor unions, replacing them with organized groups or corporations of employers, workers, and professionals to settle grievances and determine conditions of work. Mussolini drew praise from business leaders when he announced cuts in women's wages, and later he won the approval of civil servants, lawyers, and professors by banning women from those professions. Mussolini did not want women out of the workforce altogether but aimed to confine them to low-paying jobs as part of his scheme for reinvigorating men.

Mussolini's admirers were numerous across the West and included Adolf Hitler, who throughout the 1920s had been building a paramilitary group of storm troopers and a political organization called the National Socialist German Workers' Party, or Nazis.

During his brief stint in jail for the Beer Hall Putsch in 1923, Hitler wrote *Mein Kampf* (*My Struggle,* 1925), which expressed both his vicious anti-Semitism and his political psychology for manipulating the masses. Hitler was fascinated by the details of Mussolini's success: the dramatic march on Rome, Mussolini's legal accession to power, and his triumph over all opposition. Although Hitler was welding the Nazi Party into a strong political instrument, the Weimar parliamentary government was actually working well as the decade neared its end.

REVIEW How did the postwar cultural atmosphere encourage both beneficial innovations and the trend toward dictatorship?

Conclusion

The year 1929 was to prove just as fateful as 1914 had been. In 1914, an orgy of death had begun, causing tens of millions of casualties, the destruction of major dynasties, and the collapse of aristocratic classes. For four years, war promoted military technology, fierce nationalism, and the control of everyday life by a bureaucracy. While dynasties fell at the war's end, the centralization of power increased the scope of the nation-state. The Peace of Paris treaties of 1919–1920 left Germans bitterly resentful, while in eastern and central Europe the intense mingling of ethnicities, religions, and languages in the new states created by the treaties failed to guarantee a peaceful future. Massive migrations provoked additional chaos as some new nations expelled minority groups.

War furthered the development of mass society. It leveled social classes on the battlefield and in the graveyard, standardized political thinking through wartime propaganda, and extended many political rights to women to reward their wartime effort. Production techniques, improved during wartime, were used in peacetime for manufacturing consumer goods. Technological innovations, such as the prostheses built by Jules Amar, air transport, and films and radio, became available to more people. Modernity in the arts intensified, probing the nightmarish war that continued to haunt the population.

The war had so militarized politics that by the end of the 1920s, strongmen had come to power in Hungary, Poland, Romania, the Soviet Union, and Italy, with Adolf Hitler waiting in the wings in Germany. Many Westerners were impressed

Mapping the West Europe and the World, 1929
This map reflects the partitions and nations that came into being as a result of war and revolution, while it obscures the increasing movement toward throwing off colonial rule. The year 1929 was the true high point of empire: the drive for overseas empire would diminish thereafter, except in Italy, which still craved colonies, and in Japan, which continued searching for land and resources to fuel its rapid growth. Observe the League of Nations membership also depicted in the map. What common bonds, if any, united these nations?

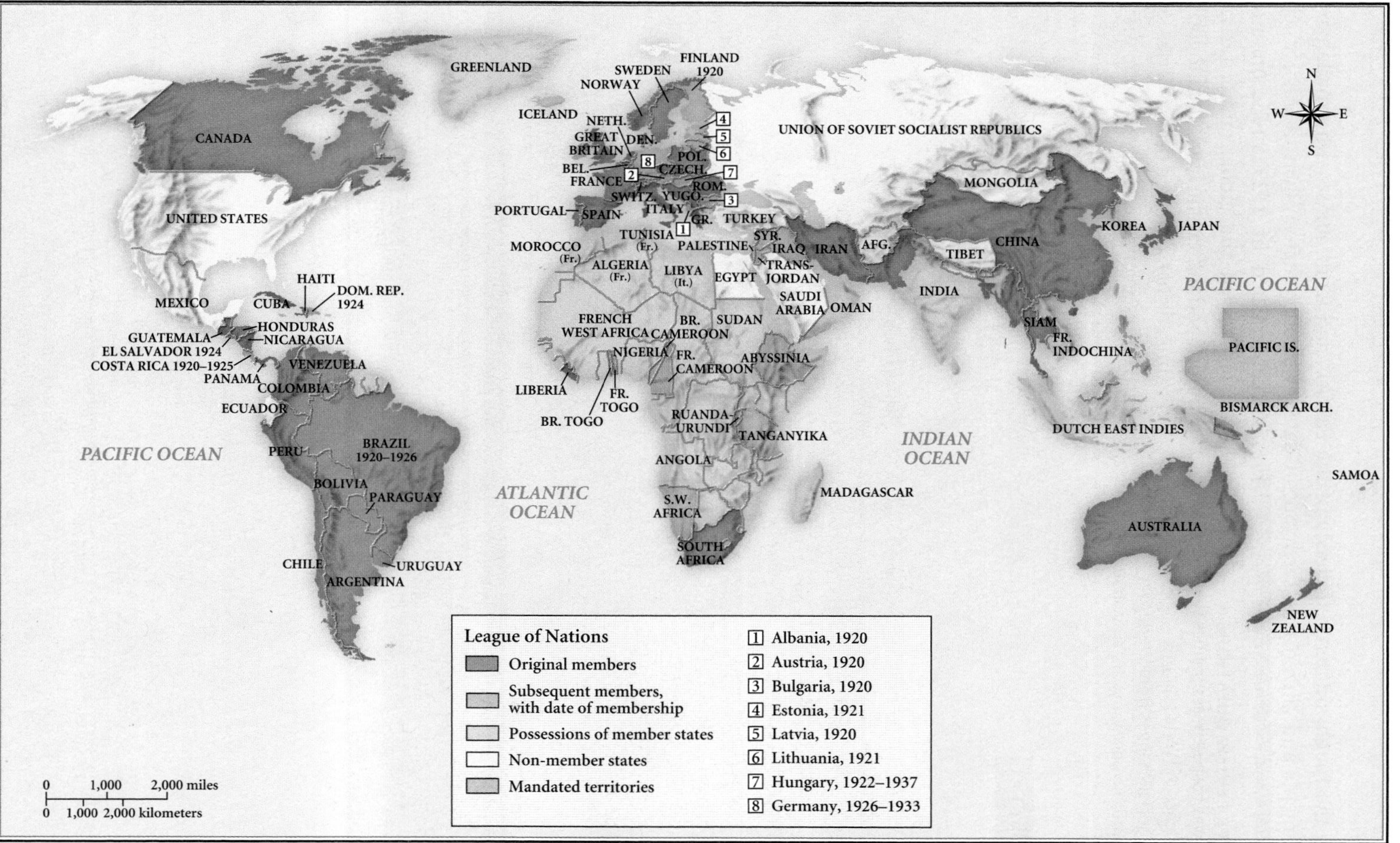
GREENLAND
FINLAND 1920
SWEDEN
NORWAY
ICELAND
NETH.
GREAT BRITAIN
DEN.
BEL.
FRANCE
POL.
CZECH.
ROM.
SWITZ.
YUGO.
PORTUGAL
SPAIN
ITALY
GR.
TURKEY
UNION OF SOVIET SOCIALIST REPUBLICS
MONGOLIA
CHINA
KOREA
JAPAN
TIBET
INDIA
AFG.
IRAN
IRAQ
SYR.
PALESTINE
TRANS-JORDAN
SAUDI ARABIA
OMAN
CANADA
UNITED STATES
MEXICO
CUBA
HAITI
DOM. REP. 1924
GUATEMALA
HONDURAS
EL SALVADOR 1924
NICARAGUA
COSTA RICA 1920–1925
PANAMA
VENEZUELA
COLOMBIA
ECUADOR
PERU
BRAZIL 1920–1926
BOLIVIA
PARAGUAY
CHILE
ARGENTINA
URUGUAY
MOROCCO (Fr.)
ALGERIA (Fr.)
TUNISIA (Fr.)
LIBYA (It.)
EGYPT
FRENCH WEST AFRICA
BR. CAMEROON
SUDAN
NIGERIA
FR. CAMEROON
ABYSSINIA
LIBERIA
FR. TOGO
BR. TOGO
RUANDA-URUNDI
TANGANYIKA
ANGOLA
S.W. AFRICA
SOUTH AFRICA
MADAGASCAR
PACIFIC OCEAN
ATLANTIC OCEAN
INDIAN OCEAN
PACIFIC OCEAN
SIAM
FR. INDOCHINA
PACIFIC IS.
BISMARCK ARCH.
DUTCH EAST INDIES
AUSTRALIA
SAMOA
NEW ZEALAND
N
W
E
S
League of Nations
Original members
Subsequent members, with date of membership
Possessions of member states
Non-member states
Mandated territories
1 Albania, 1920
2 Austria, 1920
3 Bulgaria, 1920
4 Estonia, 1921
5 Latvia, 1920
6 Lithuania, 1921
7 Hungary, 1922–1937
8 Germany, 1926–1933
0 1,000 2,000 miles
0 1,000 2,000 kilometers

by the tough, modern efficiency of the Fascists and Communists, who made parliaments and citizen rule seem out-of-date, even effeminate. When the U.S. stock market crashed in 1929 and economic disaster circled the globe, authoritarian solutions and militarism continued to look appealing. What followed was a series of catastrophes even more devastating than World War I.

CHAPTER REVIEW QUESTIONS

1. How was postwar mass politics shaped by the experience of World War I?
2. What social changes from World War I carried over into the postwar years and why?

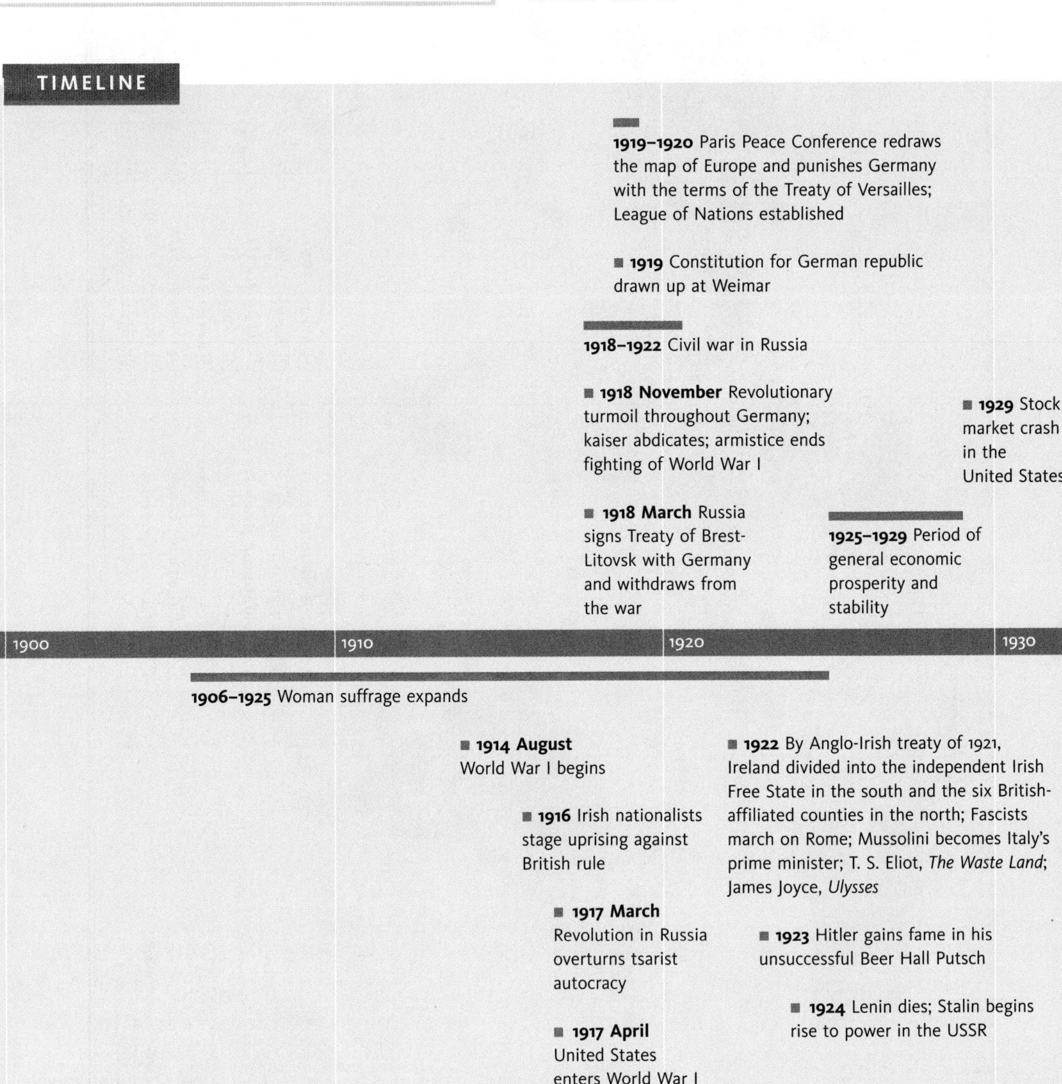

For practice quizzes and other study tools, see the Online Study Guide at bedfordstmartins.com/huntconcise.

For primary-source material from this period, see Chapter 25 of *Sources of* THE MAKING OF THE WEST, Third Edition.

Suggested References

The most recent histories of the Great War consider its military, technological, psychic, social, and economic aspects. This vision of the war as a phenomenon occurring both on and off the battlefield characterizes the newest scholarship. Histories of the war's end show deprivation, ongoing mass slaughter, the eruption of revolutions, and the complexities of peacemaking.

Barry, John. *The Great Influenza: The Epic Story of the Greatest Plague in History*. 2004.

Hanna, Martha. *Your Death Would Be Mine: Paul and Marie Pireaud in the Great War*. 2006.

Healy, Maureen. *Vienna and the Fall of the Habsburg Empire: Total War and Everyday Life in World War I*. 2004.

Holquist, Peter. *Making War, Forging Revolution: Russia's Continuum of Crisis, 1914–1921*. 2002.

Horne, John, ed. *State, Society, and Mobilization in Europe during the First World War*. 2002.

Kent, Susan Kingsley. *Aftershocks: The Politics of Trauma in Britain, 1918–1931*. 2009.

Liulevicius, Vejas Gabriel. *War Land on the Eastern Front: Culture, National Identity and German Occupation in World War I*. 2000.

Makaman, Douglas, and Michael Mays, eds. *World War I and the Cultures of Modernity*. 2000.

Marks, Sally. *The Ebbing of European Ascendancy: An International History of the World*. 2002.

Northrup, Douglas. *Veiled Empire: Gender and Power in Stalinist Central Asia*. 2004.

Panchasi, Roxanne. "Reconstructions: Prosthetics and the Rehabilitation of the Male Body in World War I." *Differences*. 1995.

Robb, George. *British Culture and the First World War*. 2002.

Roshwald, Aviel. *Ethnic Nationalism and the Fall of Empires: Central Europe, Russia and the Middle East, 1914–1923*. 2001.

Scales, Rebecca. "Radio Broadcasting, Disabled Veterans, and Politics of National Recovery in Interwar France." *French Historical Studies*. 2008.

Weitz, Eric D. *Weimar Germany: Promise and Tragedy*. 2007.

World War I Documents Archive: http://www.lib.byu.edu/%7Erdh/wwi

21

An Age of Catastrophes

1929–1945

When Etty Hillesum moved to Amsterdam from the Dutch provinces in 1932 to attend law school, an economic depression gripped the world. A resourceful young woman, Hillesum pieced together a living as a housekeeper and part-time language teacher. The pressures and pleasures of everyday life blinded her, however, to Adolf Hitler's spectacular rise to power in Germany, even when he demonized her fellow Jews as responsible for the economic slump. In 1939, the outbreak of World War II awakened her to reality. The German conquest of the Netherlands in 1940 led to the persecution of Dutch Jews and brought Hillesum to this shattering thought, noted in her diary: "What they are after is our total destruction." The Nazis started relocating Jews to camps in Germany and Poland. Hillesum went to work for Amsterdam's Jewish Council, which was forced to organize the transport of Jews to the east. Changing from self-absorbed student to heroine, she did what she could to help other Jews and began carefully recording the deportation. When she was taken prisoner and deported in turn, she smuggled out letters from the transit camps, describing the brutal treatment and inhumane conditions. "I wish I could live for a long time so that one day I may know how to explain it," she wrote. Etty Hillesum never got her wish; she died at Auschwitz in November 1943.

Nazis on Parade
By the time Adolf Hitler came to power in 1933, Germany was mired in the global economic depression. Hated by Communists, Nazis, and conservatives alike, the German republic had few supporters. To Germans still reeling from their defeat in World War I, the Nazis looked as though they would restore national power by defeating enemies both within and beyond Germany's borders. Hitler took his cue from Benito Mussolini by presenting showy parades such as this one and by promising an end to democracy and tolerance. **For more help analyzing this image, see the visual activity for this chapter in the Online Study Guide at** bedfordstmartins.com/huntconcise. *(Time Life Pictures/ Getty Images.)*

The economic recovery of the late 1920s came to a crashing halt with the collapse of the U.S. stock market in 1929. The financial collapse in the United States became part of the worldwide Great Depression. Economic distress intensified social grievances. In Europe, people turned to military-style strongmen for solutions to their problems. Among these dictators was Adolf Hitler, who called on the German masses to restore the national glory that had been damaged by defeat in World War I. He urged them to scorn democratic rights and root out those he considered to be inferior, including Jews, Slavs, and Gypsies. Authoritarian and militaristic regimes also took hold in Portugal, Spain, Poland, Hungary, Japan, China, and countries of Latin America, crushing representative institutions. In the Soviet Union, Joseph Stalin justified the killing of millions of people as being necessary for the USSR's industrialization and the survival of communism. For millions of hard-pressed people in the difficult 1930s, dictatorship had great appeal.

Elected leaders in the democracies reacted cautiously to both economic depression and the dictators' aggressive acts. In an age of mass media, leaders following democratic procedures appeared timid, while dictators dressed in uniforms looked bold and decisive. Only the German invasion of Poland in 1939 finally pushed the democracies to respond, as World War II erupted in Europe. By the end of 1941, the war had spread across the globe, with the United States, Great Britain, and the Soviet Union allied in combat against Germany, Italy, and Japan. Tens of millions of people would perish in this war because both technology and ideology had become even more deadly than they had been just two decades earlier. More than half of those killed were civilians, among them Etty Hillesum, whose only crime was being Jewish.

CHAPTER FOCUS QUESTION What were the main economic, social, and political challenges of the years 1929–1945, and how did governments and individuals respond to them?

The Great Depression

The U.S. stock market crash of 1929 and economic developments around the world triggered the Great Depression of the 1930s. Rural and urban folk alike suffered as tens of millions lost their jobs. The whole world felt the depression's impact: commerce and investment in industry fell off, social order and gender roles were upset, and the birthrate sank. From peasants in Asia to industrial workers in Germany and the United States, the Great Depression shattered the lives of millions.

Economic Disaster Strikes

In the 1920s, U.S. corporations and banks as well as millions of individual Americans had optimistically invested their money in the stock market or, more often, borrowed money to invest. Confident that prices would always rise, they used easy credit to buy shares in popular new companies based on electric, automotive, and other new technologies with full confidence in ever-rising stock prices. By the end of the decade, the Federal Reserve Bank—the nation's central bank, which controlled financial policy—tried to slow speculation by limiting credit availability. To meet the new restrictions on credit, brokers had to demand that their clients immediately repay the money they had borrowed to buy stocks. When millions of shares of stocks were sold to raise the necessary cash, the market collapsed. Between early October and mid-November 1929, the value of businesses listed on U.S. stock exchanges dropped from $87 billion to $30 billion. For individuals and for the economy as a whole, it was the beginning of catastrophe.

The crash helped bring on a global depression because the United States, a leading international creditor, had financed the economic growth of the previous five years. Suddenly lacking credit, U.S. financiers cut back on loans and called in debts, undermining businesses at home and abroad. Europe faced a decline in consumer buying, overproduction, and competition from low-cost U.S. and Japanese goods, which further slowed the European economy, including the new factories of eastern Europe.

The Great Depression hurt all sectors of the world economy, and government actions made the situation worse. Governments instituted budget cuts and high tariffs against foreign goods to restart their economies, but these policies further reduced individual spending and dampened trade. By 1933, almost six million German workers, about one-third of the workforce, were unemployed, and many other Germans were underemployed. Even in France, which had a more self-sufficient economy based on small businesses, firms began to fail, and by the mid-1930s more than 800,000 French people had lost their jobs.

Agricultural prices had been declining for several years because of technological innovation and abundant harvests around the world. Now creditors confiscated farms and equipment. With incomes declining, millions of small farmers had no money to buy the chemical

Unemployed in Germany (1932)
"I'm looking for work of any kind," this respectably dressed unemployed man announces on his sign. Germans were among those hardest hit by the Great Depression, and when demagogues pointed to such sights as evidence that democracy didn't work, it helped pull down the rule of republics based on constitutions, representative government, and guaranteed rights.
(ullstein bild/The Granger Collection, NY.)

fertilizers and motorized machinery they needed to remain competitive, and they too went under. Eastern and southern European peasants, who had pressed for the redistribution of land after World War I, could not afford to operate their newly acquired farms. In Poland, many of the 700,000 new landowners fell into debt trying to improve their farms. Eastern European governments often ignored the farmers' plight as they poured available funds into industrialization—a policy that increased tensions in rural society.

Social Effects of the Depression

The depression had complex effects on society. First, life was not uniformly bleak in the 1930s. Despite the slump, modernization continued. Bordering English slums, one traveler in the mid-1930s noticed, were "filling stations and factories that look like exhibition buildings, giant cinemas and dance halls and cafés, bungalows with tiny garages, cocktail bars, Woolworth's [and] swimming pools." Municipal and national governments continued road construction and sanitation projects. Running water, electricity, and sewage pipes were installed in many homes for the first time. New factories manufactured synthetic fabrics, electrical products such as stoves, and automobiles—all of them in demand. With government assistance, eastern European industry developed: Romanian industrial production, for example, increased by 55 percent between 1929 and 1939.

Second, the majority of Europeans and Americans had jobs throughout the 1930s, and people with steady employment benefited from a drastic drop in prices. Service workers, managers, and business leaders often prospered. In towns with heavy industry, however, sometimes more than half the population was out of work. In Britain in the mid-1930s, close to 20 percent of the population lacked adequate food, clothing, or housing. In a 1932 school assignment, a German youth wrote, "My father has been out of work for two and a half years. He thinks that I'll never find a job." Despite the prosperity of many people, the Great Depression spread fear beyond the unemployed.

Economic catastrophe upset gender relations and weakened social ties. Women often found low-paying jobs doing laundry and cleaning houses, while unemployed men sometimes stayed home all day. Men who stayed home sometimes took over the housekeeping chores but often felt that this "women's work" chipped away at their masculinity. As many women became breadwinners, though at low wages, men could be seen standing on street corners begging—a change in gender roles that fed discontent. Young men in cities faced severe unemployment. With nothing to do but loiter in parks, they became ripe for movements like Nazism. As the number of farmworkers decreased, rural men faced the erosion of patriarchal authority, once central to the organization of labor and to decisions about distributing property to offspring. Demagogues everywhere attacked parliamentary politicians for their failure to stop the collapse of traditional values, clearing the way for Nazi and fascist politicians who promised to restore male dignity.

Politicians from all parties also attacked the low birthrate, which despite a brief postwar upturn, had steadily declined. The reason was clear: in difficult economic times, people chose to have fewer children. In addition, compulsory education and more years of required schooling, enforced more strictly after World War I, reduced the income children earned for poorer families, resulting in increased costs for each additional child. Family planning centers opened, receiving many clients, and knowledge of birth control spread to the working and lower middle classes, who continued the half-century-long trend of cutting family size.

Many politicians used the population "crisis" to arouse fear of national decline and to gain votes by igniting racism. "Superior" peoples were selfishly failing to breed, they charged, and "inferior" peoples were poised to take their place. This racism took a violent form in eastern Europe, where the rural population was growing because of increased life expectancies despite the declining birthrates. As financial hardships increased, eastern European peasant political parties blamed Jewish bankers for farm foreclosures and Jewish civil servants (of whom there were actually very few) for new taxes and inadequate relief programs. Thus, population issues along with economic misery produced discord, especially in the form of ethnic hatred and anti-Semitism, opening the way for dictators who promised that eliminating Jews and other undesirables would restore individual and national prosperity.

Global Dimensions of the Crash

The effects of the depression extended beyond the West, spreading discontent in European empires. World War I and postwar investment had produced economic growth, a rising population, and explosive urbanization in Asia, Africa, and Latin America. Japan in particular had become a formidable economic rival between 1920 and 1940. The depression, however, cut the demand for copper, tin, and other raw materials and for the finished products made in urban factories worldwide. Rising agricultural productivity drove down the prices of foodstuffs like rice and coffee—a disaster for people who had been forced to grow a single cash crop. Just as in Europe, however, the economic picture was uneven. For instance, established industrial sectors of the Indian economy such as textiles gained strength, with India achieving virtual independence from British cloth imports.

Economic distress fueled anger, and anger led to action. Colonial farmers withheld produce like cocoa from imperial trade, and colonial workers went on strike to protest wage cuts imposed by imperial landlords. The colonial governments' response to the depression added to ordinary people's grievances. They insisted that all taxes and loans be paid and manipulated currency rates in favor of the mother country so that those taxes were even higher than before. As a result, the millions of African and Asian colonial veterans of World War I were more than ever determined to be free from colonial rule.

In India anger toward the British boiled over. Millions of working people, including hundreds of thousands of veterans, joined with upper-class Indians who had organized to gain rights from Britain in the late nineteenth century. Mohandas Gandhi (1869–1948; called Mahatma, or "great-souled") emerged as the charismatic leader for Indian independence. Trained in England as a Western-style lawyer, Gandhi preached Hindu self-denial, rejecting elaborate British manners and ceremonies. He wore simple clothing made of thread he had spun himself and advocated **civil disobedience**—intentionally but peacefully breaking the law—a tactic he claimed to have taken from British suffragists and from the teachings of spiritual leaders such as Jesus and Buddha. Boycotting British-made goods and disobeying British laws, he aimed to end Indians' respect toward the British. The British jailed Gandhi repeatedly and tried to split the independence movement by encouraging the rival Muslim League and promoting Hindu-Muslim conflict. Instead, Indian commitment to independence grew.

The end of the Ottoman Empire following World War I led to efforts to build nations in the Middle East. Mustafa Kemal (1881–1938), known as Atatürk (first among Turks), led the Turks to found the independent republic of Turkey in 1923 and to craft a capitalist economy. Kemal moved the national capital from Constantinople to Ankara in 1923 and officially changed the ancient Greek *Constantinople* to the Turkish *Istanbul* in 1930. In an effort to Westernize Turkish culture and the new Turkish state, Kemal mandated Western dress for men and women, introduced

A Historic Act of Civil Disobedience
Mohandas Gandhi used nonviolent resistance to challenge British rule. Because of the British government's monopoly on salt, Indians were prohibited from gathering this natural product, and every Indian family had to pay a tax on salt. In 1930, Gandhi led his supporters on a two-hundred-mile march to India's salt flats, on the coast, to protest the hated salt tax and to extract salt from seawater. Gandhi was arrested and jailed, but his followers continued their march to the sea. (© Bettmann/Corbis.)

the Latin alphabet, and abolished polygamy. In 1936, women received the vote and became eligible to serve in the Turkish parliament. Like Atatürk, nationalist leaders in Persia and Egypt sought to loosen the financial and political grip of Europeans on their countries.

France made few concessions in its colonies. Like all imperial powers during the depression, it depended increasingly on the profits it could make from its colonies. Thus, French trade with them increased as trade with Europe lagged. France also depended on the colonies for sheer numbers of people, and the rising colonial population boosted French morale. One official estimated what colonial population numbers could mean for national security: "One hundred and ten million strong, France can stand up to Germany." Like other Western-educated anti-colonial leaders, Ho Chi Minh, founder of the Indochinese Communist Party, protested this subjection, but in 1930 the French crushed a peasant uprising he led. Needing their empires, Britain and France strengthened their military positions around the world. As a result, totalitarian forces went largely unchecked in Europe during the 1930s.

REVIEW How did the Great Depression affect society and politics?

Totalitarian Triumph

Representative government collapsed in many countries under the weight of social and economic crisis. After 1929, Italy's Benito Mussolini, the Soviet Union's Joseph Stalin, and Germany's Adolf Hitler were able to mobilize vast support for their regimes. Many admired Mussolini and Hitler for the discipline they brought to social and economic life. Desperate for economic relief, citizens supported political violence as key to restoring well-being. The common use of violence has led some scholars to apply the term **totalitarianism** to the Fascist, Communist, and Nazi regimes of the 1930s. The term refers to highly centralized systems of government that attempt to control society and ensure conformity through a single party and police terror. Born during World War I and gaining strength in its aftermath, these regimes broke with the liberal principles of the rule of law and basic rights and came to wage war on their own citizens.

The Rise of Stalinism

In the 1930s, Joseph Stalin led the remarkable transformation of the USSR from a rural society into an industrial power. Stalin ended Lenin's New Economic Policy (NEP) and in 1929 laid out the first of several **five-year plans** for industrializing the country. The first plan outlined a program for massive increases in the output of coal, steel, and industrial goods. Without an end to economic backwardness, Stalin warned, "the advanced countries . . . will crush us." He thus established central economic planning—a policy used on both sides in World War I and increasingly favored by bureaucrats around the world. Between 1928 and 1940, the number of

Soviet workers in industry, construction, and transportation grew from 4.6 million to 12.6 million, and factory output soared. Stalin's first five-year plan helped make the USSR a leading industrial nation.

A new elite of bureaucrats put the plans into operation. Mostly party officials and technical experts, these managers dominated Soviet workers by limiting their ability to change jobs or move from place to place. Despite these limitations, skilled workers benefited substantially from the redistribution of privileges that accompanied industrialism and central planning. Compared with people working the land, both managers and industrial workers had better housing and higher wages. Communist officials enjoyed additional rewards, such as country homes and luxurious vacations.

Unskilled workers enjoyed no such benefits. Newcomers from the countryside were herded into barracks-like dwellings, even tents, and subjected to dangerous factory conditions. Despite the hardships, many took pride in their new skills: "We mastered this profession—completely new to us—with great pleasure," a female lathe operator recalled. More often, workers fresh from the countryside lacked the technical knowledge to accomplish the goals of the five-year plans. Because meeting these goals had top priority as a measure of progress toward the Communist utopia, official lying about productivity became part of the economic system. The attempt to turn an illiterate peasant society into an advanced industrial economy in a single decade brought intense suffering. Hardship was tolerated because Soviet workers believed that in the process of achieving a Communist society, as one worker put it, "man himself is being rebuilt."

In country and city alike, politics influenced work. Stalin demanded output from industry and more grain from peasants, both to feed the urban workforce and to provide exports to finance industrialization. Peasants resisted government demands by cutting production or withholding produce from the market, prompting Stalin to demand a "liquidation of the kulaks." *Kulak,* which means "fist," was a negative term for prosperous peasants, but in practice it applied to almost anyone. Party workers searched villages, forcing residents to identify the kulaks among them. Propagandists stirred up hatred. One Russian remembered believing that kulaks were "bloodsuckers, cattle, swine, loathsome, repulsive: they had no souls; they stank." Denounced as "enemies of the state," whole families and even entire villages were robbed of their possessions and left to starve, or even murdered outright. Confiscated kulak land formed the basis of the new collective farm, or kolkhoz, where the remaining peasants were to create a Communist agricultural system of cooperative farming using shared machinery.

Economic disaster followed collectivization and rapid industrialization, producing violent **purges**, because success in work life was defined as central to communism. Failures were common because factory workers and party officials were too inexperienced with advanced industrialization to meet quotas. The experiment with collectivization, combined with the murder of farmers, resulted in a drop in the grain harvest from 83 million tons in 1930 to 67 million in 1934. Soviet citizens starved. Blaming all failures on "wreckers" deliberately plotting against communism, Stalin instituted purges—state violence in the form of widespread arrests, imprisonment in labor camps, and executions. These purges touched nearly all segments of society, beginning with engineers who were condemned for causing low productivity. Starting in 1936, the government charged prominent Bolshevik leaders with conspiring to overthrow Soviet rule in a series of "show trials"—trials based on trumped-up charges, phony evidence, and coerced confessions. Some of the top leaders accepted their fate, seeing the purges—a "great and bold political idea," one of the accused wrote—as good for the future of communism. Tortured and forced to confess in court, most of those found guilty were shot.

The spirit of purge swept through society. One woman poet described the scene: "Great concert and lecture halls were turned into public confessionals. . . . People did penance for [everything]. . . . Beating their breasts, the 'guilty' would lament that they had 'shown political short-sightedness' and 'lack of vigilance' . . . and were full of 'rotten liberalism.'" In 1937 and 1938, military leaders were arrested and executed without public trials; some ranks were entirely wiped out. Simultaneously, the government centralized and vastly expanded the number of prison camps stretching several thousand miles from Moscow to Siberia. Called the Gulag—an acronym for the administrative arm of the camps founded under Lenin—the system held millions of prisoners under deadly conditions. Prisoners aided the economy by doing every kind of work, from digging canals to building apartment buildings. Some one million Gulag prisoners died annually as a result of insufficient food and housing and twelve- to sixteen-hour workdays of crushing physical labor. Regular beatings and murders contributed to the harsh conditions of Gulag life, becoming another aspect of totalitarian violence.

The 1930s also marked an end to toleration in Soviet social life, as social and sexual freedom began to disappear. As in the rest of Europe, the birthrate in the USSR declined rapidly in the 1930s. The Soviet Union needed to replace the millions of people lost since 1914, motivating Stalin to restrict access to birth-control information and abortion. More lavish wedding ceremonies came back into fashion, divorces became difficult to obtain, and the state made homosexuality a crime. The Bolsheviks had once scorned the family as a "bourgeois" institution; now propaganda referred to the family as a "school for socialism." At the same time, women in rural areas made gains in literacy and received improved health care. As the purges continued, positions in the lower ranks of the party were opened to women, and more women were accepted into the professions. However, women, particularly those in the industrial workforce, faced increased stress. After putting in a long workday, they had to wait in long lines to obtain scarce consumer goods and perform all household and child-care tasks.

Avant-garde experimentation in the arts ended under Stalin. He called artists and writers "engineers of the soul" and, recognizing their influence, controlled their

N. J. Altman, *Anna Akhmatova* This modernist painting portrays the poet Anna Akhmatova (1889–1966) in 1914, when she was a centerpiece of literary salon life in Russia. In the 1930s and 1940s, Akhmatova refused to follow the optimistic socialist realist style and instead gave poetic voice to Soviet suffering, recording in her verse ordinary people's endurance of purges and warfare. As she encouraged people to resist the Nazis during World War II, Stalin allowed her to revive Russian patriotism instead of promoting socialist internationalism. (© State Russian Museum, St. Petersburg, Russia/The Bridgeman Art Library. Art © Estate of N. J. Altman/RAO, Moscow/VAGA, New York, NY.)

output through the Union of Soviet Writers. The union not only assigned housing, office space, equipment, and secretarial help but also determined the types of books authors could write. In return, the "comrade artist" adhered to the official style of "socialist realism," derived from the 1920s focus on the common worker as a type of social hero. Although some artists and writers went underground, secretly creating works that are still coming to light, many others found ways to adjust to the state's demands. Sergei Prokofiev, for example, composed music for the delightful *Peter and the Wolf* and for Sergei Eisenstein's 1938 film *Alexander Nevsky,* a work that flatteringly compared Stalin with the towering medieval rulers of the Russian people. Aided by adaptable artists, workers, and bureaucrats, Stalin stood triumphant as the 1930s drew to a close. He was, as two different workers put it, "our beloved Leader" and "a god on earth."

Hitler's Rise to Power

A different but no less violent system emerged when Adolf Hitler put an end to democracy in Germany. Since the early 1920s, he had ranted that the German people should crush the fragile Weimar Republic and had spread a message of anti-Semitism and the rebirth of the German "race." When the Great Depression struck Germany in 1929, his Nazi Party began to pass its rivals in elections. Film and press mogul Alfred Hugenberg's newspapers helped, constantly slamming the Weimar government and blaming it for the disastrous economy and the loss of German pride after World War I. Nazi supporters attacked young Communist groups agitating on behalf of the new Soviet experiment. Hugenberg's newspapers always reported such incidents as the work of Communist thugs who had assaulted blameless Nazis, thus building sympathy for the Nazis among the middle classes.

Parliamentary government in Germany practically ground to a halt in the face of economic crisis. The Reichstag failed to approve emergency plans to improve the economy. As a result of its inaction, sympathetic media coverage, and its own street tactics, the Nazi Party, which had received only slightly more than 2 percent of the vote in the Reichstag elections of 1928, won almost 20 percent in 1930 and more than doubled its representation in 1932. Members of every age group and class supported Hitler, but he especially attracted young people. In 1930, 70 percent of Nazi Party members were under forty. Full of idealism, the young had faith that a better world was possible if Hitler took control. The largest number of supporters came from the industrial working class, but many white-collar workers and members of the lower middle class also joined the party in percentages out of proportion with their numbers in the population. The inflation that had wiped out their savings had left them especially bitter and open to Hitler's rhetoric, even if he did seem rough around the edges.

Hitler used modern propaganda techniques to build his following. Nazi Party members passed out thousands of recordings of Hitler's speeches and other Nazi mementos to German citizens. Teenagers painted their fingernails with swastikas, and soldiers flashed metal match covers with Nazi insignia. Nazi rallies were masterful displays in which Hitler captivated the crowds, who saw him as their strong, superior *Führer,* or leader. Frenzied and inspirational, he seemed neither a calculating politician nor a wooden bureaucrat but a "creative element," as one poet put it. In reality, however, Hitler viewed the masses with contempt. In *Mein Kampf,* he discussed how to deal with them:

> The receptivity of the great masses is very limited, their intelligence is small. In consequence of these facts, all effective propaganda must be limited to a very few points and must harp on those in slogans until the last member of the public understands what you want him to understand.

Hitler's media techniques were so successful that they continue to influence political campaigns today, particularly in the use of sound bites and simple, often hate-filled and threatening messages.

In the 1932 elections, both the Nazis and Communists did very well, making the leader of one of those parties the logical choice as chancellor. Influential conservative politicians loathed the Communists for their opposition to private property and favored Hitler as someone they could manipulate. When Hitler was invited to become chancellor in January 1933, he accepted.

Toys Depicting Nazis
As a totalitarian ideology, Nazism permeated everyday life. Nazi insignia decorated clothing, dishes, cigarette lighters, and even toys. Men and women became husbands and wives in accordance with Nazi rules and enrolled their children in Nazi clubs and organizations. Nazi songs, Nazi parades and festivals, and Nazi radio filled Germans' leisure time. (Imperial War Museum, London.)

The Nazification of German Politics

Millions of Germans celebrated Hitler's ascent to power. One recalled that upon hearing of Hitler's selection as chancellor, "my father went down to the cellar and brought up our best bottles of wine . . . and my mother wept for joy." Tens of thousands of Hitler's paramilitary supporters, called storm troopers (SA or Stürmabteilung), paraded through the streets with blazing torches. Instead of being easy to control, however, Hitler took command brutally, closing down representative government with an ugly show of force.

Within a month of his taking power, the Nazi state was in place. When the Reichstag building was gutted by fire in February 1933, Nazis used the fire as an excuse for suspending civil rights, imposing censorship of the press, and prohibiting meetings of other political parties. Indeed, Hitler had always claimed to hate democracy and differing political opinions. "Our opponents complain that we National Socialists, and I in particular, are intolerant," he declared. "They are right, we are intolerant! I have set myself one task, namely to sweep those parties out of Germany."

The storm troopers' violence became a way of life, silencing democratic politicians. At the end of March, intimidated Reichstag delegates let pass the **Enabling Act**, which suspended the constitution for four years and allowed Nazi laws to take effect without parliamentary approval. Solid middle-class Germans approved the Enabling Act as a way to advance the creation of a *Volksgemeinschaft* (people's community) of like-minded, racially pure Germans—"Aryans" in Nazi terms. Heinrich Himmler headed the elite SS (Schutzstaffel), an organization that protected Hitler, and he commanded the political police system. The Gestapo, a political police force organized by Hermann Goering, enforced complete obedience to Nazism. These organizations had vast powers to arrest, execute, or imprison people in concentration camps, the first of which opened at Dachau near Munich in March 1933. The Nazis filled it and later camps with socialists, homosexuals, Jews, and others said to interfere with the Volksgemeinschaft. One Nazi leader proclaimed:

> [National socialism] does not believe that one soul is equal to another, one man equal to another. It does not believe in rights as such. It aims to create the German man of strength, its task is to protect the German people, and all . . . must be subordinate to this goal.

Hitler deliberately blurred authority in the government and the Nazi Party so that confusion and bitter competition reigned. He then settled disputes that arose among them, often with violence. When Ernst Roehm, leader of the SA and Hitler's longtime collaborator, called for a "second revolution" to end the business and military elites' influence on top Nazis, Hitler ordered Roehm's assassination. The bloody Night of the Long Knives (June 30, 1934), during which hundreds of SA leaders and innocent civilians were killed, enhanced Hitler's support among conservatives. They saw that he would deal ruthlessly with those favoring a leveling of social privilege. Nazism's terrorist politics served as the foundation of Hitler's Third Reich—a German empire he described as succeeding the empires of Charlemagne and William II.

Like violence, new economic and social programs, especially those putting people back to work, were crucial to the survival of Hitler's regime. Economic revival built popular support, strengthened military industries, and provided the basis for German expansion. The Nazi government pursued **pump priming**—stimulating the economy through government spending on tanks and airplanes and on the Autobahn, the German highway system. Unemployment declined from a peak of almost 6 million in 1932 to 1.6 million by 1936. As labor shortages appeared in some areas, the government drafted single women into forced service as farmworkers and domestics. The Nazi Party closed down labor unions, and government managers determined work procedures and set pay levels, rating women's jobs lower than men's regardless of the level of skill required. Imitating Stalin, Hitler announced a four-year plan in 1936 with the secret aim of preparing Germany for war by 1940. His programs produced large deficits, but he was already planning to conquer and loot neighboring countries to recover the costs.

The Nazi government set policies to control everyday life, including gender roles. In June 1933, a bill took effect that encouraged Aryans to marry and have children. The bill provided for loans to Aryan newlyweds, but only to those couples in which the wife left the workforce. The loans were forgiven on the birth of a couple's fourth child. The ideal woman gave up her job, gave birth to many children, and surrendered her will to that of her husband, allowing him to feel powerful despite military defeat and economic depression. A good wife "joyfully sacrifices and fulfills her fate," one Nazi leader explained.

The government also controlled culture, destroying the rich creativity of the Weimar years. Although 70 percent of households had "people's radios" by 1938, programs were severely censored. In May 1933, a huge book-burning ceremony rid libraries of works by Jews, socialists, homosexuals, and modernist writers. Modern art in museums and private collections was destroyed or confiscated. In the Hitler Youth organization, which boys and girls over age ten were required to join, children learned to report to Nazi authorities those adults they suspected of disloyalty to the government, even their own parents. Germans boasted that they could leave their bicycles outdoors at night without fear of the bicycles being stolen, but their world was filled with informers—some 100,000 of whom were on the Nazi payroll. In general, the improved economy led many to believe that Hitler was working an economic miracle while restoring both national pride and the harmonious community of an imaginary past. For hundreds of thousands if not millions of Germans, however, Nazi rule brought anything but harmony and community.

Nazi Racism

Hitler attacked many ethnic and social groups, but he propelled the nineteenth-century politics of anti-Semitism to new and frightening heights. The Nazis defined Jews as an inferior "race" dangerous to the superior Aryan or Germanic "race" and responsible for most of Germany's problems, including its defeat in World War I and the economic depression. In the rhetoric of Nazism, Jews were "vermin," "abscesses," "parasites," and "Bolsheviks," whom the Germans would have to eliminate to create a true Volksgemeinschaft. By defining the Jews as evil financiers and businessmen and as working-class Bolsheviks, Hitler fashioned an enemy for many segments of the German population to hate.

Nazis insisted that terms such as *Aryan* and *Jewish* (a religious category) were scientific racial classifications that could be determined by physical characteristics such as the shape of one's nose. In 1935, the government enacted the **Nuremberg Laws**, which deprived Jews of citizenship and prohibited marriage between Jews and other Germans. Abortions and birth-control information were easily available to outcast groups, including Jews, Gypsies, Slavs, and mentally or physically disabled people. In the name of improving the Aryan race, German doctors helped organize the T4 project, which used carbon monoxide poisoning and other means to kill 200,000 elderly and disabled people—in the late 1930s. Killing people with disabilities was necessary, the Nazis argued, to eliminate those whose "inferiority" endangered Aryans. These murders prepared the way for the even larger mass exterminations in the future.

Jews were forced into slave labor, evicted from their apartments, and prevented from buying most clothing and food. In 1938, a Jewish teenager, reacting to such harassment of his parents, killed a German official. In retaliation, on the night of November 9–10, Nazis attacked some two hundred synagogues, smashed windows of Jewish-owned stores, ransacked apartments of known or suspected Jews, and threw more than twenty thousand Jews into prisons and concentration camps. That event became known as Kristallnacht, the "Night of Broken Glass." Faced with this relentless persecution, more than half of Germany's 500,000 Jews fled the country before the outbreak of World War II in 1939. Their enormous emigration fees helped finance Germany's economic recovery; their neighbors and individual Nazis used anti-Semitism to justify taking the personal possessions and jobs they left behind.

REVIEW What role did violence play in the Soviet and Nazi regimes?

Democracies on the Defensive

Nazism, communism, and fascism offered bold new approaches to modern politics. These ideologies maintained that democracy wasted precious time in building consensus and that additionally it was effeminate. Totalitarian leaders' energetic, military style of mobilizing the masses made the democratic values of the United States, France, and Great Britain appear feeble—a sign that these societies were on the decline in the struggle for survival. The appeal of totalitarianism put democracies on the defensive as they aimed to uphold individual rights and the rule of law while restoring economic well-being.

Confronting the Economic Crisis

As the depression wore on through the 1930s, some governments experimented with ways to solve social and economic crises while preserving democracy. In the early days of the slump, U.S. president Herbert Hoover opposed direct federal help to the unemployed and even ordered the army to use tanks to break up a march of unemployed World War I veterans in Washington, D.C. With unemployment close to fifteen million, Franklin Delano Roosevelt (1882–1945), the wealthy, patrician governor of New York, defeated Hoover in the presidential election of 1932 on the promise of relief and recovery. Roosevelt pushed through a torrent of legislation known collectively as the New Deal: relief for businesses, price supports for hard-pressed farmers, and public works programs for unemployed youths. The Social Security Act of 1935 set up a fund to which employers and employees contributed. It provided retirement benefits for workers, unemployment insurance, and payments to dependent mothers, their children, and people with disabilities.

Roosevelt's New Deal advanced the trend toward the **welfare state**—that is, a government that guarantees a certain level of economic well-being for individuals and businesses—that was taking shape across the West. The New Deal angered some businesspeople and wealthy Americans, who saw it as socialist, but Roosevelt maintained widespread support. Like other successful politicians of the 1930s, he was an expert at using the mass media, especially in his "fireside chats," broadcast by radio to the American people. Unlike Mussolini and Hitler, Roosevelt used the media to make speeches that promoted rather than attacked faith in democratic

Fireside Chat with FDR
President Franklin Delano Roosevelt was a master of words, uttering many memorable phrases that inspired Americans during the depression and World War II. Here he addresses the nation on August 23, 1938, over a radio hookup while his wife, Eleanor (left), and his mother, Sarah, observe. Although Roosevelt was disabled by polio, wore leg braces, and could not walk unassisted, the press never showed or mentioned his impairment, even on the rare occasions when he used crutches or a wheelchair in public. (Hulton Archive/Getty Images.)

rights and popular government. The participation of First Lady Eleanor Roosevelt contrasted sharply with the antiwoman ideology of the fascists, and the Roosevelts insisted that justice and human rights not be surrendered in difficult times. "We Americans of today . . . are characters in the living book of democracy," President Roosevelt told a group of teenagers in 1939. "But we are also its author." Even so, lynching of blacks and other racial violence continued to cause enormous suffering in the United States during the Roosevelt administration, and the economy did not recover fully. The president, however, was able to keep Americans' faith in democracy strong.

Sweden also developed a coherent program for solving economic and population problems, assigning government a central role in promoting social welfare and economic democracy. Sweden instituted central planning in the 1930s and devalued the currency to make Swedish exports more attractive on the international market. Thanks to pump-priming programs, Swedish productivity rose 20 percent between 1929 and 1935, a time when other democracies were still experiencing an economic decline.

Sweden addressed the population problem with government programs but without racist and antidemocratic coercion. Alva Myrdal, a leading member of parliament, believed that boosting the birthrate depended on both the economy and individual well-being. Acting on Myrdal's advice to promote "voluntary parenthood," the government started a loan program for married couples in 1937 and introduced prenatal care, free childbirth in a hospital, a food relief program, and subsidized housing for large families. By the end of the decade, almost 50 percent of all Swedish mothers received government aid. Long a concern of feminists and other social reformers, support of families became an important task of the modern state, which took on increasing responsibility for citizen welfare in hard times.

The most powerful democracy, the United States, had withdrawn from world leadership by refusing to participate in the League of Nations, leaving Britain and France with greater responsibility for maintaining international peace than their postwar resources could sustain. When the Great Depression hit, British prime minister Ramsay MacDonald faced a drop in government income. Although he was the leader of the Labour Party, he reduced payments to the unemployed, and Parliament denied unemployment insurance to women even though they had contributed to the unemployment fund. To protect jobs, the government imposed huge protective tariffs on imported goods, but that only discouraged a revival of international trade. Finally, in 1933, with the economy continuing to worsen, the government undertook massive programs of slum clearance, new housing construction, and health insurance for the needy. Previously, British leaders had seen pump priming of the economy as untested and thus resorted to it only when all else had failed.

Depression struck later in France than elsewhere, but the country endured a decade of public strife in the 1930s due to severe postwar demoralization and stagnant population growth. Deputies with opposing views on the economic crisis frequently came to blows in the Chamber of Deputies, and administrations were voted in and out with dizzying speed. Parisians took to the streets to protest the government's belt-tightening policies, and Nazi-style paramilitary groups flourished, attracting the unemployed, students, and veterans to the cause of ending representative government. In February 1934, these paramilitary groups joined Communists and other outraged citizens in starting riots around the parliament building. "Let's string up the deputies," chanted the crowd. "And if we can't string them up, let's beat in their faces, let's reduce them to a pulp." Hundreds of demonstrators were wounded or killed, but the antirepublican right lacked both substantial support outside Paris and a charismatic leader like Hitler or Mussolini.

Shocked into action by fascist violence, French liberals, socialists, and Communists established an antifascist coalition known as the Popular Front. Until that time, such a merging of groups had been impossible in democratic countries because Stalin directed Communist parties across Europe not to cooperate with other parties. As fascism spread throughout Europe, however, Stalin reversed course and allowed Communists to join such efforts to protect democracy. For just over a year in 1936–1937 and again briefly in 1938, the French Popular Front led the government, with the socialist leader Léon Blum as premier. Like the American New Dealers and the Swedish reformers, the French Popular Front instituted social welfare programs, including family subsidies and welfare benefits. Blum appointed women to his government (though women in France still were not allowed to vote). In June 1936, the government guaranteed workers a two-week paid vacation, a forty-hour workweek, and the right to bargain collectively. Working people would long remember Blum as the man who improved their living standards and provided them with the right to vacations.

During its brief life, the Popular Front offered the masses a youthful but democratic political culture. "In 1936 everyone was twenty years old," one man recalled, evoking the atmosphere of idealism. To express their opposition to fascism, citizens celebrated democratic holidays like Bastille Day with new enthusiasm. Not everyone liked the Popular Front, however. Powerful business leaders sent their money out of the country, leaving France financially strapped. "Better Hitler Than Blum" was the slogan of the upper classes. Blum's government fell when it lost crucial support from pro–Popular Front voters for refusing to aid the fight against fascism in Spain. Because of antiwar sentiment, France, like Britain, kept its military budgets small and refused to engage in military confrontations, even to help the cause of democratic government in Spain. The collapse of the antifascist Popular Front showed the difficulties that democratic societies had in the face of economic crisis and militaristic nationalism.

Fledgling democracies in central Europe, hit hard by the depression, also fought the twin struggle for economic survival and representative government, but less successfully. In 1932, Engelbert Dollfuss came to power in Austria, dismissing the parliament and ruling briefly as a dictator. Despite his authoritarian views, Dollfuss would not submit to the Nazis, who assassinated him in 1934. In Hungary, where outrage over the Peace of Paris remained intense, a crippled economy allowed right-wing general Gyula Gömbös to take over in 1932. Gömbös reoriented his country's foreign policy toward Mussolini and Hitler. He stirred up anti-Semitism and ethnic hatreds and left behind considerable pro-Nazi feeling after his death in 1936. President Tomas Masaryk worked to maintain a democratic Czechoslovakia, but the Slovaks, who were both poorer and less educated than the urbanized Czechs, built the strong Slovak Fascist Party, while the Communists also attacked democratic government there. In many of the new states created by the Peace of Paris, the appeal of fascism and communism flourished during the Great Depression.

Cultural Visions in Hard Times

Responding to the crisis of economic hard times and political menace, cultural leaders produced art that captured the spirit of everyday struggle. Some sympathized with the situations of factory workers, homemakers, and shopgirls straining to support themselves or their families. Others identified more with the ever-growing numbers of the unemployed and destitute. Artists portrayed the inhuman regimented side of modern life. In 1931, French director René Clair's film *À nous la liberté* (*Give Us*

Liberty) related the routine of prison life to working on a factory assembly line. In the film *Modern Times* (1936), the Little Tramp character created by Charlie Chaplin is a factory worker who has been so influenced by his monotonous job that he assumes anything he sees, even a coworker's body, needs mechanical adjustment.

Media sympathy poured out to other victims of the crisis, with women portrayed alternately as the cause and the cure for society's problems. *The Blue Angel* (1930), a German film starring Marlene Dietrich, contrasted a vital and seductive modern woman with an impractical, bumbling professor, showing how mixed-up gender roles could destroy a man—and ultimately civilization. Such films worked to strengthen fascist claims. In comedies and musicals, by comparison, heroines behaved bravely, pulling their men out of the depths of despair and setting things right again. In films such as *Keep Smiling* (1938), the British comedienne Gracie Fields portrayed spunky working-class women who remained cheerful despite hard times.

To drive home their antifascist, pacifist, or pro-worker beliefs, writers created realistic studies of human misery and the threat of war, which haunted life in the 1930s. British writer George Orwell described his experiences among the poor of Paris and London, wrote investigative pieces about the unemployed in the north

Gracie Fields Keeps Smiling

Like Roosevelt and many cultural leaders during the Great Depression, British film stars such as Gracie Fields, shown here in the hit film *Shipyard Sally* (1939), urged viewers to be courageous and maintain their self-respect as workers and citizens despite hard times. This was in stark contrast to fascist advocacy of conquest, war, and violence toward neighbors at home and abroad. (20th Century Fox/The Kobal Collection.)

of England, and published an account of atrocities committed by both sides during the Spanish Civil War (1936–1939). German writer Thomas Mann, a Christian, was so outraged by Hitler's rise to power that he went into voluntary exile. Mann's series of novels based on the Old Testament hero Joseph convey the struggle between humane values and barbarism. The fourth volume, *Joseph the Provider* (1944), praises Joseph's welfare state, in which the granaries are full and the rich pay taxes so the poor might live decent lives. In *Three Guineas* (1938), English writer Virginia Woolf directly attacked militarism, poverty, and the oppression of women, claiming they were interconnected parts of a single, devastating set of values undermining Europe in the 1930s.

While writers renewed moral concerns, scientists in research institutes and universities continued to point out limits to human understanding—limits that seemed at odds with the megalomaniacal pronouncements of dictators. Astronomer Edwin Hubble in California determined in the early 1930s that the universe was an expanding entity and thus an unpredictably changing one. Czech mathematician Kurt Gödel maintained that all mathematical systems contain some propositions that are undecidable. German physicist Werner Heisenberg developed the uncertainty, or indeterminacy, principle. Scientific observation of atomic behavior, according to this theory, itself disturbs the atom, thereby making precise formulations impossible. Even scientists, Heisenberg asserted, had to settle for statistical probability. Probability and limits to understanding were not concepts that dictators welcomed, and even people in democracies had a difficult time reconciling these new ideas with science's reputation for certainty.

Religious leaders helped foster a spirit of resistance to dictatorship among the faithful. Swiss theologian Karl Barth encouraged rebellion against the Nazis, teaching that religious people had to take seriously biblical calls for resistance to oppression. In his 1931 address to the world on social issues, Pope Pius XI condemned the failure of modern societies to provide their citizens with a decent, moral life. To critics, the proclamation seemed to endorse the heavy-handed intervention of the fascists. In Germany, nonetheless, Catholics frequently opposed Hitler, and religious commitment inspired many other individuals to contest the rising tide of fascism.

REVIEW How did the democracies work to maintain their values while facing the twin challenges of economic depression and the rise of fascism?

The Road to Global War

The economic crash intensified competition among the major powers and made external colonies more important than ever. Hitler, Mussolini, and Japan's military leaders believed that their nations deserved to rule far larger territories. At first, statesmen in Britain and France hoped that sanctions imposed by the League of Nations would stop aggression. Others, still traumatized by memories of World War I, wanted to turn a blind eye to German, Italian, and Japanese expansionism and to the fascist attack on the Spanish republic. The unchecked brutality of these states in the 1930s led to another, more deadly war.

The Road to World War II

1929	Global depression begins with the U.S. stock market crash
1931	Japan invades Manchuria
1933	Hitler comes to power in Germany
1935	Italy invades Ethiopia
1936	Civil war breaks out in Spain; Hitler remilitarizes the Rhineland
1937	Japan invades China
1938	Germany annexes Austria; European leaders meet in Munich to negotiate with Hitler
1939	Germany seizes Czechoslovakia; Hitler and Stalin sign a nonaggression pact; Germany invades Poland; Britain and France declare war on Germany

A Surge in Global Imperialism

The surging global imperialism of the 1930s ultimately led to a thoroughly global war. The British, French, and other European powers increased their grip on the colonies, while in Palestine European Jews continued to arrive and claim the area from local people, especially as Hitler enacted his harsh anti-Jewish policies. Also troubled economically, Japan, Germany, and Italy increased the competition for land and wealth in areas both close at hand and far away.

Japan, which had once borrowed from European institutions to become modern and powerful, now decided to chase Europeans out of Asia. Japan's military and business leaders wanted to control more of Asia and saw China, the Soviet Union, and the Western powers as obstacles to the empire's prosperity and the fulfillment of its destiny. Japan suffered from a weak monarchy in the person of Hirohito, just twenty-five years old when he became emperor in 1926, leading military and other groups to seek control of the government. Nationalists encouraged these leaders to pursue military success for Japan as the key to pulling agriculture and small business out of the depths of economic depression. A belief in racial superiority linked Japan with Germany and Italy in the 1930s, laying the groundwork for a global alliance.

The Japanese army swung into action in 1931, when Japanese officers blew up a train in the Chinese province of Manchuria, where Japanese businesses had invested heavily. Making the incident look like a Chinese plot, the army used the explosion as an excuse to invade Manchuria, set up a puppet government, and push farther into China. The Japanese public agreed with journalistic calls for aggressive expansion, and from 1931 on, Japan continued to attack China, angering the United States, on which Japan depended for natural resources and markets. Advocating Asian conquest as part of Japan's "divine mission," the military extended its influence in the government. By 1936–1937, Japan was spending 47 percent of its budget on arms.

The situation in East Asia affected international politics. The League of Nations condemned the invasion of Manchuria, but it imposed no sanctions on Japan to back up its condemnation. Yet, the league's condemnation outraged Japanese citizens and goaded the government to ally with Hitler and Mussolini. In 1937, Japan attacked China again, justifying its offensive as the first step toward liberating the region from Western imperialism. Hundreds of thousands of Chinese were massacred in the Rape of Nanjing—an atrocity so named because of the brutality toward girls and women and other acts of torture perpetrated by the Japanese. President Roosevelt immediately announced a U.S. embargo on the exportation of airplane parts to Japan and later drastically cut the flow of crucial raw materials that supplied Japanese industry. Nonetheless, the Western powers, including the Soviet Union, did not effectively resist Japan's territorial expansion in Asia and the Pacific.

Like Japanese leaders, Mussolini and Hitler called their countries "have-nots" and demanded land and resources more in line with those of the other imperial powers. Mussolini threatened "permanent conflict" to expand Italy's borders, and Hitler's agenda included breaking free from the Versailles treaty's military restrictions on Germany and gaining *Lebensraum*—"living space" in which superior Aryans could thrive. This space would be taken from the "inferior" Slavic peoples and Bolsheviks, who would be moved to Siberia or serve as slaves. Both dictators portrayed themselves as peace-loving men who resorted to extreme measures only to benefit their countries and humanity. Their anticommunism appealed to statesmen across Europe, and Hitler's anti-Semitism found widespread support as well.

Both leaders moved to plunder other countries boldly and openly. In the autumn of 1933, Germany withdrew from the League of Nations. In 1935, Hitler loudly rejected the clauses of the Treaty of Versailles that limited German military strength as he reintroduced military conscription and started openly rearming. (Germany had been rearming in secret for years.) Mussolini chose 1935 to invade Ethiopia, one of the few African states not overwhelmed by European imperialism. He wanted to demonstrate his regime's youth and vigor and to raise Italy's standing in the world. "The Roman legionnaires are again on the march," one soldier exulted. The poorly equipped Ethiopians resisted, but their capital, Addis Ababa, fell in the spring of 1936. The League of Nations voted sanctions against Italy; Britain and France, however, opposed an embargo on oil, thus keeping the sanctions from being effective while also suggesting a lack of resolve to fight aggression.

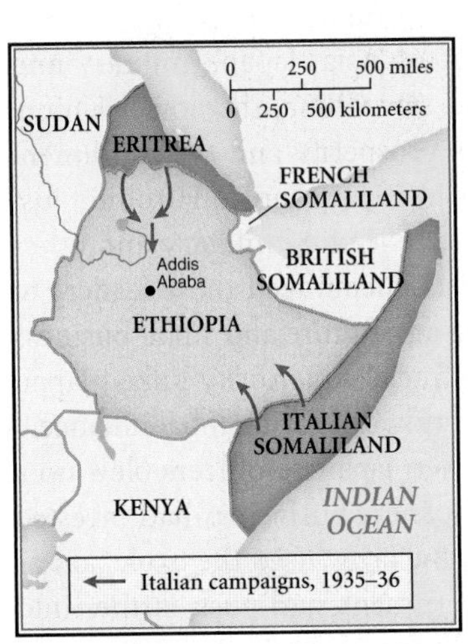

The Ethiopian War, 1935–1936

In March 1936, Hitler, profiting from world attention on Italy's attack on Ethiopia, defiantly sent his troops into the Rhineland (bordering France), which was supposed to be a permanently demilitarized zone. The inhabitants greeted the Germans with wild enthusiasm, and the French, whose security was most endangered by this action, protested to the League of Nations instead of occupying the region. The British simply accepted the remilitarization. Hitler and Mussolini thus appeared as powerful military heroes, creating, in Mussolini's muscular phrase, the "Rome-Berlin Axis." Next to them, the politicians of France and Great Britain looked timid and weak.

The Spanish Civil War, 1936–1939

Spain seemed to be headed toward democracy in the early 1930s. In 1931, Spanish republicans overthrew the monarchy and the dictatorship that ruled in its name. For centuries the Spanish state had backed the rule of large landowners and the Catholic clergy over the countryside. With cities like Barcelona and Bilbao industrializing, these ruling elites kept the impoverished peasantry in their grip, making Spain a country of economic extremes. Urban groups reacted enthusiastically to the end of the dictatorship and began debating the course of change, with Communists, socialists, anarchists, constitutionalists, and other groups all disagreeing on how to create a democratic nation. Democratic groups so battled one another that the republic had a hard time putting in place a political program that would gain it support in the countryside. Instead of building popular loyalty and reducing the strength of the political right through land redistribution, republicans failed to mount a unified effort against their reactionary opponents. In 1936, pro-republican groups temporarily banded together in the Popular Front coalition to win elections and prevent the republic from collapsing under the weight of growing monarchist opposition.

In response to the Popular Front victory, the forces of the right drew closer together, using their considerable wealth to undermine the government. In 1936, a group of army officers staged an uprising against the republican government in Madrid (Map 21.1). The rebel officers soon found a determined leader, General Francisco Franco (1892–1975), and an alliance of monarchists, landowners, the clergy, and the fascist Falange Party soon gained support from fascists in other parts of Europe. Spain became a training ground for World War II. Hitler and

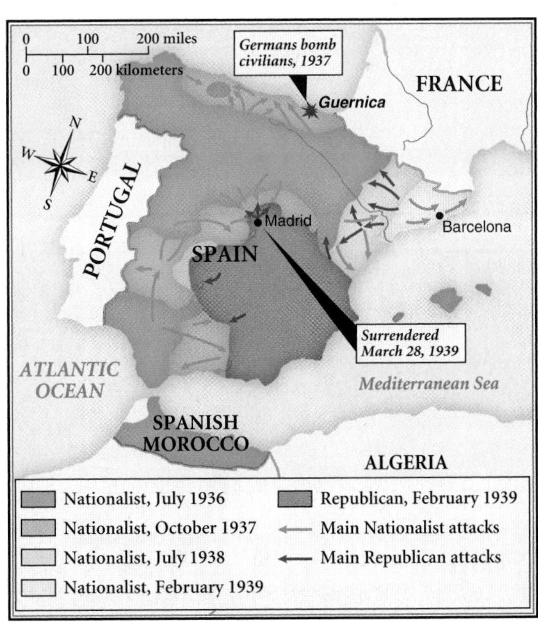

Map 21.1 The Spanish Civil War, 1936–1939
Pro-republican and antirepublican forces fought one another to determine whether Spain would be a democracy or an authoritarian state. Germany and Italy sent opponents of the Spanish republic military assistance, notably airplanes to experiment with bombing civilians, while volunteers from around the world arrived to fight for the republic. Defeating these ill-organized groups, General Francisco Franco instituted a pro-fascist government that sent many people to jail and into exile.

Mussolini sent military personnel to support Franco, gaining an opportunity to test new weapons and to practice the terror bombing of civilians. In 1937, low-flying German planes attacked the Spanish town of Guernica on market day, mowing down civilians in the streets. This useless slaughter inspired Pablo Picasso's memorial mural to the dead, *Guernica* (1937), in which the intense suffering is starkly displayed in monochromatic grays and whites.

The Spanish republic appealed everywhere for assistance, but only the Soviet Union answered. In 1938, as the Spanish government's position weakened, Stalin withdrew his support. Britain and France showed their war-wariness by refusing to provide crucial aid. Instead, a few thousand volunteers from a variety of countries—including students, journalists, and artists—remained to fight for the republic. These volunteers believed that with Mussolini and Hitler on a rampage in Europe, "Spain was the place to stop fascism." The conflict was bitter and bloody, with atrocities committed on both sides, but the splinter groups and citizen armies with which the Spanish republic defended itself could not hold. Franco's troops, bolstered decisively by aid from Hitler and Mussolini, defeated the republicans in 1939, strengthening the cause of military authoritarianism in Europe. Tens of thousands fled, while many others found themselves jailed or killed by Franco's new pro-fascist government.

The Spanish Republic Appeals for Aid
The government of the Spanish republic sent out modern advertising and propaganda to attract support from the democracies, especially Great Britain and France. Antiwar sentiment remained high among the British and French, however, and despite the horrifying and deliberate bombing of civilians by Franco's German allies, aid for the republic failed to arrive. (Imperial War Museum, London.)

Hitler's Conquest of Central Europe, 1938–1939

The next step toward World War II was Germany's annexation of Austria in 1938 (Map 21.2). Many Austrians had actually wished for such a merger, or *Anschluss,* after the Paris peace settlement had stripped them of their empire, and Hitler himself had been born in Austria. So Hitler's troops easily entered Austria, and the enthusiasm of Nazi sympathizers made the Anschluss appear to reflect the Wilsonian

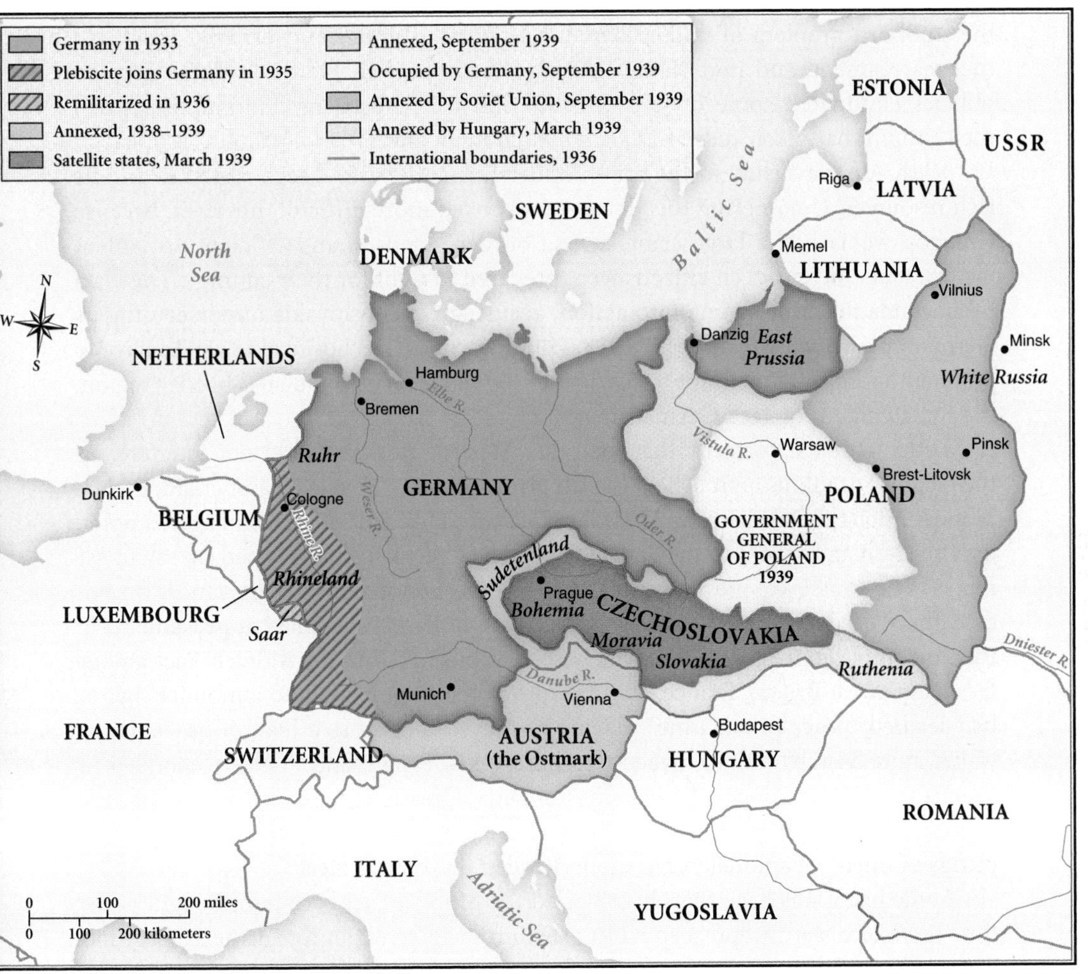

Map 21.2 The Growth of Nazi Germany, 1933–1939
German expansion was rapid and surprising, as Hitler's forces and Nazi diplomacy brought about the annexation of the new states of central and eastern Europe. Though committed to defending the sovereignty of these states through the League of Nations, French and British diplomats were more interested in satisfying Hitler because they believed that doing so would prevent his claiming even more of Europe. They were mistaken, and Hitler proceeded to take the human and material resources of adjacent countries to support the Third Reich. **For more help analyzing this map, see the map activity for this chapter in the Online Study Guide at** bedfordstmartins.com/huntconcise**.**

idea of self-determination. The annexation began the so-called unification of Aryan peoples into one greater German nation, and Hitler's seizure of Austrian gold supplies marked the next step in taking over central and eastern Europe. Austria was declared a German province, and Nazi thugs ruled once cosmopolitan Vienna. An observer later commented on the scene: "University professors were obliged to scrub the streets with their naked hands, pious white-bearded Jews were dragged into the synagogue by hooting youths and forced to do knee-exercises and to shout 'Heil Hitler' in chorus." The Nazis gained additional support in Austria by solving the stubborn problem of unemployment. Factories sprang up overnight, mostly to fuel rearmament, and new "Hitler housing" became available to workers. German policies eliminated some of the psychological pain Austrians had suffered when their empire had been reduced to a small country after World War I.

With Austria firmly in his grasp, Hitler turned next to Czechoslovakia and its rich resources. Conquering this democracy looked more difficult, however, because Czechoslovakia had a large army, strong border defenses, and efficient armament factories, and most Czech citizens were prepared to fight for their country. The Nazi propaganda machine swung into action, accusing Czechoslovakia of persecuting its German minority. By October 1, 1938, Hitler warned, Czechoslovakia would have to grant autonomy (tantamount to Nazi rule) to the German-populated border region, the Sudetenland, or face German invasion.

Hitler gambled correctly that the other Western powers would not interfere. As the October deadline approached, British prime minister Neville Chamberlain, French premier Edouard Daladier, and Mussolini met with Hitler in Munich and agreed not to oppose Germany's claim to the Sudetenland. The Czechs themselves had no say in the matter. The strategy of preventing a war by making concessions for grievances (in this case, the alleged affront to Germans in the Peace of Paris) was called **appeasement**. At the time, these concessions were widely seen as positive, and the Munich Pact among Germany, Great Britain, France, and Italy prompted Chamberlain to announce that he had secured "peace in our time." Having portrayed himself as a man of peace, Hitler waited until March 1939 to invade Czechoslovakia. Britain and France responded by promising military support to Poland, Romania, Greece, and Turkey in case of Nazi invasion. In May 1939, Hitler and Mussolini countered this agreement by signing a pledge of offensive and defensive support called the Pact of Steel.

Some historians have sharply criticized the Munich Pact because it bought Hitler time to build his army and seemed to give him the green light for further aggression. They believe that a confrontation might have stopped Hitler and that even if war had resulted, the democracies would have triumphed at less cost than they later did. According to this view, each military move by Germany, Italy, and Japan should have been met with stiff opposition, and the Soviet Union should have been made a partner in this resistance. Others counter that appeasement gave France and Britain precious time to beef up their own armies, which the Munich crisis prompted them to do.

Stalin, excluded from the Munich deliberations, saw that the democracies were not going to fight to protect eastern Europe. He took action. To the astonishment of people in the West, on August 23, 1939, Germany and the USSR signed a nonaggression agreement. The **Nazi-Soviet Pact** provided that if one country became involved in war, the other country would remain neutral. Moreover, the two dictators secretly agreed to divide Poland and the Baltic states—Latvia, Estonia, and Lithuania—at some future date. The Nazi-Soviet Pact ensured that if war came, the democracies would be fighting a Germany with no fear of attack on its eastern borders. The pact also benefited the USSR. Despite Hitler's ambition to wipe Bolshevism from the face of the earth, the pact allowed Stalin time to rebuild his officer corps, which had been destroyed in the purges. Believing that Great Britain and perhaps even France would continue not to resist him, Hitler moved to enlarge his empire further and aimed his forces at Poland.

REVIEW How did the aggression of Japan, Germany, and Italy create the conditions for global war?

World War II, 1939–1945

World War II officially began when Germany launched an all-out attack on Poland on September 1, 1939. In contrast to 1914, no jubilation in Berlin accompanied the invasion; when Britain and France declared war two days later, the mood in their capitals was similarly grim. Although Japan, Italy, and the United States did not join the battle immediately, their eventual participation spread the fighting throughout the world. By the time World War II ended in 1945, millions were starving, entire countries lay in ruins, and unparalleled atrocities, including technological genocide, had killed six million Jews and six million Slavs, Gypsies, homosexuals, and other civilian enemies of fascism.

The German Onslaught

German forces quickly defeated the ill-equipped Polish troops by launching an overpowering **Blitzkrieg** (lightning war). The Germans concentrated airplanes, tanks, and motorized infantry to encircle Polish defenders and capture the capital, Warsaw, with blinding speed. Allowing the German army to conserve supplies, Blitzkrieg assured Germans at home that the human costs of gaining Lebensraum would be low. On September 17, 1939, Soviet forces invaded Poland from the east. By the end of the month, the Polish army was in shambles, and the victors had divided Poland according to the Nazi-Soviet Pact. Within the Reich, Hitler sold the war as one of self-defense, especially from what German propagandists called the "warlike menace" of world Jewry.

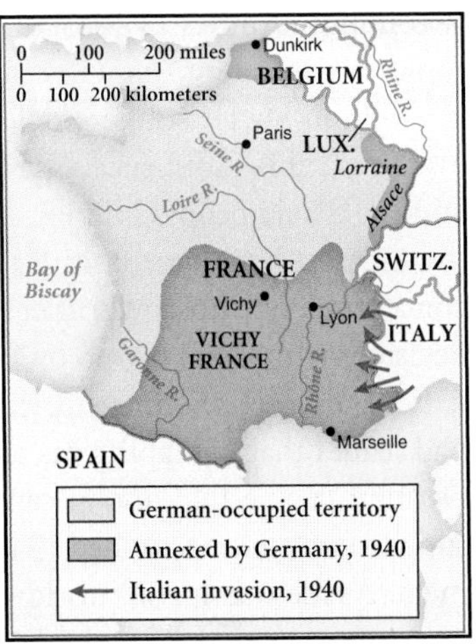

The Division of France, 1940

Hitler ordered an attack on France in November 1939, but his generals, who feared that Germany was ill prepared for total war, were able to postpone the offensive until the spring of 1940. In April 1940, Blitzkrieg crushed Denmark and Norway; the battles of Belgium, the Netherlands, and France followed in May and June. On June 5, Mussolini, eyeing future spoils for Italy, invaded France from the southeast. The French and their British allies could not withstand the German onslaught. Trapped on the beaches of Dunkirk in northern France, 370,000 British and French soldiers were rescued in a heroic effort by an improvised fleet of naval ships, fishing boats, and pleasure craft. A dejected French government surrendered on June 22, 1940, leaving Germany to rule the northern half of France, including Paris. In the south, known as Vichy France after the spa town where the government sat, Germany allowed the reactionary and aged World War I hero Henri Philippe Pétain to govern. Stalin used the diversion in western Europe to annex the Baltic states.

Britain now stood alone. Blaming Germany's rapid victories on Chamberlain's policy of appeasement, British voters swept him out of office and replaced him as prime minister with Winston Churchill (1874–1965), an early advocate of resistance to Hitler. After Hitler ordered the bombardment of Britain in the summer of 1940, Churchill rallied the nation by radio—now in more than nine million British homes—to protect the ideals of liberty with their "blood, toil, tears, and sweat." In the battle of Britain, or Blitz as the British called it, the German air force (Luftwaffe) bombed public buildings, monuments, weapons depots, and factories. Using the wealth of its colonies, Britain poured resources into antiaircraft weapons, a highly successful code-breaking group called Ultra, and the development of radar. At year's end, the British air industry was outproducing the Germans by 50 percent.

By the fall of 1940, German air losses forced Hitler to abandon his plan for a naval invasion of Britain. By forcing Hungary, Romania, and Bulgaria to join the Axis powers, Germany gained access to more food and oil. Hitler then made his fatal decision to attack the Soviet Union—the "center of judeobolshevism," as he called it. In June 1941, the German army crossed the Soviet border, breaking the Nazi-Soviet Pact, while Hitler promised to "raze Moscow and Leningrad to the ground." Three million German and other troops quickly penetrated Soviet lines along a two-thousand-mile front, and by July the German army had rolled to within two hundred miles of Moscow, eventually reaching its suburbs. Using a strategy of rapid encirclement, the Germans killed, captured, and wounded more than half the 4.5 million Soviet soldiers defending the border.

Amid this rapid success, Hitler blundered. Considering himself a military genius and the Slavic people inferior, he proposed attacking Leningrad, the Baltic states, and the Ukraine simultaneously, a plan that went against his generals' recommendation to concentrate on Moscow. Hitler's grand scheme cost precious time without achieving a decisive victory, and driven by Stalin and local party members, the Soviet people fought back. The onset of winter turned Nazi soldiers into frostbitten wretches because Hitler had feared that equipping his army for the harsh Russian winter would suggest to the German people that a long campaign lay in store, as in fact it did. Germany's poorly supplied armies succumbed to the weather, disease, and ultimately a shortage of equipment. As the war spread worldwide, Germany continued to have an inflated sense of its own power even though the Russian campaign suggested the limits of that power.

The War Expands: The Pacific and Beyond

With the outbreak of war in Europe, Japan took territories in the British Empire, bullied the Dutch in Indonesia, and invaded French Indochina to procure raw materials for its industrial and military expansion. The militarist Japanese government decided to settle matters with the United States, which was trying to block Japan's expansion, and launched an all-out attack on Pearl Harbor in Hawaii on December 7, 1941. After bombing Pearl Harbor, Japanese planes decimated a fleet of U.S. airplanes in the Philippines. Roosevelt immediately summoned Congress to declare war on Japan. By the spring of 1942, the Japanese had conquered Guam, the Philippines, Malaya, Burma, Indonesia, Singapore, and much of the southwestern Pacific. Like Hitler's early conquests, these victories strengthened the Japanese military's confidence. "The era of democracy is finished," the foreign minister announced.

Within days of Pearl Harbor, Germany joined its Japanese ally and declared war on the United States—an enemy, Hitler proclaimed, that was "half Judaized and the other half Negrified." Mussolini followed suit. The United States was not prepared for a long struggle, partly because isolationist sentiment remained strong. Its armed forces numbered only 1.6 million, and no plan existed for producing the necessary guns, tanks, and airplanes. In addition, the United States and the Soviet Union did not trust each other. Despite these obstacles to cooperation, Hitler's four enemies came together in the Grand Alliance of Great Britain, the Free French (a government in exile in London led by General Charles de Gaulle), the Soviet Union, and the United States. The Grand Alliance formed a larger coalition with twenty other countries, which became known as the Allies. Given the urgency of war and the partners' competing interests, the Allies had much internal strife to overcome in their struggle against the Axis powers (Germany, Italy, and Japan). Yet in the long run, the Allies had distinct advantages: their vast potential for war in terms of manpower and resources and their experience in waging war on many continents. Meeting frequently, the Allied leaders worked hard to wage an effective war, while the Axis rulers paid less attention to cooperation and to the material realities of waging total war.

The War against Civilians

Far more civilians than soldiers died in World War II. The Axis powers and Allies alike bombed cities simply to destroy civilians' will to resist—a tactic that seemed to backfire by inspiring defiance rather than surrender. Two such Allied attacks were the firebombing of Dresden and Tokyo, which killed tens of thousands of civilians, though Axis attacks were far more widespread. As the German army swept through eastern Europe, it slaughtered Jews, Communists, Slavs, and others whom the Nazis deemed "racial inferiors" and enemies. In Poland, the SS murdered hundreds of thousands of Polish citizens or relocated them to forced labor camps, with confiscated Polish land and homes being given to "racially pure" Aryans from Germany and other central European countries. Literate people in conquered areas were the most vulnerable, because Hitler, like Stalin, saw them as leading members of the people he wanted to destroy. Because many in the German army initially rebelled at killing innocent civilians simply because they could read, special Gestapo forces took charge of herding their victims into woods and ravines, or even against town walls, where they would be shot en masse. The Japanese did the same in China, Southeast Asia, and the islands of the Pacific. The number of casualties in China alone has been estimated at thirty million, with untold millions murdered elsewhere.

The Nazis focused on the extermination of the Jews, herding them first into urban ghettos with minimal provisions. Around captured Soviet towns, Jews were usually shot in pits, some of which they had been forced to dig themselves. After shedding their clothes and putting them in orderly piles for later Nazi use, ten thousand or more at a time were killed, often with the help of anti-Semitic villagers. In Jedwabne, Poland, some eight hundred citizens on their own initiative beat and burned their Jewish neighbors to death and took their property—evidence that the **Holocaust** was not simply a Nazi program. At this time, however, the "Final Solution"—the Nazis' evil plan to exterminate all of Europe's Jews—was not yet fully under way.

Life in the Warsaw Ghetto
The occupying Nazis resettled Warsaw's Jews into a minuscule area of the city in order, the Germans explained, to bring "moral purification" and to keep Germans from being infected by these "carriers of the bacteria of epidemics." Surviving on extremely small amounts of food and fuel, Warsaw's Jews died daily on the streets. Corpses were a common sight for the average citizen—young or old. (ullstein bild/The Granger Collection, NY.)

A more organized, technological system for rounding up Jews and transporting them to extermination sites had taken shape by the fall of 1941. Hitler had long predicted "the destruction of the Jewish race in Europe," so although no order written by Hitler exists, his responsibility for it is clear. He discussed the Final Solution's progress, issued oral directives for it, and made violent anti-Semitism a basis for Nazism from the beginning. Efficient scientists, doctors, lawyers, and government workers also made the Holocaust work. Six camps in Poland were developed specifically for the purpose of mass murder, although some, like Auschwitz-Birkenau, served as both extermination and labor camps (Map 21.3). Using techniques developed in the T4 project in the late 1930s, the camp at Chelmno first gassed Christian Poles and Soviet prisoners of war. Specially designed crematoria for the mass burning of corpses started functioning in 1943. By then, Auschwitz had the capacity to burn 1.7 million bodies per year. About 60 percent of new arrivals—particularly children, women, and the elderly—were selected for immediate murder in the gas chambers; the other 40 percent labored until, utterly used up, they too were gassed.

Victims from all over Europe were sent to the extermination camps. In the ghettos of various European cities, councils of Jewish leaders, such as the one in Amsterdam where Etty Hillesum worked, were ordered to decide on those to be "resettled in the east." For weakened, poorly armed ghetto inhabitants, open resistance meant certain death. When Jews rose up against their Nazi captors in Warsaw in 1943, they were mercilessly butchered. The Nazis also took pains to cloak their true purposes in the extermination camps. Bands played to greet incoming trainloads of victims; some new arrivals were given postcards with reassuring messages to mail home. Those not

Map 21.3 Concentration Camps and Extermination Sites in Europe
This map shows the major extermination sites and concentration camps in Europe, but the entire continent was dotted with thousands of lesser camps to which the Nazis' victims were transported. Some of these lesser camps were merely way stations on the path to ultimate extermination. In focusing on the major camps, historians often lose sight of the other deportation and extermination centers that blanketed Europe.

chosen for immediate murder had their heads shaved, were disinfected, and were given prison garments. So began life in "a living hell," as one survivor wrote.

The camps were scenes of the struggle for life in the face of torture and death. Overworked inmates were extremely undernourished, usually receiving less than five hundred calories per day. This left them vulnerable to typhus and other diseases that swept through the camps. Prisoners sometimes went mad, as did many of the guards. In the name of advancing "racial science," doctors performed unbelievably cruel experiments with no anesthesia on pregnant women, twins, and others. Despite the harsh conditions, some people maintained their spirit: prisoners forged new friendships, and women in particular observed religious holidays and celebrated birthdays—all of which helped in the struggle for survival. Thanks to those sharing a bread ration and doing him favors, wrote the Auschwitz survivor Primo Levi, "I managed not to forget that I myself was a man." Yet part of the horror of the Holocaust was how systematically and efficiently mass murder was carried out. Ordinary, supposedly civilized people committed this vast genocidal crime, whose planned, bureaucratic organization still shocks and outrages the world.

Societies at War

Even more than World War I, World War II depended on industrial productivity aimed totally toward war and mass killings. The Axis countries remained at a disadvantage throughout the war, for the Allies simply outproduced them. Even while Germany occupied the Soviet industrial heartland and besieged many of its cities, the USSR increased its production of weapons. Both Japan and Germany made the most of their lower capacity, especially in the use of the Blitzkrieg. Hitler had to avoid imposing wartime austerity because he had come to power promising to end economic suffering, not increase it. The use of millions of slave laborers and foreign resources from occupied areas helped, but both Japan's and Germany's belief in their racial superiority worked against them by preventing them from accurately estimating the capabilities of the enemies they held in contempt.

The Allied governments were overwhelmingly successful in mobilizing civilians, especially women. In the Axis countries, where government policy particularly exalted motherhood and kept women out of good jobs, officials realized too late that women were desperately needed in the workforce. They could not change their propaganda effectively enough to convince women to take the low-paid work offered them. In contrast, Soviet women constituted more than half the workforce by war's end, and 800,000 volunteered for the military, even serving as pilots. As the Germans invaded the USSR, Soviet citizens moved entire factories eastward. In a dramatic about-face, the government encouraged devotion to the Russian Orthodox church as a way of inspiring patriotism.

Even more than in World War I, civilians were bombarded with huge amounts of propaganda when they went to the movies or listened to the radio. People were glued to their radios for war news, but much of it was tightly controlled. The totalitarian powers often withheld news of defeats and high casualty numbers to keep civilian support. Wartime films depicted aviation heroes and infantrymen as well as the working women and wives left behind. Government agencies monitored filmmaking and allocated supplies only to approved films.

Between 1939 and 1945, governments organized many aspects of everyday life—a necessity because resources such as food had to be shifted away from civilians toward soldiers and military needs. In most countries, it was simply taken for granted that civilians would not receive what they needed to survive in good health. A high number of Soviet children and old people were among the one million residents who starved to death during the German siege of Leningrad. Government agencies regulated the production and distribution of clothing and household products, all of which were rationed and generally of low quality. They gave hints for preparing meals without meat, sugar, fat, and other staples and urged women and children to embrace deprivation so that fighting men could have more. With governments standardizing items such as food, clothing, and entertainment, World War II furthered the development of a mass society in which people lived and thought in similar ways.

On both sides, propaganda and government policies promoted racial thinking. Since the early 1930s, the German government had published ugly caricatures of Jews, Slavs, and Gypsies. Similarly, Allied propaganda during the war depicted Germans as perverts and "Japs" as insectlike fanatics. The U.S. government forced citizens of Japanese origin into internment camps. In the Soviet Union, Muslims and minority ethnic groups were uprooted and relocated away from the front lines as potential Nazi collaborators. Both sides drew colonized peoples into the war through forced labor and conscription into their armies. Some two million Indians served the Allied cause, as did several hundred thousand Africans. As the Japanese swept through the Pacific and parts of East Asia, they too conscripted men into their army.

From Resistance to Allied Victory

Resistance to fascism and Nazi control began early in the war. General Charles de Gaulle directed the Free French government and its forces from England. The Free French were a mixed organization of troops of colonized Asians and Africans, French troops who had been evacuated from Dunkirk, and volunteers from Axis-occupied countries. Less well known than the Free French were Communist-dominated groups of resisters throughout occupied Europe, some of whom gathered information to aid a planned Allied landing on the French coast. Rural partisans in many countries not only plotted assassinations of traitors and German officers but also bombed bridges, rail lines, and military facilities in German-occupied areas. The Polish resistance worked tirelessly against the Nazis, as did individuals such as Swedish diplomat Raoul Wallenberg, whose dealings with Nazi officials saved thousands of Hungarian Jews.

People fought back through everyday activities. Homemakers circulated newsletters urging demonstrations at prisons where civilians were detained. In central Europe, hikers smuggled Jews and others through dangerous mountain passes.

Danish villagers created vast escape networks, while women resisters used stereotypes to good advantage, often carrying weapons to assassination sites in the correct belief that the Nazis were not likely to suspect or search them. They also seduced and murdered enemy officers. Other actions subtly undermined the demands of fascist leaders. "Naturally the Germans didn't think that a woman could have carried a bomb," explained one Italian resister, "so this became the woman's task." Resistance kept alive the liberal ideal of individual political action in the face of tyranny.

Both subtle and dramatically visible resistance took place in fascist countries. Couples in Germany and Italy limited family size in defiance of pro-birth policies. German teenagers danced the forbidden American jitterbug, thus disobeying the Nazis and forcing the use of scarce manpower to police their groups. More spectacularly, in July 1944 a group of German military officers, fearing their country's military humiliation, tried but failed to assassinate Hitler—one of several such attempts. Some ask whether the assassination attempt came too late in the war to count as true resistance. However, some five million Germans alone, and millions more people of other nationalities, lost their lives in the last nine months of the war. Had Hitler died even as late as the summer of 1944, the relief to humanity would have been considerable.

Amid civilian resistance, Allied forces turned the frontline war against the Axis powers beginning in mid-1942 at the battle of Stalingrad (Map 21.4)—a battle to gain access to Soviet oil. Months of ferocious fighting ended when the Soviet army captured the ninety thousand German survivors in February 1943. Allied victories in North Africa in 1942, where British code-breaking capabilities foiled German general Erwin Rommel's innovative tactics, were followed in July 1943 by an Allied landing in Sicily, provoking a German invasion and takeover of Italy's war effort. A slow, bitter fight for the Italian peninsula lasted until April 1945, when Allied forces finally triumphed. After Italy's liberation, partisans shot Mussolini and his mistress and hung their dead bodies for public display.

The victory at Stalingrad marked the beginning of the Soviet drive westward, during which the Soviets bore the brunt of the Nazi war machine. From the air, Britain and the United States bombed German cities, aiming to destroy war industries and demoralize citizens. But it was an invasion from the west that Stalin wanted from his allies. Finally, on June 6, 1944, the combined Allied forces under the command of U.S. general Dwight Eisenhower landed on the heavily fortified beaches of Normandy and then fought their way through the German-held territory of western France. In late July, Allied forces broke through German defenses and a month later helped liberate Paris. The Soviets meanwhile captured the Baltic states and entered Poland, pausing

Map 21.4 World War II in Europe and North Africa
The Axis and Allied powers waged war in Europe and Africa, inflicting massive loss of life on civilians and armies alike and widespread destruction of property, including the infrastructure—factories, equipment, and agriculture—needed to wage total war. The war affected the entire European continent, as well as areas of Africa colonized by or allied with the major powers. Ultimately, the Allies crushed the Axis powers by squeezing them from the east, west, and south.

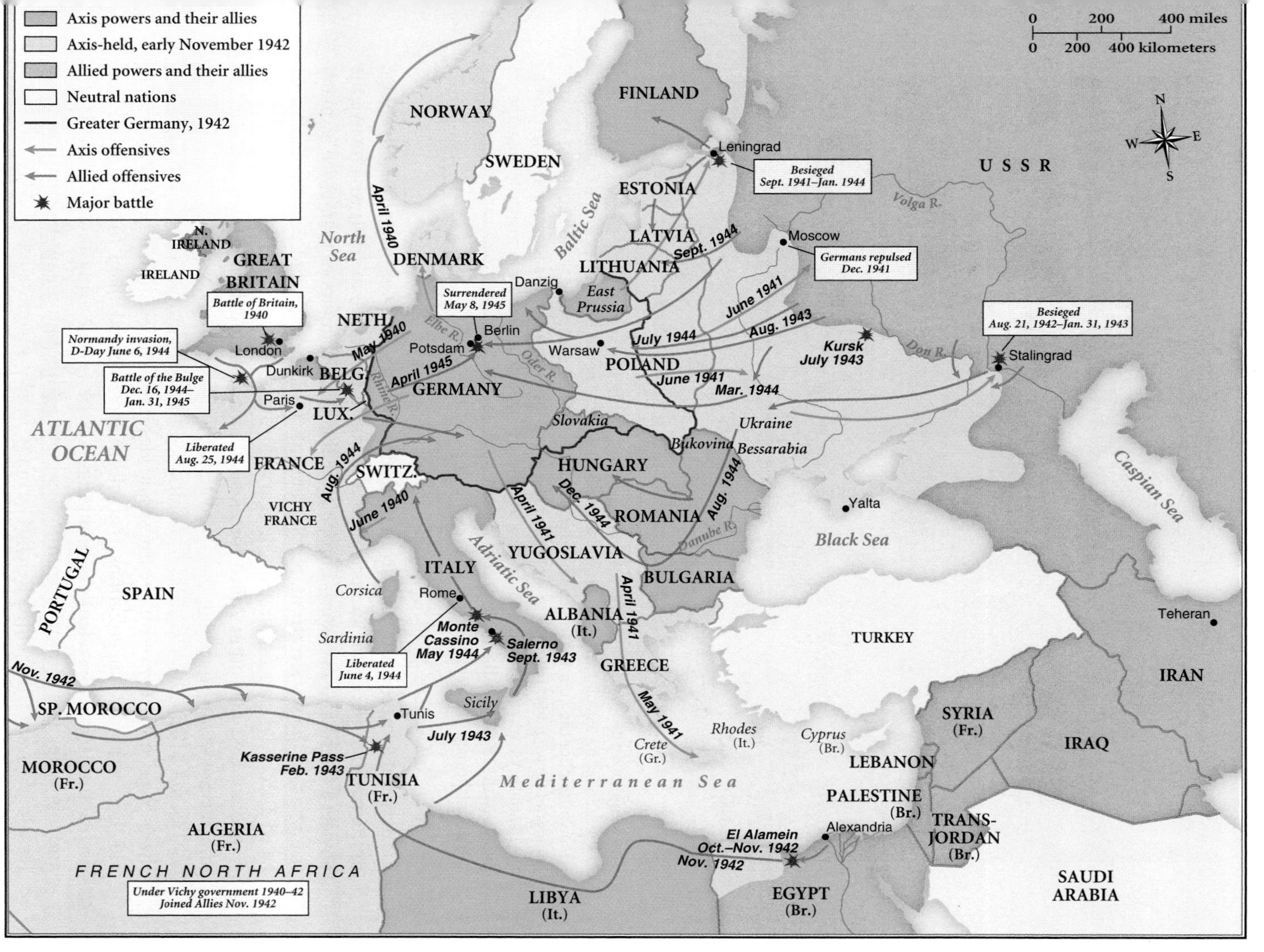

Axis powers and their allies
Axis-held, early November 1942
Allied powers and their allies
Neutral nations
Greater Germany, 1942
Axis offensives
Allied offensives
Major battle
0 200 400 miles
0 200 400 kilometers
N
W
E
S
USSR
FINLAND
NORWAY
SWEDEN
DENMARK
ESTONIA
LATVIA
LITHUANIA
East Prussia
POLAND
GERMANY
NETH.
BELG.
LUX.
FRANCE
VICHY FRANCE
SWITZ.
ITALY
YUGOSLAVIA
ALBANIA (It.)
GREECE
BULGARIA
ROMANIA
HUNGARY
Slovakia
Bukovina
Bessarabia
Ukraine
TURKEY
SYRIA (Fr.)
LEBANON
PALESTINE (Br.)
TRANS-JORDAN (Br.)
IRAQ
IRAN
SAUDI ARABIA
EGYPT (Br.)
LIBYA (It.)
TUNISIA (Fr.)
ALGERIA (Fr.)
MOROCCO (Fr.)
SP. MOROCCO
SPAIN
PORTUGAL
GREAT BRITAIN
N. IRELAND
IRELAND
FRENCH NORTH AFRICA
Under Vichy government 1940–42
Joined Allies Nov. 1942
ATLANTIC OCEAN
North Sea
Baltic Sea
Adriatic Sea
Black Sea
Caspian Sea
Mediterranean Sea
Volga R.
Don R.
Oder R.
Elbe R.
Rhine R.
Danube R.
Corsica
Sardinia
Sicily
Crete (Gr.)
Rhodes (It.)
Cyprus (Br.)
Leningrad
Besieged Sept. 1941–Jan. 1944
Moscow
Germans repulsed Dec. 1941
Stalingrad
Besieged Aug. 21, 1942–Jan. 31, 1943
Kursk July 1943
Yalta
Teheran
Warsaw
Danzig
Berlin
Potsdam
Surrendered May 8, 1945
London
Battle of Britain, 1940
Dunkirk
Paris
Liberated Aug. 25, 1944
Normandy invasion, D-Day June 6, 1944
Battle of the Bulge Dec. 16, 1944–Jan. 31, 1945
Rome
Liberated June 4, 1944
Monte Cassino May 1944
Salerno Sept. 1943
Tunis
Kasserine Pass Feb. 1943
Alexandria
El Alamein Oct.–Nov. 1942
Nov. 1942
April 1940
May 1940
June 1940
April 1941
May 1941
June 1941
Aug. 1943
Mar. 1944
July 1944
Sept. 1944
Aug. 1944
Dec. 1944
April 1945
July 1943

The Siege of Leningrad
In the face of the Nazi invasion in 1941, Soviet citizens reacted heroically, moving entire factories to the interior of the country and building fortifications. Nowhere was their resolve so tested as in Leningrad (now St. Petersburg). For more than two years, the German army besieged the city, causing the deaths of hundreds of thousands of people. Before the Allied landing at Normandy in 1944, the people of the USSR bore the brunt of Nazi military might in Hitler's attempt to defeat what he called "judeobolshevism." (Sovfoto/Eastfoto.)

for desperately needed supplies from behind their lines. The Germans took advantage of the pause to put down an uprising of the Polish resistance in 1944, which gave the Soviets a freer hand in eastern Europe after the war. Facing more than twice as many troops as on the western front, the Soviet army took Bulgaria and Romania and then faced fierce German fighting in Hungary during the winter of 1944–1945. British, Canadian, U.S., and other Allied forces simultaneously fought their way eastward to join the Soviets in squeezing the Third Reich to its final defeat.

As the Allies advanced, Hitler maintained that the German people were proving themselves unworthy of his greatness and deserved to perish in a bloody downfall. He thus refused all negotiations that might have spared them further death and destruction from the relentless bombing. As the Soviet army took Berlin, Hitler and his wife, Eva Braun, committed suicide. Although many German soldiers remained loyal to the Third Reich, Germany finally surrendered on May 8, 1945.

The Allies had followed a "Europe first" strategy in conducting the war. They had nonetheless pursued the Japanese in the Pacific without pause (Map 21.5). In 1940 and 1941, Japan had ousted the Europeans from many colonial holdings in Asia,

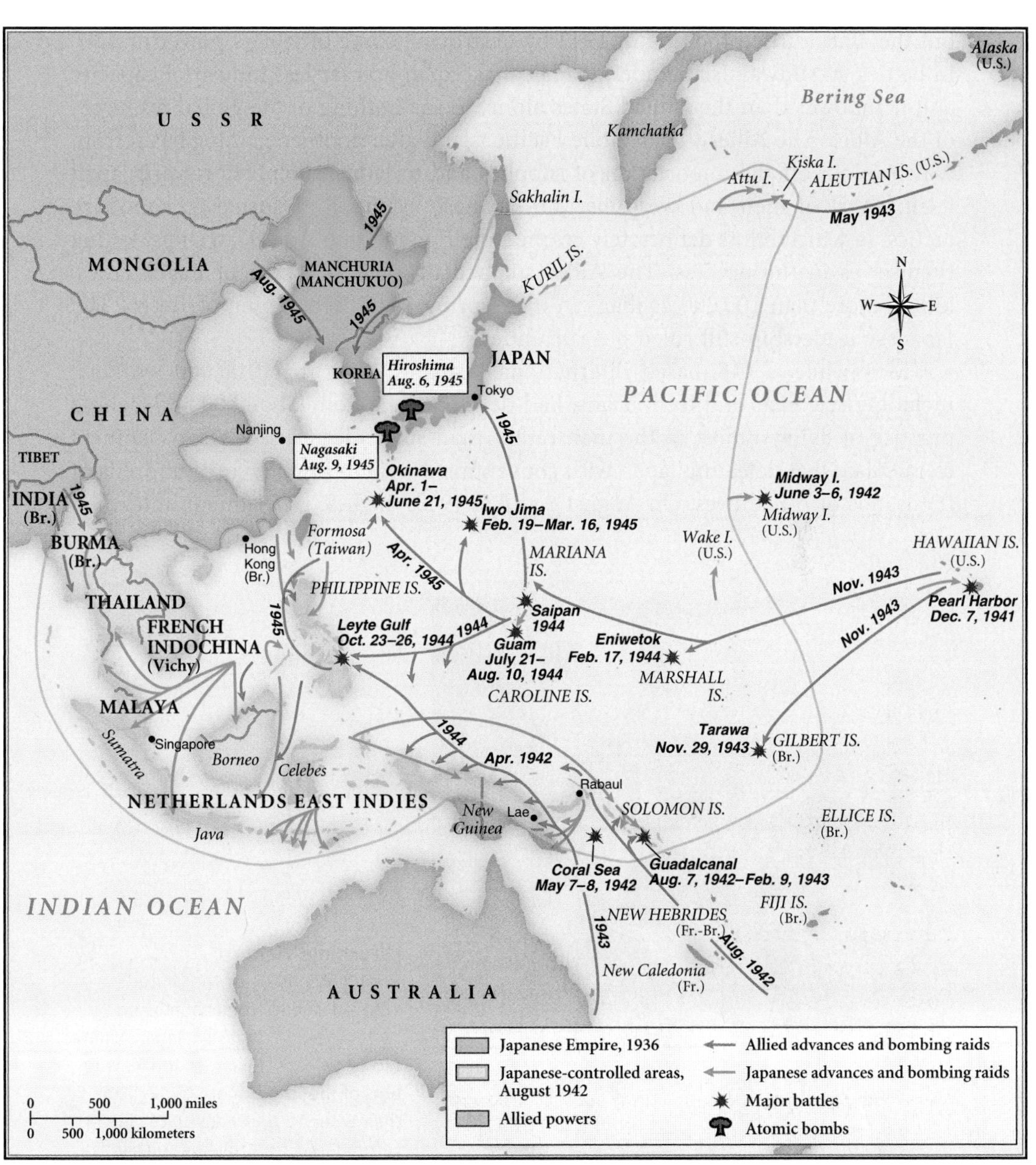

Map 21.5 World War II in the Pacific

As in Europe, the early days of World War II gave the advantage to the Axis powers in the Pacific, as Japan took the offensive in conquering islands and parts of Asia, many of them colonies of Allied states. Britain countered by mobilizing a vast Indian army. After the disastrous losses at Pearl Harbor and in the Philippines, the Allies gradually gained the upper hand by conducting costly assaults, island by island. The Japanese strategy of fighting to the last person instead of surrendering when a loss was in sight was one factor in the decision to drop the atomic bombs in August 1945.

but the allies turned the tide in 1942 by destroying some of Japan's powerful navy in battles at Midway Island and Guadalcanal. Japan had far less industrial capacity and manpower than the United States alone, to say nothing of the global resources of the Allies. The Allies stormed one Pacific island after another, gaining bases from which to cut off the importation of supplies and to launch bombers toward Japan itself. Short of men and weapons, the Japanese eventually resorted to kamikaze tactics, in which pilots deliberately crashed their planes into American ships, killing themselves in the process. The Allies stepped up their bombing of major cities, killing more than 100,000 civilians in their spring 1945 firebombing of Tokyo. The Japanese leadership still ruled out surrender.

Meanwhile, a U.S.-based international team of more than 100,000 workers, including scientists and technicians, had developed an atomic bomb. The Japanese practice of dying almost to the man rather than surrender caused Allied planners to calculate that defeating Japan with conventional weapons might cost hundreds of thousands of Allied lives. On August 6 and 9, 1945, the U.S. government unleashed

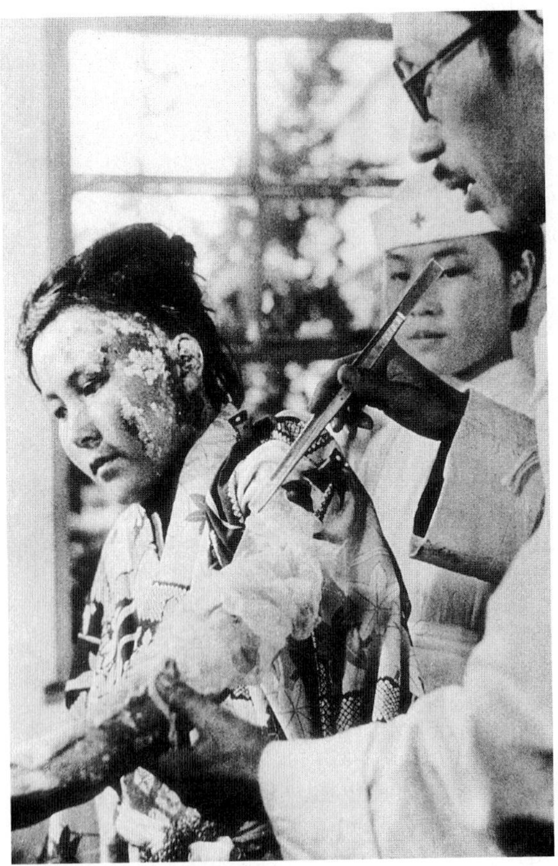

Hiroshima Victim

In early August 1945, the United States dropped atomic bombs on Hiroshima and Nagasaki, Japan, killing 140,000 people instantly and leaving tens of thousands more to die from their wounds. A few days later, Japan surrendered. Controversy still swirls around the decision to drop the bombs. People who see it as a racist act point out that no atomic weapons were dropped on Germany. People who see it as a justified act of warfare point out that Japan's no-surrender policy increased the likelihood of countless more casualties. (Tokyo/Fuji/Sumiko Kurita/Gamma.)

its new atomic weapon on Hiroshima and Nagasaki, respectively, killing 140,000 people instantly; tens of thousands later died from burns, wounds, and other afflictions. Hard-liners in the Japanese military still wanted to continue the war, but on August 14, 1945, Japan surrendered.

An Uneasy Postwar Settlement

Throughout the war, Allied leaders had met not only to plan strategy but also to resolve postwar issues. Unlike after World War I, however, there was neither a celebrated peace conference nor a definitive, formal agreement among all the Allies about the final terms for peace. Yet peace and recovery were more important than ever: Europe lay in ruins, and tens of millions were starving. Because the victorious Allies distrusted one another in varying degrees, with the United States and Soviet Union moving toward another war, the future looked grim.

Wartime agreements among members of the Grand Alliance about the future reflected their differences and became the subject of intense postwar debate. In 1941, Roosevelt and Churchill crafted the Atlantic Charter, which condemned aggression and supported collective security and the right of all peoples to choose their governments. Not only did the Allies support these ideals, but so did colonized peoples to whom, Churchill had said, the charter was not meant to apply. In October 1944, Churchill and Stalin agreed on the postwar distribution of territories. The Soviet Union would control Romania and Bulgaria, Britain would control Greece, and they would oversee Hungary and Yugoslavia together. These agreements went against Roosevelt's faith in collective security, self-determination, and open doors in trade. In February 1945, the "Big Three"—Roosevelt, Churchill, and Stalin—met in the Crimean town of Yalta. Roosevelt advocated for the formation of the United Nations to replace the League of Nations as a global peace mechanism, and he supported future Soviet influence in Korea, Manchuria, Sakhalin Island, and the Kuril Islands. The last meeting of the Allied leaders, with Harry Truman replacing Roosevelt, who had died in April, took place in Potsdam, Germany, in the summer of 1945. At Potsdam, they agreed to give the Soviets control of eastern Poland, to give a large stretch of eastern Germany to Poland, and to finalize a temporary four-way occupation of Germany, set out at Yalta, that would include France as one of the supervising powers.

The Great Depression had inflicted global suffering, while World War II had left an estimated 100 million people dead worldwide, more than 50 million refugees without homes, and one of the most abominable moral legacies in human history. Forced into armies or labor camps for war production, colonial peoples in Asia and Africa were in full rebellion or close to it. For a second time in three decades, they had seen their imperial masters killing one another, slaughtered by the very technology that was supposed to show European superiority. Deference to Europe was virtually finished, with independence only a matter of time.

The war weakened and even destroyed standards of decency and truth. Democratic Europe had given in to continuous wartime values, and it was this Europe that George Orwell captured in his novel *1984* (1949). Orwell had worked for Britain's wartime Ministry of Information (called the Ministry of Truth in the novel), where he made up phony news for wartime audiences. Truth hardly mattered: *battle fatigue* substituted for *insanity*, and *liberating* a country could mean invading it and murdering its civilians. Poor food, ragged clothing, and careworn people walking grimy streets—all characterized both wartime London and Orwell's fictional state, Oceania. Millions cheered the end of Nazi evil in 1945, but Orwell saw the war as killing prosperity, deadening creativity, and bringing big government into everyday life. For Orwell, bureaucratic domination depended on continuing conflict, and fresh conflict was indeed brewing even before the war ended. As the Allied powers competed for territory, a new struggle called the cold war was beginning.

REVIEW What were the major events and consequences of World War II?

Conclusion

The Great Depression, which brought fear, hunger, and joblessness to millions, created a setting in which dictators thrived because they promised to restore prosperity by destroying democracy and representative government. Desperate people believed the promises of dynamic new leaders—Mussolini, Stalin, and Hitler—and often forgave the brutality of their regimes. In the USSR, Stalin's program of rapid industrialization was an amazing achievement, but it cost the lives of millions. With the democracies preoccupied with economic recovery while preserving the rule of law and still haunted by memories of World War I, Hitler and Mussolini menaced Europe unchallenged. At the same time, Japan began a program of conquest aimed at ending Western domination. The coalition of Allies that finally formed to stop the Axis powers of Germany, Italy, and Japan was an uneasy alliance among Britain, Free France, the Soviet Union, and the United States. World War II ended European domination. Its economies were shattered, its colonies were on the verge of independence, and its peoples were starving and homeless.

The costs of a bloody war—one waged against civilians as well as armies—taught these powers different lessons. The United States, Britain, and France were convinced that a minimum of citizen well-being was necessary to prevent a return of fascism. The devastation of the USSR's population and resources made Stalin increasingly obsessed with national security and compensation for the damage inflicted by Germany. Britain and France faced the end of their imperial might, underscoring Orwell's insight that the war had utterly transformed society. The

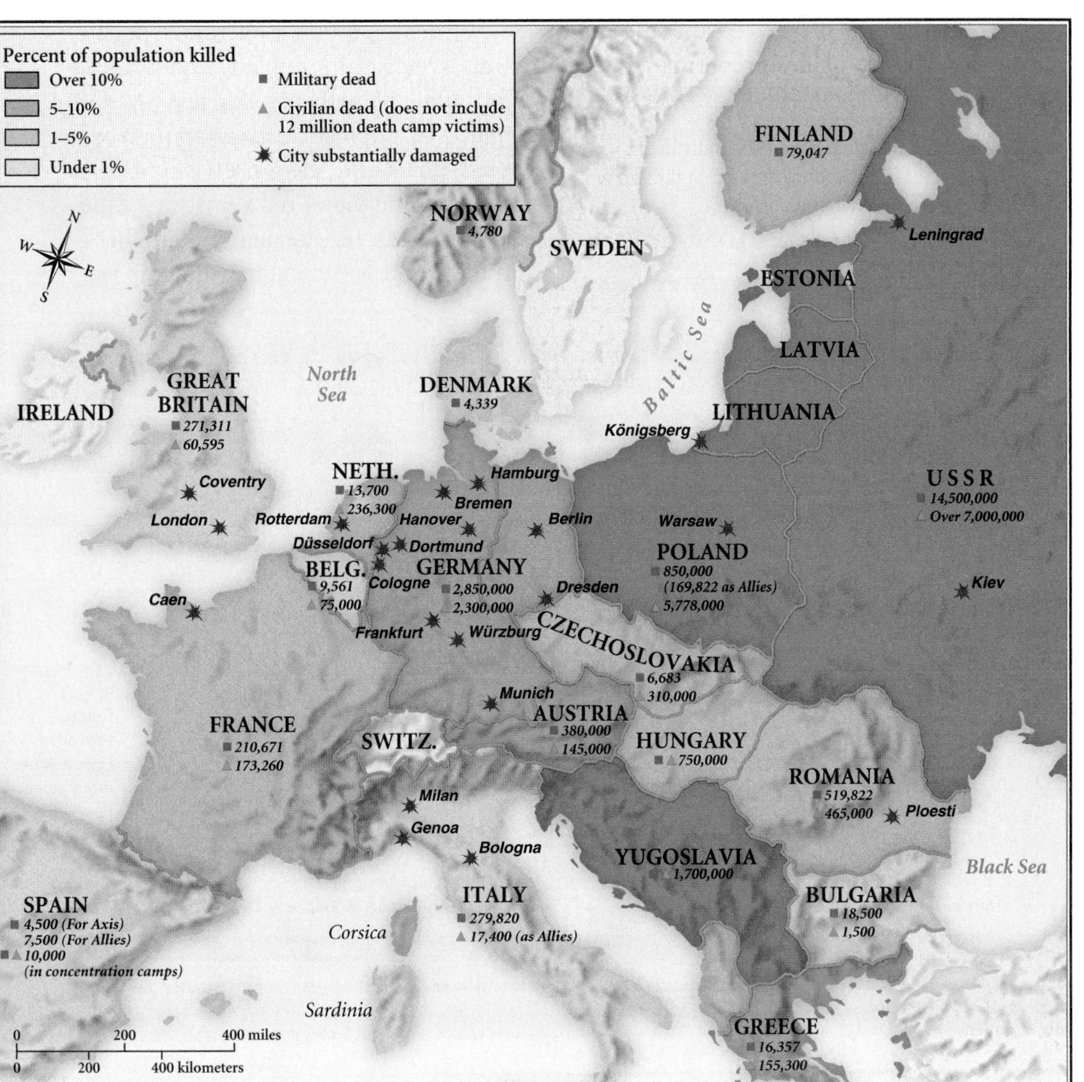

Mapping the West Europe at War's End, 1945

All of Europe was severely shocked during the age of catastrophes, and wartime damage left scars that would last for decades. Major German cities were bombed to bits. The Soviet Union suffered an unimaginable toll of perhaps as many as forty-five million deaths due to the war alone. In addition to the vast civilian and military losses shown on this map, historians estimate that no less than twelve million people were murdered in the Nazi death camps. Everything from politics to family life needed rebuilding.

militarization of society and the deliberate murder of millions of innocent citizens like Etty Hillesum permanently injured the West's claim to being an advanced civilization. Nonetheless, backed by vast supplies of sophisticated weaponry, the United States and the Soviet Union used their opposing views on a postwar settlement to justify threatening one another—and the world—with another horrific war.

CHAPTER REVIEW QUESTIONS

1. Compare fascist ideas about the individual with the idea of individual rights that drove the American and French revolutions.
2. What are the major differences between World War I and World War II?

For practice quizzes and other study tools, see the Online Study Guide at bedfordstmartins.com/huntconcise.

For primary-source material from this period, see Chapter 26 of *Sources of The Making of the West,* Third Edition.

TIMELINE

- **1920s–1930s** Movement for Indian Independence
- **1929** U.S. stock market crashes; global depression begins; Soviet leaders launch a war against the kulaks
- **1930s** Sweden constructs a welfare state
- **1930** Nationalist ruler Mustafa Kemal changes the name of Turkey's capital from Constantinople to Istanbul; French crush a peasant uprising in Indochina; Marlene Dietrich stars in *The Blue Angel*
- **1933** Hitler comes to power in Germany
- **1935** Nazis enact the Nuremberg Laws, denying rights to Jews in Germany
- **1936** Stalin starts purges of top Communist Party officials and later military leaders in show trials; Spanish Civil War begins
- **1938** Nazi attacks on Jews in Kristallnacht; Virginia Woolf, *Three Guineas*
- **1939** Germany invades Poland; World War II begins; Spanish Civil War ends
- **1940** France falls to the German army; British air force fends off German attacks in the battle of Britain
- **1941** Germany invades the USSR; Japan attacks Pearl Harbor; United States enters the war
- **1941–1945** Holocaust
- **1942–1943** Siege of Stalingrad
- **1944** Allied forces land at Normandy
- **1945** Germany surrenders; United States drops atomic bombs on Hiroshima and Nagasaki; World War II ends

1929 | 1933 | 1937 | 1941 | 1945

Suggested References

The vicious dictators Stalin, Hitler, and Mussolini and the intricacies of World War II are among the most popular subjects for historians and readers alike. Recent historical works have moved beyond this fascination to investigate their mobilization of art and the mass media and to consider the public's engagement with both totalitarian regimes and democracies.

Alvarez, Luis. *The Power of the Zoot: Youth Culture and Resistance during World War II.* 2008.

Balderston, Theo, ed. *The World Economy and National Economies in the Interwar Slump.* 2003.

Ben-Ghiat, Ruth. *Fascist Modernities: Italy, 1922–1945.* 2001.

Burleigh, Michael. *The Third Reich: A New History.* 2000.

Chickering, Roger, et al., eds. *A World at Total War: Global Conflict and the Politics of Destruction, 1937–1945.* 2005.

*Dawidowicz, Lucy S., ed. *A Holocaust Reader.* 1976.

Fenner, Angelica, and Eric D. Weitz. *Fascism and Neofascism: Critical Writings on the Radical Right in Europe.* 2004.

Fink, Carole. *Defending the Rights of Others: The Great Powers, the Jews, and International Minority Protection, 1878–1938.* 2004.

Helstosky, Carol. *Garlic and Oil: The Politics of Food in Italy.* 2004.

Maas, Ad, and Hans Hooimaijers, eds. *Scientific Research in World War II: What Scientists Did in the War.* 2009.

Pennington, Reina, and John Erickson. *Wings, Women, and War: Soviet Airwomen in World War II.* 2004.

Petrone, Karen. *Life Has Become More Joyous, Comrades: Celebrations in the Time of Stalin.* 2000.

Rose, Sonya O. *Which People's War: National Identity and Citizenship, 1939–1945.* 2003.

Siegel, Mona L. *The Moral Disarmament of France: Education, Pacifism, and Patriotism, 1914–1940.* 2004.

South Asia and Gandhi: http://www.columbia.edu/cu/libraries/indiv/area/sarai

U.S. Holocaust Museum: http://www.ushmm.org

Weinberg, Gerhard. *A World at Arms: A Global History of World War II.* 2005.

A LOVE CAUGHT IN THE FIRE OF REVOLUTIO

Turbulent were the times
and fiery was
the love story
of Zhivago,
his wife...
and the
passionate,
tender
Lara.

METRO-GOLDWYN-MAYER PRESENTS A CARLO PONTI PRODUCTION

DAVID LEAN'S FILM OF BORIS PASTERNAK'S

DOCTOR ZHIVAGO

STARRING
GERALDINE CHAPLIN · JULIE CHRISTIE · TOM COURTENAY
ALEC GUINNESS · SIOBHAN McKENNA · RALPH RICHARDSON
OMAR SHARIF (AS ZHIVAGO) ROD STEIGER · RITA TUSHINGHAM

SCREEN PLAY BY ROBERT BOLT · DIRECTED BY DAVID LEAN IN PANAVISION® AND METROCOLOR MGM

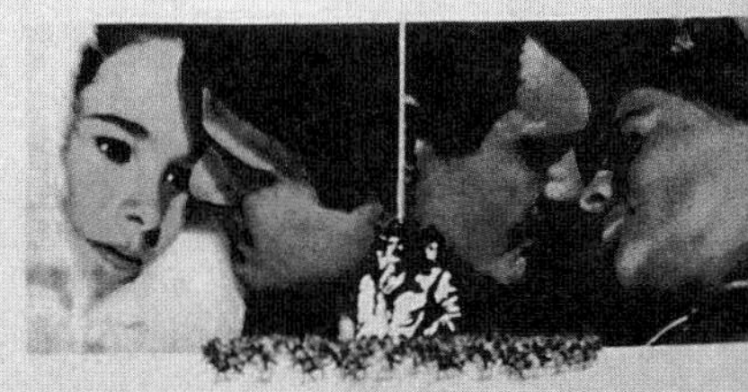

22

The Cold War and the Remaking of Europe

1945–1960s

LATE IN 1945, WITH THE USSR still reeling from the devastation of World War II, Soviet poet Boris Pasternak set out on a new project—*Doctor Zhivago,* a novel about a thoughtful medical man caught up in the Russian Revolution. Like others in the USSR, Pasternak expected the postwar era to bring about, as he put it, "a great renewal of Russian life," ending the violence and famine of the past three decades. He struggled on with his epic work even as **cold war** tensions between the United States and the USSR began. In 1953, Stalin's sudden death raised Pasternak's hopes that a more tolerant political climate would allow his masterwork to receive a warm reception. Those hopes were dashed, however, when the Soviets forbade the book's publication.

Doctor Zhivago
As soon as Boris Pasternak's forbidden novel *Doctor Zhivago* was published in Italy in 1957, Hollywood's MGM studio went after the rights for the film. Finally completed in 1965, the movie was a cold war blockbuster—an epic of life and love in postrevolutionary Russia. The story is more or less summarized in this advertising poster: two incredibly attractive people fall in love and are torn apart by the crushing Bolshevik system. *(MGM/The Kobal Collection.)*

A determined Pasternak bypassed Soviet authorities and published *Doctor Zhivago* in 1957 in Italy—now an anti-Soviet ally of the United States in the cold war. The book became a best seller, showing its readers that the Russian Revolution was far from perfect and so angering the Soviet establishment that Stalin's successor, Nikita Khrushchev, forced Pasternak to decline the Nobel Prize for Literature awarded him in 1958. But if the Soviets tried to suppress *Doctor Zhivago* for cold war reasons and frightened people into denouncing its author, it was the cold war that allowed *Doctor Zhivago* to live on. Soon after the novel appeared, the famed Hollywood studio MGM bought the rights to the book and turned it into a blockbuster film (1965), seen by tens of millions of people. By that time, however, Pasternak was dead—a broken victim of cold war persecutions that continued long after the tragic years of World War II had ended.

As the cold war opened, people in Europe, Japan, and much of East and Southeast Asia were starving and homeless. Evidence of genocide and other inhumanity was everywhere, and nuclear annihilation menaced the world. The old international order was gone, replaced by the rivalry of the United States and the Soviet Union for control of a shattered Europe. The nuclear arsenals of the two superpowers grew massively in the 1950s, but they were enemies who did not fight outright. Thus their terrifying rivalry was called the cold war. The cold war divided the West and led to political persecution in many areas, even the wealthy and secure United States.

At the same time, the defeat of Nazism inspired cautious optimism like Pasternak's. A heroic effort had defeated fascism, and that defeat raised hopes that a new age would begin. Atomic science promised advances in medicine, and nuclear energy was seen as a replacement for coal and oil. The creation of the **United Nations (UN)** suggested the beginning of real international cooperation. Around the globe, colonial peoples won independence from European masters, while in the United States the civil rights movement grew in strength. The welfare state expanded, and by the end of the 1950s economic rebirth had made much of Europe more prosperous than ever before. An "economic miracle" had occurred.

The postwar period was one of redefinition, as the experience of total war transformed both society and the international order. Gone was the definition of a West composed of Europe and its cultural relatives such as the United States and an East comprising Asian countries such as India, China, and Japan. During the cold war, the word *West* came to stand for the United States and its allies in western Europe, while *East* meant the Soviet Union and its bloc of satellites in eastern Europe. Still another terminology arose in the 1950s, one that divided the globe into the first world, or capitalist bloc of countries; the second world, or socialist bloc; and the **third world**, or countries emerging from imperial domination. This last term initially aimed to compare those rising nations to the Third Estate—the rising citizens of the French Revolution—but it is now considered an insult. As the world's people redefined themselves, the superpowers took the world to the brink of nuclear disaster when the United States discovered Soviet missile sites on the island of Cuba. From the dropping of atomic bombs on Japan in 1945 to the **Cuban missile crisis** of 1962, fear and personal anguish like that of Pasternak gripped much of the world, even in the midst of prosperity and Europe's rebirth.

CHAPTER FOCUS QUESTION How did the cold war shape the politics, economy, social life, and culture of post–World War II Europe?

World Politics Transformed

World War II ended Europe's global leadership. Many countries lay in ruins by the summer of 1945, and conditions would deteriorate before they got better. Continuing turmoil destroyed the lives of millions in eastern and central Europe. In contrast, the United States, whose territory was virtually untouched in the war, emerged as the world's sole economic giant, and the Soviet Union, despite suffering immense destruction, was an impressive military power. Occupying Europe as part of the victorious alliance against Nazism and fascism, the two superpowers used Germany—at the heart of the continent—to divide Europe in two. By the late 1940s, the USSR had imposed Communist rule throughout most of eastern Europe, and western Europeans found themselves at least partially controlled by the very U.S. economic power that helped them rebuild, especially because the United States maintained air bases and nuclear weapons on their soil. The new age of bipolar world politics made Europe its testing ground.

Chaos in Europe

In contrast to the often stationary trench warfare of World War I, armies in World War II had fought a war of movement on the ground and in the air. Massive air strikes had leveled thousands of square miles of territory, whole cities were clogged with rubble, and homeless survivors wandered the streets. On the Rhine River, almost no bridge remained standing; in the Soviet Union, seventy thousand villages and more than a thousand cities lay in shambles. Everywhere people were suffering. In the Netherlands, the severity of Nazi occupation left the Dutch population close to death, relieved only by a U.S. airlift of supplies. Allied troops in Germany were often the only source of food. "To see the children fighting for food," one British soldier noted, "was like watching animals being fed in a zoo." There was social disorder, even chaos, at the war's end but no mass uprisings as after World War I. Until the late 1940s, people were too exhausted by the struggle for bare survival to protest.

The tens of millions of refugees and homeless people suffered the most, as they wandered a continent where resources were slim and the dangers of assault and robbery great. An estimated thirty million Europeans, many of German ethnicity, were forced from Poland, Czechoslovakia, and Hungary (Map 22.1). Often refugees fled to western Europe, making it one of the world's most densely populated regions. Others ultimately found homes in countries that experienced little or no war damage, such as Denmark, Sweden, Canada, and Australia. The USSR lobbied hard for the return of several million Soviet prisoners of war, only to execute many of the returnees for being "contaminated" by Western ideas.

Survivors of the concentration camps also discovered that their suffering had not ended with Germany's defeat. Many returned home diseased and disoriented, while others had no home to return to, as property had been confiscated and entire communities destroyed. Anti-Semitism—official policy under the Nazis—lingered in popular attitudes. In the summer of 1946, a vicious crowd in Kielce, Poland, attacked 250 returning Jewish survivors, killing at least 40. The use of violence as a way to maintain the wealth and upward mobility gained from fascist anti-Semitism was common throughout eastern Europe. Meanwhile, some officials across the continent even denied that unprecedented atrocities had been committed and refused Jews any help. Survivors hoped to escape to Palestine, where Zionists had been settling for half a century. Many European countries seemed simply to have lost their moral bearings.

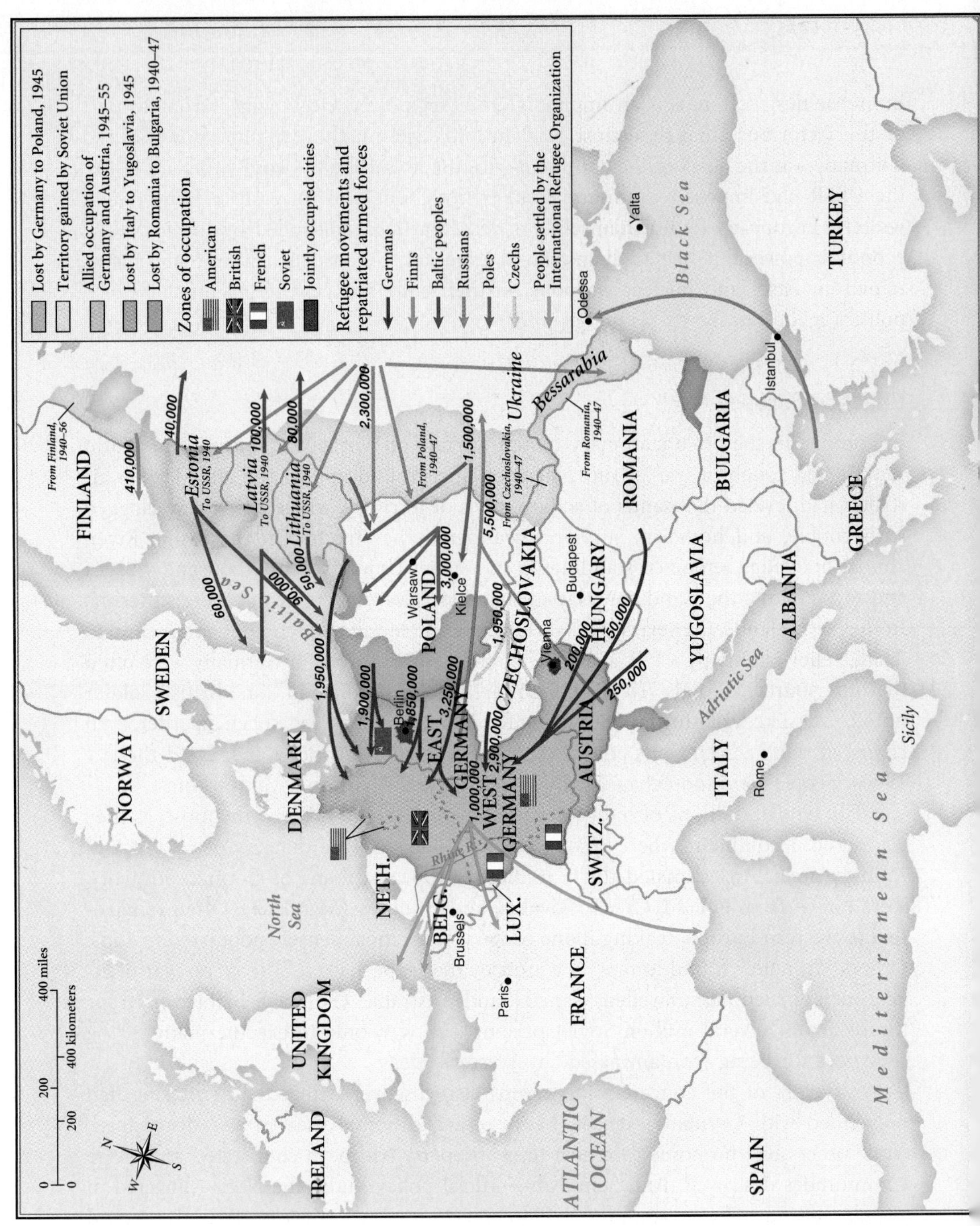

Map 22.1 The Impact of World War II on Europe
European governments, many of them struggling to provide food and other necessities for their populations, found themselves responsible for hundreds of thousands, if not millions, of refugees. At the same time, millions of prisoners of war, servicemen, and slave laborers were returned to the Soviet Union, many of them by force. This situation unfolded amid political instability and even violence.

New Superpowers: The United States and the Soviet Union

Only two powerful countries were left in 1945: the United States and the Soviet Union. The United States was now the richest country in the world. Its industrial output had increased by a remarkable 15 percent annually between 1940 and 1944. By 1947, it controlled almost two-thirds of the world's gold bullion and more than half of the world's commercial shipping. Continued spending on industrial and military research added to its prosperity, boosting the confident mood that now swept the country. In contrast to the post–World War I policy of isolationism, Americans embraced global leadership. Many had learned about the world while tracking the war's progress; hundreds of thousands of soldiers, government officials, and relief workers had had direct experience of Europe, Africa, and Asia.

The Soviets also emerged from the war with a well-justified sense of accomplishment. Despite horrendous losses, they had resisted the most massive onslaught ever launched against a nation. Instead of being outcasts as they had been after World War I, the Soviets expected respect and influence on the world stage, and many Europeans and Americans gratefully acknowledged their leadership in Hitler's defeat. Ordinary Soviet citizens believed that their wartime sacrifices, especially the loss of as many as forty-five million lives, would lead to improvements in everyday conditions. Rumors spread among the peasants that the collective farms would be divided and returned to them as individual property now that the war had been won. "Life will become pleasant," one writer prophesied. "There will be much coming and going, and a lot of contacts with the West." Boris Pasternak was among those who expected an end to decades of hardship and repression.

Stalin took a different view and moved ruthlessly to reassert control. In 1946, his new five-year plan increased production goals and mandated harsher collectivization of agriculture. For him, rapid recovery meant more work, not less, and more order, not greater freedom. Stalin turned his attention to the low birthrate, a result of wartime male casualties and women's long working days, which discouraged them from adding child care to their already heavy responsibilities. He introduced an intense propaganda campaign emphasizing that women should hold down jobs and also fulfill their "true nature" by producing many children. A crackdown on freedom took place, and a new round of purges began. Jews were especially targeted, and in 1953 the government announced that doctors—most of them Jews—had long been assassinating Soviet leaders and murdering newborns and patients in hospitals. Hysteria gripped the nation, as people feared for their lives. "I am a simple worker and not an anti-Semite," one Moscow resident wrote, "but I say . . . it's time to clean these people out." This atmosphere of fear fed the cold war.

Origins of the Cold War

The cold war between the United States and the Soviet Union, which began immediately after World War II, would afflict the world for more than four decades. No peace conference or treaties officially ended the war to document what went

The Cold War, to 1962

1945–1949	USSR establishes satellite states in eastern Europe
1947	Truman Doctrine announces U.S. commitment to contain communism; U.S. Marshall Plan provides massive aid to rebuild Europe
1948–1949	Soviet troops blockade Berlin; United States airlifts provisions to Berliners
1949	Western democracies form the North Atlantic Treaty Organization (NATO); Soviet bloc establishes the Council for Mutual Economic Assistance (COMECON); USSR tests its first nuclear weapon
1950–1953	Korean War
1950–1954	U.S. senator Joseph McCarthy leads the hunt for American Communists
1953	Stalin dies
1955	USSR and eastern-bloc countries form a military alliance called the Warsaw Pact
1956	Khrushchev denounces Stalin in the "secret speech" to a Communist Party congress; Hungarians revolt unsuccessfully against Soviet domination
1959	Castro comes to power in Cuba
1961	Berlin Wall begun
1962	Cuban missile crisis

wrong. As a result, the origins of the cold war remain a matter of debate, with historians faulting both sides for starting the dangerous rivalry. Some point to consistent U.S., British, and French hostility toward the Soviets, which began as far back as the Bolshevik Revolution of 1917 and continued through the depression. Others stress Stalin's aggressive policies, notably the Nazi-Soviet Pact in 1939 and Stalin's seizure of Polish territory and the Baltic states when World War II broke out. In this view, the Western countries naturally feared unlimited Soviet expansionism.

Suspicions ran deep among the Allied leaders during World War II. Stalin believed that Churchill and Roosevelt were deliberately letting the USSR bear the brunt of Hitler's rampage across the continent as part of their anti-Communist policy. He rightly viewed Churchill in particular as interested mainly in preserving Britain's imperial power, no matter what the cost in Soviet lives. At the time, some Americans believed that dropping the atomic bombs on Japan would frighten the Soviets and discourage them from making any more landgrabs. In addition, the new U.S. president, Harry Truman, cut off aid to the Soviets as the last gun was fired, fueling Stalin's belief that the United States was aiming for his country's utter collapse. Seeing a threat to his west, Stalin judged that the USSR needed a permanent "buffer zone" of European states loyal to it. Across the Atlantic, Truman saw the Soviet occupation of eastern Europe as the beginning of a series of Communist takeovers around the world. Members of the U.S. State Department increased U.S. fears by describing Stalin as a neurotic Asian tyrant thirsting for world domination.

The cold war thus became a series of moves and countermoves by two very different countries that jointly occupied the rich but devastated European heartland. In line with the view of its geopolitical needs, the USSR repressed democratic coalition governments of liberals, socialists, Communists, and peasant parties in central and eastern Europe between 1945 and 1949. It imposed Communist rule almost immediately in Bulgaria and Romania. In Romania, Stalin cited citizen violence in 1945 as the excuse for removing all non-Communists from government. In Poland, the Communists rigged the elections in 1945 and 1946 to create the illusion of popular support for communism. Nevertheless, between 1945 and 1947 the Communists there had to share power with the popular Peasant Party, which had a large following of rural workers and peasant landowners.

The United States now put its new interventionist spirit to work, promoting American influence. It acknowledged the USSR's authority in Soviet-occupied areas of central and eastern Europe but worried that Communist power would spread to western Europe, where memories of Communist leadership in the resistance to fascism gave it a powerful appeal. In Greece, for example, the Communists had enough of a following to threaten the right-wing monarchy the British had installed in 1944. In March 1947, Truman reacted to this threat by announcing what quickly became known as the **Truman Doctrine**—the use of economic and military aid to block communism. The president asked the U.S. Congress for $400 million in military aid for Greece and Turkey, where the Communists were also exerting pressure. Fearing that Americans would resist backing nondemocratic Greece, Congress would agree to the program only if, as one congressman put it, Truman would "scare the hell out of the country." Truman thus publicized an expensive aid program as necessary to prevent Soviet conquest of the world. The show of American support convinced the Communists to back off, and in 1949 the Greek rebels declared a cease-fire.

In 1947, the United States also devised the **Marshall Plan**, a program of massive economic aid to alleviate the daily hardships that were making communism attractive to Europeans. "The seeds of totalitarian regimes are nurtured by misery and want," Truman warned. Named after Secretary of State George C. Marshall, who announced the plan, the program's direct aid would immediately improve everyday life, while its loans and financial credits would restart international trade. The government claimed that the Marshall Plan was not directed "against any country or doctrine but against hunger, poverty, desperation, and chaos." By the early 1950s, the United States had sent Europe more than $12 billion in food, equipment, and services, reducing the appeal of communism in the countries of western Europe that received the aid.

Stalin saw the Marshall Plan as a U.S. political trick because the devastated USSR had nothing similar to offer. He thus clamped down even harder on eastern and central European governments, preventing them from responding to the U.S. offer of assistance and eliminating the last remnants of democracy in Hungary and Poland. In the autumn of 1947, a purge of non-Communist officials began in Czechoslovakia. By June 1948, Czechoslovakia's socialist president, Edvard Beneš, had resigned and been replaced by a Communist figurehead. The Czech people accepted the change so passively that Communist leaders said the takeover was "like cutting butter with a knife."

The only exception to the Soviet sweep in eastern Europe was Yugoslavia, ruled by the Communist leader known as Tito (Josip Broz). During the war, Tito had led the powerful anti-Nazi Yugoslav "partisans." After the war, he drew on support from Serbs, Croats, and Muslims to mount a Communist revolution in 1948. His revolution, however, was explicitly meant to avoid Soviet influence. "We study and take as an example the Soviet system," Tito remarked, "but we are developing socialism in our country in somewhat different forms." Stalin was furious at Tito's independence. Nonetheless, Yugoslavia emerged from its revolution as a culturally diverse federation of six republics and two independent provinces within Serbia. Tito's break with Stalin intensified the purges in the USSR, because the Soviet government could point to Tito as a vivid example of the treachery supposedly at work in the heart of the Communist world. Tito used his forceful personality and strong organization to hold diverse groups of south Slavs together until his death in 1980.

Yugoslavia after the Revolution, 1948

The Division of Germany

The superpowers' struggle for control of Germany took the cold war to a menacing level. The agreements reached at the Yalta and Potsdam conferences in 1945 divided Germany into four occupied zones, each of which was controlled by one of the four principal victors in World War II—the United States, the Soviet Union, Britain, and France (Map 22.2). However, the superpowers disagreed on how to treat Germany. First, many in the United States had come to believe that there was something wrong with the German character—a fatal flaw that had resulted in two world wars and the Holocaust. After the war, U.S. occupation forces undertook a reprogramming of German attitudes by censoring all media in the U.S. zone to ensure that they did not perpetuate fascist values. In contrast, Stalin believed that Nazism was merely an extreme form of capitalism. His solution was to confiscate the estates of wealthy Germans and redistribute them to ordinary people and Communist supporters.

A second disagreement, concerning the economy, led to Germany's partition. According to the American plan for coordinating the German economy, surplus produce from the Soviet-occupied areas would feed urban populations in the western zones; in turn, industrial goods would be sent to the USSR. The Soviets upset this plan. Following the Allied agreement that the USSR would receive reparations from German resources, the Soviets simply seized German equipment and shipped it to the Soviet Union. They transported skilled German workers, engineers, and scientists to the USSR to work as forced laborers. The Soviets also manipulated the currency in their zone, enabling the USSR to buy German goods at unfairly low prices.

In response, in 1948 the Western Allies merged their individual zones into one West German state, escalating cold war tensions. Instead of limiting Germany's power, as the wartime agreements called for, the United States also began an economic buildup of the western zone under the Marshall Plan. By 1948, notions of

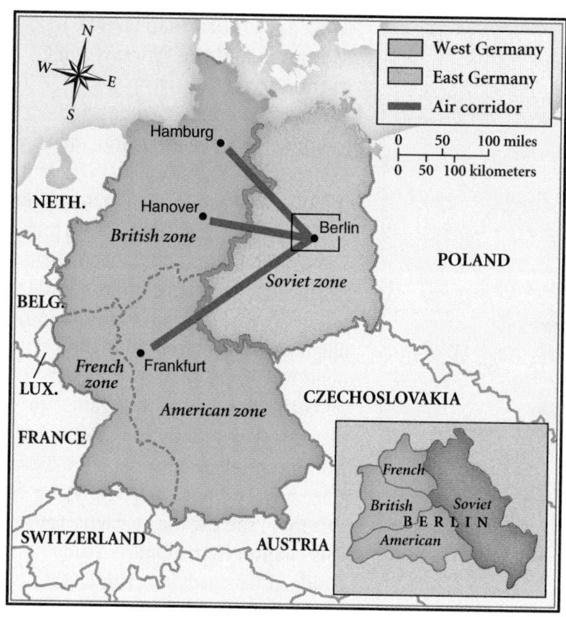

Map 22.2 Divided Germany and the Berlin Airlift, 1946–1949 Berlin, controlled by the United States, Great Britain, France, and the Soviet Union, was deep in the Soviet zone of occupation and became a major point of contention among the former Allies. When the USSR blockaded the western half of the city, the United States responded with a massive airlift. To stop movement between the two zones, the USSR built a wall in 1961 and used troops to patrol it.

a permanently weakened Germany ended, and the United States enlisted many former Nazi officials as spies and bureaucrats to pursue the cold war.

On July 24, 1948, Stalin retaliated by blockading Germany's capital, Berlin. Like Germany as a whole, the city—located more than one hundred miles inside the Soviet zone and thus cut off from western territory—had been divided into four occupation zones. Expecting the United States and its allies to give up Berlin, the Soviets declared that the city was now part of their zone of occupation and refused to allow western vehicles from outside their bloc to travel through the Soviet zone to reach it. The United States responded decisively, flying in millions of tons of provisions to Berliners. During the winter of 1948–1949, the Berlin airlift—"Operation Vittles," as U.S. pilots called it—even funneled in coal to warm some two million isolated citizens. Given the limited number of planes involved, pilots kept the engines running so that they could turn around quickly and thus ensure the delivery of enough provisions. The Soviets ended their blockade in May 1949, but cold war rhetoric made the divided capital a symbol of the capitalist-communist divide—of good versus evil.

The creation of competing institutions, military alliances, and entirely new nations added to cold war tensions. A few months after the establishment of the West German state, the USSR created an East German state. In 1949, the United States, Canada, and their allies in western Europe and Scandinavia formed the **North Atlantic Treaty Organization (NATO)**, which provided a unified military force for its member countries (Map 22.3). In 1955, after the United States forced France and Britain to invite West Germany to join NATO, the Soviet Union retaliated by establishing with its satellite countries the military organization commonly called

Map 22.3 European NATO Members and the Warsaw Pact in the 1950s
The two superpowers intensified their rivalry by creating large military alliances: NATO, formed in 1949, and the Warsaw Pact, formed in 1955 after NATO invited West Germany to join. The United States and Canada also were NATO members. International politics revolved around these two alliances, which faced off in the heart of Europe. Military planners on both sides devised war games to plan strategies for fighting a massive war in central Europe over control of Germany. **For more help analyzing this map, see the map activity for this chapter in the Online Study Guide at** bedfordstmartins.com/huntconcise.

the **Warsaw Pact**. By that time, both the United States and the USSR had accelerated the buildup of arms. The Soviets had exploded their own atomic bomb in 1949, and both nations had then tested increasingly powerful nuclear weapons. These two massive regional alliances, armed to the teeth, backed cold war politics with military muscle, definitively outstripping the individual might of the European powers.

REVIEW What major events led to and widened the cold war?

Political and Economic Recovery in Europe

The cold war served as a backdrop to the remarkable recovery that took place in Europe. The first two items on the political agenda were the eradication of the Nazi past and the creation of peacetime governments. While western Europe revived its democratic political structures, its individualistic culture, and its productive capabilities, eastern Europe was far less prosperous and far more repressive under the Stalinism of the postwar period. Even to the east, however, the conditions of everyday life improved as peasant societies were forced to modernize and as basic consumer goods became available. By the 1960s, people across the continent were enjoying a higher standard of living than ever before. Governments took increasing responsibility for the health and well-being of citizens, making the cold war era also the age of the welfare state.

Dealing with the Nazi Past

In May 1945, Europeans lived under a complex system in which local resistance leaders, Allied armies of occupation, international relief workers, and the remnants of bureaucracies—among them Nazi sympathizers—competed for authority. The goals of feeding civilians, dealing with millions of refugees, and purging Nazis all needed attention. Governments in exile returned to claim their rightful share of power, but they often ran up against occupying armies that covered much of the continent and were a law unto themselves. The Soviets were especially feared for inflicting rape and robbery—abuses they justified by pointing to tens of millions of Soviet deaths at the hands of the Nazis. The desire for revenge against the Nazis hardened with the discovery of the death camps' skeletal survivors and the remains of the millions murdered there. Civilians released pent-up rage by themselves punishing collaborators for occupation crimes. In France, villagers often shaved the heads of women suspected of associating with Germans and made some of them parade naked through the streets. Members of the resistance executed tens of thousands of Nazi officers and collaborators on the spot.

The Punishment of Collaborators
Women in France who had romantic involvements with German occupiers were called "horizontal" collaborators to suggest that they were traitorous prostitutes. After the war, they were often forced to parade through cities and towns enduring verbal and other abuse with their heads shaved and sometimes stripped of their clothing. The public shaming of these women served as the basis for the film *Hiroshima Mon Amour,* which gripped audiences in the late 1950s. (© Robert Capa/Magnum Photos Inc.)

Allied representatives undertook what they claimed to be a more systematic "denazification" that ranged from forcing German civilians to view the death camps to prosecuting major Axis leaders, most notably at the Nuremberg trials, held in the fall of 1945. Although international law lacked a precedent for defining genocide as a crime, the judges at Nuremberg found sufficient evidence from the Nazis' own records to impose death sentences on half of the twenty-four defendants, among them Hitler's closest associates, and to send the rest to prison. The Nuremberg trials introduced today's notion of prosecuting crimes against humanity.

Allied prosecution of Axis leaders was hardly thorough or evenhanded. Some of the leaders most responsible for war crimes simply disappeared and were not pursued, leaving many citizens skeptical about Allied intentions. As women in Germany faced violence at the hands of occupying troops, endured starvation, and were forced to do the rough manual labor of clearing rubble in bombed-out cities, Germans came to believe that they themselves were the main victims of the war. They interpreted the trials of Nazis as simple payback rather than honest punishment of the guilty. Distrust mounted when Allied officials hired former high-ranking Nazis and Fascists in the service of the cold war. Soon the new West German government proclaimed that the war's real casualties were the German prisoners of war still being held in Soviet camps.

Rebirth of the West

Following the immediate postwar chaos, Europe's revival accelerated in the 1950s. In western Europe, reform-minded civilian governments reflected the broad membership of the resistance movements to the Nazis. They conspicuously emphasized democratic values to show their rejection of the totalitarian regimes that had earlier attracted so many Europeans. Rebuilding devastated towns and cities spurred recovery, while bold projects for economic cooperation produced a brisk trade in consumer goods in western Europe by the late 1950s. Memories of the war remained vivid, but prosperity restored confidence.

Resistance leaders made the first claim on political offices in post-fascist western Europe. In France, the leader of the Free French, General Charles de Gaulle, governed briefly as chief of state. In 1946, the French approved a constitution that established the Fourth Republic and finally granted the vote to women. De Gaulle wanted a more conservative political system with a strong executive, and failing to get that, he soon resigned in favor of leftist and centrist parties. Meanwhile, Italy replaced its constitutional monarchy with a full parliamentary system that also allowed women the vote. As in France, a resistance-based government initially took control. Then, in late 1945, socialist and labor politicians were replaced by a coalition headed by the conservative Christian Democrats, descended from the traditional Catholic centrist parties of the prewar period. Other countries likewise saw the growing influence of Christian parties because of their participation in the resistance.

Many voters in western Europe also favored the Communist Party. Symbol of the common citizen, the Soviet soldier was a hero to many western Europeans outside occupied Germany. People also remembered the common man's struggle in the depression of the 1930s. Thus, in Britain, despite the wartime successes of Winston Churchill's Conservative Party leadership, the Labour Party of Clement Attlee won elections because it seemed more likely to fulfill promises to share prosperity fairly across the classes through expanded social welfare programs. The extreme difficulties of the immediate postwar years added to the appeal of politicians who appeared to represent the millions of ordinary people who had suffered, fought, and worked so hard during the war.

In West Germany, however, with the Communist takeovers going on directly to the east, communism and the left in general had little appeal. In 1949, centrist politicians helped govern the new state, the German Federal Republic, whose constitution aimed to prevent the reemergence of a dictator and to guarantee individual rights. West Germany's first chancellor was the seventy-three-year-old Catholic anti-Communist Konrad Adenauer, who allied himself with the economist Ludwig Erhard. Erhard stabilized the postwar German currency so that people would have enough confidence in its soundness to begin normal trade and other economic activity. Successfully guiding Germany away from both fascism and communism, the economist and the politician restored the representative government that Hitler had destroyed.

Paradoxically, given its leadership in the fight against fascism, the United States was a country in which individual freedom and democracy were imperiled after the war. As the cold war intensified in 1947 and 1948, the media and several politicians fanned a growing fear that American Communists were working as secret domestic spies in support of the Soviet Union. As during the Soviet purges, people of all occupations, including government workers, film stars, and union leaders, were called before congressional panels to testify against friends or to admit having held Communist thoughts or sympathies.

Two events in 1949—the Soviet Union's successful test of an atomic bomb and the Communist revolution in China—soon brought to the fore Joseph McCarthy, a U.S. senator from Wisconsin who was unknown outside his state. To make a name for himself and to tap into the nervous public mood, McCarthy warned of a great Communist conspiracy to overthrow the United States. The atmosphere was electric with confusion, for only five years before, the mass media had run glowing stories about Stalin and the Soviet system. During the war, Americans were told to think of Stalin as a friendly "Uncle Joe." By 1952, however, millions of Americans had been investigated, imprisoned, or fired from their jobs. McCarthy had books such as Thomas Paine's *Common Sense,* written in the eighteenth century to support the American Revolution, removed from government shelves, and he personally oversaw book burnings. Although the Senate finally voted to censure McCarthy in the winter of 1954, the assault on freedom had been devastating, and anticommunism had come to dominate political life.

Given the wartime destruction, the economic rebirth of western Europe was even more surprising than the revival of democracy. In the first months after the war, the job of rebuilding often involved menial physical labor that mobilized entire populations. Initially governments directed labor and capital into rebuilding infrastructure—transportation, communications, and industrial capacity—and away from producing consumer goods. In the midst of growing discontent over the lack of basic necessities, however, the Marshall Plan boosted recovery with American dollars; food became more plentiful; and demand for automobiles, washing machines, and vacuum cleaners drove economic growth. Increased production wiped out most unemployment.

The postwar recovery also featured the adaptation of wartime technology to consumer industry. Civilian travel expanded as nations organized their own airline industries based on improved airplane technology. Developed to relieve wartime shortages, synthetics such as nylon now became part of peacetime civilian life. Factories churned out a vast assortment of plastic products, ranging from pipes to rainwear. In the climate of cold war, military needs also remained high; governments ordered bombs, fighter planes, tanks, and missiles and sponsored military research. The outbreak of the Korean War in 1950 increased U.S. orders for manufactured goods to wage that war, further sustaining economic growth in Europe. Ultimately, the cold war prevented a repeat of the 1920s, when reduced military spending threw people out of their jobs and the resulting financial insecurity fed the growth of fascism.

Large and small states alike developed and redeveloped modern economies in short order. In the twelve principal countries of western Europe, the annual rate of economic growth had been 1.3 percent per inhabitant between 1870 and 1913. Those countries almost tripled that rate between 1950 and 1973, attaining an annual per capita growth rate of 3.8 percent. Among the larger powers, West Germany surprisingly became the economic leader by the 1960s. The smaller Scandinavian countries also achieved a notable recovery. Sweden succeeded in the development of automobile, truck, and shipbuilding industries. Finland modernized its industry in order to pay the reparations demanded by the Soviet Union for resisting its invasion. It also modernized its agricultural sector, which in turn forced the surplus farm population to seek factory work. Scandinavian women joined the workforce in record numbers, which also boosted economic growth and expanded prosperity. The thirty years after World War II were a golden age of European economic growth (see "Taking Measure," page 883).

The creation of the Common Market, which evolved over time to become the European Union, was the final ingredient in the postwar recovery. In 1951, Italy, France, Germany, Belgium, Luxembourg, and the Netherlands took a major step toward cooperation when they formed the European Coal and Steel Community (ECSC), an organization to manage the joint production of basic resources. Importantly, it arranged for West Germany's abundant output of coal and steel to benefit all of western Europe. According to the ECSC's principal architect, Robert Schuman,

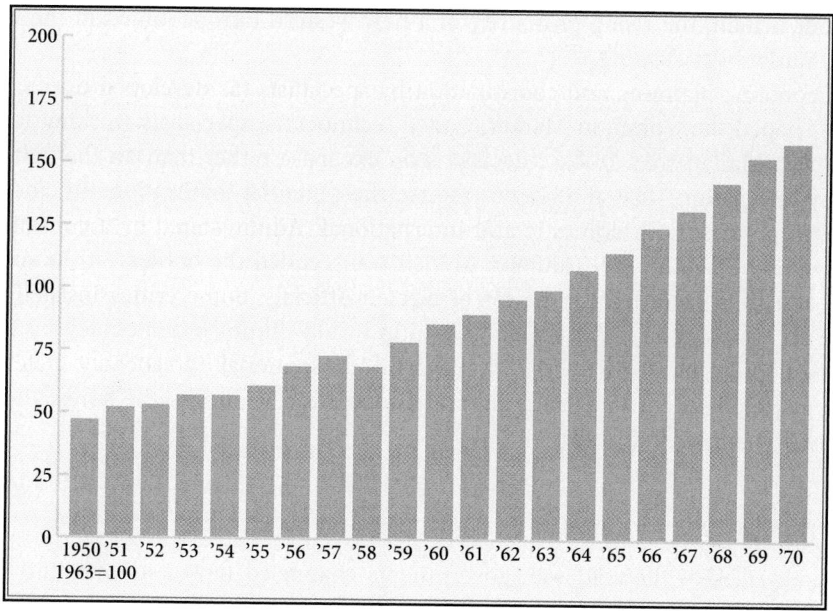

Taking Measure World Manufacturing Output, 1950–1970
During the "long boom" from the 1950s through the early 1970s, the world experienced increased industrial output, better agricultural production, and rising consumerism. This era of prosperity resulted from both the demand generated by the need to rebuild Europe and the adaptation of war technology to peacetime uses. The General Agreement on Trade and Tariffs (GATT) was also implemented after the war, lowering tariffs and thus advancing trade.

this economic cooperation would make another war "materially impossible." Simply put, the bonds of common production and trade would keep France and Germany from another cataclysmic conflict.

The success of the ECSC led to a momentous step. In 1957, the six ECSC members signed the Treaty of Rome, which provided for a more general trading partnership called the **European Economic Community (EEC)**, known popularly as the Common Market. The EEC reduced tariffs among the six partners and developed common trade policies. It brought under one cooperative economic umbrella more than 200 million consumers and would eventually add several hundred million more. According to one of its founders, the EEC aimed to "prevent the race of nationalism, which is the true curse of the modern world." Increased cooperation produced great economic rewards for the six members, whose rates of economic growth soared. Britain pointedly refused to join the partnership at first, since membership would have required surrendering certain imperial trading rights among its Commonwealth partners such as Canada and Australia. Since 1945, British statesmen had shunned the developing continental trading bloc because, as one of them put it, participation would make Britain "just another European country." Even without Britain, the rising prosperity of a new western Europe joined in the Common Market was striking.

Economic planning and coordination by specialists (as developed during wartime) shaped the Common Market. Called technocrats, specialists working for the Common Market were to base decisions on expertise rather than on the demands of any one nation. The aim was to reduce the potential for irrationality and violence in politics, both domestic and international. Administered by a commission in Brussels, Belgium, the Common Market transcended the borders of the nation-state and thus exceeded the power of elected officials. Some critics insisted (and some still insist today) that expert planning would diminish democracy by transferring power from legislatures to a powerful transnational bureaucracy. Defenders were just as insistent that planning and cooperation would be the surest tools of prosperity and lasting peace.

The Welfare State: Common Ground East and West

On both sides of the cold war, governments channeled new resources into state-financed programs such as pensions, disability insurance, and national health care. These social programs became known as the welfare state, indicating that states were no longer interested solely in maintaining order and building their power. Veterans' pensions were primary, but the welfare state extended beyond those who had fought in the war. Because the European population had declined during the war, almost all countries now desperately wanted to boost the birthrate and thus gave couples direct financial aid for having children. Imitating the sweeping Swedish programs of the 1930s, nations expanded or created family allowances and programs for pregnant women and new mothers. The French gave larger family allowances for each birth after the first; for many French families, this allowance provided as much as a third of the household income.

Some welfare-state policies had a strong bias against women. Britain's maternity benefits and child allowances provided little coverage for working women. The West German government passed strict legislation that forced employers to give women maternity leave, in effect discouraging them from hiring women at all. It also cut or eliminated benefits to married women. West Germans bragged about removing women from the workforce, claiming that this distinguished democratic practices from Communist ones. The refusal to build day-care centers or to allow stores to remain open in the evening so that working women could buy food for their families led West Germany to have among the lowest rates of female employment of any industrial country and the highest rate of female poverty in old age.

By contrast, in eastern Europe and the Soviet Union, where wartime loss of life had been enormous, women worked nearly full-time and usually outnumbered men in the workforce. As in many western European countries, however, child-care programs, family allowances, and maternity benefits were designed to encourage pregnancies by working women. A national health program provided medical

The Welfare State in Action, 1947 The Danish *crèche,* or day-care center, here shows the welfare state in action. Government programs to maintain the well-being of citizens became almost universally available in Europe, Canada, and (to a lesser extent) the United States. Children were seen as particularly important given the loss of life in the war. Governments encouraged couples to have more children through up-to-date health care systems, day-care centers, and generous family allowances. (Getty Images.)

services, as in most countries to the west, but the hardships of everyday life undermined the drive to increase population. The scarcity of consumer goods, the housing shortages, and the lack of household conveniences discouraged working women in Communist countries from having large families no matter what the government wanted. Because women bore the sole burden of domestic duties under such conditions on top of their paying jobs, they rarely wanted more children. As a result, the birthrate in the eastern bloc stagnated.

Across Europe, welfare-state programs aimed to improve people's health. State-funded health care systems covered medical needs in most industrial nations except the United States. The combination of better material conditions and state provision of health care dramatically extended life expectancies and lowered rates of infant mortality. Contributing to the overall progress, the number of doctors and dentists more than doubled between the end of World War I and 1950, and vaccines greatly reduced the death toll from diseases such as tuberculosis, diphtheria, measles, and polio. In England, schoolchildren stood on the average an inch taller than children the same age had a decade earlier.

State initiatives in other areas played a role in raising the standard of living. A growing network of government-built atomic power plants brought more thorough electrification of eastern Europe and the Soviet Union. Governments legislated more leisure time for workers. Beginning in 1955, Italian workers received twenty-eight paid holidays annually; in Sweden, workers received twenty-nine vacation days, a number that grew in the 1960s. Housing shortages brought on by three decades of economic depression and destructive war meant that postwar Europeans often lived with three generations sharing one or two rooms. To rebuild, governments sponsored a postwar housing boom. New suburbs and even entire cities formed around the edges of major urban areas in both the East and West. Many buildings went up slapdash, and although some cities were said to scar the environment, they dramatically improved living conditions for postwar refugees, workers, and immigrants.

Recovery in the East

To create a Soviet bloc according to Stalin's vision, Communists revived the harsh methods that had transformed peasant economies earlier in the century. In Hungary, for example, Communists reapportioned all estates over twelve hundred acres. Having gained support of the poorer peasants through this redistribution, Communists later took away their prized lands and pushed them into cooperative farming. Only in Poland did a substantial number of private farms remain. The process of collectivization was brutal, and rural people later looked back on the 1950s as dreadful. But some among those in the countryside felt that their lives and their children's lives had improved. "Before we peasants were dirty and poor, we worked like dogs. . . . Was that a good life? No sir, it wasn't. . . . I was a miserable sharecropper and my son is an engineer," said one Romanian peasant. Despite modernization, government investment in agriculture was never high enough to produce the bumper crops of western Europe, and even the USSR depended on produce from the small plots that enterprising farmers cultivated on the side.

Stalin prodded the Communist economies to match U.S. productivity. The Soviet Union formed regional organizations like those in the West, instituting the Council for Mutual Economic Assistance (COMECON) in 1949 to coordinate economic relations among the satellite countries and Moscow. The terms of COMECON actually worked against development of the satellite states, however, for the USSR was allowed to buy goods from these states at bargain prices and to sell products to them at exorbitant ones. Nonetheless, these formerly peasant states became oriented toward technology and bureaucratically directed industrial economies, thus creating opportunities for new careers. Tired of the struggles on the land, rural people moved to cities, where they received better education, health care, and ultimately jobs, albeit at the price of repression. The Roman Catholic church, which often protested the imposition of communism, was subdued as much as possible or infiltrated by government agents. Communists discriminated against agrarian elites, intellectuals, and other members of the middle class or imprisoned them. Political prisoners in East German camps did hard labor in uranium and other dangerous mines.

Culture, along with science, was a building block of Stalinism in the satellite countries. State-instituted programs aimed to build loyalty to the modernizing regime, and thus citizens found themselves obliged to attend adult education classes, women's groups, and public ceremonies. An intense program of Russification and de-Christianization forced students in eastern Europe to read histories of the war that ignored their own countries' resistance and gave the Red Army sole credit for fighting the Nazis. Rigid censorship resulted in what one staunchly socialist writer in the USSR characterized as "a dreary torrent of colorless, mediocre literature." Stalin also purged prominent wartime leaders to ensure conformity. Marshal Zhukov, a popular leader of the Soviet armed forces, was shipped to a distant command, while Anna Akhmatova, the great poet whose widely admired writing had emphasized perseverance during the war, was confined to a crowded hospital room because she refused to glorify Stalin in her postwar poetry.

In March 1953, amid growing repression, Stalin died, and it soon became clear that the old ways would not hold. Political prisoners in the labor camps rebelled, leading to the release of more than a million people from the Gulag. At the other end of the social order, many Soviet officials, despite enjoying luxury goods and plentiful food, had come to distrust Stalinism and now favored change. As protests took place across the Soviet bloc, governments stepped up the production of consumer goods—a policy called "goulash communism" after the Hungarian stew, because it provided more food for ordinary people. The future remained uncertain, however.

In 1955, Nikita Khrushchev (1894–1971), an illiterate coal miner before the revolution, became the undisputed leader of the Soviet Union, but he did so without

Re-creating Hungarian Youth
"Forward for the Congress of the Young Fighters of Peace and Socialism," exhorts this poster informing Hungarian youth about a conference to be held in June 1950. After World War II, people across Europe focused on the well-being of young people, and regimes in the Soviet sphere took steps to provide education in communism. Youth groups like those in the early Stalinist USSR served this end, and vivid posters in the Soviet realist style carried inspirational messages. **For more help analyzing this image, see the visual activity for this chapter in the Online Study Guide at** bedfordstmartins.com/huntconcise. (Magyar Nemzeti Múzeum, Budapest [Hungarian National Museum].)

executing his rivals. Khrushchev listened to popular complaints about conditions in both city and countryside and then made the surprising move of openly attacking Stalin. At a party congress in 1956, Khrushchev denounced the "cult of personality" Stalin had built about himself and announced that Stalinism did not equal communism. Khrushchev thus cagily attributed problems with communism to a single individual. The "secret speech"—it was not published in the USSR but became widely known—was a bombshell. People experienced, in the words of one writer, "a holiday of the soul." Debates broke out in public, and books championing the ordinary worker against the party bureaucracy appeared. The climate of relative tolerance for free speech was called "the thaw."

Protest erupted once more in the summer of 1956 when discontented Polish railroad workers struck for better wages. Popular support for their cause brought about policies providing new resources for ordinary people's needs. Inspired by the Polish example and angry at living under communism, Hungarians rebelled against forced collectivization in October 1956. As in Poland, economic issues and reports of Stalin's crimes sparked violence against the entire Communist system. Tens of thousands of protesters filled the streets of Budapest and succeeded in returning a popular hero, Imre Nagy, to power. When Nagy announced that Hungary might leave the Warsaw Pact, however, Soviet troops moved in, killing tens of thousands and causing hundreds of thousands more to flee to the West. Nagy was hanged. Crushing the Hungarian Revolution vividly displayed the limits to the thaw. Despite a rhetoric of democracy, the United States refused to intervene in Hungary, choosing not to risk World War III by challenging the Soviet sphere of influence.

The failure of eastern European uprisings overshadowed significant changes following Stalin's death. While defeating his rivals, Khrushchev ended the Stalinist purges and reformed the courts, which came to function according to procedures instead of staging show trials. The gates of the Gulag opened further, and the secret police lost many of its arbitrary powers. "It has become more interesting to visit and see people," Boris Pasternak said of the changes. "It has become easier to work." In 1957 the Soviets successfully launched the first artificial earth satellite, *Sputnik*, and in 1961 they put the first cosmonaut, Yuri Gagarin, in orbit around the earth. The Soviets' edge in space technology shocked the Western bloc and motivated the United States to create the National Aeronautics and Space Administration (NASA). For Soviets, such successes indicated that the USSR had achieved Stalin's goal of modernization and might inch closer to freedom.

Khrushchev, however, was inconsistent, showing himself open to changes in Soviet culture at one moment and then bullying honest writers at another. After condemning Pasternak because his novel *Doctor Zhivago* (1957) valued the individual, he allowed the publication of Aleksandr Solzhenitsyn's *One Day in the Life of Ivan Denisovitch* in 1961. This chilling account of life in the Gulag was useful in confirming Stalin's crimes. Under the thaw, Khrushchev made several trips to the West and was more widely seen by the public than Stalin had been. More confident and more affluent, the Soviets took steps to reduce their diplomacy's paranoid style and to expand communism's appeal in the new nations emerging from colonialism.

Despite the USSR's more relaxed posture, the cold war advanced, and the superpowers moved the world nearer to the nuclear brink.

REVIEW What factors drove economic recovery in western Europe? In eastern Europe?

Decolonization in a Cold War Climate

After World War II, activists in colonized regions used the postwar chaos in Europe and other parts of the world to achieve their long-held goal of liberation. At the war's end, the colonial powers brutally repressed nationalist groups, often with the help of the Japanese and U.S. armies, and attempted to reimpose their control. As in World War I, colonized peoples had been on the front lines defending the West, and they had witnessed the full barbarism of Western warfare. Like African American soldiers in the U.S. army, they experienced discrimination even while saving the West, and when they returned home, they did not receive the equal rights promised them. Moreover, successive wars had allowed local industries to develop outside the West, while industry in the imperial homelands fell into decline. As a result of the war, people in Asia, Africa, and the Middle East, often led by individuals steeped in Western values and experienced in war and its technology, sped toward independence.

The path to achieving independence—a process called **decolonization**—was paved with difficulties. In Africa, a continent whose peoples spoke several thousand languages and dialects, the European creation of convenient administrative units such as Nigeria and Rhodesia cut across ethnic lines and undermined local cultures. Religion played a divisive role in independence movements. In India, Hindus, Muslims, and Sikhs battled one another even though they shared the goal of eliminating British rule. In the Middle East and North Africa, pan-Arab and pan-Islamic movements—that is, those wanting to bring together all Arabs or all Muslims—might seem to have been unifying forces. Yet many Muslims were not Arab, many Arabs were not Muslim, and Islam itself encompassed competing beliefs and sects. Religious, ethnic, and cultural differences—many of them invented or promoted by the colonizers to divide and rule—worked against political unity. Despite these complications, various peoples in what was coming to be called the third world were able to overthrow imperialism, while the United States and the Soviet Union rushed to gain their support in the cold war.

The End of Empire in Asia

At the end of World War II, leaders in Asia succeeded in mobilizing mass discontent to drive out foreign rulers. Declining from an imperial power to a small island nation, Britain was the biggest loser. In 1947, it parted with India, whose independence it had promised in the 1930s. During World War II, some two million Indian men were mobilized to fight for the Allies in the Middle East and Asia, and India's domestic industries became important suppliers of war goods. Also during the war, Indian business leaders bought out local British entrepreneurs short of cash. Once the war ended, armed with economic might and military experience, Indians began to confront the British in strikes and other protests.

Britain quickly faced reality. So great was the mistrust the British had sown between the Indian National Congress and the Muslim League, however, that Britain decreed that two countries should emerge from the old colony. In 1947, India was created for Hindus, and Pakistan (itself later subdivided into two parts) was established for Muslims. During the independence year, tensions exploded between these two religious groups. The Sikhs, who felt totally ignored in the settlement, also contributed to the violence. Hundreds of thousands were massacred in the great shift of populations between India and Pakistan. In 1948, a radical Hindu assassinated Gandhi, who though a Hindu himself had continued to champion reconciliation among all the groups. Elsewhere, as some half a billion Asians gained their independence, Britain's sole notable colony was Hong Kong.

In 1949, after a lengthy civil war, a Communist victory in China brought into power a government led by Mao Zedong (1893–1976) that was no longer the plaything of the colonial powers. The new People's Republic of China under communism emphasized above all the welfare of the peasantry, rather than the industrial proletariat, and was thus distinct from Marxism and Stalinism. At the same time, backed by Stalin, Mao instituted reforms such as civil equality for women but also imposed Soviet-style collectivization, industrialization, and repression.

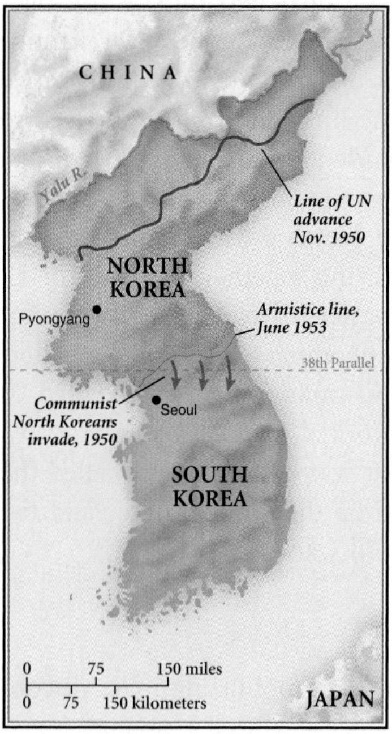

The Korean War, 1950–1953

The United States and the Soviet Union were deeply interested in East Asia—the United States because of the region's economic importance and the USSR because of its shared borders. The victory of the Chinese Communists spurred both superpowers to increase their involvement in Asian politics, where they faced off first in Korea, which had been split at the thirty-eighth parallel after World War II. In 1950, North Korea, with the support of the Soviet Union, invaded U.S.-backed South Korea, whose agents had been stirring up tensions with raids across the border. The United States maneuvered the United Nations into approving a "police action" against North Korea, and UN forces quickly drove well into North Korean territory, where they were met by the Chinese army. After two and a half years of a horribly destructive stalemate, the opposing sides finally agreed to a settlement in 1953: Korea would remain split at its prewar border, the thirty-eighth parallel. As a result of the Korean War, the United States increased its military spending from $10.9 billion in 1948 to almost $60 billion in 1953. The expansion of the cold war to Asia prompted the creation of an Asian counterpart to NATO—the Southeast Asia Treaty Organization (SEATO), established in 1954. Another important effect of the Korean War was the rapid reindustrialization of Japan to provide the United States with supplies.

The cold war then spread to Indochina, where nationalists had struggled against the postwar revival of French imperialism. Their leader, the European-educated Ho Chi Minh (1890–1969), built a powerful organization, the Viet Minh, to fight colonial rule. He advocated the redistribution of land held by big landowners, especially in the rich agricultural area in southern Indochina, where some six thousand owners possessed more than 60 percent of the land. Viet Minh peasant guerrillas ultimately defeated the technologically advanced French army, which was receiving aid from the United States, in the bloody battle of Dien Bien Phu in 1954. Later that year, the Geneva Conference carved out an independent Laos and divided Vietnam into North and South, each free from French control. The Communist-backed Viet Minh ruled in the north, while the United States supported an unpopular regime in the south, leaving the call for an independent Vietnamese nation basically unsettled.

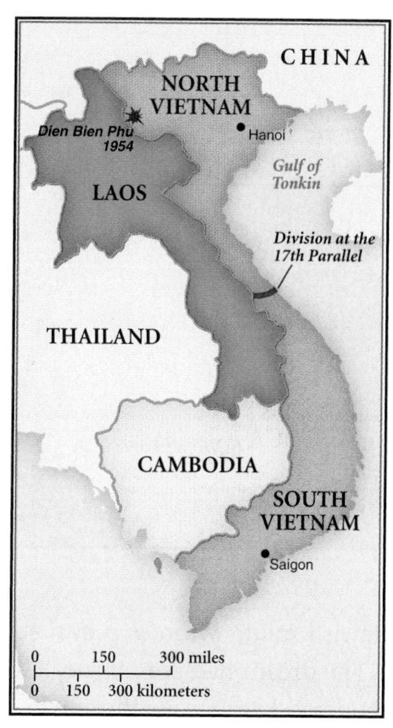

Indochina, 1954

The Struggle for Identity in the Middle East

Independence struggles in the Middle East highlighted the world's growing need for oil and showed the ability of small countries to maneuver between the superpowers. As in other regions dominated by the West, Middle Eastern peoples resisted attempts to reimpose imperial control after 1945. Weakened by the war, British oil companies wanted to tighten their grip on profits, as the value of this energy source soared. But British leaders arrogantly behaved as if they were still dominant, leading Middle Eastern states to increase their economic and political clout by renegotiating higher payments for drilling rights from Western companies.

The legacy of the Holocaust complicated the Middle Eastern political scene. Western commitment to securing a Jewish nation in the Middle East stirred Arab determination not to be pushed out of their homeland. When World War II broke out, 600,000 Jewish settlers and twice as many Arabs lived tensely in British-controlled Palestine. In 1947, an exhausted Britain turned the area over to the United Nations, which in the aftermath of the Holocaust voted to partition Palestine into an Arab region and a Jewish one (Map 22.4). Conflicting claims, however, led to a war in which

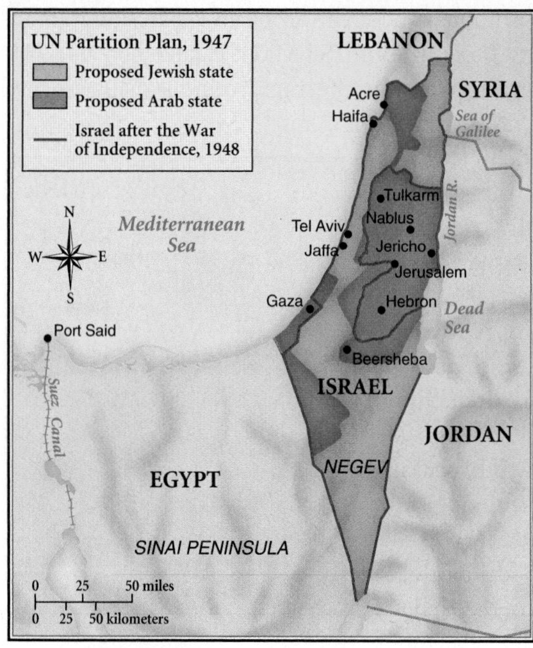

Map 22.4 The Partition of Palestine and the Creation of Israel, 1947–1948
The creation of the Jewish state of Israel in 1948 against a backdrop of ongoing wars among Jews and indigenous Arab peoples made the Middle East a powder keg. The struggle to secure resources and establish the borders of viable nation-states was at the heart of these bitter contests threatening to pull the superpowers into a third world war.

Jewish military forces prevailed. On May 14, 1948, the state of Israel came into being. "The dream had come true," Golda Meir, the future prime minister of Israel, observed, but "too late to save those who had perished in the Holocaust." Israel opened its gates to immigrants, whose ambition for land pressured their Arab neighbors.

One of those neighbors, Egypt, had gained its independence from Britain at the end of the war. Britain, however, retained its dominance in shipping to Asia through its control of the Suez Canal, which was owned by a British-run company. In 1952, Colonel Gamal Abdel Nasser became Egypt's president on a platform of economic modernization and true national independence—meaning Egyptian control of the canal. In July 1956, Nasser nationalized the canal. "I am speaking in the name of every Egyptian Arab," he remarked in his speech explaining the takeover, "and in the name of all those who believe in liberty and are ready to defend it." Nasser became a hero to Arabs, especially when Britain, Israel, and France attacked Egypt while the Hungarian revolt was in full swing. The British branded Nasser another Hitler and hoped that the Hungarian revolt would distract the superpowers. But the United States, fearing that Egypt would turn to the USSR, made the British back down. Nasser's triumph inspired confidence that colonized peoples around the world could force the imperial powers to surrender not just political but economic power.

New Nations in Africa

In sub-Saharan Africa, nationalist leaders roused their people to challenge Europe's increasing demands for resources and labor, which resulted in poverty for most African peoples. "The European Merchant is my shepherd, and I am in want," went one African version of the Twenty-third Psalm. Many Africans flocked to shantytowns in cities during World War II, where they kept themselves alive doing menial labor for whites and scavenging. At the war's end, as veterans returned home, protests mounted. Kwame Nkrumah (1909–1972) led the inhabitants of the British-controlled West African Gold Coast in Gandhian-style passive resistance, finally driving the British to withdraw and bringing the state of Ghana into being in 1957. Nigeria, the most populous African colony, achieved independence from Britain in 1960, and many other African states also became free (Map 22.5).

Where the population was mostly black, independence came less violently than in mixed-race territory with large settler populations. The east coast of Africa, as well as

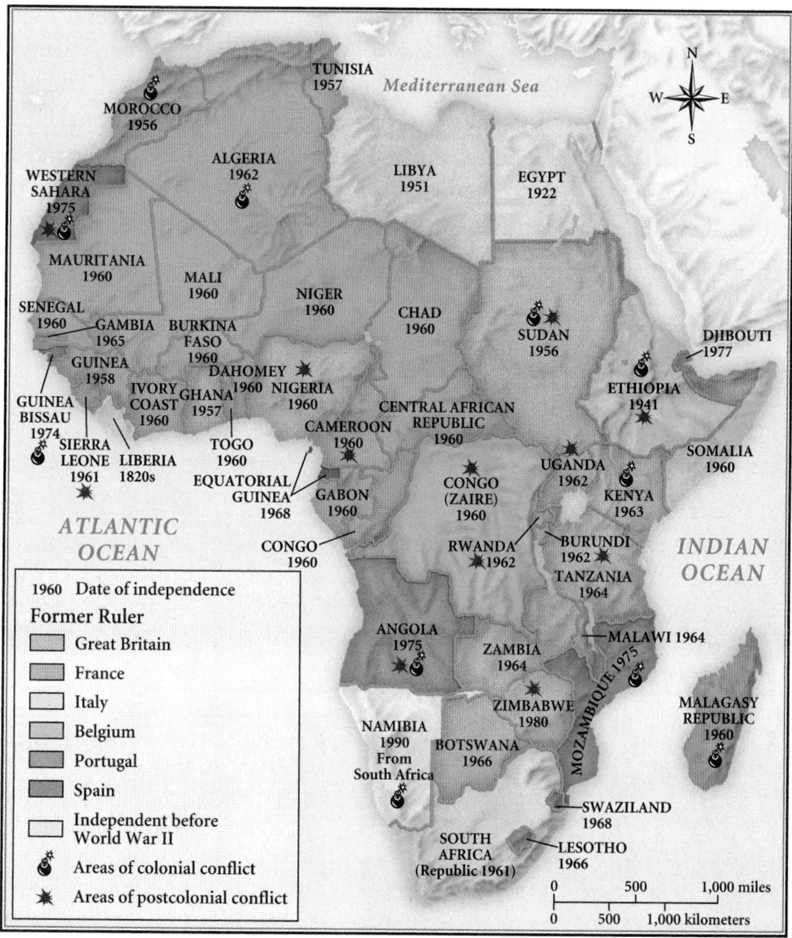

Map 22.5 The Decolonization of Africa, 1951–1990
The liberation of Africa from European rule was an uneven process, sometimes occurring peacefully and at other times demanding armed struggle to drive out European settlers, governments, and armies. After liberation, the difficult process of nation building—forming governments, educating children, providing social services, and the like—began. Creating national unity also proved challenging, except in places where the struggle against colonialism had already brought people together.

southern and central areas, had numerous European settlers, who violently resisted independence movements. In British East Africa, where white settlers ruled in splendor and blacks lacked both land and economic opportunity, violence erupted in the 1950s. African men formed rebel groups collectively called the Land Freedom Army, nicknamed the Mau Mau. With women serving as provisioners, messengers, and weapon stealers, Mau Mau bands, composed mostly of war veterans from the Kikuyu ethnic group, tried to recover land from whites. In 1963, Kenya gained formal independence, but only after the British had put hundreds of thousands of Kikuyus in concentration camps, called the "British Gulag" by those tortured there, and murdered tens of thousands more.

France granted independence with relatively little bloodshed to territories such as Tunisia, Morocco, and West Africa, where there were fewer white settlers. In Algeria, however, which had one million settlers of European descent, the French fought bitterly to keep control. At the end of World War II, the French army massacred tens of thousands of Algerian nationalists seeking independence. The liberation group resurfaced with new intensity in 1954 as the Front for National Liberation (FNL). The French dug in, sending more than 400,000 troops to Algeria. Neither side fought according to the accepted rules of warfare. The French savagely tortured Algerian Arabs; Algerian women, shielded by gender stereotypes, planted bombs in European cafés and carried weapons to assassination sites. The FNL, far less powerful than France, took its case to the court of world opinion. Reports of the

Jomo Kenyatta, First President of the New Kenyan Nation
Educated in England, Kenyatta wrote *Facing Mount Kenya,* a work that explained his native Kikuyu culture to Westerners. After a costly struggle during which he was imprisoned by the British, Kenyatta became president (1964–1978) of the new republic of Kenya. He stifled political debate by outlawing opposition parties. His one-party government brought social calm, which made Kenya a good place for Western investment. (© Bettmann/Corbis.)

French army's barbarous practices against Algeria's Muslim population prompted protests in Paris and around the globe.

France's Fourth Republic collapsed over Algeria, and Charles de Gaulle returned to power in 1958. While promising an end to the Algerian nightmare, he demanded the creation of a new republican government in France (the Fifth Republic), one with a strong president who chose the prime minister and could exercise emergency power. As de Gaulle's plans to decolonize Algeria unfolded, the French military, which had staked its prestige on keeping Algeria, launched a campaign of terrorism within metropolitan France. By 1962, de Gaulle had negotiated independence with the Algerian nationalists, and hundreds of thousands of *pieds noirs*—"black feet," as the French condescendingly called Europeans in Algeria—along with their Arab supporters, fled to France.

Violent resistance to the return of colonial rule also ended the Dutch and Belgian empires, and as newly independent nations emerged in Asia, Africa, and the Middle East, structures arose to promote international security and worldwide deliberations that included representation from the new states. Foremost among these was the United Nations, which convened for the first time in 1945. One notable change ensured the UN a greater chance of success than the League of Nations: both the United States and the Soviet Union were active members from the outset. The UN's charter outlined a collective global authority that would resolve conflicts and provide military protection if any members were threatened by aggression. In 1955, the Indonesian president Sukarno, who had succeeded in wrenching Indonesian independence from the Dutch, sponsored the Bandung Conference of nonaligned nations to set a common policy for achieving modernization and facing the superpowers. Both UN deliberations and meetings of emerging nations such as the Bandung Conference began raising major global issues such as human rights and inequities between countries of the north, which had prospered through colonial plunder, and those of the south, which had been plundered.

Newcomers Arrive in Europe

Amid the uncertainties of wars of liberation and independence, people from the former colonies began migrating to Europe—a reversal of the nineteenth-century trend of migration out of Europe. The first non-European newcomers came from Britain's Caribbean possessions right after the war. Next, labor shortages in northern Europe drove governments to negotiate with southern European countries for temporary workers. The German situation was especially serious because in 1950, the working-age population (people between the ages of fifteen and sixty-four) was composed of 15.5 million men and 18 million women. In an ideological climate that wanted women out of the workforce, the government desperately needed immigrant labor. After southern European reserves proved insufficient, Germany and France turned to North African and then to sub-Saharan countries in the 1960s. Countries in the Soviet bloc took in refugees from war-torn Southeast Asia. By the late 1970s, clandestine workers from Africa and Asia began entering countries such as Italy that had formerly exported labor. Scandinavia received immigrants from around the world, who flocked there because of reportedly greater opportunity and social programs to integrate newcomers. By the 1980s, some 8 percent of the European population was foreign-born, compared with 6 percent in the United States.

According to negotiated agreements, immigrant workers would have only temporary resident status and then return to their homeland. Initially, these workers were housed in barracks-like dormitories, and few Europeans paid any attention to the quality of their lives. Instead of settling into wider communities, they kept to themselves. Temporary workers made economic sense: virtually none of the welfare-state benefits applied to them, because their menial work was often off the books. "As they are young," one French business publication explained, "the immigrants often pay more in taxes than they receive in allowances." Most immigrants did jobs that people in the West avoided: they collected garbage, built roads, and cleaned homes. Although men predominated among immigrant workers, women performed undesirable jobs for even less pay.

The First "New" Europeans (1949)
Many immigrants from around the world came to Europe after World War II in search of economic well-being. Some of the first people to arrive in the late 1940s were from the Caribbean (like the men in the photograph looking for work in Britain) and from South Asia. Expanding welfare states hired some of them to do menial work in hospitals, clinics, and construction, no matter what their qualifications. But when race riots erupted and immigration continued to increase in the 1950s, the British House of Commons began debating the rights of these new Europeans. While governments and businesses in western Europe needed new laborers to rebuild after the war, some Europeans questioned whether they—or their wives and children—should be allowed to become citizens. (© Hulton Deutsch Collection/Corbis.)

Immigrants saw Europe as a land of relatively good government, wealth, and opportunity, and they appreciated the decent living conditions. As one Chinese immigrant to Spain put it, "If you want to be a millionaire, you must go to Singapore; if you want to be rich, you must go to Germany; but if you want good weather and an easy life, go to Spain." As empires collapsed, the composition of the European population became more diverse in terms of race, religion, and ethnicity. Whether in Europe or the United States, many of these newcomers eventually became citizens, and their children achieved good positions in government, business, education, and the professions.

REVIEW What were the results of decolonization?

Daily Life and Culture in the Shadow of Nuclear War

Both World War II and the cold war shaped postwar leisure and political culture. People engaged in heated debates over who had been responsible for Nazism, the subject of ethnic and racial justice, and the merits of the two superpowers. During this period of intense self-scrutiny, Europeans discussed the Americanization that seemed to accompany the influx of U.S. dollars, consumer goods, and cultural media. Were they becoming too materialistic like the Americans or too intolerant like the Soviets? As Europeans examined their war-filled past and their renewed prosperity, the cold war menaced hopes for peace and stability. In October 1962, the world held its breath while the leaders of the Soviet Union and the United States nearly provoked a nuclear conflagration over the issue of missiles on the island of Cuba. In hindsight, the existence of an extreme nuclear threat in an age of unprecedented prosperity seems utterly bewildering, but for those who lived with the threat of global annihilation, the dangers were all too real.

Restoring "Western" Values

After the inhumanity of Nazism, cultural currents in Europe and the United States reemphasized universal values and spiritual renewal. Some saw the churches as central to the restoration of values through an active commitment to "re-Christianizing" not only the West but the world. Responding to what he saw as a crisis in faith, Pope John XXIII (r. 1958–1963) in 1962 convened the Second Vatican Council, known as **Vatican II**. The Council modernized the liturgy, democratized many church procedures, and during the last session in 1965 renounced church doctrine that condemned the Jewish people as guilty of killing Jesus. Vatican II promoted ecumenism—cooperation among the world's faiths—and outreach to the world, which differed from the church's old spirit of missionary crusading on behalf of empire.

Despite religious reform, the trend toward a more secular culture continued. In the early postwar years, people in the U.S. bloc emphasized the triumph of "Western" civilization and "Western" values over fascism, and they characterized the war as one "to defend civilization [from] a conspiracy against man." This definition of the West often emphasized the heritage of Greece and Rome and the rise of national governments in Britain, France, and western Europe as these societies struggled against "barbaric" forces, be they nomadic tribes, Nazi armies, Communist agents, or national liberation movements in Asia and Africa. University courses in Western civilization flourished after the war to reaffirm those values.

Readers around the world snapped up memoirs of the death camps and tales of resistance to fascism. Rescued from the Third Reich in 1940, Nelly Sachs won the Nobel Prize for Literature in 1966 for her poetry about the Holocaust. Anne Frank's *Diary of a Young Girl* (1947), the moving record of a teenager hidden with her family in an Amsterdam house, showed the survival of Western values in the face of Nazi persecution. Amid the menacing evils of Nazism, Anne wrote that she never stopped believing that "people are really good at heart." Governments erected permanent plaques at spots where resisters had been killed, and organizations of resisters publicly commemorated their role in winning the war, hiding the fact of widespread collaboration in the mythical story of resistance.

By the end of the 1940s, **existentialism** was all the rage among the cultural elites and students in universities. This philosophy explored the meaning of human existence in a world where evil flourished. Two of its leaders, Albert Camus and Jean-Paul Sartre, had written for the resistance during the war, and in its aftermath they raised the question of "being," given what they perceived as the absence of God and the breakdown of morality during the war. Their answer was that being, or existing, was not the automatic process of either God's creation or humans' birth into the natural world. One was not born with spiritual goodness in the image of a creator, but instead one created an "authentic" existence through action and choice. Camus's novels, such as *The Stranger* (1942) and *The Plague* (1947), explored the responsibility of humans living under an evil and corrupt political order. Sartre's writings emphasized political activism and resistance under totalitarianism. Even though they never faced the enormous problems of making choices while living under fascism, young people in the 1950s found existentialism gripping and made it the most fashionable philosophy of the day.

In 1949, Simone de Beauvoir, Sartre's lifelong companion, published the twentieth century's most important work on the condition of women, *The Second Sex.* Beauvoir believed that most women had failed to take the kind of action necessary to lead authentic lives. Instead they lived in the world of biological necessity, devoting themselves exclusively to reproduction and motherhood. Failing to create an authentic self through action and accomplishment, they had become its opposite—an object, or "Other." Moreover, instead of struggling to define themselves and assert their freedom, women passively accepted their lives as defined by men. Beauvoir's classic book was a smash hit, in large part because people thought Sartre had written it. Both writers became celebrities, as the media spread the new commitment to humane values.

People of color in Africa and Asia contributed new theories of humanity by exploring topics of liberation and racial difference. During the 1950s, Frantz Fanon, a black psychiatrist from the French colony of Martinique, began analyzing liberation movements.

He wrote that the mental functioning of the colonized person was "traumatized" by the brutal imposition of an outside culture. Ruled by guns, the colonized person knew only violence and would thus naturally decolonize by means of violence. Translated into many languages, Fanon's *Black Skin, White Masks* (1952) and *The Wretched of the Earth* (1961) posed the question of how to decolonize one's culture and mind.

Simultaneous with decolonization, the commitment of such long-standing organizations as the National Association for the Advancement of Colored People (NAACP, founded 1909) to the cause of civil rights intensified in the 1950s. African Americans had fought in the war to defeat the Nazi idea of white racial superiority; as civilians, they now hoped to advance their ideals in the United States. With its ruling in *Brown v. Board of Education* (1954), the U.S. Supreme Court declared that segregated education violated the U.S. Constitution. On December 1, 1955, in Montgomery, Alabama, Rosa Parks, a part-time secretary for the local branch of the NAACP, boarded a bus and took the first available seat in the so-called colored section toward the back. When a white man found himself without a seat, the driver screamed at Parks, "Nigger, move back." By refusing to give up her seat at that moment, Parks violated discriminatory and often brutal southern laws affecting African Americans. She confronted that system through the studied practice of civil disobedience. Her action led to her arrest, followed by a community-wide boycott of public transportation by African Americans.

Civil rights groups boycotted discriminatory businesses and registered black voters disenfranchised by local regulations. Talented leaders emerged, foremost among them the great orator Martin Luther King Jr. (1929–1968), a young Baptist pastor originally from Georgia, whose speeches roused activists to nonviolent resistance and "soulforce"—Gandhi's *satyagraha,* or "holding to truth"—to counter aggression. The postwar culture of nonviolence would shape the civil rights movement for a few years, until the influence of Fanon and other anti-colonial activists turned it toward more violent measures.

Consumerism and Shifting Gender Norms

Government spending on European reconstruction and welfare helped prevent the kind of upheaval that had followed World War I. A rising birthrate and bustling youth culture boosted consumer spending, which in turn created jobs for veterans. Nonetheless, the war affected men's roles and sense of themselves. Young men who had missed World War II adopted the rough, violent style of soldiers, and roaming gangs posed as tough military types. While Soviet youths admired aviator aces, elsewhere groups such as the "teddy boys" in England (named after their Edwardian style of dress) and the *gamberros* (hooligans) in Spain took their cues from rock-and-roll music and films.

The leader of rock and roll was the American singer Elvis Presley. Sporting slicked-back hair and an aviator-style jacket, Presley bucked his hips and sang sexual lyrics to screaming and devoted fans. Rock-and-roll concerts and movies fired up young people across Europe, including in the Soviet bloc, where teens demanded the production of blue jeans and leather jackets. In a German nightclub late in the 1950s, members of a British rock group called the Quarrymen performed, yelling at and fighting with one another as part of their show. They would soon become known as the Beatles. Rebellious young American film stars like James Dean in *Rebel without a Cause* (1955) and Marlon Brando in *The Wild One* (1953) created the beginnings of a conspicuous postwar youth culture, in which the ideal was to be a bad boy.

The rebellious masculine style appeared also in literature, such as James Watson's autobiography, *The Double Helix* (1968), explaining how he and Francis Crick had discovered the structure of the gene by stealing other people's findings. German novelist Heinrich Böll, who decades later admitted to having been a Nazi soldier, protested that West Germany's postwar goal of respectability had allowed the people who had produced Nazism to become prominent once again. In Böll's novel *The Clown* (1963), a young middle-class hero leaves home and takes up life as a vagabond clown, mocking his audiences with clever pantomimes about the folly of their lives. He winds up begging in a railroad station, not a breadwinner but a bum. American "Beat" poets similarly rejected traditional ideals of the upright male breadwinner and family man.

Both high and low culture revealed that two horrendous world wars had weakened the Enlightenment view of men as rational, responsible achievers. The 1953 inaugural issue of the American magazine *Playboy,* and the hundreds of magazines that came

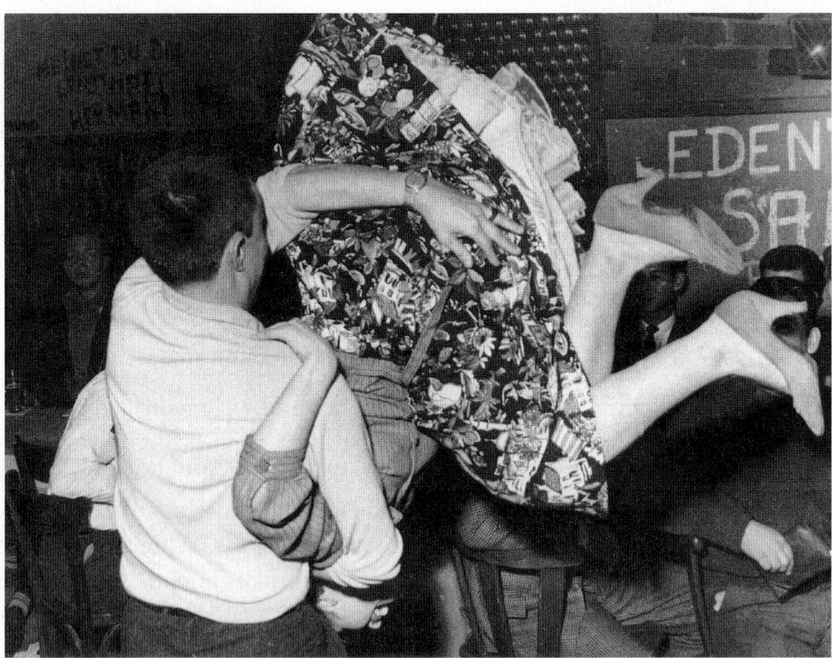

Rock and Roll

Rock and roll, born in the 1950s, spread around the world with unprecedented energy and speed. Teenage girls wore the voluminous skirts that the "new look" had made fashionable, and young men sported hairdos like Elvis Presley's. East and West, teens thronged, and even rioted, to attend rock concerts and would continue to do so despite public criticism and even police action against them. (ullstein bild/The Granger Collection, NY.)

to imitate it, ushered in a new and startling male identity. This new media presented modern man as sexually aggressive and independent of dull domestic life—just as he had been in the war. Breadwinning for a family destroyed a man's freedom and sense of self, this new male culture claimed. The definition of men's liberty came to include not just political rights but also sexual freedom outside of marriage.

In contrast, Western society promoted a postwar model for women that differed from their wartime roles. Rather than being seen as valued workers and heads of families in the absence of their men, postwar women were to symbolize the return to normalcy by leading a domestic and submissive life at home. Late in the 1940s, the fashion house of Christian Dior launched a clothing style called the "new look." It featured a pinched waist, tightly fitting bodice, and voluminous skirt. This restoration of the nineteenth-century female silhouette called for a renewal of older gender roles. Women's magazines publicized the new look and urged women to give up ambitions for themselves. Even in the hard-pressed Soviet Union, domesticity flourished: recipes for homemade face creams passed from woman to woman, and beauty parlors did a brisk business. In the West, household products such as refrigerators and washing machines raised standards for housekeeping by giving women the means to be "perfect" housewives.

However, new-look propaganda did not mesh with reality or even with all social norms. Dressmaking fabric was still being rationed in the late 1940s, and well into the next decade women could not always get enough to make voluminous skirts. In Europe, where people had barely enough to eat, the underwear needed for new-look contours simply did not exist, although the semistarved look was, for many, easy enough to achieve. In Spain, women were said to perform their role best by being religious and concerned with the spiritual well-being of their families. Spanish advertising, however, promoted physical beauty available through the consumption of cosmetics and clothing. European women continued to work outside the home after the war; indeed, mature women and mothers were working more than ever before—especially in the Soviet bloc. A major change was occurring, as the female workforce gradually became populated by wives and mothers who would hold jobs all their lives despite being bombarded with images of nineteenth-century femininity.

The advertising business helped create these cultural messages and promoted the widespread consumerism that accompanied recovery. Guided by marketing experts, western Europeans imitated Americans by driving some forty million motorized vehicles, including motorbikes, cars, buses, and trucks. They drank Coca-Cola and used American detergents, toothpaste, and soap. The number of radios in homes grew steadily, and radio remained the most influential medium throughout the 1950s, even as television loomed on the horizon. Only in the 1960s did television become an important consumer item for most Europeans.

The Culture of Cold War

Films, books, and other media added both criticism and support to the culture of cold war. Books such as George Orwell's *1984* (1949) were claimed by ideologues on both sides to support their beliefs. Ray Bradbury's popular *Fahrenheit 451* (1953), whose title indicates the temperature at which books would burn, condemned the cold war for restricting intellectual freedom. In the USSR, official writers churned out spy stories, and espionage novels topped best-seller lists in the West. *Casino Royale* (1953), by the British author Ian Fleming, introduced James Bond, who tested his wit and physical skill against Communist and other political villains. Soviet pilots would not take off when the work of Yulian Simyonov, the Russian counterpart of Ian Fleming, was playing on radio or television. Reports of Soviet- and U.S.-bloc characters—fictional or real—facing one another down became part of everyday life.

High and low culture alike contributed to the cold war climate. While many Europeans admired American innovation, the Communist Party in France led a successful campaign to ban Coca-Cola for a time in the 1950s. Soviet magazines carried fashion photos praised for their "decency" in contrast to the highly sexualized garments for women in the West. Both sides tried to win the cold war by pouring vast sums of money into high culture, although the United States did it by secretly channeling government money into foundations to award fellowships to designated artists or promote favorable journalism around the world. As leadership of the art world passed to the United States, art became part of the cold war. Abstract expressionism, practiced by American artists such as Jackson Pollock, produced nonrepresentational works by dripping, spattering, and pouring paint. Abstract expressionists spoke of the importance of the artist's self-discovery. "If I stretch my arms next to the rest of myself and wonder where my fingers are, that is all the space I need as a painter," commented one of them on his relationship with his canvas. Said to prove Western freedom, such painters were given shows in Europe and awarded commissions at the secret direction of the U.S. Central Intelligence Agency (CIA).

The USSR openly promoted an official Communist culture. When a show of abstract art opened in the Soviet Union, Khrushchev yelled at the exhibition itself that it was "dog shit." Pro-Soviet critics focused on workers and the oppressed races in the United States. In Italy, the neorealist technique was developed by filmmakers such as Vittorio De Sica in *The Bicycle Thief* (1948). Such works challenged Hollywood-style sets and costumes by using ordinary characters living in devastated, impoverished cities. They criticized both middle-class prosperity and fascist pretense. "We are in rags? Let's show everyone our rags," said one Italian director. Many of these left-leaning directors associated support for the suffering masses with the Communist cause, while on the pro-American side, the film *Doctor Zhivago* became a hit celebrating individualism and condemning the Communist way of life. Seen or unseen, the cold war entered cultural life.

The Atomic Brink

Radio was at the center of the cold war. As superpower rivalry heated up, radio's propaganda function remained strong, as it had in wartime. During the late 1940s and early 1950s, the Voice of America broadcast in thirty-eight languages from one hundred transmitters to provide an alternative source of news for people in eastern Europe.

Barbara Hepworth, *Single Form* (1961–1964)
Like others in the West, British sculptor Barbara Hepworth was strangely buoyed by the end of World War II, hoping that it meant the dawn of a new age. Full of renewed energy, Hepworth believed that art should follow pure forms, which some called "primitive," as a way of expressing enduring values. Her twenty-one-foot abstract sculpture *Single Form,* shown here as a plaster cast, was installed at the United Nations building in New York to commemorate the life of her friend Dag Hammarskjöld, who served as secretary-general of the United Nations from 1953 to 1961. (Photo Morgan-Wells, London/© Bowness, Hepworth Estate.)

The Soviet counterpart broadcast in Russian around the clock but initially spent much of its wattage jamming U.S. programming. Russian programs stressed a uniform Communist culture and values; the United States, by contrast, emphasized diverse programming and featured debate about current affairs. U.S. radio aimed to contrast the dictatorial nature of Communist society with America's commitment to choice and free speech. The public also heard reports of a nuclear buildup, while at school children rehearsed for nuclear war. At home families built bomb shelters in their backyards.

It was in this upsetting climate of cold war that John Fitzgerald Kennedy (1917–1963) became U.S. president in 1960. Kennedy represented American affluence and youth and also the nation's commitment to cold war. Kennedy's media advisers recognized how perfect a match their articulate, good-looking president was for the power of television. A war hero and early fan of the fictional cold war spy James Bond, Kennedy escalated the cold war. Some of this escalation occurred over the nearby island of Cuba, where in 1959 Fidel Castro had come to power after overthrowing a corrupt dictatorship. After being rejected by the United States, Castro allied his new government with the USSR. In the spring of 1961, Kennedy, assured of success by the CIA, launched an invasion of Cuba at the Bay of Pigs to overthrow Castro. The invasion failed miserably and humiliated the United States.

Cold war tensions increased. In the summer of 1961, the East German government directed workers to stack bales of barbed wire across miles of the city's east-west border as the beginning of the Berlin Wall. The divided city had served as an escape route by which some three million people had fled to the West. Kennedy responded by calling for increased defense spending. In October 1962, tensions came to a head in the Cuban missile crisis, when the CIA reported the installation of silos to house Soviet missiles in Cuba. Kennedy acted forcefully, ordering a naval blockade of ships headed for Cuba and demanding removal of the installations. For several days, the world stood on the brink of nuclear disaster. Then, between October 25 and 27, Khrushchev and Kennedy negotiated an end to the crisis. Kennedy spent the remainder of his short life working to improve nuclear diplomacy; Khrushchev did the same. In the summer of 1963, less than a year after the shock of the Cuban missile crisis, the United States and the Soviet Union signed a test-ban treaty outlawing the explosion of nuclear weapons in the atmosphere and the seas. Allowing the superpowers to back away from the brink, the treaty held out hope that the cold war and its culture would give way to something better.

REVIEW How did the cold war affect everyday culture and social life?

Conclusion

Nikita Khrushchev was ousted in 1964 for his erratic policies and for appearing to back down in the Cuban missile crisis. In his forced retirement, he expressed regret at his brutal treatment of Boris Pasternak. "We shouldn't have banned [*Doctor Zhivago*]," he said. "There's nothing anti-Soviet in it." But the postwar decades were bleak diplomatically. The two superpowers—the Soviet Union and the United States—each controlling atomic arsenals, overshadowed the old European powers and engaged in a menacing cold war, complete with the threat of nuclear annihilation. The cold war saturated everyday life, giving birth to bomb shelters, spies, and

Mapping the West The Cold War World, c. 1960

Superpower rivalry resulted in the division of much of the industrial world into cold war alliances. The United States and the Soviet Union also vied for the allegiance of the newly decolonized countries of Asia and Africa by providing military, economic, and technological assistance. Wars such as those in Vietnam and Korea were also products of the cold war. How might this map be said to convey the idea of a first, second, and third world?

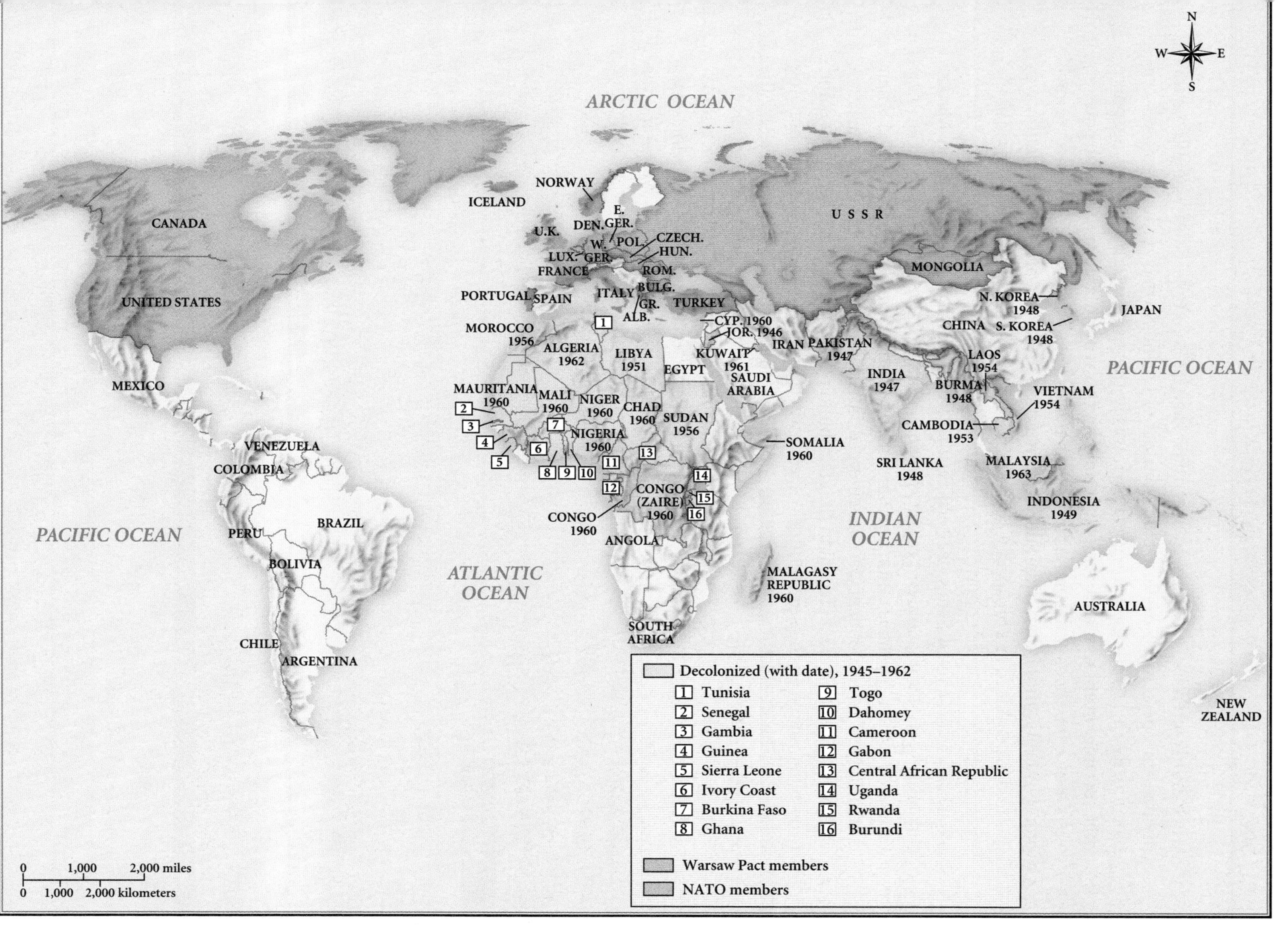

ARCTIC OCEAN
CANADA
UNITED STATES
MEXICO
ICELAND
NORWAY
U.K.
DEN.
E. GER.
W. GER.
POL.
CZECH.
HUN.
LUX.
FRANCE
ROM.
BULG.
PORTUGAL
SPAIN
ITALY
GR.
ALB.
TURKEY
U S S R
MONGOLIA
N. KOREA 1948
CHINA
S. KOREA 1948
JAPAN
PACIFIC OCEAN
MOROCCO 1956
ALGERIA 1962
LIBYA 1951
EGYPT
CYP. 1960
JOR. 1946
KUWAIT 1961
SAUDI ARABIA
IRAN
PAKISTAN 1947
INDIA 1947
LAOS 1954
BURMA 1948
VIETNAM 1954
CAMBODIA 1953
MAURITANIA 1960
MALI 1960
NIGER 1960
CHAD 1960
SUDAN 1956
NIGERIA 1960
SOMALIA 1960
SRI LANKA 1948
MALAYSIA 1963
INDONESIA 1949
VENEZUELA
COLOMBIA
BRAZIL
PERU
BOLIVIA
CHILE
ARGENTINA
PACIFIC OCEAN
ATLANTIC OCEAN
CONGO 1960
CONGO (ZAIRE) 1960
ANGOLA
SOUTH AFRICA
INDIAN OCEAN
MALAGASY REPUBLIC 1960
AUSTRALIA
NEW ZEALAND
N W E S
Decolonized (with date), 1945–1962
1 Tunisia
2 Senegal
3 Gambia
4 Guinea
5 Sierra Leone
6 Ivory Coast
7 Burkina Faso
8 Ghana
9 Togo
10 Dahomey
11 Cameroon
12 Gabon
13 Central African Republic
14 Uganda
15 Rwanda
16 Burundi
Warsaw Pact members
NATO members
0 1,000 2,000 miles
0 1,000 2,000 kilometers

witch hunts, creating a culture of fear that war was looming. Cold war diplomacy divided Europe into an eastern bloc dominated by the Soviets and a freer western bloc mostly allied with the United States. It was in this grim international atmosphere that starving, homeless, and refugee people had to rebuild a devastated Europe.

Despite the chaos at the end of 1945, both halves of Europe recovered almost miraculously in little more than a decade. Eastern Europe, where wartime devastation was greatest, experienced less prosperity. In western Europe wartime technology served as the basis for new consumer goods, while welfare-state programs improved health. Helped by aid from the United States, western Europe formed a successful Common Market that became the foundation for greater European unity. As a result of the war, Germany recovered as two countries, not one, and the weakened European powers lost their colonies. Newly independent nations emerged in Asia and Africa, leaving in question whether there would be a change in the distribution of global power. These new countries, often caught in the competition for cold war allies, faced the problem of building political and economic institutions. As the West as a whole grew in prosperity, its cultural life focused paradoxically on rethinking Western values while enjoying mass consumerism. Above all, the West—and the rest of the world—had to survive the atomic rivalry of the superpowers.

CHAPTER REVIEW QUESTIONS

1. How did the political climate after World War II differ from the political climate after World War I?
2. Why did decolonization occur so soon after World War II?

TIMELINE

- **1945** Cold war begins
- **1947** India and Pakistan win independence from Britain; U.S. president Harry Truman announces the Truman Doctrine
- **1948** State of Israel established
- **1949** Mao Zedong leads Communist revolution in China; Western allies establish NATO; Simone de Beauvoir, *The Second Sex*
- **1950** Korean War begins
- **1953** Stalin dies; Korean War ends; first issue of *Playboy*
- **1954** *Brown v. Board of Education* prohibits segregated schools in the United States; Vietnamese forces defeat the French at Dien Bien Phu
- **1955** Soviet Union establishes the Warsaw Pact
- **1956** Egyptian leader General Gamal Abdel Nasser nationalizes the Suez Canal; uprising in Hungary against the USSR
- **1957** Boris Pasternak, *Doctor Zhivago;* USSR launches *Sputnik;* European Economic Community formed
- **1958** Fifth Republic begins in France
- **1961** East German workers begin to construct the Berlin Wall
- **1962** United States and USSR face off in the Cuban missile crisis

1945 1950 1955 1960 1965

For practice quizzes and other study tools, see the Online Study Guide at bedfordstmartins.com/huntconcise.

For primary-source material from this period, see Chapter 27 of *Sources of The Making of the West*, Third Edition.

Suggested References

In the past decades, the opening of Soviet archives and careful research in U.S. records have allowed for more informed views of the diplomacy and politics of the cold war. The Cold War Files Web site, supported by the Woodrow Wilson Center and George Washington University, contains biographies of the main players, documents, and miscellaneous details of cold war events.

Cold War Files: Interpreting History through Documents: http://coldwarfiles.org

Crowley, David, and Susan E. Reid, eds. *Socialist Spaces: Sites of Everyday Life in the Eastern Bloc*. 2002.

Frommer, Benjamin. *National Cleansing: Retribution against Nazi Collaborators in Postwar Czechoslovakia*. 2005.

Gaddis, John. *The Cold War: A New History*. 2006.

Grossman, Atina. *Jews, Germans, and Allies: Close Encounters in Occupied Germany, 1945–1949*. 2007.

Herzog, Dagmar. *Sex after Fascism: Memory and Morality in Twentieth-Century Germany*. 2005.

Jobs, Richard I. *Riding the New Wave: Youth and the Rejuvenation of France after World War II*. 2007.

Judt, Tony. *Postwar: A History of Europe since 1945*. 2006.

Milward, Alan S. *The United Kingdom and the Economic Community*. 2002.

Moeller, Robert. *War Stories: The Search for a Usable Past in the Federal Republic of Germany*. 2001.

Naimark, Norman, and Leonid Gbianshii, eds. *The Establishment of Communist Regimes in Eastern Europe*. 1997.

Poiger, Uta. *Jazz, Rock, and Rebels: Cold War Politics and American Culture in a Divided Germany*. 2000.

Shepard, Todd. *The Invention of Decolonization: The Algerian War and the Remaking of France*. 2006.

Spector, Ronald H. *In the Ruins of Empire: The Japanese Surrender and the Battle for Postwar Asia*. 2007.

Statler, Kathryn, and Andrew Johns, eds. *The Eisenhower Administration, the Third World, and the Globalization of the Cold War*. 2006.

PALACH
Havel

23

Postindustrial Society and the End of the Cold War Order

1965–1989

In January 1969, Jan Palach, a twenty-one-year-old philosophy student, drove to a main square in Prague, doused his body with gasoline, and set himself ablaze. Before that, he had put aside his coat with a message in it demanding an end to Communist repression in Czechoslovakia. It promised more such suicides unless the government lifted state censorship. The manifesto was signed "Torch No. 1." Palach's suicide stunned his nation. Black flags hung from windows, and close to a million people flocked to his funeral. In the next months, more Czech youth followed Palach's grim example and became torches for freedom.

Shrine to Jan Palach
Jan Palach was a martyr to the cause of an independent Czechoslovakia, free to pursue a non-Soviet destiny. His self-immolation on behalf of that cause in 1969 roused the nation. As makeshift shrines sprang up and multiplied throughout the 1970s and 1980s, they served as common rallying points that ultimately contributed to the overthrow of Communist rule. Václav Havel, the future president of a liberated Czechoslovakia, was arrested early in the momentous year of 1989 for commemorating Palach's sacrifice at the shrine. In light of so many other deaths in the Soviet bloc, why did Palach's death become so powerful a force? *(© Marc Garanger/Corbis.)*

Before his self-immolation, Jan Palach was an ordinary, well-educated citizen of an increasingly technological society. Having recovered from World War II, the West shifted from a manufacturing economy based on heavy industry to a service economy that depended on technical knowledge in fields such as engineering, health care, and finance. This new service economy has been labeled "postindustrial." To staff it, institutions of higher education sprang up at a dizzying rate and attracted more students than ever before. Young men like Palach—along with women, minorities, and many other activists in the 1960s and 1970s—struck out against war and cold war, inequality and repression, and even against knowledge and technology. From Czechoslovakia to the United States and around the world, protesters warned that postindustrial nations in general and the superpowers in particular were becoming technological monsters. Before long, countries in both the Soviet and U.S. blocs were close to political revolution.

The challenge posed by young reformers came at a bad time for the superpowers and other leading European states. An agonizing war in Vietnam weakened the United States, and China confronted the Soviet Union on its borders. In a dramatic turn of events, the oil-producing states of the Middle East formed a cartel and reduced the flow of oil to the leading industrial nations in the 1970s. The resulting price increases helped bring on a recession, threatening the postindustrial economy. Extremists turned to **terrorism** to achieve their goals, and there was no guarantee that the superpowers—despite their wealth and military might—would emerge victorious in this age of increasingly global competition. As the USSR experienced economic decay, a reform-minded leader, Mikhail Gorbachev, directed his nation to change course. It was too late: in 1989, the Soviet bloc collapsed, helped by countless acts of protest, not the least of them the individual heroism of Jan Palach and his fellow human torches.

CHAPTER FOCUS QUESTION How did technological, economic, and social change contribute to increased activism, and what were the political results of that activism?

The Revolution in Technology

The protests of the 1960s and after took place in the midst of astonishing technological advances. These advances steadily boosted prosperity and changed daily life in the West, where people awoke to instantaneous radio and television news, worked with computers, and used revolutionary contraceptives to control reproduction. Satellites orbiting the earth relayed telephone signals and collected military intelligence. Smaller gadgets—electric popcorn poppers, portable radios and tape players, automatic garage door openers—made life more pleasant. The reliance of humans on machines led one philosopher to insist that people were no longer self-sufficient individuals but rather cyborgs—humans who needed machines for ordinary life processes.

The Information Age: Television and Computers

Information technology brought about change in the postindustrial period just as innovations in textile making and the spread of railroads had in the nineteenth century. This technology's ability to transmit knowledge, culture, and political information globally appeared even more revolutionary. In the first half of the twentieth century, mass journalism, radio, and films had created a more uniform society based on shared information and images. In the last third of the century, television, computers, and telecommunications made information even more accessible and standardized. Once remote villages were linked to urban capitals on the other side of the world thanks to videocassettes, satellite television, and telecommunications.

Between the mid-1950s and the mid-1970s, Europeans followed Americans in rapidly adopting television as a major entertainment and communications medium. In 1954, just 1 percent of French households had a television; by 1974, almost 80 percent did. With the average viewer tuning in about four and a half hours a day, the audience for newspapers and theater declined. "We devote more . . . hours per year to television than [to] any other single artifact," one sociologist commented in 1969. As with radio, European governments funded television broadcasting with tax dollars and controlled TV programming to avoid what they perceived as the substandard fare offered by American commercial TV. The French launched popular programs featuring philosophers and other writers; others broadcast drama, ballet, concerts, variety shows, and news. The welfare state, in Europe at least, thereby gained more power to shape daily life.

The emergence of communications satellites and video recorders in the 1960s brought competition to state-sponsored television. Worldwide audiences enjoyed broadcasts from around the globe as satellite technology allowed for the transmission of sports broadcasts and other programming. Feature films on videotape became readily available to television stations (although not yet to individuals) and competed with made-for-television movies and other programs. The competition increased in 1969 when the Sony Corporation introduced the first affordable color videocassette recorder to the consumer market. Critics complained that although TV provided more information than had ever been available before, the resulting shared culture represented the lowest common denominator.

East and West, television exercised a powerful political and cultural influence. Even in a rural area of the Soviet Union, more than 70 percent of the inhabitants watched television regularly in the late 1970s. Educational programming united the far-flung population of the USSR by broadcasting shows designed to advance Soviet culture. At the same time, with travel impossible or forbidden to many, shows about foreign lands were among the most popular. Heads of state could usually bump regular programming. In the 1960s, French president Charles de Gaulle addressed his fellow citizens frequently, employing the grandiose gestures of an imperial ruler to stir patriotism. As electoral success in western Europe increasingly depended on cultivating an appealing media image, politicians needed media experts as much as they did policy experts.

Just as revolutionary as television, the computer reshaped work in science, defense, and industry. Computers had evolved dramatically since the first electronic ones, among them the Colossus, which the British used in 1943 to decode Nazi military and diplomatic messages. After the war, computing machines shrank from the size of a gymnasium in the 1940s to that of an attaché case in the mid-1980s. They also became far less expensive and fantastically more powerful, thanks to the development of increasingly sophisticated digital electronic circuitry implanted on tiny silicon chips. Within a few decades, the computer could perform hundreds of millions of operations per second, and the price of the integrated circuit at the heart of computer technology would fall to less than a dollar.

Computers changed the pace and patterns of work not only by speeding up but also by performing many operations that workers had once done themselves. In garment making, for example, experienced workers no longer painstakingly figured out how to arrange patterns on cloth for maximum economy. Instead, a computer determined the best positioning of pattern pieces, and trained workers, usually women, followed the machine's directions. Soon, like outworkers in the eighteenth century, people could work for industries at home, connected to a central mainframe. In 1981 the French phone company launched a public Internet server, the

Minitel—a forerunner of the World Wide Web—through which individuals could make reservations, perform stock transactions, and gain information.

Whereas during the Industrial Revolution mechanical power replaced human energy, the computer technology of the information revolution added to brainpower. Many believed that computers would profoundly expand mental life, providing, in the words of one scientist, "boundless opportunities . . . to resolve the puzzles of cosmology, of life, and of the society of man." Others argued that computers programmed people, reducing human initiative and ability to solve problems. Such predictions are still untested even today, because the information revolution continues to unfold.

The Space Age

The Soviet launch of the *Sputnik* satellite in 1957 marked the start of the space race with the United States. The competition led to increasingly complex spaceflights that tested humans' ability to survive the process of space exploration, including weightlessness. Astronauts walked in space, endured weeks (and later months) in orbit, fixed satellites, and carried out experiments for the military and private industry. In addition, a series of unmanned rockets filled the earth's gravitational sphere with weather, television, intelligence, and other communications satellites. In July 1969, a worldwide television audience watched as U.S. astronauts Neil Armstrong and Edwin "Buzz" Aldrin walked on the moon's surface—the climactic moment in the space race.

Valentina Tereshkova, Russian Cosmonaut
People sent into space were heroes, representing modern values of courage, strength, and well-honed skills. Insofar as the space age was part of the cold war race for superpower superiority, the USSR held the lead during the first decade. The Soviets trained both women and men, and the 1963 flight of Valentina Tereshkova, the first woman in space, supported Soviet claims of gender equality in contrast to the all-male superstar image of the early U.S. space program. (Hulton Archive/Getty Images.)

The space race also influenced culture. Astronauts and cosmonauts were perhaps the era's most admired heroes: Yuri Gagarin, John Glenn, and Valentina Tereshkova—the first woman in space—topped the list. Children's toys and games centered increasingly on space. Films such as *2001: A Space Odyssey* (1968) portrayed space explorers answering questions about life that were formerly the domain of church leaders. Polish author Stanislaw Lem's popular novel *Solaris* (1971), later made into a film, described space age individuals engaged in personal quests for meaning and drew readers and viewers into futuristic fantasy.

The space age grew out of cold war concerns and relied on advances in the same rocket technology that powered missiles. At the same time, the space age depended on global cooperation. From the 1960s on, U.S. spaceflights often involved the participation of other countries. In 1965, an international consortium headed by the United States launched the first commercial communications satellite, *Intelsat I*, and by the 1970s some 150 countries worked together at more than four hundred stations worldwide to maintain global satellite communications. Although half of all satellites were used for spying, the rest made international communication possible and transnational cooperation a necessity.

Pure science flourished amid the space race. Astronomers used mineral samples from the moon to calculate the age of the solar system with unprecedented precision. Unmanned spacecraft provided data on cosmic radiation, magnetic fields, and infrared sources. Although the media touted the human conquerors of space, breakthroughs in space exploration and astronomy also depended on technology, including the radio telescope, which depicted space by receiving, measuring, and calculating nonvisible rays. These findings reinforced the so-called big bang theory of the origins of the universe, first outlined in the 1930s by American astronomer Edwin Hubble and given crucial support in the 1950s by the discovery of a low level of radiation permeating the universe in all directions. The big bang theory proposes that the universe began with the explosion of superdense, superhot matter some ten billion to twenty billion years ago.

Revolutions in Biology, Reproductive Technology, and Sexual Behavior

A revolution in the life sciences brought about dramatic new health benefits and ultimately changed reproduction itself. In 1952, scientists Francis Crick, an Englishman, and James Watson, an American, discovered the structure of **DNA**, the material in a cell's chromosomes that carries hereditary information. They showed how the double helix of the DNA molecule splits to form the basis of each new cell. This genetic material, biologists concluded, provides a chemical pattern for an individual organism's life. Beginning in the 1960s, genetics and the new field of molecular biology progressed rapidly. Growing understanding of nucleic acids and proteins advanced knowledge about viruses and bacteria that effectively ended the ravages of polio, tetanus, syphilis, tuberculosis, and such dangerous childhood diseases as mumps and measles in the West.

Scientists used their understanding of DNA to alter the makeup of plants and to bypass natural animal reproduction in a process called cloning—obtaining the cells of an organism and dividing or reproducing them in an exact copy in a laboratory. In 1997, one group of British researchers successfully produced a cloned sheep named Dolly, though she suffered an array of disabilities and died six years later. Cloning raised questions of whether scientists should interfere with so basic and essential a process as reproduction. The possibility of genetically altering species and even creating new ones (for instance, to control agricultural pests) led to concern about how such actions would affect the balance of nature. In 1967, Dr. Christiaan Barnard of South Africa performed the first successful heart transplant, and U.S. doctors later developed an artificial heart. As major breakthroughs like these occurred, commentators asked whether the enormous cost of new medical technology to save a few people would be better spent on helping the many who lacked even basic health care.

Technology also influenced the most intimate areas of human relations—sexuality and procreation. Matching family size to agricultural productivity no longer shaped sexual behavior in the industrialized and urbanized West. With reliable birth-control devices more readily available, young people began having sexual relations earlier, with less risk of pregnancy. These trends accelerated in the 1960s when the birth-control

Thalidomide Children

In the last third of the twentieth century, increasingly destructive side effects of powerful medicines became apparent. Women who took the sedative thalidomide while pregnant gave birth to children with severe disabilities. The race to profit from scientific and technological developments sometimes ignored human well-being, and the public condemned companies selling untested products. When children affected by thalidomide became adults, they were among those who launched the disability rights movement. **For more help analyzing this image, see the visual activity for this chapter in the Online Study Guide at bedfordstmartins.com/huntconcise.** (Deutsche Presse Agentur.)

pill, first tested on women in developing areas, came on the market. Millions also sought out voluntary surgical sterilization through tubal ligations and vasectomies. New techniques brought abortion, traditionally performed by amateurs, into the hands of medical professionals, making it a safe procedure for the first time.

Childbirth and conception were similarly transformed. Whereas only a small minority of Western births took place in hospitals in 1920, more than 90 percent did by 1970. Obstetricians now performed much of the work midwives had once done. As pregnancy and birth became a medical process, new procedures and equipment made it possible to monitor women and fetuses throughout pregnancy, labor, and delivery. In 1978, the first "test-tube baby," Louise Brown, was born to an English couple. She had been conceived when her mother's eggs were fertilized with her father's sperm in a laboratory dish and then implanted in her mother's uterus—a complex process called **in vitro fertilization**. If a woman could not carry a child to term, the laboratory-fertilized embryo could be implanted in the uterus of a surrogate, or substitute, mother. Researchers even began working on an artificial womb to allow for reproduction entirely outside the body—from storage bank to artificial embryonic environment.

REVIEW What were the technological and scientific advances of the 1960s and 1970s, and how did they change human life and society?

Postindustrial Society and Culture

Soaring investments in science and the spread of technology put Western countries on what has been called a postindustrial course. Instead of being centered on manufacturing and heavy industry, the postindustrial economy emphasized the distribution of services such as health care and education. The service sector was the leading force in the economy, and this meant that intellectual work, not industrial or manufacturing work, was central to creating jobs and profits. Moreover, all parts of society and industry interlocked, forming a system constantly in need of complex analysis, as in the nuclear industry. These characteristics of postindustrial society would carry over from the 1960s and 1970s into the next century.

A major development of the postindustrial era was the **multinational corporation**. Multinationals produced goods and services for a global market and conducted business worldwide, but unlike older kinds of international firms, they established major factories in countries other than their home bases. For example, of the five hundred largest businesses in the United States in 1970, more than one hundred did over a quarter of their business abroad, with IBM operating in more than one hundred countries. Although U.S.-based corporations led the way, European and Japanese multinationals like Volkswagen, Shell, Nestlé, and Sony also had a broad global reach.

Some multinationals had bigger revenues than entire nations. In the first years after World War II, multinationals preferred European employees, who constituted a highly educated labor pool and had well-developed consumer habits. Then, beginning in the 1960s, multinationals moved more of their operations to formerly colonized states to reduce labor costs and avoid taxes. Although these companies provided jobs in developing areas, profits usually enriched foreign stockholders and thus looked to some like imperialism in a new form.

Many firms believed that they could stay competitive only by expanding, merging with other companies, or becoming partners with government in doing business. In France, for example, a massive glass conglomerate merged with a metallurgical company to form a new group specializing in all phases of construction—a wise move given the postwar building boom. Firms also increased their investment in research and cooperated internationally to produce major new products. The British-French supersonic aircraft Concorde, which, beginning with its first flight in 1976, flew from London to New York in less than four hours, was one result. Another venture was the Airbus, a more practical series of passenger jets inaugurated in 1972 by a consortium of European firms. Both projects grew from the strong relationship among government, business, and science as well as from the international cooperation in manufacturing among members of the Common Market. Such relationships allowed for successful competition in the global business world.

The New Worker

In the early years of industry, workers often labored to exhaustion and lived in poor conditions. This scenario changed fundamentally in postwar Europe with the reduction of the blue-collar workforce, the growth of offshore manufacturing, and increased automation of industrial work. Manufacturing was simply cleaner and less dangerous than before. Within firms, the relationship of workers to bosses shifted as management started grouping workers into teams that set their own production quotas, organized and assigned tasks, and competed with other teams to produce more. As workers took on responsibilities once assigned to managers, union membership declined.

In both the U.S. and Soviet blocs, a new kind of working class of white-collar service personnel emerged. Its rise undermined economic distinctions based on the way one worked, for those who performed service work were not necessarily better paid than blue-collar workers. The ranks of service workers swelled with researchers, health care and medical workers, technicians, planners, and government staff. As the emphasis on service work grew, entire categories of employees such as flight attendants spent a good part of their time serving the psychological well-being of customers. The consumer economy provided more jobs in restaurants and personal health, fitness and grooming, and hotels and tourism. By 1969, the percentage of service-sector employees had passed that of manufacturing workers in several industrialized countries: 61.1 percent versus 33.7 percent in the United States and 48.8 percent versus 41.1 percent in Sweden.

Postindustrial work life differed somewhat in the Soviet bloc, where the percentage of farmers remained higher than in western Europe. A huge difference between professional occupations and those involving physical work also remained in socialist countries because of declining investment in advanced machinery and cleaner work processes. Men in both blocs generally earned higher pay and had better jobs than women. Somewhere between 80 and 95 percent of women in socialist countries worked, mostly under difficult conditions.

Farming changed as well, consolidating and becoming more scientific. Small landowners sold family plots to agribusinesses—that is, vast holdings devoted to commercial rather than peasant farming. Governments, farmers' cooperatives, and planning agencies influenced the decision making of the individual farmer; they set production quotas and handled an array of marketing transactions. Genetic research that yielded pest-resistant seeds and the skyrocketing use of pesticides, fertilizers, and machinery contributed to growth. Between 1965 and 1979, the number of tractors in Germany more than tripled from 384,000 to 1,340,000.

Planners played a crucial role in transforming agriculture. For example, in the 1970s French farmer Fernande Pelletier made a living on her hundred-acre farm in southwestern France in the new setting of international agribusiness. Advised by a government expert, Pelletier produced whatever foods might sell competitively in the Common Market. On expert advice, she switched from lamb and veal to foie gras and walnuts, and she joined with other farmers in her region to buy heavy machinery and sell her products. Agricultural prosperity required as much managerial effort and up-to-date information as did success in other sectors.

The Boom in Education and Research

Education and research were key to running postindustrial society and were the means by which nations maintained their economic and military might. Common sense, hard work, and creative intuition had launched the earliest successes of the Industrial Revolution. By the late twentieth century, success in business or government required a wide variety of expertise and ever-growing staffs of researchers—"the accumulation of knowledge, not of wealth," as one official put it.

Investment in research fueled military and industrial leadership. The United States funneled more than 20 percent of its gross national product into research in the 1960s, attracting many of Europe's leading intellectuals and technicians to the United States in a so-called brain drain. Complex systems—for example, nuclear power generation with its many components, from scientific conceptualization to plant construction to the publicly supervised disposal of radioactive waste—required intricate coordination and professional oversight. Scientists and bureaucrats often made more crucial decisions than did elected politicians in the realm of space programs, weapons development, and economic policy. Here, East-West differences became important: Soviet-bloc nations were less successful at linking their considerable achievements in science to actual applications because of bureaucratic red tape. In the 1960s, some 40 percent of Soviet-bloc scientific findings became obsolete before the government approved them for application to technology. An invisible backsliding from superpower effectiveness and leadership had begun in the USSR—much of it due to the lack of systems coordination and cooperation.

The centrality of sophisticated knowledge to success in postindustrial society led to unprecedented growth in education, especially universities and scientific institutes. The number of university students in Sweden rose by about 580 percent and in West Germany by 250 percent between 1950 and 1969. Great Britain established a network of technical universities to encourage the practical research that traditional elite universities often scorned. France set up administrative schools for future high-level experts in administration. The scientific establishment in the Soviet Union grew so rapidly that the number of its advanced researchers surpassed the number in the United States by the late 1970s. Meanwhile, institutions of higher learning added courses in business management, information technology, and systems analysis designed to build a new pool of postindustrial workers.

Changing Family Life and the Generation Gap

Just as education changed dramatically to meet the needs of postindustrial society, family roles and the relationship between parents and children shifted from what they had been a century earlier. Households became more varied, with many headed by a single parent, by remarried parents merging two sets of unrelated children, by unmarried couples cohabiting, or by traditionally married parents who had few or no children. Households of same-sex partners also became more common. At the end of the 1970s, the marriage rate in the West had fallen by 30 percent from its 1960s level, and the divorce rate continued to climb. After almost two decades of the baby boom, the birthrate dropped significantly. On average, a Belgian woman, for example, bore 2.6 children in 1960 but only 1.8 by the end of the 1970s. In the Soviet bloc, the birthrate was even lower. Although the birthrate fell, the percentage of children born outside of marriage soared.

Daily life within the family also changed. Technological consumer items filled the home, with radio and television often forming the basis of the household's common life. Appliances became more affordable and more widespread, reducing (in theory) the time women had to devote to household work and raising standards of cleanliness. More women worked outside the home during these years to pay for the longer economic dependence of children, but working mothers still did the housework and provided child care almost entirely themselves.

Whereas the early modern family organized labor, taught craft skills, and monitored reproductive behavior, the modern family seemed to have a primarily psychological mission, giving emotional nurturance to their children, who acquired their intellectual skills in school. Parents turned to psychologists, social workers, and other experts for advice on rearing children. Television and other media also offered advice on and models of how to deal with life in postindustrial society.

Postindustrial society transformed teenagers' lives most dramatically. A century earlier, teens had been full-time wage earners; now, in the new knowledge-based society, most were students, often financially dependent on their parents into their twenties. Despite teenagers' longer financial childhood, sexual activity began at an ever younger age, and people talked more openly about sex, prompting the Western media to announce the arrival of a "sexual revolution" where young people were concerned.

Youths simultaneously gained new roles as consumers. Seeing baby boomers as a multibillion-dollar market, advertisers and industrialists wooed them with consumer items associated with rock music—records, portable radios, stereos. Rock music celebrated youthful rebellion against adult culture in biting and often explicitly sexual lyrics. Sex roles for the young did not change, however. Despite the popularity of a few individual women rockers, promoters focused on men, whom they depicted as heroic, surrounded by worshipping female "groupies." The new models for youths, such as the Beatles, were themselves the products of savvy mass marketing to a mass youth audience. "What's your message for American teenagers?" the Beatles were asked. "Buy some more Beatles records," they responded. The mixture of high-tech music, pop-star marketing, and the youthful hysteria of fans contributed to a sense that there was a unique youth culture separating the young from their parents—the so-called generation gap.

Art, Ideas, and Religion in a Technocratic Society

Cultural trends developed alongside the march of consumer society and technology. A new style in the visual arts was called **pop art**. It featured images from everyday life and employed the glossy techniques of what these artists called admass, or mass advertising. Robert Rauschenberg, a leading U.S. practitioner, made collages from comic strips, magazine clippings, and fabric to fulfill his vision that "a picture is more like the real world when it's made out of the real world." The movement became a financial success by the early 1960s, boosted by such maverick American artists as Andy Warhol, who lampooned modern commercialism. Through images of actress Marilyn Monroe and former U.S. first lady Jacqueline Kennedy,

The Rolling Stones, 1976
The Rolling Stones were more energetic, sexual, and flamboyant than the earlier British rock sensation, the Beatles. Astute marketing experts for big record companies helped such rock groups target youth successfully. What exactly was the appeal of the Beatles, the Rolling Stones, and other celebrated rock stars who followed in their wake? (Getty Images.)

Warhol showed, for example, how the female body was used to sell products in the 1960s and 1970s. He depicted Campbell's soup cans as they appeared in advertisements and sold these works as elite artistic creations.

Swedish-born artist Claes Oldenburg portrayed the grotesque aspects of ordinary consumer products in *Giant Hamburger with Pickle Attached* (1962) and *Lipstick Ascending on Caterpillar Tractor* (1967). Capturing this mocking world of art, German artist Sigmar Polke did cartoon-like drawings of products and of those who craved them. Others practicing this "high art" picked up not merely commercial goods, but actually "low" objects such as scraps of metal, cigarette butts, dirt, and even excrement. Swiss sculptor Jean Tinguely used rusted parts of old machines—the "junk" of industrial society—to make fountains that could move. His partner Niki de Saint-Phalle then decorated them with huge, gaudy figures—many of them inspired by the folk traditions of the Caribbean and Africa. Their colorful, mobile fountains adorned main squares in Stockholm, Paris, and other cities.

American composer John Cage worked in a similar vein when he added sounds produced by everyday items such as combs, pieces of wood, and radio noise to his musical scores. Buddhist influence led Cage to include silence in his music and to compose by randomly tossing coins and then choosing notes by the corresponding numbers in the ancient Chinese *I Ching* (*Book of Changes*). These developments continued the trend away from melody in classical music that had begun with modernism. Other composers, called minimalists, simplified music by featuring repetition and sustained notes instead of producing the romantic melodies of nineteenth-century symphonies

Claes Oldenburg, *Trowel* (1971)
Claes Oldenburg captured the playful mood of pop art when he began duplicating ordinary objects such as vacuum cleaners, telephones, and even raisin bread on a larger-than-life scale. Pop art seemed to make a mockery of consumerism and everyday life, but museums and wealthy collectors snapped it up, eventually making celebrities of the artists and paying tens of millions of dollars for their work. (Nicolas Sapieha/Art Resource, NY.)

and piano music. Arvo Pärt, the famed Estonian composer, wrote minimalist pieces in the 1970s using only three or four notes in total; he called this style starvation music to underscore the lack of both freedom and goods in the Soviet bloc.

German composer Karlheinz Stockhausen introduced electronic music in classical compositions in 1953; Cage also used it soon after. Influenced by his own travels, Stockhausen continued the modern style of fully exploring non-Western musical patterns in such 1970s pieces as *Ceylon*. Even though this music echoed familiar electronic sounds, many listeners hated what seemed to them unpleasant noise. Yet improved recording technology and mass marketing brought music of all varieties to a wider home audience than ever before.

The social sciences reached the peak of their influence during these decades, often because of the increasing use of statistical models and predictions made possible by new technology. Social scientists produced detailed studies that claimed to demonstrate rules for understanding behavior with great certainty. Anthropology was among the most exciting of the social sciences, for it brought to young university students information about societies that seemed untouched by modern technology and industry. Colorful ethnographic films revealed different lifestyles and seemingly exotic practices. While studying people who came to be called "the other," young students had their sense of freedom reinforced by the vision of going back to nature. Whatever their discipline, social scientists announced that, like technicians and engineers, their specialized methods and factual knowledge were key to both managing complex postindustrial societies and setting policy for developing nations.

At the same time, the social sciences undermined Enlightenment beliefs that individuals had true freedom. French anthropologist Claude Lévi-Strauss developed a theory called structuralism, which insisted that all societies function within controlling structures—kinship and exchange, for example. By challenging existentialism's claim that humans could create a free existence, structuralism shook the social sciences' faith in the triumph of rationality. Lévi-Strauss's book *The Savage Mind* (1966) also demonstrated that people outside the West, even though they did not use Western scientific methods, had their own extremely effective systems of problem solving. In the 1960s and 1970s, the findings of social scientists echoed concerns that technology and highly managed bureaucratic systems were creating a society where people lacked freedom and individuality.

Religious leaders and the faithful responded to the changing times in a variety of ways. Pope Paul VI opposed artificial birth control while simultaneously becoming the first pontiff to put the global vision of Vatican II into action by visiting Africa, Asia, and South America. In some places, religious fervor at the grass roots surged in the face of scientific advances and the threat of nuclear annihilation. Growing numbers of U.S. Protestants joined sects that stressed the literal truth of the Bible and denied the validity of past scientific discoveries such as the age of the universe and the evolution of species. In western Europe, however, Christian churchgoing remained at a low level. In the 1970s, for example, only 10 percent of the British population went to religious services—about the same number that attended live soccer matches.

Most striking was the changing composition of the Western religious public. The immigration of people from former colonies and other parts of the world increased the strength of non-Christian religions such as Islam and varieties of Hinduism. Mosques, Buddhist temples, and shrines to other creeds appeared in cities and towns. New religious values sometimes mixed tensely with Western culture.

REVIEW How did Western society change in the postindustrial age?

Protesting Cold War Conditions

The United States and the Soviet Union reached new heights of power in the 1960s, but trouble was brewing for the superpowers. By 1965, the six nations of the Common Market had replaced the United States as the leader in worldwide trade, and they often acted in their own self-interest, not in the interest of the superpowers. In 1973, Britain joined the Common Market, followed by Ireland and Denmark, boosting the market's exports to almost three times those of the United States. The USSR faced competition, too. Communist China, along with countries in eastern Europe, contested Soviet leadership, and many decolonizing regions refused to ally with either of the superpowers. The struggle for Indochinese independence continued, and by the mid-1960s the United States waged a devastating war in Vietnam to block a Communist-led independence movement there. At the end of the 1970s, the USSR became involved in an equally devastating war in Afghanistan. Rising citizen discontent and dramatic acts of protest like that of Jan Palach presented another serious challenge to the cold war order. From the 1960s until 1989, people rose up against the consequences of technological development, the lack of fundamental rights, and the potential for nuclear holocaust.

Cracks in the Cold War Order

Across the social and political spectrum, there were calls to soften the effects of the cold war in this age of unprecedented progress and technological change. In the Soviet Union, the new middle class of bureaucrats and managers demanded a better standard of living and a reduction in the cold war tensions that made everyday life so menacing. Voters in western European countries elected politicians who promoted an increasing array of social programs designed to guarantee the economic democracy of the welfare state. A significant minority shifted their votes away from the centrist Christian Democratic coalitions that supported U.S. political goals.

The German and French governments both made visible changes in policy, which unsettled the cold war status quo. In Germany, Social Democratic politicians pushed to reallocate funds from defense spending to domestic programs. Willy Brandt, the Socialist mayor of West Berlin, became foreign minister in 1966 and worked to improve relations with Communist East Germany in order to open up trade. This anti–cold war policy, known as **Ostpolitik**, gave West German business leaders what they wanted: "the depoliticization of Germany's foreign trade," as one industrialist put it, and an opening of consumerism in the Soviet bloc. West German trade with eastern Europe grew rapidly, but it left the relatively poorer countries of the Soviet bloc burdened with a mounting debt—some $45 billion annually by 1970. Nevertheless, commerce began building a bridge across the U.S.-Soviet cold war divide.

To break the cold war stranglehold on international politics, French president Charles de Gaulle poured huge sums into French nuclear development, withdrew French forces from NATO, and signed trade treaties with the Soviet bloc. Communist China and France also grew closer. However, de Gaulle protected France's good relations with West Germany to prevent further encroachments from the Soviet bloc. At home, de Gaulle's government sponsored the construction of modern housing and ordered the exterior cleaning of all Parisian buildings—a massive project taking years—to wipe away more than a century of industrial grime and to highlight community, not cold war, values. With his haughty and stubborn pursuit of French grandeur, de Gaulle offered an alternative to submissively obeying the superpowers.

Brandt's Ostpolitik and de Gaulle's independence had their echoes in Soviet-bloc reforms. After the ouster of Soviet premier Nikita Khrushchev in 1964, the new leadership of Leonid Brezhnev (1909–1982) and Alexei Kosygin (1904–1980) initially continued attempts at reform, encouraging plant managers to turn a profit, allowing the production of televisions and household appliances and the construction of cheap housing to lessen the discontent of an increasingly educated and informed citizenry. The government also allowed more cultural and scientific meetings with Westerners. The Soviet satellite countries in eastern Europe took the opportunity presented by Moscow's relaxed posture. For example, Hungarian leader János Kádár introduced elements of a market system into the national economy by encouraging small businesses and trade to develop outside the Communist-controlled state network.

In the arts, Soviet-bloc writers continued for a time to break the hold of socialist realism on the arts and reduce their praise for the Soviet past. Dissident artists' paintings rejected the brightly colored scenes of socialist realism and instead depicted Soviet citizens as worn and tired in grays and other drab colors. Ukrainian poet Yevgeny Yevtushenko pointed out Soviet involvement in the Holocaust in *Babi Yar* (1961), a passionate protest against the slaughter of tens of thousands of Jews near Kiev during World War II. Challenging the celebratory nature of Communist literature, East Berlin writer Christa Wolf showed a couple tragically divided by the Berlin Wall in her novel *Divided Heaven* (1965). Repression of artistic thought returned later in the 1960s and 1970s, however, as the Soviet government took to bulldozing outdoor art shows, thereby forcing artists to hold secret exhibitions in their apartments. For their part, writers relied on samizdat culture, a key form of dissident activity in which novels and essays were written out by hand and passed from reader to reader, thus building a foundation for the successful resistance of the 1980s.

Other issues challenged U.S. leadership of the free world during the cold war. The assassination of President John F. Kennedy in November 1963 shocked the

Leonid Sokov, *Project to Construct Glasses for Every Soviet Person* (1976)
In the cold war era, the Soviets persecuted those who produced abstract or critical art. Dissident artists were adept, however, at incorporating Soviet icons into works critical of the regime. They might, for instance, include Lenin's portrait, but with citizens turning their backs on it instead of being inspired by it. In this sculpture, Leonid Sokov created a Communist version of rose-colored glasses. His work paralleled that of pop artists in the West, who mocked the array of consumer items that filled people's lives. (Jane Voorhees Zimmerli Art Museum, Rutgers, The State University of New Jersey, The Norton and Nancy Dodge Collection of Nonconformist Art from the Soviet Union 1991.0873/07809. Photograph by Jack Abraham.)

nation and the world, but it did not stop the rising demands for civil rights for African Americans and other minorities. White segregationists murdered and brutalized those attempting to integrate lunch counters or simply march on behalf of freedom. In response to white violence, Kennedy had introduced civil rights legislation and forced the desegregation of schools and universities. Lyndon B. Johnson, Kennedy's successor, steered the Civil Rights Act through Congress in 1964. This legislation forbade segregation in public facilities and created the Equal Employment Opportunity Commission (EEOC) to fight job discrimination based on "race, color, national origin, religion, and sex." Modeling himself on his hero Franklin Roosevelt, Johnson envisioned what he called the Great Society, which would arise from programs such as Project Head Start for disadvantaged preschool children and the Job Corps for training youth. Black novelist Ralph Ellison called Johnson "the greatest American president for the poor and the Negroes."

Still, the cold war did not go away, and the United States became increasingly embroiled in Vietnam (Map 23.1). After the Geneva Conference in 1954, which divided Vietnam into North and South, the United States escalated its support for the corrupt leaders of non-Communist South Vietnam. North Vietnam, China, and the Soviet Union backed the rebel Vietcong, or South Vietnamese Communists.

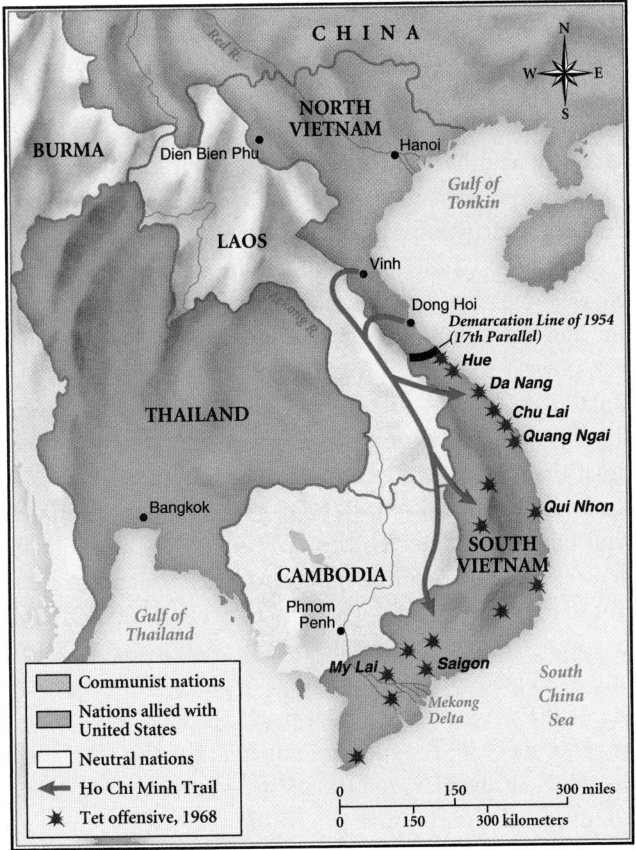

Map 23.1 The Vietnam War, 1954–1975
The local peoples of Southeast Asia had long resisted incursions by their neighbors. They also resisted French rule beginning at the end of the nineteenth century and never more fiercely than in the war that liberated them after World War II. Ill prepared by comparison with the French, the Vietnamese nonetheless triumphed in the battle of Dien Bien Phu in 1954. But the Americans soon became involved, trying to stem what they saw as the tide of Communist influence behind the Vietnamese liberation movement. The ensuing war in Vietnam in the 1960s and 1970s spread into neighboring countries, making the region the scene of vast destruction. **For more help analyzing this map, see the map activity for this chapter in the Online Study Guide at** bedfordstmartins.com/huntconcise.

By the end of 1967, the United States had nearly half a million soldiers in South Vietnam, yet the strength of the Vietcong seemed to grow daily. Despite suffering massive bombing, the insurgents, who had struggled against colonialism for decades, rejected a negotiated peace even as Johnson's advisers regularly appeared on television, telling Americans that the United States was winning the war. Faced with mounting casualties and growing antiwar sentiment, President Johnson announced in March 1968 that he would not run for reelection.

The Outbreak of Civic Activism

In the midst of cold war conflict and technological advance, a new activism emerged. Prosperity and the rising benefits of a postindustrial, service-oriented economy helped make people ever more eager for peace and justice. The U.S. civil rights movement broadened, as other minorities joined African Americans in demanding fair treatment. Meanwhile, urban riots erupted across the United States in 1965 and subsequent summers as frustrated and angry black activists turned their struggle into a militant celebration of their race under the banner "Black is beautiful." The issue they faced was one they felt they had in common with decolonizing people: how to shape an identity different from that of their white oppressors. Some urged a push for "black power" to demand rights forcefully instead of "begging" for them nonviolently. Separatism, not integration, became the goal of others. Small cadres of militants like the Black Panthers took up arms, believing that they needed to protect themselves against the violent whites around them.

As a result of the new turn in black efforts for change, white American university students who had participated in the early stages of the civil rights movement found themselves excluded from leadership positions. Many of them soon joined the swelling protests against technological change, consumerism, and the Vietnam War. European youth were also feverish for reform. In the mid-1960s, university students in Rome occupied an administration building after right-wing opponents assassinated one of their number during a protest against the university's 200-to-1 student-teacher ratio. In 1966, Prague students held carnival-like processions, commemorated the tenth anniversary of the 1956 Hungarian uprisings, and took to chanting "The only good Communist is a dead one." The "situationists" in France called on students to wake up from the slumber of mass society by jolting individuals into action with shocking graffiti and street theater.

Throughout the 1960s, students criticized the traditional university curriculum and showed off their own countercultural values. They questioned how studying Plato or Dante would help them after graduation. "How to Train Stuffed Geese" was French students' satirical version of the teaching methods they experienced in the classroom. "No professors over forty" and "Don't trust anyone over thirty" were powerful slogans of the day. Long hair, communal living, and scorn for personal cleanliness announced students' rejection of middle-class values. Widespread use of the pill made abstinence unnecessary as a method of birth control, and open promiscuity brought the sexual revolution into public view. Marijuana use became common among students, and amphetamines, hallucinogens, and barbiturates added to the drug culture, which had its own rituals, music, and gathering places. Sneered at by students, big business nonetheless made billions of dollars by selling blue jeans, dolls dressed as "hippies," natural foods, and drugs to students and by packaging and managing the rock stars of the counterculture.

Women's activism erupted across the political spectrum. Working for reproductive rights, women in France helped end the ban on birth control in 1965. American journalist Betty Friedan, author of the international best seller *The Feminine Mystique* (1963), attracted middle-class women by pointing to the stagnating talents of many housewives. Friedan helped organize the National Organization for Women (NOW) in 1966 "to bring women into full participation in the mainstream of American society now." NOW advocated equal pay and a variety of other legal and economic reforms. In Sweden, women lobbied to make tasks both at home and in the workplace less gender segregated, and a few Soviet women began speaking out against their low-paid and unpaid work, which kept the USSR running.

Women engaged in the civil rights and student movements soon realized that many protest organizations devalued women just as society at large did. Male activists adopted the leather-jacketed machismo style of their film and rock heroes, and women in the movements were often judged by the status of their activist lovers. "A woman was to 'inspire' her man," African American activist Angela Davis complained, adding that women seeking equality were accused of wanting "to rob [male activists] of their manhood." West German women students tossed tomatoes at male protest leaders to dispute male domination of the movement and standards set by men for ladylike behavior.

Women also took to the streets on behalf of issues such as abortion rights and the decriminalization of gay and lesbian sexuality. Many rebelled against social conventions in their attire, language, and attitudes and spoke openly about taboo subjects such as their sexual feelings and illegal abortions. This brand of feminist activity was meant to shock polite society, and it did. Many women of color, however, broke with feminist solidarity and spoke out against the "double jeopardy" of being "black and female." Concrete change followed: in Catholic Italy, for example, feminists won the right to

Gay Activists in London, 1974
The reformist spirit of the 1960s and 1970s changed the focus of homosexuals' activism. Instead of concentrating mostly on legal protection from criminal prosecution, gays and lesbians began affirming a special and positive identity. As other groups that had endured discrimination began making similar affirmations, "identity politics" was born. Critics charged that traditional universal values were sufficient and that homosexuals and others constituted special-interest groups. Gays, women, and ethnic and racial minorities countercharged that in practice the universal values first put forth in the Enlightenment seemed to apply only to a privileged few. (© Hulton-Deutsch Collection/Corbis.)

divorce, to gain access to birth-control information, and to obtain legal abortions. Throughout the 1970s and beyond, thousands of women's groups continued to demand equal pay, job opportunities, and protection from rape, incest, and battering.

1968: Year of Crisis

Protest and calls for reform boiled over in 1968. In January, on the first day of Tet, the Vietnamese New Year, the Vietcong and the North Vietnamese attacked more than one hundred South Vietnamese towns and American bases, inflicting heavy casualties. The Tet offensive caused many people in the United States and the rest of the West to conclude that the war might be unwinnable and fueled the antiwar movement around the world. Rising war protest intersected with African American anguish and rage when, on April 4, 1968, a white racist assassinated Martin Luther King Jr. More than a hundred cities in the United States exploded in strife. "Burn, baby, burn," chanted rioters who, rejecting King's message of nonviolent resistance, destroyed the grim inner cities around them. On campuses, bitter clashes over the intertwined issues of war, technology, racism, and sexism closed down classes.

Similar student unrest erupted around the world, most dramatically in France. In January, students at Nanterre, outside of Paris, went on strike, invading administration offices to protest what they saw as a second-rate education. They called themselves a proletariat—an exploited working class—and, rejecting the Soviet brand of communism, considered themselves part of "a new left." When students at the prestigious Sorbonne in Paris also took to the streets in protest, police assaulted them. The Parisian middle classes reacted with unexpected if temporary sympathy to the student uprising because of their own resentment of bureaucracy. They were also horrified at seeing police beating middle-class students and even passersby who expressed their support.

French workers joined in the protest. Some nine million went on strike, occupying factories and calling not only for higher wages but also for participation in everyday decision making. The combined revolt looked as if it might explode into another French Revolution, so unified were the expressions of political opposition. Charles de Gaulle sent tanks into Paris and in June announced a raise for workers, while businesses offered them more involvement in decision making. Many citizens, having grown tired of the street violence, the destruction of private property, and the breakdown of services (for example, the garbage had not been collected for weeks), began to sympathize with the government instead of the students. Although demonstrations continued throughout June, the revolutionary moment had passed.

By contrast, the 1968 revolt in Prague began within the Czechoslovak Communist Party itself. At a party congress in the fall of 1967, Alexander Dubček, head of the Slovak branch of the party, had called for more social and political openness. Attacked as an inferior Slovak by the Communist leadership, Dubček nonetheless struck a chord with frustrated party officials and intellectuals. Czechoslovaks began to dream of a new society—one based on "socialism with a human face." Party delegates elevated Dubček to the top position, where he quickly changed the Communist style of government by ending censorship, instituting the secret ballot for party elections, and allowing competing political groups to form. "Look!" one little girl in the street remarked as the new government took power. "Everyone's smiling today." The Prague Spring had begun—"an orgy of free expression," one Czech journalist called it. People bought uncensored publications, packed uncensored theater productions, and engaged in almost nonstop political debate.

Dubček faced the enormous problem of negotiating policies acceptable to the USSR, the party bureaucracy, and reform-minded citizens. His government handed down reforms with warnings about maintaining "discipline" and showing "wise behavior." Fearing change, the Polish, East German, and Soviet regimes threatened the reform government daily. When Dubček failed to attend a meeting of Warsaw Pact leaders, Soviet threats became more intense, until finally, in August 1968, Soviet tanks rolled into Prague in a massive show of force. Citizens tried to halt the return to Communist orthodoxy through sabotage. They painted graffiti on the tanks and removed street signs to confuse invading troops. Merchants refused to sell

Invasion Puts Down Prague Spring
When the Soviet Union and other Warsaw Pact members cracked down on the Prague Spring, they met determined citizen resistance. People refused assistance of any kind to the invaders and personally talked to them about the Czech cause. Despite the repression, protests small and large continued until the final fall of Communist rule two decades later. (© Bettmann/Corbis.)

food and other goods to Soviet troops. These actions did not stop the determined Soviet leadership, which removed reformers from power. Jan Palach and other university students immolated themselves the following January, but the moment of reform-minded change passed here, too.

Protest in 1968 challenged the political direction of individual nations, but little turned out the way reformers hoped, as governments worked to end criticism of the cold war status quo. In November 1968, the Soviets announced the Brezhnev Doctrine, which stated that reform movements, a "common problem" of all socialist countries, would be stamped out. As the hard-liner Brezhnev clamped down on critics, dissident morale ebbed. "The shock of our tanks crushing the Prague Spring . . . convinced us that the Soviet colossus was invincible," explained one pessimistic Soviet liberal. Other voices persisted, however. In 1974, Brezhnev expelled author Aleksandr Solzhenitsyn from the USSR after the publication of the first volume of *The Gulag Archipelago* (1973–1976) in the U.S. bloc. Composed from firsthand reports and other sources, Solzhenitsyn's story of the Gulag documented the brutal conditions endured by Soviet prisoners under Stalin. More than any other single work, *The Gulag Archipelago* disillusioned loyal Communists around the world.

The USSR also persecuted ordinary citizens who did not have Solzhenitsyn's international reputation. Soviet psychologists, working with the government, certified the "mental illness" of dissidents, who often wound up as virtual prisoners in mental institutions. In a revival of tsarist Russia's anti-Semitism, Jews faced educational restrictions (especially in university admissions), severe job discrimination, and a constant assault on their religious practices. Soviet officials commonly charged that Jews were "unreliable, they think only of emigrating. . . . It's madness to give them an education, because it's state money wasted." Ironically, dissidents blamed Jews for the Bolshevik Revolution and terror under Stalin. As attacks intensified in the 1970s, Soviet Jews sought to emigrate to Israel or the United States, often unsuccessfully.

The brain drain of eastern European intellectuals increased. Celebrated composer Gyorgy Ligeti had left Hungary in 1956, after which his work was celebrated in concert halls and in such classic films as *2001: A Space Odyssey.* From exile in Paris, Czech writer Milan Kundera enthralled audiences with *The Book of Laughter and Forgetting* (1979) and *The Unbearable Lightness of Being* (1984). His novels chronicled his own descent from enthusiasm for communism to a despair characterized by bitter humor. Kundera claimed that Communist regimes depended on making people forget by, for instance, erasing fallen leaders from history books. Individuals often tried to forget the grim reality of Communist rule by engaging in excessive sexual activity. Like the escapees from fascism in the 1930s, these newcomers to the West—from noted intellectuals to skilled craftspeople and dancers—enriched the culture of the countries that welcomed them.

In the United States the reaction against activists was different, though the impulse to restore order was strong there, too. Elected in 1968, the conservative

President Richard Nixon promised to bring peace to Southeast Asia, but in 1970 he ordered U.S. troops to invade Cambodia, the site of North Vietnamese bases. Campuses erupted again in protest, and on May 4 the National Guard killed four students and wounded eleven others at a demonstration at Kent State University in Ohio. Nixon called the victims "bums," and a growing reaction against the counterculture made many Americans agree with him. Despite signing agreements to end hostilities in 1973, the United States and North Vietnam continued fighting until 1975, when a North Vietnamese offensive defeated South Vietnam and its U.S. ally and forcibly reunified the country. The United States reeled from the defeat, having suffered the loss of thousands of young lives, turbulence at home, vast military costs, and a weakening of its reputation around the world. Yet a strong current of public opinion turned against antiwar activists, born of the belief that they—not the war, government corruption, or the huge war debt—had brought down the United States. Both superpowers were being tested, almost to the limits, creating a climate of uncertainty not only about politics but also about the future of postindustrial prosperity.

REVIEW What were the main issues for protesters in the 1960s, and how did governments address them?

The Testing of Superpower Domination and the End of the Cold War

The 1970s brought a lessening of cold war tensions called détente, during which both superpowers limited the nuclear arms race in the face of instability at home. Despite this relaxation in the cold war, internal corruption, open terrorism, competition from the oil-producing states, and continuing attempts to control the world beyond their borders threw the superpowers and their allies off balance, allowing reform-minded politicians to come to power. The two most famous innovators were Margaret Thatcher in Britain and Mikhail Gorbachev in the USSR, who introduced drastic new policies in the 1980s to keep their economies moving forward. But in the Soviet bloc, postindustrial prosperity was simply unattainable under the old system, and in 1989, astonishingly, that system collapsed.

A Changing Balance of World Power

In the midst of turmoil at home and the draining war in Vietnam, Henry Kissinger, Nixon's secretary of state and a believer—like Otto von Bismarck—in Realpolitik, decided to take advantage of the ongoing USSR-China rivalry and arranged for Nixon to visit China in 1972. The visit linked, if only tentatively, two very different great nations that both faced problems at home. Within China, the meeting helped stop the brutality and excesses of Mao's Cultural Revolution, during which Mao had incited students to decimate schools, destroy property, and injure and even kill "class enemies." The visit also helped advance the careers of Chinese pragmatists interested in technology, trade, and relations with the West who laid the groundwork for China's boom later in the century. At the same time, the diplomatic success of the visit sped up the process of détente between the United States and the Soviet Union. Fearful of the Chinese diplomatic advantage and similarly confronted by popular protest, the Soviets approached the U.S. bloc. In 1972, the superpowers signed the first Strategic Arms Limitation Treaty (SALT I), which set a cap on the number of antiballistic missiles each country could have. In 1975, in the Helsinki accords on human rights, the western bloc officially acknowledged Soviet territorial gains in World War II in exchange for the Soviet bloc's guarantee of basic human rights.

Despite these diplomatic successes, the war in Vietnam left the United States billions of dollars in debt to other countries. The international currency system collapsed under the weight of this imbalance. In the face of the resulting global economic chaos, the Common Market countries united to force the United States to relinquish its single-handed direction of Western economic strategy. Another blow to U.S. leadership followed when it was revealed that Nixon's office had worked to undermine free elections by authorizing the burglary and wiretapping of the Democratic Party headquarters in Washington's Watergate building during the 1972 election campaign. The Watergate scandal forced Nixon to resign in disgrace in the summer of 1974—the first U.S. president ever to do so. That its own leader would work to undermine democracy further weakened U.S. superpower status in the 1960s and 1970s.

Israel after the Six-Day War, 1967

Amid the instability in the United States, the Middle East's oil-producing nations dealt Western dominance yet another blow. In two wars in 1967 and 1973, U.S.-backed Israeli forces defeated Arab troops and seized Gaza and the Sinai peninsula from Egypt, the Golan Heights from Syria, and the West Bank from Jordan. Having failed militarily, the Arab nations decided to use economic force, striking at the West's weakest point—its dependence on Middle Eastern oil for its industries and postindustrial lifestyle. Arab nations in the **Organization of Petroleum Exporting Countries (OPEC)**, a relatively loose consortium before the 1973 Israeli war with Egypt, combined to quadruple the price of their oil and imposed an embargo, cutting off all exports of oil to the United States and its allies because they backed Israel. For the first time since imperialism's heyday, the producers of raw materials, not the industrial powers, controlled the flow of commodities and set prices to their own advantage (Figure 23.1). The West was now mired in an oil crisis.

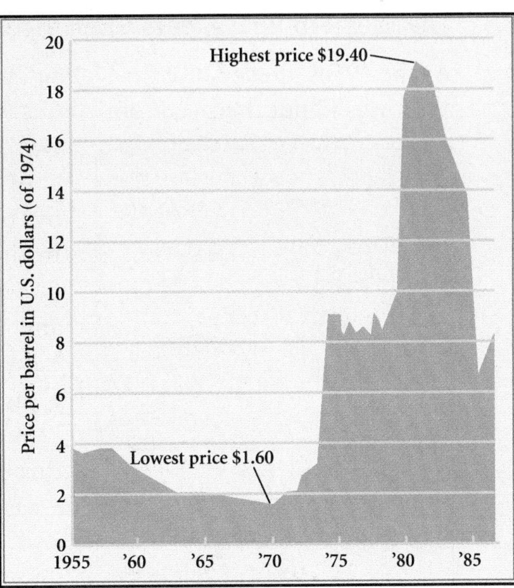

Figure 23.1 Fluctuating Oil Prices, 1955–1985 Colonization allowed the Western imperial powers to obtain raw materials at advantageous prices or even without paying at all. Even with decolonization, European and American firms were often so firmly entrenched in the newly independent economies that they were able to set the terms of trade. OPEC's oil embargo and price hikes of the 1970s were signs of change, which included the exercise of decolonized countries' control over their own resources. Not only did OPEC's action lead to a decade-long economic downturn, but it also caused some European governments to improve public transportation, encourage the production of fuel-efficient cars, and enact policies that led individual consumers to cut back on their use of oil.

Throughout the 1970s, oil-dependent Westerners watched in astonishment as OPEC upset the balance of economic power and helped provoke a recession in the West. The oil embargo and price hike not only caused inflation to soar but also caused unemployment to rise by more than 50 percent in Europe and the United States. By the end of 1973, the inflation rate had jumped to over 8 percent in West Germany, 12 percent in France, and 20 percent in Portugal. Eastern-bloc countries, dependent on Soviet oil, fared little better because the West could no longer afford their products and the Soviets boosted the price of their own oil. Skyrocketing interest rates discouraged both industrial investment and consumer buying. With prices, unemployment, and interest rates all rising—an unusual combination of economic conditions dubbed **stagflation**—western Europe drastically cut back on its oil dependence by undertaking conservation, enhancing public transportation, and raising the price of gasoline to encourage the development of fuel-efficient cars.

The U.S. bloc had farther to fall. In the late 1970s, students, clerics, shopkeepers, and unemployed men in Iran began a religious agitation that brought to power the Islamic religious leader Ayatollah Ruhollah Khomeini. Using audiocassettes to spread his message, he called for a transformation of the country into a truly Islamic society, which meant the renunciation of the Western ways advocated by the American-backed shah, who as a result was overthrown. In the autumn of 1979, revolutionary supporters of Khomeini took hostages at the American embassy in Teheran. The United States was essentially paralyzed in the face of Islamic militancy, further OPEC price hikes, and a downwardly spiraling economy.

The Western Bloc Meets Challenges with Reform

As the 1980s opened, the first agenda item for non-Communist governments in the West was to put their economic houses in order. On top of the economic challenge was the growing threat of terrorism—that is, coordinated and targeted political violence by opposition groups at home and abroad. In the 1970s, terrorist bands of young people in Europe responded to the suppression of activism and the worsening economic conditions with kidnappings, bank robberies, bombings, and assassinations. Eager to bring down the Social Democratic coalition that had led West Germany throughout the 1970s, the Red Army Faction assassinated prominent businessmen, judges, and other public officials. Italy's Red Brigades kidnapped and then murdered the head of the dominant Christian Democrats in 1978. Advocates of independence for the Basque nation in northern Spain assassinated Spanish politicians and police officers.

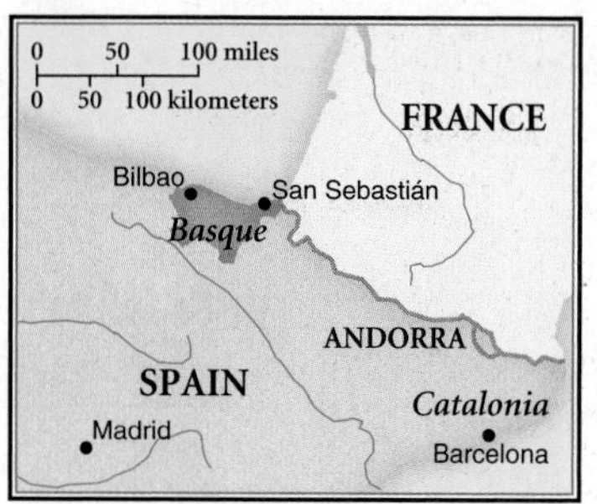

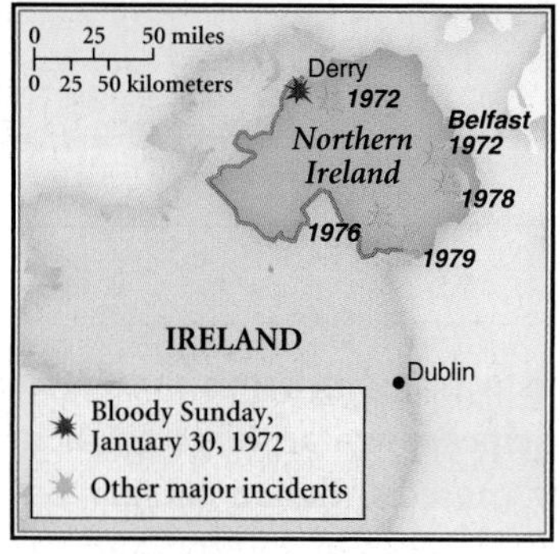

Nationalist Movements of the 1970s

In the 1970s, Catholics in Northern Ireland pitted themselves against the dominant Protestants to protest job discrimination and a lack of civil rights. Demonstrators urged union with the Irish Republic, and with protests escalating, the British government sent in troops. On January 30, 1972, which became known as Bloody Sunday, British troops fired on demonstrators and killed thirteen, setting off a cycle of violence that left five hundred dead in 1972 alone. Protestants, fearful of losing their dominant position, combated a determined Irish Republican Army (IRA), which carried out bombings and assassinations to achieve the union of the two Irelands and an end to the oppression of Catholics.

Terrorists failed in their goal of overturning the existing democracies, and battered as it was, parliamentary government scored a few important successes in the 1970s. Spain and Portugal, suffering under dictatorship since the 1930s, regained their freedom and became more prosperous. The death of Spain's Francisco Franco in 1975 ended more than three decades of dictatorial rule. Franco's handpicked successor, King Juan Carlos, surprisingly steered his nation toward a Western-style constitutional monarchy, facing down threatened military coups. Portugal and Greece also ousted right-wing dictators, thus paving the way for their integration into western Europe and for economic growth. Despite these democratic advances, the economies of the West still appeared to be troubled.

More than anyone else, Margaret Thatcher, the leader of Britain's Conservative Party and prime minister from 1979 to 1990, reshaped the West's political and economic ideas to meet the crisis. Believing that only a resurgence of private enterprise could revive the declining British economy, Thatcher lashed out at union leaders, Labour Party politicians, and people who received welfare-state benefits as enemies of British prosperity. Her anti–welfare-state policies struck a revolutionary chord, and she called herself "a nineteenth-century liberal," in reference to the economic individualism of that age. In her view, businesspeople were the key members of society. She characterized immigrants, whose low wages contributed greatly to corporate profits, as inferior. Under Thatcher, even workers blamed labor leaders or newcomers for Britain's troubles.

The policies of "Thatcherism" were based on monetarist, or supply-side, economic theory. According to monetarist theory, inflation results when government pumps money into the economy at a rate higher than a nation's economic growth rate. Thus, government should keep a tight rein on the money supply to keep prices from rising rapidly. Supply-side economists maintain that the economy as a whole flourishes when businesses grow and their prosperity "trickles down" throughout society. To implement such theories, the British government cut income taxes on the wealthy to spur new investment and increased sales taxes to compensate for the

Margaret Thatcher at a Conservative Party Conference, 1983
As British prime minister for more than a decade (1979–1990), Margaret Thatcher profoundly influenced the course of modern government by rolling back the welfare state. Thatcher was convinced—and convinced others—that the welfare state did not advance society and its citizens but made them lazy by rewarding people with handouts. Her tenure in office encouraged other leaders, from Ronald Reagan to Helmut Kohl, to make similar cuts in social programs. (© Bettmann/Corbis.)

lost revenue. The result was an increased burden on working people, who bore the brunt of the higher sales taxes. Thatcher also sold publicly owned businesses and utilities such as British Airways, refused to prop up "outmoded" industries such as coal mining, and slashed education and health programs. As Thatcher's package of economic policies spread through the West and the world, it came to be known as **neoliberalism**. The quality of universities, public transportation, highways, and hospitals deteriorated; leading scholars and scientists left the country in a new brain drain; and social unity fragmented, as blacks and Asians rioted in major cities. Although Britain had embraced welfare-state programs in the postwar period, now it was pioneering a change in course.

In the United States, President Ronald Reagan, who took office in 1981, followed a similar road to combat the economic crisis there. Dividing citizens into the good and the bad, Reagan vowed to promote the values of the "moral majority," which included a commitment to Bible-based religion, a dedication to work, and unquestioned patriotism. Those who disagreed were labeled immoral, spendthrift "liberals"—a confusing use of the word that Thatcher adopted to describe her "small government" approach. Reagan blasted "liberals" when he introduced "Reaganomics"—his program of large income-tax cuts for the wealthy combined with massive reductions in federal spending for student loans, school lunch programs, and mass transit, because these "welfare" programs only encouraged "bad" Americans to be "lazy." Like Thatcher, Reagan believed that cutting programs and cutting taxes for the wealthy would lead to investment and thus help the economy.

In foreign policy, Reagan warned of the menacing Soviet Union—the "evil empire," as he called it—and rolled back détente. He demanded huge military budgets for programs such as the Strategic Defense Initiative (SDI), known popularly as Star Wars, a costly plan to put lasers in space to defend the United States against a nuclear attack. The combination of tax cuts and military expansion had pushed the U.S. federal budget deficit to $200 billion by 1986. As in Britain, inflation was brought under control, and American prosperity returned.

Other Western leaders also limited welfare-state benefits in the face of stagflation, though without the socially divisive rhetoric of Thatcher and Reagan. West German leader Helmut Kohl, who took power in 1982, reduced welfare spending, froze government wages, and cut corporate taxes. By 1984, the inflation rate was only 2 percent, and West Germany had acquired a 10 percent share of world trade. Unlike Thatcher, Kohl did not encourage class and racial hatreds. The politics of divisiveness was particularly unwise in Germany, where terrorism on the left and on the right continued. Moreover, the legacy of Nazism loomed menacingly. When an unemployed German youth said of immigrant Turkish workers, "Let's gas 'em," the revival of Nazi language appalled many in Germany's middle class.

By 1981 stagflation had put more than 1.5 million people out of work in France, but the French took a different political path to deal with the economic slump. The French elected a socialist president, François Mitterrand, who nationalized the banks and certain industries and increased social spending to stimulate the economy—the opposite of Thatcherism. New public buildings like museums and libraries arose along with new subway lines and improved public transport. When conservative Jacques Chirac succeeded Mitterrand in 1995, he adopted neoliberal policies. As unemployment remained high, divisive politics strengthened: the politically racist National Front Party, for example, consistently won 10 percent and sometimes more of the popular vote with promises to deport African and Middle Eastern immigrants so that whites could remain dominant economically and politically.

At the same time, smaller European states without heavy defense commitments began to thrive, some of them by slashing welfare programs. Spain joined the Common Market in 1986 and used Common Market investment and tourist dollars to help rebuild its neglected infrastructure. In Ireland, new investment in education for high-tech jobs combined with low wages attracted much new business to the country in the 1990s. Austria prospered, too, in part by reducing government pensions and aid to businesses. Austrian chancellor Franz Vranitsky summed up the new focus of government: "In Austria, the shelter that the state has given to almost everyone—employee as well as entrepreneur—has led . . . a lot of people [to] think not only what they can do to solve a problem but what the state can do. . . . This needs to change." The century-long growth of the welfare state slowed by the 1990s as new economic theories took hold.

Almost alone, Sweden maintained a full array of social programs, including a wide choice of subsidized housing for immigrants. Such programs were expensive: the tax rate on income over $46,000 was 80 percent. Although the Swedes reduced their costly dependence on foreign oil by cutting consumption in half between 1976 and 1986, their welfare state came to seem extreme as Sweden's overall prosperity dropped. As elsewhere, immigrants were cast as a major threat to the country. "How long will it be before our Swedish children will have to turn their faces toward Mecca?" asked one politician in 1993.

The Collapse of Communism in the Soviet Bloc

Beginning in 1985, reform came to the Soviet Union as well. In that year, a new leader, Mikhail Gorbachev, unexpectedly opened an era of change. The son of peasants, Gorbachev had risen through the party ranks as an agricultural specialist and had traveled abroad to gain a firsthand glimpse of life in the West. At home, he saw the results of economic stagnation in the USSR. As in much of the Soviet bloc, ordinary people decided not to have children. The country was forced to import massive amounts of grain because 20 to 30 percent of the grain that was produced in the USSR rotted before it could be harvested or shipped to market, so great was the inefficiency of the state-directed economy. A massive and privileged party bureaucracy feared innovation and failed to achieve socialism's stated goal of a decent standard of living for working people. Alcoholism was rampant. To match American military growth, the Soviet Union diverted 15 to 20 percent of its gross national product (more than double the U.S. proportion) to armaments, further crippling the economy's chances of raising living standards. As these problems grew, a new generation came of age that had no memory of World War II or of Stalin's purges. "They believe in nothing," a mother said of Soviet youth in 1984.

Gorbachev quickly proposed several programs to improve the desperately inadequate Soviet system. A crucial economic reform, **perestroika** (restructuring), aimed to improve productivity, increase the rate of capital investment, encourage the use of up-to-date technology, and gradually introduce market features such as profits. The complement to economic change was the policy of **glasnost** (usually translated as "openness" or "publicity"), which called for allowing "wide, prompt, and frank information" and for giving Soviet citizens new measures of free speech. When officials complained that glasnost threatened their status, Gorbachev replaced more than a third of the Communist Party's leadership. The pressing need for glasnost became most evident after the Chernobyl catastrophe in 1986, when a nuclear reactor exploded and spewed radioactive dust into the atmosphere. Bureaucratic

Mikhail and Raisa Gorbachev
Mikhail Gorbachev and his wife, Raisa, gave a fresh look to Soviet politics. They traveled, made friends abroad, and were fashionable and modern. While the Gorbachevs became part of Western celebrity culture, average citizens back home saw their privileged lifestyle as the continuation of the Communist government's disregard for ordinary people. (© Peter Turnley/Corbis.)

cover-ups delayed the release of information about the accident, with lethal consequences for people living near the plant.

After Chernobyl, even the Communist Party and Marxism-Leninism were opened to public criticism. Party meetings suddenly included complaints about the highest leaders, and television shows adopted the outspoken methods of American investigative reporting: one program showed, for instance, the plight of Leningrad's homeless children—an admission of communism's failings. Instead of publishing made-up letters praising the great Soviet state, newspapers were flooded with real ones complaining of shortages and abuse. One outraged "mother of two" protested that the cost-cutting policy of reusing syringes in hospitals was a source of AIDS—a disease that had begun to spread rapidly around the world. "Why should little kids have to pay for the criminal actions of our Ministry of Health?" she asked. Factions arose: in the fall of 1987, Gorbachev ally Boris Yeltsin quit the governing Politburo after criticizing perestroika as inadequate. Yeltsin's political daring, which in the past might have brought harassment or prison, inspired others to oppose Communist rule, and by the spring of 1989, in a remarkably free balloting in Moscow's local elections, not a single Communist was chosen.

Gorbachev also scaled back missile production, and in early 1989, the year that ended the Soviet system and the cold war, he withdrew his country's forces from the debilitating war in Afghanistan. Meanwhile, Gorbachev's reforms in the USSR started spiraling out of his control, as dissent rose across the Soviet bloc. Already in 1980, Poles had reacted furiously to government-increased food prices by going on strike and forming an independent union, **Solidarity**, led by electrician Lech Walesa and crane operator Anna Walentynowicz of the Gdańsk shipyards. The organization soon attracted much of the adult population, including a million members of the Communist Party. They paraded through the streets, waving Polish flags and carrying giant portraits of the Virgin Mary and Pope John Paul II, a Polish native. Tens of thousands of women marched in the streets crying "We're hungry!" and protesting working conditions. The police and the army, with Soviet support, imposed a military government under General Wojciech Jaruzelski and in the winter of 1981 outlawed Solidarity. Solidarity remained alive as a force both inside and outside of Poland, as poets read dissident verse to overflow crowds, and university professors lectured to Solidarity members on such forbidden topics as Polish resistance during World War II.

Ongoing activism in Poland set the stage for the unexpected downfall of communism in 1989, but first came a surprising attack on the Communist state in China. Inspired by Gorbachev's visit to China's capital, Beijing, in the spring of 1989, thousands of students massed in the city's Tiananmen Square, the world's largest public square, to demand democracy. They used telex machines to rush their messages to the international community, and they effectively conveyed their goals through the cameras that Western television trained on them. China's aged Communist leaders, while pushing economic modernization, refused to consider the introduction of democracy. As workers began joining the pro-democracy forces, the government crushed the movement and executed as many as a thousand rebels.

The protests in Tiananmen Square were galvanizing. In June 1989, the Polish government, weakened by its own bungling of the economy and lacking Soviet support for further repression, held free parliamentary elections. Solidarity candidates won overwhelmingly, and in early 1990 Walesa became president, hastening Poland's transition to a market economy. Gorbachev openly reversed the Brezhnev Doctrine in the Polish case, refusing to interfere in the political course of another nation. When it became clear that the Soviet Union would not intervene in Poland, the fall of communism repeated itself across the Soviet bloc.

Communism collapsed first in Poland and next in Hungary in part because of those countries' early introduction of free-market measures. In Hungary, which had experimented with "market socialism" since the 1960s, officials slowly realized that political democracy had to accompany economic freedom. Citizens were protesting against ecologically unsound projects like the construction of a new dam, and they encouraged boycotts of Communist holidays. A multiparty system emerged by 1989, which, along with the popular demands for political freedom, led the Hungarian parliament to change the name of the country from the People's Republic of Hungary to simply the Republic of Hungary. People across the country tore down Soviet and Communist symbols, while free elections for parliament took place in the spring of 1990.

The most potent symbol of a divided Europe—the Berlin Wall—stood in the midst of a divided Germany. East Germans had attempted to escape over the wall for more than two decades, and since the early 1980s dissidents had held peace vigils in cities across East Germany. In the summer of 1989, crowds of East Germans flocked to the borders in hopes of escaping the crumbling Soviet bloc, and hundreds of thousands of protesters rallied throughout the fall against the regime. Satellite television brought them visions of postindustrial prosperity and of free and open public debate in West Germany. The crowds intensified in November, when Gorbachev, taken as a hero by many, visited East Germany. On November 9, guards allowed free passage through the wall to West Berlin, turning the protest into a festive holiday: as they strolled freely in the streets, East Berliners saw firsthand the goods available in a successful postindustrial society. The Communist party of East Germany finally collapsed with the elections in March 1990, while East and West Germans released years of frustration by assaulting the Berlin Wall with sledgehammers. The government finished the destruction in the fall of 1990.

In Czechoslovakia, which after 1968 had been firmly restored to Soviet-style rule, people watched the progress of glasnost expectantly. Persecuted, dissidents had maintained their critique of Communist rule, such as the accusation that Marxism-Leninism made people materialistic and indifferent to public life. In 1977, intellectuals and workers, including playwright Václav Havel, signed Charter 77, a public

Reunited Berliners Welcome the New Year
On New Year's Eve, 1989, Berliners and supporters from around the world celebrated the fall of the Berlin Wall and the prospect of a new Germany. The exuberant crowd tore the Communist seal from the flag and then hoisted the flag above the Brandenburg Gate as fireworks added to the intense emotion of the moment. The difficult transition to a reunified Germany, which included disposing of the remnants of communism, lay in the future. (ullstein bild-Boening.)

protest against the regime that resulted in the arrest of its signers. In the mid-1980s, watching Gorbachev on television calling for free speech, ordinary people took to the streets on behalf of democracy. The turning point came in November 1989 when Alexander Dubček, leader of the Prague Spring of 1968, addressed the crowds in Prague's Wenceslas Square to call for the ouster of Stalinists from the government after police had beaten student demonstrators. Almost immediately, the Communist leadership resigned. Capping the country's "velvet revolution," as it became known for its lack of bloodshed, the formerly Communist-dominated parliament elevated the dissident Havel to the presidency.

The world's attention now fastened on an unfolding political drama in Romania. From the mid-1960s on, Nicolae Ceauşescu had ruled as the harshest dictator in Communist Europe since Stalin. In the name of modernization, he destroyed whole villages; to build up the population, he outlawed contraceptives and abortion, a restriction that led to the abandonment of tens of thousands of children. He preached the virtues of a very slim body so that he could cut rations and use the savings on his pet projects, such as buying up private castles and building himself an enormous palace in Bucharest. To this end, he tore down entire neighborhoods and dozens of historical buildings, and he crushed opponents of the gaudy project so that it seemed to have unanimous support. Yet in early December 1989, an opposition movement rose up; workers demonstrated against the dictatorial government, and the army turned on Ceauşescu loyalists. On Christmas Day, viewers watched on television as the dictator and his wife were tried by a military court and then executed. For many, the death of Ceauşescu meant that the very worst of communism was over.

REVIEW What factors led to the collapse of communism in the Soviet bloc?

Conclusion

The fall of the Berlin Wall in 1989 symbolized the end of the cold war, even though the USSR still stood as a Communist power. The collapse of communism in the Soviet satellites was an utter surprise, for U.S.-bloc analysts had erroneously reported throughout the 1980s that the Soviet empire was in dangerously robust health. But no one should have been unaware of dissent or economic discontent. Since the 1960s, rebellious youths, ethnic and racial minorities, and women had condemned conditions across the West, along with criticizing the threat posed by the cold war. By the early 1980s, wars in Vietnam and Afghanistan, protests against deprivation in the Soviet bloc, the power of oil-producing states, and the growing political force of Islam had cost the superpowers their resources and reputations. Margaret Thatcher in Britain, Ronald Reagan in the United States, and Mikhail Gorbachev in the Soviet Union tried with varying degrees of success to put their postindustrial and cold war houses in order. The first two succeeded, while Gorbachev's policies of glasnost and perestroika—aimed at political and economic improvements—brought on collapse.

Glasnost and perestroika were supposed to bring about the high levels of postindustrial prosperity enjoyed outside the Soviet bloc. Across the West an unprecedented technological development had transformed businesses, the exploration of space, and the functioning of government. Technological advances also had had an enormous impact on everyday life. Work changed, as society reached a postindustrial stage in which the service sector predominated. New patterns of family life, new relationships among the generations, and revised standards of sexual behavior also characterized these years. But it was only in the United States, western Europe, and a few other Western-allied countries that the consumer benefits of postindustrialization reached ordinary people. A thoroughgoing consumer, service, and high-tech society demanded levels of efficiency, coordination, and cooperation that had not been reached in the Soviet bloc.

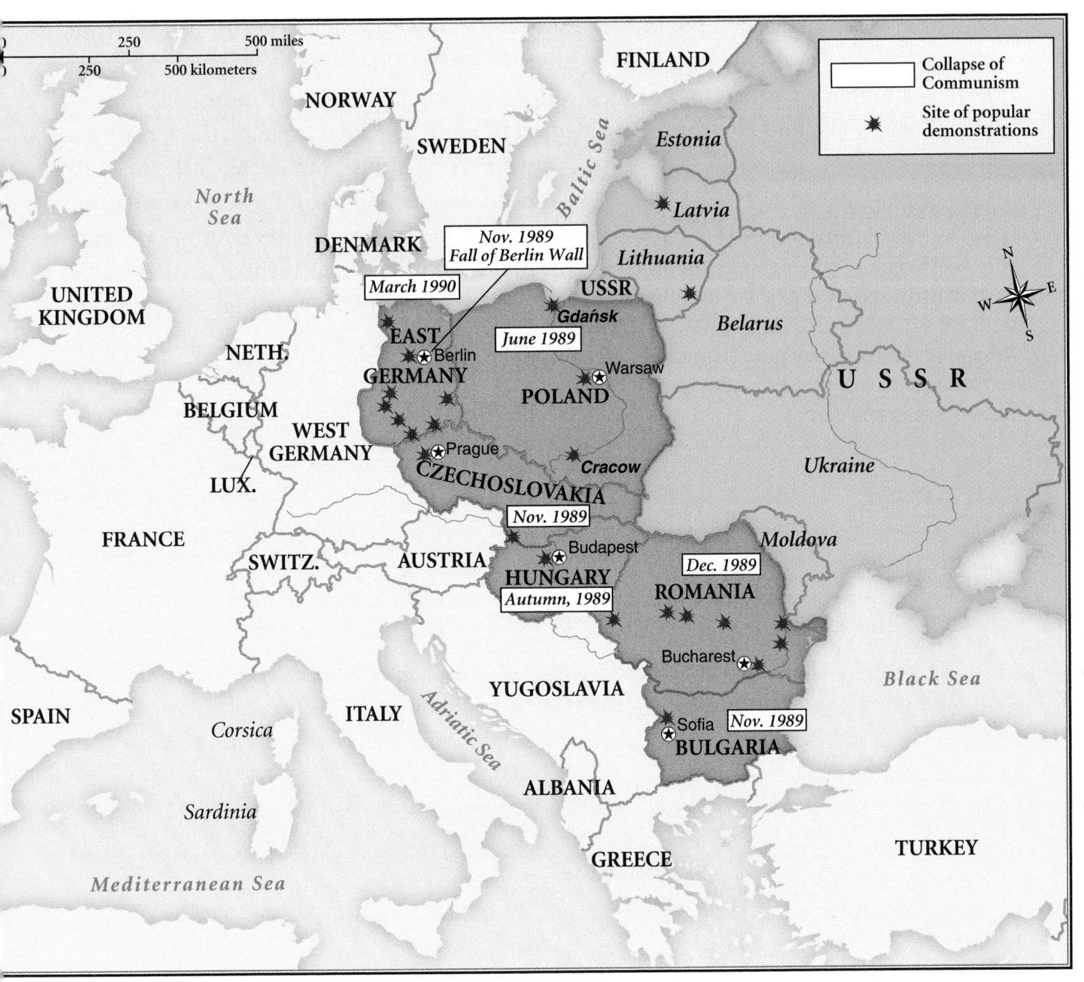

Mapping the West The Collapse of Communism in Europe, 1989–1990
The overthrow of Communist governments in the Soviet bloc occurred with surprising rapidity. The transformation began in Poland when Polish voters tossed out Communist Party leaders in June 1989 and then accelerated in September when thousands of East Germans fled to Hungary, Poland, and Czechoslovakia. Between October 1989 and March 1990, Communist regimes were replaced in Czechoslovakia, Bulgaria, Romania, and East Germany. Within three years, the Baltic states would declare their independence, the USSR itself would be dissolved, and the breakup of Yugoslavia would lead to war in the Balkans.

Many complained, nonetheless, about the dramatic changes resulting from postindustrial development. The protesters of the late 1960s addressed postindustrial society's stubborn problems: concentrations of bureaucratic and industrial power, social inequality, and environmental degradation. In the Soviet sphere, these protests were continuous but were little heeded until the collapse of Soviet domination of eastern Europe in 1989. Soon communism would be overturned in the USSR itself. However, the downfall of communism opened an era of painful adjustment, impoverishment, and even violence. Ending the cold war also hastened the process of globalization.

CHAPTER REVIEW QUESTIONS

1. How was the industrial society of the late nineteenth century different from the postindustrial society of the late twentieth century?
2. Why were there so many protests, acts of terrorism, and uprisings across the West between 1960 and 1990?

For practice quizzes and other study tools, see the Online Study Guide at bedfordstmartins.com/huntconcise.

For primary-source material from this period, see Chapter 28 of *Sources of The Making of the West*, Third Edition.

TIMELINE

1962 | 1966 | 1970 | 1974

- **1962–1965** Vatican II reforms Catholic ritual and dogma
- **1963** Betty Friedan, *The Feminine Mystique*
- **1966** West German foreign minister Willy Brandt develops Ostpolitik, a policy designed to bridge tensions between the two Germanys
- **1967** South Africa's Dr. Christiaan Barnard performs the first successful human heart transplant
- **1968** Revolution in Czechoslovakia against communism; student uprisings throughout Europe and the United States
- **1969** U.S. astronauts walk on the moon
- **1972** SALT I results in an antiballistic missile treaty between the United States and the Soviet Union
- **1973** North Vietnam and the United States sign peace agreements, but fighting continues until 1975; OPEC raises oil prices and imposes an oil embargo on the West
- **1973–1976** Aleksandr Solzhenitsyn, *The Gulag Archipelago*

Suggested References

Wartime technological development had profound consequences for the peacetime lives of individuals and for society. Technology created a postindustrial workplace, changing work and social life. The strains of an interlocked technological society along with citizen activism ultimately brought down the Soviet empire.

Bauer, Martin W., and George Gaskell, eds. *Biotechnology: The Making of a Global Controversy.* 2002.

Chaplin, Tamara. *Turning On the Mind: French Philosophers on Television.* 2007.

Dahl, Henne Marlene, and Tine Rask Eriksen, eds. *Dilemmas of Care in the Nordic Welfare State: Continuity and Change.* 2005.

Fink, Carole, et al. *1968: The World Transformed.* 1998.

*Freedman, Estelle B. *The Essential Feminist Reader,* 2007.

Green parties worldwide: http://www.greens.org

Harvey, Brian. *Europe's Space Program: To Ariane and Beyond.* 2003.

Kenney, Padraic. *Carnival of Revolution: Central Europe, 1989.* 2002.

Kotkin, Steven. *Armageddon Averted: Soviet Collapse, 1970–2000.* 2008.

Martin Luther King Jr. Papers Project at Stanford University: http://mlk-kpp01.stanford.edu/

Natalicchi, Giorgio. *Wiring Europe: Reshaping the European Telecommunications Regime.* 2001.

Ouimet, Matthew J. *The Rise and Fall of the Brezhnev Doctrine in Soviet Foreign Policy.* 2003.

Reiton, Earl A. *The Thatcher Revolution: Margaret Thatcher, John Major, Tony Blair, and the Transformation of Modern Britain.* 2002.

Siani-Davies, Peter. *The Romanian Revolution of December 1989.* 2005.

Suri, Jeremy. *Power and Protest: Global Revolution and the Rise of Détente.* 2003.

Varon, Jeremy. *Bringing the War Home: The Weather Underground, the Red Army Faction, and Revolutionary Violence in the Sixties and Seventies.* 2004.

Williams, Walter L., and Yolanda Retter. *Gay and Lesbian Rights in the United States: A Documentary History.* 2003.

- **1978** First test-tube baby born, in England
- **1978–1979** Islamic revolution in Iran; hostages taken at the U.S. embassy in Teheran
- **1980** Independent trade union, Solidarity, organizes resistance to Polish communism; Prime Minister Margaret Thatcher begins dismantling the welfare state in Britain
- **Early 1980s** AIDS epidemic strikes the West
- **1981** Ronald Reagan becomes U.S. president
- **1985** Mikhail Gorbachev comes to power in the USSR
- **1986** Explosion at a Soviet nuclear plant in Chernobyl
- **1989** Chinese students revolt in Tiananmen Square, and the government suppresses them; Communist governments ousted in eastern Europe; fall of the Berlin Wall

1978 | 1982 | 1986 | 1990

24

The New Globalism

1989 to the Present

THERESE IS A CONGOLESE IMMIGRANT TO PARIS, who arrived there in the late 1970s with the help of a brother who worked for an airline. Therese had been well known in Africa as the teenage girlfriend of pop singer Bozi Boziana, who wrote a hit song about her. But Congo's political troubles made her search for safety in Paris. Once there, Therese remained famous among African immigrants because she ran *nganda,* or informal bars. Like Therese, the immigrants who frequent her nganda are often Congolese and other Africans who have settled in Paris, many of them illegally. They flock to her nganda because they like her stylish dress, the African food she cooks, the African music she plays, and the African products she sells. Many of Therese's small bars and eateries have flourished, only to be closed down by landlords who want more of her handsome profits. Despite such obstacles, Therese keeps business going by moving her faithful clientele around her Paris neighborhood from basement to shop front to spare room. Therese is a new global citizen, working networks back home for supplies, constantly on the move because she lives on the edges of the law, and always striving to make a good living for herself and her family.

Global Citizens
The world's migrants at the turn of the twenty-first century sought safety, education, or jobs in the West's manufacturing and service occupations. Like these young immigrants from Senegal who are sharing a meal at a café in Paris, they also appreciated Western amenities. Children of immigrants were sometimes disillusioned, however, not wanting the life of extreme sacrifice that their parents had lived. Their frustrations at not being accepted as full citizens occasionally erupted into protest and even violence. *(© Directphoto .org/Alamy.)*

Therese's experience is just one example of the ease with which people in the post–cold war world crossed national boundaries while maintaining important ties around the globe. The end of the cold war rivalry between the superpowers and their allies paved the way for this more closely connected world. In the 1990s, globalization advanced with the dramatic collapse of communism in Yugoslavia and then the breakup of the Soviet Union itself. The world was no longer divided in two by the heavily guarded borders of the cold war, allowing nations and individuals more opportunity to trade and interact freely. The Common Market transformed itself into the **European Union (EU)**, which from 2004 on admitted many states from the former Soviet bloc. The telecommunications systems put in place beginning in the 1960s advanced globalization, binding peoples and cultures together in an ever more complicated social and economic web.

The global age brought vast national and international migration of tens of millions of people; an expanding global marketplace; and rapid cultural exchange of popular music, books, films, and television shows. On the negative side, greater globalization also brought widespread epidemic diseases, environmental deterioration, genocide, and terrorism. Nations in the West faced competition from the rising economic power of Japan, China, India, and Latin America. As millions of workers found new jobs in an interlinked economy, they discovered that the global age was one of opportunity and also insecurity.

While the end of superpower rivalry made global exchange easier, it also resulted in the dominance of a single power, the United States, in world affairs. As the United States exercised global power through warfare, however, the West itself seemed to fragment. European states started to resist the United States, although far less dramatically than the Soviet satellites had pulled away from the USSR. The economic power of Asian, Middle Eastern, and other countries and the cultural might of Islam created new centers of influence. Some observers predicted a huge "clash of civilizations" based on the differences between Western civilization and cultures beyond the West. Others saw a different clash—one between a Europe reborn after decades of disastrous wars as a peace-seeking group of nations defying an imperial United States, which, like Europe in the nineteenth century, increasingly waged war around the world. According to both of these models, globalization, instead of bringing connections and understanding, seemed to be a harmful development.

For historians, understanding the recent past is a challenge. Every day since 1989 receives instantaneous reporting because of global communication technology. Unlike journalists, historians do not choose from this mass the most sensational story of the moment. Rather, they are interested in judging which items from the unfiltered mass of information are actually true and, of these, which will be important in the long run. Historians want to identify social, cultural, and political events that are uniquely important or generally significant for people's everyday lives, and they need time to collect facts from more than one national source of news. They make the most reliable evaluations when phenomena are no longer "news"—that is, after a good period of time has shown their staying power and influence.

When we first started writing this book, we held our breath in the face of rapidly changing events and judged that the fall of communism and the increasing interconnectedness of the world's peoples and cultures were the challenges not only of the moment but also of history. In the second edition, we persisted in that judgment, even though the fall of communism and coming of globalism had brought greater perils than we had seen only five or six years earlier. Other forces, such as the Internet, escaped our notice altogether. Today, almost a decade after we made our first selections of important trends, we judge the gradual unification of the European continent as potentially momentous. We also see the forces of terrorism and a global economic crisis as possible events with historical staying power. As an experiment in history, you might note the important events of the months in which you take this course, put your list away for several years or more, and then see if they—along with the events discussed in this chapter—stand the test of time.

CHAPTER FOCUS QUESTION How has globalization been both a unifying and a divisive influence in the West in the twenty-first century?

Soviet Collapse Releases Global Forces

Following the fall of communism in eastern Europe and the fall of the Berlin Wall in 1989, rejection of communism spread in the early 1990s, turning events in unpredictable and often violent directions. Yugoslavia and then the Soviet Union itself fell apart, as nationality groups in both countries began to demand political and cultural autonomy. The USSR had held together more than one hundred ethnic groups, and the five republics of Soviet Central Asia were home to fifty million Muslims. Successive governments had attempted to instill Russian and Soviet culture and thus hold together this vast multicultural empire. The policy failed to build any heartfelt allegiance, leading to a swift collapse of the USSR. In Yugoslavia, Communist rulers had also enforced unity among religious and ethnic groups, and intermarriage among them occurred regularly. During the unstable years of the 1990s, however, ambitious politicians seeking to build a following whipped up ethnic hatreds. Throughout the decade, it was unclear whether peaceful, democratic nations would emerge. Amid this uncertainty, future control of the massive Soviet arsenal of nuclear weapons posed an even more dangerous threat.

The Breakup of Yugoslavia

Ethnic nationalism shaped the post-Communist future in Yugoslavia. Tensions erupted there in 1990 when Serb Communist Slobodan Milosevic became president of Serbia and began to promote Serb control of the entire Yugoslav federation as a replacement for communism. Other ethnic groups resisted Milosevic's militant pro-Serb nationalism and called for secession. "Slovenians . . . have one more reason to say they are in favor of independence," warned one of them in the face of mounting Serb pressure to take control of the other small republics that made up Yugoslavia. In the summer of 1991, two of these republics, Slovenia and Croatia, seceded, but Croatia soon lost almost a quarter of its territory when the Serb-dominated Yugoslav army, eager to enforce Serb supremacy, invaded (Map 24.1). A devastating civil war broke out in Bosnia-Herzegovina when that republic's Muslim majority tried to create a multicultural and multiethnic state. With the military support of Milosevic's government, Bosnian Serbs formed a guerrilla army and gained the upper hand.

Map 24.1 The Former Yugoslavia, c. 2000
After a decade of destructive civil war, United Nations forces and UN-brokered agreements attempted to protect the civilians of the former Yugoslavia from the brutal consequences of post-Communist rule. Ambitious politicians, most notably Slobodan Milosevic, used the twentieth-century Western strategy of fostering ethnic and religious hatreds as a powerful tool to build support for themselves while making those favoring peace look softhearted and unfit to rule. What issues of national identity does the breakup of Yugoslavia indicate? Have these changed since the nineteenth century?

Violence was inflicted on neighbors in parts of the former Yugoslavia with the aim of creating "ethnically pure" states in a region where ethnic mixture was in fact the norm. Serbs under Milosevic's leadership pursued a policy they called **ethnic cleansing**—that is, genocide—against the other ethnicities and religions. They raped women to leave them pregnant with Serb babies as a form of conquest. In 1995 Croatian forces massacred Serbs who had helped seize land from Croatia. That same year, the Serbs retaliated by slaughtering eight thousand men and boys in the town of Srebrenica, where the commander of the Serb forces ordered them to "kill the lot." Military units on all sides destroyed libraries and museums, architectural treasures like the Mostar Bridge, and cities rich with history such as Dubrovnik.

Ethnic cleansing thus involved eliminating both actual people and all traces of their complex past. Many in the West explained this violence as part of "age-old" blood feuds typical of a backward, almost "Asian" society in the Balkans. Others saw the use of genocide to achieve national power as a modern political practice employed by several politicians, including Adolf Hitler.

As with German, Italian, and Japanese aggression in the 1930s, no one stepped in to stop the violence in the former Yugoslavia. Peacekeepers were put in place, but they turned their backs on such atrocities as the Srebrenica massacre. Late in the 1990s, Serb forces moved to attack Muslims of Albanian ethnicity living in the Yugoslav province of Kosovo. From 1997 to 1999, crowds of Albanian Kosovars fled their homes as Serb militias and the Yugoslav army slaughtered the civilian population. NATO pilots bombed the region in an attempt to drive back the army and Serb militias. UN peacekeeping forces arrived to enforce an interethnic truce, but people throughout the world felt that this intervention came far too late to protect human rights and human lives. Alongside the decimated republics of Bosnia and Croatia, a new regime emerged in Serbia, and Milosevic was turned over to the International Court of Justice, or World Court, in the Netherlands to be tried for crimes against humanity. In 2003, Milosevic loyalists assassinated the new Serb president. Across a fragmenting eastern Europe, racial, ethnic, and religious hostilities were animated to shape political agendas.

The Soviet Union Comes Apart

At the beginning of January 1992, amid deteriorating conditions and the threat of violence, the Soviet Union itself collapsed. Perestroika had failed to restore the Soviet economy; people faced soaring prices, the threat of unemployment, and an even greater scarcity of goods than in the past. Although Mikhail Gorbachev announced late in 1990 that there was "no alternative to the transition to the market [economy]," his plan offered too little, too late. In 1991, the Russian parliament elected Boris Yeltsin as president of the Russian Republic over a Communist candidate. Yeltsin's election was the last straw for a group of eight antireform hard-liners, including the powerful head of the Soviet secret police, or KGB, who attempted a coup to overthrow the Soviet government. As coup leaders held Gorbachev under house arrest, Yeltsin defiantly stood atop a tank outside the Russian parliament building and called for mass resistance. Residents of Moscow and Leningrad filled the streets, and army units defected to protect Yeltsin's headquarters. People used fax machines and computers to coordinate opposition and send messages to the rest of the world. Citizen action defeated the coup and prevented a return to the Communist past.

After the failed coup, the Soviet Union disintegrated. People tore down statues of Soviet heroes; Yeltsin outlawed the Communist Party newspaper, *Pravda*. At the end of August 1991, the Soviet parliament suspended operations of the Communist Party itself. The Baltic states of Estonia, Latvia, and Lithuania declared their independence in September; other republics followed their lead. Bloody ethnic conflicts erupted in the disintegrating Soviet world. In the Soviet republic of Tajikistan, native Tajiks rioted against Armenians living there; in Azerbaijan, Azeris and Armenians clashed over contested territory; and in the Baltic states, anti-Semitism revived as a political tool. The USSR formally dissolved on January 1, 1992. Twelve of the fifteen former Soviet republics banded together in the Russian-dominated Commonwealth of Independent States, or CIS (Map 24.2).

Weakened by the coup attempt, Gorbachev abandoned politics. Yeltsin stepped in and accelerated the change to a market economy, introducing new problems as he did so. Plagued by corruption, the Russian economy entered an ever-deepening crisis. Yeltsin's political allies bought up national resources cheaply, stripped them of their value, and sent billions of dollars out of the country. By 1999, Yeltsin's own family appeared to be deeply implicated in stealing the wealth once seen as belonging to all the people. Managers, military officers, and bureaucrats took whatever goods they could lay their hands on, including weaponry, and sold it. In an attempt to consolidate support, Yeltsin launched destructive military action against the resource-rich Russian province of Chechnya, which wanted independence. Organized criminals interfered in the distribution of goods and services and assassinated businesspeople, legislators, and anyone who criticized them. As the Russian parliament pursued an investigation into the business dealings of Yeltsin, his family, and his allies, he resigned on December 31, 1999, and appointed Vladimir Putin as interim president.

Putin was a little-known member of Russia's new security force, which had evolved from the old KGB. In the presidential election of 2000, Putin surprised everyone when the electorate voted him in. Though associated with the Yeltsin family corruption, he initially stressed legality. "Democracy," he announced, "is the dictatorship of law." With a solid victory, Putin drove from power the major figures in both the regional and central governments, usually the henchmen of the robber barons. Faced with a desperate economic situation, Putin proclaimed the need to restore "strong government" and end the influence of a "handful of billionaires with only egotistical concerns." Putin's popularity rose even higher when the government arrested the billionaire head of Yukos Oil, one of Russia's largest oil companies, in 2003. The pillaging of the country—the source of ordinary citizens' suffering—was finally being punished. According to critics, however, Putin was merely transferring Russia's natural resources and other assets to his allies, while extending the vicious and destructive war in Chechnya to crush the independence movement.

Toward a Market Economy

Developing a free market and republican government brought misery to Russia and the rest of eastern Europe. The conditions of everyday life grew increasingly dire as salaries went unpaid, food remained in short supply, and essential services deteriorated. In 1994, inflation soared at a rate of 14 percent a month in Russia, while industrial production dropped by 15 percent. People took drastic steps to stay alive. Hotel lobbies became clogged with prostitutes because women were the first people fired as the economy slumped. Unpaid soldiers sold their services to

Map 24.2 Countries of the Former Soviet Union, c. 2000
The breakup of the Soviet Union in the 1990s was one of the extraordinary events of the twentieth century. As nation-states dissolved, regional alliances such as the Commonwealth of Independent States and European Union were necessary to meet the political and economic challenges of the global age with coordinated action. As the map shows, Russia remained a Goliath even after Soviet satellite countries declared their independence and dominated the politics and economy of the region. **For more help analyzing this map, see the map activity for this chapter in the Online Study Guide at** bedfordstmartins.com/huntconcise.

the Russian Mafia. Ordinary citizens stood on the sidewalks of major cities selling their household possessions. "Anything and everything is for sale," one critic noted at the time. Simultaneously, a pent-up demand for items never before available was unleashed. An enormous underground economy existed in goods such as imported automobiles stolen from people in other countries.

There were, of course, many pluses. People with enough money were able to travel freely for the first time, and the media were initially more open than ever before in Russian history. Some workers, many of them young and highly educated, profited from technology and business contacts. However, their frequent emigration to more prosperous parts of the world further drained Russia's human resources. At the same time, as the different republics of the former Soviet Union became independent, many of the hundreds of thousands of Russians whose families had decades earlier been sent there by the state as colonizers returned as refugees, putting greater demands on the chaotic Russian economy. The undoing of communism was thus more complicated and painful than anyone had imagined it would be.

For many in the former Soviet bloc, the first priority was getting economies running again—but on new terms. Replacing a government-controlled economy with a market one could not happen automatically but would require government planning. Given the growing misery, however, many opposed the introduction of

Czech Prostitute on German Border

The collapse of communism and the Soviet Union created financial disaster, particularly for women, who represented more than two-thirds of all the unemployed. Communists advocated the belief that all people, regardless of gender, should work and that they should be paid equally. While this equality never worked in practice, it did provide jobs so that women could support themselves and their children. Under the free-market system, however, women were eliminated from good jobs and paid less. Many resorted to prostitution, which often took place on borders with more prosperous countries such as Germany, as shown here. (Getty Images.)

new market-oriented measures. With collective farms up for sale, most farmers faced landlessness and starvation. The countries that experienced the most success were those in which administrators had previously introduced some ingredients of free trade, such as allowing farmers to sell their produce on the open market or encouraging independent entrepreneurs or even government factories to conduct international trade. Hungary and Poland thus emerged from the transition with less strain because both had favored market elements early on and had hired advisers to speed the transformation of the economy. These countries set up business schools and other institutions to foster trade and successfully attracted foreign capital, thus anchoring them in the world economy.

Elsewhere, however, the transition happened differently. The former Soviet Union itself, in the words of one critic, became simply one vast "kleptocracy" in the 1990s as the country's resources—theoretically the property of all the people—were stolen for personal gain. One Polish adviser noted that democracy and a successful transition to a free market went hand in hand, for unless the people were effectively represented in the government and institutionally powerful enough to prevent it, former officials would simply operate as criminals. This was especially true given the inheritance of the Soviet system of corruption, tax evasion, and off-the-books dealing. In addition to corruption, the long-standing practice of shielding the economy from global developments prevented industry from benefiting from technological change. Because plants and personnel were hopelessly out-of-date, even worthless, the introduction of competition and free trade meant closing factories and firing all the workers.

A final element in post-Soviet economic difficulties stemmed from a brain drain that struck the region. The economic chaos that followed the fall of communism set off a rush of migration from eastern Europe to western Europe, often involving those with marketable skills. Emigrants left for several reasons, including the lack of jobs, the upsurge of ethnic hatreds, and the availability of higher salaries for well-educated workers in other countries. "I knew in my heart that communism would collapse," said one ex-dissident, commenting sadly on the departure of young people from his country, "but it never crossed my mind that the future would look like this." Escaping anti-Semitism also played a role. Post-Communist politicians used the rallying cry of hatred of Jews to build a following, just as Hitler and many others had done so effectively during troubled times in the past. Banditry and violence inflicted by organized crime added to the disadvantages of remaining in eastern Europe.

The everyday advantages of living in western Europe included clean drinking water, better housing, better roads, personal safety, and at least a minimal level of social services. Although western Europe was now on a firm neoliberal course of cutting welfare-state spending, most benefits had disappeared entirely in the former Communist countries. Pensions for veterans and retired workers were rarely paid, and even when they were, they were often worthless given the countries' soaring inflation. Day-care centers, kindergartens, and homes for the elderly closed their doors, and hospitals and health care deteriorated. In these circumstances, the benefits of citizenship in western European countries were a powerful attraction.

International Politics and the New Russia

Although Gorbachev had pulled the Soviet Union out of its disastrous war with Afghanistan, his successors opened another war to prevent the secession of oil-rich Chechnya and to provide a nationalist rallying cry to shore up domestic support for the administration. For decades, Chechens had been integrated into the Soviet bureaucracy and military, but in the fall of 1991, the National Congress of the Chechen People took over the government of the region from the USSR, moving toward the same kind of independence sought by the Baltic nations and other former Soviet republics. In June 1992, Chechen rebels got control of massive numbers of Russian weapons, including airplanes, tanks, and some forty thousand automatic weapons and machine guns.

In December 1994, the Russian government sealed the Chechen borders and invaded. A high Russian official defended the war as crucial to bolstering Yeltsin's position: "We now need a small victorious war. . . . We must raise the President's rating." Despite the Russian population's opposition to the war,

Terrorist Attack on a Moscow Bus, 1996
Terrorism became more widespread from the 1970s on, taking many forms and espousing many causes. Terrorists for the most part engineered attacks on random citizens to increase the loss of life. Post-Soviet Russia experienced such attacks at the hands of various groups, among them breakaway Chechens, whose independence Russia violently resisted. Large-scale bombings also occurred in the Paris subway, on London streets, and on Spanish trains, causing these countries to cover public wastebaskets and to exhort people to be vigilant about parcels in streets, public buildings, and train and subway stations. Terrorists used the wartime strategy of targeting civilians during peacetime.
(© Ivo Lorenc/Sygma/Corbis.)

Chechnya's capital city of Grozny was pounded to bits. Casualties mounted not only among Chechen civilians but among Russians, too. In 2002, Chechen loyalists took hundreds of hostages in a Moscow theater; Chechen suicide bombers blew up airplanes, buses, and apartment buildings. Putin pursued the Chechen war into the twenty-first century, reducing the international reputation of the post-Communist government.

Putin also expanded Russian influence in Ukraine, Belarus, India, and China by taking advantage of the politics of energy. Russia had the commodities—especially oil and gas—needed to sustain the fantastic growth of emerging industries around the world. Its natural resources made Russia a major player in the global economy even after a dramatic recession struck the world in 2008. Achieving democratic values remained a more elusive goal. Putin's critics were mercilessly assassinated, newspapers and radios were closed down, and a general distrust of politics grew.

REVIEW What were the major issues facing the former Communist world in the 1990s and early 2000s?

The Nation-State in a Global Age

Although the end of the Soviet system fractured one large regional economy, it gave a boost to European unification. In the 1990s and early 2000s, the European Community was healthy in comparison to other regions of the world that were plagued with civil wars and violence. The union's economic success provoked the formation of other transnational institutions, including the North American Free Trade Agreement (NAFTA), which established a free-trade zone composed of the United States, Canada, and Mexico. As new forms of world governance and large regional blocs took shape in the 1990s, traditional Western nation-states and capital cities began to look and function differently.

Europe Looks beyond the Nation-State

From the 1990s on, Europeans worked to strengthen their shared institutions beyond those of the traditional nation-state, first by expanding the range of their common efforts. In 1992, the twelve countries of the Common Market ended national distinctions in certain business activities and border controls, effectively closing down identity checks at their common borders. Citizens of the member countries carried a uniform burgundy-colored passport, and governments, whether municipal or national, had to treat all member nations' businesses the same. In 1994, by the terms of the **Maastricht Treaty**, the European Community became the European Union, and in 1999 a common currency, the **euro**, came into being, first for transactions among financial institutions and then in 2002 for general use by the public. Some countries—most notably Britain—refused to adopt the euro, but otherwise common policies governed everything from pollution controls on automobiles to health warnings on cigarette packages. The EU parliament convened regularly in Strasbourg, France, and an EU central bank came into being to set interest rates and economic policy for the countries using the euro.

The EU was seen as key to a peaceful Europe. "People with the same money don't go to war with one another," said a French nuclear scientist about the introduction of the euro. In 2002 and 2003, Greece pushed for its traditional enemy Turkey to be admitted to the EU, despite the resistance of some who argued that a predominantly Muslim country could never fit in with the Christian traditions of EU members. Both Greece and Turkey stood to benefit by having their disputes adjudicated by the EU, principally because they would be able to cut those parts of their defense budgets used for weapons against each other. Like the rivalry between Germany and France, that between Turkey and Greece, it was hoped, would dissolve if both were bound by the strong economic and political ties of the EU. As of 2009, however, Turkey was still awaiting acceptance of its application.

Eastern European nations clamored to join the EU, working hard to meet not only the EU's budgetary requirements but also those pertaining to human rights and social policy. They saw the benefits of EU membership demonstrated in such countries as Greece, long considered the poor relative of the other EU states. Greece joined the European Community in 1981; its per capita gross domestic product was 64 percent of the European average in 1985. During the 1990s, however, Greek leaders and the EU made a real effort to bring the country closer to EU norms. By the early twenty-first century, thanks to advice from the EU and an infusion of funds, Greece had reached 80 percent of the EU per capita gross domestic product.

In 2004, the EU admitted ten new members—Estonia, Latvia, Lithuania, Poland, the Czech Republic, Slovakia, Hungary, Slovenia, Malta, and Cyprus—and in 2007 it welcomed Romania and Bulgaria (Map 24.3). Just before Poland's admission to the EU, its standard of living was 39 percent of EU standards, up from 33 percent in 1995. The Czech Republic and Hungary were at 55 and 50 percent, respectively. In all three cases, these figures masked differences between the ailing countryside and thriving cities. Citizens in eastern Europe were not always happy at the prospect of joining the EU. One retiree foresaw the cost of beer going up and said, "If I wanted to join anything in the West, I would have defected." Still others felt that having just established an independent national identity, they should not allow themselves to be swallowed up once again. People in older member states were having second thoughts, too. In the spring of 2005, a majority of voters in France and the Netherlands defeated a newly drafted constitution that would have strengthened EU ties. Commentators explained the rejection as stemming from popular anger at the EU bureaucracy's failure to consult ordinary people in its decision making.

Although still weak by comparison with most of western Europe, economic life in eastern Europe picked up considerably early in the twenty-first century. In contrast to the first bleak years of massive layoffs, soaring inflation, and unpaid salaries, purchasing power in Poland, Slovenia, and Estonia was some 40 percent higher in 2002 than in 1989. Outsourcing by international companies began to

Map 24.3 The European Union in 2009
The European Union appeared to increase the economic health of its members despite the rocky start of its common currency, the euro. The EU helped end the traditional competition among its members and facilitated trade and worker migration by providing common passports and business laws, and open borders. But many critics worried about a loss of cultural distinctiveness among peoples because of the EU, and those in the more prosperous countries came to fear that the global crisis that began in 2008 would make them financially responsible for the weak economies of eastern Europe.

flourish across the region, increasing opportunities for those with language and technical skills, and more people enjoyed consumer items such as freezers, computers, and portable telephones. The shopping malls that were built mostly around the capital cities testified to the urban nature of the benefits of the new economy. Eastern Europe was seen as a great new market consisting of 100 million customers for superstores like the Swedish furniture giant IKEA or the electronics firm Electroworld. "When Electroworld opened in Budapest [April 2002], it provoked a riot. Two hundred thousand people crowded to get in the doors," reported one observer. Critics worried that eastern Europeans had fallen prey to uncontrolled materialism and frenzied shopping, a Western disease they called "consumania."

Prague Supermarket, 2002

For people living in former eastern-bloc countries, daily life in the post-Communist world was one of extremes. Within several years, entrepreneurs opened supermarkets filled with more goods than most people had ever seen before, like the different irons available to this Prague shopper. Along with the unprecedented array of goods, the collapse of communism brought new dangers, such as bombings of public transportation and economic instability for those who did not benefit from the uneasy transition to capitalism. (Getty Images.)

Consumers themselves, however, learned to read labels and to use the superstores, where prices were lower. Proudly, many believed that they had left Communist poverty behind.

Globalizing Cities and Fragmenting Nations

After the collapse of communism, the West changed still further. It both fragmented into more nation-states than it had had fifty years earlier and developed new features—most notably the globalization of major cities. These were cities whose institutions and values were global rather than regional or national. They contained stock markets, legal firms, insurance companies, financial service organizations, and other enterprises that operated across national borders and were linked to similar enterprises in other global cities. Within these cities, high-level decision makers set global economic policy and enacted global business. The high-powered and high-priced nature of such global business operations made life in global cities extremely costly, driving middle managers and engineers to lower-priced living quarters in the suburbs that nonetheless provided good schools and other benefits for well-educated white-collar workers. Crowded into the slums of global cities and poorer suburbs were the lowest-paid service providers—the maintenance, domestic, and other workers whose menial labor was essential around the clock to attend to the needs and comfort of those at the top.

Global cities often had the best transportation and telecommunication facilities and thus became centers of migration for highly skilled and more modest workers alike. Paris, London, and New York were global spaces where workers maintained direct and constant contact with people around the world. Global cities drew criticism for their concentrated wealth, seen to be taken at the expense of poorer people in southern countries, and for their lack of patriotic focus on national causes. They contained huge diasporas of prosperous migrants, such as the estimated ninety thousand Japanese in England in the mid-1990s who staffed Japan's thriving global businesses. Because these migrants did not aim to become citizens, they made no economic or political claims on the adopted country and were thus sometimes called invisible migrants. As a result, global cities were said to produce a "deterritorialization of identities," meaning that many city dwellers lacked both a national and a local sense of themselves.

Ironically, as globalization took hold economically and culturally, there were more nations in Europe in 2000 than there had been in 1945 (Map 24.4). Belief in ethnic distinctiveness caused individual nation-states to break up. Despite two centuries aimed at unification of the Slavs, for example, in the 1990s and early 2000s, Slavs separated into their own states. In 1993, Czechoslovakia split into the Czech Republic and Slovakia. Yugoslavia came apart into several states, and Russia fought to keep Chechnya from breaking away as had many other states of the former Soviet Union.

Activists launched movements for regional independence in France, Italy, and Spain. Some Bretons and Corsicans demanded their freedom from France; Belgians threatened to split the country in two; northern Italians created an independence movement; and Basque nationalists in northern Spain assassinated tourists, police, and other public servants in an effort to gain autonomy. Although in 2005 the Basque nationalists publicly renounced terrorism, the violence did not stop. As cities globalized and nations fragmented, new combinations of local, national, and global identities took shape. Nganda manager Therese enjoyed her neighborhood in Paris, her identity as an immigrant to France, and continuing contact with friends and family in Congo. Nonetheless, these developments plus the overall expansion of the EU called into question the future of the nation-state.

Global Organizations

Supranational organizations, some of them regulating international finance and trade but others addressing social problems, had been in place for decades but became more active and powerful with globalization. Sponsored by large numbers of individual nations, the **World Bank**, International Monetary Fund, and World Trade Organization, for example, dealt with the terms of trade among countries and the economic well-being of individual peoples. Raising money from national governments, the

Map 24.4 Eastern Europe in the 1990s
In the 1990s, the countries of eastern Europe tried to forge their own destinies free from the direction of either Russia or the United States. The transition was far from easy. Old states like Czechoslovakia fragmented, and many state borders were contested. Turning definitively from Russia, the leadership of these countries began to look to western Europe, most of them eventually opting for membership in the European Union even though everyone relied on Russia's oil and natural gas. Compare this map with the sharp divisions between eastern and western Europe shown in Map 22.3 (page 878). What were the most significant changes to the region in the post–cold war era?

International Monetary Fund made loans to developing countries but only on the condition that they restructure their economies according to neoliberal principles. Other supranational organizations were charitable foundations, research institutes, or service organizations acting independently of government, many of them based in Europe and the United States. They were called **nongovernmental organizations (NGOs)**. Because some—the Rockefeller, Ford, and Open Society foundations, for example—had so much money, these NGOs often had considerable international power. After the fall of the Soviet bloc, NGOs used their resources to shape economic and social policy and the course of political reform. Some charitable and activist NGOs, like the French-based Doctors without Borders, raised money through global contributions and used it to provide medical care in places such as the war-torn former Yugoslavia. Like the EU, the larger NGOs were sometimes criticized for exercising their power with little regard for democratic processes or citizens' own preferences.

In the 1990s, there was a growing movement to attack globalization itself. In 1998, Bernard Cassen of France founded the Association for the Benefit of Citizens (ATTAC, after its French name). The organization, which soon had adherents in forty countries, stood against the control of globalization by financial institutions and held well-attended conferences to find new directions for countries suffering from global development. A globally known activist, French farmer José Bové, protested the opening of McDonald's restaurants in France and destroyed genetically modified seeds. "The only regret I have now," Bové claimed at his trial in 2003, "is that I didn't destroy more of it." Bové went to jail for his protests, but he remained a hero to antiglobalism activists, who saw him as a simple champion of, in his own words, "good food" and an enemy of standardization.

REVIEW What trends suggest that the nation-state was a declining institution at the beginning of the twenty-first century?

Global Challenges and Discontents

The rising tide of globalization brought as many challenges as opportunities. First, the health of the world's people and their environment came under a multipronged attack from nuclear disaster, acid rain, and surging population. Second, economic prosperity and physical safety continued to elude great masses of people, especially in the southern half of the globe. Third, as suprastate organizations developed, transnational allegiances and religious and ethnic movements also competed for power and influence. Growing wealth in Latin America, Asia, and the Middle East gave leaders in these regions the confidence to state that it was time for the West to surrender some of its power.

Pollution and Environmental Activism

By the early twenty-first century, many people had become aware of the dangers of industrial growth—once seen as an unqualified blessing—to the environment. In the aftermath of the 1986 nuclear explosion at Chernobyl, levels of radioactivity rose for hundreds of miles in all directions. By the 1990s cancer rates in the region were soaring, particularly among children, and thousands were perishing slowly from the effects of radiation poisoning. Fossil fuel pollutants, such as those from natural gas, coal, and oil, mixed with atmospheric moisture to produce acid rain, a poisonous brew that destroyed forests and inflicted ailments such as chronic bronchial disease on people. In less industrial areas, clearing the world's rain forests depleted the global oxygen supply and threatened the biological diversity of the planet. By the late 1980s, scientists determined that the use of chlorofluorocarbons (CFCs), chemicals found in aerosol and refrigeration products, had blown a hole in the earth's ozone layer, the part of the blanket of atmospheric gases that prevents harmful ultraviolet rays from reaching the planet. Simultaneously, automobile and industrial emissions of chemicals were adding to that thermal blanket. The result was **global warming**, an increase in the temperature of the earth's lower atmosphere. Changes in temperature and dramatic weather cycles of drought or drenching rain indicated that a "greenhouse effect" might be permanently warming the earth. Already in the 1990s, the Arctic pack ice was breaking up, allowing Finland to ship oil along the once-iced-over route in 2002. Scientists predicted dire consequences: the rate of global melting, which had more than doubled since 1988, would raise sea levels by more than ten inches by 2100, flooding coastal areas, disturbing fragile ecosystems, and harming freshwater supplies.

Activism protesting unchecked industrial growth now became an effective political force. An escapee from Nazi Germany, E. F. "Fritz" Schumacher, produced one of the bibles of the environmental movement, *Small Is Beautiful* (1973), which spelled out how technology and industrialization actually threatened the earth and its inhabitants. Behind him stood the legacy of American environmentalist Rachel Carson, author of *Silent Spring* (1962), a powerful critique that advocated the immediate rescue of rivers, forests, and the soil from the ravages of factories and chemical farming. In 1979, the Green Party was founded in West Germany, and Green Party candidates across Europe came to force other politicians to voice their concern for the environment. As the horrific effects of unchecked pollution in eastern Europe became known, protests mounted and solutions began to unfold.

Inspired by Green Party ideas, Europeans attacked environmental problems on the local and global levels. Some European cities such as Frankfurt developed car-free zones, and Venice operated completely without automobiles because of the threat they posed to the city's very existence. In Paris, whenever automobile emissions reached dangerous levels, cars were banned from city streets until the emission levels dropped. The Smart car, a very small car using less fuel than larger cars, became a fashionable way to reduce dependence on fossil fuels. Cities also developed bicycle lanes on major city streets. Parts of Europe developed wind power to such an extent that 20 percent of some countries' electricity was generated by wind. Many cities in the West began to recycle waste materials.

These were success stories, involving changing habits in some of the most industrialized countries of the world. By 1999, some eighty-four countries, including EU members, had signed the Kyoto Protocol, an international treaty whose signatories agreed to reduce their pollution levels to specified targets. The Kyoto emissions reductions finally went into effect in February 2005, but with the world's leading polluter at the time—the United States—still refusing to join the effort. In 2009, however, Barack Obama became the first African American president on a

Smart Cars in Europe
The havoc caused by the oil crisis of the 1970s spurred many European states to encourage the development of alternative sources of energy and transportation. By the twenty-first century, the landscape was dotted not only with windmills but also with tiny, fuel-efficient automobiles like the Smart car shown here. European governments also heavily taxed gasoline, with the result that it cost at least twice as much as in the United States, thus further encouraging people to buy the Smart car rather than an SUV—a far rarer sight in Europe than in the United States. (© David Cooper/Toronto Star/ZUMA/Corbis.)

platform that included a commitment to environmental responsibility, turning back the sense that the West was fragmenting over environmental issues.

Population, Health, and Disease

The issue of population was as difficult in the early twenty-first century as it had been in the 1930s. Nations with less-developed economies struggled with the pressing problem of surging populations, while Europe experienced negative population growth (more deaths than births) after 1995. The less industrially developed countries accounted for 98 percent of worldwide population growth, in part because the spread of Western medicine enabled people there to live much longer than before. By late 1999, the earth's population had reached six billion and was expected to double by 2045 (see "Taking Measure," page 966). Yet because many European countries were not replacing their populations, they were facing problems related to an aging citizenry and a shortage of younger people. In fact, Europe as a region had the lowest fertility rate in the world. The fertility rate in Italy and Spain was only 1.3 children per woman of reproductive age, far below the replacement level of 2.1 needed to maintain a steady population. Some forecasters predicted that this low rate meant that the population of Europe would fall from 725 million to 600 million by 2050.

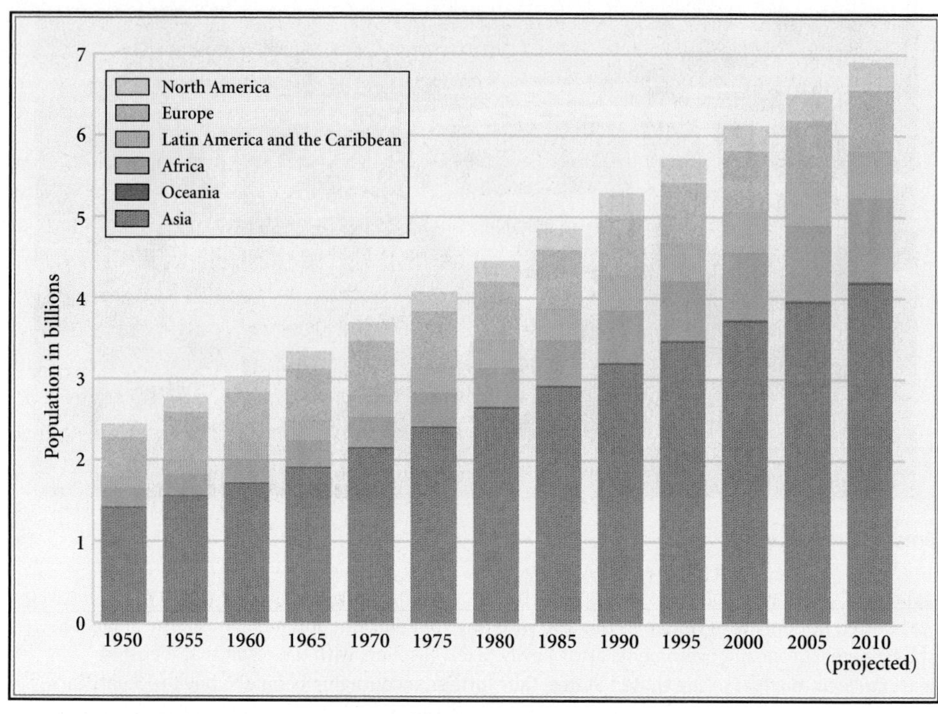

Taking Measure World Population Growth, 1950–2010
In the twenty-first century, a major question is whether the global environment can sustain billions of people indefinitely. In the early modern period, local communities had lived according to unwritten rules that balanced population size with the productive capacities of individual farming regions. Centuries later, the same need for balance had reached global proportions. As fertility dropped around the planet because of contraception, population continued to grow because of improved health.

One consequence of this decline would be fewer workers paying into the social security system to fund retirees' pensions.

Population problems were especially urgent in former Soviet-bloc countries, where life expectancy was declining at a catastrophic rate from a peak of seventy years for Russian men in the mid-1970s to fifty-one years at the beginning of the twenty-first century. Heart disease and cancer were the leading causes of male death, and these stark death rates were generally attributed to increased drinking (one in seven men in Russia was an alcoholic), smoking, drug use, poor diet, and general stress. Meanwhile, fertility rates were also declining: the lowest levels of fertility in 2003 were in the Czech Republic and Ukraine with a rate of 1.1 children, and children in eastern Europe lived on average twelve years less than their counterparts in western Europe. Between 1992 and 2002, the Russian population declined from 149 million to 144 million, with predictions that it would fall below 100 million by 2050.

Good health was spread unevenly around the world. Western medicine brought better health to many in the less-developed world through the increased use of vaccines and drugs for diseases such as malaria and smallpox. However, half of all Africans lacked basic public health facilities and safe drinking water. Drought and poverty, along with the corruption of politicians in some cases, spread famine in Sudan, Somalia, Ethiopia, and elsewhere. Around the world, the poor and the unemployed suffered more chronic illnesses than those who were better-off, but they received less care. Whereas in many parts of the world people still died from malnutrition and infectious diseases, in the West noncontagious diseases—heart and autoimmune diseases, stroke, cancer, and depression—were more deadly. The distribution of health services—heart transplants for the wealthy versus preventive health care for a wider range of people—became a hotly debated issue in the general argument about whether technological solutions could remedy global problems.

Disease, like population and technology, operated on a global terrain. In the early 1980s, both Western values and Western technological expertise were challenged by the spread of acquired immunodeficiency syndrome (AIDS). An incurable, highly virulent killer that effectively shuts down the body's immune system, AIDS initially afflicted heterosexuals in central Africa. The disease later turned up in Haitian immigrants to the United States and in homosexual men worldwide. Within a decade, AIDS became a global epidemic. The disease spread especially quickly and widely among the heterosexual populations of Africa and Asia, passed mainly by men to and through women, but in 2009 the U.S. capital, Washington, D.C., had a rate of infection as high as that in Africa. By the late 1990s, no cure had yet been discovered, although protease-inhibiting drugs helped alleviate the symptoms. The mounting death toll made some equate AIDS with the Black Death. Treatment was often not provided to poor people living in places such as sub-Saharan Africa and the slums of Asian cities, but efforts were under way to provide more lifesaving drugs to these people. In addition to the AIDS epidemic, the deadly Ebola virus and dozens of other viruses smoldered while others, such as severe acute respiratory syndrome (SARS), avian flu, and swine flu, traveled the world even as health professionals worked to contain them. Diseases as much as environmental dangers underscored the interconnectedness of the world's peoples.

North versus South?

During the 1980s and 1990s, world leaders tried to address the growing divide between the earth's northern and southern regions. Other than Australians and New Zealanders, southern peoples generally had lower living standards and poorer health than northerners. Recently emerging from colonial rule and economic exploitation by northerners, citizens in the southern regions could not yet count on their new governments to provide welfare-state services or education. Funding for such programs generally came from northern countries, with international organizations such as the World Bank and the International Monetary Fund providing loans for economic development. However, the conditions of those loans, such as cutting government spending for education and health care, led to criticism that ordinary citizens gained no real benefit from them. Some early-twenty-first-century leaders advocated that wealthy countries simply give southern countries the money they needed as reparation for centuries of imperial plunder.

Southern regions experienced various barriers to economic development. Latin American nations grappled with government corruption, multibillion-dollar debts, widespread crime, and grinding poverty, although some countries—prominent among them Brazil—began to strengthen their economies by marketing their oil and other natural resources more effectively. Africa suffered from drought, famine, and civil war. In countries such as Rwanda, Somalia, and Sudan, military rule and ethnic or religious antagonism encouraged under imperialism produced conflict and genocide in the 1990s and early 2000s. Millions perished; others were left starving and homeless due to "kleptocracies" that stole resources, including aid provided by charitable groups. Although some African countries began turning away from military dictatorship and toward constitutional government, economic advance was uneven on the continent, and in the twenty-first century the scourge of AIDS and other unchecked diseases added to the weight of Africa's problems.

Islam Meets the West

North-South antagonisms became evident in the rise of militant Islam, which often flourished where democracy and prosperity for the masses were missing. The Iranian hostage crisis (1979–1981) showed religion, nationalism, and anti-Western sentiment commanding the world's attention. The charismatic leaders of the 1980s and 1990s—Iran's Ayatollah Ruhollah Khomeini; Libya's Muammar Qaddafi; Iraq's Saddam Hussein; and Osama bin Laden, leader of the al-Qaeda transnational terrorist organization—variously promoted a pan-Arabic or pan-Islamic world order that gathered increasing support. Khomeini's program—"Neither East, nor West, only the Islamic Republic"—had wide appeal. Renouncing the Westernization that had flourished under the shah, Khomeini's regime in Iran required women once again to cover their bodies almost totally in special clothing and eliminated a range of their former rights. Aided by the prosperity that oil had brought, Islamic revolutionaries believed that a strict theocracy would restore the pride and Islamic identity that imperialism had stripped from Middle Eastern men. Khomeini built widespread support among Shi'ite Muslims by proclaiming the ascendancy of the Shi'ite clergy. Although the Shi'ites were numerous, they had long been discriminated against by Sunni Muslims.

Islamic leaders did not achieve their unifying goals (Map 24.5). Instead, war plagued the region. In 1980, Saddam Hussein, fearing a rebellion from Shi'ites in Iraq, attacked Iran, hoping to channel Shi'ite discontent into a patriotic crusade against non-Arab Iranians. The United States provided Iraq with massive aid in the struggle against Iran, but after eight years of combat and extensive loss of life

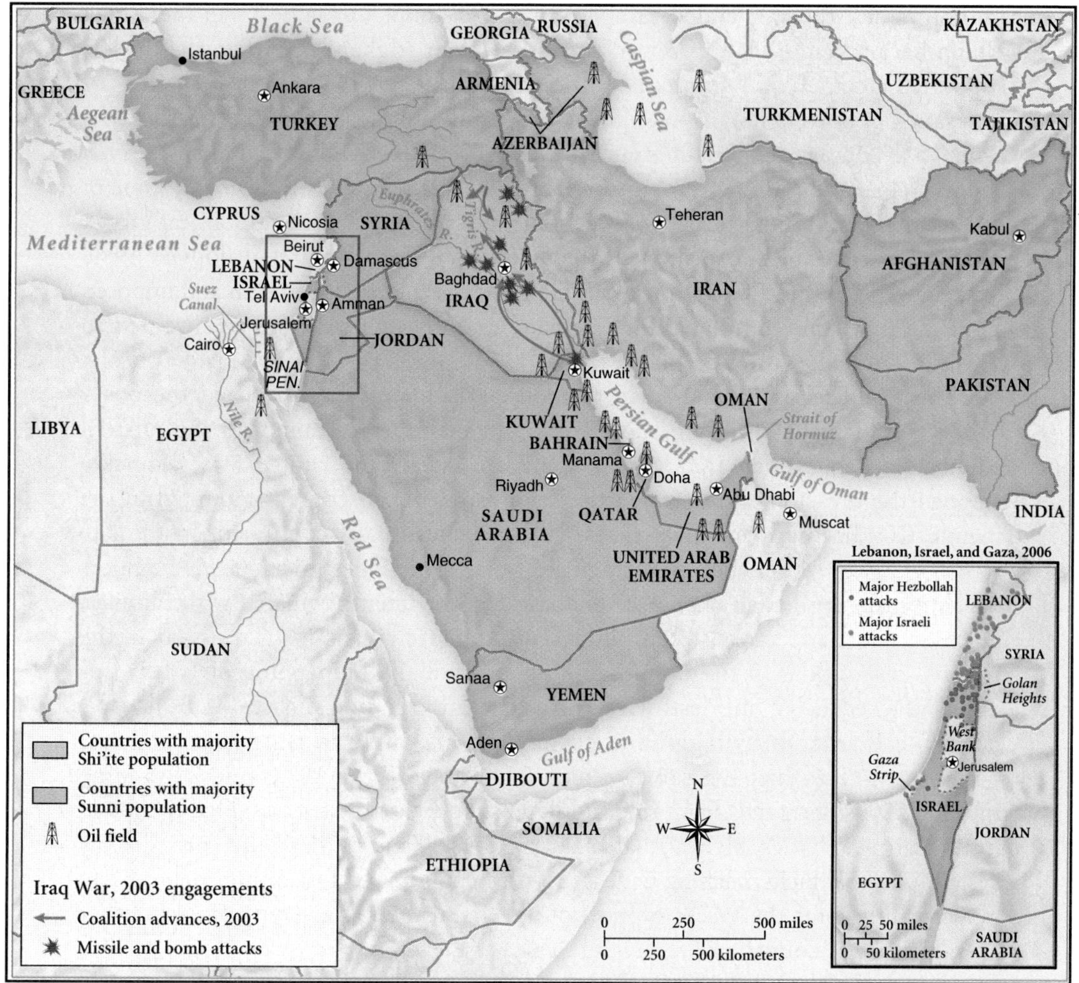

Map 24.5 The Middle East in the Twenty-first Century
Tensions among states in the Middle East, especially the ongoing conflict between the Palestinians and Israelis and animosities between Shi'ites and Sunnis, became more complicated from the 1990s on. The situation grew more uncertain in 2003 when a U.S.- and British-led invasion of Iraq deteriorated into escalating violence among competing religious and ethnic groups in the country. Additionally, for thirty-four days in the summer of 2006, Israel bombed Lebanon, including its capital city and refugee camps, with fire returned by Hezbollah and Hamas forces in the region. This violence was followed in 2009 by Israel's shelling and invading of Gaza at the end of a cease-fire and new Palestinian rocket attacks.

on both sides, the war ended in a stalemate. At about the same time, the Soviet Union became embroiled in a war against Islam in Afghanistan when the Soviets supported a coup by a Communist faction against the government in 1979. Tens of thousands of Soviets fought in Afghanistan, using the most advanced missiles and artillery to combat a powerful group of Muslim resisters. The United States, China, Saudi Arabia, and Pakistan provided weapons to this resistance movement, some of whose members united to become the Taliban—a militant Islamic political group. The war in Afghanistan so drained the USSR that it withdrew its troops in 1989. In the late 1990s, the Taliban took over the government of Afghanistan and imposed a regime that, among other things, forbade girls to attend school and women to leave their homes without a male escort.

The Middle East remained in turmoil, as Saddam Hussein tested the post–cold war waters by invading Kuwait in 1990 in hopes of annexing the oil-rich country to debt-ridden Iraq. A UN coalition, led by the United States, quickly stopped the invasion and defeated the Iraqi army, but discontent mounted in the region. Conflict between the Israelis and the Palestinians continued. In the late 1990s, as Israeli settlers began seizing Palestinian land, Palestinian suicide bombers began murdering Israeli civilians. The Israeli government retaliated with missiles, machine guns, and tanks, often killing Palestinian civilians in turn. In 2006, the Israelis, responding to the political militia Hezbollah's kidnapping of Israeli soldiers, attacked Lebanon, destroying infrastructure, sending missiles into its capital city of Beirut, and killing hundreds of civilians. In 2009, Israel's invasion and bombing of Gaza had the same results. Beginning in the 1980s and continuing into the 2000s, terrorists from the Middle East and North Africa planted bombs in many European cities, blew airplanes out of the sky, and bombed the Paris subway system. These attacks, causing widespread destruction and loss of life, were said to be punishment for the West's support of Israel and the repressive regimes in other Middle Eastern countries.

On September 11, 2001, the ongoing terrorism in Europe and around the world finally caught the full attention of the United States. In an unprecedented act, Muslim militants hijacked four commercial airplanes in the United States and flew two of them into the World Trade Center in New York City and one into the Pentagon in Virginia. The fourth plane, en route to the U.S. Capitol, crashed in Pennsylvania when passengers forced the hijackers to lose control of the aircraft. The hijackers, most of whom were from Saudi Arabia, had been inspired by the wealthy radical leader Osama bin Laden, who sought to end the presence of U.S. forces in Saudi Arabia. They had trained in bin Laden's terrorist camps in Afghanistan and learned to pilot planes in the United States. The loss of more than three thousand lives led the United States to declare a "war against terrorism." The administration of U.S. president George W. Bush forged a multinational coalition, which included the vital cooperation of Islamic countries such as Pakistan, with the main goal of driving the ruling Taliban out of Afghanistan and capturing bin Laden. After some initial

Europeans React to 9/11 Terror
On September 11, 2001, terrorists killed thousands of people from dozens of countries in airplane attacks on the World Trade Center in New York and the Pentagon outside Washington, D.C. Throughout the world, people expressed their shock and sorrow, and many, like this British tourist in Rome, remained glued to the news. Terrorism, which had plagued Europeans for several decades, easily traveled the world in these days of more open borders, economic globalization, and cultural exchange, finally reaching the sole superpower left after the collapse of the Soviet Union. **For more help analyzing this image, see the visual activity for this chapter in the Online Study Guide at** bedfordstmartins.com/huntconcise. (© Pizzoli Alberto/Sygma/Corbis.)

coalition success in Afghanistan, by 2009 the Taliban was reestablishing its authority there, and bin Laden was still at large.

At first, the September 11 attacks and other lethal bombings around the world promoted global cooperation. European countries rounded up terrorists and conducted the first successful trials of them in the spring of 2003. Ultimately, however, the West became divided when the United States claimed that Saddam Hussein was concealing weapons of mass destruction in Iraq and suggested ties between Saddam and bin Laden's terrorist group. Great Britain, Spain, and Poland were among the countries that joined the United States in invading Iraq in March 2003, but other powerful European states, including Germany, Russia, and France, refused. Many people in the United States were furious at this refusal, and some engaged in a round of "French bashing," even promoting the renaming of French fries to "freedom fries." U.S. war fever mounted with the suggestion that Syria and Iran should also be invaded, while many in the rest of the world condemned what seemed a sudden American thirst for blood. Europeans in general, including the British public, accused the United States of becoming a world military dictatorship in order to preserve its only remaining value—wasteful consumerism. The United States countercharged that the Europeans were too selfishly enjoying their democracy and creature comforts to help fund the military defense of freedom under attack. The Spanish withdrew from the U.S. occupation of Iraq after terrorists linked to al-Qaeda bombed four Madrid commuter trains on March 11, 2004. The British, too, reeled when terrorists exploded bombs in three subway cars and a bus in central London in July 2005. As the war in Iraq approached its seventh year, there was a sense that the West was coming apart, yet some felt that Obama's election as U.S. president in 2008 would lead to a quicker end to the conflict, given his campaign promise to set a timetable for troop withdrawals.

World Economies on the Rise

Amid the violence, incredible industrial and technological development took place outside the West. Just as economic change in the early modern period had redirected European affairs from the Mediterranean to the Atlantic, so explosive productivity from Japan to Singapore in the 1980s and 1990s spread economic power from the Atlantic region to the Pacific. In 1982, the Asian Pacific nations accounted for 16.4 percent of global gross domestic product, a figure that had doubled since the 1960s. By 1989, East Asia's share of world production had grown to more than 25 percent as that of the West had declined. By 2006, China alone was achieving economic growth rates of over 10 percent per year, while Japan had developed the world's second-largest national economy (after the United States). By 2009, China had edged out Germany for third place.

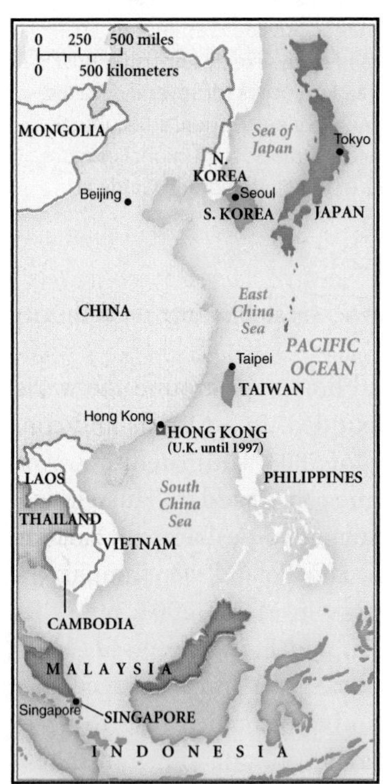

Tigers of the Pacific Rim, c. 1995

South Korea, Taiwan, Singapore, and Hong Kong were popularly called **Pacific tigers** for the ferocity of their growth in the 1980s and 1990s. By the 1990s, China, pursuing a policy of economic modernization and market orientation, had joined the surge in productivity. Japan, however, led the initial charge of Asian economies, with investment in high-tech consumer industries driving the Japanese economy. For example, in 1982 Japan had thirty-two thousand industrial robots in operation, western Europe had only nine thousand, and the United States had seven thousand. In 1989, the Japanese government and private businesses invested $549 billion to modernize Japan's industrial capacity, a full $36 billion more than U.S. public and private investment. Such spending paid off substantially, as buyers around the world snapped up automobiles, televisions, videocassette recorders, and computers from Japanese or other Asian Pacific companies. As the United States poured vast sums into its military budgets and a series of wars, Asian and Middle Eastern governments purchased U.S. government bonds, thus financing America's ballooning national debt. Forty years after its total defeat in World War II, Japan was bankrolling its former conqueror.

Despite rising national prosperity, individual workers, particularly those outside Japan, often paid dearly for this newly created wealth. For example, industrial safety standards in China were abominable, leading to horrendous mining and other disasters. Women in South Korea, Taiwan, and Central America labored in sweatshops to produce clothing for such U.S.-based companies as JCPenney and Calvin Klein. Using the lure of a low-paid and docile female workforce, governments were able to attract electronics and other industries. However, educational standards for these women did rise, along with access to birth control and other medical care.

Other emerging economies in the Southern Hemisphere continued to increase their share of the world's gross domestic product during the 1980s and 1990s, and some achieved political gains as well. In South Africa, native peoples began winning the struggle for political rights when, in 1990, the moderate government of F. W. de Klerk released political leader Nelson Mandela, imprisoned for almost three decades because of his antiapartheid activism. In free elections in 1994, Mandela was elected president. South Africa, Russia, Brazil, Iran, Saudi Arabia, Nigeria, and Chile all profited from the global need for vast quantities of raw materials such as oil and ores. India made strides in education, women's rights, and local cooperation (calming bitter rivalries), but the assassinations of prime ministers raised the question of whether India would continue to have the strong leadership necessary to attract investment and thus continue to modernize. After the brief rule of a Hindu nationalist government that often blocked development, India's economy took off in the early twenty-first century, taking business away from Western firms and making global acquisitions that gave it, for example, the world's largest steel industry. Although Western multinationals faced more competition, they also profited from increasing prosperity worldwide, which allowed more people to buy their products.

There was a downside to global development. Beginning in 1997, when speculators brought down the Thai baht, and continuing with the collapse of the ruble in 1998 and the bursting of the technology bubble in the early 2000s, the global economy suffered a series of shocks. Then in 2008, the real estate bubble burst in the United States, setting in motion a financial crisis of enormous proportions. For several years, lenders had been making home mortgages available to consumers on easy terms in the United States, which had helped prop up the economy. Financiers then distributed this U.S. debt around the world to those who hoped to make handsome profits based on rate increases written into the mortgage contracts. When people were unable to make their monthly mortgage payments and pay their ballooning credit card debt, credit became unavailable both to ordinary people and to banks and industry. A credit collapse followed, just as it had in the stock market crash of 1929. Beginning

Protesting the Global Economic Crisis, London, 2009
In the spring of 2009, citizens and activists from around the world converged on London to confront the Group of Twenty, or G-20, established to bring together the leaders of the world's twenty largest economies. These demonstrators protested the use of their tax dollars to prop up banks whose officers had brought the global economy to a virtual halt through their manipulations of finance worldwide in order to boost their profits. Protesters demanded that more humane values govern the world, even as some of them rioted and destroyed property. (© Andy Rain/epa/Corbis.)

in the United States, banks and industries became insolvent and governments around the world tried to prop them up with billions of dollars. Unemployment rose, as businesses and consumers alike stopped purchasing goods. The globalization of economic crises was another of the perils faced by the world's population.

REVIEW What were the most important challenges facing the West in the new millennium?

Global Culture and Society in the Twenty-first Century

At the beginning of the twenty-first century, increased migration and growing global communication led many to ask what would become of national cultures and Western civilization. Would the world become a uniform mass, with everyone wearing the same kind of clothing, eating the same kind of food, and watching the same films (perhaps on their cell phones)? Some critics predicted a clash of civilizations, in which antagonistic religions and cultures would lead to a global holocaust. Others asked whether the West would collapse as the United States wore itself out waging war while much of Europe turned away.

Migration, the spread of disease, global climate change, the information revolution, and the global sharing of culture argued against the cultural purity of any group, Western or otherwise. "Civilizations," Indian economist and Nobel Prize winner Amartya Sen wrote after the terrorist attacks of September 11, "are hard to partition . . . given the diversities within each society as well as the linkages among different countries and cultures." Through migration and communication, Western society changed even more rapidly in the 1980s and 1990s than it had hundreds of years earlier when it had come into intense contact with the rest of the globe. Culture transcended national boundaries, as East, West, North, and South became saturated with one another's products and customs. Some observers labeled the new century an era of denationalization—meaning that national cultures as well as national boundaries were becoming less distinct.

Redefining the West: The Impact of Global Migration

The global movement of people was massive in the last third of the twentieth century and into the twenty-first century. Uneven economic development, political persecution, and warfare (which claimed more than 100 million victims after 1945) sent tens of millions in search of opportunity and safety. By 2001, France had some 6 million Muslims within its borders, and Europe as a whole had between 35 million and 50 million. Other parts of the world also had millions of migrants from other

Headscarf Controversy in Germany
Western countries have long debated the relationship between religion and the nation-state. In particular, that debate targeted the need for religiously neutral education in order to develop citizens with undivided national loyalties. In an age of global migration, the issue of religion in the schools resurfaced, this time focusing on the headscarves worn by many Muslim women. Although in 2003 Germany upheld the right of the teacher Fereshta Ludin, pictured here, to wear the headscarf while teaching on the grounds of religious freedom, it simultaneously asserted the right of children to a religiously neutral education. (Michael Latz/ddp Berlin.)

cultures. The oil-producing nations of the Middle East employed countless foreign workers, who generally constituted one-third of the labor force. Violence in Africa sent Rwandans, Congolese, and others to South Africa, as its government became dominated by blacks. War in Afghanistan increased the number of refugees to Iran to nearly two million in 1995, while successive attacks on Iraq by the West sent millions more fleeing. By 2000, there were some 120 million migrants worldwide, many of them headed to the West.

Migrants often earned desperately needed income for family members who remained in their native countries, and in some cases they propped up the economies of entire nations. In countries as different as Yugoslavia (before its breakup), Egypt, Spain, Mexico, and Pakistan, money sent home from abroad constituted up to 60 percent of the national income. Sometimes migration was coerced; for example, many eastern European and Asian prostitutes were held in international sex rings that controlled their passports, wages, and lives. Others came to the West voluntarily, seeking opportunity and a better life. "I do not want to go back to China," said one woman restaurant owner in Hungary in the 1990s. "Some of my relatives there also have restaurants. . . . They have to have good relations with officials, . . . and sometimes they have to bribe somebody. . . . I would not be happy living like that." Like the illegal Congolese café proprietor Therese, whose story opens this chapter, many lived on the margins of the law, supporting networks of family and maintaining global economic ties from a new base in the West.

Foreign workers were often scapegoats for native peoples suffering from economic woes such as unemployment caused by downsizing. On the eve of EU enlargement in 2004, the highly respected weekly magazine *The Economist* included an article titled "The Coming Hordes," which warned of Britain's being overrun by Roma (Gypsies) from eastern Europe. Political parties with racist programs sprang to life in Europe, aided by celebrities. The Moscow rock band Corroded Metals campaigned for anti-immigrant candidates with hate-filled songs and chants in English of "Kill, kill, kill, kill the bloody foreigners" running in the background. Even citizens of immigrant descent often had a difficult time being accepted. In Austria, France, the Netherlands, Sweden, and many other Western countries, thriving anti-immigrant and white supremacist politicians challenged centrist parties. In Austria and the Netherlands, anti-immigration candidates were elected to head the government. Nonetheless, because employers sought out illegal immigrants for the low wages they could be paid, the West remained a place of opportunity.

Global Networks and the Economy

Like migration, rapid technological change also weakened traditional political, cultural, and economic borders. In 1969, the U.S. Department of Defense developed a computer network to carry communications in case of nuclear war. This system and others like it in universities, government, and business grew over the next decades into an unregulated system of more than ten thousand networks globally. These came to be known as the Internet—shorthand for *internetworking*. By 1995, users in more than 137 countries were connected to the Internet, creating new "communities" based on business needs, shared cultural interests, or other factors that went beyond the borders of a particular nation-state. An online global marketplace gradually emerged, offering goods and services ranging from books and discount airfares to advanced weaponry and organ transplants. While enthusiasts claimed that the Internet could promote world democracy, critics charged that this new communications technology favored elites and disadvantaged those without computer skills.

By 2000, as postindustrial skills spread, the Internet brought service jobs to countries that had heretofore suffered unemployment and real poverty. One of the first countries to recognize the possibilities of computing and help-desk services was Ireland, which pushed computer literacy to attract business. In 2003, U.S. firms spent $8.3 billion on outsourcing to Ireland and $7.7 billion on outsourcing to India. The Internet allowed for jobs to be apportioned anywhere. Moroccans did help-desk work for French or Spanish speakers, and in the twenty-first century Estonia, Hungary, the Czech Republic, and the Philippines were rebuilding their economies successfully by providing call-center and other business services. The Internet allowed service industries to globalize just as the manufacturing sector had done much earlier through multinational corporations.

Globalization of the economy affected the West in complex ways. Those who worked in outsourcing enterprises were more likely than those in domestic firms to participate in the global consumer economy, much of it for Western goods. Benefiting from the booming global economy of the 1990s, the Irish and eastern Europeans used their new disposable income to purchase items such as luxury automobiles, CD players, and personal computers that would have been far beyond their means a

Call Center in Bangalore, India
Modern communications have permitted the outsourcing not just of manufacturing jobs, which began after World War II, but also of service jobs to places like eastern Europe, Africa, and South Asia. These workers in southern India, who are answering a customer service hotline, are bilingual or polylingual, enabling them to service customers in Europe and the United States. What are the advantages and disadvantages of a division of labor that operates internationally? (© Jagadeesh/Reuters/Corbis.)

decade earlier. Non-Westerners may have taken jobs from the West, but they often sent funds back. A twenty-one-year-old Indian woman, working for a service provider in Bangalore under the English name Sharon, used her salary to buy Western consumer items, such as a cell phone from the Finnish company Nokia. "As a teenager I wished for so many things," she said. "Now I'm my own Santa Claus." Ordinary Western workers often discovered that this global revolution threatened their jobs. In Germany, where taxes for social security and other welfare-state financing accounted for 42 percent of payroll costs in 2003, the attraction of countries with lower costs was strong. Globalization redistributed jobs across the West and reworked economic networks, and it also contributed to the global economic crisis beginning in 2008.

A Global Culture?

As far back as the first millennium of human history, culture has crossed political boundaries. In the ancient world, Greek philosophers and traders knew of distant Asian religious beliefs, while in the eighteenth and nineteenth centuries, Western scholars immersed themselves in Asian languages. By the early 1990s, tourism had become the largest single industry in Britain and in many other Western countries, promoting cultural exchange. Chinese students in Tiananmen Square in 1989 testified to the power of the West in the world's imagination when in the name of freedom they rallied around a model of the Statue of Liberty (which itself was a gift from France to the United States). In Japan, businesspeople wore Western-style clothing and watched soccer, baseball, and other Western sports using English terms, while Europeans and Americans ate sushi, wore flip-flops, and carried umbrellas—all imports from beyond the West.

Innovations in communications integrated cultures and made the earth seem a much smaller place, though possibly one with a Western flavor. Videotapes and satellite-beamed telecasts transported American television shows to Hong Kong and Japanese movies to Europe and North America. American rock music sold briskly in Russia and elsewhere in the former Soviet bloc. When more than 100,000 Czechoslovakian rock fans, including President Václav Havel, attended a Rolling Stones concert in Prague in 1990, it was clear that despite half a century of supposedly insular Communist culture, Czechs and Slovaks had tuned in to the larger world. Young black immigrants forged transnational culture when they created hip-hop and other pop music styles by combining elements of Africa, the Caribbean, Afro-America, and Europe. Athletes like the Brazilian soccer player Ronaldo, the American golfer Tiger Woods, and the Japanese baseball star Ichiro Suzuki became better known to countless people than their own national leaders were. Film entrepreneurs marketed such international blockbusters as the Chinese *Crouching Tiger, Hidden Dragon* (2000). With their messages conveyed around the world, even today's moral leaders—Nobel Peace Prize winners Nelson Mandela, former president of South Africa; the Dalai Lama, spiritual leader of Tibet; and Aung San Suu Kyi, opposition leader in Myanmar (Burma)—are global figures.

As it had done for centuries, the West continued to devour material from other cultures—whether Hong Kong films, African textiles, Indian music, or Latin American pop culture. One of the most important influences in the West came from what was called the "boom" in Latin American literature. Latin American authors developed a style known as magical realism that melded everyday events with Latin American history and geography, while also incorporating elements of myth, magic, and religion. The novels of Colombian-born Nobel Prize winner Gabriel García Márquez were translated into dozens of languages. His lush fantasies, including *One Hundred Years of Solitude* (1967), *Love in the Time of Cholera* (1988), and many later works, portray people of titanic ambitions and passions who endure war and all manner of personal trials. García Márquez narrated the tradition of dictators in Latin America, but he also paid close attention to the effects of global business. *One Hundred Years of Solitude,* for example, closes with the machine-gunning in 1928 of thousands of workers for the American United Fruit company because they asked for one day off per week, breaks to use the toilet, and other improvements in their working conditions. Wherever they lived, readers snapped up the book, which sold thirty million copies worldwide. García Márquez's work inspired a host of other outstanding novels in the magical realism tradition, including Laura Esquivel's *Like Water for Chocolate* (1989). In the 1990s, the work was translated into two dozen languages and became a hit film because of its setting in a Mexican kitchen during the revolution of 1910, where cooking, sexuality, and brutality are intertwined. The Latin American "boom" continued into the early twenty-first century, with innumerable authors in the West adopting aspects of García Márquez's style.

Magical realism influenced a range of Western writers, including those migrating to Europe. Some described how the experience of Western culture felt to the transnational person. British-born Zadie Smith, daughter of a Jamaican mother, became a prizewinning author with her novel *White Teeth* (2000), which describes postimperial Britain through the lives of often bizarre and larger-than-life characters from many ethnic backgrounds. Odd science fiction technology, deep emotional wounds, and weird but hilarious situations guide a plot full of heartbreak. Equally drawn to aspects of the magical realist style, Indian-born Salman Rushdie published the novel *The Satanic Verses* (1988), which outraged Muslims around the world because it appeared to blaspheme the Prophet, Muhammad. From Iran, Ayatollah Khomeini issued a fatwa promising both a monetary reward and salvation in the afterlife to anyone who would assassinate the writer. Rushdie's Norwegian publisher was shot, and his Italian and Japanese translators were murdered, but in a display of Western cultural unity, international leaders took bold steps to protect Rushdie until the threat to his life was lifted a decade later.

The mainstream literary world became fraught with conflict as groups outside the accepted circles engaged in artistic production. From within the West, novelist Toni Morrison became, in 1993, the first African American woman to win the Nobel Prize for Literature. In works such as *Beloved* (1987), *Jazz* (1992), and *A Mercy* (2008), Morrison describes the nightmares, daily experiences, achievements, and dreams of those who were brought as slaves to the United States and their descendants. But some parents objected to the inclusion of Morrison's work in school curricula alongside Shakespeare and other white authors. Critics charged that unlike Shakespeare's universal Western truth, the writing of African Americans, native Americans, and

Toni Morrison
The first African American woman to receive the Nobel Prize for Literature, Toni Morrison has used her literary talent to depict the condition of blacks under slavery and after emancipation into contemporary times. Morrison also has published essays on social, racial, and gender issues in the United States. (© Deborah Feingold/Corbis.)

women represented only propaganda, not great literature. In both the United States and Europe, politicians on the right saw the presence of multiculturalism as a sign of deterioration similar to that brought about by immigration.

In the former Soviet bloc, artists and writers faced unique challenges. After the Soviet Union collapsed, classical writers like Mikhail Bulgakov (1891–1940), famous in the West for his novel *The Master and Margarita* (published posthumously in 1966–1967), became known in their homeland. At the same time, the collapse put literary dissidents out of business; having helped bring down the Soviet regime, they had lost their subject matter—the critique of a tyrannical system. State-sponsored authors, suddenly without jobs, had to sell their products on the free market in countries where economic conditions were so harsh that books were an unaffordable luxury. Eastern-bloc writers who formerly found both critical and financial success in the West seemed less heroic—and less talented—in the post-Soviet world. The work of Czech writer Milan Kundera, for example, lost its luster. It had been, according to one critic, merely about Western publishers' hype—that is, not literature but merely a "line of business." To make matters worse, there was no idea of what the post-Communist arts should be, sending artists in the former Soviet bloc scurrying for solutions.

Talented fresh voices rang out, too. Andrei Makine, an expatriate Russian author, became popular worldwide for his poignant yet disturbing novels of the collapse of communism, many of them showing the attraction of western European culture and the continuing impact of World War II and the Gulag on the imaginations of eastern-bloc people, including teenagers and older people. Both *Dreams of My*

Russian Summers (1995) and *Once Upon the River Love* (1994) describe young people bred to fantasize about the wealth, sexiness, and material goods of western Europe and America. Victor Pelevin wrote more satirically and bitingly in works such as *The Life of Insects* (1993), in which insect-humans buzz around Russia trying to discover who they are in the post-Soviet world. Pelevin, a Buddhist and former engineer, mocked politicians and the almost sacred Soviet space program, depicting it as a media sham, run from the depths of the Moscow subway system, in which hundreds of cosmonaut-celebrities are killed to prevent the truth from getting out. For him, "any politician is a TV program, and this doesn't change from one government to another." One simply judged politicians by their haircuts, ties, and other aspects of personal style, as he showed in his novel *Homo Zapiens* (2002), in which politicians are all "virtual"—that is, produced by technical effects and scriptwriters.

In music and the other arts, much energy in the former Soviet bloc was spent on recovering and absorbing all the underground works that had been hidden since 1917. The situation was utterly astonishing as the works of dozens of first-rate composers, for example, emerged. They had written their classical works in private for fear that these pieces might contain phrasings, sounds, and rhythms that would be labeled treasonous. Meanwhile, they had often earned a living writing for films, as did Giya Kancheli, who wrote immensely popular music for more than forty films but was in addition a gifted composer of classical music. Other composers simply became known to a wider world. Alfred Schnittke (1934–1998) produced dozens of operas, symphonies, chamber music pieces, concertos, and other works that were extremely sad, punctuated with anger in loud bursts of dissonance, and set in a somber bass register.

The political and economic power of the United States gave its culture an edge for many of these years. U.S. success in "marketing" culture, along with the legacy of British imperialism, helped make English the dominant international language by the end of the twentieth century. Such English words as *stop, shopping, parking, okay, weekend,* and *rock* infiltrated dozens of non-English vocabularies. English became one of the official languages of the European Union; across Europe it served as the main language of higher education, science, and tourism. In the 1960s, French president Charles de Gaulle, fearing the corruption of the French language, banned such new words as *computer* in government documents, and succeeding administrations followed his lead; this did not stop the influx of English into scientific, diplomatic, and daily life, however. In another sign of the cultural divide, the EU's parliament and national cultural ministries regulated the amount of American programming on television and in cinemas.

Nevertheless, American influence in films was dominant. Films such as *Titanic* (1997) and *The Matrix Reloaded* (2003) earned hundreds of millions of dollars from global audiences. Simultaneously, the United States itself welcomed films from around the world, including the Mexican *Y Tu Mamá También* (2001) and the Italian *Life Is Beautiful* (1997). "Bollywood" films—happy, lavish films from the Indian movie industry—had a huge following in the West, even influencing the plots of some American productions, and by the twenty-first century Bollywood had surpassed Hollywood in sales and viewers. The fastest-growing medium in the United States in the twenty-first century was Spanish-language television, just one more indication that even in the United States, culture was based on mixture and global exchange.

Some have called the global culture of the late twentieth and early twenty-first centuries **postmodernism**, defined in part as intense stylistic mixing in the arts without a central unifying theme or elite set of standards guiding them. Striking examples of postmodern art abounded in Western society, including the AT&T building (now known as the Sony Building) in New York City, which looks sleek and modern. Its entryway, however, is a Roman arch, and its cloud-piercing top suggests eighteenth-century Chippendale furniture. Postmodern buildings drew from cultural styles that spanned millennia and continents without valuing one style above others. The Guggenheim Museum in Bilbao, Spain, designed by American architect Frank Gehry and considered bizarre by classical or even "modern" standards, includes forms, materials, and perspectives that, according to the rules of earlier decades, do not belong together. Architects from around the world, working in a variety of hybrid styles, completed the postunification rebuilding of Berlin. One crowning achievement was the rebuilding of the Reichstag, whose traditional facade was given a modern dome of glass and steel. To add to the changing reality, all of these postmodern buildings could be visited virtually on the World Wide Web.

Some intellectuals defined postmodernism in political terms, as part of the decline of the eighteenth-century Enlightenment ideals of human rights, individualism, and personal freedom, which were seen as "modern." This political postmodernism included the decline of the Western nation-state. A structure like the Bilbao Guggenheim was simply an international tourist attraction rather than an institution reflecting Spanish traditions or Spain's national values. To commentators, it represented consumption, global technology, mass communications, and international migration rather than citizenship, nationalism, and rights. These qualities made it a rootless structure, unlike the Louvre in Paris, for example, which was built by the French monarchy to serve its own purposes. Critics saw the Bilbao Guggenheim as drifting, more like the nomadic businesswoman Therese, who moved between nations and cultures with no set identity. Cities and nations alike were losing their function as places providing social roots, personal identity, or human rights. For postmodernists of a political bent, computers had replaced the autonomous, free self, and transnational bureaucracies had made representative government obsolete.

The issues raised by postmodernism—whether in architecture, political thought, or the popular media—focused on the basic ingredients of Western identity as it had been defined over the past two hundred years. Postmodernism was part of the rethinking and questioning that accompanied globalization. Such critical thinking—whatever its tentative conclusions may be—is today, as in the past, a key ingredient in the making of the West.

REVIEW What social and cultural questions has globalization raised?

The German Reichstag: Reborn and Green
Nothing better symbolizes the end of the postwar era and the new millennium than the restoration of the Reichstag, the parliament building in Berlin. Like other manifestations of postmodernism, the restoration—designed by a British architect—preserves the old facade, while adding a new glass dome, complete with solar panels that make the building energy independent. As visitors walk around the dome, they can watch their elected representatives deliberating below. (© Svenja-Foto/zefa/Corbis.)

Conclusion: The Making of the West Continues

Postmodernism has not fully eclipsed Enlightenment values in the global age. Its critics point to the looming problems of contemporary life—population explosion, scarce resources, North-South inequities, global pollution, ethnic hatreds, global terrorism, and world economic crises—and find the exercise of humane values and rational thought more important than ever. Postmodernists and other philosophers counter that attempts at rational decision making fall short because of the issue of "unintended consequences"—that is, one cannot know in advance the consequences of an act. Who would have predicted, for example, the scale of human misery and rising criminality initially resulting from the fall of the Soviet empire? Reformers rationally seeking improved conditions by bringing down Soviet and Yugoslav communism unleashed bloodshed, sickness, and even genocide. Yet events from South Africa and Northern Ireland, for example, indicated that certain long-feuding groups could rationally put aside decades of bloodshed and work toward peace.

The consequences of such global change and increasing globalization are still being determined. While the Internet and migration suggest that people often relate positively to one another worldwide, militants from Saudi Arabia, Egypt, Indonesia, the Philippines, North Africa, Britain, and elsewhere have unleashed unprecedented terrorism on the world in an attempt to push back global forces. Even as globalization has raised standards of living and education in many parts of the world, in other areas—such as poorer regions of Africa and Asia—people face disease and the dramatic social and economic deterioration associated with the global age. Rational results of planning and inexplicable consequences coexist in the present world.

Western traditions of democracy, human rights, and economic equality have much to offer. Given that these were initially intended for a limited number of people—white men in powerful Western nations—debates about their value and defects are found everywhere in today's world even as many aim to achieve them. The nation-state, which protected those values for the privileged and denied them to many others, is another legacy of the West that must be rethought in an age of transnationalism. Migrants, for example, demand the dignity of citizenship, and nations often resist these demands—even though governments welcome migrants' work and tax dollars. Yet it is often supranational organizations rather than the nation-state that advocate for worldwide prosperity and human values. At the same time, the West faces questions of its own unity and cultural identity—an identity that more than ever includes people from Asia, Africa, and the Americas—areas far from Europe, the traditional center of the West. Non-Westerners of all kinds have challenged, criticized, refashioned, and made enormous contributions to Western culture; they have also served the West's citizens as slaves, servants, and menial workers. One of the greatest challenges to the West and the world in this global millennium is to determine how diverse peoples and cultures can live together on terms that are fair for everyone. In other words, how can the tradition of rights and humane values continue to advance along with globalization?

A final challenge to the West involves the inventive human spirit. Over the past five hundred years, the West has benefited from its scientific and technological advances. Longevity and improved material well-being have spread to many places. In the past

Mapping the West The World in the New Millennium

By the twenty-first century, the Internet had transformed communications and economic organizations into an interconnected global network. People in the northern half of the globe had greater access to this network in 2010 than did people in the southern half, and for the most part they enjoyed greater wealth than they had a century earlier. Despite globalization, including global economic crises, historians still find local and national conditions of political, social, and economic life important in telling the full story of peoples and cultures.

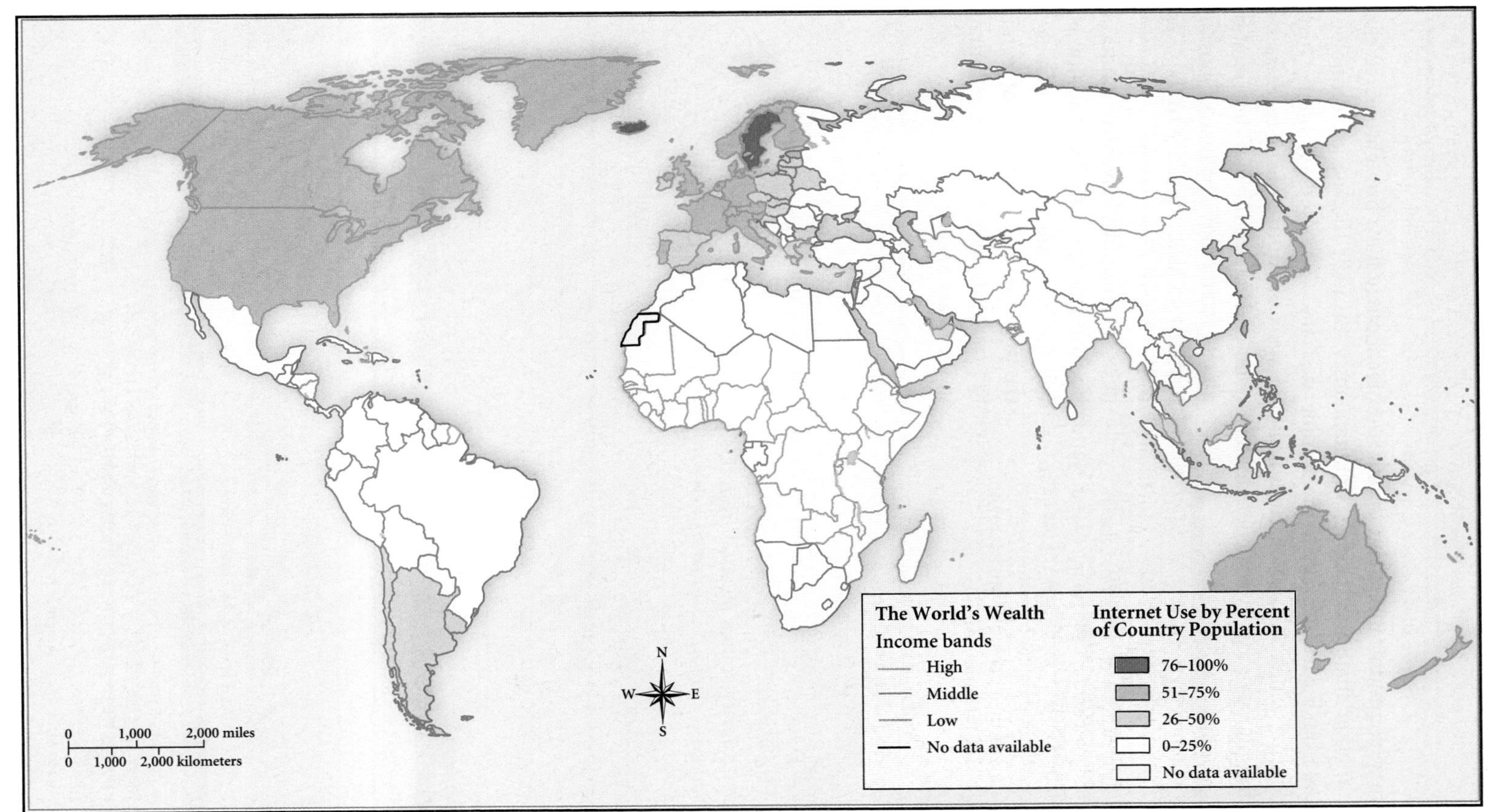
The World's Wealth
Income bands
High
Middle
Low
No data available
Internet Use by Percent of Country Population
76–100%
51–75%
26–50%
0–25%
No data available
N
W
E
S
0 1,000 2,000 miles
0 1,000 2,000 kilometers

century, communications and information technology have brought people closer to one another than ever before. Simultaneously, through the use of technology, the period from the last century to the present one is the bloodiest era in human history—one during which the use of technology threatens the future of the earth as a home for the human race. War, genocide, terrorism, and environmental deterioration are among technology's hallmarks, posing perhaps the greatest challenge to the West and to the world. The making of the West has been a constantly inventive undertaking, but also a deadly one. The question is, how will the West and the world manage both the promises and challenges of technology to protect the creativity of the human race in the years ahead?

CHAPTER REVIEW QUESTIONS

1. How did global connections at the beginning of the twenty-first century differ from global connections at the start of the twentieth century?
2. How did the Western nation-state of the early twenty-first century differ from the Western nation-state at the opening of the twentieth century?

For practice quizzes and other study tools, see the Online Study Guide at bedfordstmartins.com/huntconcise.

For primary-source material from this period, see Chapter 29 of *Sources of* THE MAKING OF THE WEST, Third Edition.

TIMELINE

- **1989** Chinese students revolt in Tiananmen Square, and the government suppresses them; fall of the Berlin Wall
- **1990s** Internet revolution
- **1990–1991** Persian Gulf War
- **1991** Civil war erupts in the former Yugoslavia; failed coup by Communist hard-liners in the Soviet Union
- **1992** Soviet Union dissolved
- **1993** Toni Morrison becomes the first African American woman to win the Nobel Prize for Literature
- **1994** Nelson Mandela elected president of South Africa; Russian troops invade Chechnya; European Union officially formed
- **1997** Collapse of Thai currency launches economic problems for the Pacific tigers
- **1999** Euro introduce[d in] the Europ[ean] Union; w[orld] populatio[n] reaches six billion

1989 | 1992 | 1995 | 1998

Suggested References

Historians see the challenges since 1989 as enormously diverse, ranging from conditions in the environment to issues of leadership in international affairs to the safety of the world's citizens in a global age. Many of these books investigate the challenges, benefits, and costs of globalization, while the European Union's Web site offers information on pending EU membership and on policies across the spectrum of its activity.

Baldwin, Peter. *Disease and Democracy: The Industrialized World Faces AIDS.* 2005.

Bass, Gary J. *Freedom's Battle: The Origins of Humanitarian Intervention.* 2008.

Benson, Leslie. *Yugoslavia: A Concise History.* 2004.

Bess, Michael. *The Light-Green Society: Economic and Technological Modernity in France.* 2003.

European Union: http://europa.eu.int

Goldman, Marshall. *The Piratization of Russia: Russian Reform Goes Awry.* 2003.

Hoerder, Dirk. *Cultures in Contact: World Migrations in the 2nd Millennium.* 2002.

Humphrey, Caroline. *The Unmaking of Soviet Life: Everyday Economies after Socialism.* 2002.

Kenney, Padraic. *The Burdens of Freedom: Eastern Europe since 1989.* 2006.

MacGaffey, Janet, et al. *Congo-Paris: Transnational Traders on the Margins of the Law.* 2000.

Osumare, Halifu. *The Africanist Aesthetic in Global Hip-Hop: Power Moves.* 2007

Rashid, Ahmed. *Jihad: The Rise of Militant Islam in Central Asia.* 2002.

Ried, T. R. *The United States of Europe: The New Superpower and the End of American Supremacy.* 2005.

Rives, Janet, and Mahmood Yousefi. *Economic Dimensions of Gender Inequality: A Global Perspective.* 1997.

Rosefielde, Steven. *Russia in the 21st Century: The Prodigal Superpower.* 2006.

Sinno, Abdulkader H., ed. *Muslims in Western Politics.* 2008.

United Nations population data: http://www.unfpa.org/swp/swpmain.htm

2001 | 2004 | 2007 | 2010

- **2000** Vladimir Putin becomes president of Russia
- **2001** Terrorist attack on the United States; United States declares "war against terrorism"
- **2003** United States–led coalition invades Iraq; West divides on this policy; European Union draft constitution rejected by France and the Netherlands
- **2004** Ten additional countries join the European Union; terrorist bombings on Madrid trains
- **2005** Terrorist bombings in central London
- **2008** Global economic crisis begins
- **2009** Barack Obama inaugurated as president of the United States

Glossary of Key Terms

This glossary of key terms contains definitions of words and ideas that are central to your understanding of the material covered in this textbook. Each term in the glossary is in **boldface** in the text when it is first defined. We have also included the page number on which the full discussion of the term appears so that you can easily locate the complete explanation to strengthen your historical vocabulary.

For words not defined here, two additional resources may be useful: the index, which will direct you to many more topics discussed in the text, and a good dictionary.

absolutism (481): A system of government in which the ruler claimed sole and uncontestable power.

agricultural revolution (532): Increasingly aggressive attitudes toward investment in and management of land that increased production of food in the 1700s; this revolution developed first in England and then spread to the continent.

Anabaptists (435): Sixteenth-century religious dissenters who believed that humans have free will and that people must knowingly select the Christian faith through rebaptism as adults. They advocated radical separation from society; though originally pacifist, some chose violent paths to religious renewal.

anarchism (715): The belief that people should not have government; it was popular among peasants and workers in the last half of the nineteenth century and the first decades of the twentieth.

appeasement (850): The strategy of preventing a war by making concessions for grievances.

art nouveau (757): A successful style in the arts, household and fashion design, and graphics that featured flowing, sinuous lines that contrasted with the mechanical influence of the early twentieth century. It borrowed many of its motifs from Asian and African art and was internationally popular.

atheists (565): People who do not believe in the existence of God.

Atlantic system (522): The triangular pattern of trade established in the 1700s that bound together western Europe, Africa, and the Americas. Europeans sold slaves from western Africa and bought commodities such as coffee and sugar that were produced by the new colonial plantations in North and South America and the Caribbean.

baroque (469): An artistic style of the seventeenth century that featured curves, exaggerated lighting, intense emotions, release from restraint, and even a kind of artistic sensationalism; like mannerism, it departed from the Renaissance emphasis on harmonious design, unity, and clarity.

Black Death (393): The term historians give to the plague that swept through Europe in 1346–1353.

Blitzkrieg (851): Literally, "lightning war"; a strategy for the conduct of war in which motorized firepower quickly and overwhelmingly attacks the enemy, leaving it in a state of shock and awe and unable to resist psychologically or militarily.

buccaneers (529): Pirates of the Caribbean who governed themselves and preyed on international shipping.

bureaucracy (486): A network of state officials carrying out orders according to a regular and routine line of authority.

Chartism (675): The movement of supporters of the People's Charter (drawn up in Britain in 1838), which demanded universal manhood suffrage, vote by secret ballot, equal electoral districts, annual elections, and the elimination of property qualifications for and the payment of stipends to members of Parliament. Chartism attracted many working-class adherents.

cholera (647): An epidemic, usually fatal disease that appeared in the 1830s in Europe; it is caused by a waterborne bacterium that induces violent vomiting and diarrhea and leaves the skin blue, eyes sunken and dull, and hands and feet ice cold.

Civil Code (627): The French legal code formulated by Napoleon in 1804 (hence also called the Napoleonic Code); it ensured equal treatment under the law to all classes of men and guaranteed religious liberty but curtailed many of the rights of women.

civil disobedience (830): Deliberately but peacefully breaking the law, a tactic used by Mohandas Gandhi in India and earlier by British suffragists to protest oppression and obtain political change.

classicism (511): A style of painting and architecture that reflected the ideals of the art of antiquity; in classicism, geometric shapes, order, and harmony of lines took precedence over the sensuous, exuberant, and emotional forms of the baroque.

cold war (869): The rivalry between the United States and the Soviet Union following World War II that led to massive growth in nuclear weapons on both sides.

communists (655): Those socialists who advocated the abolition of private property in favor of communal, collective ownership. The term was invented in 1840 but was mainly used after 1870.

conservatism (652): A political doctrine that emerged after 1815 and rejected much of the Enlightenment and the French Revolution, preferring monarchies over republics, tradition over revolution, and established religion over Enlightenment skepticism.

constitutionalism (482): A system of government in which rulers had to share power with parliaments made up of elected representatives.

consumer revolution (530): The rapid increase in consumption of new staples produced in the Atlantic system as well as of other items of daily life, such as mirrors, that were previously unavailable or beyond the reach of ordinary people.

Continental System (631): The system inaugurated by Napoleon's order in 1806 that France and its satellites boycott British goods; after some early successes in blocking British trade, the system was undermined by smuggling.

Corn Laws (653): Tariffs on grain in Great Britain that benefited landowners by preventing the import of cheap foreign grain; after agitation by the Anti–Corn Law League, the tariffs were repealed by the British government in 1846.

Cuban missile crisis (870): The confrontation in 1962 between the United States and the USSR over Soviet installation of missile sites off the American coast; both John F. Kennedy and Nikita Khrushchev backed down from using nuclear weapons to resolve the situation.

de-Christianization (616): The campaign of extremist republicans against organized churches; militants forced priests to give up their vocations and marry, sold off the buildings of the Catholic church, and set up festivals of reason to compete with Catholicism.

Declaration of the Rights of Man and of the Citizen (606): The preamble to the French constitution drafted in August 1789; it established the sovereignty of the nation and the equality of rights of citizens and granted freedom of religion, freedom of the press, equality of taxation, and equality before the law.

decolonization (889): The process—both violent and peaceful—by which colonies gained their independence from the imperial powers after World War II.

deists (565): Those who believe in God but who give God no active role in human affairs. Deists of the Enlightenment believed that a benevolent, all-knowing God had designed the universe and set it in motion but no longer intervened in the functioning of the universe. A deist might belong to no particular church (Catholic or Protestant).

DNA (913): The genetic material that forms the basis of each cell; the discovery of its structure in 1952 revolutionized genetics, molecular biology, and other scientific and medical fields.

domesticity (649): The set of beliefs, prevailing in the early to mid-nineteenth century, purporting that women should live their lives within the domestic sphere and devote themselves to their families and the home.

Dual Alliance (771): A defensive alliance forged by German chancellor Otto von Bismarck between Germany and Austria-Hungary in 1879 as part of his system of alliances to prevent or limit war; after Italy joined in 1882, it was called the Triple Alliance.

dual monarchy (697): A shared power arrangement between the Habsburg Empire and Hungary after the Prussian defeat of the Austrian Empire in 1867.

Enabling Act (836): The legislation passed in 1933 suspending constitutional government for four years in order to meet the crisis in the German economy.

enlightened despots (581): A political term that refers to rulers who tried to promote reform without giving up their own supreme political power; the best examples were Catherine the Great of Russia, Frederick the Great of Prussia, and Joseph II of Austria. Also called enlightened absolutists.

Enlightenment (522): The eighteenth-century intellectual movement whose proponents believed that human beings could apply a critical, reasoning spirit to every problem. Based on a popularization of scientific discoveries, the movement often challenged religious and secular authorities.

Entente Cordiale (771): An alliance between Britain and France that began with an agreement in 1904 to honor colonial holdings.

Estates General (601): A body of deputies from the three estates, or orders, of France; the clergy (First Estate), the nobility (Second Estate), and everyone else (Third Estate); disputes about procedures of voting in this body in 1789 opened the way to the French Revolution.

ethnic cleansing (950): The mass murder—or genocide—of people of different ethnicities.

euro (957): The common currency accepted by twelve of the fifteen members of the European Union. It went into effect gradually, becoming the denominator of business transfers in 1999 and entering public circulation in 2002.

European Economic Community (EEC or Common Market) (883): A consortium of six European countries established to promote free trade and economic cooperation among its members. Since its founding in 1957, it has expanded its membership and also its sphere of activity.

European Union (EU) (948): Formerly the European Economic Community (EEC, or Common Market), and then the European Community; instituted in 1994 by the terms of the 1992 Maastricht Treaty. Its members have political ties through the European parliament as well as common economic, legal, and business mechanisms; as of 2007, it consists of twenty-seven member countries.

existentialism (898): A philosophy prominent after World War II that stressed the importance of action in the creation of an authentic self.

Fascism (780): A doctrine advocated by Benito Mussolini that glorified the state over the people and their individual or civil rights. Beginning in the 1920s, Fascism was politically grounded in an instinctual male violence and opposed to the so-called antinationalist socialist movement and parliamentary rule.

First Consul (623): The most important of the three consuls established by the French Constitution of 1799; the title, given to Napoleon Bonaparte, was taken from the ancient Roman republic.

five-year plans (831): Centralized programs for long-range economic development first used by Joseph Stalin and copied by Adolf Hitler; these plans set production priorities and gave production targets for individual industries and agriculture.

Fourteen Points (791): A proposal by U.S. president Woodrow Wilson for peace during World War I. The Fourteen Points called for a peace based on settlement rather than on victory or a definitive conquest and thus helped bring about the surrender of the Central Powers.

Freemasons (575): Members of Masonic lodges, which were based on the rituals of stonemasons' guilds and provided a place where nobles and middle-class professionals (and even some artisans) shared interest in the Enlightenment and reform; lodges drew up constitutions and voted in elections. The movement began in Great Britain and spread eastward across Europe.

Fronde (483): A series of revolts in France, 1648–1653, that challenged the authority of young Louis XIV and his minister Mazarin.

glasnost (938): Literally, "openness" or "publicity"; a policy instituted in the 1980s by Soviet premier Mikhail Gorbachev calling for greater openness in speech and in thinking, which translated to the reduction of censorship in publishing, radio, television, and other media.

global warming (964): An increase in the temperature of the earth's lower atmosphere resulting from a buildup of chemical emissions, causing a greenhouse effect.

Glorious Revolution (504): The events when the English Parliament deposed King James II in 1688 and replaced him with William, prince of Orange, and James's daughter Mary.

Gothic (383): A style of architecture characterized by pointed arches, ribbed vaults, and large stained-glass windows.

Great Fear (603): The term used by historians to describe the rural panic of 1789; fears of an aristocratic plot to pay beggars and vagrants to burn crops or barns sometimes turned into peasant attacks on aristocrats or on seigneurial records of peasants' dues.

Great Schism (393): The term *Great Schism* refers to two different periods in the history of the Christian church. The first, in 1054, refers to the separation of the Latin Catholic church and the Greek Orthodox church; the second, to the period from 1378 to 1417, when the church had two and sometimes three popes.

Hasidim (572): A religious group within Judaism whose members pray in a highly emotional fashion; founded by the Ba'al Shem Tov in the 1740s and 1750s, and especially important in Poland-Lithuania. (The word is Hebrew for "most pious.")

Haussmannization (707): The process of urban renewal followed by many governments after the middle of the nineteenth century and named after its primary practitioner, Georges-Eugène Haussmann.

heliocentrism (472): The view articulated by Polish clergyman Nicolaus Copernicus that the earth and planets revolve around the sun; Galileo Galilei was condemned by the Catholic church for supporting this view.

Holocaust (854): A term used after World War II to name the mass murder of European Jews by the Nazis.

Huguenots (451): The name given to Calvinists in France after 1560; its linguistic origin remains uncertain.

humanism (415): A literary and intellectual movement that arose in the early fifteenth century to valorize the writings of Greco-Roman antiquity; it was so named because its practitioners studied and supported the liberal arts, or humanities.

Hundred Years' War (393): The long war between England and France, 1337–1453; it produced numerous social upheavals yet left both states more powerful than before.

ideology (640): A coherent set of beliefs (conservatism, liberalism, socialism, etc.) about the way the social and political order should be organized and changed; the word was coined during the French Revolution.

imperialism (669): European dominance of the non-West through economic exploitation and political rule (as distinct from the word *colonialism,* which usually implied establishment of settler colonies, often with slavery as the labor system).

impressionism (719): A mid- to late-nineteenth-century artistic style that captured the sensation of light in images, derived from Japanese influences and from an opposition to the realism of photographs.

indulgences (436): In Roman Catholic doctrine, a remission of sin earned by performing certain religious tasks to lessen time in purgatory after death. By the fourteenth century they could be purchased. The Catholic clergy's practice of selling indulgences came under fire during the Reformation.

industrialization (640): The process of economic transformation that began in Great Britain in the 1770s and 1780s; its most striking features were the introduction of steam engines to power machinery and the concentration of those machines in factories that mass-produced cloth from cotton grown in the British colonies.

in vitro fertilization (915): A process developed in the 1970s by which eggs are fertilized by sperm outside the human body and then implanted in a woman's uterus.

Jacobin Club (608): The first and most influential of the political clubs formed during the French Revolution; the Paris Jacobin Club inspired the formation of a national network of Jacobin clubs whose members dominated the revolutionary government during the period known as the Terror.

laissez-faire (567): An economic doctrine developed by Adam Smith based on his reading of the French physiocrats who advocated freeing the economy from government intervention and control. (The term is French for "leave alone.")

law of universal gravitation (474): Newton's law uniting celestial and terrestrial mechanics held that every body in the universe exerts over every other body an attractive force directly proportional to the product of their masses and inversely proportional to the square of the distance between them.

League of Nations (799): The international organization set up following World War I to maintain peace by arbitrating disputes and promoting collective security.

liberalism (652): An economic and political doctrine that emphasized free trade and the constitutional guarantees of individual rights such as freedom of speech and religion; liberals were favorable to the Enlightenment but critical of the violence of the French Revolution.

Maastricht Treaty (957): The agreement among the members of the European Community to have a closer alliance, including the use of common passports and eventually the development of a common currency; by the terms of this treaty, the European Community became the European Union (EU) in 1994.

mannerism (469): A late-sixteenth-century style of painting in which a distorted perspective created bizarre and theatrical effects that contrasted with the precise, harmonious lines of Renaissance painting.

march on Rome (818): The threat by Benito Mussolini and his followers in 1922 to take over the Italian government in a military convergence on Rome; the march forced King Victor Emmanuel II to make Mussolini prime minister.

Marshall Plan (875): A post–World War II program funded by the United States to get Europe back on its feet economically and thereby reduce the appeal of communism. It played an important role in the rebirth of European prosperity in the 1950s.

Marxism (715): A body of thought about the organization of production, social inequality, and the processes of revolutionary change as devised by the philosopher and economist Karl Marx.

Meiji Restoration (715): A change in the Japanese government in 1867 that reinstalled the emperor as legitimate ruler in place of the military leader, or shogun.

mercantilism (487): The doctrine that governments must intervene to increase national wealth by whatever means possible.

mestizos (528): People born to Spanish fathers and native American mothers.

Methodism (572): A religious movement founded by John Wesley that broke away from the Anglican church in Great Britain and insisted on strict self-discipline and a "methodical" approach to religious study and observance. Wesley emphasized an intense personal experience of salvation and a life of thrift, abstinence, and hard work.

mir (688): A Russian farm community fortified by the emancipation of the serfs in 1861 that provided for holding the land in common and regulating the movements of any individual by the group. The mir hindered the free movement of labor and individual agricultural enterprise, including modernization.

Mitteleuropa (772): Literally, "central Europe," but used by influential military leaders in Germany before World War I to refer to land in both central and eastern Europe that they hoped to acquire. This territory ultimately became a war aim in World War I and for Hitler thereafter.

modernism (753): Changes in the arts at the end of the nineteenth century that featured a break with realism in art and literature and with lyricism in music.

modernity (730): The accelerated pace of life, the rise of mass politics, the spread of industrial production, and the decline of a rural social order that were visible in the West from the late nineteenth century onward.

multinational corporation (915): A business that operates in many foreign countries by sending large segments of its manufacturing, finance, sales, and other business components abroad.

nationalism (656): A political doctrine that holds that all peoples derive their identities from their nations and should have states to express their common language and shared cultural traditions.

natural selection (723): Theory developed by Charles Darwin that life developed from lower forms through a primal battle for survival and through the sexual selection of mates.

Nazi-Soviet Pact (851): The agreement reached in 1939 by Germany and the Soviet Union in which both agreed not to attack the other in case of war. The agreement secretly divided up territory that would later be conquered.

neoliberalism (936): A theory promoted by Margaret Thatcher, Britain's prime minister from 1979 to 1990, and those who followed her calling for a return to liberal principles of the nineteenth century, including the reduction of welfare-state programs and the cutting of taxes for wealthy people in order to promote economic growth.

new woman (745): A woman of the turn of the twentieth century, often from the middle class, who dressed practically, moved about freely, lived apart from her family, and supported herself.

nongovernmental organizations (NGOs) (962): Charitable foundations and activist groups such as Doctors without Borders that often work internationally on political, economic, and relief issues; also, organizations such as the Rockefeller, Ford, and Open Society Foundations that shape economic and social policy and the course of political reform.

North Atlantic Treaty Organization (NATO) (877): The security alliance formed in 1949 to provide a unified military force for the United States, Canada, and their allies in western Europe and Scandinavia. The corresponding alliance of the Soviet Union and its allies was known as the Warsaw Pact.

Nuremberg Laws (838): Legislation in 1935 that deprived Jewish Germans of their citizenship and imposed many other hardships on them.

opium (669): An addictive drug derived from the heads of poppy plants; it was imported to Europe from the Ottoman Empire and India, available in various forms, and often used by ordinary people until restricted by governments after the 1860s.

Organization of Petroleum Exporting Countries (OPEC) (932): A consortium that regulated the supply and export of oil and that acted with more unanimity after the United States supported Israel against the Arabs in the wars of the late 1960s and early 1970s.

Ostpolitik (922): A policy initiated by Willy Brandt in the late 1960s in which West Germany sought better economic relations with the Communist countries of eastern Europe.

Pacific tigers (972): Countries of East Asia so named because of their massive economic growth, much of it from the 1970s and 1980s on; foremost among these were Japan and China.

Pan-Slavism (698): A movement in the nineteenth century that called for the unity of all Slavs across national and regional boundaries.

parlements (483): High courts in France (the term comes from the French *parler*, "to speak"). Each region had its parlement; the parlements could not propose laws, but they could review laws presented by the king and refuse to register them (the king could also insist on their registration).

Peace of Paris (799): The series of peace treaties that provided the settlement of World War I. These treaties were resented, especially by Germany and Hungary, as well as by states of the Middle East in which England and France took over the government.

perestroika (938): Literally, "restructuring"; an economic policy instituted in the 1980s by Soviet premier Mikhail Gorbachev calling for the introduction of market mechanisms and the achievement of greater efficiency in manufacturing, agriculture, and services.

philosophes (562): Public intellectuals of the Enlightenment who wrote on subjects ranging from current affairs to art criticism with the goal of furthering reform in society. (The word in French means "philosophers.")

physiocrats (587): French economists who advocated deregulation of the grain trade and a more equitable tax system to encourage agricultural productivity.

Pietism (540): A Protestant revivalist movement that emphasized deeply emotional individual religious experience.

plantations (522): Large tracts of land producing staple crops such as sugar, coffee, and tobacco; farmed by slave labor; and owned by a colonial settler who emigrated from western Europe.

politiques (453): Political advisers during the French Wars of Religion who argued that compromise in matters of religion—limited toleration for the Calvinists—would strengthen the monarchy.

pop art (919): A style in the visual arts that mimicked advertising and consumerism and that used ordinary objects in paintings and other compositions.

positivism (718): A theory, developed in the mid-nineteenth century, stating that the study of facts would generate accurate, or "positive," laws of society; these laws could, in turn, help formulate policy and legislation.

postmodernism (982): A term applied in the late twentieth century to both an intense stylistic mixture in the arts and a critique of Enlightenment and scientific beliefs in rationality and the possibility for precise knowledge.

predestination (442): John Calvin's doctrine that God preordained salvation or damnation for each person before creation; those chosen for salvation were considered the "elect."

Protestants (435): Members of the Christian branch that formed when Martin Luther and his followers broke from the Catholic church in 1517; the name was first used in 1529 in an imperial diet by German princes who protested Emperor Charles V's edict to repress religious dissent.

Provisional Government (792): The initial government to take control in Russia after the overthrow of the Romanov empire in 1917. The government was composed of aristocrats and members of the middle class, often deputies in the Duma—the assembly created after the Revolution of 1905.

psychoanalysis (729): Sigmund Freud's theory of human mental processes and his method for treating their malfunctioning.

pump priming (837): An economic policy used by governments to stimulate the economy through public works programs and other infusions to public funds.

purges (832): The series of attacks instituted by Joseph Stalin on citizens of the USSR in the 1930s and later. The victims were accused of being "wreckers," or saboteurs of communism, while the public grew hysterical and pliable because of its fear.

Puritans (444): Strict Calvinists who opposed all vestiges of Catholic ritual in the Church of England.

raison d'état (462): French for "reason of state." The political doctrine, first proposed by Cardinal Richelieu of France, that held that the state's interests should prevail over those of religion; Richelieu, for example, allied with the Lutheran king of Sweden even though he himself was a leading official of the Catholic church.

realism (684): An art style that arose in the mid-nineteenth century and was dedicated to depicting society realistically without romantic or idealistic overtones.

Realpolitik (683): Policies associated initially with nation building that are said to be based on hardheaded realities rather than the romantic notions of earlier nationalists. The term has come to mean any policy based on considerations of power alone.

rococo (538): A style of painting that emphasized irregularity and asymmetry, as well as movement and curvature, but on a smaller, more intimate scale than the baroque.

romanticism (571): An artistic movement of the early nineteenth century that glorified nature, emotion, genius, and imagination.

Russification (690): A program for the integration of Russia's many nationality groups involving the forced acquisition of Russian language and the practice of Russian orthodoxy as well as the settlement of ethnic Russians among other nationality groups.

salons (564): Informal gatherings, usually sponsored by middle-class or aristocratic women, that provided a forum for new ideas and an opportunity to establish new intellectual contacts among supporters of the Enlightenment; works that could not be published officially were read aloud. (The word in French means "living rooms.")

sans-culottes (608): French for "without breeches"; the name given to politically active men from the lower classes. They worked with their hands and wore the long trousers of workingmen rather than the knee breeches of the upper classes.

scientific method (472): A combination of experimental observation and mathematical deduction to determine the laws of nature; it became the secular standard of truth and as such challenged the hold of both the churches and popular beliefs.

Second International (760): A transnational organization of workers established in 1889, mostly committed to Marxian socialism.

social contract (482): The doctrine found in the writings of Hobbes and Locke that all political authority derives not from divine right but from an implicit contract between citizens and their rulers.

Solidarity (939): An outlawed Polish labor union of the 1980s that contested Communist Party programs and eventually succeeded in ousting the party from the Polish government.

soviets (792): Councils of workers and soldiers first formed in Russia during the Revolution of 1905; they took shape to represent the people in the early days of the 1917 Russian Revolution. These groups saw themselves as a more legitimate political force than the Provisional Government.

stagflation (933): The combination of a stagnant economy and soaring inflation; a period of stagflation occurred in the West in the 1970s as a result of the OPEC embargo on oil.

temperance movement (649): A movement in the United States and Europe begun in the early nineteenth century to discourage consumption of alcohol.

Terror (611): The emergency government established under the direction of the Committee of Public Safety during the French Revolution; the government aimed to establish a republic of virtue, but to do so it arrested hundreds of thousands of political suspects and executed thousands of ordinary people.

terrorism (910): Coordinated and targeted political violence by opposition groups.

Thermidorian Reaction (620): The violent backlash against the rule of Robespierre that began with his arrest and execution; most of the instruments of the Terror were dismantled, and supporters of the Jacobins were harassed or even murdered.

third world (870): A term devised after World War II to designate those countries outside either the capitalist world of the U.S. bloc or the socialist world of the Soviet bloc—most of them emerging from imperial domination.

totalitarianism (831): Highly centralized systems of government that attempt to control society in its most private details and ensure conformity through police terror and single-party rule.

total war (780): A war built on full mobilization of soldiers, civilians, and the technological capacities of the nations involved. The term also refers to a highly destructive war and one that is both a physical war and a war for ideas and ideologies.

Truman Doctrine (875): The U.S. policy to limit communism after World War II by countering political crises with economic and military aid.

United Nations (UN) (870): An organization for collective security and deliberation set up as World War II closed; it replaced the ineffective League of Nations and has proved active in resolving international conflicts both through negotiation and by the use of force.

Vatican II (897): A Catholic Council held between 1962 and 1965 to modernize some aspects of church teachings (such as condemnation of Jews), update the liturgy, and promote cooperation among the faiths (i.e., ecumenism).

Warsaw Pact (878): Military alliance established in 1955 by the Soviet Union with its satellite countries in response to West Germany's admission to the North Atlantic Treaty Organization.

Weimar Republic (797): The parliamentary republic established in 1919 in Germany to replace the imperial form of government.

welfare state (839): A system comprising state-sponsored programs for citizens, including veterans' pensions, social security, health care, family allowances, and disability insurance. Most highly developed after World War II, the welfare state intervened in society to bring economic democracy (to supplement political democracy) by setting a minimum standard of well-being.

Westernization (546): The effort, especially in Peter the Great's Russia, to make society and social customs resemble counterparts in western Europe, especially France, Britain, and the Dutch Republic.

World Bank (961): An international institution of credit created in the 1940s. With the globalization of finances and of national economies from the 1980s on, it became increasingly powerful.

Zionism (768): A movement that began in the late nineteenth century among European Jews to found a Jewish state.

Additional Acknowledgments

Chapter 12, page 463: Taking Measure: "The Rise and Fall of Silver Imports to Spain, 1550–1660." From Chart 1, "Total Imports of Treasure in Pesos (450 Maravedis) by Five-Year Intervals," page 35, in *American Revolution and the Price Revolution in Spain, 1501–1650,* edited by Earl J. Hamilton. Courtesy of Harvard University Press.

Chapter 13, page 491: Taking Measure: "The Seventeenth-Century Army." From *Armées et sociétés en Europe de 1494 à 1789* by André Corvisier. (1976, page 126). Courtesy Presses Universitaires de France.

Chapter 14, page 525: Figure 14.1: "African Slaves Imported into American Territories, 1701–1800." Adapted from *The Atlantic Slave Trade: A Census* by Philip D. Curtin. Copyright © 1969 by the Board of Regents of the University of Wisconsin System. Reprinted by permission of The University of Wisconsin Press. **Page 532:** Taking Measure: "Relationship of Crop Harvested to Seed Used, 1400–1800." Adapted from Figure 2.8, page 56, in *World Trade Since 1431: Geography, Technology, and Capitalism* by Peter J. Hugill. Copyright © 1993 The Johns Hopkins University Press. Reprinted with permission of The Johns Hopkins University Press.

Chapter 17, page 642: Taking Measure: "Railroad Lines, 1830–1850." From *European Historical Statistics 1750–1970,* edited by B. R. Mitchell. Copyright © 1975. Reprinted by permission of Macmillan Publishers, Ltd.

Chapter 18, page 710: Taking Measure: "Decline of Illiteracy, 1850–1900." From *The Birth of New Europe: State and Society in the Nineteenth Century* by Theodore S. Hamerow. Copyright © 1983 by the University of North Carolina Press. Used by permission of the publisher.

Chapter 19, page 743: Taking Measure: "Population Growth Worldwide, 1890–1910." From *International Historical Statistics: Africa, Asia, and Oceania, 1750–1993,* Third Edition, 3, 56, 57; *International Historical Statistics: The Americas, 1750–1993,* Fourth Edition, 6, 24; *International Historical Statistics: Europe, 1750–1993,* Fourth Edition, 4, 8, edited by B. R. Mitchell (London: Macmillan Reference). Copyright © 1998 Macmillan Publishers, Ltd. Reprinted by permission of the publisher.

Chapter 20, page 814: W. B. Yeats. "Sailing to Byzantium." (3 lines) From *The Collected Works of W. B. Yeats Volume I; The Poets,* revised, edited by Richard J. Finneran. Copyright © 1928 by The Macmillan Company. Copyright renewed © 1956 by George Yeats. Reprinted with the permission of Scribner, a Division of Simon and Schuster Adult Publishing Group. All rights reserved.

Index

A note about the index:
Names of individuals appear in boldface.
Letters following pages refer to:
(i) illustrations, including photographs and artifacts
(f) figures, including charts and graphs
(m) maps
(n) footnotes

Elevation
Feet
Meters
Over 13,120
Over 4,001
6,561–13,120
2,001–4,000
1,641–6,560
501–2,000
661–1640
201–500
0–660
0–200
Below sea level
Below sea level
National capital
Major city
0
250
500 miles
0
250
500 kilometers
ATLANTIC OCEAN
North Sea
Baltic Sea
English Channel
Bay of Biscay
Mediterranean Sea
Black Sea
Caspian Sea
Adriatic Sea
Tyrrhenian Sea
Ionian Sea
Aegean Sea
URAL MTS.
CAUCASUS MTS.
CARPATHIAN MTS.
ALPS
APENNINES
PYRENEES
Ural R.
Volga R.
Dnieper R.
Danube R.
Vistula R.
Oder R.
Elbe R.
Rhine R.
Seine R.
Loire R.
Rhône R.
Po R.
Ebro R.
Thames R.
Tigris R.
Euphrates R.
Nile R.
NORWAY
SWEDEN
FINLAND
ESTONIA
LATVIA
LITHUANIA
RUSSIA
RUSSIAN FEDERATION
KAZAKHSTAN
BELARUS
UKRAINE
MOLDOVA
POLAND
GERMANY
DENMARK
NETHERLANDS
BELGIUM
LUXEMBOURG
FRANCE
UNITED KINGDOM
SCOTLAND
WALES
ENGLAND
NORTHERN IRELAND
IRELAND
CZECH REP.
SLOVAKIA
AUSTRIA
HUNGARY
ROMANIA
LIECHTENSTEIN
SWITZERLAND
SLOVENIA
CROATIA
BOSNIA AND HERZEGOVINA
SERBIA
MONTENEGRO
ALBANIA
MACEDONIA
BULGARIA
GREECE
TURKEY
GEORGIA
ARMENIA
AZERBAIJAN
IRAN
IRAQ
SYRIA
CYPRUS
LEBANON
ISRAEL
JORDAN
KUWAIT
SAUDI ARABIA
EGYPT
LIBYA
TUNISIA
ALGERIA
MOROCCO
MALTA
ITALY
SAN MARINO
MONACO
ANDORRA
SPAIN
PORTUGAL
Corsica
Sardinia
Sicily
Crete
BALEARIC IS.
Bergen
Oslo
Göteborg
Stockholm
Helsinki
Tallinn
St. Petersburg
Pärnu
Riga
Jelgava
Kaunas
Vilnius
Kaliningrad
Gdánsk
Minsk
Moscow
Gomel
Brest
Warsaw
Kharkiv
Kiev
Cracow
Glasgow
Edinburgh
Belfast
Dublin
Liverpool
Cork
Birmingham
London
Aarhus
Copenhagen
Amsterdam
Rotterdam
Antwerp
Brussels
Berlin
Frankfurt
Prague
Paris
Luxembourg
Brno
Munich
Vienna
Bratislava
Miskolc
Zürich
Vaduz
Bern
Innsbruck
Graz
Budapest
Cluj
Chisinau
Tiraspol
Odessa
Lyon
Milan
Ljubljana
Zagreb
Timisoara
Bucharest
San Marino
Belgrade
Sarajevo
Split
Marseille
Andorra la Vella
Oporto
Madrid
Barcelona
Lisbon
Rome
Podgorica
Tirana
Skopje
Sofia
Plovdiv
Istanbul
Ankara
Salonica
Naples
Seville
Gibraltar (Br.)
Izmir
Athens
Palermo
Algiers
Tunis
Rabat
Valletta
Tripoli
Tbilisi
Baku
Yerevan
Baghdad
Beirut
Damascus
Amman
Tel Aviv
Jerusalem
Alexandria
Cairo